The American Express
International Traveller's Pocket
ITALIAN
Dictionary and Phrase Book

Collins/Mitchell Beazley

List of abbreviations

abbrev	–	abbreviation	*num*	–	numeral
adj	.–	adjective	*pl*	–	plural
adv	–	adverb	*pref*	–	prefix
art	–	article	*prep*	–	preposition
conj	–	conjunction	*pron*	–	pronoun
excl	–	exclamation	*vi*	–	intransitive verb
f	–	feminine noun	*vr*	–	reflexive verb
m	–	masculine noun	*vt*	–	transitive verb
n	–	noun	*vt/i*	–	transitive/intransitive verb

The asterisk * denotes an irregular verb, to which the reader is referred in the list of irregular verbs in the grammar section.

The dash — denotes that the plural is invariable.

Cross-reference letter keys occur in brackets after main section headings. Phrases are numbered in sequence following each main heading. Phrase words are cross-referenced in the English-Italian dictionary section by letter and number to their relevant phrases. An *f* after the number indicates that the cross-reference applies also to the subsequent phrase(s).

William Collins Sons & Co

Editors
Lorna Sinclair
Nicholas Rollin
with
Andrew Wilkin
Ennio Bilucaglia
Lesley Robertson
Assistant Editors
Susan Dunsmore
Valerie McNulty
Managing Editor
Richard H. Thomas

Mitchell Beazley Publishers

Editors
James Hughes
Christopher McIntosh
Designer
Philip Lord
Executive Art Editor
Douglas Wilson
Production
Julian Deeming

Edited by William Collins Sons & Co Ltd
with Mitchell Beazley International Ltd
Designed by Mitchell Beazley International Ltd
87-89 Shaftesbury Avenue
London W1V 7AD
© Mitchell Beazley Publishers 1983
© William Collins Sons & Co Ltd 1983

Typeset by Coats Dataprint Ltd, Inverness

Printed in Great Britain by William Collins Sons & Co Ltd, Glasgow.

Contents

Pronunciation

English spelling gives only an approximate idea of the Italian sounds, which can be learned only by listening to the Italians themselves. However, Italian is a fairly easy language to read. In this guide the words have been split up for greater clarity, but in fact there should be no pause between syllables.

The spellings *c* and *ch* can be confusing, because *c* is sometimes pronounced like English *ch* (see the table), while the Italian *ch* is pronounced like English *k*. Thus *c'è* (there is) is pronounced like English *check* without the final *ck*, while *chi?* (who?) is pronounced *kee*. Also, the spellings *cia*, *cie*, *cio* and *ciu* are pronounced *cha*, *chay*, *cho* and *choo*: the *i* is not pronounced unless it is part of a stressed syllable. The letter *g* behaves in a similar way, as can be seen in the table.

The vowels *a*, *e*, and *o* can be either 'long' or 'short', i.e. pronounced as either *ah* or *a*, *ay* or *e*, *oh* or *o*, depending on the circumstances. These are shown in the accompanying pronunciation scheme.

Sometimes Italian has two distinct vowel sounds next to each other, as in words like *dei*. These sounds merge into each other and should not be separated by a pause.

In English, the letter *r* is often nothing more than a sign to make the vowel sound longer, as in *more*, but in Italian all *r*'s are rolled.

Stress

Longer words are usually stressed on the penultimate (second last) syllable, but in this guide the stressed syllable is indicated each time it appears, and not only in exceptional cases. Any sound not explained here or in the table should be clear from the pronunciation shown beside each word in the dictionary section.

How to Pronounce Italian

Italian spelling	Closest English sound	Shown here by	Example	
a	pat	a	quando	**kwan**·doh
	or father	ah	comprare	kom·**prah**·ray
e	pet	e	letto	**let**·toh
	or gate	ay	per	payr
i	meet	ee	vino	**vee**·noh
	or yet	y	fieno	**fye**·noh
o	UK pot, US thought	o	soldi	**sol**·dee
	or bone	oh	cosa	**koh**·sa
u	boot	oo	luna	**loo**·na
	or won't	w	uomo	**wo**·moh
c	before e, i chat	ch	centro	**chen**·troh
	before a, o, u cat	k	cosa	**koh**·sa
ch	cat	k	chi	kee
g	before e, i gin	j or dj	giorno	**jor**·noh
	before a, h, o, u got	g	regalo	ray·**ga**·loh
gl	million	ly	figlio	**feel**·yoh
gn	companion	ny	bisogno	bee·**zon**·yoh
h	not pronounced		ho	oh
r	carrot	r	fare	**fah**·ray
s	set	s	soldi	**sol**·dee
	or phase	z	caso	**kah**·zoh
sc	before e, i shop	sh	uscita	oo·**shee**·ta
	before a, o, u scar	sk	capisco	ka·**pees**·koh
z	cats	ts	senza	**sen**·tsa
	or rods	dz	mezzo	**medz**·dzoh

Introduction

The Italian language

Italian is spoken by some 60 million as their mother tongue. The Swiss have it as one of their official languages, and it is also the local vernacular in parts of France and Yugoslavia. Italians speak it with a conscious pride and *brio*; it is a language of excitement and rhetoric, expressing joy in life. It is comparatively easy to speak adequately (though difficult to achieve excellence in), and with this book you should soon be able to make your way around.

How the book works

This is a combined phrasebook and dictionary, designed primarily for the needs of the traveller. It enables you to find easily and quickly just the phrase you need, whether you are buying a suit or trying to tell a garage mechanic what is wrong with your car. The Italian is accompanied in all cases by an instant guide to pronunciation.

Many of the phrases listed consist of a basic group of words which can be linked up with different subsidiary words to produce variations, in the way that a power tool can be fitted with extensions. With phrases of this kind the basic "tool" is shown on one side and the "extension" on the other, with a dash in between: alternative extensions are either indicated by an oblique stroke or shown on the line below. A further stock of extensions is found in the dictionary section at the back of the book, and this serves also as a cross-reference index to the phrases.

Here is an example. If you look up the word "toll" in the dictionary, you will find "il pedaggio" and a cross-reference to Section T (Travel). Here you will see, following the number shown in the cross-reference, the kind of phrase you might need in using this word.

You will soon be able to express yourself in the language with flexibility and confidence, and what you learn from this book can open the door to the whole Italian language.

Understanding what you hear

This book not only tells you what to say but also helps you to interpret some of the things that will be said to you. For example, the section on "Finding the way" anticipates the sort of directions you may be given. Fortunately, Italians usually enunciate very clearly, but it will be necessary to attune your ear to unfamiliar sounds and intonations.

As you start to hear some of the words you have learned being used by the Italians themselves, you will be able to adjust your pronunciation accordingly. Bear in mind that Italian words are heavily stressed. The stressed syllable is usually the first or second one from the end except where an accent marks it as coming on the last syllable — for example, *specialità*, "speciality". The stressed syllable is marked in the pronunciation guide by *bold* lettering (*spe·cha·lee·**ta**). When speaking, open your mouth wide and utter the words as fully and roundly as possible.

So read, listen, learn and practise. Even a limited competence in Italian will bring you great satisfaction as you travel.
Buon viaggio!

Basic equipment (B)

Here are some of the words and phrases which make up the basic coinage of Italian and which it is useful to have in your pocket for a wide variety of situations. You would be well advised to read through this whole section before starting your trip. If you can memorize any of it, so much the better.

Some essentials

Yes	No thank you
Sí	No grazie
see	*no gra·tsye*
No	Thank you (in return)
No	Grazie a Lei
no	*gra·tsye a ley*
Please	You're welcome
Per favore	Prego
payr fa·voh·re	*pre·go*
Thank you	
Grazie	
gra·tsye	

Please and thank you

Italians have rather more ritualistic conventions of common politeness than do some English-speaking races. In English one says "Thank you" and there, often, is an end to it; an Italian will almost invariably reply "Prego", which means "You're welcome" or "Not at all". You will show courtesy by doing as much yourself. Again, an Italian will often reply "Prego" to "Mi dispiace" (I'm sorry) or "Mi scusi" (Forgive me).

1 I'm sorry
  Mi dispiace
  mee dee·spyah·che

2 Excuse me/Please let me by
  Permesso
  payr·mays·soh

3 Forgive me
  Mi scusi
  mee skoo·zee

4 It doesn't matter
  Non importa
  nohn eem·por·ta

5 That's all right/That's OK
  Va bene
  va be·ne

Greetings and general exchanges

Italians use the words "Signore", "Signora" and "Signorina" much more frequently than the English use "Sir" or "Madam". It is usual to address any man, woman or girl you do not know or do not know well as "Signore", "Signora" or "Signorina", and if, for instance, you wanted to ask someone the way you would attract his or her attention by saying "Signore" or "Signora" instead of "Excuse me". Again, for example, when confronting an official, you would say "Buona sera, Signore" or "Buona sera, Signora", rather than simply "Buona sera" (Good afternoon).

Good morning —	Sir
Buon giorno —	Signore
bwon johr·noh —	*see·nyoh·re*
—	Madam
—	Signora
—	*see·nyoh·ra*
—	Miss
—	Signorina
—	*see·nyoh·ree·na*

7 Good afternoon/evening
Buona sera
bwo·na say·ra

8 Good night
Buona notte
bwo·na not·te

9 Hello (informal)
Ciao
chow

10 Hello (by telephone)
Pronto
prohn·to

11 Goodbye
Arrivederci
ar·ree·ve·dayr·chee

12 Goodbye (informal)
Ciao
chow

13 How do you do?/I'm very glad to meet you
Piacere/lieto di fare la Sua conoscenza
pya·chay·re/lye·to dee fah·ray la soo·a ko·no·shen·tsa

14 See you soon/See you later
A presto
a pre·sto

15 What is your name?
Come si chiama Lei?
koh·me see kyah·ma ley

16 My name is . . .
Mi chiamo . . .
mee kyah·mo . . .

17 How are you?
Come sta?
koh·me sta

18 I'm very well/I'm fine, thank you
Sto bene, grazie
sto be·ne gra·tsye

19 Just a minute
Un momento
oon mo·mayn·toh

20 What did you say?
Come?
koh·me

21 I understand
Capisco
ka·pee·sko

22 I do not understand
Non capisco
nohn ka·pee·sko

23 Do you understand?
Capisce?
ka·pee·she

24 I do not speak Italian
Non parlo italiano
nohn par·lo ee·ta·lyah·no

25 I do not speak Italian very well
Non parlo bene l'italiano
nohn par·lo be·ne lee·ta·lyah·no

26 Please repeat that
Vuol ripeterlo, per favore
vwol ree·pe·ter·lo payr fa·voh·re

27 Please speak more slowly
Parli più piano, per favore
par·lee pyoo pyah·no payr fa·voh·re

28 Please write that down for me
Me lo scriva, per favore
may lo skree·va payr fa·voh·re

29 Do you speak English?
Parla inglese?
par·la een·glay·se

30 I am English/American
Sono inglese/americano(a)
soh·no een·glay·se/a·me·ree·kah·no(a)

31 Really?
Vero?
vay·ro

32 Agreed
D'accordo
dak·kor·doh

33 Fine
Bene
be·ne

34 You are right
Ha ragione
a ra·joh·ne

Common questions and statements

Many of the things you will need to ask and say will involve the following groups of words. To most of them you can just add the name of the thing you need, or the place you are going to, or what you want to do or want done. Many of them will be enough on their own – "How much?", for instance.

35   Do I have to — reserve a table?
           Devo — prenotare un tavolo?
           de·vo — pre·no·tah·ray oon tah·vo·loh

36   Do we have to — pay?
        Dobbiamo — pagare?
      dob·byah·mo — pa·gah·ray

37   Do you have — any matches?
            Ha — dei fiammiferi?
           a — dey fyam·mee·fe·ree
               — the time?
               — l'ore?
               — *loh·re*

38 Could you come with me, please?
Potrebbe venire con me, per favore?
po·treb·be ve·nee·re kohn may payr fa·voh·re

39 What's the matter?
Che cosa c'è?
ke ko·sa che

40 I've made a mistake
Ho fatto uno sbaglio
o fat·to oo·no zba·lyoh

41 It's a mistake
È uno sbaglio
e oo·no zba·lyoh

42 What does that mean?
Cosa significa?
ko·sa see·nyee·fee·ka

43 What is this/that?
Cos'è questo/quello?
ko·se kway·sto/kwayl·lo

44 What time is it?
Che ora è?
ke oh·ra e

45 At what time?
A che ora?
a ke oh·ra

46 How much/many?
Quanto/quanti?
kwan·to/kwan·tee

47 How often?
Ogni quanto tempo?
oh·nyee kwan·to tem·poh

48 How long will that take?
Quanto tempo ci vorrà?
kwan·to tem·poh chee vor·ra

49 Where is?
Dov'è?
doh·ve

50 Here it is/Here you are
Eccolo/Eccoti
ek·ko·lo/ek·ko·tee

51 How do you say "..." in Italian?
Come si dice "..." in italiano?
koh·me see dee·che "..." een ee·ta·lyah·no

52 I/We need — something to drink
Ho/abbiamo bisogno di — qualcosa da bere
o/ab·byah·mo bee·zoh·nyoh dee — kwal·ko·sa da bay·re

53 I want — a cup of coffee
Voglio — una tazza di caffè
vo·lyo — oo·na tats·tsa dee kaf·fe
— to go to Florence
— andare a Firenze
— *an·dah·ray a fee·ren·tse*

54 I would like — a glass of wine
Vorrei — un bicchiere di vino
vor·rey — oon beek·kye·re dee vee·noh

55 May I borrow your pen?
Può prestarmi la penna?
pwo pre·star·mee la payn·na

56 Do you mind if — I open the window?
Le dispiace se — apro la finestra?
le dee·spyah·che se — ah·pro la fee·ne·stra

57 Whom should I see about this?
A chi devo rivolgermi per questo?
a kee de·vo ree·vol·jer·mee payr kway·sto

58 Can you — help me?
Può — aiutarmi?
pwo — a·yoo·tar·mee
— tell me the way?
— indicarmi la strada?
— *een·dee·kar·mee la strah·da*

59 Do you know — a good restaurant near here?
Conosce — un buon ristorante qui vicino?
ko·noh·she — oon bwon ree·sto·ran·te kwee vee·chee·no
— where the Hotel Ritz is?
— dov'è l'albergo Ritz?
— *doh·ve lal·ber·goh reets*

General problems and requests

60 Can you help me, please?
Può aiutarmi, per favore?
pwo a·yoo·tar·mee payr fa·voh·re

61 We need someone who can speak English
Abbiamo bisogno di qualcuno che parli inglese
ab·byah·mo bee·zoh·nyoh dee kwal·koo·no ke par·lee een·glay·se

62 Please repeat that
    Vuol ripeterlo, per favore?
    vwol ree·pe·ter·lo payr fa·voh·re
63 We are in a hurry
    Abbiamo fretta
    ab·byah·mo frayt·ta
64 Can you do it for me — at once?
    Me lo può fare — subito?
    may lo pwo fah·ray — soo·bee·to
65 The machine has broken down
    La macchina è guasta
    la mak·kee·na e gwa·sta
66   I have broken — the switch/the glass
                  Ho rotto — l'interruttore/il vetro
                  o roht·to — leen·ter·root·toh·re/eel vay·troh
67   I have spilled — the water/the wine
                  Ho versato — l'acqua/il vino
                  o ver·sah·to — lak·kwa/eel vee·noh
68   I have forgotten — my glasses/my key
                  Ho dimenticato — gli occhiali/la chiave
                  o dee·men·tee·kah·to — lyee ok·kyah·lee/la kyah·ve
69   I have left my bag — in the plane/the coach
                  Ho lasciato la mia borsa — sull'aereo/sul pullman
                  o la·shah·to la mee·a bohr·sa — sool·la·e·re·o/sool pool·man
70   I wish to leave a message
                          for — Mr Smith
        Vorrei lasciare un
            messaggio per — il Signor Smith
        *vor·rey la·shah·ray oon
            mes·saj·joh payr — eel see·nyohr smeeth*
71 Is there a message/letter for me?
    C'è un messaggio/una lettera per me?
    che oon mes·saj·joh/oo·na let·te·ra payr may
72 Go away!
    Va' via!
    va vee·a

Travel   (T)

General

1   I am leaving — tomorrow
                 Parto — domani
                 par·to — do·mah·nee
                            — on Thursday
                            — giovedí
                            — *jo·ve·dee*
2   How long will the train/flight be delayed?
    Con quanto ritardo partirà il treno/l'aereo?
    kohn kwan·to ree·tar·doh par·tee·ra eel tre·noh/la·e·re·oh
3   I have missed — my train
                 Ho perso — il treno
                 o per·so — eel tre·noh
                            — my flight
                            — il volo
                            — *eel voh·loh*
4   At what time is the next — train?
        A che ora è il prossimo — treno?
        a ke oh·ra e eel pros·see·mo — tre·noh
                            — flight?
                            — volo?
                            — *voh·loh*
                            — bus?
                            — autobus?
                            — *ow·to·boos*

5 I am a member of the American Express party travelling to Milan
Faccio parte del gruppo American Express che va a Milano
fach·cho **par**·te del **groop**·poh a·**me**·ree·kan ek·**spres** ke va a
mee·**lah**·no

6 My party has left without me
Il mio gruppo è partito senza di me
eel **mee**·o **groop**·poh e par·**tee**·to **sen**·tsa dee may

7 I have lost the rest of my party
Ho perso gli altri del mio gruppo
o **per**·so lyee **al**·tree del **mee**·o **groop**·poh

8   Where do I get the
                  connection — for Palermo?
    Dove faccio la coincidenza — per Palermo?
     doh·ve **fach**·cho la
    ko·een·chee·**den**·tsa — payr pa·**ler**·mo

9   Could you — keep my seat for me, please?
    Potrebbe — tenermi il posto, per favore?
    po·**treb**·be — te·**nayr**·mee eel **poh**·stoh payr
                fa·**voh**·re
         — keep an eye on my luggage
           for a few moments, please?
         — guardarmi un momento i
           bagagli, per favore?
         — gwar·**dar**·mee oon mo·**mayn**·toh
           ee ba·**ga**·lyee payr fa·**voh**·re

Arrival and departure

10   Here is — my passport
    Ecco — il mio passaporto
    ek·ko — eel **mee**·o pas·sa·**por**·toh
       — my driving licence
       — la mia patente
       — la **mee**·a pa·**ten**·te

11 My wife and I are on a joint passport
Mia moglie è sul mio passaporto
mee·a **moh**·lye e sool **mee**·o pas·sa·**por**·toh

12 Our children are on this passport
I bambini sono su questo passaporto
ee bam·**bee**·nee **soh**·no soo **kway**·sto pas·sa·**por**·toh

13   I am staying — for two weeks
    Sto — per due settimane
    sto — payr **doo**·e set·tee·**mah**·ne
       — at the hotel Gloria
       — all'albergo Gloria
       — al·lal·**ber**·goh **glo**·rya

14 I have nothing to declare
Non ho niente da dichiarare
nohn o **nyen**·te da dee·kya·**rah**·ray

15 I have the usual allowance of cigarettes and liquor
Ho la quantità permessa di tabacco e di alcool
o la kwan·tee·**ta** payr·**mays**·sa dee ta·**bak**·koh e dee **al**·kol

16 These are for my personal use
Questi sono per il mio uso personale
kway·stee **soh**·no payr eel **mee**·o oo·zoh payr·so·**nah**·le

17 I represent Universal Chemicals
Rappresento la Universal Chemicals
rap·pre·**zen**·to la oo·nee·ver·sal **ke**·mee·kals

18 I am looking for the representative of Alpha Engineering
Cerco il rappresentante dell'Alpha Engineering
chayr·ko eel rap·pre·zen·**tan**·te dell·**lal**·fa en·jee·**nee**·reeng

19 He/she was due to meet me here
Lui/lei doveva incontrarmi qui
loo·eelley do·**vay**·va een·kon·**trar**·mee kwee

20 The people I was to meet have not turned up
Le persone che dovevo incontrare non si sono fatte vedere
le per·**soh**·ne ke do·**vay**·vo een·kon·**trah**·ray nohn see **soh**·no
fat·te ve·**day**·re

Luggage

21	Please take these bags	— to platform 9
	Per favore porti queste	
	valigie	— al binario nove
	payr fa·voh·re por·tee	
	kway·ste va·lee·je	— *al bee·nah·ryoh no·ve*
		— to a taxi
		— ad un tassí
		— *ad oon tas·see*
22	My luggage	— has not arrived
	I miei bagagli	— non sono arrivati
	ee mee·yay ba·ga·lyee	— *nohn soh·no ar·ree·vah·tee*
23	Where is the luggage from	
	the flight	— from London?
	Dove sono i bagagli del	
	volo	— da Londra?
	doh·ve soh·no ee ba·ga·lyee	
	del voh·loh	— *da lohn·dra*

24 Is there a left-luggage office (baggage room)?
C'è un deposito bagagli?
che oon de·po·zee·toh ba·ga·lyee

25	Are there any	— porters?
	Ci sono	— dei portabagagli?
	chee soh·no	— *dey por·ta·ba·ga·lyee*
		— luggage trolleys (carriers)?
		— dei carrelli portabagagli?
		— *dey kar·rel·lee por·ta·ba·ga·lyee*

26 That bag is not mine
Quella valigia non è mia
kwayl·la va·lee·ja nohn e mee·a

27 Where is my other bag?
Dov'è l'altra mia valigia?
doh·ve lal·tra mee·a va·lee·ja

28 The contents of that bag are fragile
Il contenuto di quella valigia è fragile
eel kon·te·noo·toh dee kwayl·la va·lee·ja e frah·jee·le

29 I wish to have my luggage sent on ahead
Vorrei spedire i bagagli in anticipo
vor·rey spe·dee·re ee ba·ga·lyee een an·tee·chee·poh

30 I sent a suitcase in advance. Where do I pick it up?
Ho spedito una valigia in anticipo. Dove la posso ritirare?
o spe·dee·to oo·na va·lee·ja een an·tee·chee·poh doh·ve la pos·so ree·tee·rah·ray

31 That case is specially insured
Quella valigia è assicurata particolarmente
kwayl·la va·lee·ja e as·see·koo·rah·ta par·tee·ko·lar·mayn·te

32 I wish to leave these bags in the left-luggage office
Voglio lasciare queste valigie al deposito bagagli
vo·lyo la·shah·ray kway·ste va·lee·je al de·po·zee·toh ba·ga·lyee

33	I shall pick them up	— this evening/tomorrow
	Le riprenderò	— stasera/domani
	le ree·pren·de·ro	— *sta·say·ra/do·mah·nee*

34 How much is it per suitcase?
Quanto costa per valigia?
kwan·to ko·sta payr va·lee·ja

35 What time do you close?
A che ora chiudete?
a ke oh·ra kyoo·day·te

Airport and flight inquiries

36	Where do I get the bus	— for Leonardo da Vinci
		(Fiumicino) airport?
	Da dove parte il pullman	— per l'aeroporto di Fiumicino?
	da doh·ve par·te eel pool·man	— *payr la·e·ro·por·toh dee*
		fyoo·mee·chee·noh

Where do I get the bus — for the centre of town?
Da dove parte il pullman — per il centro della città?
da **doh**·*ve* **par**·*te eel* **pool**·*man* — *payr eel* **chen**·*troh* **del**·*la* **cheet**·**ta**

37 I wish to check in my luggage — for the Alitalia flight to Turin
Voglio registrare i miei
bagagli — per il volo Alitalia per Torino
vo·*lyo re*·*jee*·**strah**·*ray ee*
mee·**yay** *ba*·**ga**·*lyee* — *payr eel* **voh**·*loh a*·*lee*·**ta**·*lya*
payr to·**ree**·*no*

38 Where is the arrival/departure board?
Dov'è la tabella orario degli arrivi/delle partenze?
doh·**ve** *la ta*·**bel**·*la oh*·**rah**·*ryoh de*·*lyee a*·**ree**·*vee*/**del**·*le par*·**ten**·*tse*

39 At what time will the flight be called?
A che ora sarà annunciato il volo?
a ke **oh**·*ra sa*·**ra** *an*·*noon*·**chah**·*to eel* **voh**·*loh*

40 Which gate do I go to?
A quale uscita mi devo dirigere?
a **kwah**·*le oo*·**shee**·*ta mee de*·*vo dee*·**ree**·*je*·*re*

41 Is there a snack bar/duty-free shop in the departure lounge?
C'è un buffé/duty-free nella sala imbarco?
che *oon boof*·**fe**/*dyoo*·*tee*·**free** *nel*·*la* **sah**·*la eem*·**bar**·*koh*

42 Will a meal be served on the plane?
Verrà servito un pasto sull'aereo?
ver·**ra** *ser*·**vee**·*to oon pa*·*stoh sool*·*la*·*e*·*re*·*oh*

43 What are weather conditions like for the flight?
Che tempo si prevede per il volo?
ke **tem**·*poh see pre*·**vay**·*de payr eel* **voh**·*loh*
(for answers see "The weather" under "Making conversation",
p.65)

44 Can I change my seat?
Posso cambiare posto?
pos·*so kam*·**byah**·*ray* **poh**·*stoh*

I should like to be — near the front/the window
Vorrei stare — davanti/vicino al finestrino
vor·**rey** **stah**·*ray* — *da*·**van**·*tee*/*vee*·**chee**·*no al*
fee·*ne*·**stree**·*noh*

45 I suffer from airsickness
Soffro di mal d'aria
sof·*fro dee mal* **dah**·*rya*

46 I should like to speak to the airport police
Vorrei parlare con la polizia dell'aeroporto
vor·**rey** *par*·**lah**·*ray kohn la po*·*lee*·**tsee**·*a del*·*la*·*e*·*ro*·**por**·*toh*

47 I am meeting somebody arriving on a flight from Madrid
Incontro qualcuno che arriva con il volo da Madrid
een·**kohn**·*tro kwal*·**koo**·*no ke ar*·**ree**·*va kohn eel* **voh**·*loh da ma*·**dreed**

48 At what time do you expect the flight from Madrid to arrive?
A che ora è previsto l'arrivo del volo da Madrid?
a ke **oh**·*ra e pre*·**vee**·*sto lar*·**ree**·*voh del* **voh**·*loh da ma*·**dreed**

Trains

The Italian railway system is comprehensive and not expensive, so if you
are travelling from town to town it is probably the best way to go —
better than by bus, and sometimes even than by car.

Inquiring

Inquiring at large Italian stations is often difficult, with long queues
outside the English-speaking Ufficio Informazioni Turistiche. You might
be better off to read the timetables (the Italians take a delight in a code
of numerous coloured symbols) or to go straight to the ticket office. Here
are some of the questions you will want to ask. Note that the Italian
name of most major Italian (or foreign) cities is not the same as the
English one. For numerals and the time, see pp. 68, 69.

49 Where is the ticket office/
    timetable board please?
Dov'è la biglietteria/tabella
    degli orari per favore?
*doh·ve la bee·lyayt·te·ree·al
    ta·bel·la de·lyee oh·rah·ree
    payr fa·voh·re*

50 I want to go to Milan
Voglio andare a Milano
vo·lyo an·dah·ray a mee·lah·no

51 What are the times of trains
    between 8 a.m. and noon?
Qual è l'orario dei treni fra le
    otto e mezzogiorno?
*kwahl e loh·rah·ryoh dey
    tre·nee fra le ot·to e
    medz·dzo·johr·noh*

52 Which is the fastest train?
Qual è il treno piú veloce?
*kwahl e eel tre·noh pyoo
    ve·loh·che*

53 When does the next/last train
    for Genoa leave?
Quando parte il prossimo/
    l'ultimo treno per Genova?
*kwan·do par·te eel
    pros·see·mo/lool·tee·mo
    tre·noh payr je·no·va*

54 Is it an express?
È un rapido?
e oon ra·pee·doh

55 What time does the train get
    there?
A che ora ci arriva il treno?
*a ke oh·ra chee ar·ree·va eel
    tre·noh*

56 Do I have to change?
Devo cambiare?
de·vo kam·byah·ray

Tickets and reservations

Between the major cities there are special deluxe, air-conditioned trains,
called *super-rapidi*, which require reservations (for which there is an
extra charge), and in summer you would be advised to book well in
advance. Expresses are called *rapidi*, and are not to be confused with
espressi, which are sometimes not much faster than the *diretti*, while the
locali can be very slow indeed.

   Children under ten pay half-fare, and under four travel free. If you
want to travel around you can get a *biglietto chilometrico*, which allows
you to travel at a reduced rate over a specified distance. If you travel at
night you can reserve a sleeper (*vagone letto*) or, more cheaply, a
couchette (*cuccetta*), which is a simple berth with blankets in a
compartment shared by several passengers.

   Be warned that there are seldom snack bars on Italian trains. But you
can buy mineral water, wine and sandwiches (at high prices) at any
station of any size.

57   A single — to Mantua
Uno andata — per Mantova, per favore
oo·no an·dah·ta — payr man·to·va payr fa·voh·re

58   A return (round trip) — to Florence, please
Uno andata e ritorno — per Firenze, per favore
*oo·no an·dah·ta e
    ree·tohr·noh — payr fee·ren·tse payr fa·voh·re*

59   A child's return — to Venice
Uno andata e ritorno
    ridotto — per Venezia
*oo·no an·dah·ta e
    ree·tohr·noh ree·doht·to — payr ve·nay·tsya*

60 He is under ten
Ha meno di dieci anni
a may·no dee dye·chee an·nee

61   A first-class ticket — to Rome, please
Un biglietto di prima classe — per Roma, per favore
*oon bee·lyayt·toh dee
    pree·ma klas·se — payr roh·ma payr fa·voh·re*

62   I want to reserve — a seat on the *rapido* to Naples
Voglio prenotare — un posto sul rapido per Napoli
*vo·lyo pre·no·tah·ray — oon poh·stoh sool ra·pee·doh payr
    nah·po·lee*

— a couchette on the 22:00 to
    Bologna
— una cuccetta sul treno delle
    ventidue per Bologna
*— oo·na koo·chayt·ta sool tre·noh
    del·le ven·tee·doo·e payr
    bo·loh·nya*

I want to reserve	— two places on the sleeper to Sicily
Voglio prenotare	— due posti sul vagone letto per la Sicilia
***vo·*lyo pre·no·*tah·*ray**	— *doo·*e *poh·*stee sool va·*goh·*ne *let·*to payr la *see·*chee·lya

63 There are no seats left on that train
Non c'è piú nessun posto su quel treno
nohn che pyoo nes·soon poh·stoh soo kwayl tre·noh

64 Very well, when can I book a seat?
Allora, quando posso prenotare un posto?
al·loh·ra kwan·do pos·so pre·no·tah·ray oon poh·stoh

65 Write it down for me, please
Me lo scriva, per favore
may lo skree·va payr fa·voh·re

66 I'll take that, then
Prendo quello, allora
pren·do kwayl·lo al·loh·ra

67 How much does it cost to go to Bologna?
Quanto costa per andare a Bologna?
kwan·to ko·sta payr an·dah·ray a bo·loh·nya

68	I would like a place	— by the window
	Vorrei un posto	— accanto al finestrino
	*vor·***rey** oon *poh·*stoh	— ak·**kan·**to al fee·ne·**stree·**noh
		— in a smoking compartment
		— in uno scompartimento per fumatori
		— *een ***oo·**no skom·par·tee·**mayn·**toh payr foo·ma·**toh·**ree

---

Station and journey

69 Which platform do I go to for the Padua train?
A quale binario prendo il treno per Padova?
a kwah·le bee·nah·ryoh pren·do eel tre·noh payr pah·do·va

70 Is this the right platform for Florence?
È questo il binario giusto per Firenze?
e kway·sto eel bee·nah·ryoh joo·sto payr fee·ren·tse

71 Is this the Florence express?
È questo il rapido per Firenze?
e kway·sto eel ra·pee·doh payr fee·ren·tse

72 When do we get to Chiusi?
Quando arriviamo a Chiusi?
kwan·do ar·ree·vyah·mo a kyoo·see

73 Do we stop at Perugia?
Si ferma a Perugia?
see fayr·ma a pe·roo·ja

74 Is this a through train?
È un treno diretto questo?
e oon tre·noh dee·ret·to kway·sto

75 Where do I have to change for Perugia?
Dove devo cambiare per Perugia?
doh·ve de·vo kam·byah·ray payr pe·roo·ja

76 Is this seat taken?
Questo posto è occupato?
kway·sto poh·stoh e ok·koo·pah·to

77 This is my seat
Questo è il mio posto
kway·sto e eel mee·o poh·stoh

78 Can you help me with my bags, please?
Mi può aiutare con le valigie, per favore?
mee pwo a·yoo·tah·ray kohn le va·lee·je payr fa·voh·re

79 May I open/shut the window?
Posso aprire/chiudere il finestrino?
pos·so a·pree·re/kyoo·de·re eel fee·ne·stree·noh

80 This is a nonsmoking compartment
Questo è uno scompartimento per non-fumatori
kway·sto e oo·no skom·par·tee·mayn·toh payr nohn·foo·ma·toh·ree

81 Are we in Arezzo yet?
Siamo già ad Arezzo?
syah·mo ja ad a·rayts·tso

82 Are we on time?
Siamo in orario?
syah·mo een oh·rah·ryoh

83 Is a delay as long as this usual?
È normale un ritardo cosí lungo?
e nor·mah·le oon ree·tar·doh ko·see loon·go

Buses and subways

Italian towns and cities, and to a lesser degree their suburbs, are well
served by buses (or, in Venice, by boat-buses, *vaporetti*), supplemented
in Rome, Milan and Naples by a subway or underground. Usually you
are required to buy your (fixed-fare) ticket first and surrender it to the
driver or conductor when you get on; if you are using public transport at
all frequently it is well worth buying a set of these tickets, on sale near
the stop at newsstands, cafés or special booths (but sometimes
unobtainable at night).

84 One ticket, please
    Un biglietto, per favore
    oon bee-lyayt-toh payr fa-voh-re

85 A set of ten tickets, please
    Un blocchetto di dieci biglietti, per favore
    oon blok-kayt-toh dee dye-chee bee-lyayt-tee payr fa-voh-re

86 Where can I buy a ticket — for the bus?
    Dove posso comprare dei
                  biglietti — per l'autobus?
    doh-ve pos-so kom-prah-ray
    dey bee-lyayt-tee — payr low-to-boos
                       — for the subway?
                       — per la metropolitana?
                       — *payr la me-tro-po-lee-tah-na*

87 Which bus do I take — for the Piazza Navona?
    Quale autobus devo
                prendere — per Piazza Navona?
    kwah-le ow-to-boos de-vo
    pren-de-re — payr pyats-tsa na-voh-na

88 Where do I get a bus for — Leonardo da Vinci airport
                               (Fiumicino)?
    Da dove posso prendere un
                    pullman — per Fiumicino?
    da doh-ve pos-so pren-de-re
    oon pool-man — payr fyoo-mee-chee-no

89 Does this bus go — to the Vatican?
    Questo autobus va — al Vaticano?
    kway-sto ow-to-boos va — al va-tee-kah-no

90 I want to go — to Santa Maria della Salute
    Voglio andare — a Santa Maria della Salute
    vo-lyo an-dah-ray — a san-ta ma-ree-a del-la sa-loo-te

91 Where should I change?
    Dove devo cambiare?
    doh-ve de-vo kam-byah-ray

92 And then, what number do I take?
    E poi, quale numero devo prendere?
    e poy kwah-le noo-me-roh de-vo pren-de-re

93 Can you tell me when to get off?
    Può dirmi quando devo scendere?
    pwo deer-mee kwan-do de-vo shayn-de-re

94 Should I get out at the next stop for the Cathedral?
    Devo scendere alla prossima fermata per il Duomo?
    de-vo shayn-de-re al-la pros-see-ma fer-mah-ta payr eel dwo-moh

95 How long does it take to get to Fiesole?
    Quanto tempo ci vuole per andare a Fiesole?
    kwan-to tem-poh chee vwo-le payr an-dah-ray a fye-so-le

Taxis

Taxis should be picked up at a stand rather than hailed, or they can be
telephoned for. Make sure it is a proper taxi with a meter — if it is a
pirate taxi you will have to pay a lot more than the going fare. Tell the
driver where you want to go just by stating your destination and saying

"per favore" (pronounced *payr fa·voh·re* — "please"). The following phrases may also be useful:

96 Can you order me a taxi?
   Può chiamarmi un tassì?
   pwo kya·mar·mee oon tas·see
97 Where can I get a taxi?
   Dove posso prendere un tassì?
   doh·ve pos·so pren·de·re oon tas·see
98   Please take me — to this address
   Per favore mi porti — a questo indirizzo
   payr fa·voh·re mee por·tee — a kway·sto een·dee·reets·tsoh
99   How much is the fare — to/from the airport?
   Quanto costa andare — all'/dall'aeroporto?
   kwan·to ko·sta an·dah·ray — al/dal·la·e·ro·por·toh

100 Please drive us around the town
    Per favore, ci porti a fare un giro per la città
    payr fa·voh·re chee por·tee a fah·ray oon jee·roh payr la cheet·ta
101 Would you put the luggage in the boot (trunk)?
    Può mettere i bagagli nel portabagagli?
    pwo mayt·te·re ee ba·ga·lyee nel por·ta·ba·ga·lyee
102 I'm in a hurry
    Ho fretta
    o frayt·ta
103 Please wait here for a few minutes
    Per favore, aspetti qui un po'
    payr fa·voh·re a·spet·tee kwee oon po

104 Turn left/right, please
    Giri a sinistra/destra, per favore
    jee·ree a see·nee·stra/de·stra payr fa·voh·re
105 Stop here, please
    Si fermi qui, per favore
    see fayr·mee kwee payr fa·voh·re
106 How much is that, please?
    Quant'è, per favore?
    kwan·te payr fa·voh·re
107 Keep the change
    Tenga il resto
    ten·ga eel re·stoh

Motoring

There are some disadvantages to motoring in Italy. On the whole, the roads are twisty and narrow and often crowded. Much of the country is mountainous. Some of the motorways, notoriously the Florence/Bologna *autostrada*, are overused, so that driving on them is unpleasant and nerve-wracking; but others are perfectly all right and the network is fairly complete. In the cities, traffic is dense, jams are frequent and drivers are impatient — the anarchy of the Naples rush-hour is famous. Avoid driving in cities you do not know reasonably well. The Italians have a reputation for bad driving that is not justified — they take a delight in their skill, but this can look risky. Petrol and car-hire are expensive, even by European standards. On the other hand, there is no better way of seeing the Italian countryside and small towns than by car.

Renting a car

108 A hired car should be ready for me
    Ci dovrebbe essere pronta una macchina noleggiata per me
    chee do·vreb·be es·se·re prohn·ta oo·na mak·kee·na no·lej·jah·ta payr may
109 I arranged it through the Speed-Link fly-drive service
    L'ho prenotata tramite il servizio "Speed-Link/aereo più macchina"
    lo pre·no·tah·ta trah·mee·te eel sayr·vee·tsyoh speed·link/a·e·re·oh pyoo mak·kee·na
110   I want to rent a car — to drive myself
    Voglio noleggiare una macchina — da guidare personalmente
    vo·lyo no·lej·jah·ray oo·na mak·kee·na — da gwee·dah·ray per·so·nal·mayn·te

        — with a chauffeur
        — con autista
        — *kohn ow·tee·sta*

111   I want it — for five days
       La voglio — per cinque giorni
       la vo·lyo — *payr cheen·kwe johr·nee*

112   What is the charge — per day/per week?
       Quanto costa — al giorno/alla settimana?
       kwan·to ko·sta — *al johr·noh/al·la set·tee·mah·na*

113 Is the mileage unlimited?
    Il chilometraggio è illimitato?
    eel kee·lo·me·traj·joh e eel·lee·mee·tah·to

114   Do you have a car that is — larger/cheaper?
       Avete una macchina — più grande/meno cara?
       a·vay·te oo·na mak·kee·na — *pyoo gran·de/may·no kah·ra*

115 My wife/my husband will be driving as well
    Anche mia moglie/mio marito guiderà
    an·ke mee·a moh·lye/mee·o ma·ree·toh gwee·de·ra

116 I should like comprehensive insurance
    Vorrei un'assicurazione contro tutti i rischi
    vor·rey oo·nas·see·koo·ra·tsyoh·ne kohn·tro toot·tee ee ree·skee

117 Must I return the car here?
    Devo riportare la macchina qui?
    de·vo ree·por·tah·ray la mak·kee·na kwee

118 I should like to leave the car in Rimini
    Vorrei lasciare la macchina a Rimini
    vor·rey la·shah·ray la mak·kee·na a ree·mee·nee

119 I should like the car delivered to my hotel
    Vorrei che mi consegnasse la macchina al mio albergo
    vor·rey ke mee kon·se·nya·ste la mak·kee·na al mee·o al·ber·goh

120 Please show me how to operate the controls
    Mi faccia vedere come funziona la macchina, per favore
    *mee fach·cha ve·day·re koh·me foon·tsyoh·na la mak·kee·na payr
    fa·voh·re*

121 Please explain the car documents
    Per favore mi spieghi i documenti di noleggio
    payr fa·voh·re mee spee·e·gee ee do·koo·mayn·tee dee no·lej·joh

Parking

In busy towns parking is usually a headache, and sometimes impossible.
Although parking meters have appeared in Italian cities, they have not
replaced supervised parking areas, where you must pay the attendant and
park where he directs you: these are your best hope, although they are
often situated outside the centre. Sometimes you will find streets where
parking is allowed on one side only on even-numbered dates, on the
other side only on odd-numbered dates. There are also disk zones, in
which you are required to leave a special disk on your windscreen, which
shows when you arrived and so by what time you should leave.

122 Where can I park?
    Dove posso parcheggiare?
    doh·ve pos·so par·kej·jah·ray

123 Can I park here?
    Posso parcheggiare qui?
    pos·so par·kej·jah·ray kwee

124 Are you leaving?
    Va via Lei?
    va vee·a ley

125 Is there a car park (parking
    lot) nearby?
    C'è un parcheggio qui vicino?
    *che oon par·kayj·joh kwee
    vee·chee·no*

126 What time does the car park
    close?
    A che ora chiude il
    parcheggio?
    *a ke oh·ra kyoo·de eel
    par·kayj·joh*

127 How much does it cost per
    hour?
    Quanto costa all'ora?
    kwan·to ko·sta al·loh·ra

128 How long can I leave the car
    here?
    Per quanto tempo posso
    lasciare qui la macchina?
    *payr kwan·to tem·poh pos·so
    la·shah·ray kwee la
    mak·kee·na*

129 I will only be a few minutes
Non sarò che qualche minuto
nohn sa·ro ke kwal·ke mee·noo·toh

130 Do I need a parking disk?
È necessario il disco orario?
e ne·ches·sah·ryo eel dee·skoh oh·rah·ryo

131 Where can I get a parking disk?
Dove posso trovare un disco orario?
doh·ve pos·so tro·vah·ray oon dee·skoh oh·rah·ryo

132 Do I need parking lights?
Devo lasciare accesi i fari di posizione?
de·vo la·shah·ray ach·chay·see ee fah·ree dee po·zee·tsyoh·ne

Road conditions

The quickest way of travelling about Italy is by motorway (*autostrada*), on which you will periodically have to stop to pay a toll (*pedaggio*). These *autostrade* usually have two lanes in each direction and the outer (left) lane is very definitely for overtaking: keep right. The major hazard on motorways is lorries (trucks), which sometimes pull out to pass with total disregard for cars coming up behind.

Both on motorways and on ordinary roads traffic may be restricted by men working on the road (see p.18/19 for signs). In the north snow and ice are a seasonal hazard; sometimes roads further south are also slippery in winter. Road borders tend to be ill-defined, and markings are comparatively rare.

In towns, you will need to know exactly where you are going and exactly how you are going to get there through the system of one-way streets. Traffic jams and tailbacks are frequent, not only in the larger cities.

133 Is there a route that avoids the traffic?
C'è un'altra strada per evitare il traffico?
che oo·nal·tra strah·da payr e·vee·tah·ray eel traf·fee·koh

134 Is there a short-cut/detour?
C'è una scorciatoia/deviazione?
che oo·na skor·cha·to·ya/de·vya·tsyoh·ne

135 Is the traffic heavy?
Il traffico è intenso?
eel traf·fee·koh e een·ten·so

136 What is causing this hold-up?
Perché c'è questo ritardo?
payr·kay che kway·sto ree·tar·doh

137 When will the road be clear?
Quando sarà libera la strada?
kwan·do sa·ra lee·be·ra la strah·da

138 What is the speed limit?
Qual è il limite di velocità?
kwahl e eel lee·mee·te dee ve·lo·chee·ta

139 Is there a toll on this highway?
Si paga il pedaggio su quest'autostrada?
see pah·ga eel pe·daj·joh soo kway·stow·to·strah·da

140 Is the road to Geneva snowed up?
La strada per Ginevra è bloccata dalla neve?
la strah·da payr jee·nay·vra e blok·kah·ta dal·la nay·ve

141 Is the pass open?
È aperto il valico?
e a·per·to eel va·lee·koh

142 Do I need studded tyres/chains?
Devo usare le gomme chiodate/le catene?
de·vo oo·zah·ray le gohm·me kyo·dah·te/le ka·tay·ne

Road signs

Italy uses International Road Signs, but the following notices often appear without an accompanying image.

143 Alt
Stop

144 Attenzione
Danger

145 Entrata
Entrance

146 Lavori in Corso
Road Works

147 Rallentare
Slow

148 Senso Vietato
No Entry

49 Sosta Autorizzata	152 Uscita
Parking Permitted	**Exit**
(within the stated times)	153 Vietato Ingresso Veicoli
50 Sosta Vietata	**No Entry for Vehicles**
No Parking	154 Vietato Transito Autocarri
51 Svolta	**Closed to Heavy Traffic**
Bend/Curve	

Fuel

Petrol (*benzina*) comes in two grades: *normale* (2 star) and the higher-octane and more expensive *super* (4 star). Diesel fuel is also used. See conversion tables (p.72) for fuel quantities and tyre pressures.

55   15 litres of — 2 star
      Quindici litri di — normale
***kween*·dee·*chee* *lee*·tree dee — nor·*mah*·le**
           — 4 star
           — super
           — *soo*·per
           — diesel fuel
           — gasolio
           — ga·*zo*·lyoh

56 20,000 lire worth, please (for numerals, see p.68)
Ventimila lire, per favore
vayn·tee·*mee*·la *lee*·re payr fa·*voh*·re

57 Fill her up, please
Il pieno, per favore
eel *pye*·noh payr fa·*voh*·re

58   Check — the oil
      Controlli — l'olio
      kon·*trol*·lee — *lo*·lyoh
           — the water
           — l'acqua
           — *lak*·kwa
           — the tyre pressure
           — la pressione delle gomme
           — la pres·*syoh*·ne *del*·le *gohm*·me

59 The pressure is 2.3
La pressione è due virgola tre
la pres·*syoh*·ne e *doo*·e *veer*·go·la tray

60 I want some distilled water
Ho bisogno di un po' di acqua distillata
o bee·*zoh*·nyoh dee oon po dee *ak*·kwa dee·*steel*·*lah*·ta

61 Could you clean the windscreen (windshield)?
Potrebbe pulire il parabrezza?
po·*treb*·be poo·*lee*·re eel pa·ra·*braydz*·dza

62 Could you put some water in the windscreen washer?
Potrebbe mettere dell'acqua nel serbatoio dei tergicristalli?
po·*treb*·be *mayt*·te·re del·*lak*·kwa nel ser·ba·*toh*·yoh dey ter·jee·kree·*stal*·lee

63 Can I pay by credit card?
Posso pagare con una carta di credito?
pos·so pa·*gah*·ray kohn *oo*·na *kar*·ta dee *kray*·dee·toh

      Is there — a lavatory/a telephone here?
      C'è — una toilette/un telefono qui?
      che — *oo*·na twa·*let*/oon te·*le*·fo·noh
           kwee

Breakdowns and repairs

64   My car — has broken down
      La mia macchina — è guasta
      la *mee*·a *mak*·kee·na — e *gwa*·sta
           — will not start
           — non parte
           — nohn *par*·te

165 There is something wrong with my car
C'è qualcosa che non va nella mia macchina
che kwal·ko·sa ke nohn va nel·la mee·a mak·kee·na

166 I would like to telephone for emergency road service
Vorrei telefonare al servizio assistenza stradale
vor·rey te·le·fo·nah·ray al ser·vee·tsyoh as·see·sten·tsa stra·dah·le

167   Can you send — a mechanic?
               Può mandare — un meccanico?
         pwo man·dah·ray — oon mek·ka·nee·koh
                    — a breakdown van (tow truck)?
                    — un carro attrezzi?
                    — *oon kar·roh at·trayt·tsee*

168   Can you — take me to the nearest garage?
               Può — portarmi al garage piú vicino?
               pwo — por·tar·mee al ga·rahj pyoo
                    vee·chee·no
                    — give me a tow?
                    — trainarmi?
                    — *tra·ee·nar·mee*
                    — give me a push?
                    — darmi una spinta?
                    — *dar·mee oo·na speen·ta*
                    — give me a can of petrol, please?
                    — darmi una tanica di benzina, per
                      favore?
                    — *dar·mee oo·na ta·nee·ka dee*
                    ben·dzee·na payr fa·voh·re

169 Can you find the trouble?
Riesce a trovare il guasto?
ree·e·she a tro·vah·ray eel gwa·stoh

170 I have run out of petrol
Sono rimasto senza benzina
soh·no ree·ma·sto sen·tsa ben·dzee·na

171 This is broken
Questo è rotto
kway·sto e roht·to

172 It is making a funny noise
C'è un rumore strano
che oon roo·moh·re strah·no

173   The brakes — have something wrong with them
               I freni — hanno un difetto
              ee fre·nee — an·no oon dee·fet·toh

174   The windscreen wipers — are not working
               I tergicristalli — non funzionano
        ee ter·jee·kree·stal·lee — nohn foon·tsyoh·na·no

175 My windscreen has shattered
Il parabrezza è rotto
eel pa·ra·braydz·dza e roht·to

176 I have a flat tyre
Ho una gomma sgonfia
o oo·na gohm·ma zgohn·fya

177 The battery is dead
La batteria è scarica
la bat·te·ree·a e skah·ree·ka

178 The engine is overheating
Il motore surriscalda
eel mo·toh·re soor·ree·skal·da

179 There is a leak in the radiator
Il radiatore perde acqua
eel ra·dya·toh·re per·de ak·kwa

180 I have blown a fuse
Ho fuso un fusibile
o foo·zo oon foo·zee·bee·le

181 There is a bad connection
C'è un contatto difettoso
che oon kon·tat·toh dee·fet·toh·so

182 I have lost the ignition key
Ho perso la chiave di accensione
o per·so la kyah·ve dee ach·chen·syoh·ne

183   I need — a new fan belt
       Ho bisogno di — una nuova cinghia per il
                      ventilatore
       *o bee-zoh-nyoh dee — oo-na nwo-va cheen-gya payr eel
                      ven-tee-la-toh-re*

184   Can you replace — the exhaust pipe?
       Può sostituirmi — il tubo di scappamento?
       pwo so-stee-too-eer-mee — eel too-boh dee skap-pa-mayn-toh

185   Is it serious?
       È una cosa seria?
       e oo-na ko-sa se-rya

186   How long will it take to repair it?
       Quanto tempo ci vorrà per ripararlo?
       kwan-to tem-poh chee vor-ra payr ree-pa-rar-lo

187   Do you have the parts?
       Avete i pezzi di ricambio?
       a-vay-te ee pets-tsee dee ree-kam-byoh

188   Can you repair it for the time being?
       Può sistemarlo per adesso?
       pwo see-ste-mar-lo payr a-des-so

189   Can I have an itemized bill for my insurance company?
       Posso avere un conto dettagliato per la mia compagnia
       di assicurazione?
       *pos-so a-vay-re oon kohn-toh det-ta-lyah-to payr la mee-a
       kom-pa-nyee-a dee as-see-koo-ra-tsyoh-ne*

Accidents and the police

The police in Italy are on the whole well mannered and helpful, and will
naturally tend to be lenient towards foreigners. But that is not something
to take for granted, and there is nothing to be gained by being irritable,
impatient or in a hurry. Very often the police intervene in the directing of
traffic in Italy, and indicate that you should stop if you are moving or
move if you are stationary by blowing a whistle as well as or instead of
gesturing. For a traffic offence, they have the power to fine you on the
spot.

190   I'm very sorry, officer
       Mi dispiace molto, signore
       mee dee-spyah-che mohl-to see-nyoh-re

191   I am a foreigner
       Sono straniero(a)
       soh-no stra-nye-ro(a)

192   I did not see the signal
       Non ho visto il segnale
       nohn o vee-sto eel se-nyah-le

193   I did not know about that regulation
       Non conoscevo quella norma
       nohn ko-no-shay-vo kwayl-la nor-ma

194   I did not understand the sign
       Non ho capito il segnale stradale
       nohn o ka-pee-to eel se-nyah-le stra-dah-le

195   Here is — my driving licence
                       Ecco — la mia patente
       ek-ko — la mee-a pa-ten-te

196   How much is the fine?
       Quant'è la multa?
       kwan-te la mool-ta

197   I was driving at 80 km/h (50 mph) (see Conversion tables, p.72)
       Stavo guidando ad ottanta chilometri all'ora
       stah-vo gwee-dan-do ad ot-tan-ta kee-lo-me-tree al-loh-ra

198   He/she was too close
       Lui/lei era troppo vicino(a)
       loo-ee/ley e-ra trop-po vee-chee-no(a)

199   I did not see him/her
       Non l'ho visto(a)
       nohn lo vee-sto(a)

200 He was driving too fast
Stava guidando troppo forte
stah·va gwee·**dan**·do **trop**·po
for·te

201 He did not stop
Lui non si è fermato
loo·ee nohn see e fer·**mah**·to

202 He did not give way (yield)
Lui non ha dato la precedenza
loo·ee nohn a **dah**·to la
pre·che·**den**·tsa

203 He stopped very suddenly
Lui si è fermato all'improvviso
loo·ee see e fer·**mah**·to
al·leem·prov·**vee**·zo

204 He swerved
Ha sbandato
a zban·**dah**·to

205 The car turned without
signalling
La macchina ha girato senza
mettere la freccia
la **mak**·kee·na a jee·**rah**·to
sen·tsa **mayt**·te·re la
fraych·cha

206 He overtook on a bend
(passed on a curve)
Ha sorpassato in curva
a sor·pas·**sah**·to een **koor**·va

207 His car number (license
number) was . . .
Il suo numero di targa era . . .
eel **soo**·o **noo**·me·roh dee
tar·ga e·ra . . .

208 The road was wet
La strada era bagnata
la **strah**·da e·ra ba·**nyah**·ta

209 I skidded
Ho slittato
o zleet·**tah**·to

210 My brakes failed
I miei freni non hanno
funzionato
ee mee·**yay** fre·nee nohn **an**·no
foon·tsyoh·**nah**·to

211 I could not stop in time
Non ho potuto fermarmi in
tempo
nohn o po·**too**·to fer·**mar**·mee
een **tem**·poh

212 What is your name and
address?
Qual è Suo nome e indirizzo?
kwahl **e soo**·o **noh**·me e
een·dee·**reets**·tsoh

213 What is your insurance
company?
Qual'è la Sua compagnia di
assicurazione?
kwah·**le** la **soo**·a
kom·pa·**nyee**·a dee
as·see·koo·ra·**tsyoh**·ne

214 We should call the police
Dovremmo chiamare la polizia
do·**vrem**·mo kya·**mah**·ray la
po·lee·**tsee**·a

215 Will you please be a witness?
Mi vuol fare da testimone?
mee vwol **fah**·ray da
te·stee·**mo**·ne

216 Do you admit responsibility?
Ammette di essere
responsabile?
am·**mayt**·te dee es·se·re
re·spon·**sah**·bee·le

217 Could we settle in cash now?
Possiamo sistemare la cosa
ora, in contanti?
pos·**syah**·mo see·ste·**mah**·ray la
ko·sa oh·ra een kon·**tan**·tee

Finding the way (F)

Questions

The simplest way to get directions is just to say where you want to go and add "please", as you would with a taxi driver. For example, "Where is the cathedral?" would be "Il duomo, per favore". Here are some other phrases that you may need.

1 I have lost my way
Ho perso la strada
o **per**·so la **strah**·da

2 How do I get to this address?
Come ci arrivo a questo indirizzo?
koh·me chee ar·**ree**·vo a **kway**·sto een·dee·**reets**·tsoh

3   Where is — the station/the cathedral?
Dov'è — la stazione/il duomo?
doh·**ve** — la sta·**tsyoh**·ne/eel **dwo**·moh

4   I would like to go — to the town centre
Vorrei andare — al centro della città
vor·**rey** an·**dah**·ray — al **chen**·troh **del**·la cheet·**ta**

5   We are looking for — the Tourist Information Office
Cerchiamo — l'Ufficio Informazioni Turistiche
cher·**kyah**·mo — loof·**fee**·choh
een·for·ma·**tsyoh**·nee
too·**ree**·stee·ke

6   Can you tell me the way — to the castle?
         Può indicarmi la strada — per il castello?
         *pwo een·dee·**kar**·mee la*
                            *strah·da — payr eel ka·**stel**·loh*

7   Can you show me on the map?
    Può mostrarmi sulla cartina?
    *pwo mo·**strar**·mee sool·la kar·**tee**·na*

8   Where is the nearest post office?
    Dov'è l'ufficio postale piú vicino?
    *doh·ve loof·**fee**·choh po·**stah**·le pyoo vee·**chee**·no*

9   Is there a service station — near here?
         C'è una stazione di servizio — qui vicino?
         *che oo·na sta·**tsyoh**·ne dee*
                            *ser·**vee**·tsyoh — kwee vee·**chee**·no*

10   Is this the right way — to the museum?
         Va bene questa strada — per il museo?
         *va **be**·ne **kway**·sta **strah**·da — payr eel moo·**ze**·oh*

11   Is it far — to the Forum?
                È lontano — per il Foro?
                *e lon·**tah**·no — payr eel **fo**·roh*

12   How far is it — to St Mark's?
           Quant'è distante — San Marco?
           *kwan·**te** dee·**stan**·te — san **mar**·ko*

13 How long does it take to get there?
    Quanto tempo ci vuole per arrivarci?
    ***kwan**·to **tem**·poh chee **vwo**·le payr ar·ree·**var**·chee*

14 Can one walk there?
    Si può andare a piedi?
    *see pwo an·**dah**·ray a **pye**·dee*

15 Is there a bus that goes there?
    C'è un autobus che va la?
    *che oon **ow**·to·boos ke va **la***

16   Which way do I take — for Gaeta?
           Quale via devo prendere — per Gaeta?
           ***kwah**·le **vee**·a **de**·vo
                            pren·de·re — payr ga·e·ta*

17   Do I turn here — for Perugia?
           Devo girare qui — per Perugia?
           ***de**·vo jee·**rah**·ray kwee — payr pe·**roo**·ja*

18   Which is the best route — to Viterbo?
           Qual'è la strada migliore — per Viterbo?
           ***kwah**·le la **strah**·da
                            mee·**lyoh**·re — payr vee·**ter**·bo*

19 Which is the most scenic route?
    Qual'è la strada piú panoramica?
    ***kwah**·le la **strah**·da pyoo pa·no·**ra**·mee·ka*

20 How do I get back on to the motorway?
    Come faccio per rientrare sull'autostrada?
    ***koh**·me **fach**·cho payr ree·en·**trah**·ray sool·low·to·**strah**·da*

21 Where does this road go to?
    Dove porta questa strada?
    ***doh**·ve **por**·ta **kway**·sta **strah**·da*

22 Will we arrive by this evening?
    Arriveremo entro stasera?
    *ar·ree·ve·**ray**·mo **ayn**·tro sta·**say**·ra*

Answers

These are the key phrases of the answer you will receive when you ask for directions. In this case the Italian is given first, with the English below.

23   Lei va — sempre diritto
                      *ley va — **sem**·pre dee·**reet**·to*
                  You go — straight ahead
                         — a destra
                         — *a **de**·stra*
                         — right

Lei va — a sinistra
ley va — *a see·nee·stra*
You go — left

— fino a . . .
— *fee·no a*
— as far as . . .

24   Giri — a destra
jee·ree — *a de·stra*
Turn — right

— a sinistra
— *a see·nee·stra*
— left

25   Continui — verso . . .
kon·tee·nwee — *ver·so*
Keep going straight ahead — towards . . .

— fino a . . .
— *fee·no a*
— until . . .

26   Prenda — la strada per . . .
pren·da — la **strah**·da payr
Take — the road for . . .

— la prima a destra
— *la **pree**·ma a de·stra*
— the first (road) on the right

— la seconda a sinistra
— *la se·**kohn**·da a see·nee·stra*
— the second (road) on the left

27   Attraversi — la strada
at·tra·ver·see — la **strah**·da
Cross — the street

— al passaggio a livello
— *al pas·**saj**·joh a lee·**vel**·loh*
— at the level crossing

— il ponte
— *eel **pohn**·te*
— the bridge

— vicino
— *vee·**chee**·no*
— not far from here

— all'incrocio
— *al·leen·**kroh**·choh*
— at the junction (intersection)

— accanto al teatro
— *ak·**kan**·to al te·**ah**·troh*
— next to the theatre

— dopo il semaforo
— ***doh**·po eel se·**mah**·fo·roh*
— after the traffic lights

— di fronte alla chiesa
— *dee **frohn**·te **al**·la **kye**·za*
— opposite the church

— lassú
— *las·**soo***
— over there

— dietro l'angolo
— ***dye**·tro **lan**·go·loh*
— around the corner

Money (M)

General

1   How much is that — altogether?
Quanto costa — in tutto?
kwan·to **ko**·sta — een **toot**·to

2   How much is it — to get in?
Quanto costa — l'ingresso?
kwan·to **ko**·sta — leen·**gres**·soh

How much is it — for a child?
Quanto costa — per un bambino?
kwan·to ko·sta — payr oon bam·bee·noh
     — per person?
     — a persona?
     — *a per·soh·na*
     — per kilo?
     — al chilo?
     — *al kee·loh*

3 Is there any extra charge?
C'è bisogno di pagare un supplemento?
che bee·zoh·nyoh dee pa·gah·ray oon soop·ple·mayn·toh

4 Is the tip/tax (VAT) included?
È compreso(a) il servizio/l'IVA?
e kom·pray·so(a) eel ser·vee·tsyoh/lee·va

5 Is there a discount for — a group?
Si fa una riduzione per — un gruppo?
see fa oo·na
ree·doo·tsyoh·ne payr — oon groop·poh
     — students?
     — studenti?
     — *stoo·den·tee*
     — senior citizens?
     — cittadini anziani?
     — *cheet·ta·dee·nee an·tsyah·nee*

6 How much of a discount can you give me?
Che riduzione mi fa?
ke ree·doo·tsyoh·ne mee fa

7 Can you give me a 10 percent discount?
Può farmi una riduzione del dieci per cento?
pwo far·mee oo·na ree·doo·tsyoh·ne del dye·chee payr chen·to

8 Can you give me an estimate of the cost?
Può farmi un preventivo del costo?
pwo far·mee oon pre·ven·tee·voh del ko·stoh

9 Do I have to pay a deposit?
Devo pagare una cauzione?
de·vo pa·gah·ray oo·na kow·tsyoh·ne

10 Do I pay in advance or afterwards?
Pago in anticipo oppure dopo?
pah·go een an·tee·chee·po op·poo·re doh·po

11 Can I pay in instalments?
Posso pagare a rate?
pos·so pa·gah·ray a rah·te

12 Do you accept traveller's cheques?
Accettate dei travellers cheques?
ach·chet·tah·te dey tra·vel·lers cheks

13 I wish to pay by credit card
Voglio pagare con una carta di credito
vo·lyo pa·gah·ray kohn oo·na kar·ta dee kray·dee·toh

14 May I have — an itemized bill?
Posso avere — un conto dettagliato?
pos·so a·vay·re — oon kohn·toh det·ta·lyah·to
     — a receipt?
     — una ricevuta?
     — *oo·na ree·che·voo·ta*

15 You have given me the wrong change
Mi ha dato il resto sbagliato
mee a dah·to eel re·stoh zba·lyah·to

16 That's too much for me
Per me costa troppo
payr may ko·sta trop·po

17 I have no money
Non ho soldi
nohn o sol·dee

18 I do not have enough money
Non ho abbastanza soldi
nohn o ab·ba·stan·tsa sol·dee

19 That's all, thank you
Basta cosí, grazie
ba·sta ko·see gra·tsye

20　Can you change a 10,000-lire note into 1,000-lire notes?
　　Può cambiarmi diecimila lire in banconote da mille?
　　***pwo** kam·**byar**·mee dye·chee·**mee**·la **lee**·re een ban·ko·**no**·te da
　　meel·le*

21　Can you give me some small change?
　　Mi può dare degli spiccioli?
　　*mee **pwo** **dah**·ray de·lyee **speech**·cho·lee*

Banks and exchange offices

National banks are usually open from 8:30 a.m. to 1:20 p.m, Monday to
Friday. Changing money will involve two stages — checking and
calculating with a clerk, then collecting the cash from the cashier, at the
cassa. You can also change money at hotels, large stores and, of course,
uffici di cambio (exchange offices), but the rate of exchange there tends
to be less favourable; this is also true of regional banks, *casse di
risparmio*. Exchange offices at airports and major railway stations stay
open at night and over the weekend. Remember that you need your
passport when changing money. You can change not only traveller's
cheques but also draw on personal cheques with a banker's card from the
Eurocheque banks, and on credit cards.

22　　　　　　　　　Will you change — these traveller's cheques?
　　　　　　　　　　Può cambiare — questi travellers cheques?
　　　　　　　***pwo** kam·**byah**·ray — **kway**·stee **tra**·vel·lers cheks*
　　　　　　　　　　　　　　　— these notes?
　　　　　　　　　　　　　　　— queste banconote?
　　　　　　　　　　　　　　　— **kway**·ste ban·ko·**no**·te

23　　What is the exchange rate
　　　　　　　　　　　　for — sterling/dollars?
　　　　Quanto è il cambio per — la sterlina/il dollaro?
　　　***kwan**·to e eel **kam**·byoh*
　　　　　　　　　　　　*payr — la ster·**lee**·na/eel **dol**·la·roh*

24　I would like to withdraw 50,000 lire
　　Vorrei ritirare cinquantamila lire
　　*vor·**rey** ree·tee·**rah**·ray cheen·kwan·ta·**mee**·la **lee**·re*

25　I would like to cash a cheque with my Eurocheque card
　　Vorrei riscuotere un assegno con la mia carta Eurocheque
　　*vor·**rey** ree·**skwo**·te·re oon as·**say**·nyoh kohn la **mee**·a **kar**·ta
　　e·**oo**·ro·chek*

26　I would like to obtain a cash advance with my credit card
　　Vorrei ottenere un anticipo con la mia carta di credito
　　*vor·**rey** ot·te·**nay**·re oon an·**tee**·chee·poh kohn la **mee**·a **kar**·ta dee
　　kray·dee·toh*

27　What is your commission?
　　Quanto prendete di commissione?
　　***kwan**·to pren·**day**·te dee kom·mees·**syoh**·ne*

28　Can you contact my bank to arrange for a transfer of funds?
　　Può mettersi in contatto con la mia banca per organizzare un
　　trasferimento di denaro?
　　***pwo** **mayt**·ter·see een kon·**tat**·toh kohn la **mee**·a **ban**·ka payr
　　or·ga·needz·**dzah**·ray oon tras·fe·ree·**mayn**·toh dee de·**nah**·roh*

29　I have an account with the Bank of X in London/New York
　　Ho un conto aperto con la Banca X di Londra/New York
　　*o oon **kohn**·toh a·**per**·to kohn la **ban**·ka X dee **lohn**·dra/New York*

30　I have made/I wish to make an arrangement with this bank
　　Ho raggiunto/Vorrei raggiungere un accordo con questa banca
　　*o raj·**joon**·to/vor·**rey** raj·**joon**·je·re oon ak·**kor**·doh kohn **kway**·sta
　　ban·ka*

31　I would like to speak to the manager
　　Vorrei parlare con il direttore
　　*vor·**rey** par·**lah**·ray kohn eel dee·ret·**toh**·re*

Accommodation (A)

Hotel reservations and inquiries

Hotels are officially grouped into categories of 1, 2, 3 and 4 stars, plus a
small category of world-class luxury hotels, designated *de luxe*. There are
also *pensioni*, which are usually perfectly adequate, if no more than that;
they are categorized as first, second or third class. Most hotels can handle
a reservation or inquiry in English, but some *pensioni* may not be able to
do so, and if you want to take no chances, this section contains some
things you might wish to say by letter or telephone, or at the reception
desk.

1 Dear Sir

   Egregio Signore
e·gre·jo see·nyoh·re

2   I wish to stay in Perugia — from ... to ...

        Vorrei stare a Perugia — dal ... al ...
vor·rey stah·ray a pe·roo·ja — *dal ... al*
— with my wife
— con mia moglie
— *kohn mee·a moh·lye*
— with my family
— con la mia famiglia
— *kohn la mee·a fa·mee·lya*

3 I wish to stay for three nights

   Vorrei restare per tre notti
vor·rey re·stah·ray payr tray not·tee

4   Can you provide — a single room with toilet and
                                   shower/bath?

        Potreste offrire — una camera singola con
                                   doccia/bagno?
po·tre·ste of·free·re — *oo·na kah·me·ra seen·go·la kohn
dohch·cha/ba·nyoh*
— a room with twin beds?
— una camera a due letti?
— *oo·na kah·me·ra a doo·e let·tee*
— a double room, with a bed for a
   child?
— una camera matrimoniale, con
   letto aggiunto per un bambino?
— *oo·na kah·me·ra
ma·tree·mo·nyah·le kohn
let·toh aj·joon·to payr oon
bam·bee·noh*
— a suite with living room, bedroom,
   bath and toilet?
— un appartamento con salotto,
   camera da letto e bagno?
— *oon ap·par·ta·mayn·toh kohn
sa·lot·toh kah·me·ra da let·toh e
ba·nyoh*

5   I should like a room — that is quiet

      Vorrei una camera — tranquilla
vor·rey oo·na kah·me·ra — *tran·kweel·la*
— with a view
— con vista
— *kohn vee·sta*

I should like a room — on the ground/first floor
Vorrei una camera — al pianterreno/al primo piano
vor·rey oo·na kah·me·ra — *al pyan·ter·ray·noh/al pree·mo pyah·noh*
— with a TV/radio
— con TV/radio
— *kohn tee·voo/ra·dyoh*

6 Please send me a brochure about your hotel
Vogliate inviarmi un opuscolo del vostro albergo
vo·lyah·te een·vyar·mee oon o·poo·sko·loh del vo·stro al·ber·goh

7 Yours faithfully
Distinti saluti
dee·steen·tee sa·loo·tee

8 How much is the room per night?
Quanto costa la camera per una notte?
kwan·to ko·sta la kah·me·ra payr oo·na not·te

9 Is breakfast/tax (VAT) included?
È compresa la colazione/l'IVA?
e kom·pray·sa la ko·la·tsyoh·ne/lee·va

10   How much is it — with breakfast?
Quanto costa — con la prima colazione?
kwan·to ko·sta — *kohn la pree·ma ko·la·tsyoh·ne*
— with breakfast and evening meal?
— la mezza pensione?
— *la medz·dza pen·syoh·ne*
— with all meals?
— la pensione completa?
— *la pen·syoh·ne kom·ple·ta*

11 Do you have a swimming pool/sauna?
Avete la piscina/sauna?
a·vay·te la pee·shee·na/sow·na

12 Can you suggest another hotel that might have a vacancy?
Può indicarmi un altro albergo con posti liberi?
pwo een·dee·kar·mee oon al·tro al·ber·goh kohn poh·stee lee·be·ree

Checking in and out

13 I have reserved a room in the name of Smith
Ho prenotato una camera, a nome Smith
o pre·no·tah·to oo·na kah·me·ra a noh·me smeeth

14 Can I see the room, please?
Posso vedere la camera, per favore?
pos·so ve·day·re la kah·me·ra payr fa·voh·re

15   The room is too — small/noisy
La camera è troppo — piccola/rumorosa
la kah·me·ra e trop·po — *peek·ko·la/roo·mo·roh·sa*

16 When will the room be ready?
Quando sarà pronta la camera?
kwan·do sa·ra prohn·ta la kah·me·ra

17 Where is the bathroom/toilet?
Dov'è il bagno/la toilette?
doh·ve eel ba·nyoh/la twa·let

18 I want to stay an extra night
Vorrei restare un'altra notte
vor·rey re·stah·ray oo·nal·tra not·te

19 We shall be leaving at 9 o'clock tomorrow morning
Partiremo domani mattina alle nove
par·tee·ray·mo do·mah·nee mat·tee·na al·le no·ve

20 By what time do we have to vacate the room?
Per che ora dobbiamo liberare la camera?
payr ke oh·ra dob·byah·mo lee·be·rah·ray la kah·me·ra

21 I would like the bill, please
Il conto, per favore
eel kohn·toh payr fa·voh·re

22 Can I pay by credit card?
Posso pagare con una carta di credito?
pos·so pa·gah·ray kohn oo·na kar·ta dee kray·dee·toh

23   Do you accept — traveller's cheques?
              Accettate — travellers cheques?
              ach·chet·tah·te — *tra·vel·lers cheks*
                      — American Express cards/cheques?
                      — carte di credito/assegni
                           dell'American Express?
                      — *kar·te dee kray·dee·toh/as·say·nyee*
                          del·la·me·ree·kan ek·spres
24 Could you have my luggage brought down/forwarded?
Può far portare giù/spedire i miei bagagli?
pwo far por·tah·ray joo/spe·dee·re ee mee·yay ba·ga·lyee
25 Could you have any letters or messages forwarded?
Può far proseguire la mia posta od eventuali messaggi?
pwo far pro·se·gwee·re la mee·a po·sta od e·ven·twah·lee mes·saj·jee

---

Service and practical needs

26   What time is — breakfast/lunch?
             A che ora c'è — la prima colazione/il pranzo?
             a ke oh·ra che — *la pree·ma ko·la·tsyoh·ne/eel*
                          pran·dzoh
27 Can we have breakfast in our room, please?
Possiamo prendere la prima colazione in camera, per favore?
pos·syah·mo pren·de·re la pree·ma ko·la·tsyoh·ne een kah·me·ra
    payr fa·voh·re
28 Where can I park the car?
Dove posso parcheggiare la macchina?
doh·ve pos·so par·kej·jah·ray la mak·kee·na
29 What time does the hotel close?
A che ora chiude l'albergo?
a ke oh·ra kyoo·de lal·ber·goh
30 Is there a lift (elevator)?
C'è un ascensore?
che oon a·shen·soh·re
31 Can one drink the tap water?
L'acqua del rubinetto è potabile?
lak·kwa del roo·bee·nayt·toh e po·tah·bee·le
32 Please call me at 8 o'clock
Per favore, chiamatemi alle otto
payr fa·voh·re kya·mah·te·mee al·le ot·to
33 Can I leave these for safekeeping?
Posso lasciare queste cose in custodia?
pos·so la·shah·ray kway·ste ko·se een koo·sto·dya
34 Can I have my things back from the safe?
Posso avere le cose che avevo lasciato in cassaforte?
pos·so a·vay·re le ko·se ke a·vay·vo la·shah·to een kas·sa·for·te
35   Can I — make a telephone call from here?
            Posso — fare una telefonata da qui?
            pos·so — *fah·ray oo·na te·le·fo·nah·ta da*
                        kwee
                      — send a telex message from here?
                      — mandare un telex da qui?
                      — *man·dah·ray oon te·leks da kwee*
36 Are there any letters/messages for me?
Ci sono lettere/messaggi per me?
chee soh·no let·te·re/mes·saj·jee payr may
37 I should like a private room for a conference/cocktail party
Vorrei una stanza privata per una riunione/un cocktail party
vor·rey oo·na stan·tsa pree·vah·ta payr oo·na ree·oo·nyoh·ne/oon
    kok·tel par·tee
38 I am expecting a Signor Salutati
Aspetto un certo Signor Salutati
a·spet·to oon cher·to see·nyohr sa·loo·tah·tee
39 Could you call me when he arrives?
Mi può avvisare quando arriva?
mee pwo av·vee·zah·ray kwan·do ar·ree·va
40 Is the voltage 220 or 110?
Il voltaggio è duecentoventi o centodieci?
eel vol·taj·joh e doo·e·chen·to·vayn·tee o chen·to·dye·chee

41	Can I have	— my key?
	Posso avere	— la mia chiave?
	pos·so a·vay·re	— *la mee·a kyah·ve*
		— some soap?
		— del sapone?
		— *del sa·poh·ne*
		— some towels?
		— alcuni asciugamani?
		— *al·koo·nee a·shoo·ga·mah·nee*
		— some notepaper?
		— della carta da scrivere?
		— *del·la kar·ta da skree·ve·re*
		— an ashtray?
		— un portacenere?
		— *oon por·ta·chay·ne·re*
		— another blanket?
		— un'altra coperta?
		— *oo·nal·tra ko·per·ta*
		— another pillow?
		— un altro cuscino?
		— *oon al·tro koo·shee·noh*

42 Where is the socket for my electric razor?
Dov'è la presa per il mio rasoio?
doh·ve la pray·sa payr eel mee·o ra·soh·yoh

43 I cannot open the window
Non riesco ad aprire la finestra
nohn ree·e·sko ad a·pree·re la fee·ne·stra

44 The air conditioning/the heating is not working
L'aria condizionata/il riscaldamento non funziona
lah·rya kon·dee·tsyoh·nah·ta/ eel ree·skal·da·mayn·toh nohn foon·tsyoh·na

45 I cannot turn the heating off
Non riesco a spegnere il riscaldamento
nohn ree·e·sko a spe·nye·re eel ree·skal·da·mayn·toh

46 I want to turn the heating up/down
Voglio alzare/abbassare il riscaldamento
vo·lyo al·tsah·ray/ ab·bas·sah·ray eel ree·skal·da·mayn·toh

47 The lock is broken
La serratura è rotta
la ser·ra·too·ra e roht·ta

48 There is no hot water
Non c'è acqua calda
nohn che ak·kwa kal·da

49 The washbasin is dirty
Il lavandino è sporco
eel la·van·dee·noh e spor·ko

50 The plug is broken
Il tappo è rotto
eel tap·poh e roht·to

51 There is no toilet paper
Non c'è carta igienica
nohn che kar·ta ee·je·nee·ka

52 Do you have a laundry room?
C'è una lavanderia?
che oo·na la·van·de·ree·a

53 I want to iron some clothes
Voglio stirare alcuni vestiti
vo·lyo stee·rah·ray al·koo·nee ve·stee·tee

54 I want some clothes ironed
Vorrei fare stirare alcuni vestiti
vor·rey fah·ray stee·rah·ray al·koo·nee ve·stee·tee

55 Thank you, we enjoyed our stay very much
Grazie, ci siamo trovati molto bene qui
gra·tsye chee syah·mo tro·vah·tee mohl·to be·ne kwee

Rented houses

56 We have arranged to rent a house through your agency
Abbiamo preso una casa in affitto tramite la vostra agenzia
ab·byah·mo pray·so oo·na kah·sa een af·feet·toh trah·mee·te la vo·stra a·jen·tsee·a

57 Here is our reservation
Ecco la nostra prenotazione
ek·ko la no·stra pre·no·ta·tsyoh·ne

58 We need two sets of keys
Abbiamo bisogno di due mazzi di chiavi
ab·byah·mo bee·zoh·nyoh dee doo·e mats·tsee dee kyah·vee

59 Will you show us around?
Può farci vedere la casa?
*pwo far·chee ve·day·re la
kah·sa*

60 Which is the key for this door?
Qual'è la chiave di questa
porta?
*kwah·le la kyah·ve dee
kway·sta por·ta*

61 Is the cost of electricity
included in the rental?
L'elettricità è compresa
nell'affitto?
*le·let·tree·chee·ta e
kom·pray·sa nel·laf·feet·toh*

62 Where is the main switch for
the electricity?
Dov'è l'interruttore principale
dell'elettricità?
*doh·ve leen·ter·root·toh·re
preen·chee·pah·le
del·le·let·tree·chee·ta*

63 Where is the water mains
stopcock?
Dov'è la valvola principale
dell'acqua?
*doh·ve la val·vo·la
preen·chee·pah·le
del·lak·kwa*

64 Where is the water heater?
Dov'è lo scaldabagno?
doh·ve lo skal·da·ba·nyoh

65 Please show me how this
works
Può farmi vedere come
funziona questo?
*pwo far·mee ve·day·re koh·me
foon·tsyoh·na kway·sto*

66 How does the heating work?
Come funziona il
riscaldamento?
*koh·me foon·tsyoh·na eel
ree·skal·da·mayn·toh*

67 When does the maid come?
Quando viene la donna delle
pulizie?
*kwan·do vye·ne la don·na
del·le poo·lee·tsee·e*

68 Is there any spare bedding?
C'è altra biancheria per il
letto?
*che al·tra byan·ke·ree·a payr
eel let·toh*

69 Where can I contact you if
there are any problems?
Dove posso mettermi in
contatto con voi se ci sono
dei problemi?
*doh·ve pos·so mayt·ter·mee
een kon·tat·toh kohn voy se
chee soh·no dey pro·ble·mee*

70 The cooker (stove) does not
work
La cucina non funziona
*la koo·chee·na nohn
foon·tsyoh·na*

71 Where are the dustbins?
Dove sono le pattumiere?
*doh·ve soh·no le
pat·too·mye·re*

72 Where can we get logs for the
fire?
Dove possiamo trovare dei
ceppi per il fuoco?
*doh·ve pos·syah·mo
tro·vah·ray dey chayp·pee
payr eel fwo·koh*

73 I can't open the windows
Non riesco ad aprire le finestre
*nohn ree·e·sko ad a·pree·re le
fee·ne·stre*

74 We can't get any water
Non c'è acqua
nohn che ak·kwa

75 The toilet won't flush
Lo sciacquone non funziona
*lo sha·kwoh·ne nohn
foon·tsyoh·na*

76 The pipe is blocked
Il tubo è ostruito
eel too·boh e o·stroo·ee·to

77 A fuse has blown
È saltato un fusibile
e sal·tah·to oon foo·zee·bee·le

78 There is a gas leak
C'è una perdita di gas
che oo·na per·dee·ta dee gas

79 I need somebody to repair this
Ho bisogno di qualcuno per
riparare questo
*o bee·zoh·nyoh dee
kwal·koo·no payr
ree·pa·rah·ray kway·sto*

Camping

Camping in Italy is a sophisticated activity, with campers bringing lots of
home comforts with them. There are many official camping sites, many
with excellent facilities. Never camp without permission in fields or on
common land, as penalties are severe.

80 Is there anywhere for us to
camp near here?
Si può campeggiare qui vicino?
*see pwo kam·pej·jah·ray kwee
vee·chee·no*

81 Have you got a site for our
tent?
Avete un posto per la nostra
tenda?
*a·vay·te oon poh·stoh payr la
no·stra ten·da*

82 Do you mind if we camp on
your land?
Vi dispiace se campeggiamo
sul vostro terreno?
*vee dee·spyah·che se
kam·pej·jah·mo sool vo·stro
ter·ray·noh*

83 This site is very muddy
Questo posto è molto fangoso
kway·sto **poh**·stoh e **mohl**·to
fan·goh·so

84 Could we have a more
sheltered site?
Possiamo avere un posto più
riparato?
*pos·syah·mo a·vay·re oon
poh·stoh pyoo ree·pa·rah·to*

85 Can we put our caravan
(trailer) here?
Possiamo mettere la nostra
roulotte qui?
*pos·syah·mo mayt·te·re la
no·stra roo·lot kwee*

86 Is there a shop on the site?
C'è un negozio nel camping?
che oon ne·**go**·tsyoh nel
kam·peeng

87 Can I have a shower?
Posso fare una doccia?
pos·so **fah**·ray oo·na
dohch·cha

88 Where is the drinking water?
Dov'è l'acqua potabile?
doh·ve lak·kwa po·tah·bee·le

89 Where are the toilets and
washroom?
Dove sono le toilette e il
bagno?
doh·ve **soh**·no le twa·**let** e eel
ba·nyoh

90 Where can we buy ice?
Dove possiamo comprare del
ghiaccio?
doh·ve pos·**syah**·mo
kom·**prah**·ray del
gyach·choh

91 Where can we wash our
dishes/our clothes?
Dove possiamo lavare i piatti/i
vestiti?
doh·ve pos·**syah**·mo la·**vah**·ray
ee pyat·teelee ve·**stee**·tee

92 Is there another camp site near
here?
C'è un altro camping qui
vicino?
che oon **al**·tro **kam**·peeng kwee
vee·**chee**·noh

93 Are there any washing
machines?
Ci sono lavatrici?
chee soh·no la·va·tree·chee

94 We need to buy a new gas
cylinder
Dobbiamo comprare una
nuova bombola a gas
*dob·byah·mo kom·prah·ray
oo·na nwo·va bohm·bo·la a
gas*

95 I would like to change the
position of my tent
Vorrei cambiare posto
vor·rey kam·byah·ray poh·stoh

Eating out (E)

Italian food is deceptively simple, and much more varied than people
usually believe. Regional traditions of cooking are much stronger, and
more authentic, than anywhere else in Europe. Although the Italian
attitude is more straightforward than, for instance, the French, it does
not prevent them from making imaginative use of local ingredients.

The usual Italian word for restaurant is *trattoria* – which means roughly
"eating house". *Ristorante* implies more attention to the surroundings,
but this does not mean that *trattorie* are primitive. The words *tavola calda*
(literally "hot table") and *pizzeria* (pizza-house) are usually applied to
snack bars (see p.39). If you have your family with you, see "Children"
p.60.

General

1 Do you know — a good restaurant?
Conosce — un buon ristorante?
ko·noh·she — oon bwon ree·sto·ran·te

2 I would like to reserve a
table — for two people
Vorrei prenotare un tavolo — per due persone
*vor·rey pre·no·tah·ray oon
tah·vo·loh — payr doo·e per·soh·ne*
— for 8 o'clock
— per le otto
⇒ *payr le ot·to*

3　I have reserved a table in the name of...
　Ho prenotato un tavolo, a nome...
　*o pre·no·**tah**·to oon **tah**·vo·loh a **noh**·me*

4　Do you have a quiet table by the window/on the terrace?
　Avete un tavolo tranquillo accanto alla finestra/sulla terrazza?
　*a·**vay**·te oon **tah**·vo·loh tran·**kweel**·lo ak·**kan**·to al·la fee·**ne**·stra/**sool**·la ter·**rats**·tsa*

5　Is it possible to have a private room?
　È possibile avere una stanza privata?
　*e pos·**see**·bee·le a·**vay**·re oo·na **stan**·tsa pree·**vah**·ta*

6　It is for a business lunch/dinner
　È per un pranzo/una cena d'affari
　*e payr oon **pran**·dzoh/oo·na **chay**·na daf·**fah**·ree*

7　Signor Colucci is expecting me
　Sono atteso dal Signor Colucci
　*soh·no at·**tay**·so dal see·**nyohr** ko·**looch**·chee*

8　The menu, please
　Il menú, per favore
　*eel me·**noo** payr fa·**voh**·re*

Menu guide

An Italian menu is usually divided up into courses and into types of fare. You can choose the first course under the heading *antipasti* (hors d'oeuvres), *farinacei* or *paste* (different kinds of pasta) or sometimes *minestre* (soups). The main course will be subdivided into *carne* (meat dishes) and *pesce* (fish dishes), often with *contorni* (vegetables) listed separately. Desserts are sometimes called *postre*. There will normally also be specialities (*specialità*) of the day, listed separately or announced by the waiter or waitress.

There follows an alphabetical list, Italian first, English below. It is intended as a supplement to the dictionary, where basic words for beef, ham, eggs, etc are listed: it explains some of the more common specialist terms you may meet.

Hors d'oeuvres, vegetables and main dishes

Abbacchio　Baby lamb

Baccalà alla livornese　Salt cod with vegetables and tripe

Bagna calda　Literally a "hot bath", made of olive oil, butter, chopped anchovies and garlic, into which you dip raw vegetables

Bistecca alla fiorentina　A large charcoal-grilled steak

Bollito misto　Mixed boiled meats with a green sauce

Braciolette ripiene　Small stuffed veal rolls

Brodetto di pesce　Highly seasoned fish soup

Buridda　A fish stew (Liguria, Sardinia)

Cacciucco alla livornese　Fish stew flavoured with sage and garlic

Calamari in umido　Squid in oil

Calzone　A kind of pizza

Cannelloni　Large tubes of pasta, stuffed

Caponata　Aubergines (eggplants), peppers, courgettes (zucchini), onions, tomatoes, celery, pine nuts, garlic and herbs, cooked in oil

Cappelletti in brodo　Pasta stuffed with meat in broth

Cappon magro　Fish salad in a garlic and caper sauce

Carpaccio　Raw, lean beef in slices

Castrato　Mutton

Cima alla genovese　Veal with a vegetable and sausage meat stuffing, served cold

Cinghiale in agrodolce　Wild boar in a sweet-sour sauce

Cotechino　Mild pork salami, served hot in slices

Crostini di fegatini　Fried bread with chicken liver pâté

Farsu magru　Beef roll stuffed with egg, cheese and salami

Fettuccine　Flat strips of egg pasta similar to tagliatelle

Finanziera di pollo　Chicken giblet stew

Frittata　Omelette

Fritto misto　Mixed grill

Fritto misto di mare　Mixed fried shellfish

Gnocchi Dumplings of semolina or potato or maize

Granatina Fried minced beef cake

Involtini Rolls of veal, with chicken or ham filling

Lasagne A wide flat pasta, often made with spinach (*lasagne verde*)

Macaroni (maccheroni) Tubular pasta

Malfattini in brodo Grains of pasta in broth

Maniche A short tubular pasta

Mazzafegati Liver sausage

Medaglioni alla primavera Medallions of veal with a mushroom sauce

Minestrone (alla genovese) Vegetable soup (flavoured with pesto, a cheese and herb mixture)

Noce di vitello arrosto Roast top round of veal

Osso buco Shin of veal cooked in wine

Paglia e fieno Literally "straw and hay", a mixture of white and green tagliatelle with a meat sauce

Panata A kind of pancake in broth

Panzerotti Fried pasta casings, with a filling of mozzarella and ham

Pappardelle con la lepre Wide strips of pasta served in a sauce made from rabbit

Passatelli in brodo A mixture of egg, cheese and breadcrumbs, rolled into dumplings, and cooked in stock

Pasticcio Pasta cooked in a sort of pie

Penne all'arrabbiata "Quills" of pasta with tomato, bacon and red pepper sauce

Peperonata Cold sweet peppers cooked in oil

Piccata di Marsala Escalope of veal in Marsala wine

Piselli alla toscana Peas with ham

Pizza capricciosa Pizza with whatever filling the cook likes

Pizza rustica A pasta pie, with sausage, egg, cheese and vegetables

Polenta Maize flour served in various ways

Polpettone Meat roll of minced veal, ham, cheese, etc; or a fish roll

Porchetta Roast suckling pig

Prosciutto di Parma The best cured ham from Parma

Ravioli Pasta casings stuffed with spinach, ricotta and herbs or with meats

Ribollita Soup of white beans and other vegetables

Risi e bisi A soup with rice and peas in chicken stock

Sa cassola A fish stew (Sardinia)

Saltimbocca Veal with ham and sage

Salume Various types of sausages

Sa merca Rock mullet (Sardinia)

Sartù di riso A rice dish with meat, cheese and vegetables

Scaloppa milanese Thin veal cutlet in breadcrumbs

Scaloppine Thin slices of veal

Spaghetti alla carbonara Spaghetti with chopped bacon and beaten eggs

Stracciatella Consommé with eggs stirred in

Strecchini alla bolognese Fried chicken livers, sweetbreads, etc, skewered with slices of cheese, then cooked in the oven in a white sauce

Strufoli Little onion- and herb-flavoured pasties, deep-fried

Supplì Little balls of cream cheese and rice, covered in egg and breadcrumbs and fried

Taccula Small migrant birds caught and roasted (Sardinia)

Tagliatelle Ribbon-like pasta

Tortelli A kind of ravioli

Tortellini alla bolognese Little coils of egg pasta with a savoury filling, topped with either cheese and butter or cream

Trenette al pesto A variety of tagliatelle with a sauce of basil, pine nuts, garlic and pecorino cheese

Trippa alla fiorentina Tripe in tomato sauce, served with Parmesan cheese

Uccelletti di campagna Not "birds" but thin slices of rolled beef

Vermicelli Spaghetti in thin strings

Vincigrassi A pie with lasagne and meat in a smooth sauce

Vitello tonnato Cold veal in tuna sauce

Zampone Stuffed pig's trotter

Zuppa alla pavese Fried bread, eggs and Parmesan cheese in broth

Desserts

Castagnaccio Chestnut-flavoured cake

Composta di frutta Fruit salad

Crostata Flan

Gelato Ice cream

Granita An ice made with fruit syrup and water

Zabaglione Whipped egg yolks with Marsala wine

Zuppa inglese Trifle

Cheeses

Mozzarella A soft, mild, white cheese

Pecorino A hard cheese made from ewe's milk

Ricotta A soft white cheese made from ewe's milk

Taleggio A mild creamy cheese

Wines

It may surprise some readers to know that Italy produces and drinks more wine per capita than any other country in the world. Italian wines come in white (*bianco*), red (*rosso*) and rosé (*rosato*). They have two official categories: DOC (*Denominazione di Origine Controllata*), which implies a certain minimum standard but is in practice erratic; and DOCG (the above with *e garantita* added), which is awarded to only a few top wines and is the real guarantee of quality. The following list includes some of the best-known types of wine as well as a number of terms that you may find useful to know.

Abboccato Semi-sweet

Amabile Sweeter than abboccato

Amaro Bitter

Asti The sparkling Asti Spumante is well known, but several red and white wines also come from this district

Barbaresco Dry red wine

Barbera Grape used for red wine

Barolo One of the best Italian red wines

Cantina Sociale Growers' co-operative

Chianti The famous red wine sometimes sold in a wicker-covered bottle

Chiaretto Very light red

Classico Best wines of a region

Colli Hills (in wine name)

Dolce Sweet

Est! Est! Est! A well-known white wine from near Rome

Frascati A white wine from near Rome. From dry to sweet, depending on the variety

Freisa A light red wine, sweet, often sparkling

Frizzante Semi-sparkling

Lacrima Christi del Vesuvio A full-bodied red wine from Campania; there is also a white

Lambrusco A slightly sparkling red wine

Liquoroso Strong and sweet

Malvasia di Lipari One of the best-known dessert wines

Marsala Dark dessert wine from Sicily

Merlot del Trentino A dry red wine

Montepulciano, Vino Nobile di A red wine from Tuscany that ages well in bottle

Moscato A dessert wine (strictly a grape variety)

Nebbiolo d'Alba A light red wine, typically dry

Pinot Bianco A dry white wine

Riserva Wine aged in casks

Sangiovese A good red wine

Savuto A dry red wine from Calabria

Secco Dry

Soave Famous dry white wine from Verona

Spumante Sparkling

Tocai del Friuli A dry white wine

Valpolicella A light red wine

Verdicchio dei Castelli di Iesi A dry white wine from the Marche

Verduzzo A dry white wine

Vernaccia   A sweet white wine, served as an aperitif

Vino da pasto   Table wine

Ordering wine

9 May we see the wine list, please?
   Possiamo vedere la lista dei vini, per favore?
   *pos-**syah**-mo ve-**day**-re la **lee**-sta dey **vee**-nee payr fa-**voh**-re*

10 Can you recommend a good local wine?
   Ci può consigliare un buon vino locale?
   *chee pwo kon-see-**lyah**-ray oon bwon **vee**-noh lo-**kah**-le*

11 A bottle/carafe of house wine
   Una bottiglia/caraffa di vino della casa
   *oo-na bot-**tee**-lya/ka-**raf**-fa dee **vee**-noh **del**-la **kah**-sa*

12 Another bottle/half bottle, please
   Un'altra bottiglia/bottiglia da mezzo litro, per favore
   *oo-**nal**-tra bot-**tee**-lya/bot-**tee**-lya da **medz**-dzo **lee**-troh payr fa-**voh**-re*

13 Would you bring another glass, please?
   Può portare un altro bicchiere, per favore?
   *pwo por-**tah**-ray oon **al**-tro beek-**kye**-re payr fa-**voh**-re*

14 What liqueurs do you have?
   Quali liquori avete?
   *kwah-lee lee-**kwoh**-ree a-**vay**-te*

Ordering the meal and paying

15 Do you have a set menu?
   Avete un menú fisso?
   *a-**vay**-te oon me-**noo fees**-so*

16 I will take the set menu — at 20,000 lire
   Prendo il menú fisso — a ventimila lire
   ***pren**-do eel me-**noo fees**-so — a vayn-tee-**mee**-la **lee**-re*

17 What would you recommend?
   Che cosa ci consigliate?
   *ke **ko**-sa chee kon-see-**lyah**-te*

18 Is this good?
   È buono questo?
   *e **bwo**-no **kway**-sto*

19 How is this dish cooked?
   Qual'è la ricetta per questo piatto?
   *kwah-**le** la ree-**chet**-ta payr **kway**-sto **pyat**-toh*

20 Do you have a local speciality?
   Avete delle specialità locali?
   *a-**vay**-te **del**-le spe-cha-lee-**ta** lo-**kah**-lee*

21 I'll take that
   Prendo quello
   ***pren**-do **kwayl**-lo*

22 We will begin — with spaghetti with tomato sauce
   Cominceremo — con spaghetti al pomodoro
   *ko-meen-che-**ray**-mo — kohn spa-**get**-tee al po-mo-**do**-roh*

23 I will have — steak and chips (French fries)
   Prendo — una bistecca con patatine fritte
   ***pren**-do — **oo**-na bee-**stayk**-ka kohn pa-ta-**tee**-ne **freet**-te*

24 I like steak — very rare
   Mi piace la bistecca — proprio al sangue
   *mee **pyah**-che la bee-**stayk**-ka — **pro**-pryo al **san**-gwe*
   — rare
   — al sangue
   *— al **san**-gwe*
   — medium rare
   — poco cotta
   *— **po**-ko **kot**-ta*
   — well done
   — ben cotta
   *— ben **kot**-ta*

25 Are vegetables included?
È compreso anche il contorno?
e kom·pray·so an·ke eel kon·tohr·noh
26 Is this cheese very strong?
È molto forte questo formaggio?
e mohl·to for·te kway·sto for·maj·joh
27 This is not what I ordered
Non ho ordinato questo
nohn o or·dee·nah·to kway·sto
28 Does the fish come with anything else?
Servite un contorno con il pesce?
ser·vee·te oon kon·tohr·noh kohn eel pay·she
29 That is for — me
Quello è per — me
kwayl·lo e payr — may
— him/her
— il Signore/la Signora
— *eel see·nyoh·re/la see·nyoh·ra*

30 Some more bread/water, please
Ancora un po' di pane/Ancora dell'acqua, per favore
an·koh·ra oon po dee pah·ne/an·koh·ra del·lak·kwa payr fa·voh·re
31 Could I have some butter?
Posso avere del burro, per favore?
pos·so a·vay·re del boor·roh payr fa·voh·re
32 What is this called?
Come si chiama questo?
koh·me see kyah·ma kway·sto
33 This is very salty
Questo è molto salato
kway·sto e mohl·to sa·lah·to
34 I wanted cheese
Volevo del formaggio
vo·lay·vo del for·maj·joh
35 Have you forgotten the soup?
Avete dimenticato la minestra?
a·vay·te dee·men·tee·kah·to la mee·ne·stra
36 This is cold
Questo è freddo
kway·sto e frayd·do
37 This is very good
Questo è molto buono
kway·sto e mohl·to bwo·no
38 I'll have a dessert
Prenderò il dolce
pren·de·ro eel dohl·che
39 Could I have a salad instead of the cheese course?
Posso avere un'insalata invece del formaggio?
pos·so a·vay·re oo·neen·sa·lah·ta een·vay·che del for·maj·joh

40 What do you have for dessert?
Cosa avete come dolce?
ko·sa a·vay·te koh·me dohl·che
41 Nothing else, thank you — except coffee
Niente altro, grazie — salvo il caffè
nyen·te al·tro gra·tsye — sal·vo eel kaf·fe
42 Waiter, could we have the bill, please?
Cameriere, il conto, per favore
ka·me·rye·re eel kohn·toh payr fa·voh·re
43 We are in a hurry
Abbiamo fretta
ab·byah·mo frayt·ta
44 Is service included?
Il servizio è compreso?
eel ser·vee·tsyoh e kom·pray·so
45 There seems to be a mistake here
Sembra che ci sia uno sbaglio qui
saym·bra ke chee see·a oo·no zba·lyoh kwee
46 What is this item?
Cos'è questa voce?
ko·se kway·sta voh·che
47 The meal was excellent
Il pasto era ottimo
eel pa·stoh e·ra ot·tee·mo

Phrases you will hear

48 Ha scelto?
a shayl·to
Are you ready to order?
49 Che cosa prende da bere?
ke ko·sa pren·de da bay·re
What would you like to drink?

50 E come secondo?
   e koh·me se·kohn·do
   And to follow?
51 I piatti del giorno sono indicati sul cartello
   ee pyat·tee del johr·noh soh·no een·dee·kah·tee sool kar·tel·loh
   The specialities are on the blackboard
52 È finito
   e fee·nee·to
   That is not available
53 Del formaggio (grattugiato)/pepe (nero)?
   del for·maj·joh (grat·too·jah·to)/pay·pe (nay·ro)
   Some (grated) cheese/(black) pepper?

Cafés and bars

Besides selling drinks, an Italian bar usually offers several other services.
In most you will be able to get a snack; in many you will be able to buy
cigarettes and stamps and all the usual stock of a *tabaccaio* (see p.51). If
you see a yellow and black telephone sign outside you will also be able to
make telephone calls (see p.53). In many bars you will have to stand; if
you do find somewhere to sit down a waiter will come and take your
order, and there will be an additional charge. If you want to drink at the
bar you are usually expected to pay first and present your receipt when
you order. Public toilets are rare in Italy, but bars usually have toilets
available to the public.

Alcohol

54 A glass of white/red wine, please
   Un bicchiere di vino bianco/rosso, per favore
   oon beek·kye·re dee vee·noh byan·ko/rohs·so payr fa·voh·re
55 A beer
   Una birra
   oo·na beer·ra
56 A whisky/brandy/gin
   Un whisky/brandy/gin
   oon wee·skee/bran·dee/jeen
57 A Campari and soda
   Un Campari-soda
   oon kam·pah·ree·so·da
58 A Cinzano/Martini/Punt e Mes
   Un Cinzano/Martini/Punt e Mes
   oon cheen·tsah·no/mar·tee·nee/poon·te·mes
59 A Marsala/grappa/sambuca
   Una Marsala/grappa/sambuca
   oo·na mar·sah·la/grap·pa/sam·boo·ka

Cinzano, Martini and Punt e Mes are different varieties of vermouth.
Marsala is sweet and heavy like Madeira, but red; *grappa* is a kind of
marc or brandy; and *sambuca* is a clear, heavy liqueur of some strength,
which is often flavoured with the oil of roasted coffee beans.

Coffee

If you ask simply for coffee (*caffè*) in Italy you will mostly get *espresso*, a
tiny cup of very strong coffee; if you want a larger cup of the same coffee
order an *espresso doppio*. If you want something more like the coffee you
drink at home, you need to ask for *un caffè normale* (a normal coffee) or
un caffè grande (a big coffee; it will still be *espresso* but in a bigger cup
and with more water). If you ask simply for white coffee or coffee with
milk, you will probably get *cappuccino*, coffee with the milk shaken or
frothed by aeration (sometimes with shredded chocolate on top –
cioccolato). If you don't want a *cappuccino* ask for a *caffè macchiato*
(literally, "spotted" with milk).

60 Two espressos, please
    Due espressi, per favore
    doo·e e·spres·see payr fa·voh·re
61 One tea with milk/with lemon
    Un tè al latte/al limone
    oon te al lat·te/al lee·moh·ne
62 Could I have a glass of water as well, please?
    Anche un bicchiere d'acqua, per favore
    an·ke oon beek·kye·re dak·kwa payr fa·voh·re

Soft drinks

Bottled soft drinks in Italy are so sweet as to be suitable only for
children, although in many places you will be able to get American soft
drinks as well. Extremely refreshing, however, and widely available, is
fresh orange juice or lemon juice, squeezed for you there and then –
spremuta d'arancia/spremuta di limone. On a bad morning, try it with
soda.

63 Two fresh orange juices/lemon juices — with soda
    Due spremute di arancia/di limone — con soda
    doo·e spre·moo·te dee a·ran·cha/dee lee·moh·ne — kohn so·da
64 An orangeade/a lemonade/a limeade
    Una aranciata/limonata/cedrata
    oo·na a·ran·chah·ta/lee·mo·nah·ta/che·drah·ta
65 A raspberry-/strawberry-/mint-flavoured cordial
    Uno sciroppo di lampone/di fragole/di menta
    oo·no shee·rop·poh dee lam·poh·ne/dee frah·go·le/dee mayn·ta
66 Mineral water
    Acqua minerale — this comes in effervescent (*gassata*) and still
      (*naturale*) varieties
    ak·kwa mee·ne·rah·le

Snacks

The usual Italian word for a sandwich is *panino*, which is normally in fact
a bun or hard roll. A *tramezzino* is an open sandwich. The question is
academic, however: you are expected to choose from what you see on
display.

67 One of these, please, also one of those
    Uno di questi, per favore, anche uno di quelli
    oo·no dee kway·stee payr fa·voh·re an·ke oo·no dee kwayl·lee
68 A slice of pizza, please
    Una porzione di pizza, per favore
    oo·na por·tsyoh·ne dee peets·tsa payr fa·voh·re
69 A ham/cheese roll
    Un panino al prosciutto/al formaggio
    oon pa·nee·noh al pro·shoot·toh/al for·maj·joh
70 An open sandwich with anchovy paste
    Un tramezzino con pasta d'acciuga
    oon tra·medz·dzee·noh kohn pa·sta dach·choo·ga
71 A toasted sandwich
    Un toast
    oon tost
72 One of these buns/cakes
    Una di queste brioche/paste
    oo·na dee kway·ste bree·osh/pa·ste

Leisure   (L)

Sightseeing

Tourist Information Offices are rare in Italy, but people in hotels, shops
and in the street will readily direct you to the main monuments. Italian
museums are notoriously inconsistent in their opening hours, but are

usually closed one day a week and sometimes in the afternoons.
Churches are open from early in the morning but usually close for three
or four hours at noon.

1 Excuse me, can you tell me please,...
Mi scusi, può dirmi per favore,...
mee **skoo**·*zee* **pwo** *deer·mee payr fa·***voh**·*re*

2   Where is — the historic centre?
      Dov'è — il centro storico?
      doh·ve — *eel* **chen**·*troh* **sto**·*ree·ko*
         — the main square?
         — la piazza principale?
         — *la* **pyat**·*tsa preen·chee·***pah**·*le*
         — the cathedral?
         — il duomo?
         — *eel* **dwo**·*moh*
         — the (municipal) museum?
         — il museo (comunale)?
         — *eel moo·***ze**·*oh (ko·moo·***nah**·*le)*

3   Do you have — a guidebook to the town/
            area (in English)?
      Avete — una guida turistica della
            città/della zona (in inglese)?
      *a·***vay**·*te* — **oo**·*na* **gwee**·*da too·ree·***stee**·*ka*
            *del·la cheet·***ta**/*del·la* **dzo**·*na*
            *(een een·***glay**·*se)*
         — a map of the town?
         — una cartina della città?
         — **oo**·*na kar·***tee**·*na del·la cheet·***ta**
         — an audio-guide to the museum/
            church?
         — una cassetta-guida del museo/
            della chiesa?
         — **oo**·*na kas·***sayt**·*ta·***gwee**·*da del*
            *moo·***ze**·*oh/del·la* **kye**·*za*

4   Are there any — local festivals?
      Ci sono — delle feste locali?
      chee **soh**·*no* — *del·le* **fe**·*ste lo·***kah**·*lee*

5 Is there a guided tour — of the town/castle?
    C'è una gita con guida — della città/del castello?
    che **oo**·*na* **jee**·*ta kohn*
      gwee·*da* — *del·la cheet·***ta**/*del ka·***stel**·*loh*

6   Is there — a one-day excursion to Siena?
      C'è — una gita a Siena, con ritorno in
         una giornata?
      che — **oo**·*na* **jee**·*ta a* **sye**·*na kohn*
         *ree·***tohr**·*noh een* **oo**·*na*
         *johr·***nah**·*ta*

7 When does the tour begin?
Quando incomincia la gita?
kwan·*do een·ko·***meen**·*cha la* **jee**·*ta*

8 How long does it last?
Quanto dura?
kwan·*to* **doo**·*ra*

9 Where is the point of departure?
Da dove parte?
da **doh**·*ve* **par**·*te*

10 Is there an English-speaking guide?
C'è una guida che parla inglese?
che **oo**·*na* **gwee**·*da ke* **par**·*la een·***glay**·*se*

11 What is this building?
Che cos'è questo edificio?
*ke ko·***se** **kway**·*sto e·dee·***fee**·*choh*

12 What time does the museum/palace open?
A che ora apre il museo/il palazzo?
a ke **oh**·*ra* **a**·*pre eel moo·***ze**·*oh/eel pa·***lats**·*tsoh*

13 What is the admission charge?
Quanto costa l'ingresso?
kwan·*to* **ko**·*sta leen·***gres**·*soh*

14 Is one allowed to take photos with a flash/tripod?
    Si possono fare delle fotografie con il flash/treppiedi?
    see **pos·**so·no *fah·ray del·le fo·to·gra·fee·e kohn eel flash/trep·***pye·**dee
15   Where can I buy — slides?
    Dove posso comprare — delle diapositive?
    doh·ve **pos·**so
    kom·**prah·**ray — **del·**le dee·a·po·zee·**tee·**ve
                      — postcards?
                      — delle cartoline?
                      — **del·**le kar·to·**lee·**ne

Visiting churches

Sightseeing in Italy will involve visiting not only museums but also churches, which are organized not for sightseeing at all but for worship. Always be tactful, and if there is a service try to come back later. The sacristan is often helpful, and it is usual to tip him.

16   Where is — the sculpture by Michelangelo?
    Dov'è — la scultura di Michelangelo?
    *doh·*ve — *la skool·***too·**ra dee
                *mee·ke·***lan·**je·loh
                — the painting by Titian?
                — il quadro di Tiziano?
                — *eel* **kwa·**droh dee tee·**tsyah·**noh
                — the fresco by Filippo Lippi?
                — l'affresco di Filippo Lippi?
                — *laf·***fray·**skoh dee fee·**leep·**po
                *leep·*pee

17 Are you the sacristan?
    È Lei il sagrestano?
    *e ley eel sa·gre·***stah·**noh
18 Would you open this chapel
    for me, please?
    Potrebbe farmi visitare questa
    cappella, per favore?
    *po·***treb·**be *far·mee*
    *vee·zee·***tah·**ray **kway·**sta
    *kap·***pel·**la payr fa·**voh·**re
19 Could I see the Bellini in the
    sacristy?
    Potrei vedere il Bellini nella
    sagrestia?
    *po·***trey** ve·**day·**re eel
    *bel·***lee·**nee *nel·*la
    *sa·gre·***stee·**a
20 Is it possible to visit the crypt?
    È possibile visitare la cripta?
    *e pos·***see·**bee·le vee·zee·**tah·**ray
    la **kreep·**ta

21 Can we go in?
    Possiamo entrare?
    *pos·***syah·**mo en·**trah·**ray
22 Can one go to the top?
    Si può andare in cima?
    *see pwo an·***dah·**ray een
    chee·ma
23 Which way is it to the cloister?
    Per dove si va al chiostro?
    payr doh·ve see va al **kyo·**stroh
24 Is it closed for restoration?
    È chiuso(a) per restauro?
    *e kyoo·so(a) payr re·***stow·**roh
25 When will the service be over?
    Quando finisce la messa?
    kwan·do fee·**nee·**she la
    mays·sa

Beach and sports

Changing rooms as well as beach and sports items can often be rented on the main beaches, although sometimes only in private sections which you have to pay to enter.

26 Is it dangerous to swim here?
    È pericoloso nuotare qui?
    *e pe·ree·ko·***loh·**so nwo·**tah·**ray kwee
27 Can you recommend a quiet beach?
    Mi può consigliare una spiaggia tranquilla?
    *mee pwo kon·see·***lyah·**ray oo·na spyaj·ja tran·**kweel·**la
28 Where can we change?
    Dove sono gli spogliatoi?
    doh·ve **soh·**no lyee spo·lya·**toy**

29   **Can I rent — a deck chair?**
Posso prendere in affitto — una sedia a sdraio?
pos·so **pren**·de·re een
af·**feet**·toh — **oo**·na se·dya a **zdra**·yoh
            — **a sunshade?**
            — un ombrellone?
            — oon om·brel·**loh**·ne
            — **a sailing boat?**
            — una barca a vela?
            — **oo**·na **bar**·ka a **vay**·la
            — **a rowing boat?**
            — una barca a remi?
            — **oo**·na **bar**·ka a re·mee
            — **a motorboat?**
            — un motoscafo?
            — oon mo·to·**skah**·foh
            — **scuba equipment?**
            — l'attrezzatura subacquea?
            — lat·trets·tsa·**too**·ra soob·**a**·kwe·a

30   **Is it possible to go — sailing?**
Si può fare — della vela?
see pwo fah·ray — **del**·la **vay**·la
            — **water skiing?**
            — lo sci nautico?
            — lo shee **now**·tee·ko

31   **What sports can one take part in here?**
Quali sport si possono praticare qui?
kwah·lee sport see **pos**·so·no pra·tee·**kah**·ray kwee

32   **Is there a swimming pool?**
C'è una piscina?
che **oo**·na pee·**shee**·na

33   **Where can I play — tennis?**
Dove posso giocare — a tennis?
doh·ve **pos**·so jo·**kah**·ray — a **ten**·nees
            — **golf?**
            — a golf?
            — a golf

34   **Is it possible to go — gliding?**
Si può andare — in aliante?
see **pwo** an·**dah**·ray — een a·**lyan**·te

35   **Can I go fishing/riding?**
Posso andare a pescare/a cavallo?
pos·so an·**dah**·ray a pe·**skah**·ray/a ka·**val**·loh

36   **Can I rent the equipment?**
Posso noleggiare le attrezzature?
pos·so no·lej·**jah**·ray le at·trets·tsa·**too**·re

37   **Do you know any interesting walks?**
Conosce delle belle passeggiate?
ko·**noh**·she **del**·le **bel**·le pas·se·**jah**·te

38   **What are the conditions like for skiing/sailing?**
Com'è il tempo per sciare/fare della vela?
koh·**me** eel **tem**·poh payr shee·**ah**·ray/**fah**·ray **del**·la **vay**·la

39   **Are there any picnic areas near here?**
Ci sono qui vicino dei posti per fare picnic?
chee **soh**·no kwee vee·**chee**·no dey **poh**·stee payr **fah**·ray **peek**·neek

40   **Is there any interesting wildlife in this area?**
C'è della fauna interessante in questa zona?
che **del**·la **fow**·na een·te·res·**san**·te een **kway**·sta **dzo**·na

41   **What is the name of that bird/flower?**
Come si chiama quell'uccello/quel fiore?
koh·**me** see **kyah**·ma kwayl·**looch**·**chel**·loh/kwayl **fyoh**·re

---

Entertainment and night life

42   **How can we find out about local entertainment?**
Come possiamo informarci sugli spettacoli locali?
koh·**me** pos·**syah**·mo een·for·**mar**·chee **soo**·lyee spet·**ta**·ko·lee
lo·**kah**·lee

43	Where can one go	— to hear concerts/jazz?
	Dove si può andare	— per ascoltare dei concerti/del jazz?
	doh·ve see pwo an·dah·ray	— *payr a·skol·tah·ray dey kon·cher·tee/del jaz*
		— to dance?
		— a ballare?
		— *a bal·lah·ray*
		— to see cabaret?
		— a vedere il cabaret?
		— *a ve·day·re eel ka·ba·re*
44	Are there any	— films in English?
	Ci sono	— dei film in inglese?
	chee soh·no	— *dey feelm een een·glay·se*
		— good night clubs/discos?
		— dei buoni night/delle buone discoteche?
		— *dey bwo·nee nayt/del·le bwo·ne dee·sko·te·ke*
		— good concerts on?
		— dei bei concerti in programma?
		— *dey bey kon·cher·tee een pro·gram·ma*
45	Have you any seats	— for Wednesday evening?
	Avete dei posti	— per mercoledì sera?
	a·vay·te dey poh·stee	— *payr mer·ko·le·dee say·ra*
46	I should like to reserve	— a box
	Vorrei prenotare	— un palco
	vor·rey pre·no·tah·ray	— *oon pal·koh*
		— two seats in the balcony/ orchestra stalls
		— due posti in galleria/in platea
		— *doo·e poh·stee een gal·le·ree·a/ een pla·te·a*

47 What is being performed?
Che cosa danno?
ke ko·sa dan·no

48 Who is singing/playing?
Chi canta/suona?
kee kan·ta/swo·na

49 How long does the performance last?
Quanto dura lo spettacolo?
kwan·to doo·ra lo spet·ta·ko·loh

50 Where can one buy a programme?
Dove si può comprare il programma?
doh·ve see pwo kom·prah·ray eel pro·gram·ma

51	Is there	— an interval?
	C'è	— un intervallo?
	che	— *oon een·ter·val·loh*
		— a buffet/bar?
		— un buffè/un bar?
		— *oon boof·fe/oon bar*

52 When does the performance/floor-show begin?
Quando incomincia la rappresentazione/lo spettacolo?
kwan·do een·ko·meen·cha la rap·pre·zen·ta·tsyoh·ne/lo spet·ta·ko·loh

53 How much do the drinks cost?
Quanto costano le bevande?
kwan·to ko·sta·no le be·van·de

54 Is there a minimum/cover charge?
Bisogna pagare un minimo/il coperto?
bee·zohn·ya pa·gah·ray oon mee·nee·mo/eel ko·per·toh

Gambling

Without entering in detail into the language of gambling, we include here some of the phrases you might need in a casino. You will also need to recognize the following French phrases which are widely used: "Faites vos jeux" (place your bets, please), and "Les jeux sont faits" (no more bets).

55 What is the minimum/
maximum stake?
Qual'è la posta minima/
massima?
*kwah·le la po·sta
mee·nee·ma/mas·see·ma*

56 Where can I cash my chips?
Dove posso incassare le mie
fiche?
*doh·ve pos·so een·kas·sah·ray
le mee·e feesh*

57 Must one be a member to play
here?
Bisogna essere soci per poter
giocare qui?
*bee·zoh·nya es·se·re so·chee
payr po·tayr jo·kah·ray
kwee*

58 Where is the cashier's
counter?
Dov'è la cassa?
doh·ve la kas·sa

59 Excuse me, you have picked
up my stake/winnings
Scusi, Lei ha preso la mia
puntata/vincita
*skoo·zee ley ha pray·so la
mee·a poon·tah·ta/
veen·chee·ta*

60 You have miscalculated the
odds
Non ha calcolato bene le
probabilità
*nohn a kal·ko·lah·to be·ne le
pro·ba·bee·lee·ta*

61 Do you have a blackjack/
pontoon table here?
Avete un tavolo di blackjack/
di "ventuno" qui?
*a·vay·te oon tah·vo·loh dee
blak·jak/dee vayn·too·no
kwee*

62 I double (in backgammon)
Raddoppio
rad·dohp·pyo

Shopping   (s)

General

1   At what time — do you open?
     A che ora — aprite?
     a ke oh·ra — a·pree·te
          — do you close?
          — chiudete?
          — *kyoo·day·te*

2 One of these, please
Uno di questi, per favore
oo·no dee kway·stee payr fa·voh·re

3 Two of those, please
Due di quelli, per favore
doo·e dee kwayl·lee payr fa·voh·re

4 How much does that cost?
Quanto costa quello?
kwan·to ko·sta kwayl·lo

5 I am willing to pay up to 50,000 lire
Sono disposto a pagare sino a cinquantamila lire
*soh·no dee·spoh·sto a pa·gah·ray see·no a cheen·kwan·ta·mee·la
lee·re*

6   I should like to buy — some presents
     Vorrei comprare — dei regali
     vor·rey kom·prah·ray — dey re·gah·lee

7   Do you sell — sunglasses?
     Vendete — occhiali da sole?
     ven·day·te — ok·kyah·lee da soh·le

8   Do you have any — pencils?
     Avete — matite?
     a·vay·te — ma·tee·te

9   I need — some suntan oil
     Ho bisogno di — un olio abbronzante
     o bee·zoh·nyoh dee — oon o·lyoh ab·bron·dzan·te

10 Do you sell duty-free goods?
Vendete articoli esenti da dazio?
ven·day·te ar·tee·ko·lee e·zen·te da da·tsyoh

11   Where is — the shoe department?
      Dov'è — il reparto scarpe?
      doh·ve — eel re·par·toh skar·pe
           — the food department?
           — il reparto alimentari?
           — *eel re·par·toh a·lee·men·tah·ree*

12   Can I see — the hat in the window?
                          Posso vedere — il cappello in vetrina?
                          pos·so ve·**day**·re — *eel kap*·**pel**·loh een ve·**tree**·na
13   No, the other one
     No, quell'altro
     no kwayl·**lal**·tro
14   Have you anything — cheaper?
                     Avete qualche cosa — di meno caro?
                     a·**vay**·te kwal·ke *ko*·sa — *dee may*·no **kah**·ro
                                        — second-hand?
                                        — di seconda mano?
                                        — *dee se*·**kohn**·da **mah**·noh
15   I need a gadget for . . .
     Ho bisogno di un dispositivo per . . .
     o bee·**zoh**·nyoh dee oon dee·spo·zee·**tee**·voh payr
16   Can you show me how it works?
     Può mostrarmi come funziona?
     pwo mo·**strar**·mee **koh**·me foon·**tsyoh**·na
17   Have you got — a larger one?
                          Ne avete — uno piú grande?
                          nay a·**vay**·te — *oo*·no **pyoo** *gran*·de
                                        — a smaller one?
                                        — uno piú piccolo?
                                        — *oo*·no **pyoo** **peek**·ko·lo
18   I'm just looking
     Sto soltanto guardando
     sto sol·**tan**·to gwar·**dan**·do
19   I'm looking for — a blouse
                     Sto cercando — una camicetta
                     sto cher·**kan**·do — *oo*·na ka·mee·**chayt**·ta
20   I like this one
     Mi piace questo(a)
     mee **pyah**·che **kway**·sto(a)
21   I don't like it
     Non mi piace
     nohn mee **pyah**·che
22   I'll take — this one
                          Prendo — questo(a)
                          pren·do — **kway**·sto(a)
                                        — the other one
                                        — l'altro(a)
                                        — **lal**·tro(a)
23   Please wrap it
     Può incartarlo(a), per favore?
     *pwo een·kar·*tar·lo(a) payr fa·**voh**·re
24   There's no need to wrap it, thank you
     Non c'è bisogno di incartarlo(a), grazie
     *nohn che bee·**zoh**·nyoh dee een·kar·**tar**·lo(a) gra·tsye
25   Can I have a plastic bag?
     Un sacchetto di plastica, per favore
     *oon sak·**kayt**·toh dee **pla**·stee·ka payr fa·**voh**·re
26   How much would it cost to send it to England/America?
     Quanto viene a costare per mandarlo(a) in Inghilterra/America?
     kwan·to *vye*·ne a ko·**stah**·ray payr man·**dar**·lo(a) een een·geel·**ter**·ra/ a·**me**·ree·ka
27   Please send it to this address
     Lo(a) mandi a questo indirizzo, per favore
     lo(a) **man**·dee a **kway**·sto een·dee·**reets**·tsoh payr fa·**voh**·re
28   Please pack it carefully
     Lo(a) impacchetti bene, per favore
     *lo(a) eem·pak·**kayt**·tee **be**·ne payr fa·**voh**·re

Food and drink

Italy has countless small, family-run food shops which usually make for
better shopping than the new supermarkets. Most are general grocers;
others specialize not only in the normal way – as butchers, bakers,
chocolate-makers – but also in some specifically Italian ways – in fresh
pasta, for instance.

A word about weights. The usual quantities in which the Italians buy and sell are the *etto* (100 grams) and the *chilo* (1000 grams, or a kilogram). Cheese, for instance, will be sold by the *etto*, and you will find it useful to remember that one *etto* is a little less than ¼ lb, two *etti* are just under half a pound (in fact almost exactly 7 oz). If you want a full half-pound ask for two and a half *etti* (*due etti e mezzo*). Fruit, meat and vegetables are sold in units of a *chilo* or half-*chilo* (*mezzo-chilo*) and a *mezzo-chilo* of tomatoes is just over 1 lb 1 oz.

29   Where can I find — a baker/butcher?
        Dove posso trovare — un panificio/una macelleria?
      doh·ve **pos**·so tro·**vah**·ray — oon pah·nee·**fee**·choh/**oo**·na
              ma·**chel**·le·**ree**·a

30 What sort of cheese/butter do you have?
  Che tipo di formaggio/burro avete?
  ke **tee**·poh dee for·**maj**·joh/**boor**·roh a·**vay**·te

31   I would like — a kilo of apples
            Vorrei — un chilo di mele
          vor·**rey** — oon **kee**·loh dee **may**·le
               — half a kilo of tomatoes
               — mezzo chilo di pomodori
               — **medz**·dzo **kee**·loh dee
                  po·mo·**do**·ree
               — 200 grams of sugar
               — due etti di zucchero
               — **doo**·e et·tee dee **tsook**·ke·roh
               — 250 grams of ground coffee
               — due etti e mezzo di caffè macinato
               — **doo**·e et·tee e **medz**·dzo dee kaf·**fe**
                  ma·chee·**nah**·to
               — five slices of Parma ham
               — cinque fettine di prosciutto
               — **cheen**·kwe fet·**tee**·ne dee
                  pro·**shoot**·toh
               — half a dozen eggs
               — sei uova
               — sey **wo**·va

32   A packet — of salt, please
          Un pacco — di sale, per favore
        oon **pak**·koh — dee **sah**·le payr fa·**voh**·re
33   A tin — of tomatoes
          Una scatola — di pomodori
      oo·na **skah**·to·la — dee po·mo·**do**·ree
34   A litre — of milk
          Un litro — di latte
        oon **lee**·troh — dee **lat**·te
35   A bottle — of wine
         Una bottiglia — di vino
      oo·na bot·**tee**·lya — dee **vee**·noh

36 Two pork chops
  Due braciole di maiale
  doo·e bra·**cho**·le dee ma·**yah**·le
37 A joint of lamb
  Un pezzo di agnello
  oon **pets**·tsoh dee a·**nyel**·loh
38 I would like enough for two
   people
  Ne vorrei quanto basta per
   due
  nay vor·**rey** **kwan**·to **ba**·sta
  payr **doo**·e

39 Shall I help myself?
  Devo servirmi?
  de·vo ser·**veer**·mee

Chemist

In Italy a pharmacist is just that, and often does not sell toiletries and photographic equipment (see p.47), for which there are special shops. A pharmacy, marked by a red cross, will diagnose minor ailments as well as sell the appropriate medicines. Many pharmacies sell homeopathic as well as allopathic remedies.

40   I want something for — a headache
      Vorrei qualche cosa per — il mal di testa
      *vor-**rey** kwal-ke ko-sa payr* — *eel mal dee te-sta*
                              — insect bites
                              — le punture di insetti
                              — *le poon-**too**-re dee een-**set**-tee*
                              — a cold
                              — il raffreddore
                              — *eel raf-fred-**doh**-re*
                              — a cough
                              — la tosse
                              — *la **tohs**-se*
                              — hay fever
                              — la febbre da fieno
                              — *la **feb**-bre da **fye**-noh*
                              — a sore throat
                              — il mal di gola
                              — *eel mal dee **goh**-la*
                              — sunburn
                              — le scottature solari
                              — *le skot-ta-**too**-re so-**lah**-ree*
                              — an upset stomach
                              — il mal di stomaco
                              — *eel mal dee **sto**-ma-koh*

41   How many do I take?
      Quanti(e) ne devo prendere?
      kwan-tee(-te) nay **de**-vo
        pren-de-re
42   How often do I take them?
      Ogni quanto tempo dovrei
        prenderli(e)?
      *oh-nyee **kwan**-to **tem**-poh
        do-**vrey** pren-der-lee(-le)*
43   Are they safe for children to
        take?
      Vanno bene per bambini?
      *van-no **be**-ne payr
        bam-**bee**-nee*

44   Could I see a selection of
        perfume/toilet water?
      Mi fa vedere dei profumi/
        dell'acqua di colonia?
      *mee fa ve-**day**-re dey
        pro-**foo**-mee/del-**lak**-kwa dee
        ko-**lo**-nya*
45   I would like something with a
        floral scent
      Vorrei qualcosa con profumo
        di fiori
      *vor-**rey** kwal-**ko**-sa kohn
        pro-**foo**-moh dee **fyoh**-ree*
46   May I smell/try it, please?
      Posso odorarlo/provarlo?
      *pos-so o-do-**rar**-lo/pro-**var**-lo*

Cameras and film

47   I need a film — for this camera
      Ho bisogno di una pellicola — per questa macchina fotografica
      *o bee-**zoh**-nyoh dee oo-na*
        *pel-**lee**-ko-la* — *payr **kway**-sta **mak**-kee-na
                              fo-to-**gra**-fee-ka*
                              — for this cine-camera
                              — per questa cinepresa
                              — *payr **kway**-sta chee-ne-**pray**-sa*
48   I want — a black and white film
      Vorrei — una pellicola in bianco e nero
      *vor-**rey*** — *oo-na pel-**lee**-ko-la een **byan**-ko e
                      nay-ro*
                    — a 35mm film
                    — una pellicola di trentacinque
                      millimetri
                    — *oo-na pel-**lee**-ko-la dee
                      trayn-ta-**cheen**-kwe
                      meel-**lee**-me-tree*
                    — a fast/slow film
                    — una pellicola per esposizioni
                      brevi/lunghe
                    — *oo-na pel-**lee**-ko-la payr
                      e-spo-zee-**tsyoh**-nee
                      bre-vee/**loon**-ge*

I want — a colour print film
Vorrei — una pellicola a colori
vor·rey — ***oo**·na pel·**lee**·ko·la a ko·**loh**·ree*
      — a colour slide film
      — una pellicola a colori per
        diapositive
      — ***oo**·na pel·**lee**·ko·la a ko·**loh**·ree*
        *payr dee·a·po·zee·**tee**·ve*
      — batteries for the flash
      — delle batterie per il flash
      — ***del**·le bat·te·**ree**·e payr eel flash*

49 Can you develop this film please?
Può sviluppare questa pellicola per favore?
*pwo zvee·loop·**pah**·ray **kway**·sta pel·**lee**·ko·la payr fa·**voh**·re*

50 I would like two prints of this one
Vorrei due copie di questo
*vor·**rey doo**·e ko·pye dee **kway**·sto*

51 When will the photographs be ready?
Quando saranno pronte le foto?
*kwan·do sa·**ran**·no **prohn**·te le fo·toh*

52 I would like this photograph enlarged
Vorrei un ingrandimento di questa foto
*vor·**rey** oon een·gran·dee·**mayn**·toh dee **kway**·sta fo·toh*

53 There is something wrong with my camera
C'è qualcosa che non va nella mia macchina fotografica
*che kwal·**ko**·sa ke nohn va **nel**·la **mee**·a **mak**·kee·na fo·to·**gra**·fee·ka*

54 The film is jammed
La pellicola è bloccata
*la pel·**lee**·ko·la e blok·**kah**·ta*

55   I would like to buy a
           camera — with single-lens reflex
      Vorrei comprare una
      macchina fotografica — con obiettivo semplice reflex
      *vor·**rey** kom·**prah**·ray*
      ***oo**·na **mak**·kee·na*
      *fo·to·**gra**·fee·ka* — *kohn o·byet·**tee**·voh **saym**·plee·che*
                    ree·fleks

I would like to buy a
           camera — with built-in light meter
Vorrei comprare una
macchina fotografica — con esposimetro incorporato
*vor·**rey** kom·**prah**·ray*
***oo**·na **mak**·kee·na*
*fo·to·**gra**·fee·ka* — *kohn e·spo·**zee**·me·troh*
                 *een·kor·po·**rah**·to*
      — with instant developing
      — con sviluppo istantaneo
      — *kohn zvee·**loop**·poh*
        *ee·stan·**tah**·ne·o*
      — with flash attachment
      — con flash
      — *kohn flash*
      — with close-up/wide-angle lens
      — con obiettivo per primi piani/
        obiettivo grandangolare
      — *kohn o·byet·**tee**·voh payr **pree**·mee*
        ***pyah**·nee/o·byet·**tee**·voh*
        *gran·dan·go·**lah**·re*
      — with a camera case
      — con una custodia da macchina
        fotografica
      — *kohn **oo**·na koo·**sto**·dya da*
        ***mak**·kee·na fo·to·**gra**·fee·ka*

Clothes and shoes

56   I am looking for — a dress
      Sto cercando — un vestito
      *sto cher·**kan**·do* — *oon ve·**stee**·toh*

57   I would like something — informal
Vorrei qualcosa — di sportivo
vor·rey kwal·ko·sa — *dee spor·tee·vo*
— for evening wear
— da indossare la sera
— *da een·dos·sah·ray la say·ra*

58   Can you please show me
some — sun dresses?
Mi può mostrare, per favore — dei vestíti prendisole?
mee pwo mo·strah·ray payr
fa·voh·re — *dey ve·stee·tee pren·dee·soh·le*
— silk shirts?
— delle camicie di seta?
— *del·le ka·mee·che dee say·ta*

59 I would like to have a suit/pair of shoes made to measure
Vorrei farmi fare un completo/un paio di scarpe su misura
vor·rey far·mee fah·ray oon kom·ple·toh/oon pa·yoh dee skar·pe soo
mee·zoo·ra

60   I would prefer — a dark material/natural fibre
Preferirei — una stoffa scura/una fibra naturale
pre·fe·ree·rey — *oo·na stof·fa skoo·ra/oo·na*
fee·bra na·too·rah·le

61 I take a continental size 40
Porto la misura quaranta
por·to la mee·zoo·ra kwa·ran·ta

62 I take a continental shoe size 40
Calzo il numero quaranta
kal·tso eel noo·me·roh kwa·ran·ta

63 Can you measure me?
Può prendermi le misure?
pwo pren·der·mee le mee·zoo·re

64   Do you have this — in blue?
Avete questo — in blu?
a·vay·te kway·sto — *een bloo*

65 What is the material?
Che stoffa è?
ke stof·fa e

66   I like — this one
Mi piace — questo(a)
mee pyah·che — *kway·sto(a)*
— that one
— quello(a)
— *kwayl·lo(a)*
— the one in the window
— quello(a) in vetrina
— *kwayl·lo(a) een ve·tree·na*

67 May I see it in the daylight?
Posso vederlo alla luce?
pos·so ve·dayr·lo al·la loo·che

68 May I try it on?
Posso provarlo(a)?
pos·so pro·var·lo(a)

69 Where are the dressing rooms?
Dove sono i camerini di
prova?
doh·ve soh·no ee
ka·me·ree·nee dee pro·va

70 I would like a mirror
Ho bisogno di uno specchio
o bee·zoh·nyoh dee oo·no
spek·kyoh

71 I like it
Mi piace
mee pyah·che

72 I don't like it
Non mi piace
nohn mee pyah·che

73 I prefer the blue one
Preferisco quello(a) blu
pre·fe·ree·skò kwayl·lo(a) bloo

74 It does not suit me
Non mi sta bene
nohn mee sta be·ne

75 It does not fit
Non è la mia misura
nohn e la mee·a mee·zoo·ra

76   It is too — tight
È troppo — stretto(a)
e trohp·po — *strayt·to(a)*
— big
— grande
— *gran·de*
— small
— piccolo(a)
— *peek·ko·lo(a)*

77	Can you —	alter it?
	Potete —	fare delle modifiche?
	po·tay·te	*fah·ray del·le mo·dee·fee·ke*
		— take it in?
		— restringerlo(a)?
		re·streen·jer·lo(a)
		— let it out?
		— allargarlo(a)?
		al·lar·gar·lo(a)
78	I'd like one —	with a zip
	Ne vorrei uno —	con la cerniera
	nay vor·rey oo·no	*kohn la cher·nye·ra*
		— without a belt
		— senza cintura
		sen·tsa cheen·too·ra

79 Is this all you have?	82 Will it shrink?
Non ha altro?	Si restringerà?
nohn a al·tro	*see re·streen·je·ra*
80 I'll take it	83 Must it be dry-cleaned?
Lo prendo	Deve essere lavato a secco?
lo pren·do	*de·ve es·se·re la·vah·to a*
81 Is it washable?	*sayk·ko*
È lavabile?	
e la·vah·bee·le	

Jewellers, silversmiths and watchmakers

84	Have you any —	antique/modern jewellery?
	Avete —	gioielli antichi/moderni?
	a·vay·te	*jo·yel·lee an·tee·kee/mo·der·nee*
85	I am a collector of —	silverware/brooches
	Sono un collezionista di —	oggetti d'argento/spille
	soh·no oon	
	kol·le·tsyoh·nee·sta dee	*oj·jet·tee dar·jen·toh/speel·le*
86	Could you show me some —	rings/watches?
	Mi può mostrare degli —	anelli/orologi?
	mee pwo mo·strah·ray	
	de·lyee	*a·nel·lee/o·ro·lo·jee*

87 What precious stone is this?
Che pietra preziosa è questa?
ke pye·tra pre·tsyoh·sa e kway·sta

88 Is this solid gold/silver?
Questo è oro/argento massiccio?
kway·sto e o·roh/ar·jen·toh mas·seech·cho

89 Is it gold-/silver-plated?
È placcato d'oro/d'argento?
e plak·kah·to do·roh/dar·jen·toh

90	Can you repair —	this watch/necklace?
	Può riparare —	quest'orologio/questa collana?
	pwo ree·pa·rah·ray	*kway·sto·ro·lo·joh/kway·sta*
		kol·lah·na

Books, newspapers, postcards and stationery

If you want a newspaper, you will get it at a newsstand, *un'edicola*, while stationery is generally sold along with books in a *cartoleria*. Some major foreign newspapers are available on the larger stands, sometimes a day or two late. Postcards are sold usually in *edicole* (outside museums or tourist spots), also in *cartolerie*.

91	Do you have any —	English/American newspapers?
	Avete —	dei giornali inglesi/americani?
	a·vay·te	*dey johr·nah·lee een·glay·see/*
		a·me·ree·kah·nee
		— postcards?
		— delle cartoline?
		del·le kar·to·lee·ne

92	I would like	— some notepaper
	Vorrei	— della carta da lettere
	vor·rey	— *del·la **kar**·ta da **let**·te·re*
		— some envelopes
		— delle buste
		— *del·le **boo**·ste*
		— some padded envelopes
		— delle buste con l'imbottitura
		— *del·le **boo**·ste kohn leem·bot·tee·**too**·ra*
		— a ball-point pen
		— una penna biro
		— *oo·na **payn**·na **bee**·ro*
		— a pencil
		— una matita
		— *oo·na ma·**tee**·ta*
93	I need	— some airmail stickers
	Ho bisogno di	— alcune etichette indicando "Posta Aerea"
	*o bee·**zoh**·nyoh dee*	— *al·**koo**·ne e·tee·**kayt**·te een·dee·**kan**·do po·sta a·e·re·a*
		— some airmail envelopes
		— alcune buste per la Posta Aerea
		— *al·**koo**·ne **boo**·ste payr la po·sta a·e·re·a*
		— some adhesive tape
		— un nastro adesivo
		— *oon **na**·stroh a·de·**zee**·vo*
94	Do you sell	— English paperbacks?
	Vendete	— dei tascabili inglesi?
	*ven·**day**·te*	— *dey ta·**skah**·bee·lee een·**glay**·see*
		— street maps?
		— delle piante stradali?
		— *del·le **pyan**·te stra·**dah**·lee*

Tobacconist

There are numerous little shops and stalls whose main business is selling tobacco, stamps, lottery tickets and other state monopolies. They are called *tabaccherie* and are marked with a T (normally a white T on a black background). Similar things are also sold at counters in bars and supermarkets. British and American brands of cigarettes are usually available along with Italian varieties, usually of rougher Turkish or African tobacco.

95	A packet of . . . please
	Un pacchetto di . . . per favore
	*oon pak·**kayt**·toh dee payr fa·**voh**·re*
		— with filter tip
		— con filtro
		— *kohn **feel**·troh*
		— without filter
		— senza filtro
		— ***sen**·tsa **feel**·troh*

96 Do you have any American/ English brands?
Avete delle marche americane/ inglesi?
*a·**vay**·te **del**·le **mar**·ke a·me·ree·**kah**·ne/een·**glay**·see*

97 A pouch of pipe tobacco
Un pacchetto di tabacco da pipa
*oon pak·**kayt**·toh dee ta·**bak**·koh da **pee**·pa*

98 Some pipe cleaners
Degli scovolini per la pipa
*de·lyee sko·vo·**lee**·nee payr la **pee**·pa*

99 A box of matches
Una scatola di fiammiferi
*oo·na **skah**·to·la dee fyam·**mee**·fe·ree*

100 A cigar
     Un sigaro
     oon see·ga·roh
101 A cigarette lighter
     Un accendino
     oon ach·chen·dee·noh

102 A gas (butane) refill
     Una bomboletta di gas
     oo·na bom·bo·layt·ta dee gas

Presents and souvenirs

103   I am looking for a present
                       for — my wife/husband
         Sto cercando un regalo per — mia moglie/mio marito
                 sto cher·kan·do oon
                 re·gah·loh payr — mee·a moh·lye/mee·o ma·ree·toh
104 I would like to pay between 10,000 and 20,000 lire
     Vorrei pagare fra le dieci e le ventimila lire
     vor·rey pa·gah·ray fra le dye·chee e le vayn·tee·mee·la lee·re
105 Can you suggest anything?
     Mi può consigliare qualcosa?
     mee pwo kon·see·lyah·ray kwal·ko·sa
106 Have you anything suitable for a ten-year-old girl/boy?
     Avete qualcosa che vada bene per una bambina/un bambino di dieci
     anni?
     a·vay·te kwal·ko·sa ke vah·da be·ne payr oo·na bam·bee·na/oon
     bam·bee·noh dee dye·chee an·nee
107   Do you have anything — made locally?
             Avete degli articoli — locali?
                 a·vay·te de·lyee
                 ar·tee·ko·lee — lo·kah·lee
                              — hand made?
                              — lavorati a mano?
                              — *la·vo·rah·tee a mah·noh*
108 Do you have anything unusual?
     Avete qualcosa di insolito?
     a·vay·te kwal·ko·sa dee een·so·lee·to

Services and everyday needs (Sn)

Post office

Stamps can also be bought in a *tabaccheria*. Post boxes are red and
marked *poste* or *lettere*. Mail can be addressed *poste restante*, marked
Fermo Posta, to the central post office of any town, and collected on
payment of a small fee and proof of identity. Allow 7–10 days for mail
from abroad to reach Italy (or vice versa).

1   How much is a letter — to Britain?
           Quanto costa una lettera — per la Gran Bretagna?
               kwan·to ko·sta oo·na
               let·te·ra — payr la gran bre·ta·nya
                         — to the United States?
                         — per gli Stati Uniti?
                         — *payr lyee stah·tee oo·nee·tee*
2 I would like six stamps for postcards/letters to Britain/the United
   States
   Vorrei sei francobolli per cartoline/lettere per la Gran Bretagna/gli
   Stati Uniti
   vor·rey sey fran·ko·bohl·lee payr kar·to·lee·ne/let·te·re payr la gran
   bre·ta·nya/lyee stah·tee oo·nee·tee
3   I want to send — this parcel
           Vorrei spedire — questo pacco
               vor·rey spe·dee·re — kway·sto pak·koh
                             — a telegram
           Vorrei mandare — un telegramma
               vor·rey man·dah·ray — oon te·le·gram·ma

4 A telegram form, please
  Un modulo per telegrammi, per favore
  oon mo·doo·loh payr te·le·gram·mee payr fa·voh·re
5 When will it arrive?
  Quando arriverà?
  kwan·do ar·ree·ve·ra
6 I want to send this by registered mail
  Voglio mandare questo per raccomandata
  vo·lyo man·dah·ray kway·sto payr rak·ko·man·dah·ta
7 I am expecting a letter *poste restante*
  Sto aspettando una lettera fermo posta
  sto a·spet·tan·do oo·na let·te·ra fayr·mo po·sta

Telephoning

The simplest but most expensive way to telephone is from your hotel.
The next easiest, if you want to make a long-distance call, is to go to the
post office: the official will tell you (or write down for you) the code you
need and give you a token or a booth-number. You can talk in peace (the
booths are soundproof) and you pay the official after you have finished.

Otherwise you can use a public telephone (which is comparatively
rare) or a telephone in a bar. Bars with telephones display a yellow disc
with a black telephone dial, but you will only be able to make local calls
unless the sign says explicitly *interurbano* ("between cities", i.e. long-
distance). In these telephones you need to use not coins but *gettoni*,
metal tokens, worth 100 lire. Usually the bartender will be able to
provide some, but unfortunately not always; you can get them at the post
office. One *gettone* is enough for a local call, but for long-distance you
need eight or more. Insert the token or tokens first, then dial. Your
tokens are refunded if you cannot get through. (A token is acceptable
everywhere as a 100-lire coin.) The ringing tone in Italy consists of long
and fairly low bursts separated by short gaps. The engaged tone has
shorter bursts. The reply in Italy is invariably *Pronto* (Hello).

In Italian, telephone numbers are not given as single digits but in pairs,
so that 4321 would be forty-three, twenty-one. (For numerals, see p.68).

Phrases you will use

8 Hello
  Pronto
  prohn·to
9 This is Peter Williams
  Sono Peter Williams
  soh·no Peter Williams
10 Can I speak to Signor Peruzzi?
  Posso parlare col signor Peruzzi?
  pos·so par·lah·ray kol see·nyohr pe·roots·tsee
11 I would like to make a phone call to Britain/America
  Voglio fare una telefonata in Gran Bretagna/in America
  *vo·lyo fah·ray oo·na te·le·fo·nah·ta een gran bre·ta·nya/een
  a·me·ree·ka*
12 The number I want is . . .
  Voglio telefonare al numero . . .
  vo·lyo te·le·fo·nah·ray al noo·me·roh
13 I wish to make a — reversed charge call
  Voglio fare una — telefonata con la "R"
  vo·lyo fah·ray oo·na — te·le·fo·nah·ta kohn la er·re
  — person-to-person call
  — telefonata personale
  — *te·le·fo·nah·ta per·so·nah·le*
14 What is the dialling code for Pisa/Los Angeles?
  Qual è il prefisso per Pisa/Los Angeles?
  kwahl e eel pre·fees·soh payr pee·sa/los an·je·les
15 Would you write it down for me, please?
  Me lo può scrivere, per favore?
  may lo pwo skree·ve·re payr fa·voh·re

16 Could you put me through to (international) directory enquiries?
Può mettermi in comunicazione con il Servizio (internazionale) Informazioni Abbonati?
pwo mayi·ter·mee een ko·moo·nee·ka·**tsyoh**·ne kohn eel ser·**vee**·tsyoh (een·ter·na·tsyoh·**nah**·le) een·for·ma·**tsyoh**·nee ab·bo·**nah**·tee

17 May I use the phone, please?
Posso usare il telefono, per favore?
pos·so oo·**zah**·ray eel te·**le**·fo·noh payr fa·**voh**·re

18 Do I need a token?
Ho bisogno di un gettone?
o bee·**zoh**·nyoh dee oon jet·**toh**·ne

19 Can I have three tokens, please?
Posso avere tre gettoni per favore?
pos·so a·**vay**·re tray jet·**toh**·nee payr fa·**voh**·re

20 We have been cut off
Ci è stata tolta la comunicazione
chee e **stah**·ta **tol**·ta la ko·moo·nee·ka·**tsyoh**·ne

21 Is there a cheap rate?
C'è una tariffa ridotta?
che oo·na ta·**reef**·fa ree·**doht**·ta

22 What is the time now — in Hong Kong?
Che ora è adesso — a Hong Kong?
ke **oh**·ra e a·**des**·so — a hong kong

23 I cannot get through
Non riesco a ottenere la comunicazione
nohn ree·**e**·sko a ot·te·**nay**·re la ko·moo·nee·ka·**tsyoh**·ne

24 Can I check this number/code?
Posso controllare questo numero/prefisso?
pos·so kon·trol·**lah**·ray **kway**·sto **noo**·me·roh/pre·**fees**·soh

25 Do you have a directory — for Florence?
Avete l'elenco telefonico — di Firenze?
a·**vay**·te le·**len**·koh te·le·**fo**·nee·ko — dee fee·**ren**·tse

Phrases you will hear

26 Chi parla?
kee **par**·la
Who is speaking?

27 Le passo il signor Peruzzi
le **pas**·so eel see·**nyohr** pe·**roots**·tsee
I am putting you through to Signor Peruzzi

28 Resti in linea
re·stee een **lee**·ne·a
Hold the line

29 Sto cercando di metterLa in comunicazione
sto cher·**kan**·do dee **mayt**·ter·la een ko·moo·nee·ka·**tsyoh**·ne
I am trying to connect you

30 La linea è occupata
la **lee**·ne·a e ok·koo·**pah**·ta
The line is engaged

31 Richiami più tardi, per favore
ree·**kyah**·mee pyoo tar·dee payr fa·**voh**·re
Please try later

32 Questo numero è bloccato
kway·sto **noo**·me·roh e blok·**kah**·to
This number is out of order

33 Non riesco a ottenere questo numero
nohn ree·**e**·sko a ot·te·**nay**·re **kway**·sto **noo**·me·roh
I cannot obtain this number

34 È in linea — può parlare
e een **lee**·ne·a — pwo par·**lah**·ray
Please go ahead

The hairdresser

35 I'd like to make an appointment
Vorrei un appuntamento
vor·**rey** oon ap·poon·ta·**mayn**·toh

36 I want — a cut
Desidero — un taglio di capelli
de·**see**·de·ro — oon **ta**·lyoh dee ka·**payl**·lee
— a trim
— una spuntata
— **oo**·na spoon·**tah**·ta

I want — a blow-dry
Desidero — asciugarli col phon
de·see·de·ro — a·shoo·gar·lee kol fon

37 I want my hair — fairly short
Voglio i capelli — tagliati piuttosto corti
vo·lyo ee ka·payl·lee — ta·lyah·tee pyoot·to·sto kohr·tee

— not too short
— non troppo corti
— nohn trohp·po kohr·tee

— short and curly
— corti e ricci
— kohr·tee e reech·chee

— layered
— a ciocche
— a chok·ke

— in a fringe
— con la frangia
— kohn la fran·ja

38 Take more off — the front
Li tagli piú corti — davanti
lee ta·lyee pyoo kohr·tee — da·van·tee

— the back
— dietro
— dye·tro

39 Not too much off — the sides
Non tagli troppo — ai lati
nohn ta·lyee trohp·po — ay lah·tee

— the top
— sopra
— soh·pra

40 I like a parting — in the centre
Vorrei la scriminatura — al centro
vor·rey la skree·mee·na·too·ra — al chen·troh

— on the left
— a sinistra
— a see·nee·stra

— on the right
— a destra
— a de·stra

41 I'd like — a perm
Vorrei — una permanente
vor·rey — oo·na per·ma·nen·te

— a shampoo and set
— uno sciampo e messa in piega
— oo·no sham·poh e mays·sa een pye·ga

— my hair tinted
— farmi la tintura
— far·mee la teen·too·ra

— my hair streaked
— farmi le mesti
— far·mee le me·stee

42 The water is too hot/cold
L'acqua è troppo calda/fredda
lak·kwa e trohp·po kal·da/frayd·da

43 The dryer is too hot/cold
Il casco è troppo caldo/freddo
eel ka·skoh e trohp·po kal·do/frayd·do

44 I'd like — a conditioner
Vorrei — un balsamo
vor·rey — oon bal·sa·moh

— hair spray
— la lacca
— la lak·ka

45 That's fine, thank you
Va bene, grazie
va be·ne gra·tsye

Repairs and technical jobs

This section covers household jobs — from plumbing to a faulty switch —
and any other articles that could need repair, such as glasses or shoes
(cars are dealt with on p.19, clothes on p.48).

46 Where can I get this repaired?
Dove posso farlo riparare?
doh·ve pos·so far·lo ree·pa·rah·ray

47 I am having trouble — with my heating/plumbing
C'è qualcosa che non va — col riscaldamento/coi tubi
*che kwal·ko·sa ke nohn va — kol ree·skal·da·mayn·toh/koy
too·bee*

48 This — is broken
Questo — è rotto
kway·sto — e roht·to
— is not working
— non funziona
— *nohn foon·tsyoh·na*
— is damaged
— è danneggiato
— *e dan·nej·jah·to*
— is blocked
— è ostruito
— *e o·stroo·ee·to*

49 There is a leak in the pipe/roof
Il tubo/il tetto perde
eel too·boh/eel tayt·toh per·de

50 There's a gas leak
C'è una fuga di gas
che oo·na foo·ga dee gas

51 Would you have a look at this, please?
Può dare un'occhiata a questo, per favore?
pwo dah·ray oo·nok·kyah·ta a kway·sto payr fa·voh·re

52 Can you repair — my suitcase?
Può ripararmi — la valigia?
pwo ree·pa·rar·mee — la va·lee·ja

53 Can you reheel/resole these shoes?
Può rifare i tacchi/le suole a queste scarpe?
pwo ree·fah·ray ee tak·kee/le swo·le a kway·ste skar·pe

54 Have you got a replacement part?
Ha un pezzo di ricambio?
a oon pets·tsoh dee ree·kam·byoh

55 Can you get it working again?
Lo può riparare?
lo pwo ree·pa·rah·ray

56 When will it be ready?
Quando sarà pronto?
kwan·do sa·ra prohn·to

57 Can you do it quickly?
Può farlo in poco tempo?
pwo far·lo een po·ko tem·poh

58 I would like a duplicate of this key
Vorrei un doppione di questa chiave
vor·rey oon dop·pyoh·ne dee kway·sta kyah·ve

59 I have lost my key
Ho perso la chiave
o per·so la kyah·ve

60 I have locked myself out
Mi sono chiuso(a) fuori
mee soh·no kyoo·so(a) fwo·ree

61 Can you open the door?
Può aprire la porta?
pwo a·pree·re la por·ta

62 The fuse for the lights has blown
È saltata la luce
e sal·tah·ta la loo·che

63 There is a loose connection
C'è un contatto difettoso
che oon kon·tat·toh dee·fet·toh·so

64 Sometimes it works, sometimes it doesn't
A volte funziona, a volte no
a vol·te foon·tsyoh·na a vol·te no

Laundry, dry cleaners and clothes-mending

A dry cleaner's is called *una lavanderia a secco*; sometimes it is combined with *una lavanderia* (laundry), which will usually provide a fairly quick service. You will also be able to have things mended. A launderette is *una lavanderia automatica*; even in these you will usually find staff to do your laundry.

65	Will you — **clean this skirt?**
	Potete — smacchiare questa gonna?
	po·tay·te — zmak·kyah·ray kway·sta gon·na
	— **press these trousers?**
	— stirare questi pantaloni?
	— *stee·rah·ray kway·stee pan·ta·loh·nee*
	— **wash and iron these shirts?**
	— lavare e stirare queste camicie?
	— *la·vah·ray e stee·rah·ray kway·ste ka·mee·che*
	— **wash these clothes?**
	— lavare questi vestiti?
	— *la·vah·ray kway·stee ve·stee·tee*

66 Can you get this stain out?
Potete togliere questa macchia?
po·tay·te to·lye·re kway·sta mak·kya

67   This stain is — **grease/ink**
Questa è una macchia — di unto/di inchiostro
kway·sta è oo·na mak·kya — dee oon·toh/dee een·kyo·stroh

68 This fabric is delicate
Questa stoffa è delicata
kway·sta stof·fa e de·lee·kah·ta

69 When will my things be ready?
Quando saranno pronte le mie robe?
kwan·do sa·ran·no prohn·te le mee·e ro·be

70 I need them in a hurry
Ne ho assoluto bisogno
nay o as·so·loo·to bee·zoh·nyoh

71 Is there a launderette nearby?
C'è una lavanderia automatica qui vicino?
che oo·na la·van·de·ree·a ow·to·ma·tee·ka kwee vee·chee·no

72 Can I have my laundry done?
Mi potete lavare la biancheria?
mee po·tay·te la·vah·ray la byan·ke·ree·a

73 Where can I get clothes repaired?
Dove posso farmi rammendare degli indumenti?
doh·ve pos·so far·mee ram·men·dah·ray de·lyee een·doo·mayn·tee

74 Can you do invisible mending?
Potete fare un rammendo invisibile?
po·tay·te fah·ray oon ram·men·doh een·vee·zee·bee·le

75 Do you think you could repair this?
Pensate di poterlo rammendare?
pen·sah·te dee po·tayr·lo ram·men·dah·ray

76	Would you — **sew this button back on?**
	Potreste — ricucire questo bottone?
	po·tray·ste — ree·koo·chee·re kway·sto bot·toh·ne
	— **mend this tear?**
	— rammendare questo strappo?
	— *ram·men·dah·ray kway·sto strap·poh*
	— **replace this zip?**
	— cambiare questa cerniera?
	— *kam·byah·ray kway·sta cher·nye·ra*
	— **turn up/let down the hem?**
	— accorciare/allungare l'orlo?
	— *ak·kor·chah·ray/al·loon·gah·ray lohr·loh*

Police and legal matters

77	I wish to call the police	
	Voglio chiamare la polizia	
	vo·lyo kya·mah·ray la po·lee·tsee·a	
78	Where is the police station?	
	Dov'è il posto di polizia?	
	doh·ve eel poh·stoh dee po·lee·tsee·a	
79	I should like to report	— a theft
	Vorrei denunciare	— un furto
	vor·rey de·noon·chah·ray	— *oon foor·toh*
		— the loss of a camera
		— la scomparsa di una macchina fotografica
		— *la skom·par·sa dee oo·na mak·kee·na fo·to·gra·fee·ka*
80	Someone has broken into	— my car/my room
	Mi hanno rubato	— dalla macchina/in camera
	mee an·no roo·bah·to	— *dal·la mak·kee·na/een kah·me·ra*
81	Someone has stolen	— my wallet
	Mi hanno rubato	— il portafoglio
	mee an·no roo·bah·to	— *eel por·ta·fo·lyoh*
82	I have lost	— my passport
	Ho perso	— il passaporto
	o per·so	— *eel pas·sa·por·toh*
83	I wish/I demand	— to see a lawyer
	Desidero/Chiedo di	— vedere un avvocato
	de·see·de·ro/kye·do dee	— *ve·day·re oon av·vo·kah·toh*
84	My son is lost	
	Mio figlio si è perso	
	mee·o fee·lyoh see e per·so	
85	Where is the British/American Consulate?	
	Dov'è il consolato britannico/americano?	
	doh·ve eel kon·so·lah·toh bree·tan·nee·ko/a·me·ree·kah·no	

Worship

Italy is a Roman Catholic country, but all other main denominations and religions are usually represented in the larger cities.

86	Where is there	— a (Catholic) church?
	Dove c'è	— una chiesa (cattolica)?
	doh·ve che	— *oo·na kye·za (kat·to·lee·ka)*
		— a Protestant church?
		— una chiesa protestante?
		— *oo·na kye·za pro·te·stan·te*
87	What time is the service?	
	A che ora c'è l'ufficio?	
	a ke oh·ra che loof·fee·choh	
88	I'd like to see	— a priest
	Vorrei vedere	— un prete
	vor·rey ve·day·re	— *oon pre·te*
		— a minister
		— un ministro
		— *oon mee·nee·stroh*
89	Is there one	— who speaks English?
	Ce n'è uno	— che parla inglese?
	che ne oo·no	— *ke par·la een·glay·se*
90	Could you hear my confession	— in English?
	Posso confessarmi	— in inglese?
	pos·so kon·fes·sar·mee	— *een een·glay·se*

Business matters   (Bm)

Making appointments (see also Telephoning p.53)

1   My name is George Baker — of Universal Chemicals
Mi chiamo George Baker — dell'Universal Chemicals
mee kyah·mo George Baker — del·loo·nee·ver·sal ke·mee·kals

2 Here is my card
Ecco il mio biglietto da visita
ek·ko eel mee·o bee·lyayt·toh da vee·zee·ta

3   Could I see/speak to your — Managing Director/Buyer?
Potrei vedere/parlare con il
vostro — Amministratore Delegato/
Direttore agli acquisti?

*po·trey ve·day·re/par·lah·ray
kohn eel vo·stro — am·mee·nee·stra·toh·re
de·le·gah·to/dee·ret·toh·re a·lyee
ak·kwee·stee*

4 He/she is expecting me to telephone
Aspetta una mia telefonata
a·spet·ta oo·na mee·a te·le·fo·nah·ta

5 Could you put me through to Signor Peruzzi?
Mi passa il signor Peruzzi, per favore?
mee pas·sa eel see·nyohr pe·roots·tsee payr fa·voh·re

6 Is Signor Peruzzi in?
C'è il signor Peruzzi?
che eel see·nyohr pe·roots·tsee

7 Is his assistant/secretary there?
C'è la sua segretaria personale/la sua segretaria?
che la soo·a se·gre·tah·rya per·so·nah·le/la soo·a se·gre·tah·rya

8 When will he/she be back?
Quando ritornerà?
kwan·do ree·tor·ne·ra

9   I would like to make — an appointment with Signor
Peruzzi
Vorrei fissare — un appuntamento con il signor
Peruzzi
*vor·rey fees·sah·ray — oon ap·poon·ta·mayn·toh kohn eel
see·nyohr pe·roots·tsee*

10 I am free on Thursday between 9:00 and 11:00
Sono libero giovedì fra le nove e le undici
soh·no lee·be·ro jo·ve·dee fra le no·ve e le oon·dee·chee

Practicalities and fieldwork

11 I am on a business trip to Italy
Sono in viaggio d'affari in Italia
soh·no een vyaj·joh daf·fah·ree een ee·ta·lya

12   I wish to hire — a secretary/a typist
Vorrei servirmi di — una segretaria/una dattilografa a
ore
*vor·rey ser·veer·mee dee — oo·na se·gre·tah·rya/oo·na
dat·tee·lo·gra·fa a oh·re*

— a conference room
Vorrei prendere in affitto — una sala per conferenze
*vor·rey pren·de·re een
af·feet·toh — oo·na sah·la payr kon·fe·ren·tse*

13 Where can I get photocopying done?
Dove posso far fare delle fotocopie?
doh·ve pos·so far fah·ray del·le fo·to·ko·pye

14 Can I send a telex from here?
Posso mandare un telex da qui?
pos·so man·dah·ray oon te·leks da kwee

15   My firm specializes in — agricultural equipment
La mia ditta è specializzata in — macchine agricole
*la mee·a deet·ta e
spe·cha·leedz·dzah·ta een — mak·kee·ne a·gree·ko·le*

16

   I wish — to carry out a market survey
   Vorrei — fare una ricerca di mercato
   vor·rey — *fah·ray oo·na ree·chayr·ka dee*
     mer·kah·toh
   — to test the Italian market for this
     product
   — sondare il mercato italiano per
     questo prodotto
   — *son·dah·ray eel mer·kah·toh*
     ee·ta·lyah·no payr kway·sto
     pro·doht·toh

17 My firm is launching an advertising/sales campaign
La mia ditta sta lanciando una campagna pubblicitaria/di vendita
la mee·a deet·ta sta lan·chan·do oo·na kam·pa·nya
poob·blee·chee·tah·rya/dee vayn·dee·ta

18 Have you seen our catalogue?
Ha visto il nostro catalogo?
a vee·sto eel no·stro ka·tah·lo·goh

19 Can I send our sales representative to see you?
Posso mandarLe il nostro rappresentante?
pos·so man·dar·le eel no·stro rap·pre·zen·tan·te

20 I will send you a letter/telex with the details
Le manderò una lettera/un telex con i dettagli
le man·de·ro oo·na let·te·ra/oon te·leks kohn ee det·ta·lyee

21

   Can I see — a sample of your product?
   Posso vedere — un campione del Vostro prodotto?
   pos·so ve·day·re — *oon kam·pyoh·ne del vo·stro*
     pro·doht·toh
   — a selection of your goods?
   — un assortimento della Vostra
     merce?
   — *oon as·sor·tee·mayn·toh del·la*
     vo·stra mer·che

22 Can I have a copy of this document/brochure?
Posso avere una copia di questo documento/opuscolo?
pos·so a·vay·re oo·na ko·pya dee kway·sto
do·koo·mayn·toh/o·poo·sko·loh

23 Can you give me an estimate of the cost?
Può farmi un preventivo del costo?
pwo far·mee oon pre·ven·tee·voh del ko·stoh

24 What percentage of the cost is made up by transportation?
Con quale percentuale incide il trasporto sul costo?
kohn kwah·le per·chen·twah·le een·chee·de eel tra·spor·toh sool ko·stoh

25 What is the wholesale/retail price?
Qual è il prezzo all'ingrosso/al dettaglio?
kwahl e eel prets·tsoh al·leen·gros·soh/al det·ta·lyoh

26 What is the rate of inflation in Italy?
Qual è il tasso d'inflazione in Italia?
kwahl e eel tas·soh deen·fla·tsyoh·ne een ee·ta·lya

27 How high are current rates of interest?
Quali sono gli attuali tassi d'interesse?
kwah·lee soh·no lyee at·twah·lee tas·see deen·te·res·se

28 It's a pleasure to do business with you
È un piacere trattare affari con Lei
e oon pya·chay·re trat·tah·ray af·fah·ree kohn ley

Children (c)

1

   Do you have — a special children's menu?
   Avete — un menù per bambini?
   a·vay·te — *oon me·noo payr bam·bee·nee*
   — half portions for children?
   Servite — mezze porzioni per bambini?
   ser·vee·te — *medz·dze por·tsyoh·nee payr*
     bam·bee·nee

2 Can you warm this bottle for me?
   Potete riscaldarmi questo biberon?
   po·tay·te ree·skal·dar·mee kway·sto bee·be·ron
3 Do you have a highchair?
   Avete un seggiolone?
   a·vay·te oon sej·jo·loh·ne
4   Do you operate — a baby-sitting service?
               Avete — un servizio baby-sitter?
               a·vay·te — oon ser·vee·tsyoh ba·by·seet·ter
                          — a day nursery?
                          — un asilo-nido?
                          — *oon a·zee·loh·nee·doh*
5 Do you know anyone who will baby-sit for us?
   Conoscete qualcuno che ci potrebbe fare da baby-sitter?
   *ko·no·shay·te kwal·koo·no ke chee po·treb·be fah·ray da
   ba·by·seet·ter*
6 We shall be back at 11
   Torneremo alle undici
   tor·ne·ray·mo al·le oon·dee·chee
7 She/he goes to bed at 8
   Va a letto alle otto
   va a let·toh al·le ot·to
8 Are there any organized activities for the children?
   Ci sono delle attività organizzate per i bambini?
   *chee soh·no del·le at·tee·vee·ta or·ga·needz·dzah·te payr
   ee bam·bee·nee*
9   Is there — a paddling pool?
               C'è — una piscina per bambini?
               *che — oo·na pee·shee·na payr
                           bam·bee·nee*
                     — a playground?
                     — un campo-giochi?
                     — *oon kam·poh·jo·kee*
                     — an amusement park?
                     — un luna-park?
                     — *oon loo·na·park*
                     — a zoo nearby?
                     — uno zoo qui vicino?
                     — *oo·no dzo·oh kwee vee·chee·no*
10 My son has hurt himself
   Mio figlio si è fatto male
   mee·o fee·lyoh see e fat·to mah·le
11 My daughter is ill
   Mia figlia non sta bene
   mee·a fee·lya nohn sta be·ne
12 Do you have a cot (crib) for our baby?
   Avete un lettino per il bambino?
   a·vay·te oon let·tee·noh payr eel bam·bee·noh
13 Can my son sleep in our room?
   Mio figlio può dormire in camera nostra?
   mee·o fee·lyoh pwo dor·mee·re een kah·me·ra no·stra
14 Are there any other children in the hotel?
   Ci sono altri bambini nell'albergo?
   chee soh·no al·tree bam·bee·nee nel·lal·ber·goh
15 How old are your children?
   Quanti anni hanno i Suoi bambini?
   kwan·tee an·nee an·no ee swoy bam·bee·nee
16 My son is 9 years old
   Mio figlio ha nove anni
   mee·o fee·lyoh a no·ve an·nee
17 My daughter is 15 months
   Mia figlia ha quindici mesi
   mee·a fee·lya a kween·dee·chee may·see
18 Where can I feed my baby?
   Dove posso allattare il bambino?
   doh·ve pos·so al·lat·tah·ray eel bam·bee·noh
19 I need some disposable nappies (diapers)
   Ho bisogno di pannolini da buttar via
   o bee·zoh·nyoh dee pan·no·lee·nee da boot·tar vee·a

Illness and disability   (1)

The disabled

1	I suffer from	— a weak heart
	Ho	— il cuore debole
	o	*— eel **kwo**·re **day**·bo·le*
		— asthma
	Soffro	— di asma
	sof·fro	*— dee **az**·ma*
2	Do you have	— facilities for the disabled?
	Avete	— servizi per gli handicappati fisici?
	*a·**vay**·te*	*— ser·**vee**·tsee payr lyee*
		*an·dee·kap·**pah**·tee **fee**·zee·chee*
		— a toilet for the disabled?
		— una toilette per gli handicappati fisici?
		*— **oo**·na twa·**let** payr lyee*
		*an·dee·kap·**pah**·tee **fee**·zee·chee*

3 Is there a reduced rate for disabled people?
C'è una riduzione per gli handicappati fisici?
*che **oo**·na ree·doo·**tsyoh**·ne payr lyee an·dee·kap·**pah**·tee **fee**·zee·chee*

4	I am unable to	— climb stairs
	Non posso	— salire le scale
	*nohn **pos**·so*	*— sa·**lee**·re le **skah**·le*
		— walk very far
		— camminare a lungo
		*— kam·mee·**nah**·ray a **loon**·go*

5 Can you supply a wheelchair?
Avete una sedia a rotelle?
*a·**vay**·te **oo**·na **se**·dya a ro·**tel**·le*

Doctors and hospitals

If a visit to a doctor is necessary, you will have to pay on the spot. Some of the cost of medical treatment is repayable under reciprocal EEC agreements for British and Irish visitors (form E111 should be obtained before departure and taken with you), but proper accident and medical insurance is still advisable. A pharmacy (see p.46) will both prescribe and provide something for a minor ailment; for something more serious, go in the first instance to a doctor rather than a hospital. In an emergency, ambulances (which also have to be paid for) can be called by dialling 113.

Preliminary

6 I need a doctor
Ho bisogno di un dottore
*o bee·**zoh**·nyoh dee oon dot·**toh**·re*

7 I feel ill
Mi sento male
*mee **sen**·to **mah**·le*

8 Can I have an appointment with the doctor?
Posso fissare un appuntamento con il dottore?
***pos**·so fees·**sah**·ray oon ap·poon·ta·**mayn**·toh kohn eel dot·**toh**·re*

9 I would like a general checkup
Vorrei fare una visita generale
*vor·**rey** **fah**·ray **oo**·na **vee**·zee·ta je·ne·**rah**·le*

10	I would like to see	— a skin specialist
	Vorrei vedere	— un dermatologo
	*vor·**rey** ve·**day**·re*	*— oon der·ma·**to**·lo·goh*
		— an eye specialist
		— un oculista
		*— oon o·koo·**lee**·sta*

In the event of an accident

11 There has been an accident
C'è stato un incidente
che stah·to oon een·chee·den·te

12 Call an ambulance
Chiamate un'ambulanza
kya·mah·te oo·nam·boo·lan·tsa

13 Get a doctor
Chiamate un dottore
kya·mah·te oon dot·toh·re

14 He is unconscious
Ha perso conoscenza
a per·so ko·no·shen·tsa

15 He is in pain
Soffre dolore
sof·fre do·loh·re

16 He/she has been seriously
injured
È ferito(a) gravemente
e fe·ree·to(a) grah·ve·mayn·te

17 I have cut myself
Mi sono tagliato(a)
mee soh·no ta·lyah·to(a)

18 He/she has burnt
himself/herself
Si è bruciato(a)
see e broo·chah·to(a)

19 I have had a fall
Sono caduto(a)
soh·no ka·doo·to(a)

20 She has been bitten
È stata morsa
e stah·ta mor·sa

21 I have hurt my arm/my leg
Mi sono fatto(a) male ad un
braccio/ad una gamba
*mee soh·no fat·to(a) mah·le ad
oon brach·choh/ad oo·na
gam·ba*

22 I have broken my arm
Mi sono rotto(a) il braccio
*mee soh·no roht·to(a) eel
brach·choh*

23 He has dislocated his shoulder
Si è slogato una spalla
see e zlo·gah·to oo·na spal·la

24 She has sprained her ankle
Ha preso una storta alla
caviglia
*a pray·so oo·na stor·ta al·la
ka·vee·lya*

25 I have pulled a muscle
Ho uno stiramento
o oo·no stee·ra·mayn·toh

Symptoms, conditions and treatment

26 There is a swelling here
C'è un gonfiore qui
che oon gon·fyoh·re kwee

27 It is inflamed here
È infiammato qui
e een·fyam·mah·to kwee

28 I have a pain here
Mi fa male qui
mee fa mah·le kwee

29 I find it painful to walk/
breathe
Mi fa male quando cammino/
respiro
*mee fa mah·le kwan·do
kam·mee·no/re·spee·ro*

30 I have a headache/a sore
throat
Ho mal di testa/mal di gola
o mal dee te·sta/mal dee goh·la

31 I have a high temperature
Ho la febbre alta
o la feb·bre al·ta

32 I can't sleep
Non riesco a dormire
nohn ree·e·sko a dor·mee·re

33 I have sunstroke
Ho preso un'insolazione
*o pray·so
oo·neen·so·la·tsyoh·ne*

34 My stomach is upset
Ho dei disturbi di stomaco
*o dey dee·stoor·bee dee
sto·ma·koh*

35 I feel nauseous
Ho la nausea
o la now·ze·a

36 I think I have food poisoning
Penso di avere
un'intossicazione da cibo
*pen·so dee a·vay·re
oo·neen·tos·see·ka·tsyoh·ne
da chee·boh*

37 I have vomited
Ho vomitato
o vo·mee·tah·to

38 I have diarrhoea
Ho la diarrea
o la dee·ar·re·a

39 I am constipated
Sono stitico(a)
soh·no stee·tee·ko(a)

40 I feel faint
Mi sento svenire
mee sen·to zve·nee·re

41 I am allergic to penicillin/
to cortisone
Sono allergico(a) alla
penicillina/
al cortisone
*soh·no al·ler·jee·ko(a) al·la
pe·nee·cheel·lee·na/
al kor·tee·zoh·ne*

42 I have high blood pressure
Ho la pressione alta
o la pres·syoh·ne al·ta

43 I am a diabetic
Sono diabetico(a)
soh·no dya·be·tee·ko(a)

44 I am taking these drugs
Sto prendendo queste
medicine
*sto pren·den·do kway·ste
me·dee·chee·ne*

45 Can you give me an Italian prescription for them?
Può farmi una ricetta italiana per questa medicina?
pwo far·mee oo·na ree·chet·ta ee·ta·lyah·na payr kway·sta me·dee·chee·na

46 I am pregnant
Sono incinta
soh·no een·cheen·ta

47 I am on the pill
Sto prendendo la pillola
sto pren·den·do la peel·lo·la

48 My blood group is . . .
Il mio gruppo sanguigno è . . .
eel mee·o groop·poh san·gwee·nyo e

49 I don't know my blood group
Non conosco il mio gruppo sanguigno
nohn ko·noh·sko eel mee·o groop·poh san·gwee·nyo

50 Must I stay in bed?
Devo stare a letto?
de·vo stah·ray a let·toh

51 Will I be able to go out tomorrow?
Potrò uscire domani?
po·tro oo·shee·re do·mah·nee

52 Will I have to go to the hospital?
Devo andare in ospedale?
de·vo an·dah·ray een o·spe·dah·le

53 How do I get reimbursed?
Come posso essere rimborsato(a)?
koh·me pos·so es·se·re reem·bohr·sah·to(a)

Dentists

54 I need to see the dentist
Devo vedere il dentista
de·vo ve·day·re eel den·tee·sta

55 I have toothache
Ho mal di denti
o mal dee den·tee

56 It's this one
È questo
e kway·sto

57 I've broken a tooth
Mi sono spezzato(a) un dente
mee soh·no spets·tsah·to(a) oon den·te

58 The filling has come out
È uscita l'otturazione
e oo·shee·ta lot·too·ra·tsyoh·ne

59 Will you have to take it out?
Bisogna toglierlo?
bee·zoh·nya to·lyer·lo

60 Are you going to fill it?
Farà un'otturazione?
fa·ra oo·not·too·ra·tsyoh·ne

61 That hurt
M'ha fatto male
ma fat·to mah·le

62 Please give me an anaesthetic
Mi faccia un'iniezione, per favore
mee fach·cha oo·neen·ye·tsyoh·ne payr fa·voh·re

63 My gums hurt
Mi fanno male le gengive
mee fan·no mah·le le jen·jee·ve

64 My dentures are broken
La mia dentiera si è rotta
la mee·a den·tye·ra see e roht·ta

65 Can you repair them?
Può ripararla?
pwo ree·pa·rar·la

Emergencies and accidents (Ea)

Hopefully you will not need the following phrases, but it is better to know them, as they could make a difference in a critical situation. For a medical emergency, see also p.63.

1 Help!
Aiuto!
a·yoo·toh

2 Stop thief!
Alt al ladro!
alt al la·droh

3 There has been an accident
C'è stato un incidente
che stah·to oon een·chee·den·te

4 A fire has broken out
È scoppiato un incendio
e skop·pyah·to oon een·chen·dyoh

5   I have been — robbed/attacked
                   Mi hanno — derubato/assalito
                   *mee **an**·no — de·roo·**bah**·to/as·sa·**lee**·to*

6 Where is the nearest telephone/hospital?
     Dov'è il telefono/l'ospedale piú vicino?
     *doh·**ve** eel te·**le**·fo·noh/lo·spe·**dah**·le **pyoo** vee·**chee**·no*

7   Call — a doctor
                 Chiamate — un medico
                 *kya·**mah**·te — oon **me**·dee·koh*
                         — the police
                         — la polizia
                         *— lá po·lee·**tsee**·a*
                         — an ambulance
                         — un'ambulanza
                         *— oo·nam·boo·**lan**·tsa*
                         — the fire brigade
                         — i pompieri
                         *— ee pom·**pye**·ree*

8 This is an emergency
     È un caso di emergenza
     *e oon **kah**·zoh dee e·mer·**jen**·tsa*

9 It is urgent
     È urgente
     *e oor·**jen**·te*

10 Please hurry
     Fate presto, per favore
     ***fah**·te **pre**·sto payr fa·**voh**·re*

11 My address is . . .
     Il mio indirizzo è . . .
     *eel **mee**·o een·dee·**reets**·tsoh e*

Making conversation   (Mc)

Topics

The weather

Italians do not talk about the weather as much as, for example, the Americans and the English, but there are occasions when you will find the following useful.

1 It's a lovely day
     È una bella giornata
     *e **oo**·na **bel**·la johr·**nah**·ta*

2 It's hot/cold
     Fa caldo/freddo
     *fa **kal**·do/**frayd**·do*

3 It's raining
     Piove
     ***pyo**·ve*

4 It's windy
     Tira vento
     ***tee**·ra **ven**·toh*

5 It's snowing
     Nevica
     ***nay**·vee·ka*

6 It's foggy/misty
     C'è nebbia/bruma
     *che **nayb**·bya/**broo**·ma*

7 Is it going to be a nice day?
     Sarà una bella giornata?
     *sa·**ra oo**·na **bel**·la johr·**nah**·ta*

8 Is it going to rain?
     Pioverà?
     *pyo·ve·**ra***

9 What is the temperature?
     Quanti gradi ci sono?
     ***kwan**·tee **grah**·dee chee **soh**·no*

10 Is the water warm?
     È calda l'acqua?
     *e **kal**·da **lak**·kwa*

11 It's a clear night
     È una notte serena
     *e **oo**·na **not**·te se·**ray**·na*

National and regional characteristics

This is an endlessly fruitful source of material for conversation, and the main form of Italian small talk. It is an aspect of *campanilismo*, loyalty to the belfry, that is, to one's own village, town or region. Here are some points that might be raised.

12 Where do you come from?
Da dove viene?
da doh·ve vye·ne

13 Do you know the country around Florence?
Conosce i dintorni di Firenze?
ko·noh·she ee deen·tohr·nee dee fee·ren·tse

14 The wine from Orvieto/Treviso is wonderful
Il vino di Orvieto/Treviso è ottimo
eel vee·noh dee or·vye·to/tre·vee·zo e ot·tee·mo

15 Florence is a beautiful city
Firenze è una bella città
fee·ren·tse e oo·na bel·la cheet·ta

16 Have you ever been to Venice?
È mai stato(a) a Venezia?
e my stah·to(a) a ve·nay·tsya

17 The best time to go to Venice is in the spring
Il periodo migliore per andare a Venezia è in primavera
eel pe·ree·o·doh mee·lyoh·re payr an·dah·ray a ve·nay·tsya e een pree·ma·ve·ra

18 What are the people like in ...?
Com'è la gente a ...?
koh·me la jen·te a

19 Where did you spend your holidays last year?
Dove ha passato le Sue vacanze l'anno scorso?
doh·ve a pas·sah·to le soo·e va·kan·tse lan·noh skohr·so

20 Did you like it there?
Le è piaciuto?
le e pya·choo·to

21 What are the main industries of the region?
Quali sono le industrie principali della regione?
kwah·lee soh·no le een·doo·strye preen·chee·pah·lee del·la re·joh·ne

22 Is it prosperous?
È ricca?
e reek·ka

23 Does it remain unspoilt?
Il paesaggio è intatto?
eel pa·e·zaj·joh e een·tat·to

24 What sports are popular in Italy?
Quali sport sono popolari in Italia?
kwah·lee sport soh·no po·po·lah·ree een ee·ta·lya

Breaking the ice

Here are a few stock questions and answers that tend to be exchanged by people who meet casually.

25   Do you mind if — I sit here?
Le dispiace se — mi siedo qui?
le dee·spyah·che say — mee sye·do kwee
— I smoke?
— fumo?
— foo·mo

26   Can I — offer you a cigarette?
Gradisce — una sigaretta?
gra·dee·she — oo·na see·ga·rayt·ta
— buy you a drink?
— qualcosa da bere?
— kwal·ko·sa da bay·re

27 May I introduce myself?
Permetta che mi presenti
per·mayt·ta ke mee pre·zen·tee

28 Are you Italian? Where do you come from?
È italiano(a)? Da dove viene?
e ee·ta·lyah·no(a) da doh·ve vye·ne

29 I am American/English
Sono americano(a)/inglese
soh·no a·me·ree·kah·no(a)/een·glay·se

30 I live in New York/London
Abito a New York/Londra
ah·bee·to a new york/**lohn**·dra

31 Is this your first visit to Rome?
È questa la prima volta che viene a Roma?
e **kway**·sta la **pree**·ma **vol**·ta ke **vye**·ne a **roh**·ma

32 This is my third visit
Questa è la mia terza visita
kway·sta e la **mee**·a **ter**·tsa **vee**·zee·ta

33 Have you been here long?
È qui da molto?
e **kwee** da **mohl**·to

34 I have been here two days
Sono qui da due giorni
soh·no kwee da **doo**·e **johr**·nee

35 Are you staying long?
Si fermerà per molto?
see fer·me·**ra** payr **mohl**·to

36 I am staying for two weeks
Mi fermerò per due settimane
mee fer·me·**ro** payr **doo**·e set·tee·**mah**·ne

37 Where are you staying?
Dove alloggia?
doh·ve al·**loj**·ja

38 I am staying at the Hotel Gloria
Alloggio all'albergo Gloria
al·**loj**·jo al·lal·**ber**·goh **glo**·rya

39 What is your job?
Che lavoro fa?
ke la·**voh**·roh fa

40 Have you visited England/America?
Ha visitato l'Inghilterra/l'America?
a vee·zee·**tah**·to leen·geel·**ter**·ra/la·**me**·ree·ka

41 What do you think — of the people?
Cosa ne pensa — della gente?
ko·sa nay **pen**·sa — **del**·la **jen**·te
— the food?
— del cibo?
— del **chee**·boh
— the country?
— del paese?
— del pa·**ay**·ze

42 Are you married?
È sposato(a)?
e spo·**zah**·to(a)

43 Do you have any children?
Ha bambini?
a bam·**bee**·nee

44 Would you like — a cup of coffee/a drink?
Gradisce — un caffè/qualcosa da bere?
gra·**dee**·she — oon kaf·**fe**/kwal·**ko**·sa da **bay**·re
— to show me something of your city?
Le dispiacerebbe — mostrarmi qualcosa della Sua città?
le dee·spyah·che·**reb**·be — mo·**strar**·mee kwal·**ko**·sa **del**·la **soo**·a cheet·**ta**
— to have dinner/lunch with me?
Le farebbe piacere — cenare/pranzare con me?
le fa·**reb**·be pya·**chay**·re — che·**nah**·ray/pran·**dzah**·ray kohn may
— to go to the cinema/theatre with me?
— andare al cinema/a teatro con me?
— an·**dah**·ray al **chee**·ne·ma/a te·**ah**·troh kohn may
— to go out with me this evening?
— uscire insieme stasera?
— oo·**shee**·re een·**sye**·me sta·**say**·ra

Reference (R)

The alphabet

The Italian alphabet is the standard European one, although native Italian words lack J, K, W, X and Y. In the following table the names of the letters are given phonetically, and each letter (except for the five mentioned above) forms the initial of the word on the right. This is a standard system for classification, which might be used, for example, when a word is being spelled out over the telephone.

A	for	Ancona	N	for	Napoli
a		*an·**koh**·na*	*en·ne*		*nah·po·lee*
B		Bari	O		Otranto
bee		***bah**·ree*	*o*		*o·tran·to*
C		Como	P		Palermo
chee		***ko**·mo*	*pee*		*pa·**ler**·mo*
D		Domodossola	Q		quarto
dee		*do·mo·**dos**·so·la*	*koo*		***kwar**·to*
E		Empoli	R		Roma
ay		***aym**·po·lee*	*er·re*		***roh**·ma*
F		Firenze	S		Savona
ef·fe		*fee·**ren**·tse*	*es·se*		*sa·**voh**·na*
G		Genova	T		Torino
jee		***je**·no·va*	*tee*		*to·**ree**·no*
H		Hotel	U		Udine
ak·ka		*o·**tel***	*oo*		***oo**·dee·ne*
I		Imperia	V		Venezia
ee		*eem·**pe**·rya*	*voo*		*ve·**nay**·tsya*
J			W		
*ee **loon**·goh*			*voo·**dohp**·pyo*		
K			X		
***kap**·pa*			*eeks*		
L		Livorno	Y		
el·le		*lee·**vohr**·no*	*ee **gre**·ko*		
M		Milano	Z		zebra
em·me		*mee·**lah**·no*	*dze·ta*		*dze·bra*

Numbers

Cardinal numbers

0 zero	11 undici	22 ventidue
dze·ro	*oon·dee·chee*	*ven·tee·**doo**·e*
1 uno, una	12 dodici	23 ventitré
oo·noh, oo·na	*doh·dee·chee*	*ven·tee·**tray***
2 due	13 tredici	30 trenta
doo·e	*tray·dee·chee*	***trayn**·ta*
3 tre	14 quattordici	31 trentuno
tray	*kwat·**tohr**·dee·chee*	*tren·**too**·no*
4 quattro	15 quindici	40 quaranta
***kwat**·tro*	*kween·dee·chee*	*kwa·**ran**·ta*
5 cinque	16 sedici	50 cinquanta
***cheen**·kwe*	*say·dee·chee*	*cheen·**kwan**·ta*
6 sei	17 diciassette	60 sessanta
say	*dee·chas·**set**·te*	*ses·**san**·ta*
7 sette	18 diciotto	70 settanta
***set**·te*	*dee·**chot**·to*	*set·**tan**·ta*
8 otto	19 diciannove	80 ottanta
ot·to	*dee·chan·**no**·ve*	*ot·**tan**·ta*
9 nove	20 venti	90 novanta
***no**·ve*	***vayn**·tee*	*no·**van**·ta*
10 dieci	21 ventuno	100 cento
dye·chee	*ven·**too**·no*	***chen**·to*

101 centuno	300	2,000
chen·too·no	trecento	duemila
110 centodieci	*tray·chen·to*	*doo·e·mee·la*
chen·toh·dye·chee	1,000	1,000,000
200 duecento	mille	un milione
doo·e·chen·to	*meel·le*	*oon mee·lyoh·ne*

Ordinal numbers

1st	11th	20th
primo/prima	undicesimo(a)	ventesimo(a)
pree·mo/pree·ma	*oon·dee·che·zee·mo(a)*	*ven·te·zee·mo(a)*
2nd	12th	21st
secondo/seconda	dodicesimo(a)	ventunesimo(a)
se·kohn·do/	*do·dee·che·zee·mo(a)*	*ven·too·ne·zee·mo(a)*
se·kohn·da	13th	22nd
3rd	tredicesimo(a)	ventiduesimo(a)
terzo(a)	*tre·dee·che·zee·mo(a)*	*ven·tee·*
ter·tso(a)	14th	*doo·e·zee·mo(a)*
4th	quattordicesimo(a)	23rd
quarto(a)	*kwat·tor·*	ventitreesimo(a)
kwar·to(a)	*dee·che·zee·mo(a)*	*ven·tee·*
5th	15th	*tre·e·zee·mo(a)*
quinto(a)	quindicesimo(a)	30th
kween·to(a)	*kween·*	trentesimo(a)
6th	*dee·che·zee·mo(a)*	*tren·te·zee·mo(a)*
sesto(a)	16th	40th
se·sto(a)	sedicesimo(a)	quarantesimo(a)
7th	*se·dee·che·zee·mo(a)*	*kwa·ran·te·zee·mo(a)*
settimo(a)	17th	50th
set·tee·mo(a)	diciassettesimo(a)	cinquantesimo(a)
8th	*dee·chas·*	*cheen·kwan·*
ottavo(a)	*set·te·zee·mo(a)*	*te·zee·mo(a)*
ot·tah·vo(a)	18th	100th
9th	diciottesimo(a)	centesimo(a)
nono(a)	*dee·chot·te·zee·mo(a)*	*chen·te·zee·mo(a)*
no·no(a)	19th	1,000th
10th	diciannovesimo(a)	millesimo(a)
decimo(a)	*dee·chan·*	*meel·le·zee·mo(a)*
de·chee·mo(a)	*no·ve·zee·mo(a)·*	

Other numerical terms

a half	10 percent	five times
la metà	dieci per cento	cinque volte
la me·ta	*dye·chee payr chen·to*	*cheen·kwe vol·te*
a quarter	a dozen	the last (one)
un quarto	una dozzina	l'ultimo(a)
oon kwar·to	*oo·na dodz·dzee·na*	*lool·tee·mo(a)*
a third	half a dozen	
un terzo	una mezza dozzina	
oon ter·tso	*oo·na medz·dza*	
	dodz·dzee·na	

The time

In reply to the question "che ore sono?" (what time is it?) you will hear "sono" (it is), followed by the number. The 24-hour clock is often used. Otherwise one says "di mattina" (a.m.) or "di sera" (p.m.). Here are some examples.

9:00 — le nove
— *le no·ve*
9:05 — le nove e cinque
— *le no·ve ay cheen·kwe*
9:15 — le nove e un quarto
— *le no·ve ay oon kwar·to*

9:25	— le nove e venticinque	
	— le **no**·ve ay ven·tee·**cheen**·kwe	
9:30	— le nove e mezza	
	— le **no**·ve ay **medz**·dza	
9:35	— le dieci meno venticinque	
	— le **dye**·chee **may**·no ven·tee·**cheen**·kwe	
10:45	— le undici meno un quarto	
	— le **oon**·dee·chee **may**·no oon **kwar**·to	

Here are some other useful phrases connected with time.

tonight	before midnight	in an hour's time
stasera	prima di mezzanotte	fra un'ora
sta·**say**·ra	**pree**·ma dee medz·dza·**not**·te	fra oo·**noh**·ra
at night	after 3 o'clock	two hours ago
di notte	dopo le tre	due ore fa
dee **not**·te	**doh**·po le tray	**doo**·e **oh**·re fa
the morning	at half past 6	in half an hour
la mattina	alle sei e mezza	fra mezz'ora
la mat·**tee**·na	**al**·le say ay **medz**·dza	fra medz·**dzoh**·ra
this afternoon	nearly 5 o'clock	soon
questo pomeriggio	quasi le cinque	fra poco
kway·sto	**kwah**·zee le **cheen**·kwe	fra **po**·ko
po·me·**reej**·joh	at about 1 o'clock	early
at midday	circa l'una	presto
a mezzogiorno	**cheer**·ka **loo**·na	**pre**·sto
a medz·dzo·**johr**·noh		late
		tardi
		tar·dee

The calendar

Sunday	tomorrow	June
domenica	domani	giugno
do·**may**·nee·ka	do·**mah**·nee	**joo**·nyo
Monday	spring	July
lunedí	la primavera	luglio
loo·ne·**dee**	la pree·ma·**ve**·ra	**loo**·lyo
Tuesday	summer	August
martedí	l'estate	agosto
mar·te·**dee**	le·**stah**·te	a·**goh**·sto
Wednesday	autumn (fall)	September
mercoledí	l'autunno	settembre
mer·ko·le·**dee**	low·**toon**·noh	set·**tem**·bre
Thursday	winter	October
giovedí	l'inverno	ottobre
joh·ve·**dee**	leen·**ver**·noh	ot·**toh**·bre
Friday	in spring	November
venerdí	in primavera	novembre
ve·ner·**dee**	een pree·ma·**ve**·ra	no·**vem**·bre
Saturday	in summer	December
sabato	d'estate	dicembre
sa·**ba**·to	de·**stah**·te	dee·**chem**·bre
on Friday	January	in June
venerdí	gennaio	in giugno
ve·ner·**dee**	jen·**na**·yo	een **joo**·nyo
next Tuesday	February	July 6
martedí prossimo	febbraio	il sei luglio
mar·te·**dee**	feb·**bra**·yo	eel say **loo**·lyo
pros·see·mo	March	next week
yesterday	marzo	la settimana prossima
ieri	**mar**·tso	la set·tee·**mah**·na
ye·ree	April	**pros**·see·ma
today	aprile	last month
oggi	a·**pree**·le	il mese scorso
oj·jee	May	eel **may**·se **skohr**·so
	maggio	
	maj·jo	

Public holidays

New Year's Day	January 1
Easter Monday	
Liberation Day	April 25
Labour Day	May 1
Assumption	August 15
All Saints' Day	November 1
Immaculate Conception	December 8
Christmas Day	December 25
St Stephen's Day	December 26

Abbreviations

ACI	Automobile Club d'Italia (Italian Motoring Organisation)
CEE	Comunità Economica Europea (Common Market)
CIT	Compagnia Italiana del Turismo
ENIT	Ente Nazionale Italiano per il Turismo (Italian Tourist Authorities)
FS	Ferrovie dello Stato (Railways)
IVA	Imposta sul Valore Aggiunto (Value Added Tax)
PT	Poste e Telecomunicazioni (Post Office)
RAI	Radio Audizioni Italiane (Italian Radio & Television)
SIP	Società Italiana per l'esercizio telefonico (Italian Telephone Company)
TCI	Touring Club Italiano (Italian Touring Club)

Signs and notices (see also Road signs, p.18)

Ai treni	Ingresso gratuito *or*	Signori
To the trains	libero	Gentlemen
Al completo	Admission free	Si prega di attendere
Full	In restauro	Please wait
Alt	Undergoing	Sottopassaggio
Stop	restoration	Underpass
Aperto	Lavori in Corso	Spingere
Open	Men at work	Push
Ascensore	Libero	Suonare
Lift (elevator)	Vacant	Ring
Attenzione	Non toccare	Tirare
Danger	Do not touch	Pull
Avanti	Occupato	Uomini
Cross now	Occupied	Gentlemen
Cassa (in shop)	Pericoloso sporgersi	Uscita
Cashier's desk	Do not lean out	Exit
Chiuso	Polizia	Vernice fresca
Closed	Police	Wet paint
Degustazione	Saldi	Vietato il bagno
Sampling	Sale	No bathing
Donne	Servizio compreso	Vietato calpestare le
Ladies	Tip included	aiuole
Fermata	Servizio escluso	Keep off the grass
Bus stop	Tip not included	Vietato fumare
Guasto	Signore	No smoking
Out of order	Ladies	

Conversion tables

In the tables for weight and length, the central figure may be read as either a metric or a traditional measurement. So to convert from pounds to kilos you look at the figure on the right, and for kilos to pounds you want the figure on the left.

feet		metres	inches		cm	lbs		kg
3.3	1	0.3	0.39	1	2.54	2.2	1	0.45
6.6	2	0.61	0.79	2	5.08	4.4	2	0.91
9.9	3	0.91	1.18	3	7.62	6.6	3	1.4
13.1	4	1.22	1.57	4	10.6	8.8	4	1.8
16.4	5	1.52	1.97	5	12.7	11	5	2.2
19.7	6	1.83	2.36	6	15.2	13.2	6	2.7
23	7	2.13	2.76	7	17.8	15.4	7	3.2
26.2	8	2.44	3.15	8	20.3	17.6	8	3.6
29.5	9	2.74	3.54	9	22.9	19.8	9	4.1
32.9	10	3.05	3.9	10	25.4	22	10	4.5
			4.3	11	27.9			
			4.7	12	30.1			

°C	0	5	10	15	17	20	22	24	26	28	30	35	37	38	40	50	100
°F	32	41	50	59	63	68	72	75	79	82	86	95	98.4	100	104	122	212
Km	10	20	30	40	50	60	70	80	90	100	110	120
Miles	6.2	12.4	18.6	24.9	31	37.3	43.5	49.7	56	62	68.3	74.6

Tyre pressures

lb/sq in	15	18	20	22	24	26	28	30	33	35
kg/sq cm	1.1	1.3	1.4	1.5	1.7	1.8	2	2.1	2.3	2.5

Fuel

UK gallons	1.1	2.2	3.3	4.4	5.5	6.6	7.7	8.8
litres	5	10	15	20	25	30	35	40
US gallons	1.3	2.6	3.9	5.2	6.5	7.8	9.1	10.4

Basic Italian Grammar

NOUNS AND ARTICLES

Gender

This is one of the basic differences between Italian and English. In English, we say 'the knife' and 'the fork', but in Italian it is '*il coltello*' and '*la forchetta*', reflecting the fact that '*coltello*' is masculine and '*forchetta*' feminine. Equally, when using the indefinite article ('a', 'an' in English) it is '*un coltello*' but '*una forchetta*'.

While gender must be learned along with each new word you acquire, a useful guide is that:

(i) most masculine nouns end in *-o* in the singular which changes to *-i* in the plural e.g. *libro/libri*

(ii) most feminine nouns end in *-a* in the singular which changes to *-e* in the plural e.g. *casa/case*

(iii) nouns ending in *-e* in the singular can be *either* masculine *or* feminine; the *-e* becomes *-i* in the plural e.g. *padre* (m)/*padri*, *madre* (f)/*madri*

(iv) most masculine nouns ending in *-a* in the singular end in *-i* in the plural e.g. *macchinista/macchinisti*

(v) many nouns ending in *-a* in the singular can be *either* masculine *or* feminine; the *-a* becomes *-i* for the masculine plural and *-e* for the feminine plural e.g. *artista/artisti/artiste*

(vi) most masculine nouns ending in *-co* or *-go* in the singular end in *-chi* or *-ghi* in the plural; but nouns of more than two syllables where *-co* or *-go* is preceded by a vowel, end in *-ci* or *-gi* in the plural e.g. *fuoco/fuochi*, *albergo/alberghi*; *amico/amici*, *psicologo/psicologi*

(vii) nouns ending in *-ca* or *-ga* in the singular end in *-che* or *-ghe* in the plural if they are feminine and in *-chi* or *-ghi* if they are masculine e.g. *mosca/mosche*, *collega/colleghi*

(viii) most feminine nouns ending in *-cia* or *-gia* in the singular end in *-cie* or *-gie* in the plural when the *i* is stressed, and in *-ce* or *-ge* when it is not e.g. *bugia/bugie*; *provincia/province*

(ix) most masculine nouns ending in **-io** in the singular end in **-ii** in the plural
    when the *i* is stressed, and in *i* when it is not e.g. *zio/zii*; *studio/studi*
Any exceptions are clearly shown in the Italian-English dictionary section.

In Italian, the article must agree in gender (i.e. masculine or feminine) and
number (i.e. singular or plural) with the noun it accompanies. The following
table outlines the variation in article. The bracketed form is the one used with a
masculine noun beginning with *z*, *gn*, *pn*, *ps*, *x*, or *s* + consonant. See below for
examples.

	Definite article singular	**Definite article plural**	**Indefinite article**
masculine	*il (lo)*	*i (gli)*	*un (uno)*
	l' (before a vowel)	*gli* (before a vowel)	
feminine	*la*	*le*	*una*
	l' (before a vowel)		*un'* (before a vowel)
Thus:	**il** *libro*	**i** *libri*	**un** *libro*
	lo *gnomo*	**gli** *gnomi*	**uno** *gnomo*
	lo *psicologo*	**gli** *psicologi*	**uno** *psicologo*
	lo *sportello*	**gli** *sportelli*	**uno** *sportello*
	l'anello	**gli** *anelli*	**un** *anello*
	la *casa*	**le** *case*	**una** *casa*
	l'entrata	**le** *entrate*	**un'**entrata

Use of articles

1) In almost all cases where 'the' is not used in English, the article must be used
in Italian. For instance:
  apples are good for you *le mele fanno bene*
  meat is expensive *la carne è cara*
  France is beautiful *la Francia è bella*
  he likes ice cream *gli piace il gelato*

2) **a + il**, **da + il**, **su + il**, **in + il** etc
When the articles '*il*', '*lo*', '*la*', '*gli*', etc are preceded by the prepositions *a* (at; to),
da (by; from), *su* (on) and *in* (in; into), they are contracted thus:

a + il = al	*da + il = dal*	*su + il = sul*	*in + il = nel*
a + lo = allo	*da + lo = dallo*	*su + lo = sullo*	*in + lo = nello*
a + l' = all'	*da + l' = dall'*	*su + l' = sull'*	*in + l' = nell'*
a + la = alla	*da + la = dalla*	*su + la = sulla*	*in + la = nella*
a + i = ai	*da + i = dai*	*su + i = sui*	*in + i = nei*
a + gli = agli	*da + gli = dagli*	*su + gli = sugli*	*in + gli = negli*
a + le = alle	*da + le = dalle*	*su + le = sulle*	*in + le = nelle*

Thus: *alla casa* to the house *dai ragazzi* from the boys
       sul tavolo on the table *nello specchio* in the mirror

3) **di + il** etc
When the articles '*il*', '*lo*', '*gli*' etc are preceded by the preposition *di* (of), they
are contracted thus:
  di + il = del   *di + l' = dell'*   *di + i = dei*   *di + le = delle*
  di + lo = dello *di + la = della* *di + gli = degli*
NB The above forms also have the meaning 'some/any' and you should avoid
confusing this meaning with the 'of' meaning
  Thus:
  *voglio **del** pane***** I want *some* bread
  but *il titolo **del** libro* the title *of* the book
  *Note, however, that in a negative sentence, there is no article:
  non voglio pane I don't want (any) bread

4) **con + il/i**
When the articles '*il*' and '*i*' are preceded by *con* (with), they are contracted
thus:
  con + il = col *con + i = coi*
  Thus: *col maestro* with the teacher   *coi ragazzi* with the boys

ADJECTIVES

Position
Adjectives generally *follow* the noun in Italian:
  *una gonna **rossa*** a *red* skirt
  *la risposta **sbagliata*** the *wrong* answer
Among those which often *precede* the noun are some very common adjectives:
  *grande (big)   *giovane* (young)   *buono (good)
  piccolo (small)   *vecchio* (old)   *cattivo* (bad)
  lungo (long)   *bello (beautiful) *nuovo* (new)
  breve (short)   *brutto* (ugly)
*NB **Grande** becomes **gran** before a singular noun beginning with a consonant
other than z, **gn** etc, and **grand'** before a noun beginning with a vowel
  e.g. *un **gran** libro   una **gran** donna   un **grand'**uomo*
When placed before the noun, **bello** takes a form corresponding to *di + il* etc
contracted (see p.73) e.g. *un **bel** libro*, *un **bello** specchio* etc, while the singular

forms of **buono** correspond to those of the indefinite article (see p.73) e.g. *un buon libro*, *un buono sconto* etc

Agreement

In Italian, the adjective has to 'agree' in number and in gender with its noun. There are two types of adjectives: those ending in -*o* in the masculine singular and -*a* in the feminine singular, and those ending in -*e* in both the masculine and feminine singular. In the plural, as is the case for regular nouns, the -*o* becomes -*i*, the -*a* becomes -*e*, and the -*e* becomes -*i*.

Some examples:

Masculine singular	Feminine singular	Masculine plural	Feminine plural
il libro **rosso**	la porta **rossa**	i libri **rossi**	le porte **rosse**
il **piccolo** albero	la **piccola** casa	i **piccoli** alberi	le **piccole** case
il **giovane** ragazzo	la **giovane** ragazza	i **giovani** ragazzi	le **giovani** ragazze
l'uomo **inglese**	la donna **inglese**	gli uomini **inglesi**	le donne **inglesi**

Adjectives ending in -*co*, -*go*, etc follow the same pattern as the nouns (see notes iv to ix in the first section)

Possessive Adjectives

Unlike English, the possessive varies in Italian according to the gender and number of the noun it qualifies. Whether the owner is male or female, it is *il suo libro* (= *his* or *her* book), *la sua valigia* (= *his* or *her* case), *i suoi libri* (= *his* or *her* books), *le sue valigie* (= *his* or *her* cases).

There are few possessive adjectives and they can be easily summarized in, and learnt from, a table:

	SINGULAR		PLURAL	
	Masculine	**Feminine**	**Masculine**	**Feminine**
my	il mio	la mia	i miei	le mie
your (*familiar*)	il tuo	la tua	i tuoi	le tue
(*polite*)	il Suo	la Sua	i Suoi	le Sue
his/her/its	il suo	la sua	i suoi	le sue
our	il nostro	la nostra	i nostri	le nostre
your (*plural*)	il vostro	la vostra	i vostri	le vostre
(*polite*)	il loro	la loro	i loro	le loro
their	il loro	la loro	i loro	le loro

Notes

1) The '*il vostro*' form is now widely accepted as the plural form for both the '*il tuo*' and '*il Suo*' forms.

2) The definite article is omitted when any possessive (*except* **loro**) precedes a word in the singular indicating family relationship

e.g. *mio padre* my father **but** *il loro padre* their father
nostra madre our mother *la loro madre* their mother

Demonstrative Adjectives

The word for 'this' — *questo* — follows the same pattern as adjectives ending in -*o*, thus:

questo libro	this book	questi libri	these books
questa tazza	this cup	queste tazze	these cups

In addition, before a singular word beginning with a vowel, **questo** and **questa** become **quest**:

quest'albergo	this hotel	quest'arancia	this orange

The word for 'that' — *quello* — follows the same pattern as the definite article (p.73):

quel libro	that book	quei libri	those books
quello sportello	that door	quegli sportelli	those doors
quell'anello	that ring	quegli anelli	those rings
quella casa	that house	quelle case	those houses
quell'entrata	that entrance	quelle entrate	those entrances

PRONOUNS

Personal Pronouns

Subject	Direct Object	Indirect Object	In stressed position	Reflexive
SINGULAR				
1st person				
io (I)	mi (me)	mi; me* (to me)	me (me)	mi
2nd person				
tu (you: familiar)	ti (you)	ti; te* (to you)	te (you)	ti
3rd person (*m*)				
lui, egli (he)	lo, l' (him/it)	gli; glie* (to him/it)	lui (him)	si
esso (it)			esso (it)	

Subject	Direct Object	Indirect Object	In stressed position	Re-flexive
3rd person (*f*)				
lei, ella (she)	*la, l'* (her/it)	*le; glie** (to her/it)	*lei* (her)	*si*
essa (it)			*essa* (it)	
3rd person (*m/f*)				
lei (you: polite)	*la* (you)	*le; glie** (to you)	*lei* (you)	*si*
PLURAL				
1st person				
noi (we)	*ci* (us)	*ci; ce** (to us)	*noi* (us)	*ci*
2nd person				
voi (you)	*vi* (you)	*vi; ve** (to you)	*voi* (you)	*vi*
3rd person (*m*)				
loro (they)	*li* (them)	*loro* (to them)	*loro* (them)	*si*
essi (they: people/things)			*essi* (them)	
3rd person (*f*)				
loro (they)	*le* (them)	*loro* (to them)	*loro* (them)	*si*
esse (they: people/things)			*esse* (them)	
3rd person (*m/f*)				
loro (you: polite)	*li* (*m*) (you) *le* (*f*)	*loro* (to you)	*loro* (you)	*si*

*See note 2 under heading 'Order of Pronouns'.

Notes
1) The polite forms of the word 'you' are *lei* (singular) and *loro* (plural), which take the third person of the verb. You should use the familiar form of *tu* only with someone you know very well, with young children, or when invited to do so. The *voi* form is now widely accepted as the plural form for both *tu* and *lei*.
2) The form *l'* (2nd column) is used when the following word begins with a vowel or an 'h'.
3) The forms shown in the 4th column ('in stressed position') are used following prepositions e.g. *per me* for me, *con lei* with her
4) In Italian, the subject pronouns are often omitted before verbs, since the verb ending generally distinguishes the person (see p.77). They are included, however, when required for emphasis or clarity.
5) Reflexive pronouns are used with reflexive verbs (i.e. those ending in -*si*), having the value of 'oneself'. e.g.:
lavarsi

mi lavo	I wash myself
ti lavi	you wash yourself (*familiar*)
si lava	he/she washes himself/herself; you wash yourself (*polite*)
ci laviamo	we wash ourselves
vi lavate	you wash yourselves
si lavano	they wash themselves; you wash yourselves (*polite*)

Occasionally the value of 'oneself' is not reflected in the English, but if the Italian verb is reflexive, you must use the appropriate form of the pronoun, e.g.:

sedersi	to sit down	*mi siedo**	I sit down
muoversi	to move	*si muove**	it moves

*For appropriate forms of the verb, see the section on verb conjugations
Order of Pronouns
1) Direct and indirect object pronouns usually *precede* the verb:
lo vedo   I see *him*
gli legge una storia   she is reading *him* a story
Exception: *loro* which always *follows* the verb:
*scriverò **loro***   I shall write *to them/you*
However, used with an infinitive, the pronoun follows and is attached to the infinitive minus its final '*e*' (with the exception of *loro* which remains unattached).
Thus: *voglio sentirlo*   I want to hear *it*
           non vuole parlargli   she doesn't want to speak *to him*
but: *voglio dare **loro** il libro*   I want to give *them/you* the book
Similarly, the pronoun follows and is attached to the present participle (for formation see p.76) e.g. *vedendolo* on seeing *him*
The object pronoun also follows the verb and is written as one word with it, in commands of the type 'sell it', 'bring me ...' given to people *other* than those addressed as *lei* or *loro* (i.e. polite forms), in which case the pronoun *precedes* the verb.
Thus: *vendilo* (*tu*), *vendetelo* (*voi*)   sell it
but: *lo venda* (*lei*), *lo vendano* (*loro*)

portami (*tu*), portatemi (*voi*)
mi porti (*lei*), mi portino (*loro*)   bring me . . .

2) When both a direct and indirect object pronoun are used with the same verb, the indirect object pronouns *mi*, *ti*, *ci* and *vi* become *me*, *te*, *ce* and *ve* when followed by *lo*, *la*, *li* or *le*. Similarly the indirect object pronouns *gli* and *le* become *glie*, and combine with *lo*, *la*, *li* and *le* to become one single word: *glielo*, *gliela*, *glieli* and *gliele* (see table p. 74/75). With the exception of *loro*, which always *follows* the verb, the indirect object pronoun always *precedes* the direct.

Thus: *mi* parla   he talks to me
       me li dà   he gives them to me
       gli scrivo   I write to him
       glielo mando   I send it to him/her
       glieli dia (*lei*)
       date*glieli* (*voi*)   give them to him/her
       mostrando*melo*   on showing it to me
       voglio vender*glielo*   I want to sell it to him/her
but
       lo manderò *loro*   I shall send it to them/you
       lo dia *loro*   give it to them

Demonstrative Pronouns
To translate 'this (one)', 'these'/'that (one)', 'those', Italian uses
'*questo*'/'*quello*' respectively, varying the endings to indicate the gender and number of the object(s) referred to, thus:
       questo/questa this (one)   quello/quella that (one)
       questi/queste these   quelli/quelle those
'*Quello*' etc has the additional meaning of 'the one' etc as in:
       the one in the window   quello/quella in vetrina
       the ones on the shelf   quelli/quelle sullo scaffale

Possessive Pronouns
Used to translate 'mine', 'his' etc, they also depend on the number and gender of the noun described (and not on the sex of the 'possessor' — cf the possessive adjectives, above):

	with a masculine noun	with a feminine noun	with a masculine plural noun	with a feminine plural noun
mine	il mio	la mia	i miei	le mie
yours (*familiar*)	il tuo	la tua	i tuoi	le tue
(*polite*)	il Suo	la Sua	i Suoi	le Sue
his/hers/its	il suo	la sua	i suoi	le sue
ours	il nostro	la nostra	i nostri	le nostre
yours (*plural*)	il vostro	la vostra	i vostri	le vostre
(*polite*)	il loro	la loro	i loro	le loro
theirs	il loro	la loro	i loro	le loro

VERBS

Verb conjugations
The verb tables below will give you the ending patterns for the 'regular' verbs, and in a separate list you will find patterns to help you with all the irregular verbs marked with an asterisk in the dictionary section of this book. We only set out the forms for four tenses in this short grammar section, as the present, the imperfect, the future and the perfect will cater for most of your needs.

Tenses
1) As in English, an action in the present is expressed by the **present** tense. Hence: *parto* = I leave OR I am leaving
When the English has the sense of 'being in the process of doing' (rendered by the 'progressive' *-ing* form e.g. I am reading), the present tense of '*stare*' (see verb list, p.79) is used in conjunction with the present participle. To form the present participle, the infinitive endings *-are*, *-ere* and *-ire* are dropped and replaced by *-ando* for *-are* verbs and *-endo* for *-ere* and *-ire* verbs. Thus:
       stiamo mangiando   we're eating
       sto leggendo   I'm reading
       il treno sta partendo   the train is leaving
2) Past actions are shown by the **perfect** or **imperfect** tense in Italian. The latter is a simple tense, whereby endings are added to the verb stem (see table). The perfect is formed by the use of *avere* ('to have') plus the past participle (see table)
       e.g. parlavo   I was speaking   ho parlato   I spoke
Some verbs expressing the concepts of 'motion' or 'becoming' take **essere** instead of *avere* in the perfect tense. The main ones are: *andare, arrivare, cadere, divenire, diventare, entrare, essere, morire, nascere, partire, restare, rimanere, salire, scendere, stare, tornare, uscire, venire.*
Similarly, all reflexive verbs in Italian are conjugated with **essere**
       e.g. lavarsi ('to wash'): mi *sono* lavato ('I washed')
For actions in the past which happened at a specific point in time, Italian always

uses the **perfect** tense, which corresponds to our structure 'to have done'. This applies even when in English we would use a simple past tense:

I *did* it yesterday   *l'ho fatto ieri* (literally: I *have done* it . . .)

we *saw* him   *l'abbiamo visto* (literally: we *have seen* him)

The Italian perfect is also used where this tense is used in English:

I *have seen* him   *l'ho visto*   we *have done* it   *l'abbiamo fatto*

The **imperfect** tense in Italian is used only for an action or state in the past without definite limits in time, or for habitual actions in the past

e.g.

era *malata*   she *was* ill

abitavamo *a Londra durante la guerra*   we *lived* in London during the war

andavo *in ufficio alle nove*   I *went* (= used to go) to the office at nine o'clock

3) Largely used as its English counterpart, the **future** tense endings (see table) are added to the stem (see table). One particular point to note is that after **quando** ('when') and **se** ('if'), the future is used in Italian, where we use the present tense to describe a future action:

when he goes to Rome   *quando* **andrà** *a Roma*

if he comes   *se* **verrà**

Regular verb conjugations

The table below shows you how to conjugate regular verbs ending in -*are*, -*ere* and -*ire** in the infinitive (the form given in the dictionary), in all the tenses you will need for basic communication. For all other regular verbs with these endings (i.e. those NOT marked with an asterisk in the dictionary) remove the infinitive ending and add the endings shown. Since the subject pronouns are often omitted in Italian unless required for clarity or emphasis, they have been shown in brackets.

*You will note that 2 examples of the -*ire* verbs have been given, since this conjugation is divided into 2 distinct groups: those which, like **dormire**, form their present tense by removing the infinitive ending and adding the endings -*o*, -*i*, -*e*, -*iamo*, -*ite*, -*ono*; and those which, like **finire**, form their present tense by removing the infinitive ending and adding the endings -*isco*, -*isci*, -*isce*, -*iamo*, -*ite*, -*iscono*

INFINITIVE:	parl**are**	vend**ere**	dorm**ire**	fin**ire**
PRESENT				
(io)	parl**o**	vend**o**	dorm**o**	fin**isco**
(tu)	parl**i**	vend**i**	dorm**i**	fin**isci**
(lui/lei)	parl**a**	vend**e**	dorm**e**	fin**isce**
(noi)	parl**iamo**	vend**iamo**	dorm**iamo**	fin**iamo**
(voi)	parl**ate**	vend**ete**	dorm**ite**	fin**ite**
(loro)	parl**ono**	vend**ono**	dorm**ono**	fin**iscono**
FUTURE				
(io)	parl**erò**	vend**erò**	dorm**irò**	fin**irò**
(tu)	parl**erai**	vend**erai**	dorm**irai**	fin**irai**
(lui/lei)	parl**erà**	vend**erà**	dorm**irà**	fin**irà**
(noi)	parl**eremo**	vend**eremo**	dorm**iremo**	fin**iremo**
(voi)	parl**erete**	vend**erete**	dorm**irete**	fin**irete**
(loro)	parl**eranno**	vend**eranno**	dorm**iranno**	fin**iranno**
IMPERFECT				
(io)	parl**avo**	vend**evo**	dorm**ivo**	fin**ivo**
(tu)	parl**avi**	vend**evi**	dorm**ivi**	fin**ivi**
(lui/lei)	parl**ava**	vend**eva**	dorm**iva**	fin**iva**
(noi)	parl**avamo**	vend**evamo**	dorm**ivamo**	fin**ivamo**
(voi)	parl**avate**	vend**evate**	dorm**ivate**	fin**ivate**
(loro)	parl**avano**	vend**evano**	dorm**ivano**	fin**ivano**
PERFECT*				
(io)	**ho** parl**ato**	**ho** vend**uto**	**ho** dorm**ito**	**ho** fin**ito**
(tu)	**hai** parl**ato**	**hai** vend**uto**	**hai** dorm**ito**	**hai** fin**ito**
(lui/lei)	**ha** parl**ato**	**ha** vend**uto**	**ha** dorm**ito**	**ha** fin**ito**
(noi)	**abbiamo** parl**ato**	**abbiamo** vend**uto**	**abbiamo** dorm**ito**	**abbiamo** fin**ito**
(voi)	**avete** parl**ato**	**avete** vend**uto**	**avete** dorm**ito**	**avete** fin**ito**
(loro)	**hanno** parl**ato**	**hanno** vend**uto**	**hanno** dorm**ito**	**hanno** fin**ito**

*If a verb takes **essere** in the perfect instead of **avere** as shown here, the relevant part of **essere** (see p.78) replaces that of **avere**, and the past participle agrees in number and gender with its subject:

sono **andato**   *siamo* **partiti**
        andata   **partite**

Irregular Verb Forms

To identify the pattern of a verb marked with an asterisk in the dictionary and not shown here, refer to the verb with the identical ending. This may take the form of the whole word (e.g. for **promettere** see **mettere**, for **supporre** see *porre*) or only part of the word (e.g. for *ardere* see *prendere*, for *scegliere* see *cogliere*).

The irregular forms shown below are: 1) the present tense in full 2) the first person of the future tense 3) the first person of the imperfect tense 4) the past participle used with '*avere*' or '*essere*' to give the perfect tense 5) the present participle where irregular. For the future and imperfect tenses use the form shown but alternate the endings as in the table of regular verbs with the first person ending given here.

aggiungere 1) aggiungo, aggiungi, aggiunge, aggiungiamo, aggiungete, aggiungono 2) aggiungerò 3) aggiungevo 4) aggiunto

andare 1) vado, vai, va, andiamo, andate, vanno 2) andrò 3) andavo 4) andato

apparire 1) appaio, appari/apparisci, appare/apparisce, appariamo, apparite, appaiono/appariscono 2) apparirò 3) apparivo 4) apparso

aprire 1) apro, apri, apre, apriamo, aprite, aprono 2) aprirò 3) aprivo 4) aperto

assistere 1) assisto, assisti, assiste, assistiamo, assistete, assistono 2) assisterò 3) assistevo 4) assistito

assumere 1) assumo, assumi, assume, assumiamo, assumete, assumono 2) assumerò 3) assumevo 4) assunto

avere 1) ho, hai, ha, abbiamo, avete, hanno 2) avrò 3) avevo 4) avuto

bere 1) bevo, bevi, beve, beviamo, bevete, bevono 2) berrò 3) bevevo 4) bevuto 5) bevendo

cadere 1) cado, cadi, cade, cadiamo, cadete, cadono 2) cadrò 3) cadevo 4) caduto

chiedere 1) chiedo, chiedi, chiede, chiediamo, chiedete, chiedono 2) chiederò 3) chiedevo 4) chiesto

cogliere 1) colgo, cogli, coglie, cogliamo, cogliete, colgono 2) coglierò 3) coglievo 4) colto

conoscere 1) conosco, conosci, conosce, conosciamo, conoscete, conoscono 2) conoscerò 3) conoscevo 4) conosciuto

correre 1) corro, corri, corre, corriamo, correte, corrono 2) correrò 3) correvo 4) corso

costruire 1) costruisco, costruisci, costruisce, costruiamo, costruite, costruiscono 2) costruirò 3) costruivo 4) costruito/costrutto

crescere 1) cresco, cresci, cresce, cresciamo, crescete, crescono 2) crescerò 3) crescevo 4) cresciuto

cuocere 1) cuocio, cuoci, cuoce, cociamo, cocete, cuociono 2) cuocerò 3) cuocevo 4) cotto

dare 1) do, dai, dà, diamo, date, danno 2) darò 3) davo 4) dato

dipingere 1) dipingo, dipingi, dipinge, dipingiamo, dipingete, dipingono 2) dipingerò 3) dipingevo 4) dipinto

dire 1) dico, dici, dice, diciamo, dite, dicono 2) dirò 3) dicevo 4) detto 5) dicendo

dirigere 1) dirigo, dirigi, dirige, dirigiamo, dirigete, dirigono 2) dirigerò 3) dirigevo 4) diretto

discutere 1) discuto, discuti, discute, discutiamo, discutete, discutono 2) discuterò 3) discutevo 4) discusso

distinguere 1) distinguo, distingui, distingue, distinguiamo, distinguete, distinguono 2) distinguerò 3) distinguevo 4) distinto

dolere 1) dolgo, duoli, duole, doliamo, dolete, dolgono 2) dorrò 3) dolevo 4) doluto

dovere 1) devo/debbo, devi, deve, dobbiamo, dovete, devono/debbono 2) dovrò 3) dovevo 4) dovuto

esigere 1) esigo, esigi, esige, esigiamo, esigete, esigono 2) esigerò 3) esigevo 4) esatto

esprimere 1) esprimo, esprimi, esprime, esprimiamo, esprimete, esprimono 2) esprimerò 3) esprimevo 4) espresso

essere 1) sono, sei, è, siamo, siete, sono 2) sarò 3) ero, eri, era, eravamo, eravate, erano 4) stato

fare 1) faccio, fai, fa, facciamo, fate, fanno 2) farò 3) facevo 4) fatto 5) facendo

fondere 1) fondo, fondi, fonde, fondiamo, fondete, fondono 2) fonderò 3) fondevo 4) fuso

immergere 1) immergo, immergi, immerge, immergiamo, immergete, immergono 2) immergerò 3) immergevo 4) immerso

leggere 1) leggo, leggi, legge, leggiamo, leggete, leggono 2) leggerò 3) leggevo 4) letto

mentire 1) mento/mentisco, menti/mentisci, mente/mentisce, mentiamo, mentite, mentono/mentiscono 2) mentirò 3) mentivo 4) mentito

mettere 1) metto, metti, mette, mettiamo, mettete, mettono 2) metterò 3) mettevo 4) messo

morire 1) muoio, muori, muore, moriamo, morite, muoiono 2) morirò/morrò 3) morivo 4) morto

muovere 1) *muovo, muovi, muove, moviamo, movete, muovono* 2) *muoverò* 3) *muovevo* 4) *mosso*

nascere 1) *nasco, nasci, nasce, nasciamo, nascete, nascono* 2) *nascerò* 3) *nascevo* 4) *nato*

nascondere 1) *nascondo, nascondi, nasconde, nascondiamo, nascondete, nascondono* 2) *nasconderò* 3) *nascondevo* 4) *nascosto*

offrire 1) *offro, offri, offre, offriamo, offrite, offrono* 2) *offrirò* 3) *offrivo* 4) *offerto*

parere 1) *paio, pari, pare, paiamo, parete, paiono* 2) *parrò* 3) *parevo* 4) *parso*

perdere 1) *perdo, perdi, perde, perdiamo, perdete, perdono* 2) *perderò* 3) *perdevo* 4) *perso/perduto*

piacere 1) *piaccio, piaci, piace, piacciamo, piacete, piacciono* 2) *piacerò* 3) *piacevo* 4) *piaciuto*

piovere 1) *piove* 2) *pioverà* 3) *pioveva* 4) *piovuto* (used in 3rd person singular only)

porre 1) *pongo, poni, pone, poniamo, ponete, pongono* 2) *porrò* 3) *ponevo* 4) *posto* 5) *ponendo*

potere 1) *posso, puoi, può, possiamo, potete, possono* 2) *potrò* 3) *potevo* 4) *potuto*

prendere 1) *prendo, prendi, prende, prendiamo, prendete, prendono* 2) *prenderò* 3) *prendevo* 4) *preso*

prudere like *vendere*, but defective: no past participle

ridurre 1) *riduco, riduci, riduce, riduciamo, riducete, riducono* 2) *ridurrò* 3) *riducevo* 4) *ridotto* 5) *riducendo*

riempire 1) *riempio, riempi, riempie, riempiamo, riempite, riempiono* 2) *riempirò* 3) *riempivo* 4) *riempito* 5) *riempiendo*

riflettere 1) *rifletto, rifletti, riflette, riflettiamo, riflettete, riflettono* 2) *rifletterò* 3) *riflettevo* 4) *riflettuto/riflesso*

rimanere 1) *rimango, rimani, rimane, rimaniamo, rimanete, rimangono* 2) *rimarrò* 3) *rimanevo* 4) *rimasto*

risolvere 1) *risolvo, risolvi, risolve, risolviamo, risolvete, risolvono* 2) *risolverò* 3) *risolvevo* 4) *risolto*

rispondere 1) *rispondo, rispondi, risponde, rispondiamo, rispondete, rispondono* 2) *risponderò* 3) *rispondevo* 4) *risposto*

rompere 1) *rompo, rompi, rompe, rompiamo, rompete, rompono* 2) *romperò* 3) *rompevo* 4) *rotto*

salire 1) *salgo, sali, sale, saliamo, salite, salgono* 2) *salirò* 3) *salivo* 4) *salito*

sapere 1) *so, sai, sa, sappiamo, sapete, sanno* 2) *saprò* 3) *sapevo* 4) *saputo*

scrivere 1) *scrivo, scrivi, scrive, scriviamo, scrivete, scrivono* 2) *scriverò* 3) *scrivevo* 4) *scritto*

scuotere 1) *scuoto, scuoti, scuote, scotiamo, scotete, scuotono* 2) *scoterò* 3) *scotevo* 4) *scosso* 5) *scotendo*

sedere 1) *siedo/seggo, siedi, siede, sediamo, sedete, siedono/seggono* 2) *sederò* 3) *sedevo* 4) *seduto*

spargere 1) *spargo, spargi, sparge, spargiamo, spargete, spargono* 2) *spargerò* 3) *spargevo* 4) *sparso*

sparire 1) *sparisco, sparisci, sparisce, spariamo, sparite, spariscono* 2) *sparirò* 3) *sparivo* 4) *sparito*

spegnere 1) *spengo, spegni, spegne, spegniamo, spegnete, spengono* 2) *spegnerò* 3) *spegnevo* 4) *spento*

stare 1) *sto, stai, sta, stiamo, state, stanno* 2) *starò* 3) *stavo* 4) *stato*

stringere 1) *stringo, stringi, stringe, stringiamo, stringete, stringono* 2) *stringerò* 3) *stringevo* 4) *stretto*

succedere 1) *succedo, succedi, succede, succediamo, succedete, succedono* 2) *succederò* 3) *succedevo* 4) *successo*

tenere 1) *tengo, tieni, tiene, teniamo, tenete, tengono* 2) *terrò* 3) *tenevo* 4) *tenuto*

trarre 1) *traggo, trai, trae, traiamo, traete, traggono* 2) *trarrò* 3) *travo* 4) *tratto* 5) *traendo*

uscire 1) *esco, esci, esce, usciamo, uscite, escono* 2) *uscirò* 3) *uscivo* 4) *uscito*

valere 1) *valgo, vali, vale, valiamo, valete, valgono* 2) *varrò* 3) *valevo* 4) *valso*

vedere 1) *vedo/veggo, vedi, vede, vediamo, vedete, vedono/veggono* 2) *vedrò* 3) *vedevo* 4) *visto/veduto*

venire 1) *vengo, vieni, viene, veniamo, venite, vengono* 2) *verrò* 3) *venivo* 4) *venuto*

vincere 1) *vinco, vinci, vince, vinciamo, vincete, vincono* 2) *vincerò* 3) *vincevo* 4) *vinto*

vivere 1) *vivo, vivi, vive, viviamo, vivete, vivono* 2) *vivrò* 3) *vivevo* 4) *vissuto*

volere 1) *voglio, vuoi, vuole, vogliamo, volete, vogliono* 2) *vorrò* 3) *volevo* 4) *voluto*

ITALIAN–ENGLISH DICTIONARY

a *a prep* at; in; to; **a scuola** *a skwo·la* at/to school; **a Londra** *a lohn·dra* at/in/to London; **alla stazione** *al·la sta·tsyoh·ne* at/to the station; **alla televisione** *al·la te·le·vee·zee·oh·ne* on television; **alla parete** *al·la pa·ray·te* on the wall; **a sinistra/destra** *a see·nee·stra/de·stra* on/to the left/right; **alle 4** *al·le 4* at 4 o'clock; **a 30 chilometri** *a 30 kee·lo·me·tree* 30 kilometres away; **da lunedì a venerdì** *da loo·ne·dee a ve·ner·dee* Monday through Friday; **due volte al giorno** *doo·ay vol·tay al jor·noh* twice a day; **uno a uno** *oo·no a oo·no* one by one

abbagliare *ab·bal·yah·ray* vt dazzle

abbaiare *ab·ba·yah·ray* vi bark

abbandonare *ab·ban·do·nah·ray* vt abandon

abbassare *ab·bas·sah·ray* vt lower; turn down; dip (*headlights*)

abbastanza *ab·ba·stan·tsa* adv enough; quite; **ce ne sono abbastanza** *che nay soh·no ab·ba·stan·tsa* there are quite a few; **abbastanza tempo/libri** *ab·ba·stan·tsa tem·poh/lee·bree* enough time/books; **abbastanza grande** *ab·ba·stan·tsa gran·de* big enough

abbattere *ab·bat·te·re* vt knock down

abbazia *ab·ba·tsee·a* f abbey

abbigliamento *ab·beel·ya·mayn·toh* m clothes; **l'abbigliamento per uomo** *ab·beel·ya·mayn·toh payr wo·moh* menswear

abbonamento *ab·bo·na·mayn·toh* m subscription (*to periodical*); season ticket

abbonarsi *a ab·bo·nar·see* a vr subscribe to (*periodical*)

abbonato(a) *ab·bo·nah·to(a)* m/f subscriber

abbozzare *ab·bots·tsah·ray* vt sketch

abbozzo *ab·bots·tsoh* m sketch; draft (*rough outline*)

abbracciare *ab·brach·chah·ray* vt embrace; cuddle; hug

abbreviazione *ab·bre·vya·tsyoh·ne* f abbreviation

abbronzarsi *ab·bron·dzar·see* vr tan

abbronzato(a) *ab·bron·dzah·to(a)* adj sun-tanned

abbronzatura *ab·bron·dza·too·ra* f suntan

abete *a·bay·te* m fir (tree)

abilità *a·bee·lee·ta* f — ability; cleverness; skill

abitante *a·bee·tan·te* m/f inhabitant

abitare *a·bee·tah·ray* vi live (*reside*)
□ vt live in

abito *ah·bee·toh* m dress; suit (*man's*); **l'abito da sposa** *ah·bee·toh da spo·za* wedding dress; **l'abito da sera** *ah·bee·toh da say·ra* evening dress (*woman's*)

abituale *a·bee·too·ah·le* adj usual

abituarsi *a·bee·twar·see* a vr get used to

abitudine *a·bee·too·dee·ne* f habit

abolire *a·bo·lee·re* vt abolish

aborto *a·bor·toh* m miscarriage; abortion

accademia *ak·ka·de·mya* f academy

accadere* *ak·ka·day·re* vi happen

accamparsi *ak·kam·pahr·see* vr camp

accanto *ak·kan·to* adv nearby; **accanto a** *ak·kan·to* a beside

accappatoio *ak·kap·pa·toh·yoh* m bathrobe

accarezzare *ak·ka·rets·tsah·ray* vt stroke

accasciarsi *ak·ka·shar·see* vr collapse (*person*)

accelerare *ach·che·le·rah·ray* vt/i accelerate; speed up

acceleratore *ach·che·le·ra·toh·re* m accelerator

accendere* *ach·chen·de·re* vt turn on; light (*fire, cigarette*); switch on; **accendere* un fiammifero** *ach·chen·de·re con fyam·mee·fe·roh* to strike a match; **mi fa accendere?** *mee fa ach·chen·de·re* have you got a light?

accendino *ach·chen·dee·noh* m cigarette lighter

accenditore *ach·chen·dee·toh·re* m pilot light (*gas*)

accensione *ach·chen·syoh·ne* f ignition (*car*)

accento *ach·chen·toh* m accent; stress; **l'accento acuto** *ach·chen·toh a·koo·to* acute (accent); **l'accento grave** *ach·chen·toh grah·vay* grave (accent)

accentuare *ach·chen·too·ah·ray* vt emphasize (*syllable etc*)

acceso(a) *ach·chay·so(a)* adj on (*light, radio*)

accessibile *ach·ches·see·bee·le* adj accessible

accesso *ach·ches·soh* m access; fit

accessori *ach·ches·so·ree* mpl accessories

accettare *ach·chet·tah·ray* vt accept

accettazione *ach·chet·ta·tsyoh·ne* f acceptance

acchiappare *ak·kyap·pah·ray* vt catch

acciaio *ach·cha·yoh* m steel

accidentale *ach·chee·den·tah·le* adj accidental

acciuga *ach·choo·ga* f anchovy

accoglienza *ak·kol·yen·tsa* f welcome

accogliere* *ak·kol·ye·ray* vt receive (*guest*); welcome

accomodarsi *ak·ko·mo·dar·see* vr make oneself comfortable; **si accomodi** *see ak·ko·mo·dee* take a seat

accompagnare *ak·kom·pan·yah·ray* vt escort; accompany; **accompagnare qualcuno a casa** *ak·kom·pan·yah·ray kwal·koo·no a kah·sa* to see someone home; **accompagnare qualcuno alla porta** *ak·kom·pan·yah·ray kwal·koo·no al·la por·ta* to show someone out

accompagnatore *ak·kom·pan·ya·toh·re* m escort

acconciatura *ak·kon·cha·too·ra* f hairstyle

acconto *ak·kohn·toh* m down payment

accorciare *ak·kor·chah·ray* vt shorten

accordare *ak·kor·dah·ray* vt tune (*instrument*); grant (*wish*)

accordo *ak·kor·doh* m agreement; **l'accordo globale** *ak·kor·doh glo·bah·le* package deal; **essere* d'accordo con qualcuno** *es·se·re dak·kor·doh kon kwal·koo·no* to agree with someone; **mettersi* d'accordo su** *mayt·ter·see dak·kor·doh soo* to agree on

accreditare *ak·kre·dee·tah·ray* vt credit

accrescimento ak·kre·shee·mayn·toh m increase (in size)

accumularsi ak·koo·moo·lar·see vr accumulate

accusa ak·koo·za f charge (accusation)

accusare ak·koo·zah·ray vt accuse

acerbo(a) a·cher·bo(a) adj unripe; sour (sharp)

aceto a·chay·toh m vinegar

acido ah·chee·doh m acid □ adj acido(a) ah·chee·do(a) sour (milk)

acne ak·ne f acne

acqua ak·kwa f water; l'acqua corrente ak·kwa kor·ren·te running water; l'acqua potabile ak·kwa po·tah·bee·le drinking water; l'acqua distillata ak·kwa dee·steel·lah·ta distilled water; l'acqua minerale ak·kwa mee·ne·rah·lay mineral water; l'acqua tonica ak·kwa to·nee·ka tonic water; l'acqua di Colonia ak·kwa dee ko·lon·ya cologne; fare* acqua fah·ray ak·kwa to leak (boat)

acquaio ak·kwa·yoh m sink (basin)

acquario ak·kwah·ryoh m aquarium

acquazzone ak·kwats·tsoh·ne m shower (rain)

acquirente ak·kwee·ren·te m/f buyer (customer)

acquisizione ak·kwee·zee·tsyoh·ne f acquisition

acquistare ak·kwee·stah·ray vt acquire

acquisti ak·kwee·stee mpl shopping

acquisto ak·kwee·stoh m purchase

acrilico(a) a·kree·lee·ko(a) adj acrylic

acuto(a) a·koo·to(a) adj acute

adattare a·dat·tah·ray vt adapt

adatto(a) a·dat·to(a) adj suitable

addebitare ad·day·bee·tah·ray vt debit; lo addebiti al mio conto loh ad·de·bee·tee al mee·oh kohn·toh charge it to my account

addebito ad·day·bee·toh m debit

addestrare ad·de·strah·ray vt train

addizione ad·dee·tsyoh·ne f addition

addobbi ad·dob·bee mpl decorations

addome ad·do·me m abdomen

addormentato(a) ad·dor·men·tah·to(a) adj asleep; essere* profondamente addormentato(a) es·se·re pro·fohn·da·mayn·te ad·dor·men·tah·to(a) to be fast asleep

adolescente a·do·le·shen·te m/f teenager

adottare a·dot·tah·ray vt adopt

Adriatico a·dree·a·tee·koh m Adriatic (Sea)

adulto a·dool·toh m adult □ adj adulto(a) a·dool·toh(a) adult; grown-up

aereo a·e·re·oh m plane; aircraft; in aereo een a·e·re·oh by plane

aereo(a) a·e·re·o(a) adj air; per via aerea payr vee·a a·e·re·a by air

aerobus a·e·ro·boos m air bus

aerodinamico(a) a·e·ro·dee·na·mee·ko(a) adj streamlined (car)

aeroplano a·e·ro·plah·noh m aeroplane, airplane

aeroporto a·e·ro·por·toh m airport

affamato(a) af·fa·mah·to(a) adj starving

affare af·fah·re m affair (matter); deal; per affari payr af·fah·ree on business; fare* affari con qualcuno fah·ray af·fah·ree kohn kwal·koo·no to do business with someone

affari af·fah·ree mpl business (dealings, work); affairs

affascinante af·fa·shee·nan·te adj fascinating; glamorous

affatto af·fat·toh adv at all

afferrare af·fer·rah·ray vt seize; grab

affettare af·fayt·tah·ray vt slice

affetto af·fet·toh m affection

affettuosamente af·fet·too·oh·sa·mayn·te adv love from (on letter)

affettuoso(a) af·fet·twoh·so(a) adj affectionate

affidabilità af·fee·da·bee·lee·ta f reliability (of car)

affievolirsi af·fye·vo·leer·see vr grow weak; fade

affiggere* af·feej·je·re vt put up (notice)

affilato(a) af·fee·lah·to(a) adj sharp (knife)

affiliato(a) af·fee·lyah·to(a) adj subsidiary

affittare af·feet·tah·ray vt rent (house etc); let (rent out)

affittasi af·feet·ta·see to let (house etc)

affitto af·feet·toh m lease; rent

affogato(a) af·fo·gah·to(a) adj drowned; poached

affollato(a) af·fol·lah·toh(a) adj crowded

affondare af·fohn·dah·ray vt/i sink (in water)

affrancare af·fran·kah·ray vt stamp (letter)

affrettarsi af·fret·tar·see vr hurry

affrontare af·fron·tah·ray vt tackle (problem)

affumicato(a) af·foo·mee·kah·to(a) adj smoked (salmon etc)

afoso(a) a·foh·soh(a) adj close (stuffy)

Africa a·free·ka f Africa

africano(a) a·free·kah·no(a) adj African

agenda a·jen·da f diary

agente a·jen·te m agent; broker; l'agente marittimo a·jen·te ma·reet·tee·mo shipping agent; l'agente di viaggi a·jen·te dee vee·aj·jee travel agent; l'agente immobiliare a·jen·te eem·mo·bee·lyah·re estate agent; realtor; l'agente di polizia a·jen·te dee po·lee·tsee·a officer (police); l'agente di cambio a·jen·te dee kam·byoh stockbroker

agenzia a·jen·tsee·a f agency (office); l'agenzia pubblicitaria a·jen·tsee·a poob·blee·chee·tah·rya advertising agency; l'agenzia di viaggi a·jen·tsee·a dee vee·aj·jee travel agency

aggiornare aj·johr·nah·ray vt update

aggiungere* aj·joon·je·re vt add

aggiustare aj·joo·stah·ray vt adjust

aggressivo(a) ag·gres·see·vo(a) adj aggressive

aggrovigliare ag·gro·veel·yah·ray vt tangle

agile ah·jee·le adj agile

agire a·jee·re vi act; work

agitare a·jee·tah·ray vt shake; agitare la mano a·jee·tah·ray la mah·noh to wave

agitato(a) a·jee·tah·to(a) adj rough (sea); restless; upset

agli = a + gli

aglio ah·lyoh m garlic

agnello an·yel·loh m lamb

ago ah·goh m needle

agosto a·goh·sto m August

agricolo(a) a·gree·ko·lo(a) adj agricultural

agricoltore a·gree·kol·toh·re m farmer

agricoltura a·gree·kol·too·ra f agriculture

ai = a + i

aia a·ya f farmyard

aiuola a·yoo·wo·la f flowerbed

aiutare *a·yoo·tah·ray vt* help; mi può aiutare? *mee pwo a·yoo·tah·ray* can you help me?

aiuto *a·yoo·toh m* help; aiuto! *a·yoo·toh* help!

ala *ah·la f* ali wing

alba *al·ba f* dawn

albergo *al·ber·goh m* hotel

albero *al·be·roh m* tree; mast (*ship's*); l'albero di Natale *al·be·roh dee na·tah·lay* Christmas tree; l'albero a camme *al·be·roh a kam* camshaft

albicocca *al·bee·kok·ka f* apricot

album *al·boom m* album (*for photos etc*)

alcol *al·kol m* alcohol

alcolici *al·ko·lee·chee mpl* liquor

alcolico *al·ko·lee·koh m* alcoholic drink □ adj alcolico(a) *al·ko·lee·ko(a)* alcoholic (*drink*)

alcolizzato(a) *al·ko·leedz·dzah·to(a) m/f* alcoholic

alcool *al·kol m* alcohol; l'alcool denaturato *al·kol day·na·too·rah·toh* methylated spirits

alcova *al·ko·va f* alcove

alcuni(e) *al·koo·nee(·ne) art, pron* some

alcuno(a) *al·koo·no(a) adj* any

alfabeto *al·fa·be·toh m* alphabet

Algeri *al·je·ree f* Algiers

Algeria *al·je·ree·a f* Algeria

algerino(a) *al·je·ree·no(a) adj* Algerian

alghe *al·ge fpl* seaweed

aliante *a·lee·an·tay m* glider

allacciare *al·lach·chah·ray vt* fasten

Allah *al·la m* Allah

allarmare *al·lar·mah·ray vt* alarm

allarmarsi *al·lar·mar·see vr* panic

allarme *al·lar·me m* alarm (*signal, apparatus*); l'allarme antincendio *al·lar·me an·teen·chen·dyoh* fire alarm

alleanza *al·le·an·tsa f* alliance

allegato *al·le·gah·toh m* enclosure (*in letter*)

allegro(a) *al·lay·groh(a) adj* cheerful

allenamento *al·le·na·mayn·toh m* training (*for sports*)

allenarsi *al·le·nar·see vr* train (*sportsman*)

allenatore *al·le·na·toh·ray m* coach (*instructor*)

allergia *al·ler·jee·a f* allergy

allergico(a) a *al·ler·jee·ko(a) a adj* allergic to

allevare *al·le·vah·ray vt* raise (*family*); rear (*children, cattle*)

alleviare *al·le·vyah·ray vt* ease (*pain*)

alloggiare *al·loj·jah·ray vt* put up (*accommodate*) □ vi live (*reside*)

alloggio *al·loj·joh m* lodgings; accommodation

allora *al·loh·ra adv* then; d'allora in poi *dal·loh·ra een poy* from then on; da allora è sempre lì *da al·loh·ra e sem·pre lee* he's been there ever since

alludere* *a al·loo·de·ray a vi* refer to (*allude to*)

alluminio *al·loo·meen·yoh m* aluminium, aluminum

allungare *al·loon·gah·ray vt* lengthen

almeno *al·may·no adv* at least

Alpi *al·pee fpl* Alps

alpinismo *al·pee·nee·zmoh m* mountaineering; fare* l'alpinismo *fah·ray del·lal·pee·nee·zmoh* to go mountaineering

alpino(a) *al·pee·no(a) adj* alpine

altalena *al·ta·lay·na f* swing; seesaw

altare *al·tah·re m* altar

alterare *al·te·rah·ray vt* alter

alternatore *al·ter·na·toh·re m* alternator (*in car*)

altezza *al·tayts·tsa f* height

altitudine *al·tee·too·dee·ne f* altitude

alto *al·to adv* high; aloud; in alto *een al·to* high; up, upward(s)

alto(a) *al·to(a) adj* high; tall; alto(a) 6 metri *al·to(a) 6 me·tree* 6 metres high; quanto è alto lei? *kwan·to e al·to ley* how tall are you?; l'alta stagione *al·ta sta·joh·ne* high season

altoparlante *al·to·par·lan·te m* loudspeaker

altrimenti *al·tree·mayn·tee adv* otherwise

altro(a) *al·tro(a) adj* other □ pron l'altro(a) *lal·tro(a)* the other; l'altro sesso *al·tro ses·soh* the opposite sex; l'altro giorno *lal·tro johr·noh* the other day

altrove *al·troh·ve adv* somewhere else

alunno(a) *a·loon·no(a) m/f* pupil

alzare *al·tsah·ray vt* raise; turn up (*heat*)

alzarsi *al·tsahr·see vr* get up; stand up; rise

amaca *a·mah·ka f* hammock

amante *a·man·tay m/f* lover; mistress

amare *a·mah·ray vt* love

amaro(a) *a·mah·ro(a) adj* bitter

ambasciata *am·ba·shah·ta f* embassy

ambasciatore *am·ba·sha·toh·re m* ambassador

ambedue *am·be·doo·e adj, pron* both

ambiente *am·byen·te m* environment

ambizione *am·bee·tsyoh·ne f* ambition

ambizioso(a) *am·bee·tsyoh·so(a) adj* ambitious

ambulanza *am·boo·lan·tsa f* ambulance

ambulatorio *am·boo·la·to·ree·oh m* consulting room

America *a·me·ree·ka f* America; l'America del Sud *a·me·ree·ka del sood* South America; l'America del Nord *a·me·ree·ka del nord* North America

America Latina *a·me·ree·ka la·tee·na f* Latin America

americano(a) *a·me·ree·kah·no(a) adj* American

ametista *a·me·tee·sta f* amethyst

amianto *a·myan·toh m* asbestos

amichevole *a·mee·kay·vo·le adj* friendly

amico(a) *a·mee·ko(a) m/f* friend

amido *ah·mee·doh m* starch

ammaccatura *am·mak·ka·too·ra f* dent; bruise

ammaestrare *am·ma·e·strah·ray vt* train (*animal*)

ammettere* *am·met·te·ray vt* admit

amministrazione *am·mee·nee·stra·tsyoh·nay f* administration; l'amministrazione statale *am·mee·nee·stra·tsyoh·nay sta·tah·lay* civil service

ammirare *am·mee·rah·ray vt* admire

ammobiliare *am·mo·bee·lyah·ray vt* furnish (*room etc*)

ammontare a *am·mohn·tah·ray a vi* amount to

ammortizzare *am·mor·teedz·dzah·ray vt* absorb (*shock*)

ammortizzatore *am·mor·teedz·dza·toh·re m* shock absorber

ammucchiare *am·mook·kyah·ray vt* pile up

amo *ah·moh m* hook (*fishing*)

amore *a·moh·re m* love

ampère *am·pehr m* amp

ampio(a) *am·pyo(a) adj* loose (*clothing*)

amplificatore *am·plee·fee·ka·toh·re* m amplifier

analcolico(a) *a·nal·ko·lee·koh(a)* adj nonalcoholic; soft (*drink*)

analisi *a·nah·lee·see* f — analysis

analista-programmatore *a·na·lee·sta· pro·gram·ma·toh·re* m systems analyst

analizzare *a·na·leedz·dzah·ray* vt analyse

ananas *a·na·nas* m — pineapple

anatra *ah·na·tra* f duck

anca *an·ka* f hip

anche *an·ke* adv too; also; even

ancora *an·koh·ra* adv still (*up to this time*); yet; again; c'è ancora mine-stra? *che an·koh·ra mee·ne·stra* is there any more soup?; ancor più ve-loce *an·kohr pyoo ve·loh·che* even faster; ancora del formaggio *an·koh·ra del for·maj·joh* more cheese; gra-direi ancora un po' *gra·dee·ray an·koh·ra oon po* I'd like (some) more!; ancora una birra, per favore! *an·koh·ra oo·na beer·ra payr fa·voh·re* another beer please!

ancora *an·ko·ra* f anchor

andare* *an·dah·ray* vi go; andiamo *an·dyah·mo* let's go; andiamo alla spiag-gia *an·dyah·mo al·la spyaj·ja* we are going to the beach; va bene *va be·ne* O.K., okay (*agreement*); it's OK; il mio orologio va avanti *eel mee·o o·ro·lo·joh va a·van·tee* my watch is fast; andare* in macchina *an·dah·ray een mak·kee·na* to drive; andare* via *an·dah·ray vee·a* to go away; andare* in bicicletta *an·dah·ray een bee·chee·klayt·ta* to cycle; andare* alla deriva *an·dah·ray al·la de·ree·va* to drift (*boat*); andarsene* *an·dar·se·ne* to go away

anello *a·nel·loh* m ring (*on finger*); l'a-nello di fidanzamento *a·nel·loh dee fee·dan·tsa·mayn·toh* engagement ring

anemico(a) *a·ne·mee·ko(a)* adj an(a)emic

anestetico *a·ne·ste·tee·koh* m an(a)es-thetic

angelo *an·je·loh* m angel

angolo *an·go·loh* m corner; angle; è dietro l'angolo *e dye·tro lan·go·loh* it's round the corner

angora *an·go·ra* f angora (*fabric*)

angoscia *an·go·sha* f distress

anguille *an·gweel·lay* fpl eels

anguria *an·goo·ree·a* f watermelon

anima *ah·nee·ma* f soul

animale *a·nee·mah·le* m animal; l'ani-male domestico *a·nee·mah·le do·me·stee·ko* pet

animato(a) *a·nee·mah·to(a)* adj busy (*place*)

annata *an·nah·ta* f vintage; year (*as duration*)

annegare *an·ne·gah·ray* vi drown

anniversario *an·nee·ver·sah·ryoh* m an-niversary

anno *an·noh* m year; quanti anni ha? *kwan·tee an·nee a* how old are you?; all'anno *al·lan·noh* per annum

annodare *an·no·dah·ray* vt tie (*string, ribbon*); knot

annoiare *an·no·yah·ray* vt bore; annoy

annotare *an·no·tah·ray* vt write down

annuale *an·noo·ah·le* adj annual; yearly

annualmente *an·noo·al·mayn·te* adv yearly

annullare *an·nool·lah·ray* vt cancel

annuncio *an·noon·choh* m announce-ment; advertisement

annunziare *an·noon·tsyah·ray* vt an-nounce

ansia *an·see·a* f concern (*anxiety*)

ansimare *an·see·mah·ray* vi pant

Antartide *an·tar·tee·de* f Antarctic

antenato(a) *an·te·nah·to(a)* m/f ances-tor

antenna *an·tayn·na* f aerial; antenna; l'antenna trasmittente *an·tayn·na tras·meet·ten·tay* mast (*radio*)

anteprima *an·te·pree·ma* f preview

anteriore *an·te·ryoh·re* adj front

antiappannante *an·tee·ap·pan·nan·te* m demister

antibiotico *an·tee·bee·o·tee·koh* m anti-biotic

antichità *an·tee·kee·ta* f — antique; antiquity

anticipare *an·tee·chee·pah·ray* vt ad-vance (*money*)

anticipo *an·tee·chee·poh* m advance (*loan*); Lei è in anticipo *lay e een an·tee·chee·poh* you're early; in anticipo *een an·tee·chee·poh* in advance

antico(a) *an·tee·ko(a)* adj antique; an-cient

anticoncezionale *an·tee·kon·che·tsyoh·nah·lay* m contraceptive

anticongelante *an·tee·kon·je·lan·te* m antifreeze

antieconomico(a) *an·tee·e·ko·no·mee·ko(a)* adj uneconomic

antipasto *an·tee·pa·stoh* m hors d'œuvre

antiquario *an·tee·kwah·ryoh* m antique dealer

antiquato(a) *an·tee·kwa·to(a)* adj out of date; old-fashioned

antisettico *an·tee·set·tee·koh* m antiseptic

antistaminico *an·tee·sta·mee·nee·koh* m antihistamine

ape *ah·pe* f bee

aperitivo *a·pe·ree·tee·voh* m aperitif

aperto(a) *a·per·to(a)* adj on (*water supply*); open; all'aperto *al·la·per·to* in the open (air); open-air

apparecchiare *ap·pa·rek·kyah·ray* vt lay (*table*)

apparecchio *ap·pa·rayk·kyoh* m appliance; l'apparecchio acustico *ap·pa·rayk·kyoh a·koo·stee·ko* hearing aid

apparentemente *ap·pa·ren·te·mayn·te* adv apparently

apparire* *ap·pa·ree·re* vi appear

appartamento *ap·par·ta·mayn·toh* m flat; apartment

appartenere* a *ap·par·te·nay·re* a vi belong to

appassionato(a) *ap·pas·syoh·nah·to(a)* adj keen (*swimmer, reader*)

appena *ap·pay·na* adv scarcely; è ap-pena partito *e ap·pay·na par·tee·to* he's just left

appendere* *ap·pen·de·re* vt hang

appendicite *ap·pen·dee·chee·te* f ap-pendicitis

appetito *ap·pe·tee·toh* m appetite

appezzamento *ap·pets·tsa·mayn·toh* m plot (*of land*)

appiccicoso(a) *ap·peech·chee·koh·so(a)* adj sticky

applaudire *ap·plow·dee·ray* vt/i clap; cheer

applausi *ap·plow·zee* mpl applause

appoggiarsi a *ap·poj·jar·see* a vr lean against

apposta *ap·po·sta adv* on purpose; deliberately

apprendista *ap·pren·dee·sta m/f* apprentice; trainee

apprezzare *ap·prets·tsah·ray vt* appreciate

appropriato(a) *ap·pro·pree·ah·to(a) adj* suitable (*fitting*)

approssimativamente *ap·pros·see·ma·tee·va·mayn·tay adv* roughly (*approximately*)

approssimativo(a) *ap·pros·see·ma·tee·vo(a) adj* approximate

approvare *ap·pro·vah·ray vt* approve of

approvazione *ap·pro·vah·tsyoh·ne f* approval

appuntamento *ap·poon·ta·mayn·toh m* appointment (*rendezvous*); date

apribottiglie *ah·pree·bot·teel·ye m* — bottle opener

aprile *a·pree·le m* April

aprire* *a·pree·re vt* open; turn on □ *vi* open (*store, bank*); **aprire* con chiave** *a·pree·re kohn kyah·ve* to unlock

apriscatole *ah·pree·skah·to·lay m* — can-opener

aquila *ah·kwee·la f* eagle

aquilone *a·kwee·loh·ne m* kite

arabo(a) *a·ra·bo(a) m/f* Arab □ *adj* Arabic □ *m* **l'arabo** *a·ra·bo* Arabic

arachide *a·ra·kee·de f* peanut

aragosta *a·ra·goh·sta f* lobster

arancia *a·ran·cha f* orange

aranciata *a·ran·chah·ta f* orangeade

arancione *a·ran·choh·ne adj* orange

aratro *a·ra·troh m* plough

arbitro *ahr·bee·troh m* umpire; referee (*sports*)

arbusto *ar·boo·stoh m* shrub

architetto *ar·kee·tayt·toh m* architect

architettura *ar·kee·tet·too·ra f* architecture

archivio *ar·kee·vyoh m* file (*dossier*); filing cabinet; **l'archivio di dati** *ar·kee·vyoh dee dah·tee* data file

arco *ar·koh m* arch

arcobaleno *ar·ko·ba·lay·noh m* rainbow

ardere* *ar·de·re vi* burn

ardesia *ar·de·zya f* slate

area *ah·re·a f* area; **l'area di servizio** *ah·re·a dee ser·vee·tsyoh* service area

argenteria *ar·jen·te·ree·a f* silver (*ware*)

Argentina *ar·jen·tee·na f* Argentina

argentino(a) *ar·jen·tee·no(a) adj* Argentine

argento *ar·jen·toh m* silver (*metal*); **un braccialetto d'argento** *oon brach·cha·layt·toh dar·jen·toh* a silver bracelet

argilla *ahr·jeel·la f* clay

argomento *ar·go·mayn·toh m* topic

aria *ah·rya f* air; tune; **con aria condizionata** *kohn ah·rya kon·dee·tsyoh·nah·ta* air-conditioned; **all'aria aperta** *al·lah·rya a·per·ta* in the open (*air*); outdoor

arieggiare *a·ree·ej·jah·ray vt* air (*room*)

aringa *a·reen·ga f* herring

aritmetica *a·reet·me·tee·ka f* arithmetic

arma *ar·ma f —i* weapon; **l'arma da fuoco** *ar·ma da fwo·koh* firearm

armadietto *ar·mah·dyayt·toh m* locker

armadio *ar·mah·dyoh m* cupboard; wardrobe (*furniture*)

armi *ar·mee fpl* arms

armonioso(a) *ar·mo·nyoh·so(a) adj* harmonious

arnese *ar·nay·se m* tool

arpa *ar·pa f* harp

arrabbiato(a) *ar·rab·byah·to(a) adj* angry (*person*)

arrampicarsi su *ar·ram·pee·kahr·see soo vr* climb (*tree, wall*)

arrangiarsi *ar·ran·jahr·see vr* manage

arrestare *ar·re·stah·ray vt* arrest

arretrati *ar·re·trah·tee mpl* arrears

arrivare *ar·ree·vah·ray vi* arrive; **arrivare a** *ar·ree·vah·ray a* to reach; **come ci si arriva?** *koh·may chee see ar·ree·va* how do we get there?; **arrivare a casa** *ar·ree·vah·ray a kah·sa* to get home

arrivederci *ar·ree·ve·dayr·chee excl* goodbye

arrivo *ar·ree·voh m* arrival

arrossire *ar·ros·see·re vi* blush

arrostire *ar·ro·stee·ray vt* roast

arrosto *ar·ro·stoh m* roast meat

arrotolare *ar·ro·to·lah·ray vt* roll up (*newspaper etc*)

arruffato(a) *ar·roof·fah·to(a) adj* untidy (*hair*)

arrugginirsi *ar·rooj·jee·neer·see vr* rust

arrugginito(a) *ar·rooj·jee·nee·to(a) adj* rusty

arte *ar·te f* art; craft

arteria *ar·te·ree·a f* artery

Artico *ar·tee·koh m* Arctic

articolo *ar·tee·ko·loh m* article; **gli articoli di vetro** *ar·tee·ko·lee dee vay·troh* glass (*glassware*); **gli articoli da toeletta** *ar·tee·ko·lee da to·e·let·ta* toiletries

artificiale *ar·tee·fee·chah·le adj* artificial; man-made

artigiano *ar·tee·jah·noh m* craftsman

artista *ar·tee·sta m/f* artist

artrite *ar·tree·te f* arthritis

ascensore *a·shen·soh·re m* elevator; lift

ascesso *a·shays·soh m* abscess

asciugacapelli *a·shoo·ga·ka·payl·lee m* — hair-drier

asciugamano *a·shoo·ga·mah·noh m* towel

asciugare *a·shoo·gah·ray vt* dry; wipe

asciutto(a) *a·shoot·to(a) adj* dry

ascoltare *a·skol·tah·ray vi* listen □ *vt* listen to

Asia *ah·zee·a f* Asia

asiatico(a) *a·zee·a·tee·ko(a) adj* Asian

asilo d'infanzia *a·zee·loh deen·fan·tsya m* nursery school

asino *ah·see·noh m* donkey

asma *az·ma f* asthma

asparago *a·spa·ra·goh m* asparagus

aspettare *a·spet·tah·ray vt* wait for; expect □ *vi* wait; **fare* aspettare qualcuno** *fah·ray a·spet·tah·ray kwal·koo·no* to keep someone waiting; **aspetti!** *a·spet·tee* hang on! (*on phone*)

aspetto *a·spet·toh m* look (*appearance*)

aspirapolvere *a·spee·ra·pohl·ve·re m* — vacuum cleaner

aspirina *a·spee·ree·na f* aspirin

assaggiare *as·saj·jah·ray vt* taste (*try*)

assalire* *as·sa·lee·ray vt* attack

assassinare *as·sas·see·nah·ray vt* murder

assassino *as·sas·see·noh m* killer

asse *as·se m* axle □ *f* board (*of wood*)

assecondare *as·se·kon·dah·ray vt* back (*support*)

assegnare *as·sen·yah·ray vt* allocate

assegno *as·sayn·yoh m* allowance (*state payment*); cheque; **l'assegno per viaggiatori** *as·sayn·yoh per vyaj·ja·toh·ree* travel(l)er's cheque

assente *as·sen·te adj* absent

assenteismo *as·sen·te·ee·zmoh m* absenteeism

assetato(a) *as·se·tah·to(a) adj* thirsty

assicurare *as·see·koo·rah·ray vt* underwrite; insure

assicurarsi *as·see·koo·rar·see vr* insure oneself

assicurato(a) *as·see·koo·rah·to(a) adj* insured

assicuratore *as·see·koo·ra·toh·ray m* underwriter

assicurazione *as·see·koo·ra·tsyoh·ne f* insurance; l'assicurazione contro terzi *as·see·koo·ra·tsyoh·ne kohn·tro ter·tsee* third party insurance; l'assicurazione contro tutti i rischi *as·see·koo·ra·tsyoh·ne kohn·troh toot·tee ee ree·skee* comprehensive insurance

assistente *as·see·sten·te m/f* assistant; l'assistente sociale *as·see·sten·te so·chah·le* social worker

assistere* *as·see·ste·re vt* assist; assistere* a *as·see·ste·re a* to attend (*meeting etc*)

asso *as·soh m* ace (*cards*)

associazione *as·so·cha·tsyoh·ne f* society; association

assoluto(a) *as·so·loo·to(a) adj* absolute

assomigliare *as·so·meel·yah·ray a vi* resemble

assorbente *as·sor·ben·te adj* absorbent □ m l'assorbente igienico *as·sor·ben·te ee·je·nee·ko* sanitary towel

assorbire *as·sor·bee·re vt* absorb (*fluid*)

assortito(a) *as·sor·tee·to(a) adj* assorted

assumere* *as·soo·me·ray vt* recruit (*personnel*); assumere* il controllo di una ditta *as·soo·me·ray eel kon·trol·loh dee oo·na deet·ta* to take over a firm

assurdo(a) *as·soor·do(a) adj* absurd

asta *a·sta f* auction; l'asta dell'olio *a·sta del·lol·yoh* dipstick

astenersi* *a·ste·nayr·see vr* abstain

astratto(a) *a·strat·to(a) adj* abstract

astronave *a·stro·nah·ve f* spacecraft

astuccio *a·stooch·choh m* case (*for jewel(l)ery etc*)

astuto(a) *a·stoo·to(a) adj* shrewd

Atene *a·te·ne f* Athens

atlante *at·lan·te m* atlas

Atlantico *at·lan·tee·ko m* Atlantic Ocean

atleta *at·le·ta m/f* athlete

atout *a·too m* trump (*cards*)

attaccapanni *at·tak·ka·pan·nee m —* peg (*for coat*); hat stand; coat hanger

attaccare *at·tak·kah·ray vt* attach; attack; fasten; attaccare un cane ad un palo *at·tak·kah·ray oon kah·ne ad oon pah·loh* to tie a dog to a post

attacco *at·tak·koh m* raid (*military*); attack; l'attacco cardiaco *at·tak·koh kar·dee·a·ko* heart attack

atteggiamento *at·tej·ja·mayn·toh m* attitude

attendere* *at·ten·de·re vt* wait for

attenzione *at·ten·tsyoh·nay f* attention; attenzione allo scalino *at·ten·tsyoh·nay al·loh ska·lee·noh* mind the step; attenzione! *at·ten·tsyoh·nay* look out!

atterraggio *at·ter·raj·joh m* landing (*of plane*); l'atterraggio di emergenza *at·ter·raj·joh dee e·mer·jen·tsa* emergency landing; l'atterraggio di fortuna *at·ter·raj·joh dee for·too·na* crash-landing

atterrare *at·ter·rah·ray vi* land (*plane*)

attico *at·tee·koh m* attic; penthouse

attività *at·tee·vee·ta f* activity

attivo(a) *at·tee·vo(a) adj* active □ m l'attivo *at·tee·voh* asset (*financial*)

atto *at·toh m* act; action; deed; l'atto di nascita *at·toh dee na·shee·ta* birth certificate

attore *at·toh·re m* actor

attraversamento pedonale *at·tra·vayr·sa·mayn·toh pe·do·nah·lay m* pedestrian crossing, crosswalk

attraversare *at·tra·ver·sah·ray vt* cross (*road, sea*); attraversare la Manica a nuoto *at·tra·ver·sah·ray la mah·nee·ka a nwo·toh* to swim the Channel; abbiamo attraversato la Francia in macchina *ab·byah·mo at·tra·ver·sah·to la fran·cha een mak·kee·na* we drove across France

attraverso *at·tra·ver·so prep* through

attrezzatura *at·trets·tsa·too·ra f* tackle (*gear*)

attrice *at·tree·che f* actress

attuale *at·twah·le adj* present

audace *ow·dah·che adj* bold

audioguida *ow·dyo·gwee·da f* audioguide

audiovisivo(a) *ow·dyo·vee·zee·vo(a) adj* audio-visual

auguri *ow·goo·ree mpl* wishes

aumentare *ow·men·tah·ray vt* increase; turn up (*volume*) □ vi increase; aumentare di valore *ow·men·tah·ray dee va·loh·re* to appreciate (*in value*)

aumento *ow·mayn·toh m* increase (*in number*); rise; raise; growth (*in amount etc*)

Australia *ow·strah·lya f* Australia

australiano(a) *ow·stra·lyah·no(a) adj* Australian

Austria *ow·strya f* Austria

austriaco(a) *ow·stree·a·ko(a) adj* Austrian

autentico(a) *ow·ten·tee·koh(a) adj* genuine

autista *ow·tees·ta m* chauffeur

autobus *ow·to·boos m —* bus

autogrú *ow·to·groo f* breakdown van

automaticamente *ow·to·ma·tee·ka·mayn·te adv* automatically

automatico(a) *ow·to·ma·tee·ko(a) adj* automatic; la macchina automatica *mak·kee·na ow·to·ma·tee·ka* automatic (*car*)

automatizzare *ow·to·ma·teedz·dzah·ray vt* computerize (*system*)

automazione *ow·to·ma·tsyoh·ne f* automation

automobile *ow·to·mo·bee·lay f* car; l'automobile decappottabile *ow·to·mo·bee·lay de·kap·pot·tah·bee·lay* convertible

automobilista *ow·to·mo·bee·lee·sta m/f* motorist

autonomo(a) *ow·to·no·mo(a) adj* self-employed

autopompa *ow·to·pohm·pa f* fire engine

autore *ow·toh·re m* author

autorimessa *ow·toh·ree·mes·sa f* garage (*for parking*)

autostop *ow·to·stop m* hitchhiking; fare* l'autostop *fah·ray low·to·stop* to hitchhike

autostoppista *ow·to·stop·pee·sta m/f* hitchhiker

autostrada *ow·to·strah·da f* motorway; freeway; l'autostrada a pedaggio *ow·to·strah·da a pe·daj·joh* toll road

autunno *ow·toon·noh m* autumn

avanti *a·van·tee* adv in front; forward(s); il sedile è troppo in avanti *eel se·dee·le e trop·po een a·van·tee* the seat is too far forward

avanzare *a·van·tsah·ray* vi remain (*be left over*); advance; ci avanza un po' di panna *chee a·van·tsa oon po dee pan·na* there's some cream left

avaria *a·va·ree·a* f breakdown (*of car*); failure (*mechanical*)

avena *a·vay·na* f oats

avere* *a·vay·re* vt have; non abbiamo pane *nohn ab·byah·mo pah·ne* we haven't any bread; ha del pane? *a del pah·ne* have you any bread?; ho fame *o fah·me* I am hungry; ha quarant'anni *a kwa·ran·tan·nee* he's forty

aviazione *a·vya·tsyoh·ne* f air force; aviation

aviogetto *a·vyo·jet·toh* m jet (*plane*)

avocado *a·vo·kah·doh* m avocado (*pear*)

avorio *a·vo·ryoh* m ivory

avvenimento *av·ve·nee·mayn·toh* m event

avventura *av·ven·too·ra* f adventure

avvertire *av·vayr·tee·re* vt warn

avviarsi *av·vee·ar·see* vr set off

avvicinarsi *av·vee·chee·nar·see* vr approach; avvicinarsi ad un luogo *av·vee·chee·nar·see ad oon lwo·goh* to approach a place

avvisare *av·vee·zah·ray* vt inform; warn

avviso *av·vee·zoh* m warning; announcement; advertisement; notice

avvocato *av·vo·kah·toh* m barrister; solicitor; lawyer; attorney

avvolgere* *av·vol·je·re* vt wind; wrap

azione *a·tsyoh·ne* f action (*movement*); share (*finance*); le azioni privilegiate *a·tsyoh·nee pree·vee·le·jah·te* preference shares

azionista *a·tsyoh·nee·sta* m/f investor; shareholder

azzurro(a) *adz·dzoor·ro(a)* adj blue

B

babysitter *bay·bee·see·ter* f baby-sitter

bacca *bak·ka* f berry

baccarà *bak·ka·ra* m baccarat

baciare *ba·chah·ray* vt kiss

baciarsi *ba·char·see* vr kiss (each other)

bacino *ba·chee·noh* m dock; pond (*artificial*)

bacio *bah·choh* m kiss

badare a *bah·dah·ray a* vi look after; pay attention to

baffi *baf·fee* mpl moustache

bagagli *ba·gal·yee* mpl luggage

bagagliaio *ba·gal·ya·yoh* m boot (*of car*); luggage van

bagaglio a mano *ba·gal·yoh a mah·noh* m hand-luggage

bagliore *bal·yoh·re* m flash; glare (*of light*)

bagnare *ban·yah·ray* vt wet

bagnarsi *ban·yar·see* vr get wet; bathe

bagnato(a) *ban·yah·to(a)* adj wet

bagnino *ban·yee·noh* m lifeguard

bagno *ban·yoh* m bathroom (*lavatory*); bath

baia *ba·ya* f bay (*on coast*)

balcone *bal·koh·ne* m balcony

balena *ba·lay·na* f whale

balenare *ba·le·nah·ray* vi flash (*light*)

ballare *bal·lah·ray* vi dance

balletto *bal·layt·toh* m ballet

ballo *bal·loh* m ball; dance

balsamo *bal·sa·moh* m conditioner (*for hair*)

bambinaia *bam·bee·na·ya* f nurse(maid)

bambino(a) *bam·bee·noh(a)* m/f child; baby

bambola *bam·bo·la* f doll

bambú *bam·boo* m bamboo

banana *ba·nah·na* f banana

banca *ban·ka* f bank (*finance*); la banca commerciale *ban·ka kom·mayr·chah·lay* merchant bank; la banca dei dati *ban·ka de·ee dah·tee* data bank, data base

bancarella *ban·ka·rel·la* f stall; stand

bancarotta *ban·ka·roht·ta* f bankruptcy

banchetto *ban·kayt·toh* m banquet

banchiere *ban·kye·re* m banker

banchina *ban·kee·na* f platform (*in station*); quay; quayside

banco *ban·koh* m bar (*counter*); bench (*seat, work table*); counter (*in shop*); il banco di sabbia *ban·koh dee sab·bya* sandbank

bancogiro *ban·ko·jee·roh* m bank giro (system)

banconota *ban·ko·no·ta* f bank note

banda *ban·da* f gang; band (*musical*)

bandiera *ban·dye·ra* f banner; flag

bandito *ban·dee·toh* m gunman

bar *bar* m — bar; pub

bara *bah·ra* f coffin

barattolo *ba·rat·to·loh* m tin; jar

barba *bar·ba* f beard

barbabietola *bar·ba·bye·to·la* f beetroot

barbecue *bar·ba·kyoo* m barbecue

barbiere *bar·bye·re* m barber

barca *bar·ka* f boat

barcollare *bar·kol·lah·ray* vi stagger; sway

barella *ba·rel·la* f stretcher

barile *ba·ree·le* m barrel

barista *ba·ree·sta* m/f barman; barmaid

barra *bar·ra* f rod

barricata *bar·ree·kah·ta* f barricade

barriera *bar·rye·ra* f barrier

basare *ba·zah·ray* vt base

base *bah·ze* f base; basis; di base *dee bah·ze* basic

baseball *bays·bol* m baseball

basso(a) *bas·so(a)* adj low; short (*person*); in basso *een bas·so* downward(s)

bastare *ba·stah·ray* vi be enough; grazie, basta cosí *gra·tsye ba·sta ko·see* thank you, that's plenty; basta cosí? *ba·sta ko·see* will it do?

bastoncini *ba·ston·chee·nee* mpl chopsticks

bastone *ba·stoh·ne* m stick; walking stick; il bastone da passeggio *ba·stoh·ne da pas·sayj·joh* walking stick

battaglia *bat·tal·ya* f battle

battello *bat·tel·loh* m boat; il battello da diporto *bat·tel·loh da dee·por·toh* pleasure boat; il battello di salvataggio *bat·tel·loh da sal·va·tahj·joh* lifeboat

battere *bat·te·re* vt hit; beat; break (*record*) □ vi beat (*heart*); l'orologio ha battuto le tre *lo·ro·lo·joh a bat·too·to le tray* the clock struck three; battere le palpebre *bat·te·re le pal·pe·bre* to blink

batteria *bat·te·ree·a* f battery (*in car*); heat (*sports*)

battersi *bat·ter·see* vr fight; battersi la testa *bat·ter·see la te·sta* to bang one's head

battesimo bat·tay·zee·moh m baptism

baule ba·oo·le m trunk

bazar ba·dzar m — bazaar

beccare bek·kah·ray vt peck

beige bayzh adj beige

bellezza bel·layts·tsa f beauty

bello(a) bel·lo(a) adj beautiful; handsome; lovely; fine (weather); **fa bello** fa bel·lo the weather's fine

benché ben·ke conj although

benda ben·da f blindfold; bandage

bene be·ne adv well; all right; **stare* bene** stah·ray be·ne to be well; **il latte ti fa bene** eel lat·te tee fa be·ne milk is good for you; **molto bene!** mohl·to be·ne (that's) fine!; **va bene** va be·ne all right

benedire* be·ne·dee·re vt bless

beneficiario be·ne·fee·chah·ryoh m payee

Benelux be·ne·looks m Benelux

beni be·nee mpl goods; property

benvenuto(a) ben·ve·noo·to(a) adj welcome

benzina ben·dzee·na f petrol; gas(oline)

bere* bay·re vt drink; **prenda qualcosa da bere!** pren·da kwal·ko·sa da bay·re have a drink!

berlina ber·lee·na f saloon (car)

bernoccolo ber·nok·ko·loh m bump (lump)

berretto ber·rayt·toh m cap (hat)

bersaglio ber·sal·yoh m target

bestemmiare be·stem·myah·ray vi swear (curse)

bestiame be·stee·ah·may m cattle

betulla be·tool·la f birch (tree)

bevanda be·van·da f drink

biancheria byan·ke·ree·a f linen (for beds, table); **la biancheria da letto** byan·ke·ree·a da let·toh bedding; **la biancheria intima** byan·ke·ree·a een·tee·ma underwear

bianchetti byan·kayt·tee mpl whitebait

bianco(a) byan·ko(a) adj white; blank; **l'assegno in bianco** as·sayn·yoh een byan·ko blank cheque; **lasciate in bianco per favore** la·shah·te een byan·ko payr fa·voh·re please leave blank

Bibbia beeb·bya f Bible

biberon bee·be·ron m bottle (baby's)

bibita bee·bee·ta f soft drink

biblioteca bee·blee·o·te·ka f library; bookcase

bicchiere beek·kye·re m glass (tumbler); **il bicchiere da vino** beek·kye·re da vee·noh wineglass

bicicletta bee·chee·klayt·ta f bicycle; **andare* in bicicletta** an·dah·ray een bee·chee·klayt·ta to cycle

bidone bee·doh·ne m ashcan; dustbin

bigliettaio beel·yet·ta·yoh m conductor (on bus)

biglietteria beel·yet·te·ree·a f ticket office

biglietto beel·yayt·toh m note (letter); ticket; card; **il biglietto di abbonamento** beel·yayt·toh dee ab·bon·a·mayn·toh season ticket; **il biglietto di andata e ritorno** beel·yayt·toh dee an·dah·ta e ree·tohr·noh return ticket; **il biglietto di solo andata** beel·yayt·toh dee soh·lo an·dah·ta single ticket

bigodino bee·go·dee·noh m curler (for hair)

bikini bee·kee·nee m — bikini

bilancia bee·lan·cha f scales (for weighing); **la bilancia dei pagamenti** bee·lan·cha de·ee pa·ga·mayn·tee balance of payments; **la bilancia com-**

merciale bee·lan·cha kom·mer·chah·le balance of trade

bilanciare bee·lan·chah·ray vt balance

bilancio bee·lan·choh m balance sheet; **il bilancio preventivo** bee·lan·choh pre·ven·tee·vo budget

bilia beel·ya f marble (ball)

biliardo bee·lyar·doh m billiards

bilingue bee·leen·gwe adj bilingual

binario bee·nah·ryoh m track (for trains); line; platform

binocolo bee·no·ko·loh m binoculars

biologia bee·o·lo·jee·a f biology

biondo(a) byohn·do(a) adj blond(e); fair

birra beer·ra f beer; **la birra alla spina** beer·ra al·la spee·na draught beer; **la birra con limonata** beer·ra kohn lee·mo·nah·ta shandy; **la birra chiara** beer·ra kyah·ra lager

birreria beer·re·ree·a f brewery

bis bees m — encore; bis! bees encore!

biscotto bee·skot·toh m biscuit

bisognare bee·zohn·yah·ray vi to have to

bisogno bee·zohn·yoh m need; avere* **bisogno di** a·vay·ray bee·zohn·yoh dee to need

bistecca bee·stayk·ka f steak; **la bistecca di filetto** bee·stayk·ka dee fee·layt·toh fillet steak

bivio bee·vyoh m fork (in road)

bloccare blok·kah·ray vt block; **bloccare un assegno** blok·kah·ray oon as·sayn·yoh to stop a cheque

bloccarsi blok·kar·see vr jam (machine)

blocco blok·koh m block (of stone); pad (notepaper); **il blocco dei salari** blok·koh de·ee sa·lah·ree wage freeze

blu marina bloo ma·ree·na adj navy blue

blue-jeans bloo·jeenz mpl jeans

blusa bloo·za f smock

boa bo·a f buoy

bocca bohk·ka f mouth

bocciolo boch·cho·loh m bud

boccone bok·koh·ne m bite (of food)

boicottare boy·kot·tah·ray vt boycott

bolla bol·la f bubble; blister

bollettino bol·let·tee·noh m bulletin

bollicina bol·lee·chee·na f pimple

bollire bol·lee·re vi boil; fare* **bollire** fah·ray bol·lee·re to boil (water)

bollitore bol·lee·toh·re m kettle

bomba bohm·ba f bomb

bombetta bom·bayt·ta f bowler hat

bombola bohm·bo·la f cylinder (for gas); **la bombola spray** bohm·bo·la spray spray (container)

bombolone bom·bo·loh·ne m doughnut

boom boom m boom (economic)

bordo bohr·doh m border; edge; **il bordo del marciapiede** bohr·doh del mar·cha·pye·de kerb; curb; **a bordo** a bohr·doh on board (ship, plane); salire* **a bordo** sa·lee·re a bohr·doh to go aboard; **a bordo della nave** a bohr·doh del·la nah·ve aboard the ship

borghese bor·gay·say adj middle-class

borgo bohr·goh m district

borsa bohr·sa f handbag; holdall; bag; briefcase; **la borsa dell'acqua calda** bohr·sa del·lak·kwa kal·da hot-water bottle; **la borsa per la spesa** bohr·sa payr la spay·sa shopping bag; **la borsa da toletta** bohr·sa da to·layt·ta sponge-bag; **la borsa di studio** bohr·sa dee stoo·dee·oh grant (to student); **la Borsa** bohr·sa stock market; stock

exchange; la borsa nera *bohr·sa nay·ra* black market
borsellino *bor·sel·lee·noh m* purse (*for money*)
borsetta *bor·sayt·ta f* handbag
bosco *bo·skoh m* wood (*forest*)
bottega *bot·te·ga f* shop
botteghino *bot·te·gee·noh m* box office
bottiglia *bot·teel·ya f* bottle
bottoncino *bot·ton·chee·noh m* stud (*for collar*)
bottone *bot·toh·ne m* button; il bottone automatico *bot·toh·ne ow·to·ma·tee·ko* press-stud
boutique *boo·teek f* boutique
box *boks m* playpen
bozzetto *bots·tsayt·toh m* sketch (*drawing*)
braccialetto *brach·cha·layt·toh m* bracelet
bracciata *brach·chah·ta f* stroke (*swimming*)
braccio *brach·choh m* —a arm (*of person*)
braciola *bra·cho·la f* chop (*food*)
a brandelli *a bran·del·lee adv* ragged (*clothes*)
brandina *bran·dee·na f* camp-bed
brandy *bran·dee m* brandy
brano *bra·no m* passage (*from book*)
bretelle *bre·tel·le fpl* braces
breve *bre·ve adj* brief
brevetto *bre·vayt·toh m* patent
brezza *bredz·dza f* breeze
briciola *bree·cho·la f* crumb
bridge *breej m* bridge (*game*)
briglia *breel·ya f* rein; bridle
brillare *breel·lah·ray vi* shine
brindare a *breen·dah·ray a vi* toast (*drink to*)
brindisi *breen·dee·zee m* — toast (*drink, speech*)
britannico(a) *bree·tan·nee·ko(a) adj* British
brocca *brok·ka f* jug
broccoli *brok·ko·lee mpl* broccoli
brodo *bro·doh m* stock (*for soup etc*)
bronchite *bron·kee·te f* bronchitis
brontolare *bron·to·lah·ray vi* grumble
bronzo *brohn·dzoh m* bronze
bruciare *broo·chah·ray vt/i* burn; mi sono bruciato il braccio *me soh·no broo·chah·to eel brach·choh* I've burnt my arm
bruciore di stomaco *broo·choh·re dee sto·ma·koh m* heartburn
bruno(a) *broo·no(a) adj* brown; dark
brusco(a) *broo·sko(a) adj* abrupt; sharp (*bend*)
brutto(a) *broot·toh(a) adj* ugly
Bruxelles *brook·sel f* Brussels
buca *boo·ka f* hole; la buca per le lettere *boo·ka payr le let·te·re* letter box
bucato *boo·kah·toh m* washing; laundry; fare* il bucato *fah·ray eel boo·kah·toh* to do the washing
buccia *booch·cha f* peel, skin
buco *boo·koh m* hole; il buco della serratura *boo·koh del·la ser·ra·too·ra* keyhole
bufera *boo·fe·ra f* storm; la bufera di neve *boo·fe·ra dee nay·ve* blizzard
buffè *boof·fe m* buffet
bugia *boo·jee·a f* lie (*untruth*)
buio(a) *boo·yo(a) adj* dark
bulbo *bool·boh m* bulb
bulldozer *bool·do·zer m* bulldozer
bulletta *bool·layt·ta f* tack (*nail*)
buongustaio *bwon·goos·ta·ee·yoh m* gourmet
buono *bwo·noh m* voucher; coupon;

token; il buono premio *bwo·noh pre·myoh* trading stamp
buono(a) *bwo·noh(a) adj* good; buon giorno! *bwon johr·noh* good morning/afternoon!; buona sera! *bwo·na say·ra* good evening!; buona notte! *bwo·na not·tay* good night!; a buon mercato a *bwon mer·kah·toh* cheap
buono-regalo *bwo·noh·re·gah·loh m* gift token
burrasca *boor·ra·ska f* storm
burrascoso(a) *boor·ras·koh·so(a) adj* gusty (*wind*); rough (*weather*)
burro *boor·roh m* butter
bussare *boos·sah·ray vi* knock
bussola *boos·so·la f* compass
busta *boo·sta f* envelope
bustina *boo·stee·na f* sachet; la bustina di tè *boo·stee·na dee te* tea bag
busto *boo·stoh m* bust
butano *boo·tah·noh m* Calor gas
buttare via *boot·tah·ray vee·a vt* throw away

C

cabaret *ka·ba·ray m* cabaret
cabina *ka·bee·na f* cabin (*in ship*); cubicle; la cabina telefonica *ka·bee·na te·le·fo·nee·ka* telephone booth
cabinato *ka·bee·nah·toh m* cabin cruiser
cacao *ka·kow m* cocoa
caccia *kach·chah f* hunting; shooting
cacciagione *kach·cha·joh·nay f* game (*hunting*)
cacciare *kach·chah·ray vt* hunt; chase away
cacciavite *kach·cha·vee·te m* — screwdriver
cachemire *kash·meer m* cashmere
cacto *kak·toh m* cactus
cadavere *ka·dah·ve·re m* body (*corpse*)
caddie *kad·dee m* caddie
cadere* *ka·day·re vi* fall; fall over; fall down; drop; fare* cadere *fah·ray ka·day·re* to knock over; lasciare cadere *la·shah·ray ka·day·re* to drop (*let fall*)
caduta *ka·doo·ta f* fall
caffè *kaf·fe m* — café; coffee; il caffè nero *kaf·fe nay·roh* black coffee
caffellatte *kaf·fel·lat·tay m* — white coffee
caffettiera *kaf·fet·tye·ra f* coffeepot
calamita *ka·la·mee·ta f* magnet
calare *ka·lah·ray vi* fall
calcestruzzo *kal·che·stroots·tsoh m* concrete
calciare *kal·chah·ray vt* kick (*ball*)
calcio *kal·choh m* kick; football (*game*); calcium; dare* un calcio a *dah·ray oon kal·choh a* to kick
calcolare *kal·ko·lah·ray vt* calculate; calcoli 10 minuti per arrivarci *kal·ko·lee 10 mee·noo·tee payr ar·ree·var·chee* allow 10 minutes to get there
calcolatrice *kal·ko·la·tree·chay f* calculator
calcolo *kal·ko·loh m* calculation; un calcolo approssimativo *oon kal·ko·loh ap·pros·see·ma·tee·vo* a rough estimate
caldo(a) *kal·do(a) adj* warm; hot; fa caldo oggi *fa kal·do oj·jee* it's warm/hot today; ho caldo *o kal·do* I'm warm/hot
calendario *ka·len·dah·ree·oh m* calendar
callo *kal·loh m* corn (*on foot*)
calma *kal·ma f* peace (*calm*)

calmante *kal·man·te m* painkiller

calmarsi *kal·mar·see vr* calm down

calmo(a) *kal·moh(a) adj* calm

calore *ka·loh·re m* warmth; heat

caloria *ka·lo·ree·a f* calorie

calpestare *kal·pes·tah·ray vt* tread on

calvo(a) *kal·vo(a) adj* bald

calza *kal·tsa f* stocking; sock

calzatura *kal·tsa·too·ra f* footwear

calzino *kal·tsee·noh m* sock

calzoncini *kal·tson·chee·nee mpl* shorts

calzoni *kal·tsoh·nee mpl* slacks

cambiale *kam·bee·ah·le f* draft *(financial)*

cambiamento *kam·bya·mayn·toh m* change; un cambiamento del tempo *oon kam·bya·mayn·toh del tem·poh* a change in the weather

cambiare *kam·byah·ray vi* change ◻ *vt* change; exchange; cambiare treno a Marsiglia *kam·byah·ray tre·noh a Mahr·seel·ya* to change trains at Marseilles; cambiare casa *kam·byah·ray kah·sa* to move house; cambiare qualcosa per qualcos'altro *kam·byah·ray kwal·ko·sa payr kwal·ko·sal·tro* to exchange something for something; cambiare marcia *kam·byah·ray mar·cha* to change gear

cambiarsi *kam·bee·ahr·see vr* change one's clothes

cambio *kam·byoh m* change; exchange; rate of exchange; gears; il cambio sincronizzato *kam·byoh seen·kro·needz·dzah·to* synchromesh

camera *kah·me·ra f* room; la camera (da letto) *kah·me·ra (da let·toh)* bedroom; una camera singola *oo·na kah·me·ra seen·go·la* a single room; la camera matrimoniale *kah·me·ra ma·tree·mo·nyah·le* double room; la camera blindata *kah·me·ra bleen·dah·ta* strongroom; la camera dei bambini *kah·me·ra dey bam·bee·nee* nursery; la camera degli ospiti *kah·me·ra del·yee o·spee·tee* guest-room; la camera di commercio *kah·me·ra dee kom·mer·choh* Chamber of Commerce; la camera libera *kah·me·ra lee·be·ra* vacancy *(in hotel etc)*

cameriera *ka·me·rye·ra f* waitress; chambermaid; la cameriera al banco *ka·me·rye·ra al ban·koh* barmaid

cameriere *ka·me·rye·re m* waiter; il cameriere di bordo *ka·me·rye·re dee bohr·doh* steward

camicetta *ka·mee·chayt·ta f* blouse

camicia *ka·mee·cha f* shirt; la camicia da notte *ka·mee·cha da not·tay* nightdress

caminetto *ka·mee·nayt·toh m* mantelpiece

camino *ka·mee·noh m* chimney; fireplace

camion *ka·myon m* — truck; lorry; il camion di traslochi *ka·myon dee tra·zlo·kee* removal van; il camion cisterna *ka·myon chee·ster·na* tanker *(truck)*

camionista *ka·myo·nee·sta m* lorry driver

cammello *kam·mel·loh m* camel

camminare *kam·mee·nah·ray vi* walk

campagna *kam·pan·ya f* country; countryside; campaign; la campagna di pubblicità *kam·pan·ya dee poob·blee·chee·ta* publicity campaign; la campagna giornalistica *kam·pan·ya johr·na·lee·stee·ka* press-campaign; in campagna *een kam·pan·ya* in the country

campana *kam·pah·na f* bell

campanello *kam·pa·nel·loh m* bell; doorbell

campeggio *kam·payj·joh m* camping; camp(ing) site; fare* da campeggio *fah·ray del kam·payj·joh* to go camping

campione *kam·pyoh·ne m* sample *(of goods)*; specimen; champion

campo *kam·poh m* field; il campo da gioco *kam·poh da jo·koh* playing field; il campo di golf *kam·poh des golf* golf course; il campo della fiera *kam·poh del·la fye·ra* fairground; il campo da tennis *kam·poh da ten·nees* tennis court

camposanto *kam·po·san·toh m* graveyard; churchyard

Canada *ka·na·da m* Canada

canadese *ka·na·day·say adj* Canadian

canale *ka·nah·lay m* canal

canasta *ka·na·sta f* canasta

cancellare *kan·chel·lah·ray vt* rub out; cancel; cancellare un debito *kan·chel·lah·ray oon de·bee·toh* to write off a debt

cancellata *kan·chel·lah·ta f* railings

cancelleria *kan·chel·le·ree·a f* stationery

cancelliere *kan·chel·lyay·ray m* chancellor

Cancelliere dello Scacchiere *kan·chel·lyay·ray del·loh skak·kye·ray m* Chancellor of the Exchequer

cancello *kan·chel·loh m* gate *(of garden)*

cancro *kan·kroh m* cancer

candela *kan·day·la f* spark(ing) plug; candle

candidato(a) *kan·dee·da·toh(a) m/f* candidate

cane *kah·nay m* dog; il cane per ciechi *kah·nay payr che·kee* guide dog

canestro *ka·ne·stroh m* basket

canna da pesca *kan·na da pay·ska f* fishing rod

cannella *kan·nel·la f* cinnamon

cannone *kan·noh·nay m* gun; cannon

canoa *ka·no·a f* canoe; fare* della canoa *fah·ray del·la ka·no·a* to go canoeing

canottaggio *ka·not·taj·joh m* rowing *(sport)*

canottiera *ka·not·tye·ra f* vest; undershirt

canovaccio *ka·no·vach·choh m* teacloth

cantare *kan·tah·ray vt/i* sing

cantiere *kan·tye·re m* building site; il cantiere navale *kan·tye·re na·vah·le* shipyard

cantilena *kan·tee·le·na f* jingle *(advertising)*

cantina *kan·tee·na f* cellar; wine cellar

canto *kan·toh m* song; singing; il canto di Natale *kan·toh dee na·ta·lay* carol; il canto folcloristico *kan·toh fol·klo·ree·stee·ko* folk song

canzone *kan·tsoh·ne f* song

capace *ka·pah·chay adj* capable

capacità *ka·pa·chee·ta f* ability

capanna *ka·pan·na f* hut *(shed)*

capelli *ka·payl·lee mpl* hair

capello *ka·payl·loh m* hair *(single strand)*

capezzale *ka·pets·tsah·le m* bolster

capire *ka·pee·ray vt* understand

capitale *ka·pee·tah·lay f* capital *(city)* ◻ *m* capital *(finance)*; il capitale d'esercizio *ka·pee·tah·lay de·zer·chee·tsyoh* working capital

capitalismo *ka·pee·ta·lee·zmoh m* capitalism

capitalista *ka·pee·ta·lee·sta m/f* capitalist

capitano *ka·pee·tah·noh m* captain; **il capitano di porto** *ka·pee·tah·noh dee por·toh* harbo(u)r master

capitolo *ka·pee·toh·loh m* chapter

capo *kah·poh m* head; leader; boss

capocuoco *ka·po·kwoh·koh m* chef

Capodanno *kah·po·dan·noh m* New Year's Day

capolavoro *kah·po·la·voh·roh m* masterpiece

capolinea *kah·po·lee·ne·a m* terminal (buses)

caposquadra *kah·po·skwa·dra m* foreman

capotreno *kah·po·tre·noh m* guard (on train)

cappa *kap·pa f* cape

cappella *kap·pel·la f* chapel

cappello *kap·pel·loh m* hat; **il cappello da sole** *kap·pel·loh da soh·le* sun-hat; **il cappello a cilindro** *kap·pel·loh a chee·leen·droh* top hat

cappio *kap·pyoh m* loop

cappotto *kap·pot·toh m* overcoat

cappuccino *kap·pooch·chee·no m* frothy white coffee

cappuccio *kap·pooch·choh m* hood

capra *ka·pra f* goat

capretto *ka·prayt·toh m* kid

capsula *kap·soo·la f* capsule

caraffa *ka·raf·fa f* decanter; carafe

caramella *ka·ra·mel·la f* sweet; toffee; **la caramella alla menta** *ka·ra·mel·la al·la mayn·ta* mint

caramello *ka·ra·mel·loh m* caramel

carato *ka·ra·toh m* carat

carattere *ka·rat·te·ray m* character

carbone *kahr·boh·nay m* coal

carbonio *kar·boh·nyoh m* carbon

carburante *kar·boo·ran·te m* fuel; **la pompa del carburante** *pom·pa del kar·boo·ran·te* fuel pump

carburatore *kar·boo·ra·toh·ray m* carburet(t)or

carcere *kar·che·re m* prison

carciofo *kar·cho·foh m* artichoke

cardigan *kahr·dee·gan m* — cardigan

cardinale *kar·dee·nah·le m* cardinal

cardio *kahr·dee·oh m* cockle

carenza *ka·ren·tsa f* shortage

carezzare *ka·rets·tsah·ray vt* load; caress

caricare *ka·ree·kah·ray vt* load; **caricare un orologio** *ka·ree·kah·ray oon o·ro·lo·joh* to wind up a clock

carico *kah·ree·koh m* shipment; cargo; load

carino(a) *ka·ree·no(a) adj* lovely; pretty; nice

carnagione *kahr·na·joh·nay f* complexion

carne *kar·nay f* meat; flesh; **la carne di maiale** *kar·nay dee ma·yah·le* pork; **la carne di manzo** *kar·nay dee man·zoh* beef; **la carne di cervo** *kar·nay dee cher·voh* venison; **la carne tritata** *kar·nay tree·tah·ta* mince; **la carne di montone** *kar·nay dee mon·toh·nay* mutton

carnevale *kahr·ne·vah·lay m* carnival

caro(a) *kah·ro(a) adj* dear □ *m/f* darling

carota *ka·ro·ta f* carrot

carreggiata doppia *kar·rej·jah·ta dop·pya f* dual carriageway; divided highway

carrello *kar·rel·loh m* trolley; **il car-** rello per bagagli *kar·rel·loh payr ba·gal·yee* luggage trolley

carriera *kar·ree·e·ra f* career

carriola *kar·ryo·la f* wheelbarrow

carro *kar·roh m* cart; **il carro armato** *kar·roh ar·mah·to* tank (military)

carrozzina *kar·rots·tsee·na f* pram

carta *kar·ta f* paper; card; **alla carta** *al·la kar·ta* à la carte; **la carta di credito** *kar·ta dee kray·dee·toh* credit card; **la carta d'identità** *kar·ta dee·den·tee·ta* identity card; **la carta d'imbarco** *kar·ta deem·bar·koh* boarding pass; **la carta carbone** *kar·ta kar·boh·nay* carbon paper; **la carta velina** *kar·ta ve·lee·na* tissue paper; **la carta da gioco** *kar·ta da jo·koh* playing card; **la carta verde** *kar·ta vayr·day* green card; **la carta geografica** *kar·ta jay·oh·gra·fee·ka* map (of country); **la carta nautica** *kar·ta now·tee·ka* chart (map); **la carta stradale** *kar·ta stra·dah·le* road map; **la carta d'imballaggio** *kar·ta deem·bal·laj·joh* wrapping paper; **la carta da parati** *kar·ta da pa·rah·tee* wallpaper; **la carta increspata** *kar·ta en·kre·spah·ta* corrugated paper; **la carta da lettere** *kar·ta da let·te·ray* notepaper; **la carta da scrivere** *kar·ta da skree·ve·re* writing paper; **la carta igienica** *kar·ta ee·je·nee·ka* toilet paper

cartella *kar·tel·la f* folder; briefcase; schoolbag

cartello *kahr·tel·loh m* sign; signpost; cartel

cartoleria *kar·to·le·ree·a f* stationer's (shop)

cartolina *kar·to·lee·na f* postcard; greetings card; **la cartolina di Natale** *kar·to·lee·na dee na·tah·lay* Christmas card

cartone *kahr·to·nay m* cardboard; **il cartone animato** *kahr·to·nay a·nee·mah·toh* cartoon (animated)

cartuccia *kahr·tooch·cha f* cartridge

casa *kah·sa f* house; home; **a casa** *a kah·sa* at home; **andare* a casa** *an·dah·ray a kah·sa* to go home; **a casa mia** *a kah·sa mee·a* at my house; **offerto(a) dalla casa** *of·fer·to(a) dal·la kah·sa* on the house; **la casa di cura** *kah·sa dee koo·ra* nursing home; **la casa colonica** *kah·sa ko·lo·nee·ka* farmhouse; **la casa dello studente** *kah·sa del·lo stoo·den·te* student hostel; **la Casa Bianca** *kah·sa byan·ka* White House; **l'indirizzo di casa** *een·dee·reets·tsoh dee kah·sa* home address

casalinga *ka·sa·leen·ga f* housewife

casamento *ka·sa·mayn·toh m* block of flats, apartment block

cascata *ka·skah·ta f* waterfall

casco *ka·skoh m* helmet; crash helmet

casella postale *ka·sel·la po·stah·le f* post-office box

caserma *ka·ser·ma f* barracks; **la caserma dei pompieri** *ka·ser·ma dey pom·pye·ree* fire station

casinò *ka·see·noh m* — casino

caso *kah·zoh m* case (instance); **nel caso che** *nel kah·zoh kay* in case; **in caso di** *een kah·zoh dee* in case of; **a caso** *a kah·zoh* at random; **per caso** *payr kah·zoh* by accident; by chance

cassa *kas·sa f* cashdesk; till (cash register); checkout (in store); crate; **la cassa di pensionamento** *kas·sa dee pen·syoh·na·mayn·toh* pension fund; **la cassa di risparmio** *kas·sa dee ree-*

spar·myoh savings bank; **la cassa da imballaggio** *kas·sa da eem·bal·laj·joh* packing case

cassaforte *kas·sa·for·te* f **casseforti** strongbox; safe

casseruola *kas·ser·wo·la* f saucepan; casserole (*dish*)

cassetta *kas·sayt·ta* f box; cartridge (*of tape*); cassette; **la cassetta di pronto soccorso** *kas·sayt·ta dee prohn·to sok·kohr·soh* first-aid kit; **la cassetta per le lettere** *kas·sayt·ta payr le let·te·re* post-box

cassetto *kas·sayt·toh* m drawer

cassiere(a) *kas·sye·ray(a)* m/f cashier; teller

castagna *ka·stan·ya* f chestnut

castano(a) *ka·stah·no(a)* adj brown (*hair*)

castello *ka·stel·loh* m castle

casuale *ka·zoo·ah·le* adj chance

catalogo *ka·tah·lo·goh* m catalog(ue)

catarifrangente *ka·ta·ree·fran·jen·tay* m reflector (*on cycle, car*)

catena *ka·tay·na* f chain; range (*of mountains*); **la catena di montaggio** *ka·tay·na dee mon·taj·joh* assembly line

catrame *ka·trah·me* m tar

cattedrale *kat·te·drah·lay* f cathedral

cattivo(a) *kat·tee·vo(a)* adj bad; nasty; evil; naughty

cattolico(a) *kat·to·lee·ko(a)* adj Roman Catholic

catturare *kat·too·rah·ray* vt capture

causa *kow·za* f cause; case (*lawsuit*); **a causa di** *a kow·za dee* because of

causare *kow·zah·ray* vt cause

cauzione *kow·tsyoh·ne* f security (*for loan*); bail (*for prisoner*); deposit (*for key etc*); **su cauzione** *soo kow·tsyoh·ne* on bail

cava *kah·va* f quarry

cavalcare *ka·val·kah·ray* vt/i ride

cavalcata *ka·val·kah·ta* f ride (*on horse*); riding

cavalcavia *ka·val·ka·vee·a* m — flyover (*road*)

cavaliere *ka·va·lye·re* m partner (*dancing*)

cavalletto per il bucato *ka·val·layt·toh payr eel boo·kah·toh* m clotheshorse

cavallo *ka·val·loh* m horse; **il cavallo da corsa** *ka·val·loh da kohr·sa* racehorse

cavare *ka·vah·ray* vt take out; **cavarsela** *ka·var·se·la* to manage

cavatappi *ka·va·tap·pee* m — corkscrew

caverna *ka·ver·na* f cave

caviale *ka·vee·ah·lay* m caviar(e)

caviglia *ka·veel·ya* f ankle

cavo *kah·voh* m cable

cavo(a) *kah·vo(a)* adj hollow

cavolfiore *ka·vol·fyoh·ray* m cauliflower

cavolini di Bruxelles *kah·vo·lee·nee dee brook·sel* mpl Brussels sprouts

cavolo *kah·vo·loh* m cabbage; **il cavolo rapa** *kah·vo·loh rah·pa* kohlrabi

c'è *che* there is

ce *che* pron, adv before lo, la, li, le, ne = **ci**

Cecoslovacchia *che·ko·slo·vak·kya* f Czechoslovakia

cecoslovacco(a) *che·ko·slo·vak·koh(a)* adj Czech(oslovakian)

cedere *che·de·ray* vi give in (*yield*)

cedro *chay·droh* m cedar; lime (*fruit*); **il succo di cedro** *sook·koh dee chay·droh* lime juice

C.E.E. *che·e* f E.E.C.

celebrare *che·le·brah·ray* vt celebrate

celibe *che·lee·be* adj single (*not married: man*)

cella *chel·la* f cell (*in prison*)

cellofan *chel·lo·fan* m cellophane

Celsius *chel·syoos* adj Celsius

cemento *che·mayn·toh* m cement

cena *chay·na* f dinner; supper; dinner party

cenere *chay·ne·re* f ash (*cinders*)

cenno *chen·no* m sign; nod; wave

centenario *chen·te·na·ree·oh* m centenary

centesimo *chen·te·zee·moh* m cent
□ adj **centesimo(a)** *chen·te·zee·mo(a)* hundredth

centigrado *chen·tee·gra·doh* adj centigrade

centilitro *chen·tee·lee·troh* m centilitre

centimetro *chen·tee·me·troh* m centimetre

centinaio *chen·tee·na·yoh* m a hundred; about a hundred; **centinaia di libri** *chen·tee·na·ya dee lee·bree* hundreds of books

cento *chen·to* num hundred; **cento persone** *chen·to per·soh·ne* a hundred people

centrale *chen·trah·le* adj central □ f **la centrale** *chen·trah·le* exchange (*telephone*); **la centrale telefonica** *chen·trah·le te·le·fo·nee·ka* telephone exchange

centralinista *chen·tra·lee·nee·sta* m/f switchboard operator

centralino *chen·tra·lee·noh* m switchboard

centro *chen·troh* m centre; **il centro commerciale** *chen·troh kom·mer·chah·le* shopping centre; **il centro di Chicago** *chen·troh dee chee·kah·go* downtown Chicago; **il centro della città** *chen·troh del·la cheet·ta* city centre; **il centro per il giardinaggio** *chen·troh payr eel jar·dee·naj·joh* garden centre

ceppo *chayp·poh* m log (*of wood*); **il ceppo del freno** *chayp·poh del fre·noh* shoe (*of brake*)

cera *chay·ra* f wax; polish (*for floor*)

ceramica *che·ra·mee·ka* f pottery; **la fabbrica di ceramiche** *fab·bree·ka dee che·ra·mee·ke* pottery (*workshop*)

cercare *cher·kah·ray* vt look for; look up (*word*); **cercare di fare qualcosa** *cher·kah·ray dee fah·ray kwal·ko·sa* to try to do something

cerchio *chayr·kyoh* m ring; hoop; circle

cereale *che·re·ah·lay* m cereal

cerimonia *che·ree·mo·nee·a* f ceremony

cerniera lampo *cher·nye·ra lam·poh* f zip(-fastener), zipper

cerotto *che·rot·toh* m sticking-plaster; bandaid

certamente *cher·ta·mayn·tay* adv definitely; certainly

certificato *cher·tee·fee·kah·toh* m certificate; **il certificato di morte** *cher·tee·fee·kah·toh dee mor·te* death certificate

certo(a) *cher·toh(a)* adj certain; sure; definite

cerume *che·roo·me* m wax (*in ear*)

cervello *cher·vel·loh* m brain; brains (*as food*)

cervo *cher·voh* m deer

cespuglio *che·spool·yoh* m bush

cesta *chay·sta* f hamper

cestino *che·stee·noh* m waste paper basket

cetriolino *che·tree·oh·lee·noh* m gherkin

cetriolo *che·tree·o·loh* m cucumber

chalet *sha·le* m — chalet

che *ke* conj that; than □ pron who; whom; which, that; what; l'uomo che... *lwo·moh ke* the man who...; l'uomo che vede *lwo·moh ke ve·de* the man whom you see; il libro, che è lungo *eel lee·broh ke e loon·go* the book, which is long; la mela che ha mangiato *la may·la ke a man·jah·to* the apple which you ate; la foto che Le ho dato *la fo·to ke le o dah·to* the photo that I gave you; dopo di che *doh·po dee ke* after which; che c'è? *ke che* what's wrong?; che cos'è successo? *ke ko·se sooch·ches·so* what's happened?; che disordine! *ke dee·zohr·dee·ne* what a mess!; spero che... *spe·ro ke* I hope that...; non era che un errore *nohn e·ra ke oon er·roh·re* it was just a mistake

cherosene *ke·ro·ze·ne* m kerosene

chi *kee* pron who; whom; di chi è questo libro? *dee ke e kway·sto lee·broh* whose book is this?; io so di chi è *o so dee kee e* I know whose it is; chi di voi? *kee dee voy* which one of you?; chi è? *kee e* who's that?

chiacchiera *kya·kye·ra* f gossip (chatter)

chiacchierare *kya·kye·rah·ray* vi chat; gossip

chiamare *kya·mah·ray* vt call; fare* chiamare *fah·ray kya·mah·ray* to page

chiamarsi *kya·mar·see* vr to be called; come Si chiama? *koh·may see kya·ma* what is your name?; mi chiamo Paul *mee kya·moh Paul* my name is Paul

chiamata *kya·mah·ta* f call (on phone); una chiamata urbana *oo·na kya·mah·ta oor·bah·na* a local call

chiaretto *kya·rayt·toh* m claret

chiaro(a) *kyah·roh(a)* adj clear; light (bright, pale)

chiatta *kyat·ta* f barge

chiave *kyah·ve* f key; spanner; la chiave dell'accensione *kyah·ve del·lach·chen·syoh·ne* ignition key

chiavistello *kya·vee·stel·loh* m bolt; chiudere* a chiavistello *kyoo·de·re a kya·vee·stel·loh* to bolt (door, gate)

chiedere* *kyay·de·re* vt ask; ask for; chiedere* l'ora a qualcuno *kyay·de·re loh·ra a kwal·koo·no* to ask someone the time

chiesa *kye·za* f church

chile *kee·lay* m chili

chilo *kee·loh* m kilo

chilogrammo *kee·lo·gram·moh* m kilogram(me)

chilometraggio *kee·lo·me·traj·joh* m ≈ mileage

chilometro *kee·lo·me·troh* m kilometer, kilometre

chilowatt *kee·lo·vat* m kilowatt

chimica *kee·mee·ka* f chemistry

chimico(a) *kee·mee·koh(a)* adj chemical

chinarsi *kee·nar·see* vr bend (person)

chiocciola *kyoch·cho·la* f snail

chiodo *kyo·do* m nail (metal); stud; il chiodo di garofano *kyo·do dee ga·ro·fa·noh* clove

chiosco *kyo·sko* m kiosk

chip *cheep* m chip (electronics)

chirurgia *kee·roor·jee·a* f surgery (operation); la chirurgia estetica *kee·roor·jee·a e·ste·tee·ka* cosmetic surgery; la chirurgia plastica *kee·roor·jee·a pla·stee·ka* plastic surgery

chirurgo *kee·roor·goh* m surgeon

chitarra *kee·tar·ra* f guitar

chiudere* *kyoo·de·re* vt shut; close; turn off; chiudere* l'elettricità/l'acqua al contatore *kyoo·de·re le·let·tree·chee·ta/lak·kwa al kon·ta·toh·re* to turn the electricity/water off at the mains; chiudere* a chiave *kyoo·de·re a kyah·ve* to lock

chiudersi* *kyoo·der·see* vr shut; la porta si chiuse *la por·ta see kyoo·say* the door closed; a che ora si chiudono i negozi? *a kay oh·ra see kyoo·do·no ee ne·go·tsee* when do the shops close?

chiunque *kee·oon·kwe* pron whoever; anybody

chiusa *kyoo·sa* f lock (in canal)

chiuso(a) *kyoo·so(a)* adj shut; off (tap, light etc)

ci *chee* pron us; to us; ourselves; one another; ci sono *chee soh·no* there are; ci è andato *chee e an·dah·to* he went there

cialda *chal·da* f waffle

ciao *chow* excl hello; goodbye

ciascuno(a) *cha·skoo·no(a)* adj, pron each

cibo *chee·boh* m food; i cibi naturali *chee·bee na·too·rah·lee* health foods

cicatrice *chee·ka·tree·che* f scar

ciclismo *chee·klee·zmoh* m cycling; fare* del ciclismo *fah·ray del chee·klee·zmoh* to go cycling

ciclista *chee·klee·sta* m/f cyclist

ciclomotore *chee·klo·mo·toh·ray* m moped

cicoria *chee·ko·rya* f endive; chicory

cieco(a) *chee·ko(a)* adj blind

cielo *che·loh* m sky

cifra *chee·fra* f figure (number); la cifra tonda *chee·fra tohn·da* round figure/number

ciglio *cheel·yoh* m —a eyelash

cigno *cheen·yoh* m swan

ciliegia *chee·lee·ay·jah* f cherry

ciliegio *chee·lee·ay·joh* m cherry (tree)

cilindro *chee·leen·droh* m cylinder

cima *chee·ma* f peak (of mountain); top (of mountain, ladder)

cimice *chee·mee·che* f bug (insect)

cimitero *chee·mee·te·roh* m cemetery

Cina *chee·na* f China

cincin *cheen·cheen* excl cheers!

cinema *chee·ne·ma* m — cinema

cinepresa *chee·ne·pray·sa* f cinecamera

cinese *chee·nay·say* adj Chinese □ m il cinese *chee·nay·say* Chinese

cinghia *cheen·gya* f strap; la cinghia della ventola *cheen·gya del·la ven·to·la* fanbelt

cinquanta *cheen·kwan·ta* num fifty

cinque *cheen·kwe* num five

cintura *cheen·too·ra* f belt (for waist); la cintura di sicurezza *cheen·too·ra dee see·koo·rayts·tsa* seat belt; safety belt; la cintura di salvataggio *cheen·too·ra dee sal·va·taj·joh* lifebelt

cinturato(a) *cheen·too·rah·to(a)* adj radial(-ply)

ciò *cho* pron this; that; ciò che *cho ke* what

cioccolata *chok·ko·lah·ta* f chocolate

cioccolato *chok·ko·lah·toh* m choco-

late; il cioccolato scuro *chok·ko·lah·
toh skoo·ro* plain chocolate
cioè *cho·e* adv that is (to say)...
ciottolo *chot·to·loh* m pebble
cipolla *chee·pohl·la* f onion
cipollina *chee·pol·lee·na* f spring onion
cipria *chee·prya* f powder (*cosmetic*)
Cipro *chee·proh* m Cyprus
circa *cheer·ka* adv, prep about
circo *cheer·koh* m circus
circolare *cheer·ko·lah·ray* vi move
(*traffic*)
circolo *cheer·ko·loh* m circle; il circolo
della gioventú *cheer·ko·loh del·la jo·
ven·too* youth club; il circolo ricreativo *cheer·ko·loh ree·kre·a·tee·vo*
leisure centre
circondare *cheer·kon·dah·ray* vt surround
circonvallazione *cheer·kon·val·la·
tsyoh·nay* f ring road; bypass
circoscrizione *cheer·ko·skree·tsyoh·ne* f
district (*administrative*); precinct
circostanze *cheer·ko·stan·tsay* fpl circumstances
circuito *cheer·koo·ee·toh* m circuit
(*electric*)
citare *chee·tah·ray* vt quote (*passage*);
sue
citazione *chee·ta·tsyoh·ne* f quotation
(*passage*); summons
citofono *chee·to·foh·noh* m intercom
città *cheet·ta* f — town; city; andare*
in città *an·dah·ray een cheet·ta* to go
to town; le città gemelle *chee·ta je·
mel·le* twin towns
civilizzazione *chee·vee·leed·za·tsee·oh·
nay* f civilization
clacson *klak·son* m — horn (*of car*)
classe *klas·say* f grade; class; la classe
alta *klas·say al·ta* the upper class; la
classe turistica *klas·say too·ree·stee·
ka* tourist class
classico(a) *klas·see·koh(a)* adj classical
clausola *klow·zo·la* f clause (*in contract*)
cliente *klee·en·tay* m/f customer; guest
(*at hotel*); client
clima *klee·ma* m climate
clinica *klee·nee·ka* f clinic
club *kloob* m — club (*society*); il club
di golf *kloob dee golf* golf club
cocco *kok·koh* m coconut
coccodrillo *kok·koh·dreel·loh* m crocodile
cocktail *kok·tail* m cocktail (*drink*)
cocomero *ko·koh·me·roh* m watermelon
coda *koh·da* f tail; queue; train (*of
dress*); fare* la coda *fah·ray la koh·
da* to queue; to stand in line
codeina *ko·de·ee·na* f codeine
codice *ko·dee·che* m code; il codice postale *ko·dee·che po·stah·le* post-
code; zip code; il codice stradale *ko·
dee·che stra·dah·le* Highway Code
cofano *ko·fa·noh* m bonnet, hood (*of
car*)
cogliere* *kol·ye·re* vt pick (*flower*)
cognac *kon·yak* m cognac
cognata *kon·yah·ta* f sister-in-law
cognato *kon·yah·toh* m brother-in-law
cognome *kon·yoh·me* m surname; il
cognome da nubile *kon·yoh·me da
noo·bee·lay* maiden name
coincidenza *ko·een·chee·den·tsa* f connection (*train etc*); coincidence; questo treno fa coincidenza con quello
delle 16.45 *kway·stoh tre·noh fa ko·
een·chee·den·tsa kohn kwayl·loh del·*

lay 16.45 this train connects with the
16.45
coincidere* *ko·een·chee·de·ray* vi
coincide
colapasta *koh·la·pa·sta* m — colander
colare *ko·lah·ray* vi strain (*tea etc*)
colazione *ko·la·tsyoh·ne* f breakfast
colesterina *koh·lay·stay·ree·na* f
cholesterol
colica *ko·lee·ka* f colic
colino *ko·lee·noh* m strainer; il colino
da tè *ko·lee·noh da te* tea strainer
colla *kol·la* f glue; paste
collaborare *kol·la·bo·rah·ray* vi collaborate
collana *kol·lah·na* f necklace
collant *kol·loñ* m tights; panty hose
collare *kol·lah·ray* m collar (*for dog*)
collaudare *kol·low·dah·ray* vt test
(*product*)
collega *kol·le·ga* m/f colleague
collegio *kol·le·joh* m college
collera *kol·le·ra* f anger; andare* in
collera *an·dah·ray een kol·le·ra* to
lose one's temper
colletto *kol·layt·toh* m collar
collezionare *kol·le·tsyo·nah·ray* vt collect (*stamps etc*)
collezione *kol·le·tsyoh·ne* f collection
collina *kol·lee·na* f hill
collinoso(a) *kol·lee·noh·so(a)* adj hilly
collo *kol·loh* m neck; il collo alto *kol·
loh al·to* polo neck; il collo a V *kol·
loh a vee* V-neck
collocare *kol·lo·kah·ray* vt place
colloquio *kol·lo·kwee·oh* m interview
(*for job*)
colmo *kol·mo* adj full up
colomba *ko·lohm·ba* f dove
colonia *ko·lo·nee·a* f colony; holiday
camp
colonna *ko·lohn·na* f column; la colonna sonora *ko·lohn·na so·no·ra*
sound track; la colonna dello sterzo
ko·lohn·na del·lo ster·tsoh steering
column
colore *ko·loh·ray* m colo(u)r; di colore
dee ko·loh·ray colo(u)red (*person*);
color turchese *ko·lohr toor·kay·se*
turquoise
colpa *kohl·pa* f fault (*blame*); di chi è
la colpa? *dee kee è la kohl·pa* whose
fault is it?; non è colpa mia *nohn e
kohl·pa mee·a* it's not my fault
colpevole *kol·pay·vo·lay* adj guilty; essere* colpevole *es·se·re kol·pay·vo·
lay* to be to blame
colpevolezza *kol·pay·vo·layts·tsa* f
guilt
colpire *kol·pee·re* vt hit; beat; strike;
knock
colpo *kohl·poh* m knock; blow; hit;
shot (*from gun*); stroke; bang (*of
gun etc*); thump (*noise*); il colpo di
stato *kohl·poh dee stah·toh* coup
d'état
coltello *kol·tel·loh* m knife
coltivare *kol·tee·vah·ray* vt grow
(*plants*); cultivate
coma *koh·ma* m coma
comandante *ko·man·dan·tay* m captain
comandi *ko·man·dee* mpl controls
combattimento *kom·bat·tee·mayn·toh*
m fight
combustibile *kom·boo·stee·bee·le* m
fuel
come *koh·me* adv, conj like; as; how;
come? *koh·me* pardon?; com'è?
kohm·e what's it like?; come è andato? *koh·me e an·dah·toh* how did it
go?; come va? *koh·me va* how are

you getting on?; come si chiama? *koh·me see kyah·ma* what's it called?; come si dice "dog" in italiano? *koh·me see dee·che dog een ee·ta·lyah·no* what's the Italian for "dog"?; faccia come le dico *fach·cha koh·me le dee·ko ee·o* do as I say; come se *koh·me say* as if. as though

comico *ko·mee·koh m* comedian

cominciare *ko·meen·chah·ray vt/i* start; begin

comitato *ko·mee·tah·toh m* committee

commedia *kom·me·dya f* comedy; play

commento *kom·mayn·toh m* comment

commerciale *kom·mer·chah·lay adj* commercial

commercializzato(a) *kom·mer·cha·leedz·dzah·to(a) adj* commercialized

commerciante *kom·mayr·chan·te m/f* dealer; trader

commerciare in *kom·mayr·chah·ray een vi* deal in

commercio *kom·mer·choh m* commerce; trade

commesso(a) *kom·mays·so(a) m/f* sales assistant; clerk (*in store*); il commesso viaggiatore *kom·mays·so vyaj·ja·toh·re* salesman (*rep*)

commettere* *kom·mayt·te·ray vt* commit (*crime*)

commissariato *kom·mees·sa·ryah·toh m* police station

commissione *kom·mees·syoh·ne f* errand; commission; fare* una commissione *fah·ray oo·na kom·mees·syoh·ne* to run an errand

commosso(a) *kom·mos·so(a) adj* excited

comodità *ko·mo·dee·ta fpl* amenities

comodo(a) *ko·mo·doh(a) adj* comfortable

compagnia *kom·pan·yee·a f* company; la compagnia aerea *kom·pan·yee·a a·e·re·a* airline; la compagnia di navigazione *kom·pan·yee·a dee na·vee·ga·tsyoh·ne* shipping company

compartecipazione agli utili *kom·par·te·chee·pa·tsyoh·ne al·yee oo·tee·lee f* profit-sharing

compassione *kom·pas·syoh·ne f* pity; sympathy

compensato *kom·pen·sah·toh m* plywood

competente *kom·pe·ten·tay adj* competent

competizione *kom·pe·tee·tsyoh·nay f* competition

compiti *kohm·pee·tee mpl* homework

compito *kohm·pee·toh m* job; duty; task

compleanno *kom·ple·an·noh m* birthday

complesso pop *kom·ples·soh pop m* pop group

completamente *kom·ple·ta·mayn·tay adv* completely

completare *kom·ple·tah·ray vt* complete

completo *kom·ple·toh m* suit; outfit; two-piece □ *adj* completo(a) *kom·ple·toh(a)* complete; full up (*bus etc*); al completo *al kom·ple·toh* full; no vacancies

complicato(a) *kom·plee·kah·toh(a) adj* complex; elaborate; complicated

complimento *kom·plee·mayn·toh m* compliment; complimenti! *kom·plee·mayn·tee* congratulations!

comporre* *kom·pohr·re vt* dial (*number*)

comportamento *kom·por·ta·mayn·toh m* behavio(u)r

comportarsi *kom·por·tar·see vr* behave; act; comportati bene! *kom·por·ta·tee be·ne* behave yourself!

compositore *kom·po·zee·toh·ray m* composer

comprare *kom·prah·ray vt* buy; purchase; comprare qualcosa per corrispondenza *kom·prah·ray kwal·ko·sa payr kor·ree·spon·den·tsa* to buy something by mail order

compratore *kom·pra·toh·re m* buyer

compratrice *kom·pra·tree·che f* buyer

comprensione *kom·pren·syoh·nay f* understanding

comprensivo(a) *kom·pren·see·vo(a) adj* understanding

compreso(a) *kom·pray·so(a) adj* including; servizio compreso *ser·vee·tsyoh kom·pray·so* inclusive of service; ... non compreso(a) *nohn kom·pray·so(a)* exclusive of...

comproprietà *kom·pro·pree·e·ta f* joint ownership

computer *kom·pyoo·ta m* — computer

comune *ko·moo·nay adj* common

comunicare *ko·moo·nee·kah·ray vi* communicate

comunicazione *ko·moo·nee·ka·tsyoh·ne f* communication; la comunicazione telefonica *ko·moo·nee·ka·tsyoh·ne te·le·fo·nee·ka* telephone call; non sono riuscito ad ottenere la comunicazione *nohn soh·no ree·oo·shee·to ad ot·te·nay·re la ko·moo·nee·ka·tsyoh·ne* I couldn't get through (*on phone*)

comunista *ko·moo·nee·sta m/f* Communist □ *adj* Communist

comunque *ko·moon·kwe adv* in any case; nevertheless □ *conj* however

con *kohn prep* with

concernere *kon·cher·ne·re vt* concern

concerto *kon·cher·toh m* concert; il concerto pop *kon·cher·toh pop* pop concert

concessionario *kon·ches·syoh·nah·ryoh m* agent; dealer

conchiglia *kon·keel·ya f* shell

conciliatore *kon·chee·lya·toh·re m* trouble-shooter (*political*)

concorrente *kon·kor·ren·tay adj* rival □ *m/f* il/la concorrente *kon·kor·ren·tay* competitor; contestant

concorrenza *kon·kor·ren·tsa f* competition

concorso *kon·kohr·soh m* contest (*competition*)

condannare *kon·dan·nah·ray vt* sentence; condemn

condimenti *kon·dee·mayn·tee mpl* condiments

condimento *kon·dee·mayn·toh m* dressing; seasoning; il condimento per l'insalata *kon·dee·mayn·toh payr leen·sa·lah·ta* salad dressing

condizionamento dell'aria *kon·dee·tsyoh·na·mayn·toh del·lah·rya m* air-conditioning

condizione *kon·dee·tsyoh·nay f* condition; proviso; a condizione che... *a kon·dee·tsyoh·nay kay* on condition that...

condizioni *kon·dee·tsyoh·nee fpl* terms (*of contract*)

conducente *kon·doo·chen·te m* driver (*of taxi, bus*)

condurre* *kon·door·re vt/i* lead

conduttori elettrici *kon·doot·toh·ree e·let·tree·chee mpl* jump leads

confarsi* a *kon·far·see see a vr* suit; agree with

conferenza *kon·fe·ren·tsa f* lecture; conference

confermare *kon·fer·mah·ray vt* confirm

confessare *kon·fes·sah·ray vt* confess

confessarsi *kon·fes·sahr·see vr* confess

confessione *kon·fes·syoh·nay f* confession

confezionato(a) *kon·fe·tsyoh·nah·to(a) adj* ready-made (*clothes*)

confidenza *kon·fee·den·tsa f* confidence

confidenziale *kon·fee·den·tsyah·lay adj* confidential; private

confine *kon·fee·ne m* boundary; border

conflitto *kon·fleet·toh m* dispute (*industrial*)

confondere* *kon·fohn·de·ray vt* mix up; confuse; **confondere* una cosa con un'altra** *kon·fohn·de·ray oo·na ko·sa kohn oo·nal·tra* to confuse one thing with another

conforto *kon·for·toh m* comfort

confrontare *kon·fron·tah·ray vt* compare

confuso(a) *kon·foo·zoh(a) adj* confused

congedo *kon·je·doh m* leave (*holiday*); **in congedo** *een kon·je·doh* on leave

congelare *kon·je·lah·ray vt* freeze (*food*)

congelato(a) *kon·je·lah·to(a) adj* frozen (*food*)

congelatore *kon·je·la·toh·re m* deep-freeze; freezer

congetturare *kon·jet·too·rah·ray vi* guess

congratularsi con *kon·gra·too·lahr·see kohn vr* congratulate; **congratularsi con qualcuno per qualcosa** *kon·gra·too·lahr·see kohn kwal·koo·noh payr kwal·ko·sa* to congratulate someone on something

coniglio *ko·neel·yoh m* rabbit

connazionale *kon·na·tsyoh·nah·le m/f* fellow countryman/woman

cono *ko·noh m* cone

conoscenza *ko·no·shen·tsa f* acquaintance; knowledge; **fare* la conoscenza di** *fah·ray la ko·no·shen·tsa dee* to meet (*make acquaintance of*)

conoscere* *ko·noh·she·re vt* know; **conoscere* bene qualcosa** *ko·noh·she·re be·ne kwal·ko·sa* to be familiar with something

conoscersi* *ko·noh·sher·see vr* meet

conoscitore *ko·no·shee·toh·ray m* connoisseur

consegna *kon·sayn·ya f* delivery; consignment

consegnare *kon·sen·yah·ray vt* deliver (*goods*)

conseguenza *kon·se·gwen·tsa f* consequence (*result*)

conservarsi *kon·ser·var·see vr* keep

conservatore *kon·sayr·va·toh·ray adj* conservative

conservatorio *kon·ser·va·to·ryoh m* academy of music

conservatrice *kon·sayr·va·tree·chay adj* conservative

considerare *kon·se·de·rah·ray vt* consider

consigliare *kon·seel·yah·ray vt* advise; **consigliare a qualcuno di fare qualcosa** *kon·seel·yah·ray a kwal·koo·no dee fah·ray kwal·ko·sa* to advise someone to do something

consiglio *kon·seel·yoh m* advice; **il consiglio comunale** *kon·seel·yoh ko·moo·nah·lay* corporation (*of town*); council; **il consiglio d'amministrazione** *kon·seel·yoh dam·mee·nee·stra·tsyoh·ne* board (*of directors*)

consistere* in *kon·see·ste·ray een vi* consist of

consolato *kon·so·lah·toh m* consulate

console *kon·so·lay m* consul

consommé *kon·som·may m* consommé

consulente *kon·soo·len·tay m* consultant

consultare *kon·sool·tah·ray vt* consult; **refer to**

consumatore *kon·soo·ma·toh·ray m* consumer

contachilometri *kon·ta·kee·lo·me·tree m* ≈ milometer

contagioso(a) *kon·ta·joh·soh(a) adj* infectious; contagious

container *kon·tay·ner m* container (*for shipping etc*)

contante *kon·tan·te m* cash; **pagare qualcosa in contanti** *pa·gah·ray kwal·ko·sa een kon·tan·tee* to pay cash for something

contare *kon·tah·ray vt/i* count; **contare su** *kon·tah·ray soo* to rely on (*person*); **contare fino a 10** *kon·tah·ray fee·no a 10* to count up to 10

contatore *kon·ta·toh·ray m* meter

contattare *kon·tat·tah·ray vt* reach (*contact*)

contatto *kon·tat·toh m* contact; **mettersi* in contatto con** *mayt·ter·see een kon·tat·toh kohn* to contact

contea *kon·te·a f* county

contemporaneo(a) *kon·tem·po·rah·ne·oh(a) adj* contemporary

contenere* *kon·te·nay·re vt* hold; contain

contento(a) *kon·tayn·to(a) adj* happy; pleased; content(ed)

contenuto *kon·te·noo·toh m* contents

contestare *kon·te·stah·ray vt* dispute

continentale *kon·tee·nen·tah·lay adj* continental

continente *kon·tee·nen·tay m* mainland; continent

continuamente *kon·tee·noo·a·men·tay adv* continuously

continuare *kon·tee·noo·ah·ray vt/i* continue; **continuare a fare** *kon·tee·noo·ah·ray a fah·ray* to continue to do

continuo(a) *kon·tee·nwoh(a) adj* continuous; continual

conto *kohn·toh m* check; bill; account; **il conto per favore** *eel kohn·toh payr fa·voh·ray* can I have the bill please?; **il conto deposito** *kohn·toh de·po·zee·toh* deposit account; **il conto corrente** *kohn·toh kor·ren·tay* current account; checking account; **il conto bancario** *kohn·toh ban·kah·ryo* bank account; **per conto di** *payr kohn·toh dee* on behalf of

contrabbandare *kon·trab·ban·dah·ray vt* smuggle

contrabbando *kon·trab·ban·doh m* contraband

contrario *kon·trah·ryoh m* opposite; **al contrario** *al kon·trah·ryoh* on the contrary

contrattazione *kon·trat·ta·tsyoh·ne f* bargaining (*negotiation*)

contratto *kon·trat·toh m* contract

contravvenzione *kon·trav·ven·tsyoh·ne f* fine

contribuire *kon·tree·boo·ee·ray vi* contribute

contro *kohn·tro* prep against; versus

controllare *kon·trol·lah·ray* vt check; control; inspect (ticket)

controllo *kon·trol·loh* m check; control; il controllo improvviso *kon·trol·loh eem·prov·vee·zo* spot check

controllore *kon·trol·loh·re* m inspector (of tickets)

contusione *kon·too·zyoh·ne* f bruise

convalescenza *kon·va·le·shen·tsa* f convalescence

conveniente *kon·ve·nyen·te* adj convenient

convenire* *kon·ve·nee·re* vi be suitable; Le conviene giovedì? *le kon·vye·ne jo·ve·dee* does Thursday suit you?

convento *kon·ven·toh* m monastery; convent

conversazione *kon·ver·sa·tsyoh·ne* f talk; conversation

convincere* *kon·veen·che·ray* vt convince

cooperativa *koh·o·pay·ra·tee·va* f cooperative

coperchio *ko·per·kyoh* m cover; lid

coperta *ko·per·ta* f cover; blanket; la coperta elettrica *ko·per·ta e·let·tree·ka* electric blanket

coperte *ko·per·te* fpl bedclothes

copertina *ko·payr·tee·na* f cover (of book)

coperto *ko·per·toh* m place setting; al coperto *al ko·per·toh* indoor (games)

copia *ko·pya* f copy; print (photographic); la copia carbone *ko·pya kar·boh·nay* carbon copy

copiare *ko·pyah·ray* vt copy

coppa *kop·pa* f cup (trophy); la coppa dell'olio *kop·pa del·lo·lyoh* sump (in car)

coppia *kop·pya* f pair (of people); couple

coprire* *ko·pree·ray* vt cover

copyright *ko·pee·rite* m copyright

coraggio *ko·raj·joh* m nerve; courage

coraggioso(a) *ko·raj·joh·so(a)* adj brave

corallo *ko·ral·loh* m coral

corda *kor·da* f cord (twine); rope; string

cordiale *kor·dyah·lay* m cordial

cordialmente *kor·dyal·mayn·te* adv yours sincerely

cornamusa *kor·na·moo·za* f (bag)pipes

cornetto *kor·nayt·toh* m cornet (of ice cream)

cornice *kor·nee·che* f frame (of picture)

corno *kor·noh* m horn

coro *koh·roh* m choir

corona *ko·roh·na* f crown

corpo *kor·poh* m body

correggere* *kor·rej·je·ray* vt correct

corrente *kor·ren·te* f power (electricity); current; la corrente d'aria *kor·ren·te dah·ree·a* draught (wind)

correntemente *kor·ren·te·mayn·te* adv fluently

correre* *kohr·re·re* vi run (person, animal); correre* dietro a qualcuno *kohr·re·re dye·tro a kwal·koo·no* to run after someone

correttamente *kor·ret·ta·mayn·te* adv properly

corretto(a) *kor·rayt·to(a)* adj right; correct; proper

correzione *kor·re·tsyoh·nay* f correction

corrida *kor·ree·da* f bullfight

corridoio *kor·ree·doh·yoh* m corridor

corrimano *kor·ree·mah·noh* m handrail (on stairs); rail

corrispondente *kor·ree·spon·den·te* m/f correspondent; pen pal

corrispondenza *kor·ree·spon·den·tsa* f correspondence

corrispondere* *kor·ree·spohn·de·re* vi correspond

corrodere* *kor·roh·de·ray* vt corrode

corrompere* *kor·rohm·pe·re* vt corrupt; bribe

corrotto(a) *kor·ro·toh(a)* adj corrupt

corruzione *kor·roo·tsee·oh·nay* f corruption

corsa *kohr·sa* f race (sport); le corse ippiche *kohr·se eep·pee·ke* horse-racing

corsetto *kor·sayt·toh* m girdle; corset

corsia *kor·see·a* f lane; ward (in hospital); la corsia di emergenza *kor·see·a dee e·mer·jen·tsa* hard shoulder; la corsia di sorpasso *la kor·see·a dee sor·pas·soh* the outside lane (in road)

Corsica *kor·see·ka* f Corsica

corso *kohr·soh* m course; il corso intensivo *kohr·soh een·ten·see·voh* crash course; il corso per corrispondenza *kohr·soh payr kor·ree·spon·den·tsa* correspondence course

corso del cambio *kohr·soh del kam·byoh* m exchange rate

corteccia *kor·taych·cha* f bark (of tree)

corteo *kor·te·oh* m parade

cortile *kor·tee·lay* m courtyard; yard; playground

corto(a) *kohr·to(a)* adj short; essere* a corto di qualcosa *es·se·re a kohr·to dee kwal·ko·sa* to be short of something

cosa *ko·sa* f thing; cosa vuole? *ko·sa vwo·le* what do you want?

coscia *ko·sha* f thigh; drumstick (of chicken); la coscia di pollo *ko·sha dee pohl·loh* chicken leg

coscienza *ko·shen·tsa* f conscience

coscienzioso(a) *ko·shen·tsyoh·zo(a)* adj conscientious; thorough (work)

cosciotto *ko·shot·toh* m leg; il cosciotto d'agnello *ko·shot·toh dan·yel·loh* leg of lamb

così *ko·see* adv so; thus (in this way); così contento(a) che... *ko·see kon·ten·to(a)* so pleased that...; e così siamo partiti *e ko·see syah·mo par·tee·tee* and so we left; così grande come *ko·see gran·de koh·me* as big as

cosmetici *koz·me·tee·chee* mpl cosmetics

cosmopolita *koz·mo·po·lee·ta* adj cosmopolitan

cospargere* di *ko·spar·je·re dee* vt sprinkle with

costa *ko·sta* f coast

Costa Azzurra *ko·sta adz·dzoor·ra* f Riviera

costare *ko·stah·ray* vt cost; costare il doppio *ko·stah·ray eel dop·pyoh* to cost double; quanto costa? *kwan·to ko·sta* how much is it?

costo *ko·stoh* m cost; il costo della vita *ko·stoh del·la vee·ta* cost of living; il costo di esercizio *ko·stoh dee e·zayr·chee·tsyoh* running costs

costola *ko·sto·la* f rib

costoso(a) *ko·stoh·so(a)* adj expensive; poco costoso(a) *po·ko ko·stoh·so(a)* inexpensive

costringere* *ko·streen·je·re* vt force (compel)

costruire* *ko·stroo·ee·re* vt build; construct

costruzione ko·stroo·tsyoh·ne f construction; **la costruzione navale** ko·stroo·tsyoh·ne na·vah·le shipbuilding

costume ko·stoo·may m custom; fancy dress; costume; **il costume da bagno** ko·stoo·may da ban·yoh swimsuit; swimming trunks; **il costume nazionale** ko·stoo·may na·tsyoh·nah·lay national dress

costura ko·stoo·ra f seam

cotoletta ko·to·layt·ta f cutlet

cotone ko·toh·nay m cotton (fabric); **il cotone idrofilo** ko·toh·nay ee·dro·fee·lo absorbent cotton

cotto(a) kot·to(a) adj done (cooked); **insufficientemente cotto(a)** een·soof·fee·chen·te·mayn·tay kot·to(a) undercooked; underdone

cottura kot·too·ra f cooking; baking

coupé koo·pay m — coupé (car)

cozza kots·tsa f mussel

crampo kram·poh m cramp

cravatta kra·vat·ta f tie; necktie; **la cravatta a farfalla** kra·vat·ta a far·fal·la bow tie

crawl krol m crawl (swimming)

creare kray·ah·ray vt create

credenza kre·den·tsa f sideboard; belief (tenet)

credere kre·de·re vt/i believe; **credere a** kray·de·re a to believe in; **credo di sì** kre·do dee see I think so; I expect so

credito kre·dee·toh m credit; **a credito** a kray·dee·toh on credit; **fare* credito a qualcuno** fah·ray kray·dee·toh a kwal·koo·noh to give somebody credit

creditore kre·dee·toh·ray m creditor

creditrice kray·dee·tree·chay f creditor

crema kre·ma adj cream □ f **la crema** kre·ma cream (cosmetic); custard; **la crema per il viso** kre·ma payr eel vee·zoh face cream; **la crema per le mani** kre·ma payr le mah·nee hand cream; **la crema per barba** kre·ma payr bar·ba shaving cream

crepuscolo kre·poo·sko·lo m dusk

crescere* kre·she·ray vi grow; grow up

crescione kre·shoh·nay m cress

crescita kray·shee·ta f growth

crespo di cotone kray·spoh dee ko·toh·ne m seersucker

Creta kray·ta f Crete

cric kreek m — jack (for car)

criminale kree·mee·nah·lay adj, m/f criminal

crimine kree·mee·ne m crime

crisantemo kree·zan·te·moh m chrysanthemum

crisi kree·zee f — crisis

cristallo kree·stal·loh m crystal (glass)

cristiano(a) kree·stee·ah·noh(a) m/f Christian

criticare kree·tee·kah·ray vt criticize

croccante krok·kan·tay adj crisp

crocchetta krok·kayt·ta f croquette

croce kroh·chay f cross

crocevia kroh·chay·vee·a m — crossroads

crociera kro·che·ra f cruise; **fare* una crociera** fah·ray oo·na kro·che·ra to go on a cruise

croco kroh·koh m crocus

croissant krwah·soň m croissant

crollare krol·lah·ray vi collapse; slump

crollo krol·loh m collapse; slump

cromo kro·moh m chrome

cronaca kro·na·ka f news

cronista kro·nee·sta m/f reporter (press)

cronometro kro·no·me·troh m stopwatch

crosta kro·sta f crust; scab

crostacei kros·ta·che·ee mpl shellfish

crostino kro·stee·noh m crouton

croupier kroo·pyay m croupier

crudele kroo·de·lay adj cruel

crudo(a) kroo·do(a) adj raw (uncooked)

crumiro kroo·mee·roh m strikebreaker

cruscotto kroos·kot·toh m dash(board)

cubetto di ghiaccio koo·bayt·toh dee gyach·choh m ice cube

cubo koo·boh m cube

cuccetta koo·chayt·ta f couchette; berth; bunk

cucchiaia kook·kee·a·ya f tablespoon

cucchiaiata kook·kee·a·yah·ta f tablespoon (measure); spoonful

cucchiaino kook·kee·a·ee·noh m teaspoon

cucchiaio kook·kee·a·yoh m spoon; dessertspoon

cucina koo·chee·na f kitchen; cooker; stove; cuisine; cooking; **la cucina a gas** koo·chee·na a gas gas cooker

cucinare koo·chee·nah·ray vt cook

cucire koo·chee·re vt sew

cucitrice koo·chee·tree·che f stapler

cuffia koof·fya f headphones; **la cuffia da bagno** koof·fya da ban·yoh bathing cap

cugino(a) koo·jee·noh(a) m/f cousin

cui koo·ee pron that, which; whose; **il ragazzo con cui...** eel ra·gats·tsoh kohn koo·ee the boy with whom...; **l'uomo, il cui figlio** lwo·moh, eel koo·ee feel·yoh the man, whose son; **il giorno in cui noi...** eel johr·noh een koo·ee noy the day when we...

culla kool·la f cradle

cullare kool·lah·ray vt rock

cultura kool·too·ra f culture; **la cultura generale** kool·too·ra je·ne·rah·lay general knowledge

cumulo koo·moo·loh m pile; **il cumulo di neve** koo·moo·loh dee nay·ve snowdrift

cunetta koo·nayt·ta f gutter (in street)

cuocere* kwo·che·re vt/i cook; **cuocere al forno** kwo·che·re al fohr·noh to bake; **cuocere ai ferri** kwo·che·re ai fer·ree to grill

cuoco(a) kwo·koh(a) m/f cook

cuoio kwo·yoh m leather; **il cuoio verniciato** kwo·yoh ver·nee·chah·to patent leather; **il cuoio capelluto** kwo·yoh ka·pel·loo·to scalp

cuore kwo·ray m heart; **nel cuore della notte** nel kwo·ray del·la not·tay in the middle of the night

cuori kwo·ree mpl hearts (cards)

cura koo·ra f care; treatment (medical)

curare koo·rah·ray vt treat; cure; look after; nurse; take care of

curato koo·rah·to m vicar

curioso(a) koo·ree·oh·soh(a) adj curious; funny; quaint

curva koor·va f bend; corner; curve; **prendere* la curva** pren·de·ray la koor·va to corner; **la curva a gomito** koor·va a goh·mee·toh hairpin bend; **la curva a S** koor·va a es·se double bend; **la curva senza visibilità** koor·va sen·tsa vee·zee·bee·lee·ta blind corner

curvare koor·vah·ray vt/i bend

cuscinetti koo·shee·nayt·tee mpl bearings (in car)

cuscino koo·shee·noh m cushion

custode *koo·sto·day* m caretaker
custodire *koo·sto·dee·ray* vt guard (*prisoner*)

D

da *da* prep from; by; since; **cadere* da un muro** *ka·day·re da oon moo·roh* to fall off a wall; **vado dal giornalaio** *va·do dal johr·na·la·yoh* I'm going to the newsagent's; **l'uomo dal cappello grigio** *lwo·moh dal cap·pel·loh gree·joh* the man with the grey hat; **da quando siamo arrivati** *da kwan·do syah·mo ar·ree·vah·tee* since we arrived
dadi *dah·dee* mpl dice
dagli = da + gli, dai = da + i
dama *dah·ma* f draughts, checkers; partner (*dancing*)
danese *da·nay·se* adj Danish □ m il danese *da·nay·se* Danish
Danimarca *da·nee·mar·ka* f Denmark
danneggiare *dan·nej·jah·ray* vt spoil; damage
danni *dan·nee* mpl damages
danno *dan·noh* m damage; harm
dappertutto *dap·per·toot·to* adv everywhere
dapprima *dap·pree·ma* adv at first
dardo *dar·doh* m dart (*to throw*); **il gioco dei dardi** *jo·koh de·ee dar·dee* game of darts
dare* *dah·ray* vt give; **dare* qualcosa a qualcuno** *dah·ray kwal·koh·sa a kwal·koo·no* to give someone something; **me lo dia** *me lo dee·a* give it to me; **glielo dia** *lye·lo dee·a* give it to him/her; **dare* la precedenza** *dah·ray la pre·che·den·tsa* to give way (*traffic*); **dare* un passaggio a qualcuno** *dah·ray oon pas·saj·joh a kwal·koo·no* to give somebody a lift; **dare* una festa** *dah·ray oo·na fes·ta* to give a party; **questa porta dà sul giardino** *kway·sta por·ta da sool jar·dee·noh* this door leads into the garden; **dare* uno sguardo a** *dah·ray oo·no zgwar·doh a* to glance at; **dare* un esame** *dah·ray oon e·zah·me* to take an exam
data *dah·ta* f date (*day*)
dati *dah·tee* mpl data
datore di lavoro *da·toh·re dee la·voh·roh* m employer
dattero *dat·te·roh* m date (*fruit*)
dattilografo(a) *dat·tee·lo·gra·fo(a)* m/f typist
dattiloscritto(a) *dat·tee·lo·skreet·to(a)* adj typewritten
dattiloscrivere* *dat·tee·lo·skree·ve·re* vt type (*letter*)
davanti *da·van·tee* adv in front; opposite; **davanti a** *da·van·tee a* in front of; opposite; **davanti agli altri** *da·van·tee al·yee al·tree* ahead of the others
dazio *da·tsyoh* m customs duty
debito *day·bee·toh* m debt; debit; **un debito insolvibile** *oon day·bee·toh een·sol·vee·bee·le* a bad debt; **avere* dei debiti** *a·vay·re de·ee day·bee·tee* to be in debt
debole *day·bo·le* adj weak; dim (*light*); faint (*sound etc*)
decaffeinizzato(a) *de·kaf·fe·ee·needz·dzah·to(a)* adj decaffeinated
decennio *de·chen·nyoh* m decade
decente *de·chen·te* adj decent
decidere* *de·chee·de·re* vi decide; **decidere* di fare qualcosa** *de·chee·de·re*

dee fah·ray kwal·ko·sa to decide to do something
decidersi* *de·chee·der·see* vr make up one's mind; decide
decimale *de·chee·mah·le* adj decimal □ m il decimale *de·chee·mah·le* decimal
decimo(a) *de·chee·mo(a)* adj tenth
decisione *de·chee·zyoh·nay* f decision
deciso(a) *de·chee·zo(a)* adj determined; **essere* deciso a fare qualcosa** *es·se·re de·chee·zo a fah·ray kwal·ko·sa* to be determined to do something
decollare *de·kol·lah·ray* vi take off (*plane*)
decollo *de·kol·loh* m takeoff (*of plane*)
decorare *de·ko·rah·ray* vt decorate
decoratore *de·ko·ra·toh·re* m painter (*decorator*)
deficienza *de·fee·chen·tsa* f shortage
deficit *de·fee·cheet* m — deficit
deflazione *de·fla·tsyoh·ne* f deflation
deforme *de·fohr·me* adj deformed
degli = di + gli
degustare *de·goo·stah·ray* vt sample (*wine*)
dei = di + i, del = di + il
delegare *de·le·gah·ray* vt delegate
delegazione *de·le·ga·tsyoh·nay* f delegation
deliberatamente *de·lee·be·ra·ta·mayn·te* adv deliberately
delicato(a) *de·lee·kah·to(a)* adj delicate; dainty
delitto *de·leet·toh* m crime
delizioso(a) *de·lee·tsyoh·so(a)* adj delightful; delicious
deludere* *de·loo·de·re* vt disappoint
deluso(a) *de·loo·zo(a)* adj disappointed
denaro *de·nah·roh* m money
denso(a) *den·so(a)* adj thick; dense
dente *den·te* m tooth; **il mal di denti** *mal dee den·tee* toothache; **avere* il mal di denti** *a·vay·re eel mal dee den·tee* to have toothache
dentiera *den·tye·ra* f false teeth; dentures
dentifricio *den·tee·free·choh* m toothpaste
dentista *den·tee·sta* m/f dentist
dentro *dayn·tro* adv, prep in; inside; **stare*/andare* dentro** *stah·ray/an·dah·ray dayn·tro* to be/go inside
deodorante *de·o·do·ran·te* m deodorant
deporre* *de·pohr·re* vt lay down; put down; **deporre* il ricevitore** *de·pohr·re eel ree·che·vee·toh·re* to hang up (*phone*)
depositare *de·po·zee·tah·ray* vi settle (*wine*) □ vt deposit; bank
deposito *de·po·zee·toh* m deposit; **il deposito bagagli** *de·po·zee·toh ba·gal·yee* left luggage office
derubare *de·roo·bah·ray* vt rob (*person*)
descrivere* *de·skree·ve·re* vt describe
descrizione *de·skree·tsyoh·ne* f description
deserto *de·zer·toh* m desert
desiderare *de·see·de·rah·ray* vt wish for; desire
desiderio *de·see·de·ryoh* m wish; desire
desideroso(a) *de·see·de·roh·so(a)* adj eager
destinare *de·stee·nah·ray* vt intend
destinazione *de·stee·na·tsyoh·ne* f destination; **con destinazione per** *kohn*

de·stee·na·tsyoh·ne payr bound for (*ship*)

destra *de·stra* f right (*right-hand side*); **a destra** *a de·stra* on/to the right; **girare a destra** *jee·rah·ray a de·stra* to turn right

destro(a) *de·stro(a)* adj right (*not left*)

detersivo *de·ter·see·voh* m soap powder; detergent

detrarre* *de·trar·re* vt deduct

dettagliante *det·tal·yan·te* m retailer

dettagliatamente *det·tal·yah·ta·mayn·tay* adv in detail

dettagliato(a) *det·tal·yah·to(a)* adj detailed; itemized (*bill etc*)

dettaglio *det·tal·yoh* m detail

dettare *det·tah·ray* vt dictate

deviare *de·vee·ah·ray* vt reroute; divert □ vi swerve

deviazione *de·vee·a·tsyoh·ne* f diversion; detour; **fare* una deviazione** *fah·ray oo·na de·vee·a·tsyoh·ne* to make a detour

di *dee* prep of; **l'acqua di rubinetto** *ak·kwa dee roo·bee·nayt·toh* water from the tap; **tre di loro** *tray dee loh·ro* 3 of them; **di pietra** *dee pye·tra* made of stone; **di giorno/notte** *dee johr·noh/not·tay* by day/night; **meglio di lui** *mel·yo dee loo·ee* better than him; **L.20000 di benzina** *L20000 dee ben·dzee·na* L.20000 worth of petrol/gas; **del pane** *del pah·ne* some bread; **dei soldi** *de·ee sol·dee* some money

diabete *dee·a·be·te* m diabetes

diabetico(a) *dee·a·be·tee·ko(a)* m/f diabetic

diagnosi *dee·an·yo·zee* f diagnosis

diagonale *dee·a·go·nah·le* adj diagonal

diagramma *dee·a·gram·ma* m diagram

dialetto *dee·a·let·toh* m dialect

diamante *dee·a·man·te* m diamond

diametro *dee·a·me·troh* m diameter

diapositiva *dee·a·po·zee·tee·va* f slide (*photo*)

diarrea *dee·ar·re·a* f diarrh(o)ea

dibattito *dee·bat·tee·toh* m debate

dicembre *dee·chem·bre* m December

dichiarare *dee·kya·rah·ray* vt declare; state; **niente da dichiarare** *nyen·te da dee·kya·rah·ray* nothing to declare

dichiarazione *dee·kya·ra·tsyoh·ne* f declaration; statement

diciannove *dee·chan·no·vay* num nineteen

diciassette *dee·chas·set·te* num seventeen

diciassettesimo(a) *dee·chas·set·te·zee·mo(a)* adj seventeenth

diciotto *dee·chot·to* num eighteen

dieci *dye·chee* num ten

diesel *dee·zel* m diesel

dieta *dee·e·ta* f diet (*slimming*); **stare* a dieta** *stah·ray a dee·e·ta* to be on a diet

dietro *dye·tro* adv behind □ prep behind; after

difendere* *dee·fen·de·re* vt defend

difesa *dee·fay·sa* f defence

difetto *dee·fet·toh* m defect; fault

difettoso(a) *dee·fet·toh·so(a)* adj defective; faulty; imperfect

differente *deef·fe·ren·te* adj different

differenza *deef·fe·ren·tsa* f difference

difficile *deef·fee·chee·le* adj difficult; hard

difficoltà *deef·fee·kol·ta* f — difficulty

diffondere* *deef·fohn·de·re* vt spread (*news*)

diga *dee·ga* f dam; dyke

digitale *dee·jee·tah·le* adj digital

dilatare *dee·la·tah·ray* vt expand

dilatarsi *dee·la·tar·see* vr expand

dilettante *dee·let·tan·te* m amateur

diluire *dee·loo·ee·re* vt dilute

dimagrire *dee·ma·gree·ray* vi lose weight

dimenare *dee·me·nah·ray* vt wave; wag (*tail*)

dimensioni *dee·men·syoh·nee* fpl size; dimensions

dimenticare *dee·men·tee·kah·ray* vt forget; **ho dimenticato di fare…** *o dee·men·tee·kah·to dee fah·ray* I forgot to do…

dimettersi* *dee·mayt·ter·see* vr resign

diminuire *dee·mee·noo·ee·re* vt reduce; diminish

diminuzione *dee·mee·noo·tsyoh·ne* f fall (*decrease*)

dimissioni *dee·mees·syoh·nee* fpl resignation

dimostrazione *dee·mo·stra·tsyoh·ne* f demonstration

dinamico(a) *dee·na·mee·ko(a)* adj dynamic

dinamo *dee·na·mo* f — dynamo

dinghy *din·gee* m — dinghy

dintorni *deen·tohr·nee* mpl surroundings

di nuovo *dee nwo·vo* adv again

dio *dee·oh* m **dei** god; **Dio** *dee·oh* God

dipendere* da *dee·pen·de·re da* vi depend on; **dipende** *dee·pen·de* it depends

dipingere* *dee·peen·je·re* vt/i paint

diploma *dee·plo·ma* m diploma

diplomatico *dee·plo·ma·tee·koh* m diplomat

diramazione *dee·ra·ma·tsyoh·ne* f fork

dire* *dee·re* vt tell (*fact, news*); say; **dire* qualcosa a qualcuno** *dee·re kwal·ko·sa a kwal·koo·no* to tell someone something; **dire* a qualcuno di fare qualcosa** *dee·re a kwal·koo·no dee fah·ray kwal·ko·sa* to tell someone to do something; **dire* sciocchezze** *dee·re shok·kayts·tse* to talk nonsense; **si dice che…** *see dee·che ke…* they say that… (*people in general*)

direttamente *dee·ret·ta·mayn·te* adv straight

diretto(a) *dee·ret·to(a)* adj direct; **il treno diretto** *tre·noh dee·ret·to* through train

direttore *dee·ret·toh·re* m conductor (*of orchestra*); governor (*of institution*); manager; president (*of company*); director (*of firm*); **il direttore di banca** *dee·ret·toh·re dee ban·ka* bank manager; **il direttore del personale** *dee·ret·toh·re del per·so·nah·le* personnel manager; **il direttore di marketing** *dee·ret·toh·re dee mahr·ke·ting* marketing manager; **il direttore delle vendite** *dee·ret·toh·re del·le vayn·dee·te* sales manager; **il direttore generale** *dee·ret·toh·re je·ne·rah·lay* managing director, M.D.

direttrice *dee·ret·tree·chay* f manageress

direzione *dee·rets·yo·nay* f management; direction

dirigere* *dee·ree·je·ray* vt manage (*business*); run (*a business, country*); direct

dirimpetto *dee·reem·pet·to* adv opposite

diritto *dee·reet·toh* m right (*entitlement*); right side (*of cloth etc*) □ adv straight □ adj **diritto(a)** *dee·reet·to(a)* straight

dirottare *dee·rot·tah·ray* vt hijack

dirottatore *dee·rot·ta·toh·re* m hijacker

disapprovare *dee·zap·pro·vah·ray* vt disapprove of

disarcionare *dee·zar·cho·nah·ray* vt throw (rider)

disarmato(a) *dee·zar·mah·toh(a)* adj unarmed (person)

disastro *dee·za·stroh* m disaster

discesa *dee·shay·sa* f descent; in discesa *een dee·shay·sa* downhill

disciplina *dee·shee·plee·na* f discipline

disc-jockey *deesk·jok·kee* m disc jockey

disco *dee·sko* m disc; record; il disco orario *dee·sko o·rah·ryo* parking disc

discorso *dee·skohr·soh* m speech (oration)

discoteca *dee·sko·te·ka* f disco(thèque)

discreto(a) *dee·skray·to(a)* adj discreet; fair

discriminazione *dee·skree·mee·na·tsyoh·ne* f discrimination

discussione *dee·skoos·syoh·ne* f discussion; fuori discussione *fwo·ree dee·skoos·syoh·ne* out of the question

discutere* *dee·skoo·te·re* vt discuss

disdire* *dees·dee·re* vt cancel

disegnare *dee·sen·yah·ray* vt draw; design

disegnatore *dee·sen·ya·toh·re* m designer; draughtsman

disegno *dee·sayn·yoh* m plan; design; pattern; drawing

disfare* *dee·sfah·ray* vt unpack (case); undo; unwrap

disgelare *dee·zje·lah·ray* vt/i defrost; thaw; fare* disgelare *fah·ray dee·zje·lah·ray* to thaw (food)

disgusto *dee·zgoo·stoh* m disgust

disinfettante *dee·zeen·fet·tan·te* m disinfectant

disinfettare *dee·zeen·fet·tah·ray* vt disinfect

disinteressare *dee·zeen·te·res·sah·ray* vt buy out (partner etc)

disoccupati *dee·zok·koo·pah·tee* mpl the unemployed

disoccupato(a) *dee·zok·koo·pah·to(a)* adj unemployed

disoccupazione *dee·zok·koo·pa·tsyoh·nay* f unemployment

disonesto(a) *dee·zo·ne·sto(a)* adj dishonest

disordinato(a) *dee·zor·dee·nah·to(a)* adj untidy

disordine *dee·zohr·dee·nay* m mess; in disordine *een dee·zohr·dee·nay* in a muddle

dispari *dee·spa·ree* adj odd (number)

dispensa *dee·spen·sa* f larder

disperato(a) *dee·spe·rah·to(a)* adj desperate

disperso(a) *dee·spayr·soh(a)* adj missing (person)

dispetto *dee·spet·toh* m spite

dispiacere* a *dee·spya·che·re* a vi displease; non mi dispiace il caldo *nohn mee dee·spyah·che eel kal·doh* I don't mind the heat; mi dispiace *mee dee·spyah·che* (I'm) sorry; mi dispiace ma non posso farlo *mee dee·spyah·che ma nohn pos·so far·lo* I'm afraid I can't do it

disponibile *dee·spo·nee·bee·le* adj available

disporre* *dee·spohr·re* vt arrange (flowers, furniture)

dispositivo *dees·po·see·tee·vo* m gadget

disposto(a) *dee·spoh·sto(a)* adj willing

disputa *dee·spoo·ta* f dispute

dissenso *dees·sen·soh* m disagreement

distante *dee·stan·te* adj distant

distanza *dee·stan·tsa* f distance; a poca distanza dal mare *a po·ka dee·stan·tsa dal mah·re* within easy reach of the sea

distilleria *dee·steel·le·ree·a* f distillery

distinguere* *dee·steen·gwe·re* vt distinguish; non posso distinguere* tra di loro *nohn pos·so dee·steen·gwe·re tra dee loh·ro* I can't tell the difference between them

distintivo *dee·steen·tee·voh* m badge

distinto(a) *dee·steen·to(a)* adj distinct

distorsione *dee·stor·syoh·ne* f sprain

distrarre* *dee·strar·re* vt distract

distretto postale *dee·strayt·toh po·stah·le* m postal district

distribuire *dee·stree·boo·ee·re* vt distribute; deliver (mail)

distributore *dee·stree·boo·toh·re* m distributor; il distributore di benzina *dee·stree·boo·toh·re dee ben·dzee·na* petrol pump; il distributore automatico *dee·stree·boo·toh·re ow·to·ma·tee·ko* slot machine; vending machine

distribuzione *dee·stree·boo·tsyoh·ne* f distribution; delivery (of mail)

distruggere* *dee·strooj·je·re* vt destroy

disturbare *dee·stoor·bah·ray* vt disturb; pregasi non disturbare *pre·ga·see nohn dee·stoor·bah·ray* do not disturb

disturbarsi *dee·stoor·bar·see* vr put oneself out; non si disturbi per favore *nohn see dee·stoor·bee payr fa·voh·re* please don't bother

disturbo *dee·stoor·boh* m trouble; i disturbi allo stomaco *dee·stoor·bee al·lo sto·ma·koh* stomach trouble

disubbidiente *dee·zoob·bee·dyen·te* adj disobedient

disubbidire *dee·zoob·bee·dee·re* vi disobey

dito *dee·toh* m —a finger; il dito del piede *dee·toh del pye·de* toe

ditta *deet·ta* f business; firm; company

divano *dee·vah·noh* m couch; sofa; divan

diventare *dee·ven·tah·ray* vi become; diventare professionista *dee·ven·tah·ray pro·fes·syoh·nee·sta* to turn professional

diversi(e) *dee·ver·see(·se)* adj several

diversificare *dee·ver·see·fee·kah·ray* vt diversify

diverso(a) *dee·ver·so(a)* adj different

divertente *dee·ver·ten·te* adj funny (amusing)

divertire *dee·ver·tee·re* vt amuse

divertirsi *dee·ver·teer·see* vr enjoy oneself; have a good time

dividendo *dee·vee·den·doh* m dividend

dividere* *dee·vee·de·re* vt divide; share; split

divieto di ... *dee·vye·toh dee* no ..., ... prohibited

divisa *dee·vee·za* f uniform; la divisa estera *dee·vee·za e·ste·ra* foreign currency

divo(a) *dee·vo(a)* m/f star (celebrity)

divorziato(a) *dee·vor·tsyah·to(a)* adj divorced

divorzio *dee·vor·tsyoh* m divorce

dizionario *dee·tsyoh·nah·ree·oh* m dictionary

doccia *dohch·cha* f shower (bath); fare* una doccia *fah·ray oo·na dohch·cha* to have a shower

documentazione *do·koo·men·ta·tsyoh· nay f* record (*register*)

documenti *do·koo·mayn·tee mpl* papers (*passport etc*)

documento *do·koo·mayn·toh m* document

dodicesimo(a) *do·dee·che·zee·mo(a) adj* twelfth

dodici *doh·dee·chee num* twelve

dogana *do·gah·na f* customs; **esente da dogana** *e·zen·te da do·gah·na* duty-free

doganiere *do·ga·nye·ray m* customs officer

dolce *dohl·che m* dessert; cake □ *adj* sweet; mild

dolciumi *dol·choo·mee mpl* sweets

dolere* *do·lay·re vi* hurt

dollaro *dol·la·roh m* dollar

dolore *do·loh·re m* ache; grief; pain

doloroso(a) *do·lo·roh·so(a) adj* sore; painful

domanda *do·man·da f* question; demand; application (*for job*); **fare* una domanda** *fah·ray oo·na do·man· da* to ask a question; **fare* domanda per** *fah·ray do·man·da payr* to apply for

domandare *do·man·dah·ray vt* ask; ask for; demand

domandarsi *do·man·dar·see vr* wonder

domani *do·mah·nee adv* tomorrow

domattina *do·mat·tee·na adv* tomorrow morning

domenica *do·me·nee·ka f* Sunday

domestico(a) *do·me·stee·ko(a) adj* domestic □ *m/f* **il/la domestico(a)** *do· me·stee·ko(a)* servant

dominare *do·me·nah·ray vt* dominate; control

donare *do·nah·ray vt* donate

dondolare *don·do·lah·ray vi* swing

donna *don·na f* woman; **la donna delle pulizie** *don·na del·lay poo·lee·tsee·ay* cleaner (*of house etc*); **la donna poliziotto** *don·na po·lee·tsyot·toh* policewoman; **la donna d'affari** *don·na daf· fah·ree* businesswoman

dono *doh·noh m* gift; donation

dopo *doh·po prep after* □ *adv* afterward(s); **4 anni dopo** *4 an·nee doh·po* 4 years later; **dopo che fummo partiti** *doh·po ke foom·mo par·tee·tee* after we had left

dopobarba *doh·po·bar·ba m* — aftershave (lotion)

dopodomani *doh·po·do·mah·nee adv* the day after tomorrow

doppio(a) *dop·pyo(a) adj* double

dorato(a) *do·rah·toh(a) adj* golden

dormire *dor·mee·re vi* sleep

dormitorio *dor·mee·to·ryoh m* dormitory (*room*)

dosaggio *do·zaj·joh m* dosage

dose *do·ze f* dose; **la dose eccessiva** *do· ze ech·ches·see·va* overdose

dotato(a) *do·tah·toh(a) adj* gifted

dottore *dot·toh·re m* doctor

dove *doh·ve adv* where; **di dove è?** *dee doh·ve e* where are you from?

dovere* *do·vay·re m* duty (*obligation*)

dovere* *do·vay·re vt* owe □ *vi* to have to; **mi deve L.50000** *mee de·ve L50000* he owes me L.50000; **deve farlo** *de·ve far·lo* she has to do it; **devo andare** *de·voh an·dah·ray* I must go; **dovrebbe vincere** *do·vreb·be veen·che·re* he ought to win; **dovremmo comprarlo** *do·vrem·mo kom·prar·lo* we should buy it

dovunque *do·voon·kwe adv* wherever; everywhere; **la porterò dovunque voglia** *la por·te·ro do·voon·kwe vol·yah* I'll take you anywhere you like

dozzina *dodz·dzee·na f* dozen; **4 dozzine di uova** *4 dodz·dzee·ne dee wo· va* 4 dozen eggs

dramma *dram·ma m* drama; play (*theatrical*)

drammatico(a) *dram·ma·tee·ko(a) adj* dramatic

drastico(a) *dra·stee·ko(a) adj* drastic

droga *dro·ga f* drug (*narcotic*)

drogheria *dro·ge·ree·a f* grocery shop

droghiere *dro·gye·ray m* grocer

dubbio *doob·byoh m* doubt; **senza dubbio** *sen·tsa doob·byoh* no doubt; **senza alcun dubbio** *sen·tsa al·koon doob·byoh* without (a) doubt

dubitare *doo·bee·tah·ray vi* doubt; **ne dubito** *ne doo·bee·to* I doubt it

duca *doo·ka m* duke

due *doo·e num* two; **tutte e due le ragazze** *toot·te e doo·e le ra·gats·tse* both girls; **tutti(e) e due** *toot·tee(·te) e doo·e* both

dumping *dum·peeng m* dumping (*of goods*)

duna *doo·na f* dune

dunque *doon·kwe conj* so

durante *doo·ran·te prep* during; **durante tutto l'anno** *doo·ran·te toot·to lan·noh* (all) through the year

durare *doo·rah·ray vi* last; **quanto dura il programma?** *kwan·to doo·ra eel pro·gram·ma* how long is the programme?

duro(a) *doo·ro(a) adj* hard; tough (*meat etc*)

E

e *ay conj* and

ebreo *e·bre·oh m* Jew □ *adj* **ebreo(a)** *e· bre·o(a)* Jewish

ecc *ech·che·te·ra abbrev* etc

eccedente *ech·che·den·te adj* excess

eccedenza *ech·che·den·tsa f* excess; surplus; **in eccedenza** *een ech·che· den·tsa* overweight (*baggage*)

eccellente *ech·chel·len·te adj* excellent

eccentrico(a) *ech·chen·tree·ko(a) adj* eccentric

eccesso *ech·ches·soh m* excess; **l'eccesso di velocità** *ech·ches·soh dee ve· lo·chee·ta* speeding (*in car*)

eccezionale *ech·che·tsyoh·nah·le adj* exceptional

eccezione *ech·che·tsyoh·ne f* exception

eccitazione *ech·chee·ta·tsyoh·ne f* excitement

ecco *ek·ko adv* here is/are; **ecco mia sorella** *ek·ko mee·a so·rel·la* here's my sister; **eccola che viene** *ek·ko·la ke vye·ne* here she comes; **eccolo** *ek· ko·lo* here/there he/it is; **eccola** *ek· ko·la* here/there she/it is; **eccoli(e)** *ek·ko·lee(·le)* here/there they are

eco *e·koh m/f* echo

economia *e·ko·no·mee·a f* economy; economics

economico(a) *e·ko·no·mee·ko(a) adj* economic; economical (*use, method*)

economista *e·ko·no·mee·sta m/f* economist

eczema *ek·ze·ma m* eczema

edicola *e·dee·ko·la f* newsstand

edificio *e·dee·fee·choh m* building

editore *e·dee·toh·re m* publisher

editrice *e·dee·tree·che f* publisher

edizione *e·dee·tsyoh·ne f* edition

educato(a) *e·doo·kah·toh(a)* adj well-mannered

effetto *ef·fet·toh* m effect; avere* effetto *a·vay·re ef·fet·toh* to take effect; gli effetti personali *ef·fet·tee per·so·nah·lee* belongings

efficace *ef·fee·kah·che* adj effective (*remedy etc*)

efficiente *ef·fee·chen·te* adj efficient

Egitto *e·jeet·toh* m Egypt

egiziano(a) *e·jee·tsyah·no(a)* adj Egyptian

egli *ayl·yee* pron he; egli stesso *ayl·yee stays·so* (he) himself

egoistico(a) *e·go·ee·stee·ko(a)* adj selfish

egregio(a) *e·gre·jo(a)* adj distinguished; Egregio Signor Smith *e·gre·joh seen·yohr smith* Dear Mr. Smith

elaborazione dei dati *e·la·bo·ra·tsyoh·nay de·ee dah·tee* f data processing

elastico *e·la·stee·koh* m elastic; elastic band

elefante *e·le·fan·te* m elephant

elegante *e·le·gan·te* adj stylish; elegant; smart

eleggere* *e·lej·je·re* vt elect

elementare *e·le·men·tah·ray* adj junior (*class, pupil*)

elemento *e·le·mayn·toh* m unit (*of machinery, furniture*); element

elencare *e·len·kah·ray* vt list

elenco *e·len·koh* m list; l'elenco di indirizzi *e·len·koh dee een·dee·ree·tsee* mailing list; l'elenco telefonico *e·len·koh te·le·fo·nee·ko* telephone directory

elettricista *e·let·tree·chee·sta* m electrician

elettricità *e·let·tree·chee·ta* f electricity

elettrico(a) *e·let·tree·ko(a)* adj electric(al)

elettronica *e·let·tro·nee·ka* f electronics

elettronico(a) *e·let·tro·nee·ko(a)* adj electronic

elevare *e·le·vah·ray* vt raise

elevatore *e·le·va·toh·ray* m ramp (*in garage*)

elezione *e·le·tsyoh·ne* f election; le elezioni politiche *e·le·tsyoh·nee po·lee·tee·kay* general election

elicottero *e·lee·kot·te·roh* m helicopter

eliminato(a) *e·lee·mee·nah·to(a)* adj out (*team, player*)

ella *ayl·la* pron she; you

embargo *em·bar·goh* m embargo

emergenza *e·mer·jen·tsa* f emergency

emicrania *e·mee·krah·nee·a* f migraine

emigrare *e·mee·grah·ray* vi emigrate

emissione *e·mees·syoh·ne* f issue

emorragia nasale *e·mor·ra·jee·a na·sah·lay* f nosebleed

emorroidi *e·mor·roy·dee* fpl h(a)emorrhoids

emozionante *e·mo·tsyoh·nan·te* adj exciting

emozione *e·mo·tsyoh·ne* f emotion

enciclopedia *en·chee·klo·pe·dee·a* f encyclop(a)edia

energia *e·ner·jee·a* f energy

energico(a) *e·ner·jee·ko(a)* adj energetic

enfasi *en·fa·zee* f stress; emphasis; l'enfasi su qualcosa *len·fa·zee soo kwal·ko·sa* emphasis on something

enorme *e·nor·me* adj enormous

entrambi(e) *en·tram·bee(·be)* adj, pron both

entrare *en·trah·ray* vi come in; enter; go in; entrare in *en·trah·ray een* to enter (*room*)

entrata *en·trah·ta* f entrance; admission

entrate *en·trah·te* fpl takings; income

entusiasmo *en·too·zee·a·zmoh* m enthusiasm

entusiasta *en·too·zee·a·sta* adj enthusiastic

epidemia *e·pee·de·mee·a* f epidemic

epilessia *e·pee·les·see·a* f epilepsy

epoca *e·po·ka* f age (*era*)

eppure *ep·poo·re* conj and yet

equatore *e·kwa·toh·re* m equator

equilibrio *e·kwee·lee·bree·oh* m balance; perdere* l'equilibrio *per·de·re le·kwee·lee·bree·oh* to lose one's balance; l'equilibrio politico *e·kwee·lee·bree·oh po·lee·tee·ko* balance of power

equipaggiamento *e·kwee·paj·ja·mayn·toh* m equipment; gear

equipaggio *e·kwee·paj·joh* m crew (*of ship, plane*)

equitazione *e·kwee·ta·tsyoh·ne* f horse-riding; fare* dell'equitazione *fah·ray del·le·kwee·ta·tsyoh·ne* to go horse-riding

equivalente *e·kwee·va·len·te* adj equivalent

erba *er·ba* f grass

erbaccia *er·bach·cha* f weed

erbe *er·be* fpl herbs

ereditare *e·re·dee·tah·ray* vt inherit

ermetico(a) *er·me·tee·ko(a)* adj airtight

ernia *er·nee·a* f hernia; l'ernia al disco *er·nee·a al dee·sko* slipped disc

erotico(a) *e·ro·tee·ko(a)* adj erotic

erpete zoster *er·pe·te zo·ster* m shingles (*illness*)

errare *er·rah·ray* vi wander

errore *er·roh·re* m error; l'errore di stampa *er·roh·re dee stam·pa* misprint

eruzione *e·roo·tsyoh·nay* f rash

esagerare *e·za·je·rah·ray* vt exaggerate

esagerazione *e·za·je·ra·tsyoh·ne* f exaggeration

esame *e·zah·me* m examination; exam; l'esame di guida *e·zah·me dee gwee·da* test (*driving test*)

esaminare *e·za·mee·nah·ray* vt examine; test (*sight, hearing*)

esatto(a) *e·zat·toh(a)* adj exact (*time etc*); accurate

esaurimento *e·zow·ree·mayn·toh* m exhaustion; l'esaurimento nervoso *e·zow·ree·mayn·toh ner·voh·so* nervous breakdown

esaurito(a) *e·zow·ree·to(a)* adj exhausted; out of print; sold out

esausto(a) *e·zow·sto(a)* adj exhausted

esca *ay·ska* f bait

esclamare *e·skla·mah·ray* vi exclaim

escludere* *e·skloo·de·re* vt exclude

esclusiva *e·skloo·zee·va* f exclusive rights

esclusivo(a) *e·skloo·zee·vo(a)* adj exclusive (*club, shop*)

escrescenza *es·kre·shen·tsa* f growth (*anatomical*)

escursione *e·skoor·syoh·ne* f excursion; l'escursione a piedi *e·skoor·syoh·ne a pye·dee* hike

eseguire *e·ze·gwee·ray* vt carry out (*order*)

esempio *e·zem·pyoh* m example; per esempio *payr e·zem·pyoh* for example

esente *e·zen·te* adj exempt; esente da tasse *e·zen·te da tas·se* tax-free

esercitarsi *e·zer·chee·tar·see* vr practise; esercitarsi nel correre *e·zer·chee·*

tar *see nel kohr·re·re* to practise running; esercitarsi al pianoforte *e·zer·chee·tar·see al pya·no·for·te* to practise the piano

esercito *e·zer·chee·toh m* army

esercizio *e·zer·chee·tsyoh m* exercise

esigenza *e·zee·jen·tsa f* requirement

esigere* *e·zee·je·re* vt demand

esistenza *e·zee·sten·tsa f* existence

esistere* *e·zee·ste·re* vi exist

esitare *e·zee·tah·ray* vi hesitate; **esitare a fare qualcosa** *e·zee·tah·ray a fah·ray kwal·ko·sa* to hesitate to do something

esito *e·zee·toh m* result; **avere* buon esito** *a·vay·re bwon e·zee·toh* to be successful

esotico(a) *e·zo·tee·ko(a) adj* exotic

esperanto *e·spe·ran·toh m* Esperanto

esperienza *e·spe·ree·en·tsa f* experience

esperimento *e·spe·ree·mayn·toh m* experiment

esperto *e·sper·toh m* expert □ *adj* **esperto(a)** *e·sper·to(a)* expert; experienced

esplodere* *e·splo·de·re* vi explode

esplorare *e·splo·rah·ray* vt explore

esplosione *e·splo·zyoh·ne f* explosion

esporre* *es·pohr·re* vt expose; explain; display

esportare *e·spor·tah·ray* vt export

esportatore *e·spor·ta·toh·re m* exporter

esportazione *e·spor·ta·tsyoh·ne f* export

esposto(a) *e·spo·sto(a) adj* exposed; **esposto(a) a nord** *e·spo·sto(a) a nord* facing north

espressione *e·spres·syoh·ne f* expression

espresso *e·spres·soh m* express letter; express train; espresso (coffee)

esprimere* *e·spree·me·re* vt express

essenziale *es·sen·tsyah·le adj* essential (*necessary*)

essere* *es·se·re* vi be; **sono** *soh·no* I am; **è** *e* you are; he/she/it is; **siamo** *syah·mo* we are; **siete** *sye·te* you are; **sono** *soh·no* they are; **è medico e medee·koh** he is a doctor; **sono 5 chilometri** *soh·no 5 kee·lo·me·tree* it's 5 kilometres; **sono le 4** *soh·no le 4* it's 4 o'clock; **sono qui dalle 4** *soh·no kwee dal·le 4* I've been here since 4 o'clock; **sono io** *soh·no ee·o* it's me; **che c'è?** *ke che* what's the matter?; **non c'è di che!** *nohn che dee ke* don't mention it

essi(e) *es·see(·se) pron* they; them

essa(o) *es·so(a) pron* it

est *est m* east; **ad est** *ad est* east

estate *e·stah·te f* summer

esterno *e·ster·noh m* outside □ *adj* **esterno(a)** *e·ster·no(a)* exterior; external

estero(a) *e·ste·ro(a) adj* foreign; **all'estero** *al·le·ste·roh* abroad

estintore *e·steen·toh·re m* fire extinguisher

estremamente *e·stre·ma·mayn·te adv* extremely

estremo(a) *e·stre·mo(a) adj* extreme

Estremo Oriente *e·stre·mo o·ryen·te m* the Far East

età *e·tah f* age (*of person*)

etichetta *e·tee·kayt·ta f* etiquette; tag; label

etichettare *e·tee·ket·tah·ray* vt label

etico(a) *e·tee·ko(a) adj* ethical

etnico(a) *et·nee·ko(a) adj* ethnic

Europa *e·oo·ro·pa f* Europe; **l'Europa**

continentale *e·oo·ro·pa kon·tee·nen·tah·lay* the Continent

europeo(a) *e·oo·ro·pe·o(a) adj* European

evaporare *e·va·po·rah·ray* vi evaporate

eventuale *e·ven·too·ah·le adj* possible

evitare *e·vee·tah·ray* vt avoid

evoluzione *e·vo·loo·tsyoh·ne f* evolution

ex- *eks pref* ex-

eye-liner *eye·line·er m* eyeliner

F

fa *fa adv* ago

fabbrica *fab·bree·ka f* factory; works

fabbricante *fab·bree·kan·tay m* manufacturer

fabbricare *fab·bree·kah·ray* vt manufacture; **fabbricare in serie** *fab·bree·kah·ray een ser·ye* to mass-produce

fabbricazione *fab·bree·ka·tsyo·nay f* manufacturing

facchino *fak·kee·noh m* porter (*for luggage*)

faccia *fach·cha f* face

facile *fah·chee·le adj* easy

facilmente *fah·cheel·mayn·te adv* easily

facoltà *fa·kol·ta f* — faculty

faggio *faj·joh m* beech

fagiano *fa·jah·noh m* pheasant

fagioli *fa·jo·lee mpl* beans

fagiolini *fa·jo·lee·nee mpl* runner beans

falciare *fal·chah·ray* vt mow

falciatrice *fal·cha·tree·che f* lawn mower

falegname *fa·len·yah·may m* carpenter; joiner

falena *fa·le·na f* moth

fallimento *fal·lee·mayn·toh m* failure; bankruptcy

fallire *fal·lee·re* vi fail; go bankrupt

fallito(a) *fal·lee·to(a) m/f* failure (*person*) □ *adj* bankrupt

fallo *fal·loh m* error; **senza fallo** *sen·tsa fal·loh* without fail

falò *fa·lo m* — bonfire

falsificazione *fal·see·fee·ka·tsyoh·ne f* forgery

falso(a) *fal·so(a) adj* fake; false

fama *fah·ma f* fame; reputation

fame *fah·me f* hunger; **avere* fame** *a·vay·re fah·me* to be hungry

famiglia *fa·meel·ya f* family; household

famoso(a) *fa·moh·so(a) adj* famous

fanale *fa·nah·lay m* light (*on car*); **i fanali di posizione** *fa·nah·lee dee po·zee·tsyoh·ne* parking lights; sidelights; **i fanali dei freni** *fa·nah·lee dey fre·nee* stoplights

fango *fan·goh m* mud

fangoso(a) *fan·goh·soh(a) adj* muddy

fantascienza *fan·ta·shen·tsa f* science fiction

fantasma *fan·taz·ma m* ghost

fante *fan·te m* jack (*cards*)

fantino *fan·tee·noh m* jockey

farcito(a) *far·chee·to(a) adj* stuffed (*chicken*)

fare* *fah·ray* vt do; make; **dovremo fare a meno del latte** *do·vray·moh fah·ray a may·noh del lat·tay* we'll have to go without milk; **gli spinaci fanno bene alla salute** *lyee spee·nah·chee fan·no be·nay al·la sa·loo·tay* spinach is good for you; **le farà bene** *lay fa·ra be·nay* it'll do you good; **ce la fa?** *chay la fa* can you manage?; **faccia pure!** *fach·cha poo·ray* go ahead!; **fa caldo** *fa kal·do* it is warm/hot; **fare* 10 km a piedi** *fah·ray 10* *km a pye·dee* to walk 10 km; **far* fare qualcosa a qualcuno** *far fah·ray kwal·koh·sa a kwal·koo·noh* to make someone do something; **far* fare qualcosa** *far fah·ray kwal·ko·sa* to have something done; **fare* da** *fah·ray da* to act as; **non fa niente** *nohn fa nyen·tay* it doesn't matter

farfalla *far·fal·la f* butterfly

farina *fa·ree·na f* flour; **la farina di granturco** *fa·ree·na dee gran·toor·koh* cornflour

farmacia *far·ma·chee·a f* drugstore; pharmacy; chemist's shop

farmacista *far·ma·chee·sta m/f* pharmacist; druggist

faro *fah·roh m* headlamp, headlight; lighthouse

farsa *far·sa f* farce

fascino *fa·shee·noh m* charm

fascio *fa·shoh m* bundle

fastidio *fa·stee·dyoh m* bother; **dare* fastidio a** *dah·ray fa·stee·dyoh a* to annoy

fata *fah·ta f* fairy

fatale *fa·tah·le adj* fatal

fatelo da voi *fah·te·lo da voy m* do-it-yourself

fattezze *fa·tayts·tse fpl* features

fattibilità *fat·tee·bee·lee·ta f* feasibility

fatto *fat·toh m* fact

fattore *fat·toh·re m* factor

fattoria *fat·to·ree·a f* farm

fattorino d'albergo *fat·to·ree·noh dal·ber·goh m* bellboy

fattura *fat·too·ra f* invoice

favore *fa·voh·re m* favour; **per favore** *payr fa·voh·re* please; **fare* un favore a qualcuno** *fah·ray oon fa·voh·re a kwal·koo·no* to do someone a favour; **non sono a favore di quell'idea** *nohn soh·no a fa·voh·re dee kwayl·lee·de·a* I'm not in favour of that idea

favorito(a) *fa·vo·ree·to(a) adj* favourite

fazzolettino di carta *fats·tso·let·tee·noh dee kar·ta m* tissue (*handkerchief*)

fazzoletto *fats·tso·layt·toh m* handkerchief; scarf (*head*)

febbraio *feb·bra·yoh m* February

febbre *feb·bre f* fever; **avere* la febbre** *a·vay·re la feb·bre* to have a temperature; **la febbre da fieno** *feb·bre da fye·noh* hay fever

fede *fay·de f* faith; belief; wedding ring

fedeltà *fe·del·ta f* faithfulness; **ad alta fedeltà** *ad al·ta fe·del·ta* hi-fi

federa *fe·de·ra f* pillowcase, pillowslip

federale *fe·de·rah·le adj* federal

feed-back *feed·bak m* feedback

fegato *fay·ga·toh m* liver

felce *fayl·che f* fern; bracken

felice *fe·lee·chay adj* glad

felicissimo(a) *fe·lee·chees·see·mo(a) adj* delighted

felicità *fe·lee·chee·ta f* happiness

felicitazioni *fe·lee·chee·ta·tsyoh·nee fpl* congratulations; **felicitazioni!** *fe·lee·chee·ta·tsyoh·nee* congratulations!

feltro *fayl·troh m* felt (*cloth*)

femmina *faym·mee·na f* female (*animal*)

femminile *fem·mee·nee·le adj* feminine; **il sesso femminile** *eel ses·soh fem·mee·nee·le* the female sex

feriale *fe·ree·ah·le adj* working, week

ferie *fay·ree·ay fpl* holiday(s)

ferire *fe·ree·re vt* injure; wound

ferita *fe·ree·ta f* wound; injury; cut

ferito(a) *fe·ree·to(a) adj* injured

fermare *fer·mah·ray vt* stop

fermarsi *fer·mar·see vr* stop; stall (*car engine*)

fermata *fer·mah·ta f* stop; **la fermata autobus** *fer·mah·ta ow·to·boos* bus stop; **la fermata facoltativa** *fer·mah·ta fa·kol·ta·tee·va* request stop

fermo(a) *fayr·mo(a) adj* firm; steady; stationary; off (*machine*)

feroce *fe·roh·che adj* fierce

ferramenta *fer·ra·mayn·ta fpl* hardware

ferro *fer·roh m* iron (*material, golf club*); **il ferro da calza** *fer·roh da kal·tsa* knitting needle; **il ferro da stiro** *fer·roh da stee·roh* iron (*for clothes*)

ferrovia *fer·ro·vee·a f* railroad, railway; **per ferrovia** *payr fer·ro·vee·a* by rail

fertile *fer·tee·le adj* fertile (*land*)

fessura *fes·soo·ra f* slot; crack (*split*)

festa *fe·sta f* party (*celebration*); holiday (*day*); **fare* festa** *fah·ray fe·sta* to celebrate

festeggiare *fes·tej·jah·ray vt* celebrate

festival *fe·stee·val m —* festival

fetta *fayt·ta f* slice

fiacco(a) *fyak·ko(a) adj* slack (*business*)

fiamma *fyam·ma f* flame; **la casa è in fiamme** *la kah·sa e een fyam·me* the house is on fire

fiammifero *fyam·mee·fe·roh m* match

fiammingo(a) *fyam·meen·go(a) adj* Flemish □ *m* **il fiammingo** *fyam·meen·goh* Flemish

fiato *fyah·toh m* breath

fibbia *feeb·bya f* clasp; buckle

fibra *fee·bra f* fibre

fico *fee·koh m* fig

fidanzamento *fee·dan·tsa·mayn·toh m* engagement (*betrothal*)

fidanzato(a) *fee·dan·tsah·to(a) m/f* fiancé(e) □ *adj* engaged (*betrothed*)

fidarsi di *fee·dar·see dee vr* trust

fidato(a) *fee·dah·to(a) adj* reliable (*person*)

fiducia *fee·doo·cha f* confidence (*trust*)

fiducioso(a) *fee·doo·choh·so(a) adj* confident

fieno *fye·noh m* hay

fiera *fye·ra f* fair

fiero(a) *fye·ro(a) adj* proud

figlia *feel·ya f* daughter

figliastra *feel·ya·stra f* stepdaughter

figliastro *feel·ya·stroh m* stepson

figlio *feel·yoh m* son

figura *fee·goo·ra f* figure (*of human*); court-card

fila *fee·la f* row; queue

filare *fee·lah·ray vt* spin (*wool*)

filetto *fee·layt·toh m* fillet (*of meat, fish*)

filiale *fee·lyah·le f* branch; subsidiary (*company*)

film *feelm m —* film; movie; **il film d'orrore** *feelm dor·roh·re* horror film, horror movie

filo *fee·loh m* thread; lead (*electrical*); edge (*of blade*); **il filo elettrico** *fee·loh e·let·tree·ko* wire (*electrical*); **il filo di cotone** *fee·loh dee ko·toh·nay* cotton (*thread*)

filo di ferro *fee·loh dee fer·roh m* wire; **il filo di ferro spinato** *fee·loh dee fer·roh spee·nah·to* barbed wire

filtrare *feel·trah·ray vt* filter

filtro *feel·troh m* filter; **con filtro** *kohn feel·troh* tipped (*cigarettes*); **il filtro dell'olio** *feel·troh del·lol·yoh* oil filter; **il filtro dell'aria** *feel·troh del·lah·rya* air filter

finale *fee·nah·le* f finals (*sports*) □ adj
final

finalmente *fee·nal·mayn·te* adv finally

finanza *fee·nan·tsa* f finance

finanziare *fee·nan·tsyah·ray* vt finance;
back

finanziario(a) *fee·nan·tsy·ah·ryo(a)* adj
financial

finanziatore *fee·nan·tsya·toh·re* m
backer

finché *feen·kay* conj as long as; until;
finché egli verrà *feen·kay el·yee ver·
ra* until he comes

fine *fee·ne* f end □ m aim (*purpose*)
□ adj fine; alla fine *al·la fee·ne* at
last; eventually; il/la fine settimana
fee·ne set·tee·mah·na weekend

finestra *fee·ne·stra* f window (*in house*)

finestrino *fee·ne·stree·noh* m window
(*in car, train*)

fingere *feen·je·re* vt pretend; fingere*
di fare qualcosa *feen·je·re dee fah·ray
kwal·ko·sa* to pretend to do something

finimenti *fee·nee·mayn·tee* mpl harness

finire *fee·nee·re* vi end □ vt finish; la
partita è finita *la par·tee·ta e fee·nee·
ta* the match is over; è finito tutto il
nostro denaro *e fee·nee·toh toot·toh
eel no·stroh de·nah·roh* all our
money's gone

finlandese *feen·lan·day·se* adj Finnish

Finlandia *feen·lan·dya* f Finland

fino *fee·no* adv even; fino a *fee·no a*
until; as far as; fino a 6 *fee·no a 6* up
to 6

fino(a) *fee·no(a)* adj fine

finora *fee·noh·ra* adv up till now

fiocco *fyok·koh* m flake (*of snow*); i
fiocchi di granturco *fyok·kee dee
gran·toor·koh* cornflakes

fioraio(a) *fyoh·ra·yo(a)* m/f florist

fiore *fyoh·re* m flower

fiori *fyoh·ree* mpl clubs (*in cards*)

fiorire *fyo·ree·re* vi bloom

firma *feer·ma* f signature

firmare *feer·mah·ray* vt sign (*document*)

fiscale *fee·skah·le* adj fiscal

fischiare *fee·skyah·ray* vt/i whistle

fischietto *fee·skyayt·toh* m whistle (*object*)

fischio *fee·skyoh* m whistle (*sound*)

fisco *fee·skoh* m Inland Revenue

fisica *fee·zee·ka* f physics

fisico(a) *fee·zee·ko(a)* adj physical

fissare *fees·sah·ray* vt stare at; fix; arrange (*meeting*)

fitta *feet·ta* f stitch (*pain*)

fitto(a) *feet·to(a)* adj dense (*fog etc*)

fiume *fyoo·me* m river

flash *flash* m — flashbulb; flash (*on
camera*)

flatulenza *fla·too·len·tsa* f wind (*in
stomach*)

flauto *flow·toh* m flute

flessibile *fles·see·bee·le* adj flexible

flipper *fleep·per* m pinball

flirtare *fleer·tah·ray* vi flirt

flotta *flot·ta* f fleet

fluido *floo·ee·doh* m fluid

fluoro *floo·o·roh* m fluorine

flusso *floos·soh* m flow; il flusso di capitale *floos·soh dee ka·pee·tah·lay*
cash flow

focolare *fo·ko·lah·re* m hearth; fireplace

fodera *fo·de·ra* f lining

foglia *fol·ya* f leaf

foglio *fol·yoh* m sheet (*of paper*)

fogna *fohn·ya* f drain

folla *fol·la* f crowd

folle *fol·lay* adj mad; in folle *een fol·lay*
in neutral

fondamentalmente *fon·da·mayn·tal·
mayn·te* adv basically

fondare *fon·dah·ray* vt establish (*business*)

fondere* *fohn·de·ray* vt melt

fondersi* *fohn·der·see* vr melt; merge

fondi *fohn·dee* mpl funds

fondo *fohn·doh* m back (*of hall,
room*); bottom; i fondi di caffè *fohn·
dee dee kaf·fe* grounds (*of coffee*)

fontana *fon·tah·na* f fountain

fontanella *fon·ta·nel·la* f fountain (*for
drinking*)

fonte *fohn·te* f source

footing *foo·teeng* m jogging; fare* del
footing *fah·ray del foo·teeng* to go
jogging

forare *fo·rah·ray* vt pierce; punch
(*ticket etc*)

foratura *fo·ra·too·ra* f blow-out; puncture

forbici *for·bee·chee* fpl scissors

forchetta *for·kayt·ta* f fork

forcina *for·chee·na* f bobby pin; hairpin

foresta *fo·re·sta* f forest

forfora *for·fo·ra* f dandruff

forma *fohr·ma* f form; shape; in forma
een fohr·ma in good form; fit
(*strong, healthy*)

formaggio *for·maj·joh* m cheese

formale *for·mah·le* adj formal

formazione *for·ma·tsyoh·ne* f training
(*for job*)

formica *for·mee·ka* f ant

fornaio *for·na·yoh* m baker

fornire *for·nee·re* vt provide; supply;
fornire del capitale *for·nee·re del ka·
pee·tah·le* to put up capital; fornire
qualcosa a qualcuno *for·nee·re kwal·
ko·sa a kwal·koo·no* to supply someone with something

forno *fohr·noh* m oven; il forno a microonde *fohr·noh a mee·kro·ohn·day*
microwave oven

forse *fohr·se* adv perhaps; possibly

forte *for·te* adj strong; loud; essere*
forte nel golf *es·se·ray for·te nel golf*
to be good at golf

fortemente *for·te·mayn·te* adv loudly

fortuna *for·too·na* f fortune (*wealth*);
luck; buona fortuna! *bwo·na for·too·
na* good luck!

foruncolo *fo·roon·ko·loh* m boil (*on
skin*)

forza *for·tsa* f strength; force

foschia *fo·skee·a* f mist

fossa *fos·sa* f pit

fossato *fos·sah·toh* m ditch

foto *fo·toh* f — photo

fotocopia *fo·to·ko·pya* f photocopy

fotocopiare *fo·to·ko·pyah·ray* vt
photocopy

fotografare *fo·to·gra·fah·ray* vt photograph

fotografia *fo·to·gra·fee·a* f photography; photograph

fotografo *fo·to·gra·foh* m photographer

fotometro *fo·to·me·troh* m light meter

fra *fra* prep between; among(st); tornerà fra 2 giorni *tor·ne·ra fra 2 johr·
nee* he'll be back in 2 days

fracasso *fra·kas·soh* m crash (*noise*)

fragile *frah·jee·le* adj fragile

fragola *frah·go·la* f strawberry

fragore *fra·goh·ray* m noise (*loud*)

fragrante *fra·gran·te* adj sweet (*smell*)

frana *frah·na* f landslide

francese *fran·chay·ze* adj French □ m il francese *fran·chay·ze* French

Francia *fran·cha* f France

francobollo *fran·ko·bohl·loh* m stamp (*postage*)

frangia *fran·ja* f fringe

frantumare *fran·too·mah·ray* vt smash

frase *fra·ze* f phrase; sentence

frassino *fras·see·noh* m ash (*tree*)

fratellastro *fra·tel·la·stroh* m stepbrother

fratello *fra·tel·loh* m brother

frattura *frat·too·ra* f fracture (*of arm etc*)

freccia *fraych·cha* f arrow; indicator (*of car*)

freddo(a) *frayd·doh(a)* adj cold; ho freddo *o frayd·doh* I'm cold

fregare *fre·gah·ray* vt rub

frenare *fre·nah·ray* vt/i brake

freno *fray·noh* m brake; il freno a mano *fray·noh a mah·noh* handbrake; il freno a pedale *fray·noh a pe·dah·le* footbrake; i freni a disco *fray·nee a dee·sko* disc brakes

frequente *fre·kwen·te* adj frequent

fresco(a) *fray·skoh(a)* adj cool; fresh; wet (*paint*)

fretta *frayt·ta* f rush; haste; avere* fretta *a·vay·re frayt·ta* to be in a hurry

friggere* *freej·je·re* vt fry

frigo *free·goh* m fridge

frigorifero *free·go·ree·fe·roh* m refrigerator

frittata *freet·tah·ta* f omelette

frittella *freet·tel·la* f fritter; pancake

fritto(a) *freet·to(a)* adj fried

frizione *free·tsyoh·nay* f clutch (*of car*)

frontale *fron·tah·le* adj head-on

fronte *frohn·te* f forehead; di fronte *dee frohn·te* facing; la casa di fronte *la kah·sa dee frohn·te* the house opposite; di fronte a *dee frohn·te* a opposite; facing

frontiera *fron·tye·ra* f frontier; border (*of country*)

frullato *frool·lah·toh* m milkshake

frullatore *frool·la·toh·ray* m mixer

frullino *frool·lee·noh* m whisk

frumento *froo·mayn·toh* m wheat

frusta *froo·sta* f whip

frustino *froo·stee·noh* m crop (*whip*)

frutta *froot·ta* f fruit

frutteto *froot·tay·toh* m orchard

fruttivendolo *froot·tee·vayn·do·loh* m greengrocer

frutto *froot·toh* m fruit; i frutti di mare *froot·tee dee mah·re* seafood

fu *foo* adj late

fucile *foo·chee·le* m rifle; gun

fuga *foo·ga* f leak (*gas*)

fuggire *fooj·jee·re* vi run away; get away (*escape*)

fulvo(a) *fool·vo(a)* adj fawn

fumare *foo·mah·ray* vt/i smoke; lei fuma? *ley foo·ma* do you smoke?

fumatore *foo·ma·toh·re* m smoker (*person*)

fumo *foo·moh* m smoke

funerale *foo·ne·rah·le* m funeral

fungere* *foon·je·re* da vi act as

fungo *foon·goh* m mushroom

funzionare *foon·tsyoh·nah·ray* vi work (*clock, mechanism*); questa macchina funziona a nafta *kway·sta mak·kee·na foon·tsyoh·na a naf·ta* this car runs on diesel; fare* funzionare *fah·ray foon·tsyoh·nah·ray* to operate (*machine*)

funzionario(a) statale *foon·tsyo·nah·ree·oh(a) sta·tah·lay* m/f civil servant

fuoco *fwo·koh* m fire; focus; appiccare il fuoco a *ap·pee·kah·ray eel fwo·koh a* to set fire to; i fuochi d'artificio *fwo·kee dar·tee·fee·choh* fireworks; mettere* a fuoco *mayt·te·re a fwo·koh* to focus

fuori *fwo·ree* adv outside; out (*not at home*); fuori la mia portata *fwo·ree la mee·a por·tah·ta* beyond my reach; fuori di *fwo·ree dee* out of (*outside*); fuori della strada principale *fwo·ree del·la strah·da preen·chee·pah·le* off the main road; fuori della casa *fwo·ree del·la kah·sa* outside the house; fuori di casa *fwo·ree dee kah·sa* away from home

fuoribordo *fwo·ree·bohr·doh* m — speedboat □ adj outboard

furgone *foor·goh·nay* m van

furioso(a) *foo·ree·oh·soh(a)* adj mad (*angry*)

furto *foor·toh* m robbery

fusibile *foo·zee·bee·le* m fuse

fusione *foo·zyoh·ne* f amalgamation; merger

fuso orario *foo·soh o·rah·ryoh* m time zone

futuro *foo·too·roh* m future; pensare al futuro *pen·sah·ray al foo·too·roh* to think ahead

G

gabbia *gab·bya* f cage; crate

gabinetto *ga·bee·nayt·toh* m toilet (*lavatory*); il gabinetto medico *ga·bee·nayt·toh me·dee·ko* surgery; doctor's office

gaio(a) *ga·yoh(a)* adj merry

gala *gah·la* f gala

galleggiante *gal·lej·jan·te* m float (*for swimming, fishing*)

galleggiare *gal·lej·jah·ray* vi float

galleria *gal·le·ree·a* f tunnel; gallery; circle (*in theatre*); arcade; la prima galleria *pree·ma gal·le·ree·a* dress circle; la galleria d'arte *gal·le·ree·a dar·te* art gallery

Galles *gal·les* m Wales

gallese *gal·lay·se* adj Welsh □ m il gallese *gal·lay·se* Welsh

gallina *gal·lee·na* f hen; la gallina faraona *gal·lee·na fa·ra·oh·na* guinea fowl

gallo *gal·loh* m cock(erel)

gallone *gal·loh·nay* m gallon

galoppare *ga·lop·pah·ray* vi gallop

galoppo *ga·lop·poh* m gallop; andare* al galoppo *an·dah·ray al ga·lop·poh* to go at a gallop

gamba *gam·ba* f leg (*of person*)

gamberetto *gam·be·rayt·toh* m shrimp; prawn

gambero *gam·be·roh* m crawfish, crayfish

gamma *gam·ma* f range; la gamma di prezzi *gam·ma dee prets·tsee* price range

gancio *gan·choh* m hook; il gancio ad occhiello *gan·choh ad ok·kyel·loh* hook and eye; il gancio per rimorchio *gan·choh payr ree·mor·kyoh* tow-bar (*on car*)

gangster *gang·ster* m gangster

garage *ga·raj* m garage (*service station*)

garantire *ga·ran·tee·ray* vt guarantee

garanzia *ga·ran·tsee·a* f guarantee; warrant(y)

garofano *ga·ro·fa·noh* m carnation

garza *gar·dza f* gauze; lint

gas *gas m* gas; il gas di scappamento *gas dee skap·pa·mayn·toh* exhaust (fumes)

gassoso(a) *gas·soh·so(a) adj* fizzy

gatto *gat·toh m* cat

gelare *je·lah·ray vt/i* freeze

gelateria *je·lah·te·ree·a f* ice cream shop

gelatina *je·la·tee·na f* jello, jelly

gelato *je·lah·toh m* ice cream; il gelato alla vaniglia *je·lah·toh al·la va·neel·ya* vanilla ice cream

gelo *je·loh m* frost

geloso(a) *je·loh·so(a) adj* jealous

gemelli *je·mel·lee mpl* twins

gemello *je·mel·loh m* cuff link

gemere *je·me·ray vi* groan; moan

gemito *je·mee·toh m* groan; moan

gemma *jem·ma f* gem

generale *je·ne·rah·lay adj* general ☐ *m* il generale *je·ne·rah·lay* general (soldier); in generale *een je·ne·rah·lay* in general

generalmente *je·ne·rahl·mayn·tay adv* generally

generatore *je·ne·ra·toh·ray m* generator (electrical)

generazione *je·ne·ra·tsee·oh·nay f* generation

genere *je·ne·re m* kind (type); gender

generi alimentari *je·ne·re a·lee·men·tah·ree mpl* foodstuffs

genero *je·ne·roh m* son-in-law

generoso(a) *je·ne·roh·soh(a) adj* generous

gengiva *jen·jee·va f* gum (of teeth)

genitori *je·nee·toh·ree mpl* parents

gennaio *jen·na·yoh m* January

gente *jen·te f* people

gentile *jen·tee·le adj* kind; polite

geografia *jay·oh·gra·fee·a f* geography

geologia *jay·oh·loh·jee·a f* geology

geometra *je·o·me·tra m* surveyor (of land)

geometria *jay·oh·me·tree·a f* geometry

geranio *je·rah·nee·oh m* geranium

gergo *jer·goh m* slang

Germania *jer·mah·nya f* Germany

Germania Occidentale *jer·mah·nya och·chee·den·tah·le f* West Germany

Germania Orientale *jer·mah·nya o·ree·en·tah·le f* East Germany

gesso *jes·soh m* chalk; plaster (for limb); plaster of Paris

gesto *jes·toh m* gesture

gettare *jet·tah·ray vt* throw; gettare via *jet·tah·ray vee·a* to throw away

gettone *jet·toh·ne m* token (for machine); chip (in gambling); counter

ghetto *get·toh m* ghetto

ghiacciaia *gyach·cha·ya f* icebox

ghiaccio *gyach·choh m* ice

ghiacciolo *gyach·cho·loh m* ice lolly

ghiaia *gee·a·ya f* gravel

ghianda *gyan·da f* acorn

ghiandola *gee·an·doh·la f* gland

ghisa *gee·za f* cast iron

già *ja adv* already

giacca *jak·ka f* jacket; la giacca a vento *jak·ka a ven·toh* anorak; la giacca di salvataggio *jak·ka dee sal·va·taj·joh* life jacket; la giacca sportiva *jak·ka spor·tee·va* sports coat, sports jacket

giacere *ja·chay·re vi* lie

giallo *jal·loh m* yellow; thriller (book) ☐ *adj* giallo(a) *jal·lo(a)* yellow

Giappone *jap·poh·ne m* Japan

giapponese *jap·po·nay·se adj* Japanese

☐ *m* il giapponese *jap·po·nay·se* Japanese

giardinetta *jar·dee·nayt·ta f* estate (car)

giardiniere *jar·dee·nye·ray m* gardener

giardino *jar·dee·noh m* garden; il giardino botanico *jar·dee·noh bo·ta·nee·ko* botanical gardens

giarrettiere *jar·ret·tye·re fpl* suspenders (for stockings)

gigante *jee·gan·tay m* giant

giglio *jeel·yoh m* lily

gin *jeen m* gin (drink)

Ginevra *jee·ne·vra f* Geneva

ginnastica *jeen·nas·tee·ka f* gymnastics

ginocchio *jee·nok·kyoh m —chi, —chia* knee; mettersi* in ginocchio *mayt·ter·see een jee·nok·kyoh* to kneel down

giocare *jo·kah·ray vt* play ☐ *vi* play; gamble; giocare al calcio *jo·kah·ray al kal·choh* to play football; giocare a carte *jo·kah·ray a kahr·tay* to play cards; giocare con *jo·kah·ray kohn* to play with

giocatore *jo·ka·toh·ray m* player (in sport); il giocatore di golf *jo·ka·toh·ray dee golf* golfer; il giocatore d'azzardo *jo·ka·toh·ray dadz·dzar·doh* gambler

giocatrice *jo·ka·tree·che f* player (in sport)

giocattolo *jo·kat·to·loh m* toy

gioco *jo·ko m* game; essere* in gioco *es·se·re een jo·ko* to be at stake; il gioco della dama *jo·ko del·la dah·ma* draughts; checkers; il gioco del ventuno *jo·ko del ven·too·no* blackjack; il gioco d'azzardo *jo·ko dadz·dzar·doh* gambling; il gioco di carte *jo·ko dee kahr·tay* card game

giogo *jo·goh m* ridge

gioia *jo·ya f* joy

gioielli *jo·yel·lee mpl* jewellery

gioielliere *jo·yel·lye·re m* jeweller

gioiello *jo·yel·loh m* jewel; i gioielli di fantasia *jo·yel·lee dee fan·ta·zee·a* costume jewellery

giornalaio *johr·na·la·yoh m* newsagent

giornale *johr·nah·lay m* newspaper; il giornale della sera *johr·nah·lay del·la say·ra* evening paper; il giornale a fumetti *johr·nah·lay a foo·mayt·tee* comic

giornalista *johr·na·lee·sta m/f* journalist

giornata *johr·nah·ta f* day (length of time); tutta la giornata *toot·ta la johr·nah·ta* all day long

giorno *johr·noh m* day; di giorno in giorno *dee johr·noh een johr·noh* day by day; il giorno festivo *johr·noh fe·stee·vo* holiday; il giorno feriale *johr·noh fe·ree·ah·le* weekday; il giorno di mercato *johr·noh dee mayr·kah·toh* market-day

giostra *jo·stra f* merry-go-round

giovane *joh·va·ne adj* young

giovedì *jo·ve·dee m —* Thursday

gioventù *jo·ven·too f* youth (period)

giradischi *jee·ra·dee·skee m —* record-player

girare *jee·rah·ray vi* turn (person, car); spin (rotate) ☐ *vt* turn; girare qualcosa *jee·rah·ray kwal·ko·sa* to turn something round

giro *jee·roh m* tour; turn; rev (in engine); lap (of track); round (of golf); fare* un giro in macchina *fah·ray* *oon jee·roh een mak·kee·na* to go for a drive; **il giro d'affari** *jee·roh daf·fah·ree* turnover (*money*)

gita *jee·ta f* trip; excursion; run; outing; **fare* una gita** *fah·ray oo·na jee·ta* to go on an excursion

gittata *jeet·tah·ta f* range (*of missile*)

giú *joo* adv down; downstairs

giubileo *joo·bee·le·oh m* jubilee

giudicare *joo·dee·kah·ray vt* judge

giudice *joo·dee·che m* judge

giugno *joon·yoh m* June

giuncata *joon·kah·ta f* junket

giuntura *joon·too·ra f* joint (*of body etc*)

giurare *joo·rah·ray vt/i* swear

giustizia *joo·stee·tsya f* justice

giustiziare *joo·stee·tsyah·ray vt* execute (*kill*)

giusto(a) *joo·sto(a) adj* right (*morally good*); fair (*just*); **sì, giusto** *see joo·sto* yes, that's right

glassa *glas·sa f* icing (*on cake*)

gli *lyee art* the □ *pron* to him/it; **glielo dia** *lye·lo dee·a* give it to him/her

glicerina *glee·che·ree·na f* glycerin(e)

globale *glo·bah·le adj* inclusive (*costs*); global

globo *glo·boh m* globe

goccia *gohch·cha f* drop (*of liquid*); drip

gocciolare *goch·cho·lah·ray vi* drip

goffo(a) *gof·foh(a) adj* clumsy (*person*)

gola *goh·la f* throat

golf *golf m* — golf; cardigan

goloso(a) *go·loh·soh(a) adj* greedy

gomito *goh·mee·toh m* elbow

gomitolo *go·mee·to·loh m* ball (*of string, wool*)

gomma *gohm·ma f* rubber; tyre; **la gomma per cancellare** *gohm·ma payr kan·chel·lah·ray* rubber (*eraser*); **la gomma da masticare** *gohm·ma da ma·stee·kah·ray* chewing gum

gommone *gom·moh·ne m* dinghy (*inflatable*)

gonfiabile *gon·fyah·bee·le adj* inflatable

gonfiare *gon·fee·ah·re vt* inflate

gonfiarsi *gon·fyar·see vr* swell (up) (*limb etc*)

gonfio(a) *gohn·fyo(a) adj* swollen

gonfiore *gon·fyoh·re m* lump (*on skin*)

gonna *gon·na f* skirt

governante *go·ver·nan·te f* housekeeper

governare *go·vayr·nah·ray vt* govern (*country*); rule; steer (*boat*)

governatore *go·vayr·na·toh·ray m* governor (*of colony*)

governo *go·vayr·noh m* government

gradevole *gra·day·vo·le adj* pleasant

gradino *gra·dee·noh m* step; stair; **il gradino della porta** *gra·dee·noh del·la por·ta* doorstep

gradire *gra·dee·re vt* accept; like; **gradirei un gelato** *gra·dee·re·ee oon je·lah·toh* I'd like an ice cream

grado *grah·doh m* grade; standard; degree; **a 2 gradi sotto zero** *a 2 grah·dee soht·toh dze·roh* at minus 2 degrees; **un whisky di 40 gradi** *oon wee·skee dee 40 grah·dee* a 70° proof whisky

graduale *gra·dwa·lay adj* gradual

gradualmente *gra·doo·al·men·tay adv* gradually

graffetta *graf·fayt·ta f* paper clip; staple

graffiare *graf·fyah·ray vt* scratch

grafico *gra·fee·koh m* graph; chart (*diagram, table*)

grammatica *gram·ma·tee·ka f* grammar

grammo *gram·moh m* gram(me)

granaio *gra·na·yoh m* barn

Gran Bretagna *gran bre·tan·ya f* Great Britain

granchio *gran·kyoh m* crab

grande *gran·day adj* great; large; big; **di gran lunga** *dee gran loon·ga* by far

grandinare *gran·dee·nah·ray vi* hail

grandine *gran·dee·ne f* hail

graniglia *gra·neel·ya f* grit

granita *gra·nee·ta f* water ice

grano *grah·noh m* grain

granturco *gran·toor·koh m* maize

grasso *gras·soh m* fat; grease □ *adj* **grasso(a)** *gras·so(a)* fat (*person*); greasy

grassoccio(a) *gras·soch·cho(a) adj* plump

grata *grah·ta f* grating

grato(a) *grah·toh(a) adj* grateful

grattacielo *grat·ta·che·loh m* skyscraper; high-rise (*block*)

grattugia *grat·too·jah f* grater

grattugiare *grat·too·jah·ray vt* grate (*food*)

gratuito(a) *gra·too·ee·to(a) adj* free (*costing nothing*)

gravida *gra·vee·da adj* pregnant

grazie *gra·tsye excl* thank you; **grazie a** *gra·tsye a* thanks to

grazioso(a) *gra·tsyoh·so(a) adj* charming; sweet (*cute, pretty*); graceful

Grecia *gray·cha f* Greece

greco(a) *gre·koh(a) adj* Greek □ *m* **il greco** *gre·koh* Greek

gregge *grayj·je m* flock

grembiule *grem·byoo·le m* apron

grembo *grem·boh m* lap (*of person*)

grezzo(a) *graydz·dzo(a) adj* raw (*unprocessed*); crude (*oil etc*)

gridare *gree·dah·ray vt/i* shout

grido *gree·doh m* cry; shout

grigio(a) *gree·joh(a) adj* grey

griglia *greel·ya f* grill (*gridiron*)

grondaia *gron·da·ya f* gutter (*on building*)

groppa *grop·pa f* back (*of animal*)

grossa *gros·sa f* gross

grossista *gros·see·sta m/f* wholesaler

grosso(a) *gros·so(a) adj* big; thick

grossolano(a) *gros·so·lah·no(a) adj* rude

grottesco(a) *grot·tay·skoh(a) adj* grotesque

gru *groo f* — crane

gruccia *grooch·cha f* crutch; coat hanger

grugnire *groon·yee·ray vi* grunt

grumo *groo·moh m* lump (*in sauce*)

gruppo *groop·poh m* group; **il gruppo sanguigno** *groop·poh san·gween·yo* blood group; **il gruppo di pressione** *groop·poh dee pres·syoh·ne* pressure group

guadagnare *gwa·dan·yah·ray vt* earn; gain (*obtain*)

guadagno *gwa·dan·yoh m* earnings; return (*profit*)

guado *gwah·doh m* ford

guai *gwy mpl* trouble (*problems*); **essere* nei guai** *es·se·re nay gwy* to be in trouble

guancia *gwan·cha f* cheek

guanciale *gwan·chah·le m* pillow

guanto *gwan·toh m* glove

guardacoste *gwahr·da·ko·stay m* — coastguard

guardare *gwar·dah·ray vt* watch; look at □ *vi* look

guardaroba *gwar·da·ro·ba m* — wardrobe (*furniture*); cloakroom
guardia *gwar·dya f* guard (*soldiers*); la guardia del corpo *gwar·dya del kor·poh* bodyguard (*person*)
guardiano *gwar·dee·ah·noh m* warder; caretaker
guardrail *gard·rail m* — crash barrier
guarire *gwa·ree·re vt* cure; heal □ *vi* recover; heal
guarnizione *gwar·nee·tsee·oh·nay f* gasket
guastarsi *gwa·star·see vr* go bad (*food*); fail (*brakes*); break down (*car etc*)
guasto(a) *gwa·sto(a) adj* out of order (*machine*) □ *m* il guasto *gwa·stoh* failure (*mechanical*); il guasto al motore *gwa·stoh al mo·toh·re* engine trouble
guerra *gwer·ra f* war; la guerra civile *gwer·ra chee·vee·lay* civil war; la guerra mondiale *gwer·ra mon·dee·ah·le* world war
guida *gwee·da f* directory; courier; guide; guidebook; la guida a sinistra *gwee·da a see·nee·stra* left-hand drive
guidare *gwee·dah·ray vt* drive (*car etc*); steer (*car*); sa guidare? *sa gwee·dah·ray* do you drive?
guidatore *gwee·da·toh·re m* driver (*of car*); il guidatore principiante *gwee·da·toh·re preen·chee·pyan·te* learner(-driver)
guinzaglio *gween·tsal·yoh m* lead (*dog's*); leash
gulasch *goo·lash m* goulash
guscio *goo·shoh m* shell (*of egg*)
gustare *goo·stah·ray vt* taste; enjoy (*concert, outing*)
gusto *goo·stoh m* taste; di cattivo/buon gusto *dee kat·tee·vo/bwon goo·stoh* in poor/good taste

H

hamburger *ham·bur·gur m* — hamburger
handicap *han·dee·kap m* — handicap (*sports*)
hardware *hard·wer m* hardware (*computing*)
hockey *ho·kee m* hockey; l'hockey su ghiaccio *ho·kee soo gyach·choh* ice hockey
hostess *ho·stess f* — air hostess; stewardess
hot-dog *hot·dog m* — hot dog
hovercraft *ho·ver·kraft m* hovercraft

I

i *ee art* the
idea *ee·de·a f* idea; cambiare idea *kam·byah·ray ee·de·a* to change one's mind
ideale *ee·de·ah·le adj* ideal
identico(a) *ee·den·tee·ko(a) adj* identical
identificare *ee·den·tee·fee·kah·ray vt* identify
identità *ee·den·tee·ta f* — identity
idiota *ee·dyo·ta m/f* idiot
idraulico *ee·drow·lee·koh m* plumber
ieri *ye·ree adv* yesterday
igienico(a) *ee·je·nee·ko(a) adj* hygienic
ignorante *een·yo·ran·te adj* ignorant
ignorare *een·yo·rah·ray vt* ignore (*person*)
il *eel art* the
illegale *eel·le·gah·le adj* illegal

illegittimo(a) *eel·lay·jeet·tee·moh(a) adj* illegitimate
illimitato(a) *eel·lee·mee·tah·to(a) adj* unlimited
illuminato(a) *eel·loo·mee·nah·to(a) adj* floodlit
illuminazione *eel·loo·mee·na·tsyoh·ne f* lighting; illumination; l'illuminazione al neon *eel·loo·mee·na·tsyoh·ne al ne·on* strip-lighting
illustrazione *eel·loo·stra·tsyoh·ne f* illustration
imballaggio *eem·bal·laj·joh m* packing
imballare *eem·bal·lah·ray vt* pack (*goods*); wrap up (*parcel*); rev
imbarazzato(a) *eem·ba·rats·tsah·to(a) adj* embarrassed
imbarcarsi *eem·bar·kar·see vr* embark
imbattibile *eem·bat·tee·bee·lay adj* unbeatable (*offer*)
imbottito(a) *eem·bot·tee·to(a) adj* stuffed (*cushion etc*)
imbrogliare *eem·brol·yah·ray vt* mix up; cheat
imbucare *eem·boo·kah·ray vt* post
imitare *ee·mee·tah·ray vt* imitate
immagazzinare *eem·ma·gadz·dzee·nah·ray vt* store
immaginare *eem·ma·jee·nah·ray vt* imagine
immaginazione *eem·ma·jee·na·tsee·oh·nay f* imagination
immangiabile *eem·man·jah·bee·le adj* inedible
immediato(a) *eem·me·dyah·to(a) adj* immediate; instant
immergere* *eem·mer·je·re vt* dip (*into liquid*)
immigrante *eem·mee·gran·te m/f* immigrant
immobile *eem·mo·bee·le adj* still (*motionless*)
immondizie *eem·mon·dee·tsye fpl* rubbish; garbage
immutato(a) *eem·moo·tah·toh(a) adj* unchanged
imparare *eem·pa·rah·ray vt* learn
imparziale *eem·par·tsee·ah·lay adj* unbiased
impasto *eem·pa·stoh m* mixture
impaziente *eem·pa·tsyen·te adj* impatient; essere* impaziente di fare qualcosa *es·se·re eem·pa·tsyen·te dee fah·ray kwal·ko·sa* to be eager to do something
impedire *eem·pe·dee·re vt* hinder; impedire a qualcuno di fare qualcosa *eem·pe·dee·re a kwal·koo·no dee fah·ray kwal·ko·sa* to stop someone doing something
impegnarsi a *eem·pen·yar·see a vr* undertake
impegnativo(a) *eem·pen·ya·tee·vo(a) adj* demanding (*work*)
impegno *eem·payn·yoh m* undertaking; commitment
imperatore *eem·pe·ra·toh·re m* emperor
impermeabile *eem·payr·me·ah·bee·le adj* waterproof □ *m* l'impermeabile *eem·payr·me·ah·bee·le* raincoat
impero *eem·pe·roh m* empire
impersonale *eem·per·so·nah·le adj* impersonal
impiccare *eem·peek·kah·ray vt* hang (*criminal*)
impiegare *eem·pye·gah·ray vt* employ; spend
impiegato(a) *eem·pye·gah·to(a) m/f* employee; clerk (*in office*); l'impie-

gato(a) d'ufficio *eem·pye·gah·to(a) doof·fee·choh* office worker

impiego *eem·pye·goh* m employment; job; occupation

imponibile *eem·po·nee·bee·le* adj taxable

imporre* *eem·pohr·re* vt impose

importante *eem·por·tan·te* adj important

importanza *eem·por·tan·tsa* f importance

importare *eem·por·tah·ray* vt import □ vi matter; **non importa** *nohn eem·por·tah* it doesn't matter; **non me ne importa** *nohn me ne eem·por·tah* I don't care

importatore *eem·por·ta·toh·re* m importer

importazione *eem·por·ta·tsyoh·ne* f import

importo *eem·por·toh* m amount (total)

impossibile *eem·pos·see·bee·le* adj impossible

imposta *eem·poh·sta* f tax (on income); shutter (on window); **l'imposta sul reddito** *eem·poh·sta sool red·dee·toh* income tax; **le imposte sul consumo** *eem·poh·ste sool kon·soo·moh* excise duties; **l'imposta sul valore aggiunto** *eem·poh·sta sool va·loh·ray aj·joon·toh* value-added tax

imprenditore *eem·pren·dee·toh·ray* m contractor

impresa *eem·pray·sa* f venture; enterprise; undertaking; **l'impresa privata** *eem·pray·sa pree·vah·ta* private enterprise

impressionabile *eem·pres·syoh·nah·bee·le* adj emotional (person)

impressionante *eem·pres·syoh·nan·te* adj impressive

impressionare *eem·pres·syoh·nah·ray* vt impress (win approval)

impressione *eem·pres·syoh·ne* f impression

improbabile *eem·pro·bah·bee·lay* adj unlikely

improvvisamente *eem·prov·vee·za·mayn·te* adv suddenly

improvviso(a) *eem·prov·vee·zo(a)* adj sudden

in *een* prep in; to; into; **in Francia** *een fran·cha* in/to France; **lo metta nella scatola** *lo mayt·ta nel·la skah·to·la* put it in the box; **in maggio** *een maj·joh* in May; **in treno/macchina** *een tre·noh/mak·kee·na* by train/car; **in marmo** *een mahr·moh* made of marble; **siamo in quattro** *syah·mo een kwat·troh* there are four of us

inadatto(a) *een·a·dat·to(a)* adj unsuitable

incantevole *een·kan·tay·vo·lay* adj charming

incaricarsi di *een·ka·ree·kar·see dee* vr take charge of

incendio *een·chen·dyoh* m fire; blaze

inceneritore *een·che·ne·ree·toh·re* m incinerator

incentivo *een·chen·tee·voh* m incentive

incerto(a) *een·cher·to(a)* adj uncertain; doubtful

inchinarsi *een·kee·nar·see* vr bow

inchino *een·kee·noh* m bow

inchiodare *een·kyo·dah·ray* vt nail

inchiostro *een·kyo·stroh* m ink

inciampare *een·cham·pah·ray* vi trip (stumble)

incidente *een·chee·den·te* m accident

incinta *een·cheen·ta* adj pregnant

inclinare *een·klee·nah·ray* vt tip (tilt)

includere* *een·kloo·de·re* vt include

incluso(a) *een·kloo·zo(a)* adj included; enclosed; **dal 6 al 12 incluso** *dal 6 al 12 een·kloo·zo* from 6th to 12th inclusive

incollare *een·kol·lah·ray* vt glue

incolpare *een·kol·pah·ray* vt blame

incompleto(a) *een·kom·play·toh(a)* adj incomplete

incondizionato(a) *een·kon·dee·tsyoh·nah·toh(a)* adj unconditional

incontrare *een·kon·trah·ray* vt meet (encounter)

incoronazione *een·ko·ro·na·tsyoh·nay* f coronation

incredibile *een·kre·dee·bee·le* adj incredible

incrinarsi *een·kree·nar·see* vr crack

incrocio *een·kroh·choh* m crossroads; **l'incrocio a T** *een·kroh·choh a tee* T-junction (on road)

incubo *een·koo·boh* m nightmare

indecente *een·day·chen·tay* adj indecent

India *een·dee·a* f India

indiano(a) *een·dee·ah·no(a)* adj Indian □ m/f **l'indiano(a)** *een·dee·ah·no(a)* Indian

indicare *een·dee·kah·ray* vt show; point to

indicatore *een·dee·ka·toh·ray* m gauge (device)

indicazione *een·dee·ka·tsyoh·ne* f indication

indicazioni *een·dee·ka·tsyoh·nee* fpl directions

indice *een·dee·che* m index; contents (table in book)

indietro *een·dye·tro* adv backwards; back; **il mio orologio va indietro** *eel mee·o o·ro·lo·joh va een·dye·tro* my watch is slow; **fare* marcia indietro** *fah·ray mar·cha een·dye·tro* to reverse; **guardare indietro** *gwar·dah·ray een·dye·tro* to look behind

indigestione *een·dee·je·styoh·ne* f indigestion

indigesto(a) *een·dee·je·sto(a)* adj indigestible

indipendente *een·dee·pen·den·te* adj independent

indipendenza *een·dee·pen·den·tsa* f independence

indiretto(a) *een·dee·ret·to(a)* adj indirect

indirizzare *een·dee·reets·tsah·ray* vt send; address (letter)

indirizzo *een·dee·reets·tsoh* m address

indivia *een·dee·vya* f endive

individuale *een·dee·vee·doo·ah·le* adj individual

indomani *een·do·mah·nee* m the next day

indossare *een·dos·sah·ray* vt put on (clothes)

indossatrice *een·dos·sa·tree·chay* f model (mannequin)

indovinare *een·do·vee·nah·ray* vt guess

indumento *een·doo·mayn·toh* m garment; **gli indumenti da sport** *een·doo·mayn·tee da sport* sportswear

industria *een·doo·stree·a* f industry; **l'industria leggera** *een·doo·stree·a lej·je·ra* light industry

industriale *een·doo·stree·ah·le* adj industrial

industria terziaria *een·doo·stree·a ter·tsyah·rya* f service industry

inefficiente *een·ef·fee·chen·te* adj inefficient

inevitabile *een·e·vee·tah·bee·lay* adj unavoidable; inevitable

infangato(a) *een·fan·gah·toh(a)* adj muddy (clothes)

infatti *een·fat·tee* adv in fact; actually

infelice *een·fe·lee·chay* adj miserable; unhappy

inferiore *een·fayr·mye·ra* f adj inferior; lower

infermiera *een·fayr·mye·ra* f nurse

infettivo(a) *een·fet·tee·vo(a)* adj infectious

infezione *een·fe·tsyoh·ne* f infection

infiammabile *een·fyam·mah·bee·le* adj inflammable

infiammazione *een·fyam·ma·tsyoh·ne* f inflammation

inflazione *een·fla·tsyoh·ne* f inflation (economic)

influenza *een·floo·en·tsa* f influence; flu

influire su *een·floo·ee·re soo* vi influence

informale *een·for·mah·le* adj informal

informare *een·for·mah·ray* vt inform; informarsi (di) *een·for·mar·see (dee)* to inquire (about)

informazioni *een·for·ma·tsyoh·nee* fpl information

infrangibile *een·fran·jee·bee·lay* adj unbreakable

ingannare *een·gan·nah·ray* vt trick; deceive

inganno *een·gan·noh* m trick (malicious)

ingegnere *een·jen·ye·re* m engineer

ingegnoso(a) *een·jen·yoh·soh(a)* adj clever (plan)

Inghilterra *een·geel·ter·ra* f England

inghiottire *een·gyot·tee·re* vt swallow

inginocchiarsi *een·jee·nok·kyar·see* vr kneel

ingiusto(a) *een·joo·sto(a)* adj unfair

inglese *een·glay·se* adj English □ m l'inglese *een·glay·se* English

ingorgo *een·gohr·goh* m hold-up (traffic); bottleneck; l'ingorgo stradale *een·gohr·goh stra·dah·le* traffic jam

ingrandire *een·gran·dee·re* vt enlarge

ingredienti *een·gre·dyen·tee* mpl ingredients

ingresso *een·gres·soh* m entry (way in); entrance; il prezzo d'ingresso *prets·tsoh deen·gres·soh* admission fee

all'ingrosso *al·leen·gros·soh* adv wholesale

iniezione *een·ye·tsyoh·ne* f injection

iniziali *ee·nee·tsyah·lee* fpl initials

inizio *ee·nee·tsyoh* m start (beginning)

innamorarsi *een·na·mo·rar·see* vr fall in love

innamorato(a) *een·na·mo·rah·to(a)* adj in love

innestato(a) *een·ne·stah·toh(a)* adj in gear

inno *een·noh* m hymn; l'inno nazionale *een·noh na·tsyoh·nah·lay* national anthem

innocente *een·no·chen·te* adj innocent

innocuo(a) *een·no·kwo(a)* adj harmless

inoltre *een·ohl·tre* adv besides (moreover)

inondazione *een·on·da·tsyoh·ne* f flood

inossidabile *een·os·see·dah·bee·lay* adj rustproof; stainless (steel)

input *een·poot* m input (computing)

inquilino(a) *een·kwee·lee·no(a)* m/f tenant; lodger

inquinamento *een·kwee·na·mayn·toh* m pollution

insalata *een·sa·lah·ta* f salad; l'insalata

verde *een·sa·lah·ta vayr·day* green salad

insegna *een·sayn·ya* f sign (notice)

insegnante *een·sen·yan·te* m/f teacher

insegnare *een·sen·yah·ray* vt teach; insegnare qualcosa a qualcuno *een·sen·yah·ray kwal·ko·sa a kwal·koo·no* to teach someone something

inseguire *een·say·gwee·ray* vt chase

inserzione *een·sayr·tsyoh·ne* f advertisement

insettifugo *een·set·tee·foo·goh* m insect repellent

insetto *een·set·toh* m insect

insieme *een·sye·me* m ensemble (clothes) □ adv together

insignificante *een·seen·yee·fee·kan·te* adj insignificant; trivial

insistere* *een·see·ste·re* vi insist; insistere* su qualcosa *een·see·ste·re soo kwal·ko·sa* to insist on something

insolazione *een·so·la·tsyoh·ne* f sunstroke

insolente *een·so·len·te* adj insolent

insolito(a) *een·so·lee·to(a)* adj unusual

insopportabile *een·sop·por·tah·bee·lay* adj unbearable

installarsi *een·stal·lar·see* vr settle in

insuccesso *een·sooch·ches·soh* m failure

insulina *een·soo·lee·na* f insulin

insultare *een·sool·tah·ray* vt insult

insulto *een·sool·toh* m insult

intanto *een·tan·toh* adv meanwhile

intelligente *een·tel·lee·jen·te* adj bright; smart; intelligent; clever

intelligenza *een·tel·lee·jen·tsa* f intelligence

intenzionale *een·ten·tsyoh·nah·le* adj deliberate

intenzione *een·ten·tsyoh·ne* f intention; avere* l'intenzione di fare qualcosa *a·vay·re leen·ten·tsyoh·ne dee fah·ray kwal·ko·sa* to intend to do something

interessante *een·te·res·san·te* adj interesting

interessare *een·te·res·sah·ray* vt interest; concern (be important to)

interessarsi a *een·te·res·sar·see* a vr be interested in

interessato(a) *een·te·res·sah·to(a)* adj interested

interesse *een·te·res·se* m interest; l'interesse composto *een·te·res·se kom·poh·sto* compound interest

interiore *een·te·ryoh·re* adj interior

internazionale *een·ter·na·tsyoh·nah·le* adj international

interno(a) *een·ter·no(a)* adj internal □ m l'interno *een·ter·noh* inside

intero(a) *een·te·ro(a)* adj whole

interpretare *een·ter·pre·tah·ray* vt interpret

interpretazione *een·ter·pre·ta·tsyoh·ne* f interpretation; performance (of actor)

interprete *een·ter·pre·te* m/f interpreter; fare* da interprete *fah·ray da een·ter·pre·te* to interpret

interrompere* *een·ter·rohm·pe·re* vt interrupt

interruttore *een·ter·root·toh·re* m switch; l'interruttore dei anabbaglianti *een·ter·root·toh·re del·yee an·ab·bal·yan·tee* dip-switch

interurbano(a) *een·tayr·oor·bah·no(a)* adj long-distance (phone call)

intervallo *een·ter·val·loh* m half-time; interval (in performance)

intervento *een·tayr·ven·toh* m intervention; operation (*medical*)

intervista *een·ter·vee·sta* f interview

intesa *een·tay·sa* f understanding (*agreement*)

intirizzito(a) *een·tee·reedz·dzee·toh(a)* adj numb (*with cold*)

intonaco *een·to·na·koh* m plaster (*for wall*)

intonarsi *een·to·nahr·see* vr match; questo s'intona con il Suo vestito *kwes·toh seen·toh·na kon eel soo·oh ves·tee·toh* this goes with your dress

intorno *een·tohr·no* adv round; intorno a *een·tohr·no a* round; guardarsi intorno *gwar·dar·see een·tohr·no* to look around

intossicazione alimentare *een·tos·see·ka·tsyoh·ne a·lee·men·tah·re* f food poisoning

intraprendere* *een·tra·pren·de·ray* vt undertake

intrattenere* *een·trat·te·nay·re* vt entertain (*amuse*)

introdurre* *een·tro·door·re* vt introduce

introduzione *een·tro·doo·tsyoh·ne* f introduction (*in book*)

introiti *een·tro·ee·tee* mpl income; revenue

intromettersi* *een·tro·mayt·ter·see* vr interfere

inutile *ee·noo·tee·lay* adj unnecessary; useless

invalido(a) *een·va·lee·do(a)* adj disabled; invalid (*contract*) □ m l'invalido *een·va·lee·doh* m invalid

invano *een·vah·no* adv in vain

invece *een·vay·che* adv instead; invece di *een·vay·che dee* instead of

inventare *een·ven·tah·ray* vt invent

inventario *een·ven·tah·ryoh* m inventory; stocktaking

invenzione *een·ven·tsyoh·ne* f invention

inverno *een·ver·noh* m winter

inversione *een·vayr·syoh·nay* f U-turn (*in car*)

investigatore *een·ve·stee·ga·toh·ray* m detective

investimento *een·ve·stee·mayn·toh* m investment

investire *een·ve·stee·ray* vt run down; invest

invidia *een·vee·dya* f envy

invidiare *een·vee·dyah·ray* vt envy

invidioso(a) *een·vee·dyoh·so(a)* adj envious

invisibile *een·vee·zee·bee·lay* adj invisible

invitare *een·vee·tah·ray* vt invite

invito *een·vee·toh* m invitation

io *ee·o* pron I; sono io *so·noh ee·o* it's me; io stesso(a) *ee·o stays·so(a)* (I) myself

iodio *ee·oh·dee·oh* m iodine

iogurt *yo·goort* m yogurt

ipermercato *ee·per·mer·kah·toh* m hypermarket

ipoteca *ee·po·te·ka* f mortgage

ipotecare *ee·po·te·kah·ray* vt mortgage

ippodromo *eep·po·dro·moh* m racecourse

Irak *ee·rak* m Iraq

Iran *ee·ran* m Iran

Irlanda *eer·lan·da* f Ireland

irlandese *eer·lan·day·se* adj Irish

irragionevole *eer·ra·joh·nay·vo·le* adj unreasonable

irruzione *eer·roo·tsyoh·nay* f raid (*by police*)

iscritto *ee·skreet·to* m member; per iscritto *payr ee·skreet·to* in writing

Islanda *ee·slan·da* f Iceland

isola *ee·zo·la* f island; l'isola pedonale *ee·zo·la pe·do·nah·le* pedestrian precinct

isolato(a) *ee·zo·lah·to(a)* adj isolated

ispettore *ee·spet·toh·re* m surveyor (*of building*); l'ispettore di polizia *ee·spet·toh·re dee po·lee·tsee·a* inspector (*police*)

ispezionare *ee·spe·tsyoh·nah·ray* vt examine; inspect

ispezione *ee·spe·tsyoh·ne* f examination (*inspection*)

Israele *ee·zra·e·le* m Israel

istante *ee·stan·te* m instant

isterico(a) *ee·ste·ree·ko(a)* adj hysterical

istituto *ee·stee·too·toh* m institute

istruire *ee·stroo·ee·re* vt educate

istruttore *ee·stroot·toh·re* m instructor

istruttrice *ee·stroot·tree·chay* f instructress

istruzione *ee·stroo·tsyoh·ne* f education

istruzioni *ee·stroo·tsyoh·nee* fpl instructions; directions

Italia *ee·ta·lya* f Italy

italiano(a) *ee·ta·lyah·no(a)* adj Italian □ m l'italiano *ee·ta·lyah·noh* Italian

itinerario *ee·tee·ne·rah·ryoh* m route; l'itinerario turistico *ee·tee·ne·rah·ryoh too·ree·stee·ko* scenic route

Iugoslavia *yoo·go·slah·vya* f Yugoslavia

iugoslavo(a) *yoo·go·slah·vo(a)* adj Yugoslav(ian)

I.V.A. *ee·va* f V.A.T.

J

jazz *jazz* m jazz

jeep *jeep* f jeep

jersey *jer·zee* m jersey (*fabric*)

jolly *jol·lee* m joker (*cards*)

judo *joo·doh* m judo

juke-box *jook·boks* m — jukebox

jumbo *joom·boh* m jumbo jet

K

karatè *ka·rah·te* m karate

kebab *ke·bab* m kebab

Kenia *ken·ya* m Kenya

ketchup *ke·chup* m ketchup

kirsch *keersh* m kirsch

L

la *la* art the □ pron her; it; you; la donna *la don·na* the woman

là *la* adv there; per di là *payr dee la* that way

labbro *lab·broh* m —a lip

laboratorio *la·bo·ra·to·ryoh* m laboratory; il laboratorio linguistico *la·bo·ra·to·ryoh leen·gwee·stee·ko* language laboratory

lacca *lak·ka* f lacquer; hair spray

laccio *lach·choh* m lace (*of shoe*)

lacerare *la·che·rah·ray* vt split (*tear*)

lacrima *la·kree·ma* f tear; in lacrime *een la·kree·me* in tears

ladro *la·droh* m thief

laggiù *laj·joo* adv down there; over there

lagnarsi *lan·yahr·see* vr complain

lago *lah·goh* m lake

lama *lah·ma* f blade (*of knife*)

lamentarsi (di) *la·men·tahr·see (dee)* vr complain (*about*)

lametta *la·met·ta f* razor blade

lamiera *la·mye·ra f* sheet metal; **la lamiera di ferro ondulata** *la·mye·ra dee fer·roh on·doo·lah·ta* corrugated iron

lampada *lam·pa·da f* lamp; **la lampada a raggi ultravioletti** *lam·pa·da a raj·jee ool·tra·vyo·layt·tee* sunlamp; **la lampada a stelo** *lam·pa·da a ste·loh* standard lamp

lampadina *lam·pa·dee·na f* light bulb; **la lampadina tascabile** *lam·pa·dee·na ta·skah·bee·le* torch

lampione *lam·pyoh·ne m* streetlamp; lamppost

lampo *lam·poh m* lightning

lampone *lam·poh·nay m* raspberry

lana *lah·na f* wool; **di lana** *dee lah·na* wool(l)en; **la lana d'agnello** *lah·na dan·yel·loh* lambswool; **la lana di vetro** *lah·na dee vay·troh* fibre-glass

lancetta *lan·chayt·ta f* needle (*on dial*); hand (*of clock*)

lanciare *lan·chah·ray vt* throw; launch

lanolina *la·no·lee·na f* lanolin

lardo *lar·doh m* lard

larghezza *lar·gayts·tsa f* width; breadth

largo(a) *lar·go(a) adj* wide; broad; **largo(a) 4 cm.** *lar·go(a) 4 cm.* 4 cm. wide; **al largo di** *al lar·go* offshore

laringite *la·reen·jee·te f* laryngitis

lasciare *la·shah·ray vt* leave; let go of; let (*allow*); **lo hanno lasciato andare** *lo an·no la·shah·to an·dah·ray* they let him go; **lasci fare a me** *la·shee fah·ray a may* leave it to me; **mi lasci entrare** *mee la·shee en·trah·ray* let me in

lassativo *las·sa·tee·voh m* laxative

lassù *las·soo adv* up there

lastra *la·stra f* slab; plate (*of glass, metal*)

lastricato *la·stree·kah·toh m* pavement (*roadway*)

latino *la·tee·noh m* Latin □ *adj* latino(a) *la·tee·no(a)* Latin

latinoamericano(a) *la·tee·no·a·me·ree·kah·no(a) adj* Latin American

lato *lah·toh m* side; **a tutti e due i lati a** *toot·tee e doo·e ee lah·tee* on either side

latrato *la·trah·toh m* bark (*of dog*)

latta *lat·ta f* can

lattaio *lat·ta·yoh m* milkman

latte *lat·tay m* milk; **il latte condensato** *lat·tay kon·den·sah·toh* condensed milk; **il latte scremato** *lat·tay skre·mah·to* skim(med) milk; **il latte evaporato** *lat·tay e·va·po·rah·to* evaporated milk; **il latte in polvere** *lat·tay een pohl·ve·re* dried milk

latteria *lat·te·ree·a f* dairy (store)

lattuga *lat·too·ga f* lettuce

laurea *low·re·a f* degree (*university*)

laurearsi *low·ray·ar·see vr* graduate (*from university*)

laureato(a) *low·ray·ah·toh(a) m/f* graduate (*from university*)

lavabile *la·vah·bee·le adj* washable

lavabo *la·vah·boh m* washbasin

lavacristallo *la·va·kree·stal·loh m* windscreen washer

lavanderia *la·van·de·ree·a f* laundry (*place*); **la lavanderia automatica** *la·van·de·ree·a ow·to·ma·tee·ka* launderette

lavandino *la·van·dee·noh m* sink

lavare *la·vah·ray vt* wash; lavare a secco *la·vah·ray a sayk·ko* to dry-clean; lavare le stoviglie *la·vah·ray le sto·veel·ye* to wash up (*dishes*)

lavarsi *la·var·see vr* wash (oneself); mi sono lavato(a) *mee so·noh la·vah·toh(a)* I washed myself

lavastoviglie *la·va·sto·veel·ye m* — dishwasher

lavatrice *la·va·tree·che f* washing machine

lavorare *la·vo·rah·ray vi* work

lavoratore *la·vo·ra·toh·re m* worker

lavoratrice *la·vo·ra·tree·che f* worker

lavoro *la·voh·roh m* work; un buon lavoro *oon bwon la·voh·roh* a good piece of work; **il lavoro manuale** *la·voh·roh ma·nwah·le* unskilled labo(u)r; **il lavoro domestico** *la·voh·roh do·me·stee·ko* housework; **il lavoro a cottimo** *la·voh·roh a kot·tee·moh* piecework; **i lavori stradali** *la·voh·ree stra·dah·lee* road works

le *le art* □ *pron* them; to her/it; to you

lecca-lecca *layk·ka·layk·ka m* — lollipop

leccare *lek·kah·ray vt* lick

lega *lay·ga f* alloy

legale *le·gah·le adj* legal

legare *le·gah·ray vt* bind (*tie*); legare un pacco *le·gah·ray oon pak·koh* to tie up a parcel

legge *layj·je f* law

leggere* *lej·je·re vt/i* read

leggero(a) *lej·je·ro(a) adj* light (*not heavy*); weak (*tea*); mild (*cigarette*); slight; minor (*injury*)

legno *layn·yoh m* wood (*material*); di legno *dee layn·yoh* wooden

lei *lay pron* she; her; you; Lei *lay* you; lei stessa *lay stays·sa* (she) herself; lei stesso(a) *lay stays·so(a)* (you) yourself

lente *len·te f* lens (*of glasses*); le lenti a contatto *len·tee a kon·tat·toh* contact lenses

lenticchie *len·teek·kye fpl* lentils

lento(a) *len·to(a) adj* slow; slack (*loose*)

lenzuolo *len·tswo·loh m* sheet

leone *le·oh·ne m* lion

lepre *le·pray f* hare

lettera *let·te·ra f* letter; la lettera di accompagnamento *let·te·ra dee ak·kom·pan·ya·mayn·toh* covering letter; la lettera raccomandata *let·te·ra rak·ko·man·dah·ta* registered letter; la lettera per via aerea *let·te·ra per vee·a a·e·re·a* air letter

letteratura *let·te·ra·too·ra f* literature

lettino *let·tee·noh m* cot; il lettino portatile *let·tee·noh por·tah·tee·lay* carry-cot

letto *let·toh m* bed; a letto *a let·toh* in bed; andare* a letto *an·dah·ray a let·toh* to go to bed; un letto a una piazza *oon let·toh a oo·na pyats·tsa* a single bed; il letto matrimoniale *let·toh ma·tree·mo·nyah·le* double bed; il letto a castello *let·toh a ka·stel·loh* bunk beds; i letti gemelli *let·tee je·mel·lee* twin beds

lettura *let·too·ra f* reading

leva *le·va f* lever

levare *le·vah·ray vt* remove; take away; take off

levata *le·vah·ta f* collection (*of mail*)

levatrice *le·va·tree·chay f* midwife

lezione *le·tsyoh·ne f* lesson; lecture

li *lee pron* them

lì *lee adv* there

libbra *leeb·bra f* pound (*weight*)

liberare *lee·be·rah·ray vt* release

libero(a) *lee·be·ro(a) adj* free; clear

(*not blocked*); vacant (*seat, toilet*); un giorno libero *oon johr·noh lee·be·ro* a day off

Libia *lee·bya* f Libya

libretto *lee·brayt·toh* m booklet; il libretto di circolazione *lee·brayt·toh dee cheer·ko·la·tsyoh·ne* logbook (*of car*); il libretto di assegni *lee·brayt·toh dee as·sayn·ye* cheque-book; il libretto di banca *lee·brayt·toh dee ban·ka* bankbook

libro *lee·broh* m book; il libro di testo *lee·broh dee te·stoh* textbook; il libro di fraseologia *lee·broh dee fra·ze·o·lo·jee·a* phrase book; il libro di grammatica *lee·broh dee gram·ma·tee·ka* grammar (book); il libro tascabile *lee·broh ta·skah·bee·le* paperback; il libro paga *lee·broh pah·ga* payroll

licenziare *lee·chen·tsyah·ray* vt dismiss (*from job*); lay off (*workers*)

licenziato(a) *lee·chen·tsyah·to(a)* adj redundant (*worker*)

liceo *lee·che·oh* m high school (*for 14- to 19-year-olds*)

Liechtenstein *leekh·ten·shtine* m Liechtenstein

lieto(a) *lee·yay·to(a)* adj glad

lievito *lye·vee·toh* m yeast

lima *lee·ma* f file (*tool*)

limetta *lee·mayt·ta* f nailfile; la limetta di carta smerigliata *lee·mayt·ta dee kar·ta zme·reel·yah·ta* emery board

limitare *lee·mee·tah·ray* vt restrict

limite *lee·mee·te* m limit; boundary; oltre i limiti *ohl·tre ee lee·mee·tee* out of bounds; il limite di velocità *lee·mee·te dee ve·lo·chee·ta* speed limit

limonata *lee·mo·na·ta* f lemonade

limone *lee·moh·ne* m lemon

limousine *lee·moo·zeen* f limousine

linea *lee·ne·a* f line; la linea punteggiata *lee·ne·a poon·tej·jah·ta* dotted line

lingua *leen·gwa* f language; tongue

linguaggio *leen·gwaj·joh* m language (*way one speaks*)

lino *lee·noh* m linen (*cloth*)

linoleum *lee·no·le·oom* m lino(leum)

liquidazione *lee·kwee·da·tsyoh·ne* f liquidation; andare* in liquidazione *an·dah·ray een lee·kwee·da·tsyoh·ne* to go into liquidation

liquidità *lee·kwee·dee·ta* f liquid assets

liquido(a) *lee·kwee·doh(a)* adj liquid □ *lee·kwee·do(a)* liquid

liquirizia *lee·kwee·ree·tsya* f licorice

liquore *lee·kwoh·re* m liqueur

liquori *lee·kwoh·ree* mpl spirits (*alcohol*)

liscio(a) *lee·sho(a)* adj smooth; straight (*hair*); neat (*liquor*)

lista *lee·sta* f list; la lista dei vini *lee·sta de·ee vee·nee* wine list; la lista d'attesa *lee·sta dat·tay·sa* waiting list

listino prezzi *lee·stee·noh prets·tsee* m price list

lite *lee·te* f argument; quarrel

litigare *lee·tee·gah·ray* vi argue; quarrel

litro *lee·troh* m litre

livello *lee·vel·loh* m level; il livello del mare *lee·vel·loh del mah·re* sea level

lo *lo* art the □ *pron* him; it

locale *lo·kah·le* adj local

locanda *lo·kan·da* f inn

locomotiva *lo·ko·mo·tee·va* f engine (*of train*)

loggione *loj·joh·nay* m gallery (*in theatre*)

logoramento *lo·go·ra·mayn·toh* m wear and tear

logorare *lo·go·rah·ray* vt wear out

logorarsi *lo·go·rar·see* vr wear out

logoro(a) *loh·go·ro(a)* adj worn; worn-out (*object*)

Londra *lohn·dra* f London

longplaying *long·ple·eeng* m — L.P.

lontananza *lon·ta·nan·tsa* f distance; in lontananza *een lon·ta·nan·tsa* in the distance

lontano *lon·tah·no* adv far; è lontano *e lon·tah·no* it's a long way; più lontano *pyoo lon·tah·no* farther

lordo(a) *lohr·doh(a)* adj gross; pretax (*profit*)

loro *loh·ro* pron they; them; to them; you; to you; Loro *loh·ro* you; to you; il loro padre *eel loh·ro pah·dre* their/ your father; la loro madre *la loh·ro mah·dre* their/your mother; i loro fratelli/le loro sorelle *ee loh·ro fra·tel·lee/le loh·ro so·rel·le* their/your brothers/sisters; il/la loro *eel/la loh·ro* theirs; yours; i/le loro *ee/le loh·ro* theirs; yours; l'hanno fatto loro stessi(e) *lan·no fat·to loh·ro stays·see (·se)* they did it themselves; you did it yourselves

lotta *lot·ta* f struggle; wrestling

lottare *lot·tah·ray* vi struggle; fight

lotteria *lot·te·ree·a* f lottery

lotto *lot·toh* m lottery; lot (*at auction*)

lozione *lo·tsyoh·ne* f lotion

lubrificante *loo·bree·fee·kan·tay* m lubricant

lucchetto *look·kayt·toh* m padlock

luce *loo·che* f light; la luce rossa *loo·che rohs·sa* red light (*traffic light*)

lucidare *loo·chee·dah·ray* vt polish

lucido(a) *loo·chee·doh* m polish (*for shoes*)

luglio *lool·yoh* m July

lui *loo·ee* pron he; him; lui stesso *loo·ee stays·so* (he) himself

luna *loo·na* f moon; la luna di miele *loo·na dee mye·le* honeymoon

luna-park *loo·na·park* m — amusement park

lunedì *loo·ne·dee* m — Monday

lunghezza *loon·gayts·tsa* f length

lungo(a) *loon·go(a)* adj long; lungo la strada *loon·go la strah·da* along the street; quant'è lungo il fiume? *kwan·te loon·go eel fyoo·me* how long is the river?; lungo(a) 6 metri *loon·go(a) 6 me·tree* 6 metres long; a lungo *a loon·go* for a long time

lungomare *loon·go·mah·re* m promenade (*by sea*); seafront

lungometraggio *loon·go·me·traj·joh* m feature film

luogo *lwo·goh* m place; in qualche luogo *een kwal·ke lwo·goh* somewhere; in nessun luogo *een nes·soon lwo·goh* nowhere; sul luogo *sool lwo·goh* on the spot

lupo *loo·poh* m wolf

Lussemburgo *loos·sem·boor·goh* m Luxemburg

lusso *loos·so* m luxury; di lusso *dee loos·so* de luxe; luxury (*car, hotel*)

M

ma *ma* conj but

macadam *ma·ka·dam* m tarmac

maccheroni *mak·ke·roh·nee* mpl macaroni

macchia *mak·kya* f spot; stain; blot

macchiare *mak·kyah·ray* vt stain; mark

macchina *mak·kee·na f* car; machine; la macchina da scrivere *mak·kee·na da skree·ve·re* typewriter; la macchina per cucire *mak·kee·na payr koo·chee·re* sewing machine; la macchina fotografica *mak·kee·na fo·to·gra·fee·ka* camera; la macchina mangiasoldi *mak·kee·na ma·jol·dee* one-armed bandit; la macchina della polizia *mak·kee·na del·la po·lee·tsee·a* police car; la macchina sportiva *mak·kee·na spor·tee·va* sports car; la macchina noleggiata *mak·kee·na no·lej·jah·ta* hire car

macchinario *mak·kee·nah·ryoh m* plant (*equipment*); machinery

macchinetta per il caffè *mak·kee·nayt·ta payr eel kaf·fe f* percolator

macedonia *ma·che·don·ya f* fruit salad

macellaio *ma·chel·la·yoh m* butcher

macelleria *ma·chel·le·ree·a f* butcher's (*shop*)

macinare *ma·chee·nah·ray vt* mill; grind

macinato(a) *ma·chee·nah·toh(a) adj* ground (*coffee*)

macinino *ma·chee·nee·noh m* mill (*for coffee, pepper*)

madera *ma·de·ra m* Madeira (*wine*)

madre *mah·dray f* mother

Madrid *ma·dreed f* Madrid

madrina *ma·dree·na f* godmother

maestra *ma·ay·stra f* teacher (*primary school*)

maestro *ma·ay·stroh m* master; teacher (*primary school*)

magazzino *ma·gadz·dzee·noh m* store (*big shop*); store room; warehouse; in magazzino *een ma·gadz·dzee·noh* in stock; il grande magazzino *gran·de ma·gadz·dzee·noh* department store

maggio *maj·joh m* May

maggiorana *maj·jo·rah·na f* marjoram

maggioranza *maj·jo·ran·tsa f* majority; eletto(a) con una maggioranza di 5 voti *e·let·toh(a) kon oo·na maj·jo·ran·tsa dee 5 voh·tee* elected by a majority of 5

maggiore *maj·joh·re adj* larger; greater; largest; greatest; elder; eldest; il/la maggiore *maj·joh·re* elder; eldest; ne ha la maggior parte *nay a la maj·johr pahr·tay* he has the most

magia *ma·jee·a f* magic

magico(a) *ma·jee·koh(a) adj* magic

maglia *ma·lya f* jersey (*sweater*); lavorare a maglia *la·vo·rah·ray a mal·ya* to knit

maglieria *mal·ye·ree·a f* knitwear

maglietta *mal·yayt·ta f* T-shirt

maglio *mal·yo m* mallet

maglione *mal·yoh·ne m* sweater

magnate *man·yah·te m* tycoon

magnetofono *man·ye·to·fo·noh m* tape recorder; il magnetofono a cassetta *man·ye·to·fo·noh a kas·sayt·ta* cassette-recorder

magnifico(a) *ma·nyee·fee·koh(a) adj* great (*excellent*); magnificent; grand

magro(a) *ma·gro(a) adj* thin (*person*); lean (*meat*)

mai *ma·ee adv* never; egli non viene mai *el·yee nohn vye·nay ma·ee* he never comes; è mai stato a Londra? *e ma·ee stah·to a lohn·dra* have you ever been to London?

maiale *ma·yah·le m* pig; pork

maionese *ma·yo·nay·say f* mayonnaise

nais *ma·ees m* maize

maiuscola *ma·yoos·ko·la f* capital letter; A maiuscola *a ma·yoos·ko·la* capital A

malato(a) *ma·lah·to(a) adj* ill; sick

malattia *ma·lat·tee·a f* illness; disease

male *mah·le adv* badly (*not well*); □ *m* il male *mah·le* pain; ache; fare* male *fah·ray mah·le* to hurt; Si è fatto male *see e fat·to mah·le* you've hurt yourself; quello fa male! *kwayl·lo fa mah·le* that hurts!

malgrado *mal·grah·do prep* in spite of; despite

Malta *mal·ta f* Malta

malto *mal·toh m* malt

malva *mal·va f* mauve

malvagio(a) *mal·va·jo(a) adj* wicked

mamma *mam·ma f* mum(my)

mancanza *man·kan·tsa f* lack; shortage

mancare *man·kah·ray vt* miss (*target*); è mancato per poco *e man·kah·to payr po·ko* it only just missed; mancano alcune pagine *man·ka·noh al·koo·nay pah·jee·nay* some pages are missing

mancia *man·cha f* tip (*money given*)

mancino(a) *man·chee·no(a) adj* left-handed

mandare *man·dah·ray vt* send

mandarino *man·da·ree·noh m* tangerine

mandorla *man·dor·la f* almond

manette *ma·nayt·te fpl* handcuffs

mangiare *man·jah·ray vt* eat

manica *mah·nee·ka f* sleeve

Manica *mah·nee·ka f* Channel

manico *mah·nee·koh m* handle (*of brush, knife*)

manicure *ma·nee·koo·ray f* manicure

maniere *man·ye·ray fpl* manners

manifestazione *ma·nee·fe·sta·tsyoh·ne f* demonstration (*political*); rally

manifesto *ma·nee·fe·stoh m* poster

maniglia *ma·neel·ya f* door handle, doorknob

mano *mah·noh f —i* hand; trick (*in cards*); a mano *a mah·noh* by hand; fatto(a) a mano *fat·to(a) a mah·noh* handmade

manodopera *mah·no·do·pe·ra f* labo(u)r; manpower; work force

manopola *ma·no·po·la f* knob (*on radio etc*); mitt(en); la manopola di spugna *ma·no·po·la dee spoon·ya* facecloth

manovale *ma·no·vah·le m* labo(u)rer

manovella *ma·no·vel·la f* handle (*for winding*)

mantello *man·tel·loh m* cloak; coat; il mantello di visone *man·tel·loh dee vee·zoh·nay* mink coat

mantenere* *man·te·nay·re vt* support (*financially*); keep (*feed and clothe*)

manuale *ma·nwah·lay adj* manual □ *m* il manuale *ma·nwah·lay* manual; handbook

manubrio *ma·noo·bryoh m* handlebar(s)

manutenzione *ma·noo·ten·tsyoh·nay f* upkeep; maintenance

manzo *man·dzoh m* beef

marca *mar·ka f* brand (*of product*); brand name

marchio *mar·kyoh m* hallmark; il marchio di fabbrica *mar·kyoh dee fab·bree·ka* trademark; il marchio depositato *mar·kyoh de·po·zee·tah·to* registered trademark

marcia *mahr·cha f* march; gear (*of car*); seconda/terza marcia *se·kon·da/ tayr·tsa mahr·cha* 2nd/3rd gear;

quarta/prima marcia *kwar·ta/pree·ma mahr·cha* top/bottom gear

marciapiede *mar·cha·pye·de* m pavement; sidewalk; **il marciapiede a rulli** *mar·cha·pye·de a rool·lee* moving walkway

marciare *mahr·chah·ray* vi march

marcio(a) *mar·cho(a)* adj rotten (*wood etc*)

marcire *mar·chee·ray* vi rot; go bad

marco *mahr·koh* m mark (*currency*)

Mar dei Caraibi *mahr de·ee ka·ra·ee·bee* m Caribbean (Sea)

mare *mah·re* m sea; seaside; **avere* mal di mare** *a·vay·re mal dee mah·re* to be seasick

marea *ma·re·a* f tide; **la bassa marea** *bas·sa ma·re·a* low tide; **c'è alta/bassa marea** *che al·ta/bas·sa ma·re·a* the tide is in/out

Mare del Nord *mah·ray del nord m* North Sea

margarina *mahr·ga·ree·na* f margarine

margine *mar·jee·ne* m margin (*on page*); **il margine di profitto** *mar·jee·ne dee pro·feet·toh* profit margin

marina *ma·ree·na* f navy

marinaio *ma·ree·na·yoh* m sailor

marito *ma·ree·toh* m husband

marketing *mahr·ke·ting* m marketing

marmellata *mar·mel·lah·ta* f jam; **la marmellata d'arance** *mar·mel·lah·ta da·ran·chay* marmalade

marmitta *mar·meet·ta* f silencer (*on car*)

marmo *mahr·moh* m marble (*material*)

marocchino(a) *ma·rok·kee·noh(a)* adj Moroccan

Marocco *ma·rok·koh* m Morocco

marrone *mar·roh·ne* adj brown; **marrone rossiccio** *mar·roh·ne ros·seech·cho* tan

marsina *mar·see·na* f tailcoat

martedì *mar·te·dee* m — Tuesday

martedì grasso *mar·te·dee gras·so* m Shrove Tuesday

martello *mar·tel·loh* m hammer

marzapane *mahr·tsa·pah·nay* m marzipan

marzo *mahr·tsoh* m March

mascara *mas·ka·ra* m mascara

mascella *ma·shel·la* f jaw

maschera *mas·ke·ra* f mask; usherette

mascherare *mas·ke·rah·ray* vt mask

maschile *mas·kee·lay* adj masculine

maschio *mask·yo* adj male

massa *mas·sa* f mass

massaggiare *mas·saj·jah·ray* vt massage

massaggiatore *mas·saj·ja·toh·re* m masseur

massaggiatrice *mas·saj·ja·tree·chay* f masseuse

massaggio *mas·saj·joh* m massage

massiccio(a) *mas·see·choh(a)* adj massive

massimo *mas·see·moh* m maximum □ adj massimo(a) *mas·see·moh(a)* maximum; **al massimo** *al mas·see·moh* at the most; **sfruttare al massimo** *sfroot·tah·ray al mas·see·moh* to make the most of

mass media *mass mee·dee·a* mpl media

masticare *mas·tee·kah·ray* vt chew

mastro *ma·stroh* m ledger

matematica *ma·te·ma·tee·ka* f mathematics

materasso *ma·te·ras·soh* m mattress; **il materasso pneumatico** *ma·te·ras·soh pne·oo·ma·tee·ko* air-mattress; air bed

materia *ma·te·ree·a* f subject (*in school*); **le materie prime** *ma·te·ree·e pree·me* raw materials

materiale *ma·te·ryah·lay* m material

maternità *ma·tayr·nee·ta* f maternity hospital

matita *ma·tee·ta* f pencil

matrice *ma·tree·che* f stub (*counterfoil*)

matrigna *ma·treen·ya* f stepmother

matrimonio *ma·tree·mo·nyoh* m wedding; marriage

matterello *ma·te·rel·loh* m rolling pin

mattina *mat·tee·na* f morning

mattino *mat·tee·noh* m morning

mattone *mat·toh·ne* m brick

maturarsi *ma·too·rar·see* vr ripen; accrue

maturo(a) *ma·too·ro(a)* adj ripe (*fruit*); mature

mazza *mats·tsa* f club; bat

mazziere *mats·tsye·re* m dealer (*cards*)

mazzo *mats·tsoh* m pack (*of cards*); bunch

me *may* pron me

meccanico *mek·kan·ee·koh* m mechanic

meccanismo *mek·ka·nee·zmoh* m mechanism; works

media *me·dya* f average

medicina *me·dee·chee·na* f medicine

medicinale *me·dee·chee·nah·le* m drug (*medicine*)

medico(a) *me·dee·koh(a)* adj medical □ m **il medico** *me·dee·koh* doctor; **il medico generico** *me·dee·koh je·ne·ree·koh* general practitioner, G.P.

medio(a) *me·dee·o(a)* adj medium; average

mediocre *me·dee·o·kre* adj poor (*mediocre*)

Medio Oriente *med·yoh o·ree·en·tay* m Middle East

mediterraneo(a) *me·dee·ter·rah·nay·oh(a)* adj Mediterranean □ m **il Mediterraneo** *me·dee·ter·rah·nay·oh* the Mediterranean (Sea)

medusa *me·doo·za* f jellyfish

meglio *mel·yo* adv, adj better; best; **canta meglio di te** *kan·ta mel·yo dee te* he sings better than you; **sempre meglio** *sem·pre mel·yo* better and better

mela *may·la* f apple

melagrana *me·la·grah·na* f pomegranate

melanzana *me·lan·dzah·na* f aubergine

melassa *me·las·sa* f treacle; molasses; **la melassa raffinata** *me·las·sa raf·fee·nah·ta* (golden) syrup

melo *may·loh* m apple tree

melone *me·loh·nay* m melon

membro *mem·broh* m member

memoria *me·mo·ree·a* f memory; **a memoria** *a me·mo·ree·a* by heart

mendicante *men·dee·kan·te* m/f beggar

mendicare *men·dee·kah·ray* vi beg

meno *may·no* adv less; minus; **a meno che noi non veniamo** *a may·no ke noy nohn ve·nya·mo* unless we come; **il meno caro** *eel may·no kah·ro* the least expensive; **il meno denaro** *eel may·no de·nah·roh* the least money; **ha il meno** *a eel may·no* he has the least; **meno carne** *may·no kar·ne* less meat; **meno errori** *may·no er·roh·ree* fewer errors; **meno rapidamente** *may·no ra·pee·da·mayn·te* less quickly; **meno di** *may·no dee* less than; **meno di un chilometro** *may·no* *dee oon kee·lo·me·troh* under a kilometre

mensa *men·sa* f canteen

mensile *men·see·lay* adj monthly □ *m* il mensile *men·see·lay* monthly

menta *mayn·ta* f mint (herb); **la menta peperita** *mayn·ta pe·pe·ree·ta* peppermint (plant)

mente *mayn·tay* f mind

mentire* *men·tee·re* vi lie (tell a lie)

mento *mayn·toh* m chin

mentre *mayn·tre* conj while; whereas; **è arrivato mentre stavamo partendo** *e ar·ree·vah·to mayn·tre sta·vah·mo par·ten·do* he arrived as we left

menú *me·noo* m — menu

menzionare *men·tsyo·nah·ray* vt mention

menzione *men·tsyoh·nay* f reference (mention)

meraviglioso(a) *me·ra·veel·yoh·so(a)* adj wonderful; marvellous

mercante *mayr·kan·tay* m merchant

mercato *mer·kah·toh* m market; **il mercato delle valute estere** *mer·kah·toh del·le va·loo·te e·ste·re* foreign exchange market; **il mercato delle pulci** *mer·kah·toh del·le pool·chee* flea market

Mercato Comune *mer·kah·toh ko·moo·nay* m Common Market

merceria *mer·che·ree·a* f haberdashery

merci *mayr·chee* fpl freight; goods

mercoledì *mayr·ko·le·dee* m — Wednesday

merenda *me·ren·da* f snack

meridionale *me·ree·dyo·nah·le* adj southern

meringa *me·reen·ga* f meringue

meritare *me·ree·tah·ray* vt deserve

merlano *mer·lah·noh* m whiting

merlo *mer·loh* m blackbird

merluzzo *mayr·loots·tsoh* m cod

meschino(a) *mes·kee·noh(a)* adj mean (unkind)

mescolanza *mes·ko·lan·tsa* f mixture

mescolare *me·sko·lah·ray* vt blend; mix

mescolarsi *me·sko·lahr·see* vr mix

mese *may·say* m month

messa *mes·sa* f mass (church)

messaggero *mes·saj·je·roh* m messenger

messaggio *mes·saj·joh* m message

messicano(a) *mes·see·ka·noh(a)* adj Mexican

Messico *mes·see·koh* m Mexico

mestiere *may·stee·ay·ray* m job; trade

mestruazioni *me·stroo·a·tsyoh·nee* fpl period (menstruation)

metà *me·ta* f — half; **a metà** *a me·ta* half; **a metà prezzo** *a me·ta prets·tsoh* half-price; **a metà strada** *a me·ta strah·da* halfway; **dividere* a metà** *dee·vee·de·re a me·ta* to halve (divide in two); **ridurre* di metà** *ree·door·re dee me·ta* to halve (reduce by half)

metallo *me·tal·loh* m metal

metodo *me·to·doh* m method

metrico(a) *met·ree·koh(a)* adj metric

metro *me·troh* m metre; **il metro a nastro** *me·troh a na·stroh* tape measure

metropolitana *me·tro·po·lee·tah·na* f subway; underground railway

mettere* *mayt·te·re* vt put; put on (clothes); **mettere* qualcuno in comunicazione** *mayt·te·re kwal·koo·no een ko·moo·ne·ka·tsyoh·ne* to put someone through (on phone)

mezzanotte *medz·dza·not·tay* f midnight

mezzi *medz·dzee* mpl means

mezzo(a) *medz·dzoh(a)* adj half □ *m* il mezzo *medz·dzoh* half; middle; **nel bel mezzo** *nel bel medz·dzoh* right in the middle; **due e mezzo** *doo·e ay medz·dzoh* two and a half; **tre chilometri e mezzo** *tray kee·lo·me·tree ay medz·dzoh* three and a half kilometers; **per mezzo di** *payr medz·dzoh dee* by means of; **di mezza età** *dee medz·dza ay·ta* middle-aged; **una mezza dozzina** *oo·na medz·dza dodz·dzee·na* a half dozen

mezzogiorno *medz·dzo·johr·noh* m midday; noon

mezz'ora *medz·dzoh·ra* f half-hour

mi *mee* pron me; to me; myself

mia *mee·a* adj my □ pron mine

microbo *mee·kro·boh* m germ

microchip *mee·kro·chip* m — microchip

microcomputer *mee·kro·kom·poo·tayr* m — microcomputer

microfilm *mee·kro·feelm* m — microfilm

microfono *mee·kro·fo·noh* m microphone

microprocessor *mee·kro·pro·ches·sohr* m — microprocessor

microscheda *mee·kro·ske·da* f microfiche

mie *mee·ay* adj my □ pron mine

miei *mee·ay·ee* adj my □ pron mine

miele *mye·le* m honey

mietere *mye·te·re* vt harvest (grain)

miglio *meel·yoh* m —a mile

miglioramento *meel·yo·ra·mayn·toh* m improvement

migliorare *meel·yo·ra·ray* vt/i improve

migliore *meel·yoh·re* adj better; best; **il/la migliore** *eel/la meel·yoh·re* the best

miliardo *mee·lyar·doh* m billion

milionario *mee·lee·o·nah·ree·oh* m millionaire

milione *mee·lee·oh·nay* m million

milionesimo(a) *mee·lee·o·ne·zee·moh(a)* adj millionth

militare *mee·lee·tah·ray* adj military

mille *meel·le* num thousand

millesimo(a) *meel·le·zee·mo(a)* adj thousandth

milligrammo *meel·lee·gram·moh* m milligram(me)

millilitro *meel·lee·lee·troh* m millilitre

millimetro *meel·lee·me·troh* m millimetre

mina *mee·na* f lead (in pencil)

minaccia *mee·nach·cha* f threat

minacciare *mee·nach·chah·ray* vt threaten

minatore *mee·na·toh·ray* m miner

minestrone *mee·ne·stroh·nay* m minestrone (soup)

minicomputer *mee·nee·kom·poo·ter* m minicomputer

miniera *mee·nye·rah* f mine (for coal etc)

minigonna *mee·nee·gohn·na* f miniskirt

minimo *mee·nee·moh* m minimum □ adj minimo(a) *mee·nee·moh(a)* minimum

ministero *mee·nee·ste·roh* m ministry; **il Ministero del Tesoro** *mee·nee·ste·roh del te·zo·roh* Treasury

ministro *mee·nee·stroh* m minister; **il Ministro delle Finanze** *mee·nee·stroh del·le fee·nan·tse* Finance Minister; **il primo ministro** *pree·mo mee·nee·stroh* prime minister, P.M.

minitassi *mee·nee·tas·see* m minicab

minoranza *mee·no·ran·tsa* f minority

minore *mee·noh·re* adj less; smaller; lower; younger

minorenne *mee·no·ren·ne* adj under age

minuto *mee·noo·toh* m minute

mio *mee·oh* adj my ▢ pron mine; un mio amico *oon mee·oh a·mee·koh* a friend of mine

miope *mee·o·pe* adj shortsighted

mira *mee·ra* f aim; prendere* la mira *pren·de·re la mee·ra* to aim

mirtillo *meer·teel·loh* m cranberry

miscela *mee·she·la* f blend

mistero *mee·ster·oh* m mystery

misto(a) *mee·stoh(a)* adj mixed

misura *mee·zoo·ra* f measure; measurement; prendere* le misure per fare qualcosa *pren·de·re le mee·zoo·ra payr fah·ray kwal·ko·sa* to take steps to do something; fatto(a) su misura *fat·toh(a) soo mee·zoo·ra* made-to-measure

misurare *mee·zoo·rah·ray* vt/i measure

mite *mee·tay* adj mild; gentle

mittente *meet·ten·te* m/f sender

mobile *mo·bee·le* m piece of furniture

mobili *mo·bee·lee* mpl furniture

mochetta *mo·kayt·ta* f wall-to-wall carpet(ing)

moda *mo·da* f fashion; l'ultima moda *lool·tee·ma mo·da* the latest fashions; di moda *dee mo·da* fashionable

modellista *mo·del·lee·sta* m/f designer

modello *mo·del·loh* m model

modernizzare *mo·der·needz·dzah·ray* vt modernize

moderno(a) *mo·der·noh(a)* adj modern

modesto(a) *mo·de·stoh(a)* adj modest

modifica *mo·de·fee·ka* f modification

modificare *mo·dee·fee·kah·ray* vt modify

modo *mo·doh* m way; manner; ad ogni modo *ad ohn·yee mo·doh* in any case; in tutti i modi *een toot·tee ee mo·dee* at all costs; in qualche modo *een kwal·kay mo·doh* somehow

modulo *mo·doo·loh* m form (document); il modulo d'ordinazione *eel mo·doo·loh dor·dee·na·tsyoh·ne* order-form

mogano *mo·ga·noh* m mahogany

moglie *mohl·ye* f wife

mohair *mo·er* m mohair

molecola *mo·le·ko·la* f molecule

molla *mol·la* f spring (coil)

molletta *mol·layt·ta* f clothes-peg

molo *mo·loh* m pier

molti(e) *mohl·tee(·te)* adj, pron many

moltiplicare *mol·tee·plee·kah·ray* vt multiply

moltiplicazione *mol·tee·plee·kats·yoh·nay* f multiplication

molto *mohl·to* adv a lot; much; very; mi piace molto *mee pyah·che mohl·to* I like it very much; molto meglio *mohl·to mel·yoh* much better

molto(a) *mohl·to(a)* adj, pron much; molto latte *mohl·to lat·te* a lot of milk; molta gente *mohl·ta jen·te* lots of people

momento *mo·mayn·toh* m moment; un momento *oon mo·mayn·toh* just a minute; in questo momento *een kway·stoh mo·mayn·toh* at the moment; at present; per il momento *payr eel mo·mayn·toh* for the time being

monaca *mo·na·ka* f nun

monaco *mo·na·koh* m monk

Monaco *mo·na·koh* f Monaco

Monaco di Baviera *mo·na·koh dee Ba·vye·ra* f Munich

monastero *mo·na·ste·roh* m monastery

mondo *mohn·doh* m world

moneta *mo·nay·ta* f coin

monetario(a) *mo·ne·tah·ree·oh(a)* adj monetary

monitore *mo·nee·toh·ray* m monitor (TV)

mono *mo·noh* adj mono

monopolio *mo·no·po·lyo* m monopoly

monorotaia *mo·no·ro·ta·ya* f monorail

montagna *mon·tan·ya* f mountain

montare *mon·tah·ray* vt go up; assemble (parts of machine); whip (cream, eggs)

montatura *mon·ta·too·ra* f frames (of eyeglasses)

monumento *mo·noo·mayn·toh* m monument

mora *mo·ra* f blackberry

morbido(a) *mor·bee·do(a)* adj soft (not hard)

morbillo *mor·beel·loh* m measles

mordere *mor·de·re* vt bite

morire *mo·ree·re* vi die

morso *mor·soh* m bite (by animal)

morte *mor·te* f death

morto(a) *mor·to(a)* adj dead

mosca *moh·ska* f fly

Mosca *moh·ska* f Moscow

moscerino *mo·she·ree·noh* m gnat

moschea *mo·skay·a* f mosque

mosella *mo·zel·la* m moselle (wine)

mostarda *mo·stahr·da* f mustard

mostra *moh·stra* f show; exhibition

mostrare *mo·strah·ray* vt show

mostro *moh·stroh* m monster

motel *mo·tel* m — motel

moto *mo·toh* m motion

motocicletta *mo·to·chee·klayt·ta* f motorbike

motociclista *mo·to·chee·klee·sta* m/f motorcyclist

motolancia *mo·to·lan·cha* f launch

motore *mo·toh·re* m engine; motor; il motore diesel *mo·toh·re dee·zel* diesel engine

motorino d'avviamento *mo·to·ree·noh dav·vya·mayn·toh* m starter (in car)

motoscafo *mo·to·skah·foh* m motorboat

mousse *moos* f mousse

movimento *mo·vee·mayn·toh* m motion; movement; il movimento delle merci *mo·vee·mayn·toh del·le mer·chee* turnover (in goods)

mucchio *mook·kyoh* m pile; heap

mulino *moo·lee·noh* m mill; il mulino a vento *moo·lee·noh a ven·toh* windmill

multa *mool·ta* f fine; la multa per sosta vietata *mool·ta payr so·sta vye·tah·ta* parking-ticket

multilingue *mool·tee·leen·gway* adj multilingual

multinazionale *mool·tee·nats·yo·nah·lay* adj multinational

municipale *moo·nee·chee·pah·lay* adj municipal

municipio *moo·nee·chee·pyoh* m town hall; city hall

muovere* *mwo·ve·ray* vt move

muoversi* *mwo·ver·see* vr move

muro *moo·roh* m wall

muscolo *moo·sko·loh* m muscle

museo *moo·ze·oh* m museum

musica *moo·zee·ka* f music; la musica

leggera *moo·zee·ka lej·je·ra* light music

musicista *moo·zee·chee·sta* m/f musician

musulmano(a) *moo·sool·mah·noh(a)* adj Muslim □ m/f il/la musulmano(a) *moo·sool·mah·noh(a)* Muslim

mutande *moo·tan·day* fpl underpants

mutandine *moo·tan·dee·ne* fpl panties; pants

muto(a) *moo·to(a)* adj dumb

N

nafta *naf·ta* f diesel oil

nailon *nai·lon* m nylon

narrativa *nar·ra·tee·va* f fiction

nascere* *na·she·re* vi be born

nascita *na·shee·ta* f birth

nascondere* *na·skohn·de·re* vt hide

nascondersi* *na·skohn·der·see* vr hide

naso *nah·soh* m nose

nastro *na·stroh* m ribbon; tape; il nastro adesivo *na·stroh a·de·zee·vo* sellotape; il nastro magnetico *na·stroh man·ye·tee·koh* magnetic tape

Natale *na·tah·lay* m Christmas; il giorno di Natale *johr·noh dee na·tah·lay* Christmas Day

nativo(a) *na·tee·voh(a)* adj native

nato(a) *nah·to(a)* adj born

natura *na·too·ra* f nature

naturale *na·too·rah·lay* adj natural

naturalizzato(a) *na·too·ra·leedz·dzah·toh(a)* adj naturalized

naturalmente *na·too·ral·mayn·te* adv of course; naturally

naufragare *now·fra·gah·ray* vi be wrecked (*ship*)

naufragio *now·frah·joh* m shipwreck

nausea *now·ze·a* f sickness; nausea

navata *na·vah·ta* f nave

nave *nah·ve* f ship; la nave cisterna *nah·ve chee·ster·na* tanker (*ship*)

nave-traghetto *nah·ve·tra·gayt·toh* f ferry

navigare *na·vee·gah·ray* vi sail

navigazione *na·vee·ga·tsyoh·ne* f navigation

nazionale *na·tsyoh·nah·lay* adj national

nazionalità *na·tsyoh·na·lee·ta* f — nationality

nazionalizzare *na·tsyoh·na·leedz·dzah·ray* vt nationalize

nazione *na·tsyoh·nay* f nation

Nazioni Unite *na·tsyoh·nee oo·nee·tay* fpl United Nations Organization, UN, UNO

ne *nay* pron of him/her/it/them; about him etc; some; non ne abbiamo *nohn nay ab·byah·mo* we haven't any; ne avanzava un po' *nay a·van·tsah·va oon po* some (of it) was left

né .... né *nay ... nay* neither ... nor; né l'uno né l'altro *nay loo·noh nay lal·troh* neither

neanche *nay·an·ke* adv, conj not even; neither

nebbia *nayb·bya* f fog; c'è della nebbia *che del·la nayb·bya* it's foggy

nebbioso(a) *neb·byoh·so(a)* adj foggy

necessario(a) *ne·ches·sah·ree·oh(a)* adj necessary

negare *ne·gah·ray* vt deny

negativa *ne·ga·tee·va* f negative (*of photo*)

negli = in + gli

negoziabile *ne·go·tsyah·bee·lay* adj negotiable

negoziante *ne·go·tsyan·tay* m shopkeeper

negoziare *ne·go·tsyah·ray* vi negotiate

negozio *ne·go·tsyoh* m shop; fare* un giro dei negozi *fah·ray oon jee·roh de·ee ne·go·tsee* to go round the shops; il negozio di calzature *ne·go·tsyoh dee kal·tsa·too·re* shoeshop; il negozio a catena *ne·go·tsyoh a ka·tay·na* chain store; il negozio di giocattoli *ne·go·tsyoh dee jo·kat·to·lee* toyshop

nei = in + i, nel = in + il

nemico *ne·mee·koh* m enemy

nemmeno *nem·may·noh* adv, conj not even; io non c'ero e nemmeno lui *ee·o nohn che·ro e nem·may·noh loo·ee* I wasn't there and neither was he

nero(a) *nay·ro(a)* adj black

nervo *ner·voh* m nerve

nervoso(a) *ner·voh·soh(a)* adj nervous

nessuno(a) *nes·soo·no(a)* adj no; any □ pron nobody; none; anybody; non vedo nessuno *nohn vay·do nes·soo·no* I can't see anybody; non lo vedo in nessun luogo *nohn lo vay·do e nes·soon lwo·goh* I can't see it anywhere

netto(a) *nayt·toh(a)* adj net (*income, price*)

neutrale *ne·oo·trah·lay* adj neutral

neve *nay·ve* f snow

nevicare *ne·vee·kah·ray* vi snow; nevica *nay·vee·ka* it's snowing

nevischio *ne·vee·skyoh* m sleet

nido *nee·doh* m nest; il nido d'infanzia *nee·doh deen·fan·tsya* day nursery; crèche

niente *nyen·te* pron nothing; anything □ m nothing; non vedo niente *nohn vay·do nyen·te* I can't see anything

night-club *nait·kloob* m night club

nipote *nee·poh·tay* m grandson; nephew □ f granddaughter; niece

nipotino(a) *nee·po·tee·noh(a)* m/f grandchild

no *no* adv no (*as answer*)

nocca *nok·ka* f knuckle

nocciolo *noch·cho·loh* m stone (*in fruit*)

noce *noh·che* f walnut

nocivo(a) *no·chee·vo(a)* adj harmful

nodo *no·doh* m knot; bow (*ribbon*); fare* un nodo *fah·ray oon no·doh* to tie a knot; il nodo ferroviario *no·doh fer·ro·vee·ah·ree·oh* junction (*railway*)

noi *noy* pron we; us; siamo noi *syah·mo noy* it's us; noi stessi(e) *noy stays·see('se)* (we) ourselves

noioso(a) *no·yoh·so(a)* adj dull; boring; annoying

noleggiare *no·lej·jah·ray* vt hire; rent; charter (*plane, bus*)

noleggio *no·layj·joh* m hire; rental

nome *noh·may* m name; first name; a nome di *a noh·may dee* on behalf of; il nome di battesimo *noh·may dee bat·tay·zee·moh* Christian name

nomina *no·mee·na* f appointment (*to job*)

nominare *no·mee·nah·ray* vt appoint

non *nohn* adv not □ pref non- *nohn-* non-

nondimeno *nohn·dee·may·no* conj all the same

non-fumatore *nohn·foo·ma·toh·ray* m nonsmoker (*person*)

nonna *non·na* f grandmother

nonno *non·noh* m grandfather

nono(a) *no·noh(a)* adj ninth

nord *nord m* north; **a nord** *a nord* north

nord-est *nord·est m* northeast

nord-ovest *nord·o·vest m* northwest

norma *nor·ma f* norm; par *(golf)*

normale *nor·mah·lay adj* normal; regular

normalmente *nor·mal·mayn·tay adv* normally

nostalgia *no·stal·jee·a f* homesickness; nostalgia

nostro(a) *no·stroh(a) adj □ pron* ours; **nostri(e)** *no·stree(·stray)* our; ours

nota *no·ta f* note; memo(randum)

notare *no·tah·ray vt* notice

notevole *no·tay·vo·lay* remarkable

notizie *no·tee·tsye fpl* news

notte *not·tay f* night

novanta *no·van·ta num* ninety

nove *no·vay num* nine

novembre *no·vem·bre m* November

novità *no·vee·ta f* — novelty; news

nubile *noo·bee·le adj* single *(unmarried: woman)*

nucleare *noo·klay·ah·ray adj* nuclear

nudo(a) *noo·doh(a) adj* naked; nude; bare

nullo(a) *nool·loh(a) adj* void *(contract)*; **nullo(a) e di nessun effetto** *nool·loh(a) e dee nes·soon ef·fet·toh* null and void

numero *noo·me·roh m* number *(figure)*; act *(at circus etc)*; issue *(of magazine)*; size *(of shoes)*; **il numero telefonico** *noo·me·roh te·le·fo·nee·ko* telephone number; **il numero di immatricolazione** *noo·me·roh dee eem·ma·tree·ko·la·tsyoh·nay* registration number *(on car)*

nuora *nwoh·ra f* daughter-in-law

nuotare *nwo·tah·ray vi* swim

nuoto *nwo·toh m* swimming

nuovo(a) *nwo·voh(a) adj* new

nutrire *noo·tree·re vt* feed

nuvola *noo·vo·la f* cloud

nuvoloso(a) *noo·vo·loh·soh(a) adj* cloudy

O

o *o conj* or; **o... o...** *o o...* o either... or...

obbediente *ob·be·dyen·te adj* obedient

obbligo *ob·blee·goh m* obligation

obiettare a *o·byet·tah·ray a vi* object to

obiettivo *o·byet·tee·voh m* lens *(of camera)*; target; objective; **l'obiettivo grandangolare** *o·byet·tee·voh gran·dan·goh·lah·re* wide-angle lens

oblò *o·blo m* porthole

oblungo(a) *o·bloon·go(a) adj* oblong

oca *o·ka f* goose

occasione *ok·ka·zee·oh·ne f* opportunity; occasion; bargain *(cheap buy)*

occhiali *ok·kyah·lee mpl* glasses; goggles; **gli occhiali da sole** *ok·kyah·lee da sol·le* sunglasses; shades

occhio *ok·kyoh m* eye; **l'occhio nero** *ok·kyoh nay·ro* black eye; **strizzare l'occhio** *streets·tsah·ray lok·kyoh* to wink

occidentale *och·chee·den·tah·le adj* western

Occidente *och·chee·den·te m* the West

occorrere* *ok·kohr·re·re vi* be necessary; **non occorre che lei venga** *nohn ok·kohr·ray kay le·e ven·ga* you needn't come

occuparsi *ok·koo·par·see vr* occupy oneself; **occuparsi di qualcosa** *ok·*

koo·par·see dee kwal·ko·sa to see to something

occupato(a) *ok·koo·pah·to(a) adj* busy; engaged

oceano *o·che·a·noh m* ocean

Oceano Pacifico *o·che·a·noh pa·chee·fee·ko m* Pacific Ocean

odiare *o·dyah·ray vt* hate

odio *o·dyoh m* hatred

odore *o·doh·re m* smell; scent; **ha un odore forte** *a oon o·doh·re for·te* it has a strong smell

offendere* *of·fen·de·re vt* offend

offerente *of·fe·ren·te m/f* bidder

offerta *of·fer·ta f* bid; offer; **l'offerta e la domanda** *lof·fer·ta e la do·man·da* supply and demand; **l'offerta di acquisto** *of·fer·ta dee ak·kwee·stoh* take-over bid; **fare* un'offerta per qualcosa** *fah·ray oo·nof·fer·ta payr kwal·ko·sa* to bid for something

officina *of·fee·chee·na f* workshop

offrire* *of·free·re vt* offer; bid *(amount)*; **offrire* di fare qualcosa** *of·free·re dee fah·ray kwal·ko·sa* to offer to do something; **Le offrirò un gelato** *lay of·free·ro oon je·lah·toh* I'll treat you to an ice cream

oggetto *oj·jet·toh m* object; **l'oggetto d'antiquariato** *oj·jet·toh dan·tee·kwa·ree·ah·toh* antique

oggi *oj·jee adv* today; **quanti ne abbiamo oggi?** *kwan·tee ne ab·byah·mo oj·jee* what's the date today?

oggigiorno *oj·jee·johr·noh adv* nowadays

ogni *ohn·yee adj* every; each; **ogni due giorni** *ohn·yee doo·e johr·nee* every other day; **ogni sei giorni** *ohn·yee se·ee johr·nee* every 6th day

ognuno *o·nyoo·noh pron* everyone

Olanda *o·lan·da f* Holland

olandese *o·lan·day·se adj* Dutch □ *m* **l'olandese** *o·lan·day·se* Dutch

oleodotto *o·le·o·doht·toh m* pipeline

olio *o·lyoh m* oil; **l'olio solare** *o·lyoh so·lah·re* suntan oil; **l'olio di ricino** *o·lyoh dee ree·chee·noh* castor oil; **l'olio d'oliva** *o·lyoh do·lee·va* olive oil

oliva *o·lee·va f* olive

olmo *ohl·moh m* elm

oltre *ohl·tre prep* beyond; **oltre a lui** *ohl·tre a loo·e* besides him

oltremare *ol·tre·mah·re adv* overseas; **d'oltremare** *dol·tre·mah·re* overseas *(market)*

ombra *ohm·bra f* shadow; shade

ombrello *om·brel·loh m* umbrella

ombrellone *om·brel·loh·ne m* sunshade *(over table)*

ombretto *om·brayt·toh m* eyeshadow

omettere* *o·mayt·te·re vt* leave out *(omit)*; miss out

omicidio *o·mee·chee·dee·oh m* murder

omogeneizzato(a) *o·mo·je·ne·eedz·dzah·to(a) adj* homogenized

oncia *ohn·cha f* ounce

onda *ohn·da f* wave; **le onde medie** *ohn·day me·dee·ay* medium wave; **le onde corte** *ohn·day kohr·tay* short wave; **le onde lunghe** *ohn·day loon·ge* long wave

ondulato(a) *on·doo·lah·to(a) adj* wavy

onesto(a) *o·ne·sto(a) adj* decent *(respectable)*; honest

onorario *o·no·rah·ryoh m* fee

OPEC *oh·pek f* OPEC

opera *o·pe·ra f* work *(art, literature)*; opera; **l'opera d'arte** *o·pe·ra dar·te* work of art

operaio(a) *o·pe·ra·yo(a) adj* working-class □ *m* l'operaio *o·pe·ra·yoh* workman

operazione *o·pe·ra·tsyoh·ne f* operation

opinione *o·pee·nyoh·ne f* opinion

opuscolo *o·poo·sko·loh m* brochure

opzione *op·tsyoh·ne f* option

ora *oh·ra f* hour □ *adv* now; ogni ora *ohn·yee ora f* hourly; è arrivato proprio ora *e ar·ree·vah·to pro·pree·o oh·ra* he arrived just now; l'ora di punta *oh·ra dee poon·ta* rush hour; le ore di punta *oh·re dee poon·ta* peak hours; le ore d'ufficio *oh·re doof·fee·choh* office hours; che ora è? *ke oh·ra e* what's the time?; 100 chilometri all'ora *100 kee·lo·me·tree al·loh·ra* 100 km per hour; l'ora di pranzo *oh·ra dee pran·dzoh* lunch hour; le ore di lavoro *oh·re dee la·voh·roh* working hours; le ore straordinarie *oh·re stra·or·dee·nah·ree·e* overtime

orario *o·rah·ryoh m* timetable; schedule; in orario *een o·rah·ryoh* punctual; on schedule; l'orario delle partenze *o·rah·ryoh del·le par·ten·tse* departure timetable

orchestra *or·ke·stra f* orchestra

ordinare *or·dee·nah·ray vt* order (*goods, meal*)

ordinario(a) *or·dee·nah·ryo(a) adj* ordinary

ordinato(a) *or·dee·nah·toh(a) adj* neat; tidy

ordinazione *ohr·dee·na·tsyoh·ne f* order (*for goods*)

ordine *ohr·dee·ne m* command; order; l'ordine pubblico *ohr·dee·ne poob·blee·ko* law and order; l'ordine successivo *ohr·dee·ne soo·ches·see·vo* repeat order; l'ordine del giorno *ohr·dee·ne del jor·noh* agenda; l'ordine bancario *ohr·dee·ne ban·kah·ryo* banker's order; di prim'ordine *dee pree·mohr·dee·ne* high-class; l'ordine di pagamento automatico *ohr·dee·ne dee pa·ga·mayn·toh ow·to·ma·tee·ko* standing order

orecchino *o·rek·kee·noh m* earring

orecchio *o·rayk·kyoh m* ear; il mal d'orecchi *mal do·rayk·kee* earache; avere* mal d'orecchi *a·vay·re mal do·rayk·kee* to have earache

orecchioni *o·rek·kyoh·nee mpl* mumps

orfano(a) *or·fa·no(a) m/f* orphan

organigramma *or·ga·neez·gram·ma m* flow chart

organizzare *or·ga·needz·dzah·ray vt* organize

organizzazione *or·ga·needz·dza·tsyoh·ne f* organization

organo *or·ga·noh m* organ (*instrument*)

orgoglio *or·gohl·yoh m* pride

orgoglioso(a) *or·goh·lyoh·so(a) adj* proud

orientale *o·ree·en·tah·le adj* oriental; eastern

orientarsi *o·ree·en·tar·see vr* take one's bearings

Oriente *o·ree·en·te* the East

originale *o·ree·jee·nah·le adj* original □ *m* l'originale *o·ree·jee·nah·le* original

originariamente *o·ree·jee·nah·rya·mayn·te adv* originally (*at first*)

origine *o·ree·jee·ne f* origin

orizzontale *o·reedz·dzon·tah·le adj* level; horizontal

orizzonte *o·reedz·dzohn·te m* horizon

orlo *ohr·loh m* hem; verge

ormeggiare *or·mej·jah·ray vt* moor

ornamento *or·na·mayn·toh m* ornament

ornare *or·nah·ray vt* decorate

oro *o·roh m* gold; in oro massiccio *een o·roh mas·seech·cho* in solid gold; d'oro *do·roh* gold; placcato d'oro *plak·kah·toh do·roh* gold-plated

orologio *o·ro·lo·joh m* watch; clock; l'orologio a pendolo *o·ro·lo·joh a pen·do·loh* grandfather clock

orribile *or·ree·bee·le adj* horrible

orso *ohr·soh m* bear

ortaggi *or·taj·jee mpl* vegetables

osare *o·zah·ray vt/i dare*

oscillare *o·sheel·lah·ray vi* sway (*building, bridge*)

oscuro(a) *o·skoo·ro(a) adj* dim; obscure

ospedale *o·spe·dah·le m* hospital; l'ospedale psichiatrico *o·spe·dah·le psee·kee·a·tree·koh* mental hospital

ospitalità *o·spee·ta·lee·ta f* hospitality

ospite *o·spee·te m/f* guest; host; hostess; l'ospite pagante *o·spee·tay pa·gan·te* paying guest

osservazione *os·sayr·va·tsyoh·nay f* remark

ossessione *os·ses·syoh·ne f* obsession

ossigeno *os·see·je·noh m* oxygen

osso *os·soh m* bone

ostacolare *o·sta·ko·lah·ray vt* obstruct; hinder

ostacolo *o·sta·ko·loh m* obstacle

ostaggio *o·staj·joh m* hostage; prendere* qualcuno come ostaggio *pren·de·re kwal·koo·no kohm·e o·staj·joh* to take someone hostage

ostello *o·stel·loh m* hostel; l'ostello della gioventù *o·stel·loh del·la jo·ven·too* youth hostel

ostrica *o·stree·ka f* oyster

ostruzione *o·stroo·tsyoh·ne f* blockage

ottanta *ot·tan·ta num* eighty; gli anni ottanta *an·nee ot·tan·ta* eighties (*decade*)

ottavo(a) *ot·tah·vo(a) adj* eighth

ottenere* *ot·te·nay·re vt* obtain; get; win (*contract*); ottenere* la linea *ot·te·nay·re la lee·nay·a* to get through (*on phone*)

ottico *ot·tee·koh m* optician

ottimista *ot·tee·mee·sta adj* optimistic

otto *ot·to num* eight

ottobre *ot·toh·bre m* October

ottone *ot·toh·ne m* brass

otturatore *ot·too·ra·toh·re m* shutter (*in camera*)

otturazione *ot·too·ra·tsyoh·ne f* filling (*in tooth*)

ovale *o·vah·le adj* oval

ovatta *o·vat·ta f* cotton wool

overdrive *oh·ver·draiv m* overdrive

ovest *o·vest m* west; all'ovest *al·lo·vest* west

ovviamente *ov·vya·mayn·te adv* obviously

ovvio(a) *ov·vyo(a) adj* obvious

ozio *o·tsyoh m* leisure

P

pacchetto *pak·kayt·toh m* pack; packet

pacco *pak·koh m* package; parcel

pace *pah·che f* peace

pachistano(a) *pa·kee·stah·no(a) adj* Pakistani

padella *pa·del·la f* skillet; fry(ing) pan

padre *pah·dre m* father

padrino *pa·dree·noh m* godfather

padrona *pa·droh·na f* landlady

padrone *pa·droh·ne m* landlord

paesaggio *pa·e·zaj·joh m* scenery; countryside

paese *pa·ay·zay m* country; land

Paesi Bassi *pa·ay·zee bas·see mpl* Low Countries

paesino *pa·e·zee·noh m* village

paga *pah·ga f* pay

pagabile *pa·gah·bee·le adj* payable

pagaia *pa·ga·ya f* paddle (*oar*)

pagamento *pa·ga·mayn·toh m* payment; pagamento alla consegna *pa·ga·mayn·toh al·la kon·sayn·ya* cash on delivery; come pagamento parziale *koh·me pa·ga·mayn·toh par·tsyah·le* as a trade-in

pagare *pa·gah·ray vt* pay; pay for; pagare il conto *pa·gah·ray eel kohn·toh* to check out; fare* pagare qualcosa *fah·ray pa·gah·ray kwal·ko·sa* to make a charge for something; da pagarsi *da pa·gar·see* due (*owing*)

pagato(a) *pa·gah·to(a) adj* paid; mal pagato(a) *mal pa·gah·to(a)* underpaid; non pagato(a) *nohn pa·gah·to(a)* unpaid (*debt*)

paggio *paj·joh m* pageboy

pagina *pah·jee·na f* page

paglia *pal·ya f* straw

pagliaccio *pal·yach·choh m* clown

pagnotta *pan·yot·ta f* round loaf

paio *pa·yoh m* —a pair; paio di scarpe *pa·yoh dee skar·pe* pair of shoes; un paio di *oon pa·yoh dee* a couple of (*a few*)

Pakistan *pa·kee·stan m* Pakistan

pala *pah·la f* shovel

palazzo *pa·lats·tsoh m* mansion; palace; il palazzo di uffici *pa·lats·tsoh dee oof·fee·chee* office-block

palco *pal·koh m* platform

palcoscenico *pal·ko·she·nee·koh m* stage

Palestina *pa·le·stee·na f* Palestine

palestinese *pa·le·stee·nay·se adj* Palestinian

palestra *pa·le·stra f* gym(nasium)

paletta *pa·layt·ta f* dustpan

palla *pal·la f* ball; la palla da golf *pal·la da golf* golf ball; la palla di neve *pal·la de nay·ve* snowball

pallacanestro *pal·la·ka·ne·stroh f* basketball

pallavolo *pal·la·voh·loh f* volleyball

pallido(a) *pal·lee·do(a) adj* pale

pallone *pal·loh·ne m* balloon; football (*ball*)

pallottola *pal·lot·to·la f* bullet

palma *pal·ma f* palm-tree

palmo *pal·moh m* palm (*of hand*)

palo *pah·loh m* pole (*wooden*); post; il palo da tenda *pah·loh da ten·da* tent pole; il palo indicatore *pah·loh een·dee·ka·toh·re* signpost

palpebra *pal·pe·bra f* eyelid

palude *pa·loo·de f* swamp; bog

panca *pan·ka f* bench

pancetta *pan·chayt·ta f* bacon

panciotto *pan·chot·toh m* waistcoat

pane *pah·ne m* bread; loaf (of bread); il pane integrale *pah·ne een·te·grah·le* wholemeal bread; il pan di Spagna *pan dee span·ya* sponge (*cake*); il pane di segale *pah·ne dee say·ga·le* rye bread; il pane tostato *pah·ne to·stah·to* toast

panico *pa·nee·koh m* panic; preso(a) dal panico *pray·so(a) dal pa·nee·koh* in a panic

paniere *pa·nye·re m* basket; hamper

panificio *pah·nee·fee·choh m* bakery

panino *pa·nee·noh m* roll (*bread*); il

panino imbottito *pa·nee·noh eem·bot·tee·to* sandwich; un panino al prosciutto *oon pa·nee·noh al pro·shoot·toh* a ham sandwich

panna *pan·na f* cream; la panna montata *pan·na mon·tah·ta* whipped cream; la panna agra *pan·na a·gra* sour(ed) cream

panno *pan·noh m* cloth (*cleaning*)

pannocchia *pan·nok·kya f* corn-on-the-cob

pannolino *pan·no·lee·noh m* nappy; diaper

pantaloni *pan·ta·loh·nee mpl* pants; trousers; pair of trousers; i pantaloni da sci *pan·ta·loh·nee da shee* ski pants

pantofola *pan·to·fo·la f* slipper

papa *pah·pa m* pope

papà *pa·pa m* dad(dy)

paprica *pa·pree·ka f* paprika

parabrezza *pa·ra·brayts·tsa m* — windscreen; windshield

paracadute *pa·ra·ka·doo·te m* parachute

parafango *pa·ra·fan·goh m* mudguard

paraffina *pa·raf·fee·na f* paraffin

paragrafo *pa·ra·gra·foh m* paragraph

paralizzato(a) *pa·ra·leedz·dzah·to(a) adj* paralysed

parallelo(a) *pa·ral·le·lo(a) adj* parallel

paralume *pa·ra·loo·me m* lampshade

parasole *pa·ra·soh·le m* — parasol

paraspruzzi *pa·ra·sproots·tsee m* — mud-flap

paraurti *pa·ra·oor·tee m* — bumper (*on car*); fender

paravento *pa·ra·ven·toh m* screen (*partition*)

parcheggiare *par·kej·jah·ray vt/i* park; posso parcheggiare qui? *pos·so par·kej·jah·ray kwee* can I park here?

parcheggio *par·kayj·joh m* parking-lot; car-park

parchimetro *par·kee·me·troh m* parking meter

parco *par·koh m* park; il parco macchine *par·koh mak·kee·ne* fleet of vehicles

parecchi(ie) *pa·rayk·kee(·kye) adj* several; parecchi di noi *pa·rayk·kee dee noy* several of us

pareggiare *pa·rej·jah·ray vt* balance (*accounts*); pareggiare i costi *pa·rej·jah·ray ee ko·stee* to break even

parente *pa·ren·te m/f* relation; relative; il parente stretto *pa·ren·te strayt·toh* next of kin

parere* *pa·ray·ray vi* seem, appear □ *m* il parere *pa·ray·ray* view (*opinion*); pare che... *pa·re ke* it appears that...; a mio parere *a mee·o pa·ray·ray* in my opinion

parete *pa·ray·te f* wall

pari *pah·ree f* par (*business*); un numero pari *oon noo·me·roh pah·ree* an even number; sopra la pari *soh·pra la pah·ree* above par

Parigi *pa·ree·jee f* Paris

parlamento *par·la·mayn·toh m* parliament

parlare *par·lah·ray vt/i* talk; speak; parlare di qualcosa *par·lah·ray dee kwal·ko·sa* to talk about something; parlare a qualcuno di qualcosa *par·lah·ray a kwal·koo·no dee kwal·ko·sa* to talk to someone about something; parla inglese? *par·la een·glay·se* do you speak English?

parmigiano par·mee·jah·noh m Parmesan

parola pa·ro·la f word; **parola per parola** pa·ro·la payr pa·ro·la word for word

parrucca par·rook·ka f wig

parrucchiere par·rook·kye·re m hairdresser

parte par·te f share; part; **la parte anteriore** par·te an·te·ryoh·re front (foremost part); **l'ho visto dall'altra parte della strada** lo vee·sto dal·lal·tra par·te del·la strah·da I saw him (from) across the road; **in parte** een par·te partly; **a parte** a par·te apart (separately)

partecipare par·te·chee·pah·ray vi participate

partecipazione par·te·chee·pa·tsyoh·ne f participation

partenza par·ten·tsa f departure

particolare par·tee·ko·lah·re adj particular □ m il particolare par·tee·ko·lah·re detail; **in particolare** een par·tee·ko·lah·re in particular

particolarmente par·tee·ko·lar·mayn·te adv particularly

partire par·tee·ray vi go; leave; **i treni partono ogni ora** ee tre·nee par·to·no ohn·yee oh·ra the trains run every hour; **è partito per una settimana** e par·tee·to payr oo·na set·tee·mah·na he's away for a week

partita par·tee·ta f match (sport); round (in competition); **una partita di tennis** oo·na par·tee·ta dee ten·nees a game of tennis

partito par·tee·toh m party (political)

Pasqua pa·skwa f Easter

passaggio pas·saj·joh m passage; gangway; **il passaggio a livello** pas·saj·joh a lee·vel·loh level crossing; grade crossing; **dare* un passaggio in città a qualcuno** dah·ray oon pas·saj·joh een cheet·ta a kwal·koo·noh to give someone a ride into town; **il passaggio pedonale** pas·saj·joh pe·do·nah·le pedestrian crossing

passaporto pas·sa·por·toh m passport

passare pas·sah·ray vt pass (place); pass (hand on: object); **la strada passa davanti alla casa** la strah·da pas·sa da·van·tee al·la kah·sa the road runs past the house; **è passato un aereo** e pas·sah·to oon a·e·re·oh a plane flew by; **mi passi il Signor X** mee pas·see eel seen·yohr X put me through to Mr X (on phone); **passare correndo** pas·sah·ray kor·ren·do to run past; **mi ha passato di corsa** mee a pas·sah·to dee kohr·sa he ran past me; **mi passa lo zucchero per favore** mee pas·sa lo tsook·ke·roh payr fa·voh·re please pass the sugar

passatempo pas·sa·tem·poh m interest; hobby

passato(a) pas·sah·to(a) adj past; off (meat) □ m il passato pas·sah·toh past

passeggero(a) pas·sej·je·ro(a) m/f passenger

passeggiare pas·sej·jah·ray vi walk (for pleasure, exercise)

passeggiata pas·sej·jah·ta f walk; **fare* una passeggiata** fah·ray oo·na pas·sej·jah·ta to go for a walk

passeggiatina pas·sej·ja·tee·na f stroll

passeggino pas·sej·jee·noh m pushchair; stroller

passe-partout pas·par·too m — master key

passera pas·se·ra f plaice

passerella pas·se·rel·la f gangway (bridge)

passero pas·se·roh m sparrow

passione pas·syoh·ne f passion

passivo pas·see·voh m liabilities (on balance sheet)

passo pas·soh m pace; step; pass (in mountains); **fare* quattro passi** fah·ray kwat·tro pas·see to go for a stroll; **tenere* il passo di** te·nay·re eel pas·soh dee to keep pace with

pasta pa·sta f pastry; pasta; dough; **la pasta di mandorla** pa·sta dee man·dor·la almond paste

pastella pa·stel·la f batter (for frying)

pastello pa·stel·loh m crayon

pasticceria pa·steech·che·ree·a f cake shop

pasticciere pa·steech·che·ray m confectioner

pasticcino pa·steech·chee·noh m bun

pasticcio pa·steech·choh m muddle; pie (meat)

pastiglia pa·steel·ya f tablet (medicine); pastille; **le pastiglie per la tosse** pa·steel·yay payr la tohs·say cough drops

pastinaca pa·stee·nah·ka f parsnip

pasto pa·stoh m meal

pastore pa·stoh·ray m minister (of religion)

pastorizzato(a) pa·sto·reedz·dzah·to(a) adj pasteurized

patata pa·tah·ta f potato; **la patata dolce** pa·tah·ta dohl·che sweet potato

patatine pa·ta·tee·nay fpl crisps; **le patatine fritte** pa·ta·tee·nay freet·tay chips; french fried potatoes, french fries

pâté pa·tay m pâté

patente pa·ten·te f licence, licence; **la patente di guida** pa·ten·te dee gwee·da licence, license (for driving)

patio pa·tyoh m patio

patrigno pa·treen·yoh m stepfather

patrimonio pa·tree·mo·nyoh m property (estate)

patron pa·tron m pattern (dressmaking)

patta pat·ta f flap

pattinare pat·tee·nah·ray vi skate

pattino pat·tee·noh m skate; **il pattino a pedali** pat·tee·noh a pe·dah·lee pedalo; **i pattini a rotelle** pat·tee·nee a ro·tel·le roller skates

pattumiera pat·too·mye·ra f trash can; garbage can

paura pa·oo·ra f fear; **avere* paura di qualcosa** a·vay·re pa·oo·ra dee kwal·ko·sa to be afraid of something

pausa pow·za f pause; break; **la pausa per il caffè** pow·za payr eel kaf·fe coffee break; **la pausa per il tè** pow·za payr eel te tea-break; **fare* una pausa** fah·ray oo·na pow·za to pause

pavimento pa·vee·mayn·toh m floor

paziente pa·tsyen·te adj patient □ m/f il/la paziente pa·tsyen·te patient

pazienza pa·tsyen·tsa f patience

pazzo(a) pat·tsoh(a) adj mad (insane); crazy

peccato pek·kah·toh m sin; **che peccato!** ke pek·kah·toh what a shame!

pecora pe·ko·ra f sheep

pedaggio pe·daj·joh m toll (on road etc)

pedale pe·dah·le m pedal

pediatra pe·dee·a·tra m/f p(a)ediatrician

pedicure *pay·dee·koo·ray* m chiropodist

pedone *pe·doh·ne* m pedestrian

peggio *pej·jo* adv worse; **fare*** qualcosa di peggio *fah·ray kwal·ko·sa dee pej·jo* to do something worse; **l'ha fatto il peggio** *la fat·to eel pej·jo* he did it worst

peggiore *pej·joh·re* adj worse; **il peggiore libro** *eel pej·joh·re lee·broh* the worst book; **è peggiore (dell'altro)** *e pej·joh·re (del·lal·tro)* it's worse (than the other)

pelle *pel·le* f skin; hide (*leather*); **la pelle di montone** *pel·le dee mon·toh·ne* sheepskin; **la pelle scamosciata** *pel·le ska·mo·shah·ta* suede; **la pelle di cinghiale** *pel·le dee cheen·gyah·le* pigskin

pelliccia *pel·leech·cha* f fur coat; **la pelliccia di ermellino** *pel·leech·cha dee er·mel·lee·noh* ermine (*fur*)

pellicola *pel·lee·ko·la* f film (*for camera*)

pelo *pay·loh* m hair; fur

pena *pay·na* f sentence; sorrow; **darsi* pena di fare qualcosa** *dar·see pay·na dee fah·ray kwal·ko·sa* to go to the trouble of doing something

pendenza *pen·den·tsa* f slope

pendere *pen·de·re* vi hang; lean

pendio *pen·dee·oh* m hill; slope (*sloping ground*)

pendolare *pen·do·lah·ray* m commuter

pene *pe·ne* m penis

penetrare *pe·ne·trah·ray* vt penetrate

penicillina *pe·nee·cheel·lee·na* f penicillin

penna *payn·na* f pen; **la penna stilografica** *payn·na stee·lo·gra·fee·ka* fountain pen

pennarello *pen·na·rel·loh* m felt-tip pen

pennello *pen·nel·loh* m brush; **il pennello da barba** *pen·nel·loh da bar·ba* shaving brush

pensare *pen·sah·ray* vt/i think; **penso che...** *pen·so ke* I feel that...; **pensare a qualcosa** *pen·sah·ray a kwal·ko·sa* to think of something; **pensare a qualcuno** *pen·sah·ray a kwal·koo·no* to think about someone

pensiero *pen·sye·roh* m thought

pensionato(a) *pen·syoh·nah·to(a)* m/f pensioner; old-age-pensioner

pensione *pen·syoh·ne* f boarding house; pension; superannuation; guest-house; **andare* in pensione** *an·dah·ray een pen·syoh·ne* to retire; **la pensione completa** *pen·syoh·ne kom·ple·ta* full board; **la mezza pensione** *medz·dza pen·syoh·ne* half board

Pentecoste *pen·te·ko·ste* f Whitsun; Whitsunday

pentola *payn·to·la* f pot; saucepan; **la pentola a pressione** *payn·to·la a pres·syoh·ne* pressure cooker

pepaiola *pe·pa·yo·la* f pepper pot

pepato(a) *pe·pah·to(a)* adj peppery

pepe *pay·pe* m pepper

peperone *pe·pe·roh·ne* m pepper (*capsicum*); **il peperone verde/rosso** *pe·pe·roh·ne vayr·de/rohs·so* green/red pepper

per *payr* prep for; per; **per fare qualcosa** *payr fah·ray kwal·ko·sa* in order to do something; **per sempre** *payr sem·pre* forever; **fa caldo per marzo** *fa kal·do payr mar·tsoh* it's warm for March; **vendere qualcosa per $5000** *vayn·de·re kwal·ko·sa payr $5000* to sell something for $5000; **partire per Londra** *par·tee·re payr lohn·dra* to leave for London; **saremo lì per le 4** *sa·ray·mo lee payr le 4* we'll be there by 4 o'clock; **3 metri per 3** *3 me·tree payr 3* 3 metres square; **per via aerea** *payr vee·a a·e·re·a* by air; **per me** *payr may* for my sake; **per persona** *payr per·soh·na* per person; **20 per cento** *20 payr chen·to* 20 per cent

pera *pay·ra* f pear

percallina a quadretti *payr·kal·lee·na a kwa·dret·tee* f gingham

percentuale *payr·chen·too·ah·le* f percentage

perché *payr·kay* adv why □ conj because; **l'ha fatto perché io andassi** *la fat·to payr·kay ee·oh an·das·see* he did it so that I would go

percorrere* *per·kohr·re·re* vt travel (*a distance*)

percorso *payr·kohr·soh* m ride (*in vehicle*); **non è che un breve percorso** *nohn e ke oon bre·ve payr·kohr·soh* it's only a short ride

perdere* *per·de·re* vt lose; miss (*train*); **perdere* tempo** *per·de·re tem·poh* to waste one's time

perdita *per·dee·ta* f leak; loss

perdonare *per·do·nah·ray* vt forgive

perfetto(a) *per·fet·to(a)* adj perfect

perforare *payr·fo·rah·ray* vt drill (*hole*)

pericolo *pe·ree·ko·loh* m danger; **una nave in pericolo** *oo·na nah·ve een pe·ree·ko·loh* a ship in distress

pericoloso(a) *pe·ree·ko·loh·so(a)* adj dangerous

periferia *pe·ree·fe·ree·a* f outskirts; the suburbs

periodo *pe·ree·o·doh* m period (*of time*); **durante il suo periodo di carica** *doo·ran·te eel soo·o pe·ree·o·doh dee kah·ree·ka* during his term of office

perito *pe·ree·toh* m expert; surveyor

perizia *pe·ree·tsya* f survey (*of building*)

perla *per·la* f pearl; bead

permanente *per·ma·nen·te* adj permanent □ f la permanente *per·ma·nen·te* perm

permanentemente *per·ma·nen·te·mayn·te* adv permanently

permesso *per·mays·soh* m permission; permit; **il permesso di soggiorno** *per·mays·soh dee soj·johr·noh* residence permit; **il permesso di uscita** *per·mays·soh dee oo·shee·ta* exit permit

permettere* *per·mayt·te·re* vt permit; **permettere* a qualcuno di partire** *per·mayt·te·re a kwal·koo·no dee par·tee·re* to allow someone to go; **permettere* a qualcuno di fare qualcosa** *per·mayt·te·re a kwal·koo·no dee fah·ray kwal·ko·sa* to permit someone to do something; **non me lo posso permettere** *nohn may lo pos·so per·mayt·te·re* I can't afford it

pernice *per·nee·che* f partridge

pernottare *per·not·tah·ray* vi stay the night

perquisire *payr·kwee·zee·re* vt search

persiana *per·syah·na* f shutter

persiano(a) *per·syah·no(a)* adj Persian

persona *per·soh·na* f person; **di persona** *dee per·soh·na* in person

personale *per·so·nah·le* adj personal □ m **il personale** *per·so·nah·le* staff; personnel

personalità *per·so·na·lee·ta* f personality

personalmente *per·so·nal·mayn·te* adv personally

persuadere* *per·swa·day·re* vt persuade; **persuadere* qualcuno a fare qualcosa** *per·swa·day·re kwal·koo·no a fah·ray kwal·ko·sa* to persuade someone to do something

pertinente a *payr·tee·nen·te a* adj relevant to

pertosse *payr·tohs·se* f whooping cough

p. es. *payr e·zaym·pyoh* abbrev e.g.

pesante *pe·san·te* adj heavy; rich (food); **troppo pesante** *trop·po pe·san·te* overweight (person)

pesare *pe·sah·ray* vt/i weigh

pesca *pay·ska* f angling; fishing; peach; **andare* a pesca** *an·dah·ray a pay·ska* to go fishing

pescatore *pe·ska·toh·re* m angler

pesce *pe·she* m fish; **il pesce rosso** *pay·she rohs·soh* goldfish

pescecane *pe·she·kah·ne* m shark

pescivendolo *pe·shee·vayn·do·loh* m fishmonger

peso *pay·soh* m weight; **il peso netto** *pay·soh nayt·toh* net weight

pessimista *pes·see·mee·sta* adj pessimistic

pessimo(a) *pes·see·moh(a)* adj awful

petardo *pe·tahr·doh* m cracker (paper toy)

petroliera *pe·tro·lye·ra* f oil tanker

petrolio *pe·tro·lyoh* m oil (petroleum)

pettinare *pet·tee·nah·ray* vt comb

pettine *pet·tee·nay* m comb; scallop

petto *pet·toh* m breast (chest, of poultry); chest (of body)

pezza *pets·tsa* f patch (of material)

pezzettino *pets·tset·tee·noh* m scrap (bit)

pezzo *pets·tsoh* m piece; cut (of meat); component (for car etc); **il pezzo di ricambio** *pets·tsoh dee ree·kam·byoh* spare (part); **un pezzo di** *oon pets·tsoh dee* a bit of

pezzuola *pets·tswo·la* f cloth; rag

piacere* *pya·chay·re* vi please □ m il piacere *pya·chay·re* enjoyment; pleasure; **piacere* a** *pya·chay·re a* to like; **piacere* molto a qualcuno fare qualcosa** *pya·chay·re mohl·to a kwal·koo·no fah·ray kwal·ko·sa* to love doing something; **mi piacerebbe andare** *mee pyah·che·reb·be an·dah·ray* I'd love to go; I'd like to go

piacevole *pya·chay·vo·le* adj pleasant

pialla *pyal·la* f plane (tool)

pianerottolo *pya·ne·rot·to·loh* m landing (on stairs)

pianeta *pya·nay·ta* m planet

piangere* *pyan·je·ray* vi cry

pianificazione *pya·nee·fee·ka·tsyoh·ne* f planning (economic)

piano(a) *pyah·no(a)* adj level (surface) □ adv quietly (speak) □ m il piano *pyah·noh* storey; piano; **a piú piani** *a pyoo pyah·nee* multi-storey; **il primo piano** *pree·mo pyah·noh* 1st floor (Brit), 2nd floor (US)

pianoforte a coda *pya·no·for·tay a koh·da* m grand piano

pianta *pyan·ta* f sole (of foot); map (of town); plan; plant

piantare *pyan·tah·ray* vt plant; pitch (tent)

pianterreno *pyan·ter·ray·noh* m ground floor

pianura *pya·noo·ra* f plain

piastra riscaldante *pya·stra ree·skal·dan·te* f hotplate

piastrella *pya·strel·la* f tile

piattaforma *pyat·ta·fohr·ma* f platform; **la piattaforma petrolifera** *pyat·ta·fohr·ma pe·tro·lye·ra* oil-rig

piattino *pyat·tee·noh* m saucer

piatto(a) *pyat·to(a)* adj flat □ m il piatto *pyat·toh* dish; course (of meal); plate; **il primo piatto** *pree·mo pyat·toh* entrée

piazza *pyats·tsa* f square (in town); **la piazza del mercato** *pyats·tsa del mayr·kah·toh* market-place

piazzola *pyats·tso·la* f lay-by

piccante *peek·kan·te* adj spicy; hot

picche *peek·ke* fpl spades (cards)

picchetto *peek·kayt·toh* m peg; picket; tent peg

picchiare *peek·kyah·ray* vt hit □ vi knock (engine); pink

piccione *peech·choh·ne* m pigeon

piccolo(a) *peek·ko·lo(a)* adj little; small

piccone *peek·koh·ne* m pick; pickaxe

picnic *peek·neek* m picnic; **andare* a fare un picnic** *an·dah·ray a fah·ray oon peek·neek* to go on a picnic

pidocchio *pee·dok·kyoh* m louse

piede *pye·de* m foot (of person, measurement); bottom (of page, list)

piega *pye·ga* f crease; fare* fare la **messa in piega** *far·se fah·ray la mays·sa een pye·ga* to have one's hair set

piegare *pye·gah·ray* vt fold; bend

pieghettato(a) *pye·get·tah·to(a)* adj pleated

pieno(a) *pye·no(a)* adj full; **il pieno, per favore!** *eel pye·noh payr fa·voh·re* fill it up! (car); **pieno(a) di** *pye·no(a) dee* full of; **a tempo pieno** *a tem·po pye·noh* full-time

pietra *pye·tra* f stone; **la pietra focaia** *pye·tra fo·ka·ya* flint (in lighter)

piffero *peef·fe·roh* m pipe (musical)

pigiama *pee·jah·ma* m pyjamas; pajamas

pigro(a) *pee·gro(a)* adj lazy

pila *pee·la* f battery (for radio etc)

pilastro *pee·la·stroh* m pillar

pillola *peel·lo·la* f pill; **prendere* la pillola** *pren·de·re la peel·lo·la* to be on the pill

pilota *pee·lo·ta* m pilot

pince *pañs* f dart (on clothes)

ping-pong *peeng·pong* m ping-pong

pinne *peen·ne* fpl flippers (for swimming)

pino *pee·noh* m pine

pinze *peen·tse* fpl pliers

pinzette *peen·tsayt·te* fpl tweezers

pioggia *pyoj·jah* f rain

piombo *pyohm·boh* m lead

pioppo *pyop·poh* m poplar

piovere* *pyo·ve·re* vi rain; **piove** *pyo·ve* it's raining

pioviggine *pyo·veej·jee·ne* f drizzle

piovoso(a) *pyo·voh·so(a)* adj rainy; wet (weather, day)

pipa *pee·pa* f pipe (for smoking)

pipistrello *pee·pee·strel·loh* m bat (animal)

piramide *pee·ra·mee·de* f pyramid

Pirenei *pee·re·ne·ee* mpl Pyrenees

piroscafo *pee·ro·ska·foh* m steamer (ship)

piscina *pee·shee·na* f swimming pool; **la piscina per bambini** *pee·shee·na payr bam·bee·nee* paddling pool

piselli *pee·sel·lee* mpl peas

pista *pee·sta* f track (sports); race track; **la pista d'atterraggio** *pee·sta* *dat·ter·raj·joh* runway; **la pista di pattinaggio** *pee·sta dee pat·tee·naj·joh* skating rink; **la pista per principianti** *pee·sta payr preen·chee·pee·an·tee* nursery slope; **la pista da ballo** *pee·sta da bal·loh* dance floor; **la pista da sci** *pee·sta da shee* ski run

pistone *pee·stoh·ne* m piston

pittore *peet·toh·re* m painter

più *pyoo* adv more; most; plus □ *mpl* i più *ee pyoo* most people; **pesa più di un chilo** *pay·sa pyoo dee oon kee·loh* it weighs over a kilo; **più le spese postali** *pyoo le spay·se po·stah·lee* postage extra; **in più** *een pyoo* extra; **più di 10** *pyoo dee 10* more than 10; **il/la più bello(a)** *eel/la pyoo bel·loh(a)* the most beautiful; **più gente** *pyoo jen·tay* more people; **più pericoloso che** *pyoo pe·ree·ko·loh·soh kay* more dangerous than; **più o meno** *pyoo o may·noh* more or less; **sono più ricchi di noi** *soh·no pyoo reek·kee dee noy* they are better off than us (*richer*); **il più grande numero di macchine** *eel pyoo gran·day noo·me·roh dee mak·kee·nay* the most cars

piuma *pyoo·ma* f feather; down (*fluff*)

piumino *pyoo·mee·no* m duvet; eiderdown

piuttosto *pyoot·to·sto* adv quite; fairly; rather

pizza *peets·tsa* f pizza

pizzicare *peets·tsee·kah·ray* vt pinch

pizzico *peets·tsee·koh* m pinch; sting

pizzo *peets·tsoh* m lace

placcare *plak·kah·ray* vt tackle (*in sports*)

placcato(a) di *plak·kah·to(a) dee* adj plated (*with metals*)

plaid *plahd* m plaid

planetario *pla·ne·tah·ryoh* m planetarium

plastica *pla·stee·ka* f plastic; **in plastica** *een pla·stee·ka* plastic

platano *pla·ta·noh* m plane (*tree*)

platea *pla·te·a* f stalls (*in theatre*)

platino *pla·tee·noh* m platinum

plexiglas *plek·see·glas* m plexiglas; Perspex

plico *plee·koh* m parcel; bundle; in plico a parte *een plee·koh a par·te* under separate cover

pneumatico *pne·oo·ma·tee·koh* m tyre; tire; lo pneumatico rimodellato *pne·oo·ma·tee·koh ree·mo·del·lah·toh* retread

po' *see* **poco(a)**

pochi(e) *po·kee(·ke)* adj few; pochi libri *po·kee lee·bree* a few books

poco(a) *po·ko(a)* adj little □ adv poco *po·ko* little □ pron little, not much; un po' *oon po* a little; un po' di X *oon po de X* a small amount of X; poco sopra il gomito *po·ko soh·pra eel go·mee·toh* just above the elbow; fra poco *fra po·ko* shortly (*soon*)

poesia *po·e·zee·a* f poem; poetry

poggiatesta *poj·ja·te·sta* m headrest

poi *poy* adv then

poiché *poy·kay* conj because; poiché è malato *poy·kay e ma·lah·to* since he's ill

poker *po·ker* m poker (*card game*)

polacco(a) *po·lak·ko(a)* adj Polish □ m/f il/la polacco(a) *po·lak·ko(a)* Pole □ m il polacco *po·lak·koh* Polish

polaroid *po·la·royd* adj Polaroid

poliestere *po·lee·e·ste·re* m polyester

polietilene *po·lee·e·tee·le·ne* m polythene

polio *po·lyoh* f polio

politica *po·lee·tee·ka* f policy; politics; la politica estera *po·lee·tee·ka e·ste·ra* foreign policy

politico(a) *po·lee·tee·ko(a)* adj political; l'uomo politico *wo·moh po·lee·tee·ko* politician

polizia *po·lee·tsee·a* f police

poliziotto *po·lee·tsyot·toh* m policeman

polizza *po·leets·tsa* f policy; la polizza di assicurazione *po·leets·tsa dee as·see·koo·ra·tsyoh·ne* insurance policy

pollame *pol·lah·me* m poultry

pollice *pol·lee·che* m thumb

pollo *pohl·loh* m chicken

polmone *pol·moh·ne* m lung

polmonite *pol·mo·nee·te* f pneumonia

polo *po·loh* m polo; terminal (*electricity*)

Polonia *po·lo·nya* f Poland

Polo Nord *po·loh nord* m North Pole

Polo Sud *po·loh sud* m South Pole

polsino *pol·see·noh* m cuff (*of shirt*)

polso *pohl·soh* m wrist

poltrona *pol·troh·na* f armchair

polvere *pohl·ve·re* f dust; powder

polveroso(a) *pol·ve·roh·so(a)* adj dusty

pomeriggio *po·me·reej·joh* m afternoon

pomo *poh·moh* m knob (*on door*)

pomodoro *po·mo·do·roh* m tomato

pompa *pohm·pa* f pump

pompare *pohm·pah·ray* vt pump

pompelmo *pom·pel·moh* m grapefruit

pompiere *pom·pye·re* m fireman

ponce *pon·che* m punch (*drink*)

ponte *pohn·te* m bridge; deck (*of ship*); il ponte a pedaggio *pohn·te a pe·daj·joh* toll bridge; fare* il ponte *fah·ray eel pohn·te* to take an extra day's holiday

pontile *pon·tee·le* m jetty

pony *poh·nee* m pony

pop *pop* adj pop (*music, art*)

popeline *po·pe·leen* f poplin

popolare *po·po·lah·ray* adj popular

popolazione *po·po·la·tsyoh·ne* f population

popolo *po·po·loh* m people

porcellana *por·chel·lah·na* f china; porcelain

porpora *por·po·ra* f purple

porre* *por·re* vt put

porro *por·roh* m leek

porta *por·ta* f door; goal; gate (*of building*)

portabagagli *por·ta·ba·gal·yee* m — luggage rack (*in train*); roof rack

portabottiglie *por·ta·bot·teel·yay* m — rack (*for wine*)

portacenere *por·ta·chay·ne·re* m — ashtray

portachiavi *por·ta·kyah·vee* m — key ring

portafogli *por·ta·fol·yee* m — wallet; pocketbook

portafoglio *por·ta·fol·yoh* m portfolio

portaombrelli *por·ta·om·brel·lee* m — umbrella stand

portare *por·tah·ray* vt carry; bring; wear (*clothes*); da portar via *da por·tar vee·a* take-away (*food*); portare qualcuno a teatro *por·tah·ray kwal·koo·no a te·ah·troh* to take someone out to the theatre; portare qualcuno alla stazione *por·tah·ray kwal·koo·no al·la sta·tsyoh·ne* to take someone to the station; porti questo alla posta *por·tee kway·sto al·la po·sta* take this to the post office; portare al limite

massimo *por·tah·ray al lee·mee·tay mas·see·moh* to maximize

portasigarette *por·ta·see·ga·rayt·tay m* cigarette case

portata *por·tah·ta f* range; capacity; **fuori portata** *fwo·ree por·tah·ta* out of reach

portatile *por·tah·tee·le adj* portable

portauovo *por·ta·wo·voh m* — egg cup

portavoce *por·ta·voh·che m* — spokesman

portella *por·tel·la f* hatch (*for serving*)

portellone posteriore *por·tel·loh·ne po·ste·ryoh·re m* tailgate (*of car*)

porticciolo *por·teech·cho·loh m* marina

portico *por·tee·koh m* porch

portiera *por·tye·ra f* door

portiere *por·tye·re m* porter (*doorkeeper*); janitor; **il portiere di notte** *por·tye·re dee not·tay* night porter

porto *por·toh m* port; harbo(u)r; **porto franco** *por·toh fran·koh* carriage free

Portogallo *por·to·gal·loh m* Portugal

portoghese *por·to·gay·se adj* Portuguese □ *m* **il portoghese** *por·to·gay·se* Portuguese

porzione *por·tsyoh·ne f* portion; helping

posare *po·sah·ray vt* put down; lay

posateria *po·sah·te·ree·a f* cutlery

positivo(a) *po·zee·tee·vo(a) adj* positive

posizione *po·zee·tsyoh·ne f* position

posporre *pos·pohr·re vt* postpone

possedere *pos·se·day·re vt* own (*possess*)

possibile *pos·see·bee·le adj* possible; **fare* tutto il possibile** *fah·ray toot·to eel pos·see·bee·le* to do all one possibly can

possibilità *pos·see·bee·lee·ta f* possibility; **entro le possibilità di** *ayn·tro le pos·see·bee·lee·ta dee* within the scope of; **egli ha delle buone possibilità di...** *ay·lyee a del·lay bwo·nay pos·see·bee·lee·ta dee* he has a good chance of...

posta *po·sta f* mail; stake (*in gambling*); odds (*in betting*); **per posta aerea** *payr po·sta a·e·re·a* by air mail; **la posta raccomandata** *po·sta rak·ko·man·dah·ta* registered mail; **fermo posta** *fayr·mo po·sta* poste restante; **per posta** *payr po·sta* by post

postagiro *po·sta·jee·roh m* giro (*post office*)

postale *po·stah·le adj* postal

postdatare *post·da·tah·ray vt* postdate

Poste *po·ste fpl* the Post Office

posteggio *po·stayj·joh m* car park; **il posteggio per tassi** *po·stayj·joh payr tas·see* taxi rank

posteriore *po·ste·ryoh·ray adj* rear; later (*date etc*)

postino *po·stee·noh m* mailman; postman

posto *poh·stoh m* place; position (*place, job*); seat; **a posto** *a poh·stoh* in place; **fuori posto** *fwo·ree poh·stoh* out of place (*object*); **il posto vacante** *poh·stoh va·kan·tay* vacancy (*job*)

potabile *po·tah·bee·lay adj* drinking; drinkable

potare *po·tah·ray vt* trim (*hedge*)

potente *po·ten·te adj* powerful

potenza *po·ten·tsa f* power (*of machine*)

potere* *po·tay·re vi* can □ *m* **il potere** *po·tay·re* power (*authority*); **lo potremmo fare** *loh po·trem·moh fah·ray* we could do it; **potrei avere...**

po·tre·ee a·vay·ray could I have...; **potere* fare qualcosa** *po·tay·re fah·ray kwal·ko·sa* to be able to do something; **non potere* fare qualcosa** *nohn po·tay·re fah·ray kwal·ko·sa* to be unable to do something; **posso entrare?** *pos·soh en·trah·ray* may I come in?; **potrà piovere** *po·tra pyo·ve·ray* it may rain; **potrebbe piovere** *po·treb·bay pyo·ve·ray* it might rain; **non posso farci nulla** *nohn pos·so far·chee nool·la* I can't help it; **il potere mondiale** *po·tay·re mon·dee·ah·le* world power

povero(a) *po·ve·ro(a) adj* poor

pozzanghera *pots·tsan·ge·ra f* puddle; pool

pozzo *pohts·tsoh m* well

Praga *prah·ga f* Prague

pranzo *pran·dzoh m* lunch

prassi *pras·see f* normal procedure

pratica *pra·tee·ka f* practical experience

pratico(a) *pra·tee·ko(a) adj* practical; handy (*convenient*); **poco pratico(a)** *po·ko pra·tee·ko(a)* inconvenient

prato rasato *prah·toh ra·sah·to m* lawn

precedente *pre·che·den·te adj* previous; earlier

precedenza *pre·che·den·tsa f* right of way (*on road*); **dare* la precedenza** *dah·ray la pre·che·den·tsa* to give way (*when driving*)

precipitarsi *pre·chee·pee·tar·see vr* rush

precisamente *pre·chee·za·mayn·te adv* exactly

precisione *pre·chee·zyoh·ne f* precision

preciso(a) *pre·chee·zo(a) adj* precise; exact; accurate

precotto(a) *pre·kot·to(a) adj* ready-cooked

predire* *pre·dee·re vt* predict

predizione *pre·dee·tsyoh·ne f* prediction

preferire *pre·fe·ree·re vt* prefer; **preferirei andare al cinema** *pre·fe·ree·ray an·dah·ray al chee·ne·ma* I'd rather go to the cinema

pregare *pre·gah·ray vt* pray

preghiera *pre·gye·ra f* prayer

pregiudizio *pre·joo·dee·tsyoh m* prejudice

prego *pre·go excl* don't mention it!; after you!

preliminare *pre·lee·mee·nah·re adj* preliminary

preludio *pre·loo·dee·oh m* overture

pré-maman *pray·ma·man m* maternity dress

premere *pre·me·re vt* push; press

premio *pre·myoh m* bonus (*on salary*); premium; prize; **il Gran Premio** *gran pre·myoh* Grand Prix

prendere* *pren·de·re vt* take; get (*fetch*); catch (*train, illness*); **andare* a prendere un amico** *an·dah·ray a pren·de·re oon a·mee·koh* to pick up a friend; **me lo ha preso** *me lo a pray·so* he took it from me; **andare* a prendere** *an·dah·ray a pren·de·re* to fetch; **prendere* freddo** *pren·de·re frayd·doh* to catch cold

prenotare *pre·no·tah·ray vt* book (*seat*)

prenotazione *pre·no·ta·tsyoh·ne f* reservation (*of seats, rooms etc*); **la prenotazione a gruppo** *pre·no·ta·tsyoh·ne a groop·poh* block booking

preoccupato(a) *pre·ok·koo·pah·to(a) adj* worried

preoccupazione *pre·ok·koo·pa·tsyoh· ne f* worry

prepagato(a) *pre·pa·gah·to(a)* adj prepaid

preparare *pre·pa·rah·ray vt* prepare; preparare il fuoco *pre·pa·rah·ray eel fwo·koh* to lay the fire

prepararsi *pray·pa·rahr·see vr* get ready; si prepara a partire *see pre· pah·ra a par·tee·re* he's preparing to leave

preparativi *pre·pa·ra·tee·vee mpl* preparations (*for trip*)

preparazione *pre·pa·ra·tsyoh·ne f* preparation

presa *pray·sa f* socket (*electrical*); outlet (*electric*); la presa di corrente *pray·sa dee kor·ren·te* power point

presbite *prez·bee·te adj* long-sighted

presbiteriano(a) *pre·zbee·te·ree·ah· no(a)* adj Presbyterian

presentare *pre·zen·tah·ray vt* introduce (*person*)

presentarsi *pre·zen·tahr·see vr* report; check in (*at airport*)

presentazione *pre·zen·ta·tsyoh·ne f* introduction (*social*); presentation

presente *pre·zen·te adj* present

preservativo *pre·ser·va·tee·voh m* sheath (*contraceptive*)

preside *pre·see·de m/f* headmaster; headmistress

presidente *pre·see·den·te m* president; chairman

pressione *pres·syoh·ne f* pressure; la pressione sanguigna *pres·syoh·ne san·gween·ya* blood pressure

presso *pres·soh prep* near; care of, c/o

prestare *pre·stah·ray vt* lend; loan

prestigiatore *pre·stee·ja·toh·re m* conjuror

prestigio *pre·stee·joh m* prestige

prestito *pre·stee·toh m* loan; il prestito bancario *pre·stee·toh ban·kah·ryo* bank loan; prendere* in prestito *pren·de·re een pre·stee·toh* to borrow; prendere* qualcosa in prestito da qualcuno *pren·de·re kwal·ko·sa een pre·stee·toh da kwal·koo·no* to borrow something from someone

presto *pre·sto adv* early; soon; faccia presto! *fach·cha pre·sto* hurry up!

prete *pre·te m* priest

previsione *pre·vee·zyoh·ne f* forecast; le previsioni del tempo *pre·vee·zyoh· nee del tem·poh* weather forecast

prezioso(a) *pre·tsyoh·so(a) adj* precious (*jewel etc*)

prezzemolo *prets·tsay·mo·loh m* parsley

prezzo *prets·tsoh m* price; il prezzo minimo *prets·tsoh mee·nee·mo* reserve price; il prezzo del coperto *prets·tsoh del ko·per·toh* cover charge; comprare qualcosa a prezzo di costo *kom· prah·ray kwal·ko·sa a prets·tsoh dee ko·stoh* to buy something at cost; il prezzo della corsa *prets·tsoh del·la kohr·sa* fare (*in taxi*); il prezzo fisso *prets·tsoh fees·so* flat rate; il prezzo di catalogo *prets·tsoh dee ka·tah·lo· goh* list price; il prezzo al minuto *prets·tsoh al mee·noo·toh* retail price; comprare qualcosa a prezzo ridotto *kom·prah·ray kwal·ko·sa a prets·tsoh ree·doht·to* to buy something at a reduction; il prezzo d'ingresso *prets· tsoh deen·gres·soh* entrance fee; il prezzo unitario *prets·tsoh oo·nee·tah· ree·oh* unit price

prigione *pree·joh·ne f* prison; jail; la

prigione sotterranea *pree·joh·ne sot· ter·rah·ne·a* dungeon; in prigione *een pree·joh·ne* in prison

prigioniero(a) *pree·joh·nye·ro(a) m/f* prisoner

prima *pree·ma adv* before; first; earlier □ *f* la prima *pree·ma* première; prima che *pree·ma ke* before; prima di mezzogiorno *pree·ma dee medz· dzo·johr·noh* before noon

primario(a) *pree·mah·ryo(a) adj* primary (*education*)

primato *pree·mah·toh m* record (*in sports*)

primavera *pree·ma·ve·ra f* spring (*season*)

primo(a) *pree·mo(a) adj* first; top (*in rank*); early; di prima classe *dee pree·ma klas·se* first-class (*work etc*); viaggiare in prima classe *vyaj·jah·ray een pree·ma klas·se* to travel first class; in prima *een pree·ma* in first (gear); il primo piano *pree·mo pyah· noh* first floor

principale *preen·chee·pah·lay adj* major; main

principalmente *preen·chee·pal·mayn· tay adv* mainly

principe *preen·chee·pe m* prince

principessa *preen·chee·pays·sa f* princess

principiante *preen·chee·pyan·te m/f* beginner

privato(a) *pree·vah·to(a) adj* private; personal (*private*); in privato *een pree·vah·to* in private

privo(a) di *pree·vo(a) dee adj* lacking

probabile *pro·bah·bee·le adj* probable; likely; è probabile che venga *e pro· bah·bee·le ke ven·ga* he's likely to come

probabilmente *pro·ba·beel·mayn·te adv* probably

problema *pro·ble·ma m* problem

procedimento *pro·che·dee·mayn·toh m* procedure; process (*method*)

processare *pro·ches·sah·ray vt* try (*in law*)

processo *pro·ches·soh m* trial (*in law*); process

prodotti *pro·doht·tee mpl* produce (*products*)

prodotto *pro·doht·toh m* product; commodity; il prodotto nazionale lordo *pro·doht·toh na·tsyoh·nah·le lohr·do* gross national product

produrre* *pro·door·re vt* produce; bring in (*profit*)

produttività *pro·doot·tee·vee·ta f* productivity

produttore *pro·doot·toh·re m* producer

produzione *pro·doo·tsyoh·ne f* production; output; la produzione in serie *pro·doo·tsyoh·ne een ser·ye* mass production

professionale *pro·fes·syoh·nah·le adj* professional

professione *pro·fes·syoh·ne f* profession

professore *pro·fes·soh·re m* professor; teacher (*secondary school*)

professoressa *pro·fes·sor·res·sa f* teacher (*secondary school*)

profiterole *pro·fee·te·rohl f* profiterole

profitto *pro·feet·toh m* profit

profondità *pro·fohn·dee·ta f* depth

profondo(a) *pro·fohn·do(a) adj* deep (*water, hole*); poco profondo(a) *po· ko pro·fohn·do(a)* shallow

profumo *pro·foo·moh m* scent; perfume

progettare *pro·jet·tah·ray* vt plan

progetto *pro·jet·toh* m plan; project; blueprint; scheme; **fare* dei progetti in anticipo** *fah·ray de·e pro·jet·tee een an·tee·chee·po* to plan ahead

programma *pro·gram·ma* m syllabus; schedule; program(me)

programmare *pro·gram·mah·ray* vt program(me)

programmatore *pro·gram·ma·toh·re* m programmer (*person*)

programmatrice *pro·gram·ma·tree·che* f programmer (*person*)

programmazione *pro·gram·ma·tsyoh·nay* f computer programming

progresso *pro·gres·soh* m progress; **fare* progressi** *fah·ray pro·gres·see* to make progress

proibire *pro·ee·bee·re* vt ban; prohibit; **proibire a qualcuno di fare qualcosa** *pro·ee·bee·re a kwal·koo·no dee fah·ray kwal·ko·sa* to forbid someone to do something

proibizione *pro·ee·bee·tsyoh·ne* f ban

proiettare *pro·yet·tah·ray* vt show (*movie*)

proiettore *pro·yet·toh·re* m headlight; projector; **il proiettore fendinebbia** *pro·yet·toh·re fen·dee·nayb·bya* fog-lamp

promessa *pro·mays·sa* f promise

promettere* *pro·mayt·te·re* vt promise

promosso(a) *pro·mos·so(a)* adj promoted; **essere* promosso(a)** *es·se·re pro·mos·so(a)* to pass (*exam*)

promozione *pro·mo·tsyoh·ne* f promotion

promuovere* *pro·mwo·ve·re* vt promote

pronostico *pro·no·stee·koh* m forecast

pronto(a) *prohn·to(a)* adj ready; **il pronto soccorso** *prohn·to sok·kohr·soh* first aid; **pronto!** *prohn·to!* hello! (*on telephone*)

pronuncia *pro·noon·cha* f pronunciation

pronunciare *pro·noon·chah·ray* vt pronounce

proporre* *pro·pohr·re* vt propose (*suggest*)

proposito *pro·po·see·to* m intention; **a proposito** *a pro·po·see·to* by the way

proposta *pro·poh·sta* f proposal (*suggestion*)

proprietà *pro·pree·e·ta* f ownership; property; land; **la proprietà fondiaria** *pro·pree·e·ta fon·dee·ah·ree·a* real estate

proprietario(a) *pro·pree·e·tah·ree·o(a)* m/f owner

proprio *pro·pree·o* adv just; really

proprio(a) *pro·pree·o(a)* adj own

prosciugare *pro·shoo·gah·ray* vt drain (*land*)

prosciutto *pro·shoot·toh* m ham

proseguire *pro·se·gwee·ray* vt continue; **fare* proseguire** *fah·ray pro·se·gwee·ray* to readdress

prospero(a) *pro·spe·ro(a)* adj prosperous; successful (*businessman*)

prospettiva *pro·spet·tee·va* f prospect; outlook

prospetto *pro·spet·toh* m prospectus

prossimo(a) *pros·see·moh(a)* adj next (*stop, station, week*)

proteggere* *pro·tej·je·re* vt protect; guard

proteina *pro·te·ee·na* f protein

protesta *pro·te·sta* f protest

protestante *pro·te·stan·te* adj Protestant

protestare *pro·te·stah·ray* vt/i protest

protezione *pro·te·tsyoh·ne* f protection

prototipo *pro·to·tee·poh* m prototype

prova *pro·va* f proof; evidence; rehearsal; test; **la prova su strada** *pro·va soo strah·da* road test; **mettere* alla prova** *mayt·te·re al·la pro·va* to test (*ability*); **in prova** *een pro·va* on approval

provare *pro·vah·ray* vt prove; try; **provare un vestito** *pro·vah·ray oon ve·stee·toh* to try on a dress; **provare una macchina su strada** *pro·vah·ray oo·na mak·kee·na soo strah·da* to test-drive a car

provincia *pro·veen·cha* f province (*region*)

provinciale *pro·veen·chah·le* adj provincial

provvedere* a *prov·ve·day·re a* vi provide for

provvisorio(a) *prov·vee·zo·ryo(a)* adj temporary

provvista *prov·vee·sta* f supply; store (*stock*)

prudente *proo·den·te* adj wise (*decision*); careful (*cautious*)

prudere* *proo·de·re* vi itch

prugna *proon·ya* f plum

prurito *proo·ree·toh* m itch

P.S. *pee·es·se* abbrev P.S.

psichiatra *psee·kee·a·tra* m/f psychiatrist

psichiatrico(a) *psee·kee·a·tree·ko(a)* adj psychiatric

psicologia *psee·ko·lo·jee·a* f psychology

psicologico(a) *psee·ko·lo·jee·ko(a)* adj psychological

psicologo(a) *psee·ko·lo·go(a)* m/f psychologist

pubblicare *poob·blee·kah·ray* vt publish

pubblicità *poob·blee·chee·ta* f publicity; advertising; **fare* pubblicità a** *fah·ray poob·blee·chee·ta a* to advertise (*product*)

pubblico(a) *poob·blee·ko(a)* adj public □ m **il pubblico** *poob·blee·koh* public; audience; **in pubblico** *een poob·blee·koh* in public

pugilato *poo·jee·lah·toh* m boxing

pugnalare *poon·ya·lah·ray* vt stab

pugnale *poon·yah·le* m dagger

pugno *poon·yoh* m fist; punch (*blow*); **dare* un pugno a** *dah·ray oon poon·yoh a* to punch

pulire *poo·lee·ray* vt clean; **fare* pulire un vestito** *fah·ray poo·lee·ray oon ve·stee·toh* to have a suit cleaned

pulito(a) *poo·lee·toh(a)* adj clean

pullman *pool·man* m bus (*long distance*)

pullmino *pool·mee·noh* m minibus

pullover *pool·lo·ver* m — pullover

pungere* *poon·je·re* vt prick; sting

punire *poo·nee·re* vt punish

punizione *poo·nee·tsyoh·ne* f punishment

punta *poon·ta* f point; tip

puntare *poon·tah·ray* vt point; aim (*gun etc*); **puntare su** *poon·tah·ray soo* to back (*bet on*); **puntare un fucile contro qualcuno** *poon·tah·ray oon foo·chee·le kohn·tro kwal·koo·no* to aim a gun at someone

punteggio *poon·tayj·joh* m score

puntina *poon·tee·na* f drawing pin; thumbtack

punto *poon·toh* m point; spot (*dot*); stitch (*sewing*); full stop; **il punto di**

vista *poon·toh dee vee·sta* point of view; il punto di riferimento *poon·toh dee ree·fe·ree·mayn·toh* landmark; il punto interrogativo *poon·toh een·ter·ro·ga·tee·vo* question mark; gli ha risposto punto per punto *lyee a ree·spoh·sto poon·toh payr poon·toh* he answered him point by point

puntuale *poon·too·ah·le* adj punctual

puntualmente *poon·too·al·mayn·te* adv on time

puntura *poon·too·ra* f bite; sting

pupazzo *poo·pats·tsoh* m puppet

purché *poor·kay* conj as long as (*provided that*); provided, providing; purché venga *poor·kay ven·ga* provided (that) he comes

purè *poo·re* m — purée; il purè di patate *poo·re dee pa·tah·tay* mashed potatoes

puro(a) *poo·ro(a)* adj pure

purpureo(a) *poor·poo·re·o(a)* adj purple

pustola *poo·sto·la* f spot (*pimple*)

puzzle *puz·zuhl* m jigsaw (puzzle)

Q

qua *kwa* adv here; di qua, per favore *dee kwa payr fa·voh·re* this way please

quaderno *kwa·der·noh* m exercise book

quadrato(a) *kwa·drah·to(a)* adj square □ m il quadrato *kwa·drah·toh* square; un metro quadrato *oon me·troh kwa·drah·to* a square metre

a quadretti *a kwa·drayt·tee* adv check(er)ed (*patterned*)

quadri *kwa·dree* mpl diamonds (*cards*)

quadro *kwa·droh* m picture; painting; i quadri medi *kwa·dree me·dee* middle management

quaglia *kwal·ya* f quail

qualche *kwal·kay* adj some; qualche volta *kwal·kay vol·ta* sometimes

qualcosa *kwal·ko·sa* pron something; qualcosa di più grande *kwal·ko·sa dee pyoo gran·de* something bigger; può vedere qualcosa? *pwo ve·day·re kwal·ko·sa* can you see anything?

qualcuno *kwal·koo·no* pron somebody, someone; qualcuno di voi sa cantare? *kwal·koo·no dee voy sa kan·tah·ray* can any of you sing?; può vedere qualcuno? *pwo ve·day·re kwal·koo·no* can you see anybody?; qualcun altro *kwal·koon al·troh* someone else

quale *kwah·le* adj what; which □ pron which one; qual libro? *kwahl lee·broh* what book?; non so quale prendere *nohn so kwah·le pren·de·re* I don't know which to take; quali lingue? *kwah·lee leen·gwe* which languages?

qualificarsi per *kwa·lee·fee·kar·see payr* vr qualify for (*in sports*)

qualificato(a) *kwa·lee·fee·kah·to(a)* adj qualified

qualità *kwa·lee·ta* f — quality; gli articoli di qualità *ar·tee·ko·lee dee kwa·lee·ta* quality goods

qualsiasi *kwal·see·a·see* adj any

qualunque *kwa·loon·kwe* adj any

quando *kwan·do* conj when; di quando in quando *dee kwan·do een kwan·do* occasionally

quantità *kwan·tee·ta* f — quantity

quanto(a) *kwan·to(a)* adj how much; quanto tempo? *kwan·to tem·po* how long?; quanti(e)? *kwan·tee(·te)* how

many?; quante persone? *kwan·te per·soh·ne* how many people?; quanto latte? *kwan·to lat·te* how much milk?; quanto dista da qui a…? *kwan·to dee·sta da kwee a* how far is it to…?; quanto a questo *kwan·to a kway·sto* as for this

quaranta *kwa·ran·ta* num forty

quarantena *kwa·ran·te·na* f quarantine

quartiere *kwar·tye·re* m district (*of town*); il quartiere luce rossa *kwar·tye·re loo·che rohs·sa* red light district

quarto(a) *kwar·toh* m quarter □ adj quarto(a) *kwar·to(a)* fourth; la quarta (marcia) *kwar·ta (mar·cha)* top (gear); un quarto d'ora *oon kwar·toh doh·ra* a quarter of an hour

quarzo *kwar·tsoh* m quartz

quasi *kwah·zee* adv nearly; almost

quattordici *kwat·tor·dee·chee* num fourteen

quattro *kwat·troh* num four

quei *kway* adj those

quel(la) *kwayl(·la)* adj that

quelli(e) *kwayl·lee(·le)* adj those □ pron those; ecco quelli(e) che voglio *ek·ko kwayl·lee(·le) ke vol·yo* those are what I want; quelle donne *kwayl·le don·ne* those women

quello *kwayl·lo* pron that; quello(a) lì *kwayl·lo(a) lee* that one; ho visto quello che è successo *o kwe·sto kwayl·lo e sooch·ches·so* I saw what happened; quello(a) sulla tavola *kwayl·lo(a) sool·la tah·vo·la* the one on the table; ecco quello che voglio *ek·ko kwayl·lo ke vol·yo* this is what I want; che cos'è quello? *ke ko·se kwayl·lo* what's that?

quercia *kwer·cha* f oak

questi(e) *kway·stee(·ste)* adj, pron these

questionario *kwe·styoh·nah·ryoh* m questionnaire

questione *kwe·styoh·ne* f issue; question; è questione di e *kwe·styoh·ne dee* it's a question of

questo(a) *kway·sto(a)* adj this □ pron this one

qui *kwee* adv here; venga qui *ven·ga kwee* come over here; è qui in vacanza e *kwee een va·kan·tsa* he's over here on holiday; proprio qui *pro·pree·o kwee* just here

quiche *keesh* f quiche

quindi *kween·dee* adv then

quindici *kween·dee·chee* num fifteen

quindicina di giorni *kween·dee·chee·na dee johr·nee* f fortnight

quinto(a) *kween·to(a)* adj fifth

quota *kwo·ta* f subscription; quota

quotare *kwo·tah·ray* vt quote (*price*)

quotazione *kwo·ta·tsyoh·ne* f quotation (*price*)

quotidiano(a) *kwo·tee·dee·ah·no(a)* adj daily □ m il quotidiano *kwo·tee·dee·ah·noh* daily (*newspaper*)

R

rabarbaro *ra·bar·ba·roh* m rhubarb

rabbia *rab·bya* f anger; rabies

rabbino *rab·bee·noh* m rabbi

rabbrividire *rab·bree·vee·dee·re* vi shiver

racchetta *rak·kayt·ta* f racket (*tennis*); bat (*table tennis*)

raccogliere* *rak·kol·ye·ray* vt gather (*assemble*); collect; pick up (*object*)

raccolto *rak·kol·toh* m crop; harvest

raccomandare *rak·ko·man·dah·ray vt* recommend

raccontare *rak·kon·tah·ray vt* tell (*story*)

raccordo *rak·kor·doh m* adapter, adaptor (*electrical*)

radar *ra·dar m* radar; il controllo radar *kon·trol·loh ra·dar* radar trap

raddoppiare *rad·dop·pyah·ray vt/i* double

radersi* *rah·der·see vr* shave

radiatore *ra·dya·toh·ray m* radiator

radice *ra·dee·chay f* root

radio *ra·dyoh f —* radio; alla radio *al·la ra·dyoh* on the radio

radiografare *ra·dyo·gra·fah·ray vt* X-ray

radiografia *ra·dyo·gra·fee·a f* X-ray (*photo*)

radunarsi *ra·doo·nahr·see vr* gather (*crowd*)

raffermo(a) *raf·fayr·mo(a) adj* stale (*bread*)

raffica *raf·fee·ka f* squall; gust

raffinare *raf·fee·nah·ray vt* refine

raffineria *raf·fee·ne·ree·a f* refinery

raffreddamento *raf·fred·da·men·toh m* cooling

raffreddare *raf·fred·dah·ray vt* chill (*wine, food*)

raffreddore *raf·frayd·doh·ray m* cold (*illness*)

ragazza *ra·gats·tsa f* girl (*young woman*); girlfriend; la ragazza squillo *ra·gats·tsa skwee·loh* call girl

ragazzo *ra·gats·tsoh m* boy; boyfriend

raggio *raj·joh m* beam (*of light*); ray

raggiungere* *raj·joon·je·ray vt* reach

ragione *ra·joh·nay f* reason

ragioneria *ra·jo·ne·ree·a f* accountancy

ragionevole *ra·jo·nay·vo·le adj* sensible; reasonable

ragioniere *ra·jo·nye·re m* accountant; il ragioniere diplomato *ra·jo·nye·re dee·plo·mah·toh* chartered accountant

ragno *ran·yoh m* spider

rallentare *ral·len·tah·ray vt/i* to slow down *or* up

rally *ral·lee m* rally (*sporting*)

ramaiolo *ra·ma·yo·loh m* ladle

rame *rah·may m* copper (*metal*)

rammendare *ram·men·dah·ray vt* darn

ramo *rah·moh m* branch (*of tree*)

ramoscello *ra·mo·shel·loh m* twig

rampa *ram·pa f* ramp (*slope*)

rana *rah·na f* frog

rango *ran·goh m* rank (*status*)

rapa *ra·pa f* turnip; la rapa svedese *ra·pa zve·day·se* swede

rapidamente *ra·pee·da·mayn·te adv* quickly

rapido(a) *ra·pee·do(a) adj* high-speed; quick □ *m* il rapido *ra·pee·doh* express train

rapire *ra·pee·re vt* kidnap

rapporto *rap·por·toh m* ratio; report; relationship; i rapporti interrazziali *rap·por·tee een·tayr·rats·tsyah·lee* race relations; i rapporti sessuali *rap·por·tee ses·soo·ah·lee* sexual intercourse

rappresentante *rap·pre·zen·tan·te m/f* representative; il rappresentante sindacale *rap·pre·zen·tan·te seen·da·kah·le* shop steward

rappresentare *rap·pre·zen·tah·ray vt* represent

rappresentazione *rap·pre·zen·ta·tsyoh·ne f* performance (*of play*); production

raramente *rah·ra·mayn·te adv* seldom

raro(a) *rah·ro(a) adj* rare; scarce

raso *rah·soh m* satin

rasoio *ra·soh·yo m* razor; il rasoio elettrico *ra·soh·yo e·let·tree·ko* shaver

rassomigliare *ras·so·meel·yah·ray vi* look like; resemble; rassomiglia a suo padre *ras·so·meel·ya a soo·o pah·dre* he resembles his father

rastrello *ra·strel·loh m* rake

rata *rah·ta f* instal(l)ment

rateizzare *ra·te·eed·dzah·ray vt* spread (*payments*)

ratto *rat·toh m* rat

rattristare *rat·tree·stah·ray vt* sadden

ravanello *ra·va·nel·loh m* radish

ravioli *ra·vee·o·lee mpl* ravioli

razionalizzare *ra·tsyoh·na·leedz·dzah·ray vt* rationalize

razionalizzazione *ra·tsyoh·na·leedz·dza·tsyoh·nay f* rationalization

razza *rats·tsa f* race; breed

razzia *rats·tsee·a f* raid

razziale *rats·tsyah·lay adj* racial

razzo *radz·dzoh m* rocket

re *ray m* king

reale *re·ah·le adj* royal

realizzare *re·a·leedz·dzah·ray vt* carry out; realize (*assets*)

realmente *re·al·mayn·tay adv* in real terms

reattore *re·at·toh·ray m* reactor

reazione *re·a·tsyoh·nay f* reaction; backlash

recapito *re·ka·pee·toh m* address; delivery; il recapito dei bagagli *re·ka·pee·toh de·ee ba·gal·yee* baggage claim

recensione *re·chen·syoh·nay f* review (*of book etc*)

recente *re·chen·tay adj* recent

recentemente *re·chen·te·mayn·te adv* lately; recently

recessione *re·ches·syoh·nay f* recession

recinto *re·cheen·toh m* fence

recipiente *re·chee·pyen·tay m* container

réclame *ray·klam f* commercial; advertisement

reclamo *re·klah·moh m* complaint (*dissatisfaction*)

recluta *re·kloo·ta f* recruit

reclutamento *re·kloo·ta·mayn·toh m* recruitment

redditizio(a) *red·dee·tee·tsyo(a) adj* profitable

reddito *red·dee·toh m* income; yield (*financial*)

redigere* *re·dee·je·re vt* draw up (*document*)

referenza *re·fe·ren·tse fpl* reference (*testimonial*)

regalare *ray·ga·lah·ray vt* give away; present

regalo *re·gah·loh m* present; gift; il regalo di nozze *re·gah·loh dee nots·tse* wedding present

regata *re·gah·ta f* regatta

reggere* *rej·je·re vt* support (*hold up*)

reggiseno *rej·jee·say·noh m* bra

regina *re·jee·na f* queen

regione *re·joh·nay f* region; district (*in country*); area

regista *re·jee·sta m/f* producer (*of play*); director (*of film*)

registrare *re·jee·strah·ray vt* tape record; register; record

registrarsi *re·jee·strahr·see vr* check in (*at hotel*)

registro *re·jee·stroh m* register

Regno Unito *rayn·yoh oo·nee·to m* United Kingdom, U.K.

regola *re·go·la* f rule (*regulation*)

regolamento *re·go·la·mayn·toh* m regulation (*rule*)

regolare *re·go·lah·ray* adj regular; steady (*pace*) □ vt settle (*argument*)

regolo *re·go·loh* m ruler (*for measuring*); il regolo calcolatore *re·go·loh kal·ko·la·toh·re* slide rule

relativo(a) *re·la·tee·vo(a)* adj relevant; relative

relazione *re·la·tsyoh·nay* f relationship; report; le pubbliche relazioni *poob·blee·ke re·la·tsyoh·nee* public relations

religione *re·lee·joh·nay* f religion

religioso(a) *re·lee·joh·so(a)* adj religious

remare *re·mah·ray* vi row (*sport*)

remo *re·moh* m oar

rendere* *ren·de·re* vt yield (*investment*); rendersi* conto di *ren·der·see kohn·toh dee* to realize

rendimento *ren·dee·mayn·toh* m performance (*of car*); profitability; output

rendita *ren·dee·ta* f unearned income; revenue; la rendita vitalizia *ren·dee·ta vee·ta·lee·tsya* annuity

rene *re·ne* m kidney (*of person*)

Reno *re·no* m Rhine

reparto *re·par·toh* m department (*in store*); unit; il reparto contabile *re·par·toh kon·tah·bee·le* accounts department

repubblica *re·poob·blee·ka* f republic

repubblicano(a) *re·poob·blee·kah·no(a)* adj republican

residenza *re·see·den·tsa* f residence

residenziale *re·see·den·tsyah·le* adj residential (*area*)

resistente *re·see·sten·te* adj hard-wearing; durable (*fabric, article*); tough (*material*)

resistenza *re·see·sten·tsa* f resistance (*to illness*); strength (*of girder, rope etc*)

resistere* *re·see·ste·ray* vi resist

respingere* *re·speen·je·ray* vt reject

respirare *re·spee·rah·ray* vt/i breathe

responsabile *re·spon·sah·bee·lay* adj responsible; è lui il responsabile del dipartimento *e loo·ee eel re·spon·sah·bee·lay del dee·par·tee·mayn·toh* he's responsible for the department; essere* responsabile per *es·se·ray re·spon·sah·bee·lay payr* to be in charge of

responsabilità *re·spon·sa·bee·lee·ta* f responsibility; questo è di Sua responsabilità *kway·stoh e dee soo·a re·spon·sa·bee·lee·ta* this is your responsibility

restare *res·tah·ray* vi remain; le uova mi restano sullo stomaco *le wo·va mee re·sta·no sool·lo sto·ma·koh* eggs disagree with me

restituire *re·stee·too·ee·ray* vt return (*give back*)

resto *re·sto* m remainder; change

restringersi* *re·streen·jer·see* vr shrink

restrizione *re·stree·tsyoh·nay* f restriction; la restrizione del credito *re·stree·tsyoh·nay del kray·dee·toh* credit squeeze; la restrizione economica *re·stree·tsyoh·nay e·ko·no·mee·ka* squeeze (*financial*)

rete *ray·tay* f goal (*sport*); net; string bag

retro *re·troh* m back; Vedi retro P.T.O.

retrodatare *re·tro·da·tah·ray* vt back-date (*letter*)

retromarcia *re·tro·mar·cha* f reverse (*gear*); in retromarcia *een re·tro·mar·cha* in reverse (*gear*); entrare nel garage in retromarcia *en·trah·ray nel ga·raj een re·tro·mar·cha* to reverse into the garage

retrospettivamente *re·tro·spet·tee·va·mayn·tay* adv in retrospect

reumatismo *re·oo·ma·tee·zmoh* m rheumatism

revisione *re·vee·zee·oh·nay* f review; service (*for car*)

revisore dei conti *re·vee·zoh·re de·ee kohn·tee* m auditor

riaddestramento *ree·ad·de·stra·mayn·toh* m retraining

riaddestrare *ree·ad·de·strah·ray* vt retrain

riaddestrarsi *ree·ad·de·strar·see* vr retrain

rialzare *ree·al·tsah·ray* vt raise (*price*)

rialzo *ree·al·tso* m upturn (*in business*); rise (*in prices, wages*); in rialzo *een ree·al·tso* buoyant (*market*)

rianimare *ree·a·nee·mah·ray* vt revive (*person*)

riattaccare *ree·at·tak·kah·ray* vt reattach; riattaccare il telefono *ree·at·tak·kah·ray eel te·le·fo·no* to ring off

ribassare *ree·bas·sah·ray* vt fall (*prices etc*)

ribasso *ree·bas·soh* m reduction (*in price*)

ribes *ree·bes* m blackcurrant; il ribes rosso *ree·bes rohs·so* red currant

ricamato(a) *ree·ka·mah·to(a)* adj embroidered

ricamo *ree·kah·moh* m embroidery

ricchezza *reek·kayts·tsa* f wealth

ricciolo *reech·cho·loh* m curl

ricciuto(a) *reech·choo·toh(a)* adj curly

ricco(a) *reek·ko(a)* adj wealthy; rich

ricerca *ree·chayr·ka* f research; la ricerca di mercato *ree·chayr·ka dee mayr·ka·toh* market research

ricetta *ree·chet·ta* f prescription; recipe

ricevere *ree·chay·ve·re* vt entertain (*give hospitality*); receive (*letter*)

ricevimento *ree·che·vee·mayn·toh* m reception; reception desk

ricevitore *ree·che·vee·toh·ray* m receiver (*phone*)

ricevuta *ree·che·voo·ta* f receipt; accusare ricevuta di *ak·koo·zah·ray ree·che·voo·ta dee* to acknowledge (*letter*); con ricevuta di ritorno *kohn ree·che·voo·ta dee ree·tohr·noh* by recorded delivery

richiesta *ree·kye·sta* f request

ricompensa *ree·kom·pen·sa* f reward

riconoscere* *ree·ko·noh·she·ray* vt recognize

ricordare *ree·kor·dah·ray* vt remind; ricordare qualcosa a qualcuno *ree·kor·dah·ray kwal·ko·sa a kwal·koo·no* to remind someone of something; ricordarsi di *ree·kor·dar·see dee* to remember

ricordo *ree·kor·doh* m souvenir; un mio ricordo *oon mee·oh ree·kor·doh* one of my memories

ricorrere* *ree·kohr·re·ray* a vi resort to

ricuperare *ree·koo·pe·rah·ray* vt recover; retrieve (*data*)

ridere* *ree·de·re* vi laugh; ridere* di qualcuno *ree·de·re dee kwal·koo·no* to laugh at somebody

ridicolo(a) *ree·dee·ko·lo(a) adj* ridiculous

ridistribuire *ree·dee·stree·boo·ee·ray vt* redistribute

ridistribuzione *ree·dee·stree·boo·tsyoh·nay f* redistribution

ridurre* *ree·door·re vt* turn down (*heat*); reduce

riduzione *ree·doo·tsyoh·nay f* reduction

riempire* *ree·em·pee·re vt* fill; fill in/out/up

riesaminare *ree·e·za·mee·nah·ray vt* review

rifare* *ree·fah·ray vt* do again; repair; **rifare* i letti** *ree·fah·ray ee let·tee* to make the beds

riferimento *ree·fe·ree·mayn·toh m* reference

rifiutare *ree·fyoo·tah·ray vt* refuse; reject; **rifiutarsi di fare qualcosa** *ree·fyoo·tar·see dee fah·ray kwal·ko·sa* to refuse to do something

rifiuti *ree·fyoo·tee mpl* rubbish; waste

rifiuto *ree·fyoo·toh m* refusal

riflettere* *ree·flet·te·re vt* reflect; **riflettere* su qualcosa** *ree·flet·te·re soo kwal·ko·sa* to think something over

riflettore *ree·flet·toh·re m* spotlight; floodlight

rifugio *ree·foo·joh m* refuge; shelter

rigido(a) *ree·jee·do(a) adj* stiff

riguardare *ree·gwar·dah·ray vt* concern; **ciò non la riguarda** *cho nohn la ree·gwahr·da* that doesn't concern you

riguardo *ree·gwar·do m* care; respect; **senza riguardo a** *sen·tsa ree·gwar·do* a regardless of

rilassarsi *ree·las·sar·see vr* relax

rilievo *ree·lye·voh m* survey (*of land*)

rimandare *ree·man·dah·ray vt* send back; postpone

rimanere* *ree·ma·nay·re vi* stay; remain

rimbalzare *reem·bal·tsah·ray vi* bounce (*ball*)

rimbombare *reem·bom·bah·ray vi* roar (*engine*)

rimborsare *reem·bohr·sah·ray vt* repay; refund

rimborso *reem·bohr·soh m* refund

rimedio *ree·me·dyoh m* remedy

rimescolare *ree·me·sko·lah·ray vt* shuffle (*cards*); stir

rimessa *ree·mays·sa f* remittance; garage

rimettere* *ree·mayt·te·re vt* replace (*put back*)

rimettersi* *ree·mayt·ter·see vr* recover (*from illness*)

rimorchiare *ree·mor·kyah·ray vt* tow

rimorchio *ree·mor·kyoh m* trailer (*for goods*); **a rimorchio a** *ree·mor·kyoh* on tow

rinchiudere* *reen·kyoo·de·re vt* shut up

rincrescere* *reen·kray·she·ray vi* regret

rinforzare *reen·for·tsah·ray vt* strengthen

rinfreschi *reen·fray·skee mpl* refreshments

ringhiare *reen·gyah·ray vi* growl

ringhiera *reen·gye·ra f* rail (*on bridge, balcony*)

ringraziare *reen·gra·tsyah·ray vt* thank

rinnovare *reen·no·vah·ray vt* renew (*subscription, passport*)

rinunciare *ree·noon·chah·ray vi* quit (*give up*)

rinviare *reen·vyah·ray vt* shelve (*project*); return (*send back*); delay

(*postpone*); rinviare la seduta *reen·vyah·ray la se·doo·ta* to adjourn the meeting

rinvio *reen·vee·oh m* adjournment; return

riordinare *ree·or·dee·nah·ray vt* reorder (*goods*)

riorganizzare *ree·or·ga·needz·dzah·ray vt* reorganize

riorganizzazione *ree·or·ga·needz·dza·tsyoh·nay f* reorganisation

ripagare *ree·pa·gah·ray vt* repay

riparare *ree·pa·rah·ray vt* mend; repair

ripararsi *ree·pa·rar·see vr* shelter (*from rain etc*)

riparazione *ree·pa·ra·tsyoh·nay f* repair

ripassare *ree·pas·sah·ray vt* revise

ripetere *ree·pe·te·re vt* repeat; **può ripetere quello?** *pwo ree·pe·te·re kwayl·lo* could you say that again?

ripetizione *ree·pe·tee·tsyoh·nay f* repetition

ripido(a) *ree·pee·do(a) adj* abrupt; steep

ripieno *ree·pye·noh m* stuffing (*in chicken etc*)

riportare *ree·por·tah·ray vt* report

riposarsi *ree·po·sar·see vr* rest

riposo *ree·po·soh m* rest

riprendere* *ree·pren·de·re vt* take back; resume; **riprendere* i sensi** *ree·pren·de·re ee sen·see* to come round (*recover*)

risa *ree·sa fpl* laughter

risarcimento *ree·sar·chee·mayn·toh m* compensation

riscaldamento *ree·skal·da·mayn·toh m* heating; **il riscaldamento centrale** *ree·skal·da·mayn·toh chen·trah·lay* central heating

riscaldatore *ree·skal·da·toh·re m* heater

rischiare *ree·skyah·ray vt* risk

rischio *ree·skyoh m* risk

risciacquare *ree·shak·kwah·ray vt* rinse

riscuotere* *ree·skwo·te·ray vt* cash (*cheque*)

riserva *ree·ser·va f* reserve (*for game*); stock (*supply*); reservation (*doubt*)

riservare *ree·ser·vah·ray vt* reserve (*seat, room*)

riserve *ree·ser·ve fpl* reserves

riso *ree·soh m* laugh; rice

risolvere* *ree·sol·ve·re vt* solve; work out

risorse *ree·sohr·se fpl* resources

risotto *ree·sot·toh m* risotto

risparmiare *ree·spar·myah·ray vt* save

rispettabile *ree·spet·tah·bee·lay adj* respectable

rispettare *ree·spet·tah·ray vt* respect

rispetto *ree·spet·toh m* respect

risplendere *ree·splen·de·re vi* blaze (*lights*)

rispondere* *ree·spohn·de·ray vi* reply
□ *vt/i* answer; **rispondere* a una domanda** *ree·spohn·de·ray a oo·na do·man·da* to reply to a question; **rispondere* al telefono** *ree·spohn·de·ray al te·le·fo·noh* to answer the phone; **rispondere* a** *ree·spohn·de·ray a* to meet (*demand*)

risposta *ree·spoh·sta f* reply; answer

ristabilirsi *ree·sta·bee·leer·see vr* recover; get well; **si ristabilisca presto** *see ree·sta·bee·lee·ska pre·sto* get well soon

ristorante *ree·sto·ran·te m* restaurant

risultato *ree·sool·tah·toh m* result

ritardare *ree·tar·dah·ray* vt delay □ vi be late; lose (*clock, watch*)

ritardo *ree·tar·doh* m delay; **essere*** in ritardo *es·se·re een ree·tar·doh* to be late; **il treno ha un ritardo** *eel tre·no a oon ree·tar·doh* the train has been delayed

ritelefonare *ree·te·le·fo·nah·ray* vt ring back

ritenere* *ree·te·nay·re* vt hold back; consider; **lo si ritiene un ingegnere** *lo see ree·tye·ne oon een·jen·ye·re* he's supposed to be an engineer

ritirare *ree·tee·rah·ray* vt withdraw

ritirarsi *ree·tee·rar·see* vr withdraw; retire; **ritirarsi da un affare** *ree·tee·rar·see da oon af·fah·re* to pull out of a deal

ritiro *ree·tee·ro* m retirement; withdrawal

ritmo *reet·moh* m rhythm; **al ritmo di** *al reet·moh dee* at the rate of

ritorno *ree·tohr·noh* m return

riunione *ree·oon·yoh·nay* f meeting; conference

riuscire* *ree·oo·shee·re* vi succeed; **è riuscito a farlo** *e ree·oo·shee·to a far·lo* he succeeded in doing it; **riuscire* a fare qualcosa** *ree·oo·shee·re a fah·ray kwal·ko·sa* to manage to do something; **ci sono appena riuscito** *chee so·no ap·pay·na ree·oo·shee·to* I just managed it; **non riuscire*** *nohn ree·oo·shee·re* to fail (*person*)

riva *ree·va* f bank (*of river, lake*)

rivale *ree·vah·le* m/f rival

rivedere* *ree·ve·day·re* vt revise (*estimate etc*)

rivendere *ree·ven·de·ray* vt resell

rivendita *ree·vayn·dee·ta* f resale; retailer's shop; **rivendita proibita** *ree·vayn·dee·ta pro·ee·bee·ta* not for resale

rivista *ree·vee·sta* f magazine (*journal*); revue

rivoltare *ree·vol·tah·ray* vt turn over; turn inside out

rivoluzione *ree·vo·loo·tsyoh·nay* f revolution

roba *ro·ba* f stuff (*things*)

robot *ro·bot* m robot

roccia *roch·cha* f rock

rodare *ro·dah·ray* vt run in (*engine, car*)

rognone *ron·yoh·ne* m kidney

rollino *rol·lee·noh* m spool. cartridge (*for camera*)

Roma *roh·ma* f Rome

Romania *ro·ma·nee·a* f Rumania

romano(a) *ro·mah·no(a)* adj Roman

romantico(a) *ro·man·tee·ko(a)* adj romantic

romanzo *ro·man·dzoh* m novel (*book*)

rombare *rom·bah·ray* vi rumble

rombo *rohm·boh* m turbot; roar (*of engine*); rumble

romeno(a) *ro·me·no(a)* adj Rumanian □ m il romeno *ro·me·noh* Rumanian

rompere* *rohm·pe·re* vt break

rompersi* *rohm·per·see* vr break; **rompersi* il braccio** *rohm·per·see eel brach·choh* to break one's arm

rompicapo *rom·pee·kah·poh* m puzzle; worry

rosa *ro·za* adj — pink □ f la rosa *ro·za* rose

rosé *ro·zay* m rosé

rossetto *ros·sayt·toh* m lipstick

rosso(a) *rohs·so(a)* adj red; **dai capelli rossi** *dai ka·pel·lee rohs·see* red-haired; **passare con il rosso** *pas·sah·*

---

ray kohn eel rohs·soh to go through a red light

rosticceria *ro·steech·che·ree·a* f grill-room

rotaie *ro·ta·ye* fpl rails (*for train*)

rotolare *ro·to·lah·ray* vi roll; **fare* rotolare** *fah·ray ro·to·lah·ray* to roll (*on wheels*)

rotolo *ro·to·loh* m roll

rotonda *ro·tohn·da* f roundabout

rotondo(a) *ro·tohn·do(a)* adj round

roulette *roo·let* f roulette

roulotte *roo·lot* f caravan

routine *roo·teen* f routine

rovesciare *ro·ve·shah·ray* vt pour; spill; **rovesciare qualcosa** *ro·ve·shah·ray kwal·ko·sa* to turn something upside down; to turn something over

rovesciarsi *ro·ve·shar·see* vr spill

rovescio *ro·ve·shoh* m back (*reverse side*); the wrong side

rovina *ro·vee·na* f ruin

rovinare *ro·vee·nah·ray* vt wreck (*plans*); ruin

rovine *ro·vee·ne* fpl ruins

R.S.V.P. *abbrev* R.S.V.P.

rubare *roo·bah·ray* vt steal; **rubare qualcosa a qualcuno** *roo·bah·ray kwal·ko·sa a kwal·koo·no* to steal something from someone

rubinetto *roo·bee·nayt·toh* m tap (*for water*); **il rubinetto di arresto** *roo·bee·nayt·toh dee ar·re·stoh* stopcock

rubino *roo·bee·noh* m ruby

rudemente *roo·de·mayn·tay* adv roughly

ruga *roo·ga* f wrinkle

rugby *roog·bee* m rugby

ruggine *rooj·jee·ne* f rust

ruggire *rooj·jee·ray* vi roar

ruggito *rooj·jee·toh* m roar

rum *room* m rum

rumore *roo·moh·ray* m noise

rumoroso(a) *roo·mo·roh·soh(a)* adj noisy

ruota *rwo·ta* f wheel; **la ruota di scorta** *rwo·ta dee skor·ta* spare wheel

rurale *roo·rah·le* adj rural

ruscello *roo·shel·loh* m stream

russare *roos·sah·ray* vi snore

Russia *roos·sya* f Russia

russo(a) *roos·so(a)* adj Russian □ m il russo *roos·soh* Russian

ruvido(a) *roo·vee·do(a)* adj rough; coarse (*texture, material*)

S

sabato *sah·ba·toh* m Saturday

sabbia *sab·bya* f sand

sabbioso(a) *sab·byoh·so(a)* adj sandy (*beach*)

saccarina *sak·ka·ree·na* f saccharin(e)

sacchetto *sak·kayt·toh* m bag (*of paper*); **il sacchetto di plastica** *sak·kayt·toh dee pla·stee·ka* polythene bag

sacco *sak·koh* m bag; sack; **il sacco a pelo** *sak·koh a pay·loh* sleeping bag; **il sacco in plastica** *sak·koh een pla·stee·ka* plastic bag

saggio(a) *saj·jo(a)* adj wise □ m il saggio *saj·joh* essay

saia *sa·ya* f twill

sala *sah·la* f hall (*room*); auditorium; **la sala d'aspetto** *sah·la da·spet·toh* waiting room (*at station*); lounge (*at airport*); **la sala d'esposizione** *sah·la de·spo·zee·tsyoh·ne* showroom; **la sala da pranzo** *sah·la da pran·dzoh* dining room; **la sala di partenza** *sah·*

la dee par·ten·tsa departure lounge;
la sala di transito sah·la dee tran·see·
toh transit lounge

salame sa·lah·me m salami; **il salame
all'aglio** sa·lah·me al·lal·yoh garlic
sausage

salariato sa·la·ree·ah·toh m wage
earner

salario sa·lah·ryoh m wage, wages

salato(a) sa·lah·to(a) adj salted; salty;
savo(u)ry (not sweet); **non salato(a)**
nohn sa·lah·to(a) unsalted

saldare sal·dah·ray vt settle (bill); weld

saldi sal·dee mpl sales (cheap prices)

saldo sal·doh m balance (remainder
owed); **il saldo bancario** sal·doh ban·
kah·ryo bank balance

sale sah·le m salt

saliera sa·lye·ra f salt cellar

salire* sa·lee·ray vi rise □ vt/i go up;
salire* su una collina sa·lee·ray soo
oo·na kol·lee·na to go up a hill; **sali·
re* su** sa·lee·ray soo to board (train,
bus)

saliscendi sa·lee·shayn·dee m — latch

saliva sa·lee·va f saliva

salmone sal·moh·ne m salmon

salone sa·loh·ne m lounge (in hotel); **il
salone dell'automobile** sa·loh·ne del·
low·to·mo·bee·lay motor show

salotto sa·lot·toh m living room; sitting
room

salsa sal·sa f gravy; sauce; **la salsa vinaigrette** sal·sa vee·nay·gret vinaigrette (sauce); **la salsa di pomodoro**
sal·sa dee po·mo·do·roh tomato
sauce; **la salsa tartara** sal·sa tar·ta·ra
tartar sauce

salsiccia sal·seech·cha f sausage

saltare sal·tah·ray vi blow (fuse) □ vt/i
jump; **saltare un muricciolo** sal·tah·
ray oon moo·reech·cho·loh to jump
(over) a wall

saltato(a) sal·tah·to(a) adj sauté

salumeria sa·loo·me·ree·a f delicatessen

salutare sa·loo·tah·ray vt greet

salute sa·loo·te f health

saluto sa·loo·toh m greeting; **distinti
saluti** dee·steen·tee sa·loo·tee yours
sincerely

salvagente pedonale sal·va·jen·te pe·
do·nah·le m island (traffic)

salvaguardia sal·va·gwar·dya f safeguard

salvare sal·vah·ray vt save; rescue

salvataggio sal·va·taj·joh m rescue

salvia sal·vya f sage (herb)

salvo(a) sal·vo(a) adj safe

sanatorio sa·na·to·ryoh m sanatorium

sandalo san·da·loh m sandal

sangue san·gwe m blood; **al sangue** al
san·gwe rare (steak)

sanguinare san·gwee·nah·ray vi bleed

sano(a) sah·no(a) adj healthy

santo(a) san·to(a) adj holy □ m/f il/la
santo(a) san·to(a) saint

sanzioni san·tsyoh·nee fpl sanctions

sapere* sa·pay·re vt know (fact, subject); **sa di pesce** sa dee pay·she it
tastes of fish; **sapere* di aglio** sa·pay·
re dee al·yoh to smell of garlic; **sape·
re* fare qualcosa** sa·pay·re fah·ray
kwal·ko·sa to know how to do something; **per quanto io sappia** payr
kwan·to ee·o sap·pya as far as I
know

sapone sa·poh·ne m soap; **il sapone in
scaglie** sa·poh·ne een skal·ye soap-
flakes; **il sapone da barba** sa·poh·ne
da bar·ba shaving soap

saponetta sa·po·nayt·ta f bar of soap

sapore sa·poh·re m flavo(u)r; taste

sarcastico(a) sar·ka·stee·ko(a) adj sarcastic

Sardegna sar·dayn·ya f Sardinia

sardella sar·del·la f pilchard

sardina sar·dee·na f sardine

sarto sar·toh m tailor

sassoso(a) sas·soh·so(a) adj stony

satellite sa·tel·lee·te m satellite

satira sa·tee·ra f satire (play)

saturare sa·too·rah·ray vt saturate

sauna sow·na f sauna

sbadigliare zba·deel·yah·ray vi yawn

sbagliarsi zbal·yahr·see vr make a mistake

sbagliato(a) zbal·ya·toh(a) adj incorrect; wrong

sbaglio zbal·yoh m mistake; **per sbaglio**
payr zbal·yoh by mistake; in error

sbalordire zba·lor·dee·re vt amaze

sbandare zban·dah·ray vi swerve

sbarcare zbar·kah·ray vi land

sbarra zbar·ra f bar (metal)

sbarrare zbar·rah·ray vt cross (cheque)

sbattere zbat·te·re vt slam; whisk
(cream, eggs) □ m **lo sbattere** zbat·te·
re bang (of door)

sbiadire zbee·a·dee·re vi fade

sbloccare zblok·kah·ray vt clear

sbornia zbor·nya f drunkenness; **avere***
mal di testa dopo una sbornia a·vay·
re mal dee te·sta doh·po oo·na zbor·
nya to have a hangover

sbrinare zbree·nah·ray vt defrost (refrigerator)

sbucciare zbooch·chah·ray vt peel

scacchi skak·kee mpl chess

scadenza ska·den·tsa f maturity; **a
lunga scadenza** a loon·ga ska·den·tsa
long-term

scadere* ska·day·re vi expire

scaduto(a) ska·doo·to(a) adj out-of-
date (passport, ticket)

scaffale skaf·fah·le m shelf

scaglia skal·ya f scale (of fish); flake

scala skah·la f scale; ladder; staircase;
la scala portatile skah·la por·tah·tee·
le stepladder; **la scala mobile** skah·la
mo·bee·le escalator

scaldabagno skal·da·ban·yoh m immersion heater; water heater

scaldare skal·dah·ray vt warm

scale skah·le fpl stairs

scalfire skal·fee·ray vt graze; scratch

scalfittura skal·feet·too·ra f graze

scalinata ska·lee·nah·ta f flight of steps

scalino ska·lee·noh m step

scalo skah·loh m stopover (air travel)

scalogno ska·lohn·yoh m shallot

scaloppina ska·lop·pee·na f escalope

scalzo(a) skal·tsoh(a) adj barefoot

scamiciato ska·mee·chah·toh m
pinafore dress

scampi skam·pee mpl scampi

Scandinavia skan·dee·nah·vya f Scandinavia

scandinavo(a) skan·dee·nah·vo(a) adj
Scandinavian

scantinato skan·tee·nah·toh m cellar

scapolo skah·po·loh m bachelor

scappare skap·pah·ray vi escape

scarafaggio ska·ra·faj·joh m beetle

scaricare ska·ree·kah·ray vt unload

scaricato(a) ska·ree·kah·to(a) adj dead
(battery)

scarico(a) skah·ree·ko(a) adj flat (battery); **il luogo di scarico** lwo·go dee
skah·ree·ko dump (for rubbish)

scarlatto(a) skar·lat·to(a) adj scarlet

scarpa skar·pa f shoe

scarpetta da tennis *skar·payt·ta da ten·nees f* tennis shoe

scarpette *skar·payt·te fpl* sneakers

scarpone da sci *skar·poh·ne da shee m* ski boot

scassinatore *skas·see·na·toh·re m* burglar

scatola *skah·to·la f* box; carton; in scatola *een skah·to·la* canned; tinned (food); la scatola di fiammiferi *skah·to·la dee fyam·mee·fe·ree* matchbox; la scatola del cambio *skah·to·la del kam·byoh* gearbox; la scatola di cartone *skah·to·la dee kar·toh·ne* box (cardboard)

scattare *skat·tah·ray vt* take (photograph)

scavalcare *ska·val·kah·ray vt* climb over

scavare *ska·vah·ray vt* dig (hole); dig up

scegliere* *shayl·ye·ray vt* choose; pick

scelta *shayl·ta f* range (variety); selection; choice

scena *she·na f* scene; mettere* in scena *mayt·te·re een she·na* to produce (play)

scendere* *shayn·de·ray vt/i* go down □ *vi* go downhill

sceriffo *she·reef·foh m* sheriff

scheda *ske·da f* slip (of paper)

schedario *ske·dah·ree·oh m* card index; file

scheggia *skayj·ja f* splinter (wood)

schermo *skayr·moh m* screen (TV, movie)

scherzo *skayr·tsoh m* joke

schiacciare *skya·chah·ray vt* crush; squash; mash

schiaffeggiare *skyaf·fej·jah·ray vt* smack; slap

schiaffo *skyaf·foh m* smack

schiamazzo *skya·mats·tsoh m* row (noise)

schiantarsi *skyan·tar·see vr* shatter

schiavo(a) *skyah·vo(a) m/f* slave

schiena *skye·na f* back (of person); il mal di schiena *mal dee skye·na* backache

schienale *skye·nah·le m* back (of chair)

schiocco *skee·ok·koh m* crack (noise)

schiuma *skyoo·ma f* foam

schizzare *skeets·tsah·ray vt/i* splash

sci *shee m* ski; skiing; lo sci nautico *shee now·tee·ko* water-skiing; fare* dello sci nautico *fah·ray del·lo shee now·tee·ko* to go water-skiing; fare* dello sci *fah·ray del·lo shee* to go skiing

scialbo(a) *shal·bo(a) adj* drab

scialle *shal·le m* shawl; wrap

scialuppa di salvataggio *sha·loop·pa dee sal·va·taj·joh f* lifeboat (on ship)

sciampagna *sham·pan·ya m* champagne

sciampo *sham·poh m* shampoo

sciare *shee·ah·ray vi* ski

sciarpa *shar·pa f* scarf

sciatore *shee·a·toh·re m* skier

sciatrice *shee·a·tree·che f* skier

scientifico(a) *shen·tee·fee·ko(a) adj* scientific

scienza *shen·tsa f* science

scienziato(a) *shen·tsyah·to(a) m/f* scientist

scimmia *sheem·mya f* ape; monkey

scintilla *sheen·teel·la f* spark

scintillare *sheen·teel·lah·ray vi* sparkle

sciocchezze *shok·kayts·tse fpl* nonsense; rubbish

sciogliere* *shol·ye·re vt* untie; dissolve

sciogliersi *shol·yer·see vr* dissolve; melt

sciolto(a) *shol·to(a) adj* loose

scioperante *sho·pe·ran·te m/f* striker

scioperare *sho·pe·rah·ray vi* strike (workers)

sciopero *sho·pe·roh m* walkout; strike (industrial); lo sciopero bianco *sho·pe·roh byan·koh* go-slow; lo sciopero non ufficiale *sho·pe·roh nohn oof·fee·chah·lay* unofficial strike; in sciopero *een sho·pe·roh* on strike; paralizzato(a) da uno sciopero *pa·ra·leedz·dzah·to(a) da oo·no sho·pe·roh* strikebound

sciorinare *sho·ree·nah·ray vt* air (clothes)

sciovia *shee·o·vee·a f* ski lift

sciroppo *shee·rop·poh m* syrup; lo sciroppo per la tosse *shee·rop·poh payr la tohs·say* cough medicine

sciupato(a) *shoo·pah·to(a) adj* ruined; spoilt; shop-soiled

scivolare *shee·vo·lah·ray vi* slip; slide; glide

scodella *sko·del·la f* bowl; basin

scogliera *skol·ye·ra f* cliff

scoiattolo *sko·yat·to·loh m* squirrel

scolapiatti *sko·la·pyat·tee m —* draining-board

scolare *sko·lah·ray vt* drain

scommessa *skom·mays·sa f* bet

scommettere* *skom·mayt·te·re vt* bet

scomodo(a) *sko·mo·doh(a) adj* uncomfortable; inconvenient (time, place)

scompartimento *skom·par·tee·mayn·toh m* compartment (on train); lo scompartimento per non-fumatori *skom·par·tee·mayn·toh payr nohn·foo·ma·toh·ree* nonsmoker (compartment); lo scompartimento per fumatori *skom·par·tee·mayn·toh payr foo·ma·toh·ree* smoker

sconfiggere* *skon·feej·je·re vt* defeat

sconfitta *skon·feet·ta f* defeat

sconosciuto(a) *sko·no·shoo·to(a) adj* unknown □ *m/f* lo/la sconosciuto(a) *sko·no·shoo·to(a)* stranger

sconto *skohn·toh m* discount; sconto del 3% *skohn·toh del 3%* 3% off; con uno sconto *kohn oo·no skohn·toh* at a discount

scontrarsi *skon·trahr·see vr* collide

scontrino *skon·tree·noh m* ticket

scontro *skohn·troh m* collision; crash; avere* uno scontro con la macchina *a·vay·ray oo·noh skohn·troh kohn la mak·kee·na* to crash one's car

sconveniente *skon·ve·nyen·te adj* improper

scooter *skoo·ter m* scooter

scopa *skoh·pa f* broom

scopare *sko·pah·ray vt* sweep (floor)

scoperto *sko·per·toh m* overdraft

scopo *skoh·po m* aim; goal; purpose

scoppiare *skop·pyah·ray vi* burst; fare* scoppiare *fah·ray skop·pyah·ray* to burst

scoppio *skop·pyoh m* blast (explosion)

scoprire* *sko·pree·re vt* discover; find out; uncover

scoraggiato(a) *sko·raj·jah·to(a) adj* discouraged

scorciatoia *skor·cha·toh·ya f* short cut

scorrere* *skohr·re·re vi* flow; pour

scortese *skor·tay·zay adj* unkind; rude

scossa *skos·sa f* shock

scottarsi *skot·tar·see vr* scald

scottato(a) *skot·tah·to(a) adj* sunburnt (painfully)

scottatura *skot·ta·too·ra f* burn; sunburn (painful)

Scozia *sko·tsya f* Scotland
scozzese *skots·tsay·se adj* Scottish □ *m/f* lo/la scozzese *skots·tsay·se* Scot
scriminatura *skree·mee·na·too·ra f* parting (*in hair*)
scrittore *skreet·toh·re m* writer
scrittrice *skreet·tree·che f* writer
scrittura *skreet·too·ra f* writing
scrivania *skree·va·nee·a f* desk
scrivere* *skree·ve·re vt/i* write; spell; **scrivere* a stampatello** *skree·ve·re a stam·pa·tel·loh* to print (*write in block letters*)
scrutinio *skroo·tee·nyoh m* ballot
scultura *skool·too·ra f* sculpture
scuola *skwo·la f* school; **la scuola elementare** *skwo·la e·le·men·tah·ray* primary school; **la scuola serale** *skwo·la se·rah·lay* night school; **la scuola privata** *skwo·la pree·vah·ta* public school; **la scuola statale** *skwo·la sta·tah·le* state school; **la scuola media** *skwo·la me·dya* secondary school
scuotere* *skwo·te·re vt* shake
scure *skoo·re f* axe
scuro(a) *skoo·ro(a) adj* dark (*colour*)
scusa *skoo·za f* excuse (*pretext*)
scusare *skoo·zah·ray vt* excuse; **mi scusi** *mee skoo·zee* excuse me
scusarsi *skoo·zar·see vr* apologize
scusate *skoo·zah·te excl* pardon
sdraiarsi *zdra·yar·see vr* lie down
sdrucciolevole *zdrooch·cho·lay·vo·le adj* slippery
se *say conj* whether; if
sé *say pron* himself; herself; itself; oneself; themselves; **in sé** *een say* conscious; **l'ha fatto da sé** *la fat·to da say* he did it on his own; **se stesso(a)** *say stays·so(a)* oneself
sebbene *seb·be·ne conj* though
seccare *sek·kah·ray vt* bother (*annoy*)
seccarsi *sek·kahr·see vr* dry up
seccatura *sek·ka·too·ra f* nuisance; bother
secchio *sayk·kyoh m* pail; bucket
secco(a) *sayk·ko(a) adj* dried (*fruit, beans*); dry
secolo *se·ko·loh m* century
secondario(a) *se·kon·dah·ryo(a) adj* secondary; minor (*road*)
secondo(a) *se·kohn·do(a) adj* second □ *prep* according to □ *m* **il secondo** *se·kohn·doh* second (*time*); **di seconda mano** *dee se·kohn·da mah·noh* secondhand (*car etc*); **di seconda classe** *dee se·kohn·da klas·se* second-class
sedano *se·da·noh m* celery
sedativo *se·da·tee·voh m* sedative
sede *se·de f* seat; head office
sedere *se·day·re m* bottom (*of person*)
sedere* *se·day·re vi* sit, be seated
sedersi *se·dayr·see vr* sit down
sedia *se·dya f* chair; **la sedia a rotelle** *se·dya a ro·tel·le* wheelchair; **la sedia a sdraio** *se·dya a zdra·yo* deckchair; **la sedia pieghevole** *se·dya pye·gay·vo·le* folding chair
sedicesimo(a) *say·dee·che·zee·mo(a) adj* sixteenth
sedici *say·dee·chee num* sixteen
sedile *se·dee·le m* bench; **il sedile del passeggero** *se·dee·le del pas·sej·je·roh* passenger seat
seduto(a) *se·doo·toh(a) adj* sitting
segale *say·ga·le f* rye
seggio *sej·joh m* seat
seggiolone *sej·jo·loh·ne m* highchair
seggiovia *sej·jo·vee·a f* chair-lift

segnale *sen·yah·le m* signal; road sign; **il segnale di linea libera** *sen·yah·le dee lee·nay·a lee·bay·ra* dial(ling) tone; **il segnale "occupato"** *sen·yah·le ok·koo·pah·to* engaged tone; **il segnale di soccorso** *sen·yah·le dee sok·kohr·soh* distress signal; **il segnale d'allarme** *sen·yah·le dal·lahr·may* communication cord
segnare *sen·yah·ray vt* mark; score (*goal*)
segno *sayn·yoh m* sign; mark
segretario(a) *se·gre·tah·ryo(a) m/f* secretary; **il segretario generale** *se·gre·tah·ryo je·ne·rah·lay* company secretary; **il/la segretario(a)** particolare *se·gre·tah·ryo(a) par·tee·ko·lah·re* personal secretary
Segretario di Stato *se·gre·tah·ryo dee stah·toh m* secretary of state
segreto(a) *se·gray·to(a) adj* secret □ *m* **il segreto** *se·gray·toh* secret
seguente *se·gwen·te adj* following
seguire *se·gwee·re vt* follow □ *vi* follow; continue; **seguire qualcuno/qualcosa** *se·gwee·re kwal·koo·no/kwal·ko·sa* to come after someone/something
sei *sey num* six
sella *sel·la f* saddle
selvaggina *sel·vaj·jee·na f* game (*hunting*)
selvaggio(a) *sel·vaj·jo(a) adj* wild (*animal, tribe*)
selvatico(a) *sel·va·tee·ko(a) adj* wild (*flower*)
selz *selts m* soda water
semaforo *se·mah·fo·roh m* traffic lights
sembrare *sem·brah·ray vi* look; seem; **sembra malato** *saym·bra ma·lah·to* he appears ill
seme *say·me m* suit (*cards*); seed
semiaperto(a) *se·mee·a·per·to(a) adj* half open
semifinale *se·mee·fee·nah·le f* semifinal
seminterrato *se·meen·ter·rah·toh m* basement
semispecializzato(a) *se·mee·spe·cha·leedz·dzah·to(a) adj* semiskilled
semplice *saym·plee·che adj* plain; simple
sempre *sem·pre adv* always; ever; **sempre meno** *sem·pre may·noh* less and less
senape *say·na·pe f* mustard
senato *se·nah·toh m* senate
senatore *se·na·toh·re m* senator
seno *say·noh m* breast
sensibilità *sen·see·bee·lee·ta f —* feeling
senso *sen·soh m* sense; **avere* senso** *a·vay·re sen·soh* to make sense; **la strada a senso unico** *strah·da a sen·soh oo·nee·ko* one-way street; **il senso comune** *sen·soh ko·moo·ne* sense (*common sense*)
sentiero *sen·tye·roh m* path; footpath
sentinella *sen·tee·nel·la f* guard (*sentry*)
sentire *sen·tee·re vt* smell □ *vt/i* hear; **sento la mancanza di Londra** *sen·to la man·kan·tsa dee lohn·dra* I miss London; **non sento l'aglio** *nohn sen·to lal·yoh* I can't taste the garlic; **non La sento** *nohn la sen·to* I can't hear (you); **mi sento meglio** *mee sen·to mel·yoh* I feel better; **mi sento male** *mee sen·to mah·le* I feel sick; **mi sento venir meno** *mee sen·to ve·neer may·no* I feel faint
senza *sen·tsa prep* without; **rimanere*** senza benzina *ree·ma·nay·re sen·tsa*

ben·dzee·na to be out of petrol; siamo rimasti senza latte *syah·mo ree·ma·stee sen·tsa lat·te* we've run out of milk

separare *se·pa·rah·ray* vt divide (*separate*)

separato(a) *se·pa·rah·to(a)* adj separate

seppellire *sep·pel·lee·re* vt bury

sera *say·ra* f evening; di sera *dee say·ra* p.m.; la sera *la say·ra* in the evening

serbatoio *ser·ba·toh·yoh* m tank (*of car*)

serie *se·ree·e* f series; round (*of talks*)

serietà *se·ree·e·ta* f seriousness; reliability (*of person*)

serio(a) *se·ryo(a)* adj serious; reliable

serpeggiare *ser·pej·jah·ray* vi twist (*road*)

serpente *ser·pen·te* m snake

serra *ser·ra* f greenhouse

serratura *ser·ra·too·ra* f lock

servire *ser·vee·re* vt attend to; serve; non ci serve *nohn chee ser·ve* it's of no benefit (to us); a che serve? *a ke ser·ve* what's the point?; si serva use *ser·va* help yourself

servizi *ser·vee·tsee* mpl facilities

servizio *ser·vee·tsyoh* m service charge; service; report (*in press*); il servizio della domestica *ser·vee·tsyoh del·la do·mes·tee·ka* maid service; il servizio di camera *ser·vee·tsyoh dee kah·me·ra* room service; in servizio *een ser·vee·tsyoh* on duty (*doctor*); fuori servizio *fwo·ree ser·vee·tsyoh* off duty; il servizio sanitario *ser·vee·tsyoh sa·nee·tah·ryo* health service; il servizio di assistenza *ser·vee·tsyoh dee as·see·sten·tsa* after-sales service; i servizi sociali *ser·vee·tsee so·chah·lee* social services; il servizio di spola *ser·vee·tsyoh dee spo·la* shuttle (service) (*airline*); il servizio autobus *ser·vee·tsyoh ow·to·boos* bus service

sessanta *ses·san·ta* num sixty

sesso *ses·soh* m sex

sesto(a) *se·sto(a)* adj sixth

seta *say·ta* f silk; un vestito di seta *oon ve·stee·toh dee say·ta* a silk dress

setacciare *se·tach·chah·ray* vt sieve; sift

setaccio *se·tach·choh* m sieve

sete *say·te* f thirst; avere* sete *a·vay·re say·te* to be thirsty

settanta *set·tan·ta* num seventy

sette *set·te* num seven

settembre *set·tem·bre* m September

settentrionale *set·ten·tree·o·nah·lay* adj northern

setticemia *set·tee·che·mee·a* f blood poisoning

settimana *set·tee·mah·na* f week; la settimana scorsa *la set·tee·mah·na skohr·sa* last week; $40 la settimana *$40 la set·tee·mah·na* $40 a week

settimanale *set·tee·ma·nah·le* adj weekly □ m il settimanale *set·tee·ma·nah·le* weekly (*periodical*)

settimanalmente *set·tee·mah·nal·mayn·te* adv weekly

settimo(a) *set·tee·mo(a)* adj seventh

settore *set·toh·re* m sector; il settore privato *set·toh·re pree·vah·to* private sector; il settore pubblico *set·toh·re poob·blee·ko* public sector

severo(a) *se·ve·ro(a)* adj harsh; strict

sfacciataggine *sfach·cha·taj·jee·nay* f cheek (*impudence*)

sfacciato(a) *sfach·chah·to(a)* adj familiar (*impertinent*); cheeky

sfinito(a) *sfee·nee·to(a)* adj worn-out

sfoderato(a) *sfo·de·rah·to(a)* adj unlined (*clothes*)

sfondo *sfohn·doh* m background

sfortuna *sfor·too·na* f bad luck

sfortunatamente *sfor·too·nah·ta·mayn·tay adv* unfortunately

sfortunato(a) *sfor·too·nah·to(a)* adj unfortunate; unlucky

sforzare *sfor·tsah·ray* vt force; sforzarsi di fare qualcosa *sfor·tsar·see dee fah·ray kwal·ko·sa* to struggle to do something

sforzo *sfor·tsoh* m effort

sfuso(a) *sfoo·zo(a)* adj in bulk (*unpackaged*)

sgabello *zga·bel·loh* m stool

sgelare *zje·lah·ray* vi thaw

sghiacciare *zgyach·chah·ray* vt de-ice

sgombro *zgom·bro* m mackerel

sgonfio(a) *zgohn·fyo(a)* adj flat (*deflated*)

sgradevole *zgra·day·vo·le* adj unpleasant

sgualcito(a) *zgwal·chee·toh(a)* adj creased

sguardo *zgwar·doh* m look; glance

sguazzare *zgwats·tsah·ray* vi splash; paddle

shock *shok* m shock

si *see* pron himself; herself; oneself; each other; themselves; si lavano *see lah·va·no* they wash themselves

sì *see* adv yes

siccità *seech·chee·ta* f drought

Sicilia *see·chee·lya* f Sicily

sicuramente *see·koo·ra·mayn·te* adv surely; verrà sicuramente *ver·ra see·koo·ra·mayn·te* he's sure to come

sicurezza *see·koo·rayts·tsa* f safety; security (*at airport*); la sicurezza sociale *see·koo·rayts·tsa so·chah·le* social security

sicuro(a) *see·koo·ro(a)* adj safe; sure; sicuro che funzionerà *see·koo·ro ke foon·tsyoh·ne·ra* it's sure to work

sidro *see·droh* m cider

siepe *sye·pe* f hedge

siesta *sye·sta* f siesta

sigaretta *see·ga·rayt·ta* f cigarette

sigaro *see·ga·roh* m cigar

significare *seen·yee·fee·kah·ray* vt mean (*signify*)

significato *seen·yee·fee·kah·toh* m meaning

Signor *seen·yohr* m Mr

signora *seen·yoh·ra* f lady; madam; Signora *seen·yoh·ra* Mrs; Gentile Signora *jen·tee·le seen·yoh·ra* Dear Madam

signore *seen·yoh·ray* m sir; gentleman; Egregio Signore *e·gre·joh seen·yoh·ray* Dear Sir

Signorina *seen·yo·ree·na* f Miss; Ms

silenzio *see·len·tsyoh* m silence

silenziosamente *see·len·tsyoh·sa·mayn·te* adv quietly (*walk, work*)

silenzioso(a) *see·len·tsyoh·so(a)* adj silent

sillaba *seel·la·ba* f syllable

simbolico(a) *seem·bo·lee·koh(a)* adj nominal (*fee*)

simbolo *seem·bo·loh* m symbol

simile *see·mee·le* adj similar; alike

simmetrico(a) *seem·me·tree·ko(a)* adj symmetrical

simpatico(a) *seem·pa·tee·ko(a)* adj pleasant; nice (*person*)

simposio *seem·po·zyoh* m symposium

sinagoga *see·na·go·ga* f synagogue

sincero(a) *seen·che·ro(a)* adj sincere

sindacato *seen·da·kah·toh m* syndicate; trade union

sindaco *seen·da·koh m* mayor

sinfonia *seen·fo·nee·a f* symphony

singhiozzo *seen·gyots·tsoh m* sob; hiccup; **avere* il singhiozzo** *a·vay·re eel seen·gyots·tsoh* to have (the) hiccups

singolarmente *seen·go·lar·mayn·te adv* individually

singolo(a) *seen·go·lo(a) adj* single

sinistra *see·nee·stra f* the left; **girare a sinistra** *jee·rah·ray a see·nee·stra* to turn left

sinistro *see·nee·stroh m* accident

sinistro(a) *see·nee·stro(a) adj* left; **il lato sinistro** *lah·to see·nee·stro* the left side

sintetico(a) *seen·te·tee·ko(a) adj* synthetic

sintomo *seen·to·moh m* symptom

sirena *se·re·na f* siren

Siria *see·rya f* Syria

siriano(a) *see·ryah·no(a) adj* Syrian

sistema *see·ste·ma m* system; **il sistema hi-fi** *see·ste·ma hi·fi* hi-fi

sistematico(a) *see·ste·ma·tee·ko(a) adj* systematic

sito *see·toh m* site

situazione *see·too·a·tsyoh·ne f* situation

slacciare *zlach·chah·ray vt* unfasten; undo

slavo(a) *zlah·vo(a) m/f* Slav

sleale *zle·ah·lay adj* unfair

slegare *zle·gah·ray vt* untie

slip *zleep m* — briefs

slitta *zleet·ta f* sledge; sleigh

slittamento *zleet·ta·mayn·toh m* skid

slittare *zleet·tah·ray vi* skid

slogan *zlo·gan m* slogan

slogare *zlo·gah·ray vt* dislocate; **slogarsi la caviglia** *zlo·gar·see la ka·veel·ya* to sprain one's ankle

smagliatura *zmal·ya·too·ra f* ladder (in stocking)

smalto *zmal·toh m* nail polish, nail varnish; enamel

smarrirsi *zmar·reer·see vr* lose one's way

smarrito(a) *zmar·ree·toh(a) adj* missing (object)

smeraldo *zme·ral·doh m* emerald

smettere* *zmayt·te·ray vi* stop; cease; **smettere* di fare qualcosa** *zmayt·te·ray dee fah·ray kwal·ko·sa* to stop doing something; **smettere* di fumare** *zmayt·te·ray dee foo·mah·ray* to give up smoking

smoking *smo·keeng m* dinner jacket; evening dress (man's)

smorfia *zmor·fee·a f* grimace

smussato(a) *zmoos·sah·to(a) adj* blunt (knife)

snack-bar *znak·bar m* snack bar

snello(a) *znel·lo(a) adj* slim

snobistico(a) *zno·bee·stee·ko(a) adj* snobbish

sobbollire *sob·bol·lee·re vi* simmer

sobborgo *sob·bohr·goh m* suburb

sociale *so·chah·le adj* social

socialismo *so·cha·lee·zmoh m* socialism

socialista *so·cha·lee·sta adj* socialist □ *m/f* **il/la socialista** *so·cha·lee·sta* socialist

società *so·che·ta f* society; corporation (firm); **la società a responsabilità limitata** *so·che·ta a re·spon·sa·bee·lee·ta lee·mee·tah·ta* private limited company; **la società immobiliare** *so·che·ta eem·mo·beel·yah·re* building

society; **la società per azioni** *so·che·ta payr a·tsyoh·nee* joint-stock company

socio(a) *so·cho(a) m/f* associate □ *m* **il socio** *so·cho* member; **diventare socio di** *dee·ven·tah·ray so·cho dee* to join (club)

soda *so·da f* soda

soddisfacente *sod·dee·sfa·chen·te adj* satisfactory

soddisfare* *sod·dee·sfah·ray vt* satisfy

sodo *so·do adv* hard □ *adj* **sodo(a)** *so·do(a)* hard-boiled (egg)

soffiare *sof·fyah·ray vi* blow; **soffiarsi il naso** *sof·fyar·see eel nah·soh* to blow one's nose

soffice *sof·fee·che adj* soft

soffitta *sof·feet·ta f* loft; attic

soffitto *sof·feet·toh m* ceiling

soffocante *sof·fo·kan·te adj* stuffy

soffrire* *sof·free·re vt/i* suffer

sofisticato(a) *so·fee·stee·kah·to(a) adj* sophisticated

soggetto(a) a *soj·jet·to(a) a adj* subject to

soggiorno *soj·johr·noh m* visit; stay

sogliola *sol·yo·la f* lemon sole

sognare *son·yah·ray vt/i* dream; **sognare di** *son·yah·ray dee* to dream about

sogno *sohn·yoh m* dream

soia *so·ya f* soya bean

solamente *soh·la·mayn·te adv* only

solare *so·lah·re adj* solar

solco *sohl·koh m* track (on record)

soldato *sol·dah·toh m* soldier

soldi *sol·dee mpl* money; **fare* soldi** *fah·ray sol·dee* to make money

sole *soh·le m* sunshine; sun; **fare* un bagno di sole** *fah·ray oon ban·yoh dee soh·le* to sunbathe

soleggiato(a) *soh·lej·jah·to(a) adj* sunny

solido(a) *so·lee·do(a) adj* strong (structure, material); solid; fast (dye)

solitario(a) *so·lee·tah·ryo(a) adj* lonely

solito(a) *so·lee·to(a) adj* usual; **di solito** *dee so·lee·to* usually

solleticare *sol·le·tee·kah·ray vt* tickle

sollevare *sol·le·vah·ray vt* raise; lift; relieve

sollievo *sol·lye·voh m* relief (from pain, anxiety)

solo *soh·lo adv* only □ *adj* **solo(a)** *so·lo(a)* alone; lonely

solubile *so·loo·bee·le adj* soluble; **il caffè solubile** *kaf·fe so·loo·bee·le* instant coffee

soluzione *so·loo·tsyoh·ne f* solution

somigliare a *so·meel·yah·ray a vi* be like; look like

somma *sohm·ma f* sum; **la somma totale** *sohm·ma to·tah·le* sum total

sommare *som·mah·ray vt* add (up) (numbers)

sommario *som·mah·ryoh m* summary; outline

sommelier *so·muh·lyay m* wine waiter

sommergibile *som·mer·jee·bee·le m* submarine

sonnecchiare *son·nek·kyah·ray vi* doze

sonnellino *son·nel·lee·noh m* nap (sleep)

sonnifero *son·nee·fe·roh m* sleeping pill

sonno *sohn·noh m* sleep

sontuoso(a) *son·too·oh·so(a) adj* luxurious

sopportare *sop·por·tah·ray vt* bear (endure); stand

sopra *soh·pra prep* on; above; over

□ *adv* on top; above; **di sopra** *dee soh·pra* upstairs

sopracciglio *so·prach·cheel·yoh m* —**a** eyebrow

soprattassa *soh·prat·tas·sa f* surcharge

sopravvivere* *soh·prav·vee·ve·re vt/i* survive

sordo(a) *sohr·do(a) adj* deaf

sorella *so·rel·la f* sister

sorellastra *so·rel·la·stra f* stepsister

sorgente *sor·jen·te f* spring (*of water*)

sorgere* *sohr·je·re vi* rise (*sun*) □ *m* **il sorgere del sole** *sohr·je·re del soh·le* sunrise

sorpassare *sor·pas·sah·ray vt* overtake (*car*)

sorprendere* *sor·pren·de·re vt* surprise

sorpresa *sor·pray·sa f* surprise

sorpreso(a) *sor·pray·so(a) adj* surprised; **sorpreso(a) da** *sor·pray·so(a) da* surprised at

sorreggere* *sor·rej·je·re vt* bear (*weight*)

sorridere* *sor·ree·de·re vi* smile

sorriso *sor·ree·soh m* smile

sorvegliante *sor·vel·yan·te m/f* supervisor

sorvegliare *sor·vel·yah·ray vt* watch; supervise

S.O.S. *es·se·o·es·se m* SOS

sospendere* *so·spen·de·re vt* suspend (*worker*)

sospensione *so·spen·syoh·ne f* suspension

sospirare *so·spee·rah·ray vi* sigh

sosta *so·sta f* stop; **divieto di sosta** *dee·vye·toh dee so·sta* no waiting (*road sign*)

sostanza *so·stan·tsa f* substance; stuff

sostanzioso(a) *so·stan·tsyoh·so(a) adj* filling (*food*)

sostegno *so·stayn·yoh m* backing; support (*moral, financial*)

sostenere* *so·ste·nay·re vt* support

sostentamento *so·sten·ta·mayn·toh m* maintenance

sostituire *so·stee·too·ee·ray vt* replace (*substitute*); **sostituire qualcosa a qualcos'altro** *so·stee·too·ee·ray kwal·ko·sa a kwal·ko·sal·tro* to substitute something for something else

sostituto *so·stee·too·toh m* substitute

sostituzione *so·stee·too·tsyoh·nay f* replacement

sottaceti *sot·ta·chay·tee mpl* pickles

sottana *sot·tah·na f* slip (*underskirt*)

sotterraneo(a) *soht·ter·rah·ne·oh(a) adj* underground (*pipe etc*)

sottile *sot·tee·le adj* sheer (*stockings*); thin; subtle

sotto *soht·toh prep* underneath; under; below □ *adv* underneath; below; **di sotto** *dee soht·toh* downstairs; **sta di sotto** *sta dee soht·toh* it's underneath; **sotto Natale** *soht·toh na·tah·lay* near (to) Christmas

sottobicchiere *sot·toh·beek·kye·re m* mat (*under a glass*)

sottocommissione *sot·toh·kom·mees· syoh·ne f* subcommittee

sottoesposto(a) *soht·to·e·spoh·stoh(a) adj* underexposed

sottolineare *soht·to·lee·ne·ah·ray vt* emphasize; underline

sottopassaggio *soht·to·pas·saj·joh m* underpass (*for pedestrians*)

sottopiatto *soht·to·pyat·toh m* place mat; table-mat

sottoporre* *soht·to·pohr·re vt* submit (*proposal*)

sottosopra *soht·to·soh·pra adv* upside down

sottosviluppato(a) *soht·to·zvee·loop· pah·toh(a) adj* underdeveloped (*country*)

sottotitolo *soht·to·tee·to·loh m* subtitle (*of movie*)

sottovalutare *soht·to·va·loo·tah·ray vt* undervalue

sottoveste *soht·to·ve·ste f* petticoat

sottovia *soht·to·vee·a f* underpass (*for cars*)

sottrarre* *soht·trar·re vt* subtract

soufflé *soo·flay m* soufflé

sovietico(a) *so·vye·tee·ko(a) adj* Soviet

sovraesposto(a) *soh·vra·e·spoh·sto(a) adj* overexposed (*photo*)

sovvenzionare *sov·ven·tsyoh·nah·ray vt* subsidize

sovvenzione *sov·ven·tsyoh·ne f* subsidy; grant (*to institution*)

spaccatura *spak·ka·too·ra f* split (*tear*)

spada *spah·da f* sword

spaghetti *spa·gayt·tee mpl* spaghetti

Spagna *span·ya f* Spain

spagnolo *span·yo·loh m* Spanish □ **spagnolo(a)** *span·yo·lo(a) m/f* Spaniard □ *adj* Spanish

spago *spah·goh m* string

spalla *spal·la f* shoulder

spallina *spal·lee·na f* strap (*of dress etc*)

spalmare *spal·mah·ray vt* spread (*butter*)

sparare *spa·rah·ray vt* fire □ *vi* fire; shoot

sparire* *spa·ree·re vi* disappear

spartitraffico *spar·tee·traf·fee·koh m* — central reservation

spatola *spa·to·la f* spatula

spaventare *spa·ven·tah·ray vt* frighten

spazio *spa·tsyoh m* space; room

spazzaneve *spats·tsa·nay·ve m* — snowplough, snowplow

spazzola *spats·tso·la f* brush (*for cleaning*); **la spazzola per capelli** *spats·tso·la payr ka·payll·lee* hairbrush

spazzolare *spats·tso·lah·ray vt* brush

spazzolino *spats·tso·lee·noh m* brush; **lo spazzolino da unghie** *spats·tso·lee· noh da oon·gyay* nailbrush; **lo spaz· zolino da denti** *spats·tso·lee·noh da den·tee* toothbrush

specchietto retrovisore *spek·kyayt·toh re·tro·vee·zoh·ray m* rear-view mirror

specchio *spek·kyoh m* mirror

speciale *spe·chah·le adj* special

specialista *spe·cha·lee·sta m/f* specialist

specialità *spe·cha·lee·ta f* — speciality

specializzarsi *spe·cha·leedz·dzar·see vr* specialize

specializzato(a) *spe·cha·leedz·dzah· to(a) adj* skilled (*workers*)

specialmente *spe·chal·mayn·te adv* especially

specie *spe·che f* — kind

specificare *spe·chee·fee·kah·ray vt* specify

specificazioni *spe·chee·fee·ka·tsyoh·nee fpl* specifications

specifico(a) *spe·chee·fee·ko(a) adj* specific

spedire *spe·dee·re vt* send; dispatch; ship (*goods*); **spedire qualcosa per posta ordinaria** *spe·dee·re kwal·ko·sa payr po·sta or·dee·nah·rya* to send something surface mail

spedizione *spe·dee·tsyoh·ne f* expedition

spegnere* *spen'ye're* vt turn off; switch off; put out

spellarsi *spel·lar·see* vr peel

spendere* *spen'de·re* vt spend (*money*)

spento(a) *spen'to(a)* adj off (*radio, light*)

speranza *spe·ran'tsa* f hope

sperare *spe·rah'ray* vt/i hope; spero di sì/no *spe'ro dee see/no* I hope so/not

spesa *spay'sa* f expense (*cost*); fare• la spesa *fah'ray la spay'sa* to go shopping; le spese postali *spay'se po·stah'lee* postage; le spese generali *spay'se je·ne·rah'lee* overheads; le spese di rappresentanza *spay'se dee rap·pre·zen·tan'tsa* business expenses; le spese bancarie *spay'se ban·kah'rye* bank charges

spese *spay'se* fpl expenditure; expenses; costs (*of production etc*)

spesso *spays'so* adv often

spesso(a) *spays·so(a)* adj thick; spesso(a) 3 metri *spays·so(a) 3 me'tree* 3 metres thick

spettacolo *spet·ta·ko·loh* m show (*in theatre*); lo spettacolo di varietà *spet·ta·ko·loh dee va·ree·e·ta* variety show; lo spettacolo di suoni e luci *spet·ta·ko·loh dee swo·nee e loo·chee* son et lumière

spezie *spe'tsye* fpl spices

spezzarsi *spets·tsar'see* vr snap (*break*)

spezzatino *spets·tsa·tee'noh* m stew

spia *spee'a* f spy

spiacente *spya·chen'te* adj sorry

spiacere* *spya·chay·re* vi be sorry; le spiace se…? *le spyah'chay se* do you mind if…?

spiacevole *spya·chay·vo·le* adj unpleasant

spiaggia *spyaj·ja* f beach; shore

spiccare *speek·kah'ray* vi stand out

spicchio d'aglio *speek'kyoh dal'yoh* m clove of garlic

spiccioli *speech'cho·lee* mpl change (*money*)

spiedino *spye·dee'noh* m skewer

spiedo *spye'doh* m spit (*for roasting*)

spiegare *spee·e·gah'ray* vt explain; unfold; spread out

spiegazione *spye·ga·tsyoh'ne* f explanation

spilla *speel'la* f brooch

spillo *speel'loh* m pin; lo spillo di sicurezza *speel·loh dee see·koo·rayts'tsa* safety pin

spina *spee'na* f bone (*of fish*); plug (*electric*); la spina dorsale *spee'na dor·sah'le* spine (*backbone*)

spinaci *spee·nah·chee* mpl spinach

spingere* *speen·je·re* vt push

spirito *spee·ree·toh* m spirit; giù di spirito *joo dee spee·ree·toh* depressed (*person*)

splendente *splen·den·te* adj shiny

splendere *splen·de·re* vi shine (*sun etc*)

splendido(a) *splen·dee·doh(a)* adj splendid

spogliarellista *spol·ya·rel·lee·sta* f stripper

spogliarello *spol·ya·rel·loh* m striptease

spogliarsi *spol·yar·see* vr undress

spogliatoio *spol·ya·to·yo* m dressing room

spolverare *spol·ve·rah·ray* vt dust (*furniture*)

sporcizia *spor·chee·tsya* f dirt

sporco(a) *spor·ko(a)* adj dirty

sport *sport* m — sport; gli sport invernali *sport een·ver·nah·lee* winter sports

sposa *spo·za* f bride

sposare *spo·zah·ray* vt marry

sposarsi *spo·zahr·see* vr marry; si sono sposati ieri *see so·noh spo·zah·tee ye·ree* they were married yesterday

sposato(a) *spo·zah·toh(a)* adj married

sposo *spo·zoh* m bridegroom

spostare *spo·stah·ray* vt move

sprecare *spre·kah·ray* vt waste

spreco *spre·koh* m waste

spremere *spre·me·re* vt squeeze (*lemon*)

spremilimoni *spre·mee·lee·moh·nee* m — lemon-squeezer

spremuta *spray·moo·ta* f fresh juice

spruzzare *sproots·tsah·ray* vt spray (*liquid*); spruzzare con acqua *sproots·tsah·ray kohn ak·kwa* to sprinkle with water

spruzzo *sproots·tsoh* m spray (*of liquid*)

spugna *spoon·ya* f sponge

spumante *spoo·man·te* adj sparkling (*wine*)

spuntare *spoon·tah·ray* vt trim (*hair*)

spuntino *spoon·tee·noh* m snack

sputare *spoo·tah·ray* vi spit

squadra *skwa·dra* f team

squalificare *skwa·lee·fee·kah·ray* vt disqualify

squash *skwosh* m squash (*sport*)

squattrinato(a) *skwat·tree·nah·to(a)* adj broke (*penniless*)

squillare *skweel·lah·ray* vi ring

S.r.l. *es·se·er·re·el·le* abbrev Ltd

stabile *stah·bee·le* adj stable; firm (*object, material*) □ m lo stabile *stah·bee·le* building

stabilimento *sta·bee·lee·mayn·toh* m plant (*factory*)

stabilire *sta·bee·lee·re* vt establish

staccarsi *stak·kahr·see* vr come off

stadio *sta·dyoh* m stadium

stagionato(a) *sta·joh·nah·to(a)* adj ripe (*cheese*); mature

stagione *sta·joh·ne* f season; la stagione di villeggiatura *la sta·joh·ne dee vee·lej·ja·too·ra* the holiday season; di bassa stagione *dee bas·sa sta·joh·ne* off-season

stagno *stan·yoh* m tin (*substance*); pond (*natural*)

stagnola *stan·yo·la* f tin foil

stalla *stal·la* f stable

stampa *stam·pa* f print; press (*newspapers, journalists*)

stampare *stam·pah·ray* vt print (*book, newspaper*)

stampatello *stam·pa·tel·loh* m block letters

stampato *stam·pah·toh* m printout

stancarsi *stan·kahr·see* vr get tired

stanco(a) *stan·ko(a)* adj tired

standard *stan·dard* adj standard

stanotte *sta·not·te* adv tonight; last night

stantio(a) *stan·tee·o(a)* adj stale; flat (*beer*)

stanza *stan·tsa* f room (*in house*); la stanza da letto *stan·tsa da let·toh* bedroom; la stanza da bagno *stan·tsa da ban·yoh* bathroom

stare* *stah·ray* vi stay; be; stare• per fare qualcosa *stah·ray payr fah·ray kwal·ko·sa* to be about to do something; stare• in piedi *stah·ray een pye·dee* to stand; mi sta bene *mee sta be·ne* it fits (me); quel cappello ti sta bene *kwayl kap·pel·loh tee sta be·ne* that hat suits you; **non ci sta** *nohn chee sta* it won't go in; **come sta?** *koh·me sta* how are you?; **sta bene** *sta be·ne* he's all right (*safe, fit*)

starnutire *star·noo·tee·re* vi sneeze

starnuto *star·noo·toh* m sneeze

stasera *sta·say·ra* adv tonight

statistica *sta·tee·stee·ka* f statistics; statistic

statistico(a) *sta·tee·stee·ko(a)* adj statistical

Stati Uniti (d'America) *stah·tee oo·nee·tee (da·me·ree·ka)* mpl United States (of America), US(A)

stato *stah·toh* m state (*condition*); **lo Stato** *stah·toh* the State

statua *sta·too·a* f statue

statura *sta·too·ra* f height (*of person*)

stazionario(a) *sta·tsyoh·nah·ryo(a)* adj stationary; unchanged

stazione *sta·tsyoh·ne* f station; resort; **la stazione di servizio** *sta·tsyoh·ne ser·vee·tsyoh* petrol station; service station; **la stazione balneare** *sta·tsyoh·ne bal·ne·ah·re* seaside resort; **la stazione autobus** *sta·tsyoh·ne ow·to·boos* bus depot; **la stazione radio** *sta·tsyoh·ne ra·dyoh* station (*radio*); **la stazione termale** *sta·tsyoh·ne ter·mah·le* spa

stecca *stayk·ka* f splint; carton

stella *stayl·la* f star

stelo *ste·loh* m stem

stendere* *sten·de·re* vt stretch; spread; hang out; lay down

stendersi* *sten·der·see* vr lie down

stenodattilografo(a) *ste·no·dat·tee·lo·gra·fo(a)* m/f shorthand typist

stenografia *ste·no·gra·fee·a* f shorthand

stereo *ste·re·oh* m stereo(phonic)

stereofonico(a) *ste·re·o·fo·nee·ko(a)* adj stereo(phonic)

sterile *ste·ree·le* adj sterile

sterilizzare *ste·ree·leedz·dzah·ray* vt sterilize (*disinfect*)

sterlina *ster·lee·na* f sterling; pound

sterzo *ster·tsoh* m steering wheel; steering (*in car*)

stesso(a) *stays·so(a)* adj same □ pron lo/la stesso(a) *lo/la stays·so(a)* the same (one); **lo stesso, per favore** *lo stays·so pyer fa·voh·re* (the) same again please!; **l'ho fatto io stesso** *loh fat·toh ee·oh stays·so* I did it myself

stile *stee·le* m style

stima *stee·ma* f estimate

stimare *stee·mah·ray* vt estimate

stinco *steen·koh* m shin

stipendio *stee·pen·dyoh* m salary; **lo stipendio netto** *stee·pen·dyoh nayt·to* take-home pay

stipula *stee·poo·la* f stipulation

stipulare *stee·poo·lah·ray* vt stipulate

stirare *stee·rah·ray* vt press; iron

stirarsi *stee·rar·see* vr strain (*muscle*); stretch

stitico(a) *stee·tee·koh(a)* adj constipated

stivale *stee·vah·le* m boot

stivalone di gomma *stee·va·loh·ne dee gohm·ma* m wellington boot

stock *stok* m stock (*in shop*)

stoffa *stof·fa* f material (*fabric*)

stola *sto·la* f stole (*wrap*)

stomaco *sto·ma·koh* m stomach; **il mal di stomaco** *mal dee sto·ma·koh* stomach ache; **ho mal di stomaco** *o mal dee sto·ma·koh* I have (a) stomach ache

stoppino *stop·pee·noh* m wick

storcere* *stor·che·re* vt twist

stordire *stor·dee·re* vt stun

storia *sto·ree·a* f history; story; **fare* delle storie** *fah·ray del·le sto·ree·e* to make a fuss

storto(a) *stor·toh(a)* adj crooked

stoviglie *sto·veel·ye* fpl crockery

straccio *strach·choh* m rag; cloth

strada *strah·da* f road; street; **la strada principale** *strah·da preen·chee·pah·le* high street; **la strada secondaria** *strah·da se·kohn·dah·rya* side-road, side-street; **la strada sussidiaria** *strah·da soos·see·dee·ah·ree·a* relief road; **la strada statale** *strah·da sta·tah·le* highway; **la strada a doppia carreggiata** *strah·da a dohp·pya kar·rej·jah·ta* dual carriageway; **strada facendo** *strah·da fa·chen·do* on the way

strangolare *stran·go·lah·ray* vt strangle

straniero(a) *stran·ye·ro(a)* adj foreign; overseas (*visitor*) □ m/f lo/la straniero(a) *stran·ye·ro(a)* foreigner

strano(a) *strah·no(a)* adj strange; odd

straordinario(a) *stra·or·dee·nah·ree·o(a)* adj extraordinary; **fare* dello straordinario** *fah·ray del·lo stra·or·dee·nah·ree·o* to work overtime

strappare *strap·pah·ray* vt tear; rip; pull off

strapparsi *strap·par·see* vr rip; split

strappo *strap·poh* m tear

strascico *stra·shee·koh* m train (*on dress*)

strato *strah·toh* m layer

stravagante *stra·va·gan·te* adj extravagant; odd (*peculiar*)

strega *stray·ga* f witch

strettamente *strayt·ta·mayn·te* adv tightly

stretto(a) *strayt·toh(a)* adj narrow; tight (*clothes*)

strillare *streel·lah·ray* vi scream

strillo *streel·loh* m scream

stringa *streen·ga* f shoelace

stringere* *streen·je·re* vt squeeze (*hand*); **stringere* la mano a qualcuno** *streen·je·re la mah·noh a kwal·koo·no* to shake hands with someone

stringersi* nelle spalle *streen·jer·see nel·le spal·le* vr shrug

striscia *stree·sha* f strip; stripe; streak

strisciare *stree·shah·ray* vt scrape □ vi crawl

strizzare *streets·tsah·ray* vt wring (*clothes*)

strofinaccio *stro·fee·nach·choh* m duster (*cloth*); **lo strofinaccio per i piatti** *stro·fee·nach·choh payr ee pyat·tee* dishcloth

strofinare *stro·fee·nah·ray* vt rub

strumento *stroo·mayn·toh* m instrument

struttura *stroot·too·ra* f structure

stucchevole *stook·kay·vo·le* adj sickly (*cake etc*)

studente *stoo·den·te* m student

studentessa *stoo·den·tays·sa* f student

studiare *stoo·dyah·ray* vt/i study

studio *stoo·dyoh* m study; studio; **lo studio della fattibilità** *stoo·dyoh del·la fat·tee·bee·lee·ta* feasibility study

stufa *stoo·fa* f stove

stufato *stoo·fah·toh* m stew □ adj stufato(a) *stoo·fah·to(a)* braised

stufo(a) *stoo·fo(a)* adj fed up

stuoia *stoo·oy·a* f mat

stupido(a) *stoo·pee·do(a)* adj stupid; dumb; silly

stupore *stoo·poh·re* m amazement

su *soo prep* on; onto; about □ *adv* up; in **su** *een soo* upwards; uphill; **sulla tavola** *sool·la tah·vo·la* on the table; **sul treno** *sool tre·noh* on the train

sua *soo·a adj* his; her; its; your □ *pron* his; hers; its; yours; **Sua** *soo·a* your; yours

subappaltatore *soo·bap·pal·ta·toh·re m* subcontractor

subappalto *soo·bap·pal·toh m* subcontract

subire *soo·bee·re vt* suffer

subito *soo·bee·to adv* at once; immediately; straight away

subordinato(a) *soo·bor·dee·nah·to(a) adj* subordinate □ *m/f* il/la **subordinato(a)** *soo·bor·dee·nah·to(a)* subordinate

subtotale *soob·to·tah·le m* subtotal

suburbano(a) *soo·boor·bah·no(a) adj* suburban

succedere* *sooch·che·de·re vi* happen; che cosa gli è successo? *ke ko·sa lyee e sooch·ches·so* what happened to him?

successo *sooch·ches·soh m* success

succhiare *sook·kyah·ray vt* suck

succhietto *sook·kyayt·toh m* dummy (baby's)

succo *sook·koh m* juice; **il succo di limone** *sook·koh dee lee·moh·ne* lemon juice; **il succo di pompelmo** *sook·koh dee pom·pel·moh* grapefruit juice

succoso(a) *sook·koh·so(a) adj* juicy

succursale *sook·koor·sah·le f* branch (of store, bank etc)

sud *sood m* south; **al sud** *al sood* south

Sud-Africa *soo·da·free·ka m* South Africa

sudafricano(a) *soo·da·free·kah·no(a) adj* South African

sudamericano(a) *soo·da·me·ree·kah·no(a) adj* South American

sudare *soo·dah·ray vi* sweat

suddito(a) *sood·dee·to(a) m/f* subject (person)

sud-est *sood·dest m* southeast

sudicio(a) *soo·dee·choh(a) adj* filthy

sudiciume *soo·dee·choo·me m* filth

sudore *soo·doh·re m* sweat

sud-ovest *sood·do·vest m* southwest

sue *soo·e adj* his; her; its; your □ *pron* his; hers; its; yours; **Sue** *soo·e* your; yours

sufficiente *soof·fee·chen·te adj* sufficient

suggerimento *sooj·je·ree·mayn·toh m* suggestion

suggerire *sooj·je·ree·re vt* suggest

sughero *soo·ge·roh m* cork

sugli = su + gli

sugna *soon·ya f* suet

sui = su + i

suicidio *soo·ee·chee·dyoh m* suicide

suo *soo·o adj* his; her; its; your □ *pron* his; hers; its; yours; **Suo** *soo·o* your; yours

suocera *swo·che·ra f* mother-in-law

suocero *swo·che·roh m* father-in-law

suoi *swoy adj* his; her; its; your □ *pron* his; hers; its; yours; **Suoi** *swoy* your; yours

suola *swo·la f* sole (of shoe)

suolo *swo·loh m* soil

suonare *swo·nah·ray vi* ring; ring the (door)bell; **suonare il violino** *swo·nah·ray eel vee·o·lee·noh* to play the violin; **suonare il clacson** *swo·nah·ray eel klak·son* to sound one's horn

suono *swo·noh m* sound

superare *soo·pe·rah·ray vt* exceed; get through (exam); overtake (car)

superbo(a) *soo·per·boh(a) adj* proud; superb

superficie *soo·per·fee·che f* surface

superiore *soo·pe·ryoh·re adj* upper; senior (in rank); superior (quality) □ *m* il **superiore** *soo·pe·ryoh·re* superior

supermercato *soo·per·mer·kah·toh m* supermarket

superpetroliera *soo·per·pe·tro·lye·ra f* supertanker

superstizione *soo·per·stee·tsyoh·ne f* superstition

supplementare *soop·ple·men·tah·re adj* extra

supplente *soop·plen·te adj* temporary; acting

supporre* *soop·pohr·re vt* suppose; figure; assume; **suppongo che verrà** *soop·pohn·go ke ver·ra* I expect he'll come

supposta *soop·poh·sta f* suppository

surfing *soor·feeng m* surfing; **fare* del surfing** *fah·ray del soor·feeng* to go surfing; **il surfing a vela** *soor·feeng a vay·la* windsurfing

surriscaldarsi *soor·ree·skal·dahr·see vr* overheat (engine)

susina *soo·see·na f* plum

sussidio *soos·see·dyoh m* subsidy; **i sussidi visivi** *soos·see·dee vee·zee·vee* visual aids

sussurrare *soos·soor·rah·ray vi* whisper

svago *zva·goh m* relaxation; pastime

svaligiare *zva·lee·jah·ray vt* rob (bank)

svalutare *zva·loo·tah·ray vt* devalue (currency)

svalutazione *zva·loo·ta·tsyoh·ne f* devaluation

svantaggiato(a) *zvan·taj·jah·to(a) adj* at a disadvantage

svantaggio *zvan·taj·joh m* disadvantage; handicap

svedese *zve·day·se adj* Swedish □ *m/f* lo/la **svedese** *zve·day·se* Swede □ *m* lo **svedese** *zve·day·se* Swedish

sveglia *zvayl·ya f* alarm (clock)

svegliare *zvel·yah·ray vt* wake; **mi svegli alle 7 di mattina** *mee zvayl·yee al·lay 7 dee mat·tee·na* call me at 7 a.m. (in hotel etc)

svegliarsi *zvel·yar·see vr* wake up

sveglio(a) *zvayl·yo(a) adj* awake; sharp (intelligent)

svelto(a) *zvel·toh(a) adj* quick

svenire* *zve·nee·re vi* faint

sventolare *zven·to·lah·ray vi* flap (sail)

svestire *zve·stee·re vt* undress

svestirsi *zve·steer·see vr* undress

Svezia *zve·tsya f* Sweden

sviluppare *zvee·loop·pah·ray vt* develop; expand (business)

svilupparsi *zvee·loop·par·see vr* expand (business); develop

sviluppo *zvee·loop·poh m* development

svincolo *zveen·ko·loh m* slip-road

svitare *zvee·tah·ray vt* unscrew

Svizzera *zveets·tse·ra f* Switzerland

svizzero(a) *zveets·tse·ro(a) adj* Swiss

svolta *zvol·ta f* turn

svuotare *zvwo·tah·ray vt* empty; drain (sump, pool)

T

tabaccaio(a) *ta·bak·ka·yoh(a) m/f* tobacconist

tabaccheria *ta·bak·ke·ree·a f* tobacconist's (shop)

tabacco ta·bak·koh m tobacco; **il tabacco da fiuto** ta·bak·koh da fyoo·toh snuff

tabella ta·bel·la f table (list)

tabellone ta·bel·loh·nay m notice board

taccheggio tak·kayj·joh m shoplifting

tacchino tak·kee·noh m turkey

tacco tak·koh m heel (of shoe); **i tacchi a spillo** tak·kee a speel·loh stiletto heels

tachimetro ta·kee·me·troh m speedometer

tafano ta·fah·noh m horsefly

taglia tal·ya f size (of clothes); **di taglia grande** dee tal·ya gran·de outsize (clothes)

tagliare tal·yah·ray vt cut; **farsi• tagliare i capelli** far·see tal·yah·ray ee ka·pel·lee to get one's hair cut; **tagliare qualcosa in due** tal·yah·ray kwal·ko·sa een doo·e to cut something in half

tagliarsi tal·yahr·see vr cut oneself

taglierini tal·ye·ree·nee mpl noodles

taglio tal·yoh m cut; **il taglio dei capelli** tal·yoh dey ka·payl·lee haircut (style)

tailleur tye·yur m suit (women's)

tailleur-pantalone tye·yur·pan·ta·loh·ne m trouser-suit

talco tal·koh m talc(um powder)

tale tah·le adj such; **un tale libro** oon tah·le lee·broh such a book; **tali libri** tah·lee lee·bree such books

talento ta·len·toh m gift (ability); talent

talloncino tal·lon·chee·noh m counterfoil

tallone tal·loh·ne m heel

tamburo tam·boo·roh m drum

tampone assorbente tam·poh·ne as·sor·ben·te m tampon

tango tan·goh m tango

tanti(e) tan·tee(·te) adj so many

tanto(a) tan·to(a) adj so much □ adv tanto tan·to so; so much; **tanto(a) quanto(a)** tan·to(a) kwan·to(a) as much/many as; **ogni tanto** on·yee tan·to now and then, now and again; **di tanto in tanto** dee tan·to een tan·to from time to time

tappa tap·pa f stage (point); **a tappe** a tap·pe in stages

tappare tap·pah·ray vt plug

tappetino tap·pe·tee·noh m rug

tappeto tap·pay·toh m carpet

tappezzare tap·pets·tsah·ray vt paper (wall)

tappo tap·poh m top (of bottle); cork; stopper; plug (for basin etc); **i tappi per gli orecchi** tap·pee payr lyee o·rayk·kee earplugs

tardi tar·dee adv late; late in the day; **piú tardi** pyoo tar·dee later

tardivo(a) tar·dee·vo(a) adj backward (child)

targa d'immatricolazione tahr·ga deem·ma·tree·ko·la·tsyoh·nay f numberplate

tariffa ta·reef·fa f tariff (list of charges); rate (price); **la tariffa ridotta** ta·reef·fa ree·doht·ta half-fare; **la tariffa doganale** ta·reef·fa do·ga·nah·le customs tariff

tartufo tar·too·foh m truffle (fungus)

tasca ta·ska f pocket

tassa tas·sa f tax; **le tasse comunali** tas·se ko·moo·nah·lee rates (local tax); **la tassa industriale** tas·sa een·doo·stryah·lay corporation tax

tassare tas·sah·ray vt tax

tassazione tas·sa·tsyoh·ne f taxation

tassi tas·see m — taxi; cab

tasso tas·soh m rate; **il tasso d'interesse** tas·soh deen·te·res·se interest rate; **il tasso di cambio** tas·soh dee kam·byoh exchange rate

tasso d'inflazione tas·soh deen·fla·tsyoh·ne m rate of inflation

tasto ta·stoh m key (of piano, typewriter)

tattica tat·tee·ka f tactics

tavola tah·vo·la f table; plank; **la tavola reale** tah·vo·la re·ah·le backgammon; **la tavola da surfing** tah·vo·la da soor·feeng surf board; **la tavola da toeletta** tah·vo·la da to·e·let·ta dressing table; **tavola calda** tah·vo·la kal·da snack bar

tavoletta tah·vo·layt·ta f bar

tazza tats·tsa f mug; cup; **la tazza da tè** tats·tsa da te teacup; **la tazza da caffè** tats·tsa da kaf·fe coffee cup

tè te m — tea; **il tè alla menta** te al·la mayn·ta mint tea

te tay pron you; **te stesso(a)** tay stays·so(a) (you) yourself

teatro te·ah·troh m theater, theatre; drama (art)

tecnica tek·nee·ka f technique

tecnico(a) tek·nee·ko(a) adj technical □ m/f il/la tecnico(a) tek·nee·ko(a) technician

tecnologia tek·no·lo·jee·a f technology

tecnologico(a) tek·no·lo·jee·ko(a) adj technological

tedesco(a) te·day·skoh(a) adj German □ m il tedesco te·day·skoh German

tee tee m — tee (in golf)

tegame te·gah·me m pan (saucepan)

tegola tay·go·la f tile (on roof)

teiera te·ye·ra f teapot

tela tay·la f cloth; canvas; **la tela di blue-jeans** tay·la dee bloo·jeens denim; **la tela impermeabile** tay·la eem·payr·may·ah·bee·lay groundsheet

telaio te·la·yoh m chassis

telecamera te·le·kah·me·ra f camera (TV)

telecomando te·le·ko·man·doh m remote control

telecomunicazioni te·le·ko·moo·nee·ka·tsyoh·nee fpl telecommunications

telefonare te·le·fo·nah·ray vt/i telephone; **telefonare ad onere del destinatario** te·le·fo·nah·ray ad o·ne·re del de·stee·na·tah·ree·oh to reverse the charges; **sta telefonando** sta te·le·fo·nan·do he's on the phone

telefonata te·le·fo·nah·ta f phone-call; **la telefonata con la R** te·le·fo·nah·ta kohn la er·re reversed charge call; **la telefonata personale** te·le·fo·nah·ta per·so·nah·le person-to-person call

telefonista te·le·fo·nee·sta m/f telephonist; operator

telefono te·le·fo·noh m telephone; **il telefono interno** te·le·fo·noh een·ter·no extension; **essere• al telefono** es·se·re al te·le·fo·noh to be on the telephone; **per telefono** payr te·le·fo·noh by telephone

telegrafare te·le·gra·fah·ray vt/i telegraph

telegramma te·le·gram·ma m telegram; wire

telemetro te·le·me·troh m range finder (on camera)

teleobiettivo te·le·o·byet·tee·voh m telephoto lens

telescopio te·le·sko·pyoh m telescope

teleselezione *te·le·se·le·tsyoh·ne f* S.T.D.

teletrasmettere* *te·le·tra·zmayt·te·re vt* televise

televisione *te·le·vee·zyoh·ne f* television; **la televisione a circuito chiuso** *te·le·vee·zyoh·ne a cheer·koo·ee·toh kyoo·soh* closed circuit television; **la televisione a colori** *te·le·vee·zyoh·ne a ko·loh·ree* colo(u)r TV; **alla televisione** *al·la te·le·vee·zyoh·ne* on television

televisore *te·le·vee·zoh·re m* television (set)

telex *te·lex* — telex

temere *te·may·ray vt/i* fear; dread; **temo di no** *te·mo dee no* I'm afraid not

temperatura *tem·pe·ra·too·ra f* temperature; **prendere* la temperatura a qualcuno** *pren·de·re la tem·pe·ra·too·ra a kwal·koo·no* to take someone's temperature

temperino *tem·pe·ree·noh m* penknife; pocketknife

tempesta *tem·pe·sta f* storm

tempestoso(a) *tem·pe·stoh·so(a) adj* stormy

tempio *tem·pyoh m* temple (building)

tempo *tem·poh m* weather; time; **a tempo parziale** *a tem·poh par·tsyah·le* part-time; **poco/molto tempo** *po·ko/mohl·to tem·poh* a short/long time; **nei tempi passati** *nay tem·pee pas·sah·tee* in times past; **il tempo libero** *tem·poh lee·be·ro* spare time; **non prenderò molto tempo** *nohn pren·de·ro mohl·to tem·poh* I shan't be long; **giusto in tempo** *joo·sto een tem·poh* just in time

temporale *tem·po·rah·le m* thunderstorm

tenda *ten·da f* curtain; drape; tent

tendenza *ten·den·tsa f* trend; tendency

tendere* *ten·de·re vt* stretch; hold out; **tendere* a fare qualcosa** *ten·de·re a fah·ray kwal·ko·sa* to tend to do something

tendina *ten·dee·na f* blind; window shade

tenere* *te·nay·re vt* keep; hold; lo **tenga fermo** *lo ten·ga fayr·mo* hold him still; **tenga il resto!** *ten·ga eel re·stoh* keep the change!; **tenere* qualcosa per più tardi** *te·nay·re kwal·ko·sa payr pyoo tar·dee* to keep something till later; **tenere* qualcosa in ordine** *te·nay·re kwal·ko·sa een ohr·dee·ne* to keep something tidy

tenero(a) *te·ne·ro(a) adj* tender

tennis *ten·nees m* tennis; **il tennis da tavolo** *ten·nees da tah·vo·loh* table tennis; **il tennis su erba** *ten·nees soo er·ba* lawn tennis

tenore di vita *te·noh·re dee vee·ta m* standard of living

tensione *ten·syoh·nay f* voltage; tension

tentare *ten·tah·ray vt* attempt; tempt

tentativo *ten·ta·tee·voh m* attempt

tenuta *te·noo·ta f* estate (property)

teoria *te·o·ree·a f* theory

teppista *tep·pee·sta m* vandal

tergicristallo *ter·jee·kree·stal·loh m* windscreen wiper

terilene *te·ree·le·ne m* terylene

terminal *ter·mee·nal m* terminal

terminare *ter·mee·nah·ray vt/i* end

termine *ter·mee·ne m* term; **a breve termine** *a bre·ve ter·mee·ne* short term

termometro *ter·mo·me·troh m* thermometer

termos *ter·mos m* — Thermos (flask)

terra *ter·ra f* ground; earth; soil; land (opposed to sea); **a terra** *a ter·ra* ashore

terrapieno *ter·ra·pye·noh m* embankment

terrazza *ter·rats·tsa f* terrace

terremoto *ter·re·mo·toh m* earthquake

terreni *ter·ray·nee mpl* grounds (land)

terribile *ter·ree·bee·le adj* awful; terrible

territorio *ter·ree·to·ryoh m* territory

terrorismo *ter·ro·ree·zmoh m* terrorism

terrorista *ter·ro·ree·sta m/f* terrorist

terzino *ter·tsee·noh m* back (in sports)

terzo(a) *ter·tso(a) adj* third; **la terza (marcia)** *ter·tsa (mar·cha)* third (gear)

Terzo Mondo *ter·tso mohn·doh m* Third World

teschio *te·skyoh m* skull

teso(a) *tay·so(a) adj* tight (rope); tense

tesoro *te·zo·roh m* treasure

tessere *tes·se·re vt* weave

tessili *tes·see·lee mpl* textiles

tessitura *tes·see·too·ra f* texture

tessuto *tes·soo·toh m* fabric

testa *te·sta f* head; **il mal di testa** *mal dee te·sta* headache; **avere* mal di testa** *a·vay·re mal dee te·sta* to have a headache; **essere* in testa** *es·se·re een te·sta* to lead (in contest)

testamento *te·sta·mayn·toh m* will (testament)

testardo(a) *te·star·do(a) adj* stubborn

testimone *te·stee·mo·ne m* witness; **il testimone dello sposo** *te·stee·mo·ne del·lo spo·zoh* best man

testimonianza *te·stee·mo·nyan·tsa f* evidence (of witness)

testo *te·stoh m* text

tetraone *te·tra·oh·nay m* grouse (bird)

tettarella *tet·ta·rel·la f* teat (for bottle); dummy

tetto *tayt·toh m* roof; **il tetto mobile** *tayt·toh mo·bee·le* sunroof

tettoia *tet·toh·ya f* shelter

thermos *ter·mos m* — flask

thriller *threel·ler m* thriller (film)

ti *tee pron* you; to you; yourself

tifoso *tee·foh·soh m* fan (supporter)

tigre *tee·gre f* tiger

timbro *teem·broh m* stamp (rubber)

timido(a) *tee·mee·do(a) adj* shy

timo *tee·mo m* thyme

timone *tee·moh·nay m* rudder

tingere* *teen·je·re vt* dye

tinta *teen·ta f* dye

tintoria *teen·to·ree·a f* dry-cleaner's

tintura *teen·too·ra f* dye; rinse (for hair)

tipico(a) *tee·pee·ko(a) adj* typical

tipo *tee·poh m* type (sort)

tipografo *tee·po·gra·foh m* printer

tirare *tee·rah·ray vt* pull; **tirare lo sciacquone** *tee·rah·ray lo shak·kwoh·ne* to flush the toilet

tirchio(a) *teer·kyoh(a) adj* mean (miserly)

titoli *tee·to·lee mpl* stocks (financial)

titolo *tee·to·loh m* headline; qualification (diploma etc); title

tizio *tee·tsyoh m* fellow

toboga *to·bo·ga m* toboggan

toccare *tok·kah·ray vt* touch; feel; handle; **tocca a Lei** *tok·ka a lay* it's your turn

toeletta *to·e·let·ta f* dressing-table; toilet

toga *to·ga* f gown (*academic*)

togliere* *tol·ye·re* vt remove; take away; **farsi* togliere un dente** *far·see tol·ye·re oon den·te* to have a tooth taken out

togliersi* *tol·yer·see* vr take off (*clothes*)

tomba *tohm·ba* f grave

tonfo *tohn·foh* m splash; thud

tonico *to·nee·koh* m tonic (*medicine*)

tonnellata *ton·nel·lah·ta* f ton

tonno *tohn·noh* m tuna(-fish)

tono *to·noh* m tone

tonsillite *ton·seel·lee·te* f tonsillitis

topinambur *to·pee·nam·boor* m Jerusalem artichoke

topo *to·poh* m mouse

torace *to·ra·che* m chest

torcere* *tor·che·re* vt twist

torcicollo *tor·chee·kol·loh* m a stiff neck

tornare *tor·nah·ray* vi return; come/go back; **tornare sui propri passi** *tor·nah·ray soo·ee pro·pree pas·see* to turn back

toro *to·roh* m bull

torre *tohr·re* f tower; **la torre di controllo** *tohr·re dee kon·trol·loh* control tower

torrone *tor·roh·nay* m nougat

torta *tohr·ta* f cake; tart; pie

torto *tor·toh* m wrong (*injustice*); **ha torto a tor·toh** you're wrong

tosse *tohs·say* f cough

tossicomane *tos·see·ko·ma·ne* m/f addict

tossire *tos·see·ray* vi cough

tostapane *to·sta·pah·ne* m — toaster

totale *to·tah·le* m total □ adj total

tovaglia *to·val·ya* f tablecloth

tovagliolo *to·val·yo·loh* m serviette; napkin

tra *tra* prep between; among(st); in

traccia *trach·cha* f trace (*mark*); track

tradizione *tra·dee·tsyoh·ne* f tradition

tradurre* *tra·door·re* vt translate

traduzione *tra·doo·tsyoh·ne* f translation

traffico *traf·fee·koh* m traffic

trafiggere* *tra·feej·je·re* vt pierce

traghetto *tra·gayt·toh* m ferry; **il traghetto per auto** *tra·gayt·toh payr ow·toh* car-ferry

tram *tram* m — tram(car)

trama *trah·ma* f plot (*in play*)

tramezzino *tra·medz·dzee·noh* m sandwich

tramezzo *tra·medz·dzoh* m partition (*wall*)

tramonto *tra·mohn·toh* m sunset

trampolino *tram·po·lee·noh* m diving-board

tranne *tran·ne* prep except (for), except(ing); **tutti tranne lui** *toot·tee tran·ne loo·ee* all but him

tranquillante *tran·kweel·lan·te* m tranquillizer

tranquillo(a) *tran·kweel·lo(a)* adj quiet; calm; peaceful

transatlantico(a) *tran·sat·lan·tee·ko(a)* adj transatlantic □ m **il transatlantico** *trans·at·lan·tee·koh* liner (*ship*)

transazione *tran·sa·tsyoh·ne* f transaction

transistore *tran·see·stoh·re* m transistor

transito *tran·see·toh* m transit

trapano *tra·pa·noh* m drill (*tool*)

trappola *trap·po·la* f trap

trapunta *tra·poon·ta* f quilt

trascinare *tra·shee·nah·ray* vt drag

trascorrere* *tra·skohr·re·re* vt pass (*time*); spend

trasferire *tras·fe·ree·re* vt transfer

trasferirsi *tra·sfe·reer·see* vr move

traslocarsi *traz·lo·kahr·see* vr move (*move house*)

trasmettere* *tra·zmayt·te·re* vt broadcast

trasmettitore *tra·zmet·tee·toh·re* m transmitter

trasmissione *tra·zmees·syoh·ne* f broadcast; transmission

trasparente *tra·spa·ren·te* adj transparent; clear

traspirare *tra·spee·rah·ray* vi perspire

trasportare *tra·spor·tah·ray* vt carry; transport

trasporto *tra·spor·toh* m transport; **il trasporto aereo** *tra·spor·toh a·e·re·o* air freight

tratta *trat·ta* f bank bill

trattamento *trat·ta·mayn·toh* m treatment

trattare *trat·tah·ray* vt treat; handle (*deal with*); process

trattative *trat·ta·tee·ve* fpl talks; negotiations

trattenere* *trat·te·nay·re* vt hold up (*delay*)

trattino *trat·tee·noh* m dash (*in writing*); hyphen

trattore *trat·toh·re* m tractor

trave *trah·ve* f beam

traversata *tra·vayr·sah·ta* f crossing (*voyage*)

travestimento *tra·ve·stee·mayn·toh* m disguise

travestito(a) *tra·ve·stee·to(a)* adj in disguise

trazione anteriore *tra·tsyoh·ne an·te·ryoh·re* f front-wheel drive

tre *tray* num three

treccia *traych·cha* f plait (*of hair etc*)

tredicesimo(a) *tre·dee·che·zee·mo(a)* adj thirteenth

tredici *tray·dee·chee* num thirteen

tremare *tre·mah·ray* vi shake

treno *tre·noh* m train; **il treno con cuccette** *tre·noh kohn kooch·chayt·te* sleeper (*train*); **il treno supplementare** *tre·noh soop·ple·men·tah·ray* relief train; **il treno merci** *tre·noh mayr·chee* freight train

trenta *trayn·ta* num thirty

trentesimo(a) *tren·te·zee·mo(a)* adj thirtieth

treppiede *trep·pye·de* m tripod

triangolo *tree·an·go·loh* m triangle

tribù *tree·boo* f — tribe

tribunale *tree·boo·nah·lay* m court (*law*)

trimestre *tree·me·stre* m term (*school etc*)

trinciare *treen·chah·ray* vt carve (*meat*)

trippa *treep·pa* f tripe

triste *tree·ste* adj sad

tritacarne *tree·ta·kahr·nay* m — mincer

tritare *tree·tah·ray* vt mince; chop

tromba *trohm·ba* f trumpet

trombone *trom·boh·ne* m trombone; daffodil

tronco *trohn·koh* m trunk (*of tree*)

tropicale *tro·pee·kah·le* adj tropical

tropici *tro·pee·chee* mpl tropics

troppo *trop·po* adv too much; too

troppo(a) *trop·po(a)* adj, pron too much; **troppi(e)** *trop·pee('pe)* too many

trota *tro·ta* f trout

trottare *trot·tah·ray* vi trot (*horse*)

trovare *tro·vah·ray* vt find

truccarsi *trook·kahr·see vr* make (oneself) up

trucco *trook·koh m* trick (*clever act*); make-up

truppa *troop·pa f* troop

trust *trust m* trust (*company*)

tu *too pron* you; **tu stesso(a)** *too stays·so(a)* (you) yourself

tua *too·a adj* your □ *pron* yours

tubo *too·boh m* pipe; tube; **il tubo fluorescente** *too·boh floo·o·re·shen·te* fluorescent light; **il tubo flessibile** *too·boh fles·see·bee·le* hose (*pipe*); **il tubo di respirazione** *too·boh dee re·spee·ra·tsyoh·ne* snorkel; **il tubo di scolo** *too·boh dee skoh·loh* drainpipe; **il tubo di scappamento** *too·boh dee skap·pa·mayn·toh* exhaust

tue *too·e adj* your □ *pron* yours

tuffarsi *toof·far·see vr* dive

tuffo *toof·foh m* dive

tulipano *too·lee·pah·noh m* tulip

tumefazione *too·me·fa·tsyoh·ne f* swelling (*lump*)

tumulto *too·mool·toh m* riot

tunica *too·nee·ka f* tunic (*of uniform*)

Tunisia *too·nee·see·a f* Tunisia

tuo *too·o adj* your □ *pron* yours

tuoi *twoy adj* your □ *pron* yours

tuono *two·noh m* thunder

turbine *toor·bee·ne m* whirlwind

Turchia *toor·kee·a f* Turkey

turco(a) *toor·ko(a) adj* Turkish □ *m* **il turco** *toor·ko* Turkish

turismo *too·ree·zmoh m* tourism

turista *too·ree·sta m/f* tourist

turno *toor·noh m* turn; shift (*of workmen*)

tuta *too·ta f* overall; dungarees; suit (*astronaut, diver*); track suit; **la tuta da lavoro** *too·ta da la·voh·roh* overalls

tutore *too·toh·ray m* guardian

tutrice *too·tree·chay f* guardian

tuttavia *toot·ta·vee·a conj* still (*nevertheless*); however

tutti *toot·tee pron* everybody, everyone; **sanno tutti che...** *san·no toot·tee ke* all of them know that...

tutti(e) *toot·tee(·te) adj* all

tutto *toot·toh pron* everything; **del tutto** *del toot·toh* quite (*absolutely*); **tutto ciò di cui ha bisogno** *toot·toh cho dee koo·ee a bee·zohn·yoh* all you need

tutto(a) *toot·to(a) adj* all; **tutta la giornata** *toot·ta la johr·nah·ta* all day; **tutto il pane** *toot·to eel pah·ne* all the bread

TV *tee·voo f* TV

U

ubbidire *oob·bee·dee·re vi* obey; **ubbidire a qualcuno** *oob·bee·dee·re a kwal·koo·no* to obey someone

ubicazione *oo·bee·ka·tsyoh·ne f* situation (*place*)

ubriaco(a) *oo·bree·ah·ko(a) adj* drunk

uccello *ooch·chel·loh m* bird

uccidere* *ooch·chee·de·ra vt* kill

ufficiale *oof·fee·chah·le m* officer (*in army etc*) □ *adj* official

ufficio *oof·fee·choh m* bureau; office; service (*in church*); **l'ufficio prenotazioni** *oof·fee·choh pre·no·ta·tsyoh·nee* booking office; **l'ufficio informazioni** *oof·fee·choh een·for·ma·tsyoh·nee* information desk/office; **l'ufficio oggetti smarriti** *oof·fee·choh oj·jet·tee zmar·ree·tee* lost property office;

l'ufficio del personale *oof·fee·choh del per·so·nah·le* personnel department; **l'ufficio turistico** *oof·fee·choh too·ree·stee·ko* tourist office; **l'ufficio postale** *oof·fee·choh po·stah·le* post office

ufficioso(a) *oof·fee·choh·so(a) adj* unofficial

uggioso(a) *ooj·joh·so(a) adj* dull (*day, weather*)

uguale *oo·gwah·le adj* equal; even

ulcera *ool·che·ra f* ulcer

ultimatum *ool·tee·mah·toom m —* ultimatum

ultimissimo *ool·tee·mees·see·mo m* the very last

ultimo(a) *ool·tee·mo(a) adj* last; **in ultimo** *een ool·tee·mo* in the last resort; **per ultimo** *payr ool·tee·mo* last; **le ultime notizie** *ool·tee·me no·tee·tsye* the latest news

umano(a) *oo·mah·no(a) adj* human

umido(a) *oo·mee·do(a) adj* wet; damp

umore *oo·moh·ray m* mood; **di buon umore** *dee bwon oo·moh·ray* in a good mood; in good spirits; **di cattivo umore** *dee kat·tee·vo oo·moh·ray* in a bad mood

un *oon art* a; an; one

unanime *oo·nah·nee·may adj* unanimous (*decision*)

uncino *oon·chee·noh m* hook

undicesimo(a) *oon·dee·che·zee·mo(a) adj* eleventh

undici *oon·dee·chee num* eleven

UNESCO *oo·ne·sko f* UNESCO

ungherese *oon·ge·ray·se adj* Hungarian □ *m* **l'ungherese** *oon·ge·ray·se* Hungarian

Ungheria *oon·ge·ree·a f* Hungary

unghia *oon·gya f* nail (*human*); **il nécessaire per unghie** *nay·ses·sayr payr oon·gye* manicure set

unguento *oon·gwen·toh m* ointment

unico(a) *oo·nee·ko(a) adj* unique; **l'unica donna là** *loo·nee·ka don·na la* the only woman there; **un figlio unico** *oon feel·yoh oo·nee·ko* an only child

unilaterale *oo·nee·la·te·rah·lay adj* unilateral

unione *oo·nyoh·nay f* union

Unione Sovietica *oo·nyoh·ne so·vye·tee·ka f* Soviet Union

unire *oo·nee·re vt* join; unite; connect

unisex *oo·nee·sex adj* unisex

unità *oo·nee·ta f —* unit

unito(a) *oo·nee·to(a) adj* united; plain (*not patterned*)

universale *oo·nee·vayr·sah·lay adj* universal

università *oo·nee·ver·see·ta f —* university

universo *oo·nee·ver·soh m* universe

uno(a) *oo·no(a) adj, num* a, an; one; **o l'uno o l'altro di voi** *o loo·no o lal·troh dee voy* either of you; **quale?** - **o l'uno o l'altro** *kwah·le* - *o loo·no o lal·troh* which one? - either; **l'un l'altro** *loon lal·tro* one another; **uno dovrebbe...** *oo·no do·vreb·be* one should...

uomo *wo·moh m* **uomini** man; **l'uomo d'affari** *wo·moh daf·fah·ree* businessman

uovo *wo·voh m —a* egg; **l'uovo di Pasqua** *wo·voh dee pa·skwa* Easter egg; **un uovo à la coque** *oon wo·voh a la kok* a boiled egg

uragano *oo·ra·gah·noh m* hurricane

urbano(a) *oor·bah·no(a) adj* urban

urgente *oor·jen·te adj* urgent

urgentemente *oor·jen·te·mayn·te adv* urgently

urlare *oor·lah·ray vi* roar (*person*)

urlo *oor·loh m* roar (*of person*)

U.R.S.S. *oo·erre·esse·esse f* U.S.S.R.

urtare *oor·tah·ray vt* bump; hit (*with car*)

urto *oor·toh m* bump (*knock*)

usare *oo·zah·ray vt* use

usato(a) *oo·za·toh(a) adj* used

uscire* *oo·shee·ray vi* come out (*person, sun*); go out; **uscire*** **con qualcuno** *oo·shee·ray kon kwal·koo·noh* to go out with somebody; **uscire*** **da** *oo·shee·ray da* to leave; **è uscito di corsa dalla casa** *e oo·shee·to dee kohr·sa dal·la kah·sa* he ran out of the house; **fare*** **uscire** *fah·ray oo·shee·ray* to release (*book, film*)

uscita *oo·shee·ta f* exit; **l'uscita di sicurezza** *oo·shee·ta dee see·koo·rayts·tsa* emergency exit; fire escape

uscite *oo·shee·te fpl* outgoings

uso *oo·zo m* use; **in uso** *een oo·zo* in use

utero *oo·te·roh m* womb

utile *oo·tee·lay adj* useful

uva *oo·va f* grapes; **l'uva passa** *oo·va pas·sa* currants; raisins; **l'uva sultanina** *oo·va sool·ta·nee·na* sultanas; **l'uva spina** *oo·va spee·na* gooseberry

V

vacante *va·kan·te adj* vacant

vacanza *va·kan·tsa f* holiday(s); **in vacanza** *een va·kan·tsa* on holiday

vacanze *va·kan·tse fpl* holiday (*period*); vacation

vacca *vak·ka f* cow

vaccinazione *vach·chee·na·tsyoh·nay f* vaccination; inoculation

vagabondo(a) *va·ga·bohn·doh(a) m/f* tramp

vaglia *val·ya m* — postal order; money order

vago(a) *va·go(a) adj* vague

vagone *va·goh·nay m* car (*of train*); **wag(g)on** (*rail*); **il vagone letto** *va·goh·nay let·to* sleeping car; **il vagone ristorante** *va·goh·nay ree·sto·ran·te* restaurant car

vaiolo *va·yo·loh m* smallpox

valanga *va·lan·ga f* avalanche

valere* *va·lay·re vi* be worth □ *vi* be valid; **vale la pena** *vah·le la pay·na* it's worth it; **tanto vale che andiamo** *tan·toh vah·le kay an·dya·moh* we might as well go

valido(a) *vah·lee·do(a) adj* valid

valigetta *va·lee·jayt·ta f* grip (*case*)

valigia *va·lee·ja f* suitcase; **fare*** **la valigia** *fah·ray la va·lee·ja* to pack one's case

valle *val·le f* valley; **a valle** *a val·le* downstream

valore *va·loh·ray m* value; **il valore di mercato** *va·loh·ray dee mayr·kah·toh* market value; **di gran valore** *dee gran va·loh·ray* valuable; **gli oggetti di valore** *oj·jet·tee dee va·loh·ray* valuables

valuta *va·loo·ta f* currency

valutare *va·loo·tah·ray vt* value

valvola *val·vo·la f* valve

valzer *val·tser m* — waltz

vanga *van·ga f* spade

vangare *van·gah·ray vt* dig (*ground*)

vaniglia *va·neel·ya f* vanilla

vanitoso(a) *va·nee·toh·soh(a) adj* conceited; vain

vano *vah·noh m* room

vantaggio *van·taj·joh m* benefit; advantage

vantaggioso(a) *van·taj·joh·so(a) adj* profitable

vantarsi *van·tar·see vr* boast

vapore *va·poh·re m* steam; **cuocere*** **a vapore** *kwo·che·re a va·poh·re* to steam (*food*)

varare *va·rah·ray vt* launch (*ship*)

variabile *va·ree·ah·bee·lay adj* variable □ *f* **la variabile** *va·ree·ah·bee·lay* variable

variare *va·ree·ah·ray vt/i* vary

variazione *va·ree·a·tsyoh·nay f* variation

varicella *va·ree·chel·la f* chicken pox

varietà *va·ree·e·ta f* — variety

vario(a) *vah·ree·oh(a) adj* various

Varsavia *var·sah·vya f* Warsaw

vasca da bagno *va·ska da ban·yoh f* bath (*tub*)

vaselina *va·ze·lee·na f* petroleum jelly; vaseline

vasellame *va·zel·la·me m* crockery; china

vasino *va·zee·noh m* pot(ty)

vaso *vah·zoh m* vase; pot

vassoio *vas·soh·yoh m* tray

Vaticano *va·tee·kah·noh m* Vatican

ve *ve pron, adv* before **lo, la, li, le, ne** = **vi**

vecchio(a) *vayk·kyo(a) adj* old

vedere* *ve·day·re vt/i* see; **non vedere*** **l'ora di** *nohn ve·day·re loh·ra dee* to look forward to

vedersi *ve·dayr·see vr* meet; show (*be visible*)

vedova *vay·do·va f* widow

vedovo *vay·do·voh m* widower

veduta *ve·doo·ta f* scene (*sight*)

vegetariano(a) *ve·je·ta·ree·ah·no(a) adj* vegetarian

vegliare *vel·yah·ray vi* stay up (*at night*)

veicolo *ve·ee·ko·loh m* vehicle

vela *vay·la f* sail; sailing

veleggiare *ve·lej·jah·ray vi* sail

veleno *ve·lay·noh m* poison

velenoso(a) *ve·le·noh·so(a) adj* poisonous

veliero *ve·lye·roh m* sail(ing) boat

velina *ve·lee·na f* tissue paper

vellutato(a) *vel·loo·tah·to(a) adj* creamy (*texture*)

velluto *vel·loo·toh m* velvet; **il velluto a coste** *vel·loo·toh a ko·stay* corduroy

velo *vay·loh m* veil

veloce *ve·loh·che adj* fast (*speedy*)

velocemente *ve·loh·che·mayn·te adv* fast

velocità *ve·lo·chee·ta f* speed

vena *vay·na f* vein

venatura *vay·na·too·ra f* grain (*in wood*)

vendemmia *ven·daym·mya f* harvest (*of grapes*); **fare*** **la vendemmia di** *fah·ray la ven·daym·mya dee* to harvest (*grapes*)

vendere *vayn·de·re vt* sell; **da vendere o rimandare** *da vayn·de·re o ree·man·dah·ray* on sale or return; **vendere al minuto** *vayn·de·re al mee·noo·toh* to retail

vendita *vayn·dee·ta f* sale; **la vendita al minuto** *vayn·dee·ta al mee·noo·toh* retail; **la vendita all'ingrosso** *vayn·dee·ta al·leen·gros·soh* wholesale; **la vendita all'asta** *vayn·dee·ta al·la·sta* auction; **la vendita a rate** *vayn·dee·ta a rah·te* hire purchase

venditore *ven·dee·toh·ray* m vendor; **il venditore a domicilio** *ven·dee·toh·ray a do·mee·cheel·yoh* door-to-door salesman

venerdì *ve·ner·dee* m — Friday; **venerdì santo** *ve·ner·dee san·toh* Good Friday; **di venerdì** *dee ve·ner·dee* on Fridays

Venezia *ve·ne·tsya* f Venice

venire* *ve·nee·re* vi come (*arrive*); **veniamo domani?** *ve·nyah·mo do·mah·nee* shall we come tomorrow?; **ella verrebbe se... ay!·la ver·reb·be say** she would come if...; **venire* incontro a qualcuno** *ve·nee·re een·kohn·tro a kwal·koo·no* to come towards someone; **verrò a prenderla alla stazione** *ver·roh a pren·dayr·la al·la sta·tsyoh·nay* I'll meet you at the station; **venga a casa nostra** *ven·ga a kah·sa no·stra* come back to our place; **venire* giú** *ve·nee·re joo* to come down

ventaglio *ven·tal·yoh* m fan (*folding*)

venti *vayn·tee* num twenty

ventilatore *ven·tee·la·toh·re* m fan (*electric*); ventilator

vento *ven·toh* m wind (*breeze*); **tira vento** *tee·ra ven·toh* it's windy

ventola *ven·to·la* f fan

ventuno *ven·too·noh* m twenty one; pontoon

veramente *ve·ra·mayn·tay* adv really

veranda *ve·ran·da* f veranda

verbale *vayr·bah·lay* adj verbal

verde *vayr·day* adj green

verdetto *vayr·dayt·toh* m verdict

verdura *vayr·doo·ra* f vegetables

vergogna *ver·gohn·ya* f shame

vergognarsi (di) *ver·gon·yar·see (dee)* vr be ashamed (of)

verificare *ve·ree·fee·kah·ray* vt check (*train time etc*); audit

verità *ve·ree·ta* f truth

verme *ver·me* m worm

vermut *ver·moot* m vermouth

vernice *vayr·nee·chay* f varnish; paint

verniciare *vayr·nee·chah·ray* vt paint; varnish

vero(a) *vayr·o(a)* adj true; real; **lo conosce, non è vero?** *lo ko·no·she, nohn e vay·ro* you know him, don't you?; **non è venuto, vero?** *nohn e ve·noo·to, vay·ro* he didn't come, did he?; **è un vero problema** *e oon vay·ro pro·ble·ma* it's a real problem

verruca *ver·roo·ka* f wart

versamento *ver·sa·mayn·toh* m payment; deposit

versare *ver·sah·ray* vt pour (*tea, milk*)

versione *ver·syoh·nay* f version

verso *ver·so* prep toward(s)

verticale *vayr·tee·kah·lay* adj vertical

vertigine *ver·tee·jee·ne* f dizziness; **preso(a) da vertigine** *pray·so(a) da ver·tee·jee·ne* dizzy (*person*)

vescica *ve·shee·ka* f bladder

vescichetta *ve·shee·kayt·ta* f blister (*on skin*)

vescovo *vay·sko·voh* m bishop

vespa *ve·spa* f wasp

vestaglia *ve·stal·ya* f housecoat; dressing gown

veste *ves·tay* f gown (*dress*)

vestiario *ve·stee·ah·ree·oh* m wardrobe

vestibolo *ve·stee·bo·loh* m hall; lobby

vestire *ve·stee·re* vt dress (*child*)

vestirsi *ve·steer·see* vr dress (*oneself*)

vestiti *ve·stee·tee* mpl clothes; **i vestiti**

sportivi *ve·stee·tee spor·tee·vee* casual clothes, casual wear

vestito *ve·stee·toh* m dress; suit (*man's*); **il vestito da spiaggia** *ve·stee·toh da spyaj·ja* sun dress

veterinario(a) *ve·te·ree·nah·ryoh(a)* m/f vet(erinary surgeon)

veto *ve·toh* m veto; **mettere* il veto a** *mayt·te·ray eel ve·toh a* to veto

vetrata *ve·trah·ta* f glass door/window; **la vetrata dipinta** *ve·trah·ta dee·peen·ta* stained glass window

vetrina *ve·tree·na* f shop window

vetro *vay·troh* m pane; glass

vettura *vet·too·ra* f coach (*of train*)

V.H.F. *voo·akka·effe* abbrev V.H.F.

vi *vee* pron you; to you; yourselves; each other □ adv there; here

via *vee·a* f street □ prep via; **passare via Londra** *pas·sah·ray vee·a lohn·dra* to go via London

viadotto *vee·a·doht·toh* m overpass; viaduct

viaggi *vee·aj·jee* mpl travel

viaggiare *vyaj·jah·ray* vi travel; **viaggiare in prima classe** *vyaj·jah·ray een pree·ma klas·say* to travel first class

viaggiatore *vyaj·ja·toh·re* m travel(l)er

viaggio *vyaj·joh* m journey; trip; drive; **il viaggio organizzato** *vyaj·joh or·ga·needz·dzah·to* package holiday; **siamo in viaggio di nozze** *syah·mo een vyaj·joh dee nots·tse* we're on our honeymoon; **il viaggio d'affari** *vyaj·joh daf·fah·ree* business trip; **il viaggio di andata e ritorno** *vyaj·joh dee an·dah·ta e ree·tohr·noh* return journey; **il viaggio aereo** *vyaj·joh a·e·re·o* air travel

viale *vyah·le* m avenue

vice- *vee·che* pref deputy (*second-incommand*)

vicenda *vee·chen·da* f event; **a vicenda** *a vee·chen·da* in turn

vicepresidente *vee·che·pre·see·den·te* m vice chairman; vice president

viceversa *vee·che·ver·sa* adv vice versa

vicinato *vee·chee·nah·toh* m neighbo(u)rhood

vicino *vee·chee·noh* adv near; close by □ m/f il/la vicino(a) *vee·chee·noh(a)* neighbo(u)r; **vicino a** *vee·chee·noh a* close to; **vicino alla casa** *vee·chee·noh al·la kah·sa* near (to) the house; **vicino(a) ai negozi** *vee·chee·noh(a) a·ee ne·go·tsee* convenient for shops; **qui vicino** *kwee vee·chee·noh* nearby

vicolo *vee·ko·loh* m alley; lane; **il vicolo cieco** *vee·ko·loh che·ko* blind alley; dead end

video *vee·de·oh* m video

videocassetta *vee·de·o·kas·sayt·ta* f videocassette

videonastro *vee·de·o·na·stroh* m videotape

videoregistratore a cassetta *vee·de·o·re·jee·stra·toh·ray a kas·sayt·ta* m videocassette recorder

Vienna *vee·en·na* f Vienna

vietare *vee·e·tah·ray* vt forbid; **è vietato(a)** *e vee·e·tah·to(a)* it is forbidden

vigile *vee·jee·le* m policeman; **i vigili del fuoco** *vee·jee·lee del fwo·koh* fire brigade; **il vigile urbano** *vee·jee·le oor·bah·no* traffic warden

vigilia *vee·jeel·ya* f eve; **la vigilia di Capodanno** *vee·jeel·ya dee kah·po·dan·noh* New Year's Eve; **la vigilia di Natale** *vee·jeel·ya dee na·tah·lay* Christmas Eve

vigliacco *veel·yak·koh* m coward

vigna *veen·ya* f vineyard

vignetta umoristica *veen·yayt·ta oo·mo·ree·stee·ka* f cartoon

villa *veel·la* f detached house; villa

villeggiante *veel·lej·jan·te* m/f holiday-maker; vacationer

vimine *vee·mee·ne* m wicker

vincere* *veen·che·re* vi win □ vt win; defeat

vincitore *veen·chee·toh·re* m winner

vincitrice *veen·chee·tree·che* f winner

vinile *vee·nee·le* m vinyl

vino *vee·noh* m wine; un vino di qualità *oon vee·noh dee kwa·lee·ta* a quality wine; il vino del Reno *vee·noh del re·noh* hock

violento(a) *vee·o·len·to(a)* adj violent

violenza *vee·o·len·tsa* f violence

violino *vee·o·lee·noh* m violin

violoncello *vee·o·lon·chel·loh* m cello

viottolo *vee·ot·to·loh* m lane (in country)

V.I.P. *voo·ee·pee* m V.I.P.

vipera *vee·pe·ra* f adder (snake)

virare di bordo *vee·rah·ray dee bohr·doh* vi tack (sailing)

virgola *veer·go·la* f comma; la virgola decimale *veer·go·la de·chee·mah·le* decimal point; 3 virgola 4 *3 veer·go·la 4* 3 point 4

visibile *vee·zee·bee·lay* adj visible

visiera *vee·zye·ra* f sun visor (in car); peak (of cap)

visione *vee·zee·oh·ne* f vision; quando è in visione il film? *kwan·do è een vee·zee·oh·ne eel feelm* when is the film on?

visita *vee·zee·ta* f visit; examination (medical); la visita con guida *vee·zee·ta kohn gwee·da* guided tour

visitare *vee·zee·tah·ray* vt visit; tour

visitatore *vee·zee·ta·toh·ray* m visitor

visitatrice *vee·zee·ta·tree·chay* f visitor

viso *vee·zoh* m face

visone *vee·zoh·nay* m mink (fur)

vista *vee·sta* f eyesight; view; avere* la vista debole *a·vay·re la vee·sta day·bo·le* to have poor sight; una bella vista *oo·na bel·la vee·sta* a lovely sight

vistare *vee·stah·ray* vt visa

visto *vee·stoh* m visa, visé; il visto di transito *vee·stoh dee tran·see·toh* transit visa

vita *vee·ta* f life; waist; guadagnarsi la vita *gwa·dan·yar·se la vee·ta* to earn one's living; l'assicurazione sulla vita *as·see·koo·ra·tsyoh·ne sool·la vee·ta* life insurance; a vita *a vee·ta* for life

vitale *vee·tah·lay* adj vital (essential)

vitamina *vee·ta·mee·na* f vitamin

vite *vee·te* f vine; screw

vitello *vee·tel·loh* m veal; calf

vittima *veet·tee·ma* f victim

vittoria *veet·to·ree·a* f victory

vivace *vee·vah·che* adj lively

vivere* *vee·ve·re* vi live

vivo(a) *vee·vo(a)* adj live; alive

viziare *vee·tsyah·ray* vt spoil (child)

vocabolario *vo·ka·bo·lah·ree·oh* m vocabulary; dictionary

voce *voh·che* f voice; ad alta voce *ad al·ta voh·che* aloud

vodka *vod·ka* f vodka

voi *voy* pron you; l'avete fatto voi stessi(e) *la·vay·te fat·to voy stays·see(·se)* you did it yourselves

volano *vo·lah·noh* m badminton

volante *vo·lan·te* m steering-wheel

volare *vo·lah·ray* vi fly □ m il volare *vo·lah·ray* flying

volere* *vo·lay·re* vt want (wish for); vuole partire *vwo·le par·tee·re* he wants to leave; vorrei potere... *vor·re·e po·tay·re* I wish I could...; ci vuole un grande sforzo/un'ora *chee vwo·le oon gran·de sfor·tsoh/oon·oh·ra* it takes a lot of effort/an hour; che cosa vorrebbe? *ke ko·sa vor·reb·be* what would you like?; volere* fare qualcosa *vo·lay·re fah·ray kwal·ko·sa* to want to do something

volo *voh·loh* m flight; il volo a vela *voh·loh a vay·la* gliding (sport); il volo charter *voh·loh char·ter* charter flight; prendere* un volo diretto per Venezia *pren·de·re oon voh·loh dee·ret·to payr ve·ne·tsya* to fly to Venice direct; il volo di linea *voh·loh dee lee·ne·a* scheduled flight

volpe *vohl·pe* f fox

volta *vol·ta* f time; qualche volta *kwal·ke vol·ta* sometimes; una volta *oo·na vol·ta* once; ancora una volta *an·koh·ra oo·na vol·ta* once more; due volte *doo·e vol·te* twice; la prima volta *la pree·ma vol·ta* the first time; quante volte? *kwan·te vol·te* how many times?

voltare *vol·tah·ray* vt turn

voltarsi *vol·tar·see* vr turn round; turn over

volume *vo·loo·me* m volume

vomitare *vo·mee·tah·ray* vt vomit

vortice *vor·tee·che* m whirlpool

vostri(e) *vo·stree(·stre)* adj your □ pron yours

vostro(a) *vo·stro(a)* adj your □ pron yours

votare *vo·tah·ray* vi vote

voto *voh·toh* m vote; mark (in school)

vulcano *vool·kah·noh* m volcano

vuotare *vwo·tah·ray* vt empty

vuoto(a) *vwo·to(a)* adj empty

W

wafer *va·fer* m wafer

watt *vat* m watt

week-end *week·end* m weekend

western *wes·tern* m western (movie)

whisky *wee·skee* m whisky; il whisky scozzese *wee·skee skots·tsay·se* Scotch (liquor); un whisky con selz *oon wee·skee kohn selts* a whisky and soda; il whisky americano *wee·skee a·me·ree·kah·no* bourbon; il whisky di segale *wee·skee dee say·ga·le* rye (whisky)

whist *weest* m whist

X

xerocopia *kse·ro·ko·pya* f Xerox

Y

yacht *yot* m yacht

yachting *yo·teeng* m yachting; fare* dello yachting *fah·ray del·lo yo·teeng* to go yachting

yoga *yo·ga* m yoga

yogurt *yo·goort* m yoghurt

Z

zaino *dza·ee·noh* m rucksack; back pack

zampa *tsam·pa* f leg (of animal); paw; foot

zanzara *dzan·dzah·ra* f mosquito

zanzariera *dzan·dza·ree·e·ra f* mosquito net
zebra *dze·bra f* zebra
zenzero *tsen·tse·roh m* ginger
zerbino *dzer·bee·noh m* doormat
zero *dze·roh m* nil; zero
zia *tsee·a f* aunt(ie)
zinco *tseen·koh m* zinc
zingaro *tseen·ga·roh m* gypsy
zio *tsee·oh m* uncle
zitto(a) *tseet·to(a) excl* be quiet!
zolletta *tsol·layt·ta f* cube; la zolletta di zucchero *tsol·layt·ta dee tsook·ke·roh* lump of sugar
zona *dzo·na f* zone; la zona residenziale *dzo·na re·see·den·tsyah·le* estate (*housing*); la zona industriale *dzo·na een·doo·stryah·le* trading estate; la

zona di concentramento *dzo·na dee kon·chen·tra·men·toh* conurbation
zoo *dzo m* zoo
zoom *zoom m* zoom lens
zoppicare *tsop·pee·kah·ray vi* limp
zoppo(a) *tsop·poh(a) m/f* cripple
zucca *tsook·ka f* pumpkin; squash (*gourd*); marrow (*vegetable*)
zuccheriera *tsook·ke·rye·ra f* sugar bowl
zucchero *tsook·ke·roh m* sugar
zucchini *tsook·kee·nee mpl* zucchini; courgettes
zuppa *tsoop·pa f* soup; la zuppa inglese *tsoop·pa een·glay·se* trifle (*dessert*); la zuppa di tartaruga *tsoop·pa dee tar·ta·roo·ga* turtle soup

ENGLISH–ITALIAN DICTIONARY

a *art* un(a) *oon(a)*; **twice a day** due volte al giorno *doo·ay vol·tay al jor·noh*; **£40 a week** £40 la settimana *£40 la se·tee·mah·na*

abbey *n* l'abbazia (*f*) *ab·ba·tsee·a*

abbreviation *n* l'abbreviazione (*f*) *ab·bre·vya·tsyoh·ne*

abdomen *n* l'addome (*m*) *ad·do·me*

ability *n* la capacità *ka·pa·chee·ta*

able *adj* □ **to be able to do something** potere* fare qualcosa *po·tay·re fah·ray kwal·ko·sa*

aboard *adv* □ **to go aboard** salire* a bordo *sa·lee·re a bohr·doh* □ *prep* **aboard the ship** a bordo della nave *a bohr·doh del·la nah·ve*

abolish *vt* abolire *a·bo·lee·re*

about *prep* □ **about £10** circa £10 *cheer·ka £10*; **about here** qui intorno *kwee een·tohr·no*; **to talk about something** parlare di qualcosa *par·lah·ray dee kwal·ko·sa* □ *adv* **things lying about** cose lasciate in giro *ko·se la·shah·te een jee·roh*; **to look about** guardarsi intorno *gwar·dar·see een·tohr·no*; **to be about to do something** stare* per fare qualcosa *stah·ray payr fah·ray kwal·ko·sa*

above *prep, adv* sopra *soh·pra*

abroad *adv* all'estero *al·le·ste·roh*

abrupt *adj* (*person*) brusco(a) *broo·sko(a)*; (*slope*) ripido(a) *ree·pee·do(a)*

abscess *n* l'ascesso (*m*) *a·shays·soh*

absent *adj* assente *as·sen·te*

absenteeism *n* l'assenteismo (*m*) *as·sen·te·ee·zmoh*

absolute *adj* assoluto(a) *as·so·loo·to(a)*

absorb *vt* (*fluid*) assorbire *as·sor·bee·re*; (*shock*) ammortizzare *am·mor·teedz·dzah·ray*

absorbent *adj* assorbente *as·sor·ben·te*

absorbent cotton *n* il cotone idrofilo *ko·toh·ne eed·ro·fee·lo*

abstain *vi* (*in voting*) astenersi* *a·ste·nayr·see*

abstract *adj* astratto(a) *a·strat·to(a)*

absurd *adj* assurdo(a) *as·soor·do(a)*

academy *n* □ **academy of music** il conservatorio *kon·ser·va·to·ryoh*; **military academy** l'accademia militare (*f*) *ak·ka·de·mya mee·lee·tah·re*

accelerate *vi* accelerare *ach·che·le·rah·ray*

accelerator *n* l'acceleratore (*m*) *ach·che·le·ra·toh·re*

accent *n* l'accento (*m*) *ach·chen·toh*

accept *vt* accettare *ach·chet·tah·ray*

acceptance *n* l'accettazione (*f*) *ach·chet·ta·tsyoh·ne*

access *n* l'accesso (*m*) *ach·ches·soh*

accessible *adj* accessibile *ach·ches·see·bee·le*

accessories *pl* gli accessori *ach·ches·so·ree*

accident *n* l'incidente (*m*) *een·chee·den·te*; **by accident** per caso *payr kah·zoh* Ill, Ea3

accidental *adj* accidentale *ach·chee·den·tah·le*

accommodation *n* l'alloggio (*m*) *al·loj·joh* Alf

accompany *vt* (*go with*) accompagnare *ak·kom·pan·yah·ray*

according to *prep* secondo *se·kohn·do*

account *n* il conto *kohn·toh* M29

accountancy *n* la ragioneria *ra·jo·ne·ree·a*

accountant *n* il ragioniere *ra·jo·nye·re*

accounts department *n* il reparto contabile *re·par·toh kon·tah·bee·le*

accrue *vi* maturarsi *ma·too·rar·see*

accumulate *vi* accumularsi *ak·koo·moo·lar·see*

accurate *adj* preciso(a) *pre·chee·zo(a)*

accuse *vt* accusare *ak·koo·zah·ray*

ace *n* (*cards*) l'asso (*m*) *as·soh*

ache *n* il dolore *do·loh·re* □ *vi* fare* male *fah·ray mah·le*

acid *n* l'acido (*m*) *ah·chee·doh*

acknowledge *vt* (*letter*) accusare ricevuta di *ak·koo·zah·ray ree·che·voo·ta dee*

acne *n* l'acne (*f*) *ak·ne*

acorn *n* la ghianda *gyan·da*

acquaintance *n* la conoscenza *ko·no·shen·tsa*

acquire *vt* acquistare *ak·kwee·stah·ray*

acquisition *n* l'acquisizione (*f*) *ak·kwee·zee·tsyoh·ne*

acre *n* l'acro (*m*) *a·kroh*

across *prep* □ **to walk across the road** attraversare la strada *at·tra·ver·sah·ray la strah·da*; **I saw him (from) across the road** l'ho visto dall'altra parte della strada *lo vee·sto dal·lal·tra par·te del·la strah·da*; **we drove across France** abbiamo attraversato la Francia in macchina *ab·byah·mo at·tra·ver·sah·to la fran·cha een mak·kee·na*

acrylic *adj* acrilico(a) *a·kree·lee·ko(a)*

act *n* (*of play*) l'atto (*m*) *at·toh*; (*at circus etc*) il numero *noo·me·roh* □ *vi* (*behave*) comportarsi *kom·por·tar·see* □ *vt* **to act Hamlet** fare* la parte di Amleto *fah·ray la par·te dee am·le·to*; **to act as X** fungere* da X *foon·je·re da X*

acting *adj* supplente *soop·plen·te*

action *n* (*movement*) l'azione (*f*) *a·tsyoh·ne*; (*act*) l'atto (*m*) *at·toh*

active *adj* attivo(a) *at·tee·vo(a)*

activity *n* l'attività (*f*) *at·tee·vee·ta*

actor *n* l'attore (*m*) *at·toh·re*

actress *n* l'attrice (*f*) *at·tree·che*

actually *adv* infatti *een·fat·tee*

acute accent *n* l'accento acuto (*m*) *ach·chen·toh a·koo·to*

adapt *vt* adattare *a·dat·tah·ray*

adapter, adaptor *n* (*electrical*) il raccordo *rak·kor·doh*

add *vt* (*comment*) aggiungere* *aj·joon·je·re*; **add (up)** (*numbers*) sommare *som·mah·ray*

adder *n* (*snake*) la vipera *vee·pe·ra*

addict *n* il/la tossicomane *tos·see·ko·ma·ne*

addition *n* l'addizione (*f*) *ad·dee·tsyoh·ne*

address *n* l'indirizzo (*m*) *een·dee·reets·tsoh* □ *vt* (*letter*) indirizzare *een·dee·reets·tsah·ray* T98, F2, S27

adjourn *vi* rinviare la seduta *reen·vee·ah·ray la se·doo·ta*

adjournment *n* il rinvio *reen·vee·oh*

adjust *vt* aggiustare *aj·joo·stah·ray*

administration *n* l'amministrazione (*f*) *am·mee·nee·stra·tsyoh·ne*

admire *vt* ammirare *am·mee·rah·ray*

admission *n* l'entrata (*f*) *en·trah·ta* L13

admission fee *n* il prezzo d'ingresso *prets·tsoh deen·gres·soh*

adopt *vt* adottare *a·dot·tah·ray*

Adriatic (Sea) *n* l'Adriatico (*m*) *a·dree·a·tee·koh*

adult *n* l'adulto (*m*) *a·dool·toh* □ *adj* per adulti *payr a·dool·tee*

advance *vt* (*money*) anticipare *an·tee·chee·pah·ray* □ *vi* avanzare *a·van·tsah·ray* □ *n* (*loan*) l'anticipo (*m*) *an·tee·chee·poh*; **in advance** in anticipo *een an·tee·chee·poh* M10

advance booking office *n* l'ufficio prenotazioni (*m*) *oof·fee·choh pre·no·ta·tsyoh·nee*

advantage *n* il vantaggio *van·taj·joh*

adventure *n* l'avventura (*f*) *av·ven·too·ra*

advertise *vt* (*product*) fare* pubblicità a *fah·ray poob·blee·chee·ta a* □ *vi* to **advertise for a secretary** fare* un'inserzione per trovare una segretaria *fah·ray oon een·sayr·tsyoh·ne payr tro·vah·ray oo·na se·gre·tah·rya*

advertisement *n* la réclame *ray·klam*; (*in small ads*) l'annuncio (*m*) *an·noon·choh*

advertising *n* la pubblicità *poob·blee·chee·ta* Bm17

advertising agency *n* l'agenzia pubblicitaria (*f*) *a·jen·tsee·a poob·blee·chee·tah·rya*

advice *n* il consiglio *kon·seel·yoh*

advice note *n* l'avviso (*m*) *av·vee·zoh*

advise *vt* consigliare *kon·seel·yah·ray*; **to advise someone to do something** consigliare a qualcuno di fare qualcosa *kon·seel·yah·ray a kwal·koo·no dee fah·ray kwal·ko·sa*

aerial *n* l'antenna (*f*) *an·tayn·na*

aeroplane *n* l'aereo (*m*) *a·e·re·oh*

aerosol *n* la bombola spray *bohm·bo·la spry*

affair *n* (*matter*) l'affare (*m*) *af·fah·re*; **affairs** gli affari *af·fah·ree*

affect *vt* influire *een·floo·ee·re*

affection *n* l'affetto (*m*) *af·fet·toh*

affectionate *adj* affettuoso(a) *af·fet·twoh·so(a)*

affiliated company *n* la filiale *feel·yah·le*

afford *vt* □ **I can't afford it** non me lo posso permettere *nohn may lo pos·so payr·mayt·te·re*

afraid *adj* □ **to be afraid of something** avere* paura di qualcosa *a·vay·re pa·oo·ra dee kwal·ko·sa*; **I'm afraid not** temo di no *te·mo de no*; **I'm afraid I can't do it** mi dispiace ma non posso farlo *mee dee·spyah·che ma nohn pos·so far·lo*

Africa *n* l'Africa (*f*) *a·free·ka*

African *adj* africano(a) *a·free·kah·no(a)*

after *prep*, *adv* dopo *doh·po*; **to come after someone/something** seguire qualcuno/qualcosa *se·gwee·re kwal·koo·no/kwal·ko·sa*; **4 years after** 4 anni dopo *4 an·nee doh·po* □ *conj* **after** dopo che *doh·po ke*; **after we had left** dopo che fummo partiti *doh·po ke foom·mo par·tee·tee*

afternoon *n* il pomeriggio *po·me·reej·joh*

after-sales service *n* il servizio di assistenza *sayr·vee·tsyoh dee as·see·sten·tsa*

aftershave (lotion) *n* il dopobarba *doh·po·bar·ba*

afterward(s) *adv* dopo *doh·po*

again *adv* ancora *an·koh·ra*; **di nuovo** *dee nwo·vo*

against *prep* contro *kohn·tro*

age *n* (*of person*) l'età (*f*) *e·ta*; (*era*) l'epoca (*f*) *e·po·ka*; **under age** minorenne *mee·no·ren·ne*

agency *n* (*office*) l'agenzia (*f*) *a·jen·tsee·a* A56

agenda *n* l'ordine del giorno (*m*) *ohr·dee·ne del johr·noh*

agent *n* l'agente (*m*) *a·jen·te*; **the Renault agent** il concessionario Renault *kon·ches·syoh·nah·ryoh re·no*

aggressive *adj* aggressivo(a) *ag·gres·see·vo(a)*

agile *adj* agile *ah·jee·le*

ago *adv* □ **4 years ago** 4 anni fa *4 an·nee fa*

agony *n* il dolore atroce *do·loh·re a·troh·che*

agree *vt/i* □ **to agree with somebody** essere* d'accordo con qualcuno *es·se·re dak·kor·doh kon kwal·koo·no*; **to agree on** (*price*) mettersi* d'accordo su *mayt·ter·see dak·kor·doh soo*; **onions don't agree with me** le cipolle non mi si confanno le *chee·pohl·le nohn mee see kon·fan·no*

agreement *n* l'accordo (*m*) *ak·kor·doh*

agricultural *adj* agricolo(a) *a·gree·ko·lo(a)*

agriculture *n* l'agricoltura (*f*) *a·gree·kol·too·ra*

ahead *adv* □ **to see something ahead** vedere* qualcosa in lontananza *ve·day·re kwal·ko·sa een lon·ta·nan·tsa*; **to plan ahead** fare* dei progetti in anticipo *fah·ray dee pro·jet·tee een an·tee·chee·po*; **to think ahead** pensare al futuro *pen·sah·ray al foo·too·roh* □ *prep* **ahead of** the others davanti agli altri *da·van·tee al·yee al·tree*

aim *vt* (*gun etc*) puntare *poon·tah·ray*; **to aim a gun at someone** puntare un fucile contro qualcuno *poon·tah·ray oon foo·chee·le kohn·tro kwal·koo·no* □ *vi* **aim** prendere* la mira *pren·de·re la mee·ra* □ *n* (*intention*) lo scopo *sko·poh*

air *n* l'aria (*f*) *ah·rya*; **by air** per via aerea *payr vee·a a·e·re·a* □ *vt* **air** (*room*) arieggiare *a·ree·ej·jah·ray*; (*clothes*) sciorinare *sho·ree·nah·ray*

air bed *n* il materasso pneumatico *ma·te·ras·soh pne·oo·ma·tee·ko*

air bus *n* l'aerobus (*m*) *a·e·ro·boos*

air-conditioned *adj* con aria condizionata *kohn ah·rya kon·dee·tsyoh·nah·ta*

air-conditioning *n* il condizionamento dell'aria *kon·dee·tsyoh·na·mayn·toh del·lah·rya* A44

aircraft *n* l'aereo (*m*) *a·e·re·oh*

air filter *n* il filtro dell'aria *feel·troh del·lah·rya*

air force *n* l'aviazione (*f*) *a·vya·tsyoh·ne*

air freight *n* il trasporto aereo *tra·spor·toh a·e·re·o*

air hostess *n* la hostess *ho·stess*

airline *n* la compagnia aerea *kom·pan·yee·a a·e·re·a*

air mail *n* □ **by air mail** per posta aerea *payr po·sta a·e·re·a*

air-mattress *n* il materasso pneumatico *ma·te·ras·soh pne·oo·ma·tee·ko*

airplane *n* l'aeroplano (*m*) *a·e·ro·plah·noh*

airport n l'aeroporto (m) *a·e·ro·por·toh* T36

airtight adj ermetico(a) *er·me·tee·ko(a)*

air travel n il viaggio aereo *vyaj·joh a·e·re·o*

à la carte adv alla carta *al·la kar·ta*

alarm n (signal, apparatus) l'allarme (m) *al·lar·me* □ vt allarmare *al·lar·mah·ray*

alarm (clock) n la sveglia *zvayl·ya*

album n (for photos etc) l'album (m) *al·boom*; (record) il longplaying *long·ple·eeng*

alcohol n l'alcol (m) *al·kol* E54f

alcoholic adj (drink) alcolico(a) *al·ko·lee·ko(a)* □ n l'alcolizzato(a) (m/f) *al·ko·leedz·dzah·to(a)*

alcove n l'alcova (f) *al·ko·va*

Algeria n l'Algeria (f) *al·je·ree·a*

Algerian adj algerino(a) *al·je·ree·no(a)*

Algiers n Algeri (f) *al·je·ree*

alike adj simile *see·mee·le*

alive adj vivo(a) *vee·vo(a)*

all adj (with singular noun) tutto(a) *toot·to(a)*; (with plural noun) tutti(e) *toot·tee(·te)*; **all day** tutta la giornata *toot·ta la johr·nah·ta*; **all the tables** tutte le tavole *toot·te le tah·vo·le*; **all the bread** tutto il pane *toot·to eel pah·ne*; **all passengers** tutti i passeggeri *toot·tee ee pas·sej·je·ree* □ pron all (singular) il tutto *eel toot·toh*; (plural) i tutti *ee toot·tee*; **le tutte** *lay toot·te*; **all you need** tutto ciò di cui ha bisogno *toot·to cho dee koo·ee a bee·zohn·yoh*; **all of them know that...** sanno tutti che... *san·no toot·tee ke*

Allah n Allah (m) *al·la*

allergic to adj allergico(a) a *al·ler·jee·ko(a) a* I41

allergy n l'allergia (f) *al·ler·jee·a*

alley n il vicolo *vee·ko·loh*

alliance n l'alleanza (f) *al·le·an·tsa*

allocate vt assegnare *as·sen·yah·ray*

allow vt □ **to allow someone to go** permettere* a qualcuno di partire *payr·mayt·te·re a kwal·koo·no dee par·tee·re*; **we will allow £10** assegneremo £10 *as·sen·ye·re·mo £10*; **allow 10 minutes to get there** calcoli 10 minuti per arrivarci *kal·ko·lee 10 mee·noo·tee payr ar·ree·var·chee*

allowance n (state payment) l'assegno (m) *as·sayn·yoh*

alloy n la lega *lay·ga*

all right adv (yes) bene *be·ne*; **he's all right** (safe, fit) sta bene *sta be·ne*; **he did it all right** (satisfactorily) l'ha fatto bene *la fat·to be·ne*

almond n la mandorla *man·dor·la*

almond paste n la pasta di mandorla *pa·sta dee man·dor·la*

almost adv quasi *kwah·zee*

alone adj solo(a) *soh·lo(a)*

along prep □ **along the street** lungo la strada *loon·go la strah·da*

aloud adv (read) ad alta voce *ad al·ta voh·che*

alphabet n l'alfabeto (m) *al·fa·be·toh*

alpine adj alpino(a) *al·pee·no(a)*

Alps pl le Alpi *al·pee*

already adv già *ja*

also adv anche *an·ke*

altar n l'altare (m) *al·tah·re*

alter vt alterare *al·te·rah·ray*

alternator n (in car) l'alternatore (m) *al·ter·na·toh·re*

although conj benché *ben·ke*

altitude n l'altitudine (f) *al·tee·too·dee·ne*

aluminium, aluminum n l'alluminio (m) *al·loo·meen·yoh*

always adv sempre *sem·pre*

a.m. adv del mattino del *mat·tee·noh*

am vi □ **I am** sono *soh·no*

amalgamation n la fusione *foo·zyoh·ne*

amateur n il dilettante *dee·let·tan·te*

ambassador n l'ambasciatore (m) *am·ba·sha·toh·re*

amber n (traffic light) il giallo *jal·loh*

ambition n (aim) l'ambizione (f) *am·bee·tsyoh·ne*

ambitious adj ambizioso(a) *am·bee·tsyoh·so(a)*

ambulance n l'ambulanza (f) *am·boo·lan·tsa* I12

amenities pl le comodità *ko·mo·dee·ta*

America n l'America (f) *a·me·ree·ka*

American adj americano(a) *a·me·ree·kah·no(a)* B30

amethyst n l'ametista (f) *a·me·tee·sta*

among(st) prep fra *fra*

amount n (total) l'importo (m) *eem·por·toh*; **a large amount of X** una grande quantità di X *oo·na gran·de kwan·tee·ta dee X*; **a small amount of X** un po' di X *oon po dee X* □ vi **it amounts to L.4000** ammonta a L.4000 *am·mohn·ta a L4000*

amp n l'ampère (m) *am·pehr*

amplifier n l'amplificatore (m) *am·plee·fee·ka·toh·re*

amuse vt divertire *dee·ver·tee·re*

amusement park n il luna-park *loo·na·park*

an art un(a) *oon(a)*

anaemic adj anemico(a) *a·ne·mee·ko(a)*

anaesthetic n l'anestetico (m) *a·ne·ste·tee·koh* 162

analyse vt analizzare *a·na·leedz·dzah·ray*

analysis n l'analisi (f) *a·nah·lee·see*

ancestor n l'antenato (m/f) *an·te·nah·to(a)*

anchor n l'ancora (f) *an·ko·ra*

anchovy n l'acciuga (f) *ach·choo·ga*

and conj e *ay*; **better and better** sempre meglio *sem·pre mel·yo*; **to go and buy** andare* a comprare *an·dah·ray a kom·prah·ray*

anemic adj anemico(a) *a·ne·mee·ko(a)*

anesthetic n l'anestetico (m) *a·ne·ste·tee·koh*

angel n l'angelo (m) *an·je·loh*

anger n la collera *kol·le·ra*

angler n il pescatore *pe·ska·toh·re*

angling n la pesca *pay·ska*

angora adj (fabric) l'angora (f) *an·go·ra*

angry adj (person) arrabbiato(a) *ar·rab·byah·to(a)*; **to be angry with someone** essere* arrabbiato con qualcuno *es·se·re ar·rab·byah·to kohn kwal·koo·no*

animal n l'animale (m) *a·nee·mah·le*

ankle n la caviglia *ka·veel·ya*

anniversary n l'anniversario (m) *an·nee·ver·sah·ryoh*

announce vt annunziare *an·noon·tsyah·ray*

annoy vt (person) dare* fastidio a *dah·ray fa·stee·dyoh a*; (thing) annoiare *an·no·yah·ray*

annual adj annuale *an·noo·ah·le*

annual general meeting, AGM n l'assemblea generale annuale (f) *as·sem·ble·a je·ne·rah·le an·noo·ah·le*

annuity n la rendita vitalizia *ren·dee·ta vee·ta·lee·tsya*

anorak n la giacca a vento *jak·ka a ven·toh*

another adj □ another beer please! ancora una birra, per favore! *an·koh·ra oo·na beer·ra payr fa·voh·re*; I want to see another shirt vorrei vedere un'altra camicia *vor·re·ee ve·day·re oo·nal·tra ka·mee·cha*

answer n la risposta *ree·spoh·sta* □ vi rispondere* *ree·spohn·de·re* □ vt to answer a question rispondere* a una domanda *ree·spohn·de·re a oo·na do·man·da*; to answer the phone rispondere* al telefono *ree·spohn·de·re al te·le·fo·noh*

ant n la formica *for·mee·ka*

Antarctic n l'Antartide (f) *an·tar·tee·de*

antenna n l'antenna (f) *an·tayn·na*

antibiotic n l'antibiotico (m) *an·tee·bee·o·tee·koh*

antifreeze n l'anticongelante (m) *an·tee·kon·je·lan·te*

antihistamine n l'antistaminico (m) *an·tee·sta·mee·nee·koh*

antique n l'oggetto d'antiquariato (m) *oj·jet·toh dan·tee·kwa·ree·ah·toh* S84

antique dealer n l'antiquario (m) *an·tee·kwah·ryoh*

antiseptic n l'antisettico (m) *an·tee·set·koh*

any adj □ give me any book mi dia qualsiasi libro *mee dee·a kwal·see·a·see lee·broh*; we haven't any bread non abbiamo pane *nohn ab·byah·mo pah·ne*; have you any bread? ha del pane? *a del pah·ne*; is there any more soup? c'è ancora minestra? *che an·koh·ra mee·ne·stra* □ pron we haven't any non ne abbiamo *nohn nay ab·byah·mo*; can any of you sing? qualcuno di voi sa cantare? *kwal·koo·no dee voy sa kan·tah·rey*

anybody, anyone pron □ can you see anybody? può vedere qualcuno? *pwo ve·day·re kwal·koo·no*; I can't see anybody non vedo nessuno *nohn vay·do nes·soo·no*; anybody at all chiunque *kee·oon·kwe*

anything pron □ can you see anything? può vedere qualcosa? *pwo ve·day·re kwal·ko·sa*; I can't see anything non vedo niente *nohn vay·do nyen·te*; anything at all qualunque cosa *kwa·loon·kwe ko·sa*

anyway adv (none the less) tuttavia *toot·ta·vee·a*

anywhere adv □ I'll take you anywhere you like la porterò dovunque voglia *la por·te·ro do·voon·kwe vol·ya*; I can't see it anywhere non lo vedo in nessun luogo *nohn lo vay·do een nes·soon lwo·goh*

apart adv (separately) a parte *a par·te*

apartment n l'appartamento (m) *ap·par·ta·mayn·toh*

ape n la scimmia *sheem·mya*

aperitif n l'aperitivo (m) *a·pe·ree·tee·voh*

apologize vi scusarsi *skoo·zar·see*

apparently adv apparentemente *ap·pa·ren·te·mayn·te*

appear vi apparire* *ap·pa·ree·re*; he appears ill sembra malato *saym·bra ma·lah·to*; it appears that... pare che... *pah·re ke*

appendicitis n l'appendicite (f) *ap·pen·dee·chee·te*

appetite n l'appetito (m) *ap·pe·tee·toh*

appetizer n qualcosa che stimola l'appetito *kwal·ko·sa ke stee·mo·la lap·pe·tee·toh*

applause n gli applausi *ap·plow·zee*

apple n la mela *may·la*

apple tree n il melo *may·loh*

appliance n l'apparecchio (m) *ap·pa·rayk·kyoh*

application n (for job) la domanda *do·man·da*

apply vi □ to apply for a job presentare una domanda d'impiego *pre·zen·tah·ray oo·na do·man·da deem·pye·goh*

appoint vt nominare *no·mee·nah·ray*

appointment n (rendezvous) l'appuntamento (m) *ap·poon·ta·mayn·toh*; (to job) la nomina *no·mee·na* Sn35, Bm9

appreciate vt apprezzare *ap·prets·tsah·ray* □ vi (in value) aumentare di valore *ow·men·tah·ray dee va·loh·re*

apprentice n l'apprendista (m/f) *ap·pren·dee·sta*

approach vi avvicinarsi *av·vee·chee·nar·see* □ vt to approach a place avvicinarsi ad un luogo *av·vee·chee·nar·see ad oon lwo·goh*

approval n l'approvazione (f) *a·pro·vah·tsyoh·ne*; on approval in prova *een pro·va*

approve of vt approvare *ap·pro·vah·ray*

approximate adj approssimativo(a) *ap·pros·see·ma·tee·vo(a)*

apricot n l'albicocca (f) *al·bee·kok·ka*

April n aprile (m) *a·pree·le*

apron n il grembiule *grem·byoo·le*

aquarium n l'acquario (m) *ak·kwah·ryoh*

Arab n l'arabo(a) (m/f) *a·ra·bo(a)*

Arabic adj arabo(a) *a·ra·bo(a)* □ n l'arabo (m) *a·ra·bo*

arcade n la galleria *gal·le·ree·a*

arch n l'arco (m) *ar·koh*

architect n l'architetto (m) *ar·kee·tayt·toh*

architecture n l'architettura (f) *ar·kee·tet·too·ra*

Arctic n l'Artico (m) *ar·tee·koh*

are vi □ we are siamo *syah·mo*; you are siete *sye·te*; they are sono *soh·no*

area n (of surface) l'area (f) *ah·re·a*; (region) la regione *re·joh·ne*

Argentina n Argentina (f) *ar·jen·tee·na*

Argentine adj argentino(a) *ar·jen·tee·no(a)*

argue vi (quarrel) litigare *lee·tee·gah·ray*

argument n (quarrel) la lite *lee·te*

arithmetic n l'aritmetica (f) *a·reet·mee·tee·ka*

arm n (of person) il braccio *brach·choh* I22

armchair n la poltrona *pol·troh·na*

arms pl le armi *ar·mee*

army n l'esercito (m) *e·zer·chee·toh*

around adv □ to look around guardarsi intorno *gwar·dar·see een·tohr·no*; things lying around cose sparse da tutte le parti *ko·se spar·se da toot·te le par·te* □ prep to go around the world andare* intorno al mondo *an·dah·ray een·tohr·no al mohn·doh*; around £10 circa £10 *cheer·ka £10*

arrange vt (flowers, furniture) disporre* *dee·spohr·re*; (meeting) fissare *fees·sah·ray*

arrears npl gli arretrati *ar·re·trah·tee*; to be in arrears with a payment essere* in arretrato con un pagamento *es·se·re een ar·re·trah·to kohn oon pa·ga·mayn·toh*

arrest vt arrestare *ar·re·stah·ray*

arrival n l'arrivo (m) ar·ree·voh

arrive vi arrivare ar·ree·vah·ray

arrow n la freccia fraych·cha

art n l'arte (f) ar·te

artery n l'arteria (f) ar·te·ree·a

art gallery n la galleria d'arte gal·le·ree·a dar·te

arthritis n l'artrite (f) ar·tree·te

artichoke n il carciofo kar·cho·foh; Jerusalem artichoke il topinambur to·pee·nam·boor

article n l'articolo (m) ar·tee·ko·loh

artificial adj artificiale ar·tee·fee·chah·le

artist n l'artista (m/f) ar·tee·sta

as conj □ as he was asleep (because) poiché dormiva poy·kay dor·mee·va; (while) mentre dormiva mayn·tre dor·mee·va; he arrived as we left è arrivato mentre stavamo partendo e ar·ree·vah·to mayn·tre sta·vah·mo par·ten·do; do as I say faccia come le dico io fach·cha koh·me le dee·ko ee·o; as big as così grande come ko·see gran·de koh·me; as for this quanto a questo kwan·to a kway·sto; as if, as though come se koh·me say; as well (too) anche an·ke; as much as tan·to quanto(a) tan·to(a) kwan·to(a)

asbestos n l'amianto (m) a·myan·toh

ash n (tree) il frassino fras·see·noh; (cinders) la cenere chay·ne·re

ashamed adj □ to be ashamed (of) vergognarsi (di) ver·gon·yar·see (dee)

ashcan n il bidone bee·doh·ne

ashore adv a terra a ter·ra

ashtray n il portacenere por·ta·chay·ne·re A41

Asia n Asia (f) ah·zee·a

Asian adj asiatico(a) a·zee·a·tee·ko(a)

ask vt/i domandare do·man·dah·ray; to ask a question fare* una domanda fah·ray oo·na do·man·da; to ask someone the time chiedere* l'ora a qualcuno kyay·de·re loh·ra a kwal·koo·no; to ask for something chiedere* qualcosa kyay·de·re kwal·ko·sa

asleep adj addormentato(a) ad·dor·men·tah·to(a)

asparagus n l'asparago (m) a·spa·ra·goh

aspirin n l'aspirina (f) a·spee·ree·na

assemble vt (parts of machine) montare mon·tah·ray

assembly line n la catena di montaggio ka·tay·na dee mon·taj·joh

asset n (financial) l'attivo (m) at·tee·voh

assistant n (in shop) il/la commesso(a) kom·mays·so(a) Bm7

associate n il/la socio(a) so·cho(a)

association n l'associazione (f) as·so·chya·tsyoh·ne

assorted adj assortito(a) as·sor·tee·to(a)

assume vt (suppose) supporre* soop·pohr·re

asthma n l'asma (f) az·ma

at prep □ at 4 o'clock alle 4 al·le 4; at my house a casa mia a kah·sa mee·a; to stop at London fermarsi a Londra fer·mar·see a lohn·dra; to throw something at someone gettare qualcosa a qualcuno jet·tah·ray kwal·ko·sa a kwal·koo·no; not at all affatto af·fat·to; at once subito soo·bee·to

Athens n Atene a·te·ne

athlete n l'atleta (m/f) at·le·ta

Atlantic Ocean n l'Atlantico (m) at·lan·tee·ko

atlas n l'atlante (m) at·lan·te

attach vt attaccare at·tak·kah·ray

attack vt attaccare at·tak·kah·ray □ n l'attacco (m) at·tak·koh

attempt vt tentare ten·tah·ray □ n il tentativo ten·ta·tee·voh

attend vt (meeting etc) assistere* a as·see·ste·re a

attic n la soffitta sof·feet·ta

attitude n l'atteggiamento (m) at·tej·ja·mayn·toh

attorney n l'avvocato (m) av·vo·kah·toh

aubergine n la melanzana me·lan·dzah·na

auction n la vendita all'asta vayn·dee·ta al·la·sta

audience n (in theatre) il pubblico poob·blee·koh

audio-guide n l'audioguida (f) ow·dyo·gwee·da L3

audio-visual adj audiovisivo(a) ow·dyo·vee·zee·vo(a)

audit vt verificare ve·ree·fee·kah·ray

auditor n il revisore dei conti re·vee·zoh·re de·ee kohn·tee

auditorium n la sala sah·la

au gratin adj au gratin ō gra·tañ

August n agosto (m) a·goh·sto

aunt(ie) n la zia tsee·a

Australia n Australia (f) ow·strah·lya

Australian adj australiano(a) ow·stra·lyah·no(a)

Austria n Austria (f) ow·strya

Austrian adj austriaco(a) ow·stree·a·ko(a)

author n l'autore (m) ow·toh·re

automatic adj automatico(a) ow·to·ma·tee·ko(a) □ n (car) la macchina automatica mak·kee·na ow·to·ma·tee·ka

automatically adv automaticamente ow·to·ma·tee·ka·mayn·te

automation n l'automazione (f) ow·to·ma·tsyoh·ne

auto(mobile) n la macchina mak·kee·na

autumn n l'autunno (m) ow·toon·noh

available adj disponibile dee·spo·nee·bee·le

avalanche n la valanga va·lan·ga

avenue n il viale vyah·le

average adj medio(a) me·dyo(a) □ n la media me·dya

aviation n l'aviazione (f) a·vya·tsyoh·ne

avocado (pear) n l'avocado (m) a·vo·kah·doh

avoid vt evitare e·vee·tah·ray

away adv □ away from home fuori di casa fwo·ree dee kah·sa; he's away for a week è partito per una settimana e par·tee·to payr oo·na set·tee·mah·na; 30 kilometres away a 30 chilometri a 30 kee·lo·me·tree

awful adj terribile ter·ree·bee·le

axe n la scure skoo·re

axle n l'asse (m) as·se

B

baby n il/la bambino(a) bam·bee·no(a) C18

baby buggy, baby carriage n la carrozzina per bambini kar·rots·tsee·na payr bam·bee·nee

babysit vi fare* da babysitter fah·ray da bay·bee·see·ter C4

baby-sitter n la babysitter bay·bee·see·ter C5

baccarat n il baccarà bak·ka·ra

bachelor n lo scapolo skah·po·loh

back n (of person) la schiena skye·na;

(of animal) la groppa grop·pa; (of chair) lo schienale skye·nah·le; (reverse side) il rovescio ro·ve·shoh; (of hall, room) il fondo fohn·doh; (in sports) il terzino ter·tsee·noh □ adv (backwards) indietro een·dye·tro; to come/go back tornare tor·nah·ray □ vt back (support) assecondare as·se·kon·dah·ray; (financially) finanziare fee·nan·tsyah·ray; (bet on) puntare su poon·tah·ray soo; to back the car fare* marcia indietro fah·ray mar·cha een·dye·tro

backache n il mal di schiena mal dee skye·na

backdate vt (letter) retrodatare re·tro·da·tah·ray

backer n il finanziatore fee·nan·tsya·toh·re

backgammon n la tavola reale tah·vo·la re·ah·le

background n lo sfondo sfohn·doh

backing n il sostegno so·stayn·yoh

backlash n la reazione re·a·tsyoh·ne

backlog □ backlog of work il lavoro accumulato la·voh·roh ak·koo·moo·lah·to

back pack n lo zaino dzy·noh

backward adj (glance) indietro een·dye·tro; (child) tardivo(a) tar·dee·vo(a)

backwards adv indietro een·dye·tro

bacon n la pancetta pan·chayt·ta

bad adj cattivo(a) kat·tee·vo(a); to go bad (food) guastarsi gwa·star·see; a bad debt un debito insolvibile oon day·bee·toh een·sol·vee·bee·le

badge n il distintivo dee·steen·tee·voh

badly adv (not well) male mah·le; to want something badly desiderare molto qualcosa de·see·de·rah·ray mohl·to kwal·ko·sa

badminton n il volano vo·lah·noh

bag n (of paper) il sacchetto sak·kayt·toh; (paper carrier) il sacco sak·koh; (handbag) la borsa bohr·sa; bags (luggage) i bagagli ba·gal·yee B69, T21f, 78, S25

baggage n i bagagli ba·gal·yee T24

baggage car n il bagagliaio ba·gal·ya·yoh

baggage check n lo scontrino per i bagagli skon·tree·noh payr ee ba·gal·yee

baggage claim n il recapito dei bagagli re·ka·pee·toh de·ee ba·gal·yee

baggage room n il deposito bagagli de·po·zee·toh ba·gal·yee T24

bail n (for prisoner) la cauzione kow·tsyoh·ne; on bail su cauzione soo kow·tsyoh·ne

bait n (in fishing) l'esca (f) ay·ska

bake vt cuocere* al forno kwo·che·re al fohr·noh

baker n il fornaio for·na·yoh S29

bakery n il panificio pah·nee·fee·choh

balance n l'equilibrio (m) e·kwee·lee·bree·oh; (remainder owed) il saldo sal·doh; balance of power l'equilibrio politico (m) e·kwee·lee·bree·oh po·lee·tee·ko; balance of payments la bilancia dei pagamenti bee·lan·cha de·ee pa·ga·mayn·tee; balance of trade la bilancia commerciale bee·lan·cha kom·mer·chah·le; to lose one's balance perdere* l'equilibrio per·de·re le·kwee·lee·bree·oh □ vt balance lanciare bee·lan·chah·ray; (accounts) pareggiare pa·rej·jah·ray □ vi pareggiare pa·rej·jah·ray

balance sheet n il bilancio bee·lan·choh

balcony n il balcone bal·koh·ne

bald adj calvo(a) kal·vo(a)

ball n la palla pal·la; (inflated) il pallone pal·loh·ne; (of string, wool) il gomitolo go·mee·to·loh; (dance) il ballo bal·loh

ballet n il balletto bal·layt·toh

balloon n il pallone pal·loh·ne

ballot n lo scrutinio skroo·tee·nyoh

bamboo n il bambú bam·boo

ban vt proibire pro·ee·bee·re □ n la proibizione pro·ee·bee·tsyoh·ne

banana n la banana ba·nah·na

band n (musical) la banda ban·da

bandage n la benda ben·da

bandaid n il cerotto che·rot·toh

bang n (of gun etc) il colpo kohl·poh; (of door) lo sbattere zbat·te·re; (blow) il colpo kohl·poh □ vt (door) sbattere zbat·te·re; to bang one's head battersi la testa bat·ter·see la testa □ vi bang (gun etc) esplodere* e·splo·de·re

bangs pl la frangia fran·jah

bank n (of river, lake) la riva ree·va; (finance) la banca ban·ka □ vt (money) depositare de·po·zee·tah·ray □ vi to bank with Smiths avere* un conto con Smiths a·vay·re oon kohn·toh kohn Smiths M28f

bank account n il conto bancario kohn·toh ban·kah·ryo M29

bank balance n il saldo bancario sal·doh ban·kah·ryo

bank bill n la tratta trat·ta

bankbook n il libretto di banca lee·brayt·toh dee ban·ka

bank charges pl le spese bancarie spay·se ban·kah·rye

banker n il banchiere ban·kye·re

banker's card n la carta d'identità bancaria kar·ta dee·den·tee·ta ban·kah·rya

banker's order n l'ordine bancario (m) ohr·dee·ne ban·kah·ryo

bank holiday n il giorno festivo johr·noh fe·stee·vo

bank loan n il prestito bancario pre·stee·toh ban·kah·ryo

bank manager n il direttore di banca dee·ret·toh·re dee ban·ka M31

bank note n la banconota ban·ko·no·ta

bankrupt adj fallito(a) fal·lee·to(a); to go bankrupt fare* fallimento fah·ray fal·lee·mayn·toh

bankruptcy n la bancarotta ban·ka·roht·ta

banner n la bandiera ban·dye·ra

banquet n il banchetto ban·kayt·toh

baptism n il battesimo bat·tay·zee·moh

Baptist adj battista bat·tee·sta

bar n (metal) la sbarra zbar·ra; (counter) il banco ban·koh; (drinking establishment) il bar bar; bar of soap la saponetta sa·po·nayt·ta; bar of chocolate la tavoletta di cioccolata tah·vo·layt·ta dee chok·ko·lah·ta E54f, L51

barbecue n il barbecue bar·bee·kyoo

barbed wire n il filo di ferro spinato fee·loh dee fer·roh spee·nah·to

barber n il barbiere bar·bye·re

bare adj (person, head) nudo(a) noo·do(a); to go barefoot andare* a piedi scalzi an·dah·ray a pye·de skal·tsee

bargain n (cheap buy) l'occasione (f) ok·ka·zyoh·ne; to make a bargain concludere* un affare kon·kloo·de·re oon af·fah·re

bargaining *n* (*negotiation*) la contrattazione *kon·trat·ta·tsyoh·ne*
barge *n* la chiatta *kyat·ta*
bark *n* (*of tree*) la corteccia *kor·taych·cha*; (*of dog*) il latrato *la·trah·toh* □ *vi* abbaiare *ab·ba·yah·ray*
barmaid *n* la cameriera al banco *ka·me·rye·ra al ban·koh*
barman *n* il barista *ba·ree·sta*
barn *n* il granaio *gra·na·yoh*
barracks *pl* la caserma *ka·ser·ma*
barrel *n* (*for beer*) il barile *ba·ree·le*
barrier *n* (*fence*) la barriera *bar·rye·ra*
barrister *n* l'avvocato (*m*) *av·vo·kah·toh*
bartender *n* il barista *ba·ree·sta*
base *n* la base *bah·ze* □ *vt* basare *ba·zah·ray*
baseball *n* il baseball *bays·bol*
basement *n* il seminterrato *se·meen·ter·rah·toh*
basic *adj* di base *dee·bah·ze*
basically *adv* fondamentalmente *fon·da·mayn·tal·mayn·te*
basin *n* (*dish*) la scodella *sko·del·la*; (*for washing*) il lavabo *la·vah·boh*
basis *n* la base *bah·ze*
basket *n* il canestro *ka·ne·stroh*
basketball *n* la pallacanestro *pal·la·ka·ne·stroh*
bat *n* (*table tennis etc*) la racchetta *rak·kayt·ta*; (*animal*) il pipistrello *pee·pee·strel·loh*
bath *n* (*tub*) la vasca da bagno *va·ska da ban·yoh* A4
bathe *vi* bagnarsi *ban·yar·see* □ *vt* (*wound etc*) bagnare *ban·yah·ray*
bathing cap *n* la cuffia da bagno *koof·fya da ban·yoh*
bathing suit *n* il costume da bagno *ko·stoo·me da ban·yoh*
bathroom *n* la stanza da bagno *stan·tsa da ban·yoh*; (*lavatory*) il bagno *ban·yoh* A17
batter *n* (*for frying*) la pastella *pa·stel·la*
battery *n* (*for radio etc*) la pila *pee·la*; (*in car*) la batteria *bat·te·ree·a* T177
battle *n* la battaglia *bat·tal·ya*
bay *n* (*on coast*) la baia *ba·ya*
bazaar *n* il bazar *ba·dzar*
be *vi* essere* *es·se·re*; I am sono *soh·no*; you are è *e*; we are siamo *syah·mo*; they are sono *soh·no*; how are you? come sta? *koh·me sta*, I am hungry ho fame *o fah·me*; what is that? che cosa è quello? *ke ko·sa è kwayl·lo*; how much is it? quanto costa? *kwan·to ko·sta*; it is hot fa caldo *fa kal·do*; we are going to the beach andiamo alla spiaggia *an·dyah·mo al·la spyaj·ja*; we have been to Paris siamo andati a Parigi *syah·mo an·dah·tee a pa·ree·jee*; he is a doctor è medico *e me·de·koh*
beach *n* la spiaggia *spyaj·ja* L27
bead *n* la perlina *per·lee·na*
beam *n* (*of wood*) la trave *trah·ve*; (*of light*) il raggio *raj·joh*
beans *pl* i fagioli *fa·jo·lee*
bear *n* l'orso (*m*) *ohr·soh* □ *vt* (*weight*) sorreggere* *sor·rej·je·re*; (*endure*) sopportare *sop·por·tah·ray*
beard *n* la barba *bar·ba*
bearings *pl* (*in car*) i cuscinetti *koo·shee·nayt·tee*; to take one's bearings orientarsi *o·ree·en·tar·see*
beat *vt* (*hit*) colpire *kol·pee·re*; (*defeat*) battere *bat·te·re* □ *vi* (*heart*) battere *bat·te·re*
beautiful *adj* bello(a) *bel·lo(a)*

beauty *n* la bellezza *bel·layts·tsa*
because *conj* perché *payr·kay*; because of a causa di *a kow·za dee*
become *vi* diventare *dee·ven·tah·ray*
bed *n* il letto *let·toh*; in bed a letto *a let·toh*; to go to bed andare* a letto *an·dah·ray a let·toh* A4, I50
bedclothes *pl* le coperte *ko·per·te*
bedding *n* la biancheria da letto *byan·ke·ree·a da let·toh* A68
bedroom *n* la camera *kah·me·ra*
bee *n* l'ape (*f*) *ah·pe*
beech *n* il faggio *faj·joh*
beef *n* la carne di manzo *kar·ne dee man·dzoh*
beer *n* la birra *beer·ra* E55
beetle *n* lo scarafaggio *ska·ra·faj·joh*
beetroot *n* la barbabietola *bar·ba·bye·to·la*
before *prep* (*in time*) prima di *pree·ma dee*; before noon prima di mezzogiorno *pree·ma dee medz·dzo·johr·noh*; before the king (*in space*) davanti al re *da·van·tee al ray* □ *adv* before prima *pree·ma*; we've met before ci siamo già conosciuti *chee syah·mo ja ko·no·shoo·tee* □ *conj* before prima che *pree·ma ke*; before I go to bed prima che io vada a letto *pree·ma ke ee·oh vah·da a let·toh*
beg *vi* mendicare *men·dee·kah·ray*
beggar *n* il/la mendicante *men·dee·kan·te*
begin *vt/i* cominciare *ko·meen·chah·ray*
beginner *n* il/la principiante *preen·chee·pyan·te*
behalf *n* □ on behalf of a nome di *a noh·me dee*
behave *vi* comportarsi *kom·por·tar·see*; behave yourself! comportati bene! *kom·por·ta·tee be·ne*
behaviou(r) *n* il comportamento *kom·por·ta·mayn·toh*
behind *adv, prep* dietro *dye·tro*; to look behind guardare indietro *gwar·dah·ray een·dye·tro*; to be behind schedule essere* in ritardo *es·se·re een ree·tar·doh*
beige *adj* beige *bayzh*
belief *n* (*faith*) la fede *fay·de*; (*tenet*) la credenza *kre·den·tsa*
believe *vt/i* credere *kray·de·re*; to believe in credere a *kray·de·re a*
bell *n* la campana *kam·pah·na*; (*electric*) il campanello *kam·pa·nel·loh*
bellboy *n* il fattorino d'albergo *fat·to·ree·noh dal·ber·goh*
belong *vi* □ to belong to someone appartenere* *ap·par·te·nay·re a qualcuno *a kwal·koo·no*; to belong to a club essere* membro di un club *es·se·re mem·broh dee oon kloob*
belongings *pl* gli effetti personali *ef·fet·tee per·so·nah·lee*
below *adv, prep* sotto *soht·to*
belt *n* (*for waist*) la cintura *cheen·too·ra* S78
bench *n* (*seat*) la panca *pan·ka*; (*work table*) il banco *ban·koh*
bend *n* la curva *koor·va* □ *vt* piegare *pye·gah·ray* □ *vi* (*person*) chinarsi *kee·nar·see*; (*road*) curvare *koor·vah·ray* T206
beneath = below
benefit *n* il vantaggio *van·taj·joh*; it's of no benefit (to us) non ci serve *nohn chee ser·ve*
Benelux *n* Benelux (*m*) *be·ne·looks*
berry *n* la bacca *bak·ka*
berth *n* la cuccetta *kooch·chayt·ta*

beside *prep* accanto a *ak·kan·to a*

besides *adv* (*moreover*) inoltre *een·ohl·tre* □ *prep* besides him oltre a lui *ohl·tre a loo·ee*

best *adj* il/la migliore *eel/la meel·yoh·re* □ **n** he's the best è il migliore *e eel meel·yoh·re* □ *adv* he can do it best lo fa meglio lui *lo fa mel·yo loo·ee*

best man *n* il testimone dello sposo *te·stee·mo·ne del·lo spo·zoh*

bet *vt/i* scommettere* *skom·mayt·te·re* □ *n* la scommessa *skom·mays·sa*

better *adj* migliore *meel·yoh·re* □ *adv* he sings better than you canta meglio di te *kan·ta mel·yo dee te*; to get better (*from illness*) migliorare *meel·yo·rah·ray*; they are better off than us (*richer*) sono piú ricchi di noi *soh·no pyoo reek·kee dee noy*

between *prep* tra *tra*

beyond *prep* oltre *ohl·tre*; beyond my reach fuori la mia portata *fwo·ree la mee·a por·tah·ta*; beyond his means fuori la sua portata *fwo·ree la soo·a por·tah·ta*

Bible *n* la Bibbia *beeb·bya*

bicycle *n* la bicicletta *bee·chee·klayt·ta*

bid *vt* (*amount*) offrire* *of·free·re* □ *vi* to bid for something fare* un'offerta per qualcosa *fah·ray oo·nof·fer·ta payr kwal·ko·sa* □ *n* bid l'offerta (*f*) *of·fer·ta*

bidder *n* l'offerente (*m/f*) *of·fe·ren·te*

big *adj* (*person, house*) grande *gran·de*; (*sum of money*) grosso(a) *gros·so(a)*

bikini *n* il bikini *bee·kee·nee*

bilingual *adj* bilingue *bee·leen·gwe*

bill *n* (*account*) il conto *kohn·toh*; (*bank note*) la banconota *ban·ko·no·ta* T189, A21, E42

billiards *n* il biliardo *bee·lyar·doh*

billion *n* il miliardo *mee·lyar·doh*

bin *n* (*for refuse*) la pattumiera *pat·too·mye·ra*

bind *vt* (*tie*) legare *le·gah·ray*

binoculars *pl* il binocolo *bee·no·ko·loh*

biology *n* la biologia *bee·o·lo·jee·a*

birch *n* (*tree*) la betulla *be·tool·la*

bird *n* l'uccello (*m*) *ooch·chel·loh* L41

birth *n* la nascita *na·shee·ta*

birth certificate *n* l'atto di nascita (*m*) *at·toh dee na·shee·ta*

birthday *n* il compleanno *kom·ple·an·noh*

biscuit *n* (*sweet*) il biscotto *bee·skot·toh*; (*savo(u)ry*) il cracker *krak·ker*

bishop *n* il vescovo *vay·sko·voh*

bit *n* (*piece*) il pezzo *pets·tsoh*; a bit of un pezzo di *oon pets·tsoh dee*

bite *vt* mordere* *mor·de·re* □ *n* (*by animal*) il morso *mor·soh*; (*by insect*) la puntura *poon·too·ra*; (*of food*) il boccone *bok·koh·ne*

bitter *adj* amaro(a) *a·mah·ro(a)* □ *n* (*beer*) la birra *beer·ra*

black *adj* nero(a) *nay·ro(a)*; a black coffee un caffè nero *oon kaf·fe nay·ro*

blackberry *n* la mora *mo·ra*

blackbird *n* il merlo *mer·loh*

blackcurrant *n* il ribes *ree·bes*

black eye *n* l'occhio nero (*m*) *ok·kyoh nay·ro*

blackjack *n* il gioco del ventuno *jo·koh del ven·too·no*

black market *n* la borsa nera *bohr·sa nay·ra*

bladder *n* la vescica *ve·shee·ka*

blade *n* (*of knife*) la lama *lah·ma*

blame *vt* (*reproach*) incolpare *een·kol·*

pah·ray; to be to blame essere* colpevole *es·se·re kol·pay·vo·le*

blank *adj* in bianco *een byan·ko*; blank cheque l'assegno in bianco (*m*) *as·sayn·yoh een byan·ko*; please leave blank lasciate in bianco per favore *la·shah·te een byan·ko payr fa·voh·re*

blanket *n* la coperta *ko·per·ta* A41

blast *n* (*explosion*) lo scoppio *skop·pyoh*

blaze *n* (*fire*) l'incendio (*m*) *een·chen·dyoh* □ *vi* ardere* *ar·de·re*; (*lights*) risplendere *ree·splen·de·re*

blazer *n* la giacca sportiva *jak·ka spor·tee·va*

bleed *vi* sanguinare *san·gwee·nah·ray*

blend *vt* mescolare *me·sko·lah·ray* □ *n* la miscela *mee·she·la*

bless *vt* benedire* *be·ne·dee·re*

blind *adj* (*person*) cieco(a) *che·ko(a)* □ *n* (*at window*) la tendina *ten·dee·na*

blind alley *n* il vicolo cieco *vee·ko·loh che·ko*

blind corner *n* la curva senza visibilità *koor·va sen·tsa vee·zee·bee·lee·ta*

blink *vi* battere le palpebre *bat·te·re le pal·pe·bre*

blister *n* (*on skin*) la vescichetta *ve·shee·kayt·ta*

blizzard *n* la bufera di neve *boo·fe·ra dee nay·ve*

block *n* (*of stone*) il blocco *blok·koh*; 3 blocks away (*streets*) alla terza strada *al·la ter·tsa strah·da*; block of flats, apartment block il casamento *ka·sa·mayn·toh* □ *vt* block bloccare *blok·kah·ray*; block letters lo stampatello *stam·pa·tel·loh*; block booking la prenotazione a gruppo *pre·no·ta·tsyoh·ne a groop·poh*

blockage *n* l'ostruzione (*f*) *o·stroo·tsyoh·ne*

blond(e) *adj* biondo(a) *byohn·do(a)*

blood *n* il sangue *san·gwe*

blood group *n* il gruppo sanguigno *groop·poh san·gween·yo* I48, 49

blood poisoning *n* la setticemia *set·tee·che·mee·a*

blood pressure *n* la pressione sanguigna *pres·syoh·ne san·gween·ya* I42

bloom *n* (*flower*) il fiore *fyoh·re* □ *vi* fiorire *fyo·ree·re*

blossom *n* i fiori *fyoh·ree*

blot *n* la macchia *mak·kya* □ *vt* (*ink*) asciugare *a·shoo·gah·ray*

blouse *n* la camicetta *ka·mee·chayt·ta* S19

blow *n* (*knock*) il colpo *kohl·poh* □ *vi* (*wind*) soffiare *sof·fyah·ray*; (*fuse*) saltare *sal·tah·ray* □ *vt* to blow one's nose soffiarsi il naso *sof·fyar·see eel nah·soh*

blow-dry *n* l'asciugatura con il fon (*f*) *a·shoo·ga·too·ra kohn eel fon*

blow-out *n* la foratura *fo·ra·too·ra*

blue *adj* azzurro(a) *adz·dzoor·ro(a)*

bluebottle *n* il moscone *mos·koh·ne*

blue chips *pl* i valori di prima classe *va·loh·ree dee pree·ma klas·se*

blueprint *n* il progetto *pro·jet·toh*

blunt *adj* (*knife*) smussato(a) *zmoos·sah·to(a)*

blush *vi* arrossire *ar·ros·see·re*

board *n* (*of wood*) l'asse (*f*) *as·se*; (*for notices*) il tabellone *ta·bel·loh·ne*; (*of directors*) il consiglio d'amministrazione *kon·seel·yoh dam·mee·nee·stra·tsyoh·ne*; on board (*ship, plane*) a bordo *a bohr·doh*; full board la pensione completa *pen·syoh·ne kom·*

ple·ta; half board la mezza pensione *medz·dza pen·syoh·ne* □ *vt* board (*train, bus*) salire* su *sa·lee·re soo*; (*ship*) salire* a bordo di *sa·lee·re a bohr·doh dee*

boarding house *n* la pensione *pen· syoh·ne*

boarding pass *n* la carta d'imbarco *kar·ta deem·bar·koh*

boast *vi* vantarsi *van·tar·see*

boat *n* la barca *bar·ka* L29

bobby pin *n* la forcina *for·chee·na*

body *n* il corpo *kor·poh*; (*corpse*) il cadavere *ka·dah·ve·re*

bodyguard *n* (*person*) la guardia del corpo *gwar·dya del kor·poh*

bog *n* la palude *pa·loo·de*

boil *vi* bollire *bol·lee·re* □ *vt* (*water*) fare* bollire *fah·ray bol·lee·re* □ *n* (*on skin*) il foruncolo *fo·roon·ko·loh*

bold *adj* audace *ow·dah·che*

bolster *n* il capezzale *ka·pets·tsah·le*

bolt *n* il chiavistello *kya·vee·stel·loh* □ *vt* (*door, gate*) chiudere* a chiavistello *kyoo·de·re a kya·vee·stel·loh*

bomb *n* la bomba *bohm·ba*

bone *n* l'osso (*m*) *os·soh*; (*of fish*) la spina *spee·na*

bonfire *n* il falò *fa·lo*

bonnet *n* (*on car*) il cofano *ko·fa·noh*

bonus *n* (*on salary*) il premio *pre· myoh*

book *n* il libro *lee·broh* □ *vt* (*seat*) prenotare *pre·no·tah·ray*

booking *n* la prenotazione *pre·no·ta· tsyoh·ne*

booking office *n* l'ufficio prenotazioni (*m*) *oof·fee·choh pre·no·ta·tsyoh·nee*

boom *n* (*noise*) il rombo *rohm·boh*; (*economic*) il boom *boom* □ *vi* business is booming gli affari vanno a gonfie vele *lyee af·fah·ree van·no a gohn·fye vay·le*

boost *vt* (*sales*) aumentare *ow·men· tah·ray*

boot *n* lo stivale *stee·vah·le*; (*of car*) il bagagliaio *ba·gal·ya·yoh*

booth *n* (*telephone*) la cabina *ka· bee·na*

border *n* (*edge*) il bordo *bohr·doh*; (*of country*) la frontiera *fron·tye·ra*

bored *adj* stufo(a) *stoo·fo(a)*

boring *adj* noioso(a) *no·yoh·so(a)*

born *adj* nato(a) *nah·to(a)*; to be born nascere* *na·she·re*

borough *n* il borgo *bohr·goh*

borrow *vt* prendere* in prestito *pren· de·re een pre·stee·toh*; to borrow something from someone prendere* qualcosa in prestito da qualcuno *pren·de·re kwal·ko·sa een pre·stee· toh da kwal·koo·no*

boss *n* il capo *kah·poh*

botanical gardens *pl* il giardino botanico *jar·dee·noh bo·ta·nee·ko*

both *adj* ambedue *am·be·doo·e*; both girls tutte e due le ragazze *toot·te e doo·e le ra·gats·tse* □ *pron* both (*of them*) tutti(e) e due *toot·tee(·te) e doo·e*

bother *vt* (*annoy*) seccare *sek·kah·ray* □ *vi* please don't bother non si disturbi per favore *nohn see dee·stoor· bee payr fa·voh·re* □ *n* bother (*nuisance*) la seccatura *sek·ka·too·ra*; (*effort*) il fastidio *fa·stee·dyoh*

bottle *n* la bottiglia *bot·teel·ya*; (*baby's*) il biberon *bee·be·ron* E11, C2

bottleneck *n* l'ingorgo (*m*) *een·gohr· goh*

bottle opener *n* l'apribottiglie (*m*) *ah· pree·bot·teel·ye*

bottom *n* il fondo *fohn·doh*; (*of page, list*) il piede *pye·de*; (*of person*) il sedere *se·day·re* □ *adj* inferiore *een·fe· ryoh·re*

bounce *vi* (*ball*) rimbalzare *reem·bal· tsah·ray*

bound *adj* □ bound for (*ship*) con destinazione per *kohn de·stee·na·tsyoh· ne payr* □ *n* out of bounds oltre i limiti *ohl·tre ee lee·mee·tee*

boundary *n* il limite *lee·mee·te*

bourbon *n* il whisky americano *wee· skee a·me·ree·kah·no*

boutique *n* la boutique *boo·teek*

bow [1] *vi* inchinarsi *een·kee·nar·see* □ *n* l'inchino (*m*) *een·kee·no*

bow [2] *n* (*ribbon*) il nodo *no·doh*

bowl *n* (*for food*) la scodella *sko·del· la*; (*for washing*) la bacinella *ba· chee·nel·la*

bowler hat *n* la bombetta *bom·bayt·ta*

bow tie *n* la cravatta a farfalla *kra·vat· ta a far·fal·la*

box *n* la scatola *skah·to·la*

boxing *n* il pugilato *poo·jee·lah·toh*

box number *n* la casella postale *ka·sel· la po·stah·le*

box office *n* il botteghino *bot·te·gee· noh*

boy *n* il ragazzo *ra·gats·tsoh*

boycott *vt* boicottare *boy·kot·tah·ray*

boyfriend *n* il ragazzo *ra·gats·tsoh*

bra *n* il reggiseno *rej·jee·say·noh*

bracelet *n* il braccialetto *brach·cha· layt·toh*

bracken *n* la felce *fayl·che*

bracket *n* (*in writing*) la parentesi *pa· ren·te·zee*

brain *n* il cervello *cher·vel·loh*; **brains** (*as food*) il cervello *cher·vel·loh*

braised *adj* stufato(a) *stoo·fah·to(a)*

brake *n* il freno *fray·noh* □ *vi* frenare *fre·nah·ray* T173, 210

brake fluid *n* il fluido per i freni *floo· ee·doh payr ee fray·nee*

branch *n* (*of tree*) il ramo *rah·moh*; (*of store, bank etc*) la succursale *sook· koor·sah·le*

brand *n* (*of product*) la marca *mar·ka* S96

brand name *n* la marca *mar·ka*

brandy *n* il brandy *bran·dee* E56

brass *n* l'ottone (*m*) *ot·toh·ne*

brave *adj* coraggioso(a) *ko·raj·joh· so(a)*

bread *n* il pane *pah·ne* E30

break *n* (*pause*) la pausa *pow·za* □ *vt* rompere* *rohm·pe·re*; (*record*) battere *bat·te·re*; to break one's arm rompersi* il braccio *rohm·per·see eel brach·choh* □ *vi* break rompersi* *rohm·per·see*; to break down (*car*) guastarsi *gwa·star·see* B65f, T164

breakdown *n* (*of car*) l'avaria (*f*) *a·va· ree·a* T164f

breakdown van *n* l'autogrú (*f*) *ow·to· groo*

break even *vi* pareggiare i costi *pa·rej· jah·ray ee ko·stee*

breakfast *n* la colazione *ko·la·tsyoh·ne* A9, 26

breast *n* il seno *say·noh*; (*chest, of poultry*) il petto *pet·toh*

breath *n* il fiato *fyah·toh*

breathe *vi* respirare *re·spee·rah·ray*

breeze *n* la brezza *bred·dza*

brewery *n* la birreria *beer·re·ree·a*

bribe *vt* corrompere* *kor·rohm·pe·re*

brick *n* il mattone *mat·toh·ne*

bride n la sposa *spo·za*
bridegroom n lo sposo *spo·zoh*
bridge n il ponte *pohn·te*; (game) il bridge *breej*
bridle n la briglia *breel·ya*
brief adj breve *bre·ve*
briefcase n la borsa *bohr·sa*
briefs pl lo slip *zleep*
bright adj chiaro(a) *kyah·ro(a)*; (clever) intelligente *een·tel·lee·jen·te*
bring vt portare *por·tah·ray*; to bring in (profit) produrre* *pro·door·re*
Britain n Gran Bretagna (f) *gran bre·tan·ya*
British adj britannico(a) *bree·tan·nee·ko(a)*
broad adj largo(a) *lar·go(a)*
broadcast vt trasmettere* *tra·zmayt·te·re* □ n la trasmissione *tra·zmees·syoh·ne*
broccoli n i broccoli *brok·ko·lee*
brochure n l'opuscolo (m) *o·poo·sko·loh* A6, Bm22
broil vt arrostire alla griglia *ar·ro·stee·re al·la greel·ya*
broke adj (penniless) squattrinato(a) *skwat·tree·nah·to(a)*
broker n l'agente (m) *a·jen·te*
bronchitis n la bronchite *bron·kee·te*
bronze n il bronzo *brohn·dzoh*
brooch n la spilla *speel·la* S85
broom n la scopa *skoh·pa*
brother n il fratello *fra·tel·loh*
brother-in-law n il cognato *kon·yah·toh*
brown adj marrone *mar·roh·ne*; (hair) castano(a) *ka·stah·no(a)*
bruise n la contusione *kon·too·zyoh·ne*
brush n (for cleaning) la spazzola *spats·tso·la*; (for painting) il pennello *pen·nel·loh*; (for hair) la spazzola per capelli *spats·tso·la payr ka·payl·lee* □ vt spazzolare *spats·tso·lah·ray*
Brussels n Bruxelles (f) *brook·sel*
Brussels sprouts n i cavolini di Bruxelles *kah·vo·lee·nee dee brook·sel*
bubble n la bollicina *bol·lee·chee·na*
bucket n il secchio *sayk·kyoh*
buckle n la fibbia *feeb·bya*
bud n il bocciolo *boch·cho·loh*
budget n il bilancio preventivo *bee·lan·choh pre·ven·tee·vo*
buffet n (snackbar) il buffè *boof·fe*
bug n (insect) la cimice *chee·mee·che*
build vt (house) costruire* *ko·stroo·ee·re*
building n l'edificio (m) *e·dee·fee·choh* L11
building society n la società immobiliare *so·che·ta eem·mo·beel·yah·re*
bulb n il bulbo *bool·boh*; (light) la lampadina *lam·pa·dee·na*
bulk n □ in bulk (in large quantities) all'ingrosso *al·leen·gros·soh*; (unpackaged) sfuso(a) *sfoo·zo(a)*; bulk buying l'acquisto all'ingrosso (m) *ak·kwee·stoh al·leen·gros·soh*
bull n il toro *to·roh*
bulldozer n il bulldozer *bool·do·zer*
bullet n la pallottola *pal·lot·to·la*
bulletin n il bollettino *bol·let·tee·noh*
bullfight n la corrida *kor·ree·da*
bump n (knock) l'urto (m) *oor·toh*; (lump) il bernoccolo *ber·nok·ko·loh* □ vt urtare *oor·tah·ray*
bumper n (on car) il paraurti *pa·ra·oor·tee*
bun n il pasticcino *pa·steech·chee·noh*
bunch n (of flowers) il mazzo *mats·tsoh*
bundle n il fascio *fa·shoh*

bungalow n il bungalow
bunk n la cuccetta *kooch·chayt·ta*; bunk beds il letto a castello *let·toh a ka·stel·loh*
buoy n la boa *bo·a*
buoyant adj (market) in rialzo *een ree·al·tsoh*
bureau n (office) l'ufficio (m) *oof·fee·choh*
burglar n lo scassinatore *skas·see·na·toh·re*
burn vt bruciare *broo·chah·ray*; I've burnt my arm mi sono bruciato il braccio *mee soh·no broo·chah·to eel brach·choh*
burst vt scoppiare *skop·pyah·ray* □ vt fare* scoppiare *fah·ray skop·pyah·ray*
bury vt (person) seppellire *sep·pel·lee·re*
bus n l'autobus (m) *ow·to·boos*; (long distance) il pullman *pool·man* T87f, F15
bush n il cespuglio *che·spool·yoh*
business n (dealings, work) gli affari *af·fah·ree*; (firm) la ditta *deet·ta*; on business per affari *payr af·fah·ree*; to do business with someone fare* affari con qualcuno *fah·ray af·fah·ree kohn kwal·koo·no* E6, Bm28
business expenses pl le spese di rappresentanza *spay·ze dee rap·pre·zen·tan·tsa*
business hours pl le ore d'ufficio *oh·re doof·fee·choh*
businessman n l'uomo d'affari (m) *moh·daf·fah·ree*
business trip n il viaggio d'affari *vyaj·joh daf·fah·ree* Bm11
businesswoman n la donna d'affari *don·na daf·fah·ree*
bus service n il servizio autobus *ser·vee·tsyoh ow·to·boos*
bus stop n la fermata autobus *fer·mah·ta ow·to·boos* T94
bust n il busto *boo·stoh*
busy adj occupato(a) *ok·koo·pah·to(a)*; (place) animato(a) *a·nee·mah·to(a)*
busy signal n il segnale "occupato" *sen·yah·le ok·koo·pah·to*
but conj ma *ma*; not this, but that non questo ma quello *nohn kway·sto ma kwayl·lo* □ prep all but him tutti tranne lui *toot·tee tran·ne loo·ee*
butcher n il macellaio *ma·chel·la·yoh*; butcher's (shop) la macelleria *ma·chel·le·ree·a* S29
butter n il burro *boor·roh* E31, S30
butterfly n la farfalla *far·fal·la*
button n il bottone *bot·toh·ne* Sn76
buy vt comprare *kom·prah·ray*; to buy out (partner etc) disinteressare *dee·zeen·te·res·sah·ray* S6
buyer n (customer) (m/f) l'acquirente *ak·kwee·ren·te*; (for shop, factory) il compratore *kom·pra·toh·re*, la compratrice *kom·pra·tree·che* Bm3
by prep (next to) accanto a *ak·kan·to a*; to go by London (via) passare via Londra *pas·sah·ray ve·a lohn·dra*; by air per via aerea *payr ve·a a·e·re·a*; by train/car in treno/macchina *een tre·noh/mak·kee·na*; we'll be there by 4 o'clock saremo lì per le 4 *sa·ray·mo lee payr le 4* □ adv a plane flew by è passato un aereo *e pas·sah·to oon a·e·re·oh*
bypass n la circonvallazione *cheer·kon·val·la·tsyoh·ne*

C

cab n (taxi) il tassì tas·see
cabaret n il cabaret ka·ba·ray L43
cabbage n il cavolo kah·vo·loh
cabin n (in ship) la cabina ka·bee·na
cabin cruiser n il cabinato ka·bee·nah·toh
cable n il cavo kah·voh
cactus n il cacto kak·toh
caddie n il caddie kad·dee
café n il caffè kaf·fe
cafeteria n il ristorante self-service ree·sto·ran·tay self·sayr·vees
cage n la gabbia gab·bya
cake n la torta tohr·ta
calcium n il calcio kal·choh
calculate vt calcolare kal·ko·lah·ray
calculator n la calcolatrice kal·ko·la·tree·chay
calendar n il calendario ka·len·dah·ree·oh
calf n il vitello vee·tel·loh
call n (shout) il grido gree·doh; (on phone) la chiamata kya·mah·ta □ vi (shout) gridare gree·dah·ray □ vt chiamare kya·mah·ray; (telephone) telefonare a te·le·fo·nah·ray a; **call me at 7 a.m.** (in hotel etc) mi svegli alle 7 di mattina mee zvayl·yee al·lay 7 dee mat·tee·na; **to be called** chiamarsi kee·ah·mar·see Sn11
call box n la cabina telefonica ka·bee·na te·le·fo·nee·ka
call girl n la ragazza squillo ra·ga·tsa skwee·loh
calm adj (sea, day) calmo(a) kal·moh(a); (person) tranquillo(a) tran·kweel·loh(a)
Calor gas n il butano boo·tah·noh
calorie n la caloria ka·lo·ree·a
camel n il cammello kam·mel·loh
camera n la macchina fotografica mak·kee·na fo·to·gra·fee·ka; (TV) la telecamera te·le·kah·me·ra S47f
camp vi accamparsi ak·kam·pahr·see A80f
campaign n la campagna kam·pan·ya Bm17
camp-bed n la brandina bran·dee·na
camping n il campeggio kam·payj·joh; **to go camping** fare* del campeggio fah·ray del kam·payj·joh
camp(ing) site n il campeggio kam·payj·joh A84
camshaft n l'albero a camme (m) al·bay·roh a kam
can¹ n (container) il barattolo ba·rat·to·loh
can² vi potere* po·tay·ray; **I can** posso pos·soh; **you can** può pwo; **he/she can** (egli/ella) può ayl·yee/ayl·la pwo; **we can** possiamo pos·syah·moh
Canada n Canadà (m) ka·na·dah
Canadian adj canadese ka·na·day·say
canal n il canale ka·nah·lay
canasta n la canasta ka·na·sta
cancel vt (reservation) annullare an·nool·lah·ray; (appointment) disdire* dees·dee·re
cancer n il cancro kan·kroh
candidate n (for election) il/la candidato(a) kan·dee·da·toh(a)
candle n la candela kan·day·la
candy n la caramella ka·ra·mel·la
cane n (walking stick) il bastone da passeggio ba·stoh·nay da pas·sayj·joh
canned adj in scatola een skah·to·la
cannon n il cannone kan·noh·nay
canoe n la canoa ka·no·a

canoeing n □ **to go canoeing** fare* della canoa fah·ray del·la ka·no·a
can-opener n l'apriscatole (m) ah·pree·skah·to·lay
canteen n la mensa men·sa
canvas n la tela tay·la
cap n (hat) il berretto ber·rayt·toh
capable adj capace ka·pah·chay; **capable of** capace di ka·pah·chay dee
cape n la cappa kap·pa
capital n (city) la capitale ka·pee·tah·lay; (finance) il capitale ka·pee·tah·lay; **in capitals** in maiuscole een ma·yoos·ko·lay; **capital A** A maiuscola a ma·yoos·ko·la
capital goods pl le materie prime ma·te·rye pree·may
capitalism n il capitalismo ka·pee·ta·lee·zmoh
capitalist n il/la capitalista ka·pee·ta·lee·sta
capital letter n la lettera maiuscola let·te·ra ma·yoos·ko·la
capsule n (of medicine) la capsula kap·soo·la
captain n il capitano ka·pee·tah·noh; (of plane) il comandante ko·man·dan·tay
capture vt catturare kat·too·rah·ray
car n la macchina mak·kee·na; (of train) il vagone va·goh·nay T108f, A28
carafe n la caraffa ka·raf·fa E11
caramel n il caramello ka·ra·mel·loh
carat n il carato ka·ra·toh
caravan n la roulotte roo·lot A85
carbon n il carbonio kar·boh·nyoh
carbon copy n la copia carbone ko·pya kar·boh·nay
carbon paper n la carta carbone kahr·ta kar·boh·nay
carburet(t)or n il carburatore kar·boo·ra·toh·ray
card n (post) la cartolina kahr·to·lee·na; (playing card) la carta da gioco kahr·ta da jo·koh; **to play cards** giocare a carte jo·kah·ray a kahr·tay S91, Bm2, M25
cardboard n il cartone kahr·to·nay
card game n il gioco di carte jo·koh dee kahr·tay
cardigan n il cardigan kahr·dee·gan
card index n lo schedario ske·dah·ree·oh
care n (carefulness) la cura koo·ra □ vi **I don't care** non me ne importa nohn me ne eem·por·tah; **to take care of** (children etc) curare koo·rah·ray
career n la carriera kar·ree·e·ra
careful adj (cautious) prudente proo·den·tay; **be careful!** attenzione! at·ten·tsyoh·nay
care of, c/o prep presso pres·soh
caretaker n il custode koo·sto·day
car-ferry n il traghetto per auto tra·gayt·toh payr ow·toh
cargo n il carico kah·ree·koh
Caribbean (Sea) n il Mar dei Caraibi mahr de·ee ka·ra·ee·bee
carnation n il garofano ga·ro·fa·noh
carnival n il carnevale kahr·ne·vah·lay
carol n il canto di Natale kan·toh dee na·ta·lay
car-park n il parcheggio pahr·kayj·joh T125
carpenter n il falegname fa·len·yah·may
carpet n il tappeto tap·pay·toh
carport n la tettoia tet·toh·ya
carriage n (railway) la vettura vet·too·

ra; **carriage free** or **paid** porto franco *por·toh fran·koh*

carriageway n (*of road*) la carreggiata *kar·rej·jah·ta*

carrot n la carota *ka·ro·ta*

carry vt (*in hands, arms*) portare *por·tah·ray*; (*transport*) trasportare *tra·spor·tah·ray*; **to carry out an order** eseguire un ordine *e·ze·gwee·ray oon ohr·dee·nay*

carry-cot n il lettino portatile *let·tee·noh por·tah·tee·lay*

carry-out adj (*food*) da portar via *da por·tar vee·a*

cart n il carro *kar·roh*

cartel n il cartello *kar·tel·loh*

carton n (*box*) la scatola di cartone *skah·to·la dee kar·to·nay*; (*of yogurt etc*) la scatola *skah·to·la*

cartoon n la vignetta umoristica *veen·yayt·ta oo·mo·ree·stee·ka*; (*animated*) il cartone animato *kahr·to·nay a·nee·mah·toh*

cartridge n (*for gun*) la cartuccia *kahr·tooch·cha*; (*for camera*) il rollino *rol·lee·noh*; (*of tape*) la cassetta *kas·sayt·tah*

carve vt (*meat*) trinciare *treen·chah·ray*

case n la valigia *va·lee·ja*; (*of wine*) la cassetta *kas·sayt·ta*; (*instance*) il caso *kah·zoh*; (*lawsuit*) la causa *kow·za*; **just in case ...** nel caso che ... *nel kah·zoh kay*; **in case of** in caso di *een kah·zoh dee*; **in any case** ad ogni modo *ad ohn·yee mo·doh*

cash n (*cheque*) riscuotere* *ree·skwo·te·ray* □ i soldi *sol·dee*; **to pay cash for something** pagare qualcosa in contanti *pa·gah·ray kwal·ko·sa een kon·tan·tee*; **cash on delivery** pagamento alla consegna *pa·ga·mayn·toh al·la kon·sayn·ya* M25, L56

cashdesk n la cassa *kas·sa*

cash flow n il flusso di capitale *floos·soh dee ka·pee·tah·lay*

cashier n il/la cassiere(a) *kas·sye·ray(a)*

cashmere n il cachemire *kash·meer*

casino n il casinò *ka·see·noh*

casserole n (*food*) lo spezzatino *spets·tsa·tee·noh*; (*dish*) la casseruola *kas·ser·wo·la*

cassette n la cassetta *kas·sayt·ta*

cassette-recorder n il magnetofono a cassetta *man·ye·to·fo·noh a kas·sayt·ta*

cast n (*of play*) gli attori *lyee at·toh·ree*

cast iron n la ghisa *gee·za*

castle n il castello *ka·stel·loh* L5, F5

castor oil n l'olio di ricino (m) *ol·yoh dee ree·chee·noh*

casual clothes, casual wear n i vestiti sportivi *ves·tee·tee spor·tee·vee*

cat n il gatto *gat·toh*

catalog(ue) n il catalogo *ka·tah·lo·goh* Bm18

catch vt (*ball, animal, fish, person*) acchiappare *ak·kyap·pah·ray*; (*train, illness*) prendere* *pren·de·ray*; **to catch cold** prendere* freddo *pren·de·ray frayd·doh*

cathedral n la cattedrale *kat·te·drah·lay* F3, L2

catholic adj cattolico(a) *kat·to·lee·koh(a)*

cattle pl il bestiame *be·stee·ah·may*

cauliflower n il cavolfiore *ka·vol·fyoh·ray*

cause n la causa *kow·za* □ vt causare *kow·zah·ray*

cave n la caverna *ka·ver·na*

caviar(e) n il caviale *ka·vee·ah·lay*

cedar n il cedro *chay·droh*

ceiling n il soffitto *sof·feet·toh*

celebrate vt fare* festa *fah·ray fe·sta* □ vt festeggiare *fes·tej·jah·ray*

celeriac n il sedano rapa *se·da·noh rah·pa*

celery n il sedano *se·da·noh*

cell n (*in prison*) la cella *chel·la*

cellar n lo scantinato *skan·tee·nah·toh*

cello n il violoncello *vee·o·lon·chel·loh*

cellophane n il cellofan *chel·lo·fan*

Celsius adj Celsius *chel·syoos*

cement n il cemento *che·mayn·toh*

cemetery n il cimitero *chee·mee·te·roh*

cent n il centesimo *chen·te·zee·moh*

centenary n il centenario *chen·te·na·ree·oh*

center n il centro *chen·troh*

centigrade adj centigrado *chen·tee·gra·doh*

centilitre n il centilitro *chen·tee·lee·troh*

centimetre n il centimetro *chen·tee·me·troh*

central adj centrale *chen·trah·lay*

central heating n il riscaldamento centrale *ree·skal·da·mayn·toh chen·trah·lay* A44

central reservation n lo spartitraffico *spar·tee·traf·fee·koh*

centre n il centro *chen·troh* F4

century n il secolo *se·ko·loh*

cereal n (*breakfast*) il cereale *che·re·ah·lay*

ceremony n la cerimonia *che·ree·mo·nee·a*

certain adj certo(a) *cher·toh(a)*

certainly adv certamente *cher·ta·mayn·tay*

certificate n il certificato *cher·tee·fee·kah·toh*

certified mail n la posta raccomandata *pos·ta rak·ko·man·dah·ta*

chain n la catena *ka·tay·na*

chain store n il negozio a catena *ne·go·tsyoh a ka·tay·na*

chair n la sedia *se·dya*; (*armchair*) la poltrona *pol·troh·na*

chair-lift n la seggiovia *sej·jo·vee·a*

chairman n il presidente *pre·see·den·tay*

chalet n lo chalet *sha·le*

chalk n il gesso *jes·soh*

Chamber of Commerce n la camera di commercio *ka·may·ra dee kom·mer·choh*

champagne n lo sciampagna *sham·pan·ya*

champion n il campione *kam·pyoh·nay*

chance n □ **by chance** per caso *payr kah·zoh*; **he has a good chance of...** egli ha delle buone possibilità di... *ay·lyee a del·lay bwo·nay pos·see·bee·lee·ta dee*

chancellor n (*in Germany, Austria*) il cancelliere *kan·chel·ye·ray*

Chancellor of the Exchequer n il Cancelliere dello Scacchiere *kan·chel·lye·ray del·loh skak·kye·ray*

change vt/i cambiare *kam·bee·ah·ray*; **to change one's clothes** cambiarsi *kam·bee·ahr·see*; **to change trains at Marseilles** cambiare treno a Marsiglia *kam·bee·ah·ray tre·noh a Mahr·seel·ya* □ n **change** (*transformation*) il cambiamento *kam·bya·mayn·toh*; (*money*) gli spiccioli *speech·cho·lee*; **a change in the weather** un cambiamento del tempo *oon kam·bya·mayn·toh del tem·poh* T91, M15, 20f

Channel n la Manica *mah·nee·ka*

chapel n la cappella *kap·pel·la*

chapter n il capitolo *ka·pee·to·loh*

character n (*nature*) il carattere *ka·rat·te·ray*

charge n (*accusation*) l'accusa (f) *ak·koo·za*; to make a charge for something fare* pagare qualcosa *fah·ray pa·gah·ray kwal·ko·sa*; free of charge gratuito(a) *gra·too·ee·toh(a)*; to be in charge of essere* responsabile per *es·se·ray res·pon·sah·bee·lay payr* □ vt charge (*money*) fare* pagare *fah·ray pa·gah·ray*; charge it to my account lo addebiti al mio conto *loh ad·de·bee·tee al mee·oh kohn·toh* M3

charm n il fascino *fa·shee·noh*

charming adj incantevole *een·kan·tay·vo·lay*

chart n (*map*) la carta nautica *kar·ta now·tee·ka*; (*diagram, table*) il grafico *gra·fee·koh*

charter vt (*plane, bus*) noleggiare *no·lej·jah·ray*

chartered accountant n il ragioniere diplomato *ra·jo·nye·ray dee·plo·mah·toh*

charter flight n il volo charter *voh·loh char·ter*

chase vt inseguire *een·say·gwee·ray*

chassis n il telaio *te·la·yoh*

cheap adj a buon mercato *a bwon mer·kah·toh* S14, S21

cheat vt imbrogliare *eem·brol·yah·ray*

check n (*banking*) l'assegno (m) *as·sayn·yoh*; (*bill*) il conto *kohn·toh*; can I have the check please? il conto per favore *eel kohn·toh payr fa·voh·ray* □ vt check controllare *kon·trol·lah·ray*; (*train time etc*) verificare *ve·ree·fee·kah·ray*; to check in (*at hotel*) registrarsi *re·jee·strahr·see*; (*at airport*) presentarsi *pre·zen·tahr·see*; to check out pagare il conto *pa·gah·ray eel kohn·toh*

checkbook n il libretto di assegni *lee·brayt·toh dee as·sayn·yee*

check(er)ed adj (*patterned*) a quadretti *a kwa·drayt·tee*

checkers pl il gioco della dama *jo·koh del·la dah·ma*

checking account n il conto corrente *kohn·toh kor·ren·tay*

checkout n (*in store*) la cassa *kas·sa*

checkroom n il deposito bagagli *de·po·zee·toh ba·gal·yee*

cheek n la guancia *gwan·cha*; (*impudence*) la sfacciataggine *sfach·cha·taj·jee·nay*

cheeky adj sfacciato(a) *sfach·chah·toh(a)*

cheer vt applaudire *ap·plow·dee·ray*; cheers! cincin! *cheen·cheen*

cheese n il formaggio *for·maj·joh* E26, S30

cheesecake n la torta di ricotta *tor·tah dee ree·kot·ta*

chef n il capocuoco *kah·po·kwo·koh*

chemical adj chimico(a) *kee·mee·koh(a)*

chemist n (*pharmacist*) il farmacista *far·ma·chee·sta*; chemist's shop la farmacia *far·ma·chee·a* S40f

chemistry n la chimica *kee·mee·ka*

cheque n l'assegno (m) *as·sayn·yoh* M12, 22f

cheque-book n il libretto di assegni *lee·brayt·toh dee as·sayn·yee*

cheque card n la carta d'identità bancaria *kahr·ta dee·den·tee·ta ban·kah·ree·a*

cherry n la ciliegia *chee·lee·ay·jah*; (*tree*) il ciliegio *chee·lee·ay·joh*

chess n gli scacchi *skak·kee*

chest n (*of body*) il petto *pet·toh*

chestnut n la castagna *ka·stan·ya*

chew vt masticare *ma·stee·kah·ray*

chewing gum n la gomma da masticare *gohm·ma da ma·stee·kah·ray*

chicken n il pollo *pohl·loh*

chicken pox n la varicella *va·ree·chel·la*

chicory n la cicoria *chee·ko·ree·a*

chief n (*boss*) il capo *kah·poh*

child n il/la bambino(a) *bam·bee·noh(a)* A4, C1, 14f

chili n il chile *kee·lay*

chill vt (*wine, food*) raffreddare *raf·fred·dah·ray*; to serve something chilled servire qualcosa freddo *sayr·vee·ray kwal·koh·sa frayd·doh*

chimney n il camino *ka·mee·noh*

chin n il mento *mayn·toh*

china n la porcellana *por·chel·lah·na*

China n Cina (f) *chee·na*

Chinese adj cinese *chee·nay·say* □ n (*language*) il cinese *chee·nay·say*

chip n (*electronics*) il chip *cheep*; (*in gambling*) il gettone *jet·toh·nay*

chips pl le patatine fritte *pa·ta·tee·nay freet·tay* E23

chiropodist n il pedicure *pay·dee·koo·ray*

chives pl l'erba cipollina (f) *er·ba chee·pol·lee·na*

chocolate n la cioccolata *chok·ko·lah·ta*

choice n la scelta *shayl·ta*

choir n il coro *koh·roh*

choke n (*of car*) la valvola dell'aria *val·voh·la del·lah·ryah*

cholesterol n la colesterina *koh·lay·stay·ree·na*

choose vt scegliere* *shayl·ye·ray*

chop vt (*food*) tritare *tree·tah·ray* □ n pork chop la braciola di maiale *bra·cho·la dee ma·yah·lay*

chopsticks pl i bastoncini *ba·ston·chee·nee*

Christian n il/la cristiano(a) *kree·stee·ah·noh(a)*

Christian name n il nome di battesimo *noh·may dee bat·tay·zee·moh*

Christmas n Natale (m) *na·tah·lay*

Christmas card n la cartolina di Natale *kahr·to·lee·na dee na·tah·lay*

Christmas Day n il giorno di Natale *johr·noh dee na·tah·lay*

Christmas Eve n la vigilia di Natale *vee·jeel·ya dee na·tah·lay*

Christmas tree n l'albero di Natale (m) *al·be·roh dee na·tah·lay*

chrome n il cromo *kro·moh*

chrysanthemum n il crisantemo *kree·zan·te·moh*

church n la chiesa *kye·za* L3, 16f, Sn86

churchyard n il camposanto *kam·po·san·toh*

cider n il sidro *see·droh*

cigar n il sigaro *see·ga·roh*

cigarette n la sigaretta *see·ga·rayt·ta* S95f

cigarette case n il portasigarette *por·ta·see·ga·rayt·tay*

cigarette lighter n l'accendino (m) *ach·chen·dee·noh* S101

cine-camera n la cinepresa *chee·ne·pray·sa*

cinema n il cinema *chee·ne·ma* Mc44

cinnamon n la cannella *kan·nel·la*

circle *n* il cerchio *chayr·kyoh*; (*in theatre*) la galleria *gal·le·ree·a*

circuit *n* (*electric*) il circuito *cheer·koo·ee·toh*

circumstances *pl* le circostanze *cheer·ko·stan·tsay*

circus *n* il circo *cheer·koh*

city *n* la città *chee·ta*; **city centre** il centro della città *chen·troh del·la cheet·ta* Mc44

city hall *n* il municipio *moo·nee·chee·pee·oh*

civilization *n* la civilizzazione *chee·vee·leed·za·tsee·oh·nay*

civil servant *n* il/la funzionario(a) statale *foon·tsyo·nah·ree·oh(a) sta·tah·lay*

civil service *n* l'amministrazione statale (*f*) *am·mee·nee·stra·tsyoh·nay sta·tah·lay*

civil war *n* la guerra civile *gwer·rah chee·vee·lay*

claim *vt* (*lost property, baggage*) chiedere* la restituzione di *kyay·de·ray la re·stee·too·tsyoh·nay dee*

clam *n* la vongola *von·go·la*

clap *vi* applaudire *ap·plow·dee·ray*

claret *n* il chiaretto *kya·rayt·toh*

clasp *n* la fibbia *feeb·bya*

class *n* la classe *klas·say*; **to travel first class** viaggiare in prima classe *vyaj·jah·ray een pree·ma klas·say*; **a second class ticket** un biglietto di seconda classe *oon beel·yay·toh dee se·kohn·da klas·say*

classical *adj* (*music, art*) classico(a) *klas·see·koh(a)*

clause *n* (*in contract*) la clausola *klow·zo·la*

clay *n* l'argilla (*f*) *ahr·jeel·la*

clean *adj* pulito(a) *poo·lee·toh(a)* □ *vt* pulire *poo·lee·ray*; **to have a suit cleaned** fare* pulire un vestito *fah·ray poo·lee·ray oon ve·stee·toh* Sn65

cleaner *n* (*of house etc*) la donna delle pulizie *don·na del·lay poo·lee·tsee·ay*

cleaner's *n* la tintoria *teen·to·ree·a*

clear *adj* (*transparent*) trasparente *tra·spa·ren·tay*; (*distinct*) chiaro(a) *kyah·roh(a)*; (*not blocked*) libero(a) *lee·be·roh(a)* □ *vt* sbloccare *zblok·kah·ray*

clerk *n* (*in office*) l'impiegato(a) (*m/f*) *eem·pye·gah·toh(a)*; (*in store*) il/la commesso(a) *kom·mays·soh(a)*

clever *adj* (*person*) intelligente *een·tel·lee·jen·tay*; (*plan*) ingegnoso(a) *een·jen·yoh·soh(a)*

client *n* il/la cliente *klee·en·tay*

cliff *n* la scogliera *skol·ye·ra*

climate *n* il clima *klee·ma*

climb *vt* (*tree, wall*) arrampicarsi su *ar·ram·pe·kahr·see soo*; **to climb over something** scavalcare qualcosa *ska·val·kah·ray kwal·ko·sa*

clinic *n* la clinica *klee·nee·ka*

cloak *n* il mantello *man·tel·loh*

cloakroom *n* il guardaroba *gwar·da·ro·ba*

clock *n* l'orologio (*m*) *o·ro·lo·joh*

close¹ *adj* (*near*) vicino(a) *vee·chee·noh(a)*; (*stuffy*) afoso(a) *a·foh·soh(a)*; **close to** vicino a *vee·chee·noh a*; **close by** vicino *vee·chee·noh* T198

close² *vt* chiudere* *kyoo·de·ray* □ *vi* **the door closed** la porta si chiuse *la por·ta see kyoo·say*; **when do the shops close?** a che ora si chiudono i negozi? *a kay oh·ra see kyoo·do·no ee ne·go·tsee* A29

closed circuit television *n* la televisione a circuito chiuso *te·le·vee·zee·oh·nay a cheer·koo·ee·toh kyoo·soh*

closet *n* l'armadio (*m*) *ahr·mah·dyoh*

cloth *n* (*cleaning*) il panno *pan·noh*

clothes *pl* i vestiti *ves·tee·tee* S56f, Sn65

clotheshorse *n* il cavalletto per il bucato *ka·val·layt·toh payr eel boo·kah·toh*

clothesline *n* la corda per stendere il bucato *cor·da payr sten·de·ray eel boo·kah·toh*

clothes-peg *n* la molletta *mol·layt·ta*

cloud *n* la nuvola *noo·vo·la*

cloudy *adj* nuvoloso(a) *noo·vo·loh·soh(a)*

clove *n* il chiodo di garofano *kyo·doh dee ga·ro·fa·noh*; **clove of garlic** lo spicchio d'aglio *speek·kyoh dal·yoh*

clown *n* il pagliaccio *pal·yach·choh*

club *n* (*society*) il club *kloob*; **clubs** (*in cards*) i fiori *fyoh·ree*

clumsy *adj* (*person*) goffo(a) *gof·foh(a)*

clutch *n* (*of car*) la frizione *free·tsyoh·nay*

coach *n* (*of train*) la vettura *vet·too·ra*; (*bus*) il pullman *pool·man*; (*instructor*) l'allenatore (*m*) *al·le·na·toh·ray*

coal *n* il carbone *kahr·boh·nay*

coarse *adj* (*texture, material*) ruvido(a) *roo·vee·doh(a)*

coast *n* la costa *ko·sta*

coastguard *n* il guardacoste *gwahr·da·ko·stay*

coat *n* il mantello *man·tel·loh*

coat hanger *n* l'attaccapanni (*m*) *at·tak·ka·pan·nee*

cock(erel) *n* il gallo *gal·loh*

cockle *n* il cardio *kahr·dee·oh*

cocktail *n* (*drink*) il cocktail *kok·tail*; **prawn cocktail** l'antipasto di gamberetti (*m*) *an·tee·pa·stoh dee gam·be·rayt·tee*

cocoa *n* il cacao *ka·kow*

coconut *n* il cocco *kok·koh*

cod *n* il merluzzo *mayr·loots·tsoh*

codeine *n* la codeina *ko·de·ee·na*

coffee *n* il caffè *kaf·fe*; **black coffee** il caffè nero *kaf·fe nay·roh*; **white coffee** il caffellatte *kaf·fel·lat·tay* B53, E60f

coffee break *n* la pausa per il caffè *pow·za payr eel kaf·fe*

coffee cup *n* la tazza da caffè *tats·tsa da kaf·fe*

coffeepot *n* la caffettiera *kaf·fet·tye·ra*

coffee table *n* il tavolino da caffè *tah·vo·lee·noh da kaf·fe*

coffin *n* la bara *bah·ra*

cognac *n* il cognac *kon·yak*

coin *n* la moneta *mo·nay·ta*

coincide *vi* coincidere* *koh·een·chee·de·ray*

coincidence *n* la coincidenza *koh·een·chee·den·tsa*

colander *n* la colapasta *koh·la·pa·sta*

cold *adj* freddo(a) *frayd·doh(a)*; **I'm cold** ho freddo *o frayd·doh* □ *n* **cold** (*illness*) il raffreddore *raf·frayd·doh·ray* E36, S40, Mc2

coleslaw *n* l'insalata di cavolo (*f*) *een·sa·lah·ta dee kah·vo·loh*

colic *n* la colica *ko·lee·ka*

collaborate *vi* collaborare *kol·la·bo·rah·ray*

collapse *vi* (*person*) accasciarsi *ak·ka·shar·see*

collar *n* il colletto *kol·layt·toh*; (*for dog*) il collare *kol·lah·ray*

colleague *n* il/la collega *kol·le·ga*

collect *vt* (*stamps etc*) collezionare *kol·*

le·tsyo·nah·ray; (*donations*) raccogliere* rak·kol·ye·ray

collect call n la telefonata con la R te·le·fo·nah·ta kohn la er·re

collection n (*of mail*) la levata le·vah·ta

college n il collegio kol·le·joh

collide vi scontrarsi skon·trahr·see

collision n lo scontro skohn·troh

cologne n l'acqua di Colonia (f) ak·kwa dee ko·lon·ya

colo(u)r n il colore ko·loh·ray; **colo(u)r TV** la telèvisione a colori te·le·vee·zyoh·nay a ko·loh·ree

colo(u)red adj (*person*) di colore dee ko·loh·ray

comb n il pettine pet·tee·nay □ vt pettinare pet·tee·nah·ray

come vi (*arrive*) venire* ve·nee·ray; **to come in** entrare en·trah·ray; **to come off** staccarsi stak·kahr·see; **to come out** (*person, sun*) uscire* oo·shee·ray; (*stain*) andare* via an·dah·ray vee·a; **to come round** (*recover*) riprèndere* i sensi ree·pren·de·ray ee sen·see

comedian n il comico ko·mee·koh

comedy n la commedia kom·me·dya

comfort n (*ease*) il conforto kon·for·toh

comfortable adj comodo(a) ko·mo·doh(a)

comfort station n i gabinetti pubblici ga·bee·nayt·tee poob·blee·chee

comic n il giornale a fumetti jor·nah·lay a foo·mayt·tee

comma n la virgola veer·go·la

command n l'ordine (m) ohr·dee·nay

comment n il commento kom·mayn·toh

commerce n il commercio kom·mer·choh

commercial adj commerciale kom·mer·chah·lay □ n (*ad*) la réclame ray·klam

commercialized adj (*resort*) commercializzato(a) kom·mer·cha·leedz·dzah·to(a)

commission n (*sum received*) la commissione kom·mees·syoh·nay

commit vt (*crime*) commèttere* kom·mayt·te·ray

committee n il comitato ko·mee·tah·toh

commodity n il prodotto pro·doht·toh

common adj (*ordinary, frequent*) comune ko·moo·nay

Common Market n il Mercato Comune mer·kah·toh ko·moo·nay

communicate vi □ **to communicate with someone** comunicare con qualcuno ko·moo·nee·kah·ray kon kwal·koo·noh

communication cord n il segnale d'allarme sen·yah·lay dal·lahr·may

Communist n il/la comunista ko·moo·nee·sta □ adj comunista ko·moo·nee·sta

commutation ticket n il biglietto di abbonamento beel·yayt·toh dee ab·bon·a·mayn·toh

commuter n il pendolare pen·do·lah·ray

company n (*firm*) la ditta deet·ta Bm15f

company secretary n il segretario generale se·gre·tah·ree·oh je·ne·rah·lay

compare vt □ **to compare something with something** confrontare qualcosa con qualcosa kon·fron·tah·ray kwal·ko·sa kohn kwal·ko·sa

compartment n (*on train*) lo scompartimento skom·pahr·tee·mayn·toh T68

compass n la bussola boos·so·la

compensation n il risarcimento ree·sar·chee·mayn·toh

competent adj competente kom·pe·ten·tay

competition n la competizione kom·pe·tee·tsyoh·nay

competitor n il/la concorrente kon·kor·ren·tay

complain vi lagnarsi lan·yahr·see; **to complain about** lamentarsi di la·men·tahr·see dee

complaint n (*dissatisfaction*) il reclamo re·klah·moh

complete adj completo(a) kom·ple·toh(a) □ vt completare kom·ple·tah·ray

completely adv completamente kom·ple·ta·mayn·tay

complex adj complicato(a) kom·plee·kah·toh(a)

complexion n la carnagione kahr·na·joh·nay

complicated adj complicato(a) kom·plee·kah·toh(a)

compliment n il complimento kom·plee·mayn·toh

component n (*for car etc*) il pezzo pets·tsoh

composer n il compositore kom·po·zee·toh·ray

compound interest n l'interesse composto (m) een·te·res·se kom·poh·stoh

comprehensive insurance n l'assicurazione contro tutti i rischi (f) as·see·koo·ra·tsyoh·nay kohn·troh toot·tee ee ree·skee T116

computer n il computer kom·pyoo·ta

computerize vt (*system*) automatizzare ow·to·ma·teedz·dzah·ray

computer programming n la programmazione pro·gram·ma·tsyoh·nay

conceited adj vanitoso(a) va·nee·toh·soh(a)

concern n (*anxiety*) l'ansia (f) an·see·a □ vt (*be important to*) interessare een·te·res·sah·ray; **that doesn't concern you** ciò non la riguarda cho nohn la ree·gwahr·da

concert n il concerto kon·cher·toh L43

concrete n il calcestruzzo kal·che·stroots·tsoh □ adj in calcestruzzo een kal·che·stroots·tsoh

condemn vt condannare kon·dan·nah·ray

condensed milk n il latte condensato lat·tay kon·den·sah·toh

condiments pl i condimenti kon·dee·mayn·tee

condition n la condizione kon·dee·tsyoh·nay; **on condition that...** a condizione che... a kon·dee·tsyoh·nay kay

conditioner n (*for hair*) il balsamo bal·sa·moh Sn44

conductor n (*on bus*) il bigliettaio beel·yet·ta·yoh; (*of orchestra*) il direttore dee·ret·toh·ray; (*on train*) il capotreno kah·po·tre·noh

cone n (*for ice cream*) il cono ko·noh

confectioner n il pasticciere pa·steech·che·ray

confectionery n i dolciumi dol·choo·mee

conference n (*meeting*) la riunione ree·oon·yoh·nay A37

confess vt confessare kon·fes·sah·ray □ vi confessarsi kon·fes·sahr·see; **to**

confess to something ammettere* qualcosa *am·met·te·ray kwal·ko·sa*

confession *n* la confessione *kon·fes· syoh·nay* Sn90

confidence *n* (*trust*) la fiducia *fee·doo· cha*; in confidence in confidenza *een kon·fee·den·tsa*

confident *adj* fiducioso(a) *fee·doo· choh·so(a)*

confidential *adj* confidenziale *kon·fee· den·tsyah·lay*

confirm *vt* (*reservation etc*) confermare *kon·fer·mah·ray*

confuse *vt* confondere* *kon·fohn·de· ray*; **to confuse one thing with another** confondere* una cosa con un'altra *kon·fohn·de·ray oo·na ko·sa kohn oo·nal·tra*

confused *adj* (*muddled*) confuso(a) *kon·foo·zoh(a)*

congratulate *vt* congratularsi con *kon· gra·too·lahr·see kohn*; **to congratu- late someone on something** congratu- larsi con qualcuno per qualcosa *kon· gra·too·lahr·see kohn kwal·koo·noh payr kwal·ko·sa*

congratulations *pl* le felicitazioni *fe· lee·chee·ta·tsyoh·nee*; **congratula- tions!** felicitazioni! *fe·lee·chee·ta· tsyoh·nee*

conjuror *n* il prestigiatore *pre·stee·ja· toh·re*

connect *vt* (*join*) unire *oo·nee·ray*; **this train connects with the 16.45** questo treno fa la coincidenza con quello delle 16.45 *kway·stoh tre·noh fa la·een· chee·den·tsa kohn kwayl·loh del·lay 16.45*

connection *n* (*train etc*) la coincidenza *ko·een·chee·den·tsa* T8

connoisseur *n* il conoscitore *ko·no· shee·toh·ray*

conscience *n* la coscienza *ko·shen·tsa*

conscious *adj* in sé *een say*

consequence *n* (*result*) la conseguenza *kon·se·gwen·tsa*

conservative *adj* conservatore *kon· sayr·va·toh·ray*, conservatrice *kon· sayr·va·tree·chay*

conservatory *n* (*greenhouse*) la serra *ser·ra*

consider *vt* considerare *kon·see·de· rah·ray*

consist of *vt* consistere* in *kon·see·ste· ray een*

consommé *n* il consommé *kon·som· may*

constipated *adj* stitico(a) *stee·tee· koh(a)*; **to be constipated** stare* stiti- co(a) *sta·ray stee·tee·koh(a)*

construct *vt* costruire* *ko·stroo·ee·ray*

consul *n* il console *kon·so·lay*

consulate *n* il consolato *kon·so·lah·toh* Sn85

consult *vt* consultare *kon·sool·tah·ray*

consultant *n* (*doctor*) lo/la specialista *spe·cha·lee·sta*; (*other specialist*) il consulente *kon·soo·len·tay*

consulting room *n* l'ambulatorio (*m*) *am·boo·la·to·ree·oh*

consumer *n* il consumatore *kon·soo· ma·toh·ray*

consumer goods *pl* i beni di consumo *ee be·nee dee kon·soo·moh*

contact *vt* mettersi* in contatto con *mayt·ter·see een kon·tat·toh kohn*

contact lenses *pl* le lenti a contatto *len· tee a kon·tat·toh*

contagious *adj* contagioso(a) *kon·ta· joh·soh(a)*

contain *vt* contenere* *kon·te·nay·ray*

container *n* il recipiente *re·chee·pyen· tay*; (*for shipping etc*) il container *kon·tay·ner*

contemporary *adj* (*modern*) contempo- raneo(a) *kon·tem·po·rah·ne·oh(a)*

content(ed) *adj* contento(a) *kon·ten· toh(a)*

contents *pl* il contenuto *kon·te·noo· toh*; (*table in book*) l'indice (*m*) *een· dee·chay*

contest *n* (*competition*) il concorso *kon·kohr·soh*

contestant *n* il/la concorrente *kon·kor· ren·tay*

continent *n* il continente *kon·tee·nen· tay*; **the Continent** l'Europa conti- nentale (*f*) *ay·oo·ro·pa kon·tee·nen· tah·lay*

continental *adj* continentale *kon·tee· nen·tah·lay*

continental breakfast *n* la colazione *ko·la·tsyoh·nay*

continental quilt *n* il piumino *pyoo· mee·noh*

continual *adj* continuo(a) *kon·tee· nwoh(a)*

continue *vt/i* continuare *kon·tee·noo· ah·ray*; **to continue to do** continuare a fare *kon·tee·noo·ah·ray a fah·ray*

continuous *adj* continuo(a) *kon·tee· nwoh(a)*

continuously *adv* continuamente *kon· tee·noo·a·men·tay*

contraband *n* il contrabbando *kon· trab·ban·doh*

contraceptive *n* l'anticoncezionale (*m*) *an·tee·kon·che·tsyoh·nah·lay*

contract *n* il contratto *kon·trat·toh*

contractor *n* l'imprenditore (*m*) *eem· pren·dee·toh·ray*

contrary *n* □ **on the contrary** al con- trario *al kon·trah·ree·oh*

contribute *vi* contribuire *kon·tree·boo· ee·ray*

control *vt* dominare *do·mee·nah·ray* □ *n* circumstances beyond our control le circostanze che non dipendono da noi *cheer·ko·stan·tsay kay nohn dee· pen·do·no da noi*

controls *pl* i comandi *ko·man·dee* T120

control tower *n* la torre di controllo *tohr·ray dee kon·trol·loh*

conurbation *n* la zona di concentra- mento *dzoh·na dee kon·chen·tra· men·toh*

convalescence *n* la convalescenza *kon· va·le·shen·tsa*

convenient *adj* utile *oo·tee·lay*; con- venient for shops vicino(a) ai negozi *vee·chee·noh(a) a·ee ne·go·tsee*

convent *n* il convento *kon·ven·toh*

conversation *n* la conversazione *kon· vayr·sa·tsyoh·nay*

convertible *n* (*car*) l'automobile de- cappottabile (*f*) *ow·to·mo·bee·lay de· kap·pot·tah·bee·lay*

convince *vt* convincere* *kon·veen·che· ray*

cook *vt* cucinare *koo·chee·nah·ray* □ *vi* the meat is cooking la carne si sta co- cendo *kahr·nay see sta ko·chen·doh* □ *n* cook il/la cuoco(a) *kwo·koh(a)*

cooker *n* la cucina *koo·chee·na* A70

cookie *n* il biscotto *bee·skot·toh*

cooking *n* la cucina *koo·chee·na*

cool *adj* fresco(a) *fray·skoh(a)*

cooling system *n* il sistema di raffred- damento *see·stay·ma dee raf·fred·da· men·toh*

co-operate *vi* collaborare *kol·la·bo· rah·ray*

co-operative *n* la cooperativa *koh·o·pay·ra·tee·va*

copper *n* (*metal*) il rame *rah·may*

copy *n* la copia *ko·pya* □ *vt* copiare *ko·pyah·ray* Bm22

copyright *n* il copyright *ko·pee·rite*

coral *n* il corallo *ko·ral·loh*

cord *n* (*twine*) la corda *kor·da*; (*fabric*) il velluto a coste *vel·loo·toh a ko·stay*

cordial *n* il cordiale *kor·dyah·lay*

corduroy *n* il velluto a coste *vel·loo·toh a ko·stay*

cork *n* il sughero *soo·ge·roh*; (*of bottle*) il tappo *tap·poh*

corkscrew *n* il cavatappi *ka·va·tap·pee*

corn *n* (*cereals*) i cereali *che·re·ah·lee*; (*on foot*) il callo *kal·loh*

corner *n* (*of streets*) l'angolo (*m*) *an·go·loh*; (*bend in road*) la curva *koor·va* □ *vi* prendere* la curva *pren·de·ray la koor·va*

cornet *n* (*of ice cream*) il cornetto *kor·nayt·toh*

cornflakes *n* i fiocchi di granturco *fyok·kee dee gran·toor·koh*

cornflour *n* la farina di granturco *fa·ree·na dee gran·toor·koh*

corn-on-the-cob *n* la pannocchia *pan·nok·kya*

cornstarch *n* la farina di granturco *fa·ree·na dee gran·toor·koh*

coronation *n* l'incoronazione (*f*) *een·ko·ro·na·tsyoh·nay*

corporation *n* (*firm*) la società *so·che·ta*; (*of town*) il consiglio comunale *kon·seel·yoh ko·moo·nah·lay*

corporation tax *n* la tassa industriale *tas·sa een·doo·stryah·lay*

correct *adj* (*accurate*) esatto(a) *e·zat·toh(a)*; (*proper*) corretto(a) *kor·ret·toh(a)* □ *vt* correggere* *kor·rej·je·ray*

correction *n* (*alteration*) la correzione *kor·re·tsyoh·nay*

correspondence *n* (*mail*) la corrispondenza *kor·ree·spon·den·tsa*

correspondence course *n* il corso per corrispondenza *kohr·soh payr kor·ree·spon·den·tsa*

corridor *n* il corridoio *kor·ree·doh·yoh*

corrode *vt* corrodere* *kor·roh·de·ray*

corrugated iron *n* la lamiera di ferro ondulata *la·mye·ra dee fer·roh on·doo·lah·ta*

corrugated paper *n* la carta increspata *kahr·ta een·kre·spah·ta*

corrupt *adj* corrotto(a) *kor·ro·toh(a)*

corruption *n* la corruzione *kor·roo·tsee·oh·nay*

corset *n* il corsetto *kor·sayt·toh*

Corsica *n* Corsica (*f*) *kor·see·ka*

cosmetics *pl* i cosmetici *koz·me·tee·chee*

cosmetic surgery *n* la chirurgia estetica *keer·oor·jee·a e·ste·tee·ka*

cosmopolitan *adj* cosmopolita *koz·mo·po·lee·ta*

cost *n* il costo *ko·stoh*; **to buy something at cost** comprare qualcosa a prezzo di costo *kom·prah·ray kwal·ko·sa a prets·tsoh de ko·stoh* □ *vt* cost costare *ko·stah·ray* S4, Bm23

cost of living *n* il costo della vita *ko·stoh del·la vee·ta*

cost price *n* il prezzo di costo *prets·tsoh dee ko·stoh*

costs *pl* (*of production etc*) le spese *spay·say*

costume *n* (*theatrical*) il costume *ko·stoo·may*

costume jewellery *n* i gioielli di fantasia *joy·yel·lee dee fan·ta·zee·a*

cot *n* il lettino *let·tee·noh* C12

cottage *n* il cottage *kot·tij*

cottage cheese *n* il formaggio magro *for·maj·joh mah·groh*

cotton *n* (*fabric*) il cotone *ko·toh·nay*; (*thread*) il filo di cotone *fee·loh dee ko·toh·nay*

cotton wool *n* l'ovatta (*f*) *o·vat·ta*

couch *n* il divano *dee·vah·noh*

couchette *n* la cuccetta *koo·chayt·ta*

cough *n* la tosse *tos·say* □ *vi* tossire *tos·see·ray* S40

cough drops *pl* le pastiglie per la tosse *pa·steel·yay payr la tohs·say*

cough medicine *n* lo sciroppo per la tosse *shee·rop·poh payr la tohs·say*

could *vi* □ **we could do it** lo potremmo fare *loh po·trem·moh fah·ray*; **could I have…** potrei avere… *po·tre·ee a·vay·ray*

council *n* (*of town*) il consiglio comunale *kon·seel·yoh ko·moo·nah·lay*

count *vt* (*objects, people*) contare *kon·tah·ray* □ *vi* **to count up to 10** contare fino a 10 *kon·tah·ray fee·no a 10*

counter *n* (*in shop*) il banco *ban·koh*; (*gambling*) il gettone *jet·toh·nay*

counterfoil *n* il talloncino *tal·lon·chee·noh*

country *n* (*land*) il paese *pa·ay·zay*; (*not town*) la campagna *kam·pan·ya*; **in the country** in campagna *een kam·pan·ya* Mc13

countryside *n* la campagna *kam·pan·ya*

county *n* la contea *kon·te·a*

coup d'état *n* il colpo di stato *kohl·poh dee stah·toh*

coupé *n* (*car*) il coupé *koo·pay*

couple *n* (*persons*) la coppia *kop·pya*; **a couple of** (*a few*) un paio di *oon pa·yoh dee*

coupon *n* il buono *bwo·noh*

courage *n* il coraggio *ko·raj·joh*

courgettes *pl* gli zucchini *tsook·kee·nee*

courier *n* la guida *gwee·da*

course *n* (*lessons*) il corso *kohr·soh*; (*of meal*) il piatto *pyat·toh*; (*for golf*) il campo *kam·poh*; **course of treatment** il trattamento *trat·ta·mayn·toh*

court *n* (*law*) il tribunale *tree·boo·nah·lay*; (*tennis etc*) il campo *kam·poh*

court-card *n* la figura *fee·goo·ra*

courtyard *n* il cortile *kor·tee·lay*

cousin *n* il/la cugino(a) *koo·jee·noh(a)*

cover *n* (*of book*) la copertina *ko·payr·tee·na*; (*blanket*) la coperta *ko·per·ta*; (*insurance*) la protezione *pro·te·tsyoh·ne*; **under separate cover** in plico a parte *een plee·koh a par·te* □ *vt* **cover** coprire* *ko·pree·ray*; (*distance*) percorrere* *payr·kohr·re·ray*

cover charge *n* il prezzo del coperto *prets·tsoh del ko·per·toh* L54

covering letter *n* la lettera di accompagnamento *layt·te·ra dee ak·kom·pan·ya·mayn·toh*

cow *n* la vacca *vak·ka*

coward *n* il vigliacco *veel·yak·koh*

cowboy *n* il cow-boy *kow·boy*

crab *n* il granchio *gran·kyoh*

crack *n* (*split*) la fessura *fes·soo·ra*; (*noise*) lo schiocco *skee·ok·koh* □ *vt* **to crack a glass** incrinare un bicchiere *een·kree·nah·ray oon beek·kye·ray* □ *vi* **the glass cracked** il bicchiere si è incrinato *eel beek·kye·ray see e een·kree·nah·toh*

cracker *n* (*crisp wafer*) il cracker *kra·ker*; (*paper toy*) il petardo *pe·tahr·doh*

cradle *n* la culla *kool·la*

craft *n* l'arte (*f*) *ahr·tay*

craftsman *n* l'artigiano (*m*) *ahr·tee·jah·noh*

cramp *n* il crampo *kram·poh*

cranberry *n* il mirtillo *meer·teel·loh*

crane *n* (*machine*) la gru *groo*

crash *n* (*noise*) il fracasso *fra·kas·soh*; (*collision*) lo scontro *skohn·troh* □ *vt* **to crash one's car** avere* uno scontro con la macchina *a·vay·ray oo·noh skohn·troh kohn la mak·kee·na* □ *vi* **to crash into something** schiantarsi contro qualcosa *skyan·tar·see kohn·tro kwal·ko·sa*

crash barrier *n* il guardrail *gard·rail*

crash course *n* il corso intensivo *kohr·soh een·ten·see·voh*

crash helmet *n* il casco *kas·koh*

crash-landing *n* l'atterraggio di fortuna (*m*) *at·ter·raj·joh dee for·too·na*

crate *n* la cassa *kas·sa*

crawfish, crayfish *n* il gambero *gam·be·roh*

crawl *vi* strisciare *stree·shah·ray* □ *n* (*swimming*) il crawl *krol*

crayon *n* il pastello *pa·stel·loh*

crazy *adj* pazzo(a) *pats·tsoh(a)*

cream *n* la panna *pan·na*; (*cosmetic*) la crema *kre·ma* □ *adj* crema *kre·ma*

cream cheese *n* il formaggio cremoso *for·maj·joh kre·moh·so*

creamy *adj* (*texture*) vellutato(a) *vel·loo·tah·to(a)*

crease *n* la piega *pye·ga*

creased *adj* sgualcito(a) *zgwal·chee·toh(a)*

create *vt* creare *kray·ah·ray*

crèche *n* il nido d'infanzia *nee·doh deen·fan·tsya*

credit *n* il credito *kray·dee·toh*; **on credit** a credito *a kray·dee·toh*; **to give somebody credit** fare* credito a qualcuno *fah·ray kray·dee·toh a kwal·koo·noh* □ *vt* **to credit L.5000 to someone's account** accreditare L.5000 al conto di qualcuno *ak·kre·dee·tah·ray L5000 al kohn·toh dee kwal·koo·noh*

credit card *n* la carta di credito *kahr·ta dee kray·dee·toh* T163, M13

creditor *n* il creditore *kray·dee·toh·ray*, la creditrice *kray·dee·tree·chay*

credit squeeze *n* la restrizione del credito *re·stree·tsyoh·nay del kray·dee·toh*

crème de menthe *n* la crème de menthe *krem duh moñt*

cress *n* il crescione *kre·shoh·nay*

Crete *n* Creta (*f*) *kray·ta*

crew *n* (*of ship, plane*) l'equipaggio (*m*) *e·kwee·paj·joh*

crib *n* (*baby's*) il lettino *let·tee·noh* C12

cricket *n* (*sport*) il cricket *kree·ket*

crime *n* il delitto *de·leet·toh*

criminal *adj* criminale *kree·mee·nah·lay*

cripple *n* lo/la zoppo(a) *tsop·poh(a)*

crisis *n* la crisi *kree·zee*

crisp *adj* croccante *krok·kan·tay* □ *pl* **crisps** le patatine *pa·ta·tee·nay*

criticize *vt* criticare *kree·tee·kah·ray*

crockery *n* le stoviglie *sto·veel·ye*

crocodile *n* il coccodrillo *kok·koh·dreel·loh*

crocus *n* il croco *kroh·koh*

croissant *n* il croissant *krwah·soñ*

crooked *adj* storto(a) *stor·toh(a)*

crop *n* (*harvest*) il raccolto *rak·kol·toh*; (*whip*) il frustino *froo·stee·noh*

croquet *n* il croquet *kroh·key*

croquette *n* la crocchetta *krok·kayt·ta*

cross *n* la croce *kroh·chay* □ *vt* (*road, sea*) attraversare *at·tra·vayr·sah·ray*; (*cheque*) sbarrare *zbar·rah·ray*; **to cross out** cancellare *kan·chel·lah·ray*

crossing *n* (*voyage*) la traversata *tra·vayr·sah·ta*

crossroads *n* l'incrocio (*m*) *een·kroh·choh*

crosswalk *n* l'attraversamento pedonale (*m*) *at·tra·vayr·sa·mayn·toh pe·do·nah·lay*

croupier *n* il croupier *kroo·pyay*

crouton *n* il crostino *kro·stee·noh*

crowd *n* la folla *fol·la*

crowded *adj* affollato(a) *af·fol·lah·toh(a)*

crown *n* la corona *ko·roh·na*

crude *adj* (*oil etc*) grezzo(a) *graydz·zoh(a)*

cruel *adj* crudele *kroo·de·lay*

cruise *n* la crociera *kro·che·ra*; **to go on a cruise** fare* una crociera *fah·ray oo·na kro·che·ra*

crumb *n* la briciola *bree·cho·la*

crush *vt* schiacciare *skya·chah·ray*

crust *n* la crosta *kro·sta*

crutch *n* la gruccia *grooch·cha*

cry *vi* piangere* *pyan·je·ray* □ *n* il grido *gree·doh*

crystal *n* (*glass*) il cristallo *kree·stal·loh*

cube *n* la zolletta *tsol·layt·ta*

cubicle *n* la cabina *ka·bee·na*

cucumber *n* il cetriolo *che·tree·o·loh*

cuddle *vt* abbracciare *ab·brach·chah·ray*

cuff *n* (*of shirt*) il polsino *pol·see·noh*

cuff link *n* il gemello *je·mel·loh*

cuisine *n* la cucina *koo·chee·na*

cul-de-sac *n* il vicolo cieco *vee·ko·loh che·koh*

cultivate *vt* coltivare *kol·tee·vah·ray*

culture *n* la cultura *kool·too·ra*

cup *n* la tazza *tats·tsa*; (*trophy*) la coppa *kop·pa*

cupboard *n* l'armadio (*m*) *ahr·mah·dyoh*

curb *n* il bordo del marciapiede *bohr·doh del mar·cha·pye·de*

cure *vt* curare *koo·rah·ray*

curious *adj* (*inquisitive*) curioso(a) *koo·ree·oh·soh(a)*; (*strange*) strano(a) *strah·noh(a)*

curl *n* il ricciolo *reech·cho·loh*

curler *n* (*for hair*) il bigodino *bee·go·dee·noh*

curly *adj* ricciuto(a) *reech·choo·toh(a)*

currant *n* l'uva passa (*f*) *oo·va pas·sa*

currency *n* la valuta *va·loo·ta*; **foreign currency** la divisa estera *dee·vee·za e·ste·ra*

current *n* (*of water, air*) la corrente *kor·ren·tay*

current account *n* il conto corrente *kohn·toh kor·ren·tay*

curry *n* il curry *kah·ree*

curry powder *n* la polvere di curry *pohl·ve·ray dee kah·ree*

curtain *n* la tenda *ten·da*

curve *n* la curva *koor·va*

cushion *n* il cuscino *koo·shee·noh*

custard *n* la crema *kre·ma*

custom *n* il costume *ko·stoo·may*

customer *n* il/la cliente *klee·en·tay*

custom-made *adj* fatto(a) su misura *fat·toh(a) soo mee·zoo·ra*

customs *n* la dogana *do·gah·na*

customs duty *n* il dazio *da·tsyoh*

customs officer *n* il doganiere *do·ga·nye·ray*

cut *vt* tagliare *tal·yah·ray*; (*reduce*) ridurre* *ree·door·ray*; (*dilute*) diluire *dee·loo·ee·ray*; to cut oneself tagliarsi *tal·yar·see* □ n cut (*wound*) la ferita *fe·ree·ta*; (*of meat*) il pezzo *pets·tsoh* Sn36

cute adj (*pretty*) grazioso(a) *gra·tsyoh·soh(a)*

cutlery n la posateria *po·sah·te·ree·a*

cutlet n la cotoletta *ko·to·layt·ta*

cut-price adj a prezzo ridotto *a prets·tsoh ree·doht·toh*

cycle vi andare* in bicicletta *an·dah·ray een bee·chee·klayt·ta*

cycling n il ciclismo *chee·klee·zmoh*; to go cycling fare* del ciclismo *fah·ray del chee·klee·zmoh*

cyclist n il/la ciclista *chee·klee·sta*

cylinder n il cilindro *chee·leen·droh*

Cyprus n Cipro (m) *chee·proh*

Czechoslovakia n Cecoslovacchia (f) *che·ko·slo·vak·kya*

Czech(oslovakian) adj cecoslovacco(a) *che·ko·slo·vak·koh(a)*

D

dacron n il terilene *te·ree·le·ne*

dad(dy) n il papà *pa·pa*

daffodil n il trombone *trom·boh·ne*

dagger n il pugnale *poon·yah·le*

daily adj quotidiano(a) *kwo·tee·dee·ah·no(a)* □ n (*newspaper*) il quotidiano *kwo·tee·dee·ah·noh*

dainty adj delicato(a) *de·lee·kah·to(a)*

dairy (store) n la latteria *lat·te·ree·a*

dam n la diga *dee·ga*

damage n il danno *dan·noh*; damages i danni *dan·nee* □ vt damage danneggiare *dan·nej·jah·ray* Sn48

damp adj umido(a) *oo·mee·do(a)*

dance vi ballare *bal·lah·ray* □ n il ballo *bal·loh* L43

dandruff n la forfora *fohr·fo·ra*

danger n il pericolo *pe·ree·ko·loh*

dangerous adj pericoloso(a) *pe·ree·ko·loh·so(a)* L26

Danish adj danese *da·nay·se* □ n il danese *da·nay·se*

dare vi □ to dare to do something osare fare qualcosa *o·zah·ray fah·ray kwal·ko·sa*

dark adj buio(a) *boo·yo(a)*; (*colour*) scuro(a) *skoo·ro(a)*; (*hair*) bruno(a) *broo·no(a)*

darling n caro(a) (m/f) *kah·ro(a)*

darn vt rammendare *ram·men·dah·ray*

dart n (*to throw*) il dardo *dar·doh*; (*on clothes*) la pince *pañs*; game of darts il gioco dei dardi *jo·koh de·ee dar·dee*

dash n (*in writing*) il trattino *trat·tee·noh*

dash(board) n il cruscotto *kroos·kot·toh*

data pl i dati *dah·tee*

data bank, data base n la banca dei dati *ban·ka de·ee dah·tee*

data file n l'archivio di dati (m) *ar·kee·vee·oh dee dah·tee*

data processing n l'elaborazione dei dati (f) *e·la·bo·ra·tsyoh·nay de·ee dah·tee*

date n (*day*) la data *dah·ta*; (*appointment*) l'appuntamento (m) *ap·poon·ta·mayn·toh*; (*fruit*) il dattero *dat·te·roh*; what's the date today? quanti ne abbiamo oggi? *kwan·tee ne ab·byah·mo oj·jee*; out of date antiquato(a) *an·tee·kwa·to(a)*

date line n la meridiana di cambiamento di data *me·ree·dee·ah·na dee kam·bya·mayn·toh dee dah·ta*

daughter n la figlia *feel·ya* C11

daughter-in-law n la nuora *nwoh·ra*

dawn n l'alba (f) *al·ba*

day n il giorno *johr·noh*; (*length of time*) la giornata *johr·nah·ta*; every day ogni giorno *ohn·yee johr·noh*; day by day di giorno in giorno *dee johr·noh een johr·noh*; the day before il giorno prima *eel johr·noh pree·ma*; the next or following day l'indomani (m) *leen·do·mah·nee* T111

day nursery n l'asilo d'infanzia *nee·doh deen·fan·tsya* C4

day-return n il biglietto di andata e ritorno lo stesso giorno *beel·yayt·toh dee an·dah·ta e ree·tohr·noh lo stes·so johr·noh*

dazzle vt abbagliare *ab·bal·yah·ray*

dead adj (*person*) morto(a) *mor·to(a)*; (*battery*) scaricato(a) *ska·ree·kah·to(a)*; the line is dead (*phone*) la linea è bloccata *la lee·ne·a e blok·kah·ta*

dead end n il vicolo cieco *vee·ko·loh che·ko*

deaf adj sordo(a) *sohr·do(a)*

deal n l'affare (m) *af·fah·ray* C11 □ vi to deal with a firm avere* rapporti d'affari con una ditta *a·vay·re rap·por·tee daf·fah·ree kohn oo·na deet·ta*; to deal with a subject trattare un argomento *trat·tah·ray oon ar·go·mayn·toh*; to deal in something commerciare in qualcosa *kom·mayr·chah·ray een kwal·ko·sa*

dealer n il commerciante *kom·mayr·chan·te*; (*cards*) il mazziere *mats·tsye·re*

dear adj caro(a) *kah·ro(a)*; Dear Sir Egregio Signore *e·gre·joh seen·yoh·ray*; Dear Madam Gentile Signora *jen·tee·le seen·yoh·ra*; Dear Mr. Smith Egregio Signor Smith *e·gre·joh seen·yohr smith*

death n la morte *mor·te*

death certificate n il certificato di morte *chayr·tee·fee·kah·toh dee mor·te*

debate n il dibattito *dee·bat·tee·toh*

debit n l'addebito (m) *ad·day·bee·toh* □ vt to debit L.5000 to someone's account addebitare L.5000 al conto di qualcuno *ad·day·bee·tah·ray L5000 al kohn·toh de·ee kwal·koo·no*

debt n il debito *day·bee·toh*; to be in debt avere* dei debiti *a·vay·re de·ee day·bee·tee*

decade n il decennio *de·chen·nyoh*

decaffeinated adj decaffeinizzato(a) *de·kaf·fee·ee·needz·dzah·to(a)*

decanter n la caraffa *ka·raf·fa*

deceive vt ingannare *een·gan·nah·ray*

December n dicembre (m) *dee·chem·bre*

decent adj (*moral*) decente *de·chen·te*; (*respectable*) onesto(a) *o·ne·sto(a)*

decide vi (*between alternatives*) decidersi* *de·chee·der·see*; to decide to do something decidere* di fare qualcosa *de·chee·de·re dee fah·ray kwal·ko·sa*

decimal adj decimale *de·chee·mah·le* □ n il decimale *de·chee·mah·le*

decimal point n la virgola decimale *veer·go·la de·chee·mah·le*

decision n la decisione *de·chee·zyoh·nay*

deck n (*of ship*) il ponte *pohn·te*; (*of cards*) il mazzo *mats·tsoh*

deckchair *n* la sedia a sdraio *se·dya·a zdra·yo* L29

declare *vt* dichiarare *dee·kya·rah·ray*; nothing to declare niente da dichiarare *nyen·te da dee·kya·rah·ray*

decorate *vt* (*adorn*) decorare *de·ko·rah·ray*; (*paint*) verniciare *vayr·nee·chah·ray*

decorations *pl* gli addobbi *ad·dob·bee*

decrease *vt* diminuire *dee·mee·noo·ee·re*

deduct *vt* detrarre* *de·trar·re*

deep *adj* (*water, hole*) profondo(a) *pro·fohn·do(a)*; (*voice*) basso(a) *bas·so(a)*

deepfreeze *n* il congelatore *kon·je·la·toh·re*

deer *n* il cervo *cher·voh*

defeat *vt* sconfiggere* *skon·feej·je·re* □ *n* la sconfitta *skon·feet·ta*

defect *n* il difetto *dee·fet·toh*

defective *adj* difettoso(a) *dee·fet·toh·so(a)*

defence *n* la difesa *dee·fay·sa*

defend *vt* difendere* *dee·fen·de·re*

deficit *n* il deficit *de·fee·cheet*

definite *adj* (*distinct*) chiaro(a) *kyah·ro(a)*; (*certain*) certo(a) *cher·to(a)*

definitely *adv* certamente *cher·ta·mayn·tay*

deflation *n* la deflazione *de·fla·tsyoh·ne*

deformed *adj* deforme *de·fohr·me*

defrost *vt* (*food*) disgelare *dee·zje·lah·ray*; (*refrigerator*) sbrinare *zbree·nah·ray*

degree *n* il grado *grah·do*; (*university*) la laurea *low·re·a*

de-ice *vt* sghiacciare *zgyach·chah·ray*

delay *vt* (*hold up*) ritardare *ree·tar·dah·ray*; (*postpone*) rinviare *reen·vee·ah·ray*; the train has been delayed il treno ha un ritardo *eel tre·no a oon ree·tar·doh* □ *n* delay (*to train, plane*) il ritardo *ree·tar·doh* T83

delegate *vt* delegare *de·le·gah·ray*

delegation *n* la delegazione *de·le·ga·tsyoh·nay*

deliberate *adj* intenzionale *een·ten·tsyoh·nah·le*

deliberately *adv* apposta *ap·po·sta*

delicate *adj* delicato(a) *de·lee·kah·to(a)*

delicatessen *n* la salumeria *sa·loo·me·ree·a*

delicious *adj* delizioso(a) *de·lee·tsyoh·so(a)*

delighted *adj* felicissimo(a) *fe·lee·chees·see·mo(a)*

deliver *vt* (*mail*) distribuire *dee·stree·boo·ee·re*; (*goods*) consegnare *kon·sen·yah·ray*

delivery *n* (*of mail*) la distribuzione *dee·stree·boo·tsyoh·ne*; (*of goods*) la consegna *kon·sayn·ya*

de luxe *adj* di lusso *dee loos·so*

demand *vt* esigere* *e·zee·je·re* □ *n* (*for goods*) la domanda *do·man·da*

demister *n* l'antiappannante (*m*) *an·tee·ap·pan·nan·te*

demonstrate *vt* (*appliance etc*) mostrare *mo·strah·ray*

demonstration *n* la dimostrazione *dee·mo·stra·tsyoh·ne*; (*political*) la manifestazione *ma·nee·fe·sta·tsyoh·ne*

denim *n* la tela di blue-jeans *tay·la dee bloo·jeens*

Denmark *n* Danimarca (*f*) *da·nee·mar·ka*

dense *adj* (*fog etc*) fitto(a) *feet·to(a)*

dent *n* l'ammaccatura (*f*) *am·mak·ka·too·ra*

dentist *n* il/la dentista *den·tee·sta* I54

dentures *pl* la dentiera *den·tye·ra* I64

deny *vt* negare *ne·gah·ray*

deodorant *n* il deodorante *de·o·do·ran·te*

department *n* (*in store*) il reparto *re·par·toh* S11

department store *n* il grande magazzino *gran·de ma·gad·zee·noh*

departure board *n* il tabellone delle partenze *ta·bel·loh·ne del·le par·ten·tse* T38

departure lounge *n* la sala di partenza *sah·la dee par·ten·tsa* T41

depend *vi* □ it depends dipende *dee·pen·de*; to depend on dipendere* da *dee·pen·de·re da*

deposit *n* (*down payment*) il deposito *de·po·zee·toh*; (*for key etc*) la cauzione *kow·tsyoh·ne* □ *vt* (*money*) depositare *de·po·zee·tah·ray* M9

deposit account *n* il conto deposito *kohn·to de·po·zee·toh*

depot *n* la stazione autobus *sta·tsyoh·ne ow·to·boos*; (*trains*) lo scalo *skah·loh*

depressed *adj* (*person*) giú di spirito *joo dee spee·ree·toh*

depth *n* la profondità *pro·fohn·dee·ta*

deputy *n* (*second-in-command*) il/la vice *vee·che*

describe *vt* descrivere* *de·skree·ve·re*

description *n* la descrizione *de·skree·tsyoh·ne*

desert *n* il deserto *de·zer·toh*

deserve *vt* meritare *me·ree·tah·ray*

design *n* il disegno *dee·sayn·yoh* □ *vt* disegnare *dee·sen·yah·ray*

designer *n* il disegnatore *dee·sen·ya·toh·re*; (*of clothes*) il/la modellista *mo·del·lee·sta*

desire *n* il desiderio *de·see·de·ree·oh*

desk *n* (*in office*) la scrivania *skree·va·nee·a*; (*cash desk*) la cassa *kas·sa*; (*reception*) il ricevimento *ree·che·vee·mayn·toh*

desperate *adj* disperato(a) *dee·spe·rah·to(a)*

despite *prep* malgrado *mal·grah·do*

dessert *n* il dolce *dohl·che*

dessertspoon *n* il cucchiaio *kook·kee·a·yoh*

destination *n* la destinazione *de·stee·na·tsyoh·ne*

destroy *vt* distruggere* *dee·strooj·je·re*

detached house *n* la villa *veel·la*

detail *n* il particolare *par·tee·ko·lah·ray*; in detail dettagliatamente *det·tal·yah·ta·mayn·tay* Bm20

detailed *adj* dettagliato(a) *det·tal·yah·to(a)*

detective *n* l'investigatore (*m*) *een·ve·stee·ga·toh·re*

detergent *n* il detersivo *de·tayr·see·voh*

determined *adj* deciso(a) *de·chee·so(a)*; to be determined to do something essere* deciso a fare qualcosa *es·se·re de·chee·so a fah·ray kwal·ko·sa*

detour *n* la deviazione *de·vee·a·tsyoh·ne*; to make a detour fare* una deviazione *fah·ray oo·na de·vee·a·tsyoh·ne* T134

devaluation *n* la svalutazione *zva·loo·ta·tsyoh·ne*

devalue *vt* (*currency*) svalutare *zva·loo·tah·ray*

develop vi svilupparsi *zvee·loop·par·see* □ vt (photo) sviluppare *zvee·loop·pah·ray*

developing country n il paese in via di sviluppo *pa·e·ze een vee·a dee zvee·loop·poh*

diabetes n il diabete *dee·a·be·te*

diabetic n/la diabetico(a) *dee·a·be·tee·ko(a)*

diagnosis n la diagnosi *dee·an·yo·zee*

diagonal adj diagonale *dee·a·go·nah·le*

diagram n il diagramma *dee·a·gram·ma*

dial vt (number) comporre* *kom·pohr·re* Sn14

dialect n il dialetto *dee·a·let·toh*

dial(ling) tone n il segnale di linea libera *sen·yah·le dee lee·nay·a lee·bay·ra*

diameter n il diametro *dee·a·me·troh*

diamond n il diamante *dee·a·man·te*; diamonds (cards) i quadri *kwa·dree*

diaper n il pannolino *pan·no·lee·noh* C19

diarrh(o)ea n la diarrea *dee·ar·re·a*

diary n l'agenda (f) *a·jen·da*

dice n i dadi *dah·dee*

dictate vt (letter) dettare *det·tah·ray*

dictionary n il dizionario *dee·tsyoh·nah·ree·oh*

die vi morire* *mo·ree·re*

diesel n il diesel *dee·zel*

diesel engine n il motore diesel *mo·toh·re dee·zel*

diesel fuel n la nafta *naf·ta*

diet n (slimming) la dieta *dee·e·ta*; to be on a diet stare* a dieta *stah·ray a dee·e·ta*

difference n la differenza *deef·fe·ren·tsa*

different adj differente *deef·fe·ren·te*; different from diverso(a) da *dee·ver·so(a) da*

difficult adj difficile *deef·fee·chee·le*

difficulty n la difficoltà *deef·fee·kol·ta*

dig vt (ground) vangare *van·gah·ray*; (hole) scavare *ska·vah·ray*; to dig up scavare *ska·vah·ray*

digital adj digitale *dee·jee·tah·le*

dike n la diga *dee·ga*

dilute vt diluire *dee·loo·ee·re*

dim adj (light) debole *day·bo·le*; (room) oscuro(a) *o·skoo·ro(a)*

dimensions pl le dimensioni *dee·men·syoh·nee*

diner n il ristorante self-service *ree·sto·ran·te self·sayr·vees*

dinghy n il dinghy *din·gee*; (inflatable) il gommone *gom·moh·ne*

dining car n il vagone ristorante *va·goh·ne ree·sto·ran·te*

dining room n la sala da pranzo *sah·la da pran·dzoh*

dinner n la cena *chay·na* E6

dinner jacket n lo smoking *smo·keeng*

dinner party n la cena *chay·na*

dip vt (into liquid) immergere* *eem·mer·je·re*; (headlights) abbassare *ab·bas·sah·ray*

diploma n il diploma *dee·plo·ma*

diplomat n il diplomatico *dee·plo·ma·tee·koh*

dipstick n l'asta dell'olio (f) *a·sta del·lol·yoh*

dip-switch n l'interruttore degli anabbaglianti (m) *een·ter·root·toh·re del·yee an·ab·bal·yan·te*

direct adj diretto(a) *dee·ret·to(a)* □ adv to fly to Venice direct prendere* un volo diretto per Venezia *pren·de·re oon vo·loh dee·ret·to payr ve·ne·tsya*

□ vt direct (traffic) dirigere* *dee·ree·je·re*

direction n la direzione *dee·re·tsyoh·ne*; in the direction of nella direzione di *nel·la dee·re·tsyoh·ne dee*; directions (to a place) le indicazioni *een·dee·ka·tsyoh·nee*; directions for use le istruzioni per l'uso *ee·stroo·tsyoh·nee payr loo·zoh*

director n (of firm) il direttore *dee·ret·toh·re*; (of film) il regista *re·jee·sta* Bm3

directory n la guida *gwee·da*; (telephone) l'elenco telefonico (m) *e·len·ko te·le·fo·nee·ko* Sn16

dirt n la sporcizia *spor·chee·tsya*

dirty adj sporco(a) *spor·ko(a)* A49

disabled adj invalido(a) *een·va·lee·do(a)* I2,3

disadvantage n lo svantaggio *zvan·taj·joh*; at a disadvantage svantaggiato(a) *zvan·taj·jah·to(a)*

disagree vi □ to disagree with somebody non essere* d'accordo con qualcuno *nohn es·se·re dak·kor·doh kohn kwal·koo·no*; eggs disagree with me le uova mi restano sullo stomaco le wo·va mee re·sta·no sool·lo *sto·ma·koh*

disagreement n il dissenso *dees·sen·soh*

disappear vi sparire* *spa·ree·re*

disappointed adj deluso(a) *de·loo·zo(a)*

disapprove vi □ to disapprove of something disapprovare qualcosa *dee·zap·pro·vah·ray kwal·ko·sa*

disaster n il disastro *dee·za·stroh*

disc n il disco *dee·sko*; slipped disc l'ernia al disco (f) *er·nee·a al dee·sko*

disc brakes pl i freni a disco *fray·nee a dee·sko*

discipline n la disciplina *dee·shee·plee·na*

disc jockey n il disc-jockey *deesk·jok·kee*

disco(thèque) n la discoteca *dee·sko·te·ka*

discount n lo sconto *skohn·toh*; at a discount con uno sconto *kohn oo·no skohn·toh* M5f

discouraged adj scoraggiato(a) *sko·raj·jah·to(a)*

discover vt scoprire* *sko·pree·re*

discreet adj discreto(a) *dee·skray·to(a)*

discrimination n (racial etc) la discriminazione *dee·skree·mee·na·tsyoh·ne*

discuss vt discutere* *dee·skoo·te·re*

disease n la malattia *ma·lat·tee·a*

disguise n il travestimento *tra·ve·stee·mayn·toh*; in disguise travestito(a) *tra·ve·stee·to(a)*

disgust n il disgusto *dee·zgoo·stoh*

disgusted adj indignato(a) *een·deen·yah·to(a)*

dish n il piatto *pyat·toh* E19

dishcloth n lo strofinaccio per i piatti *stro·fee·nach·choh payr ee pyat·tee*

dishonest adj disonesto(a) *dee·zo·ne·sto(a)*

dish up vt servire *ser·vee·re*

dishwasher n il lavastoviglie *la·va·sto·veel·ye*

disinfect vt disinfettare *dee·zeen·fet·tah·ray*

disinfectant n il disinfettante *dee·zeen·fet·tan·te*

dislocate vt slogare *zlo·gah·ray*

dismiss vt (from job) licenziare *lee·chen·tsyah·ray*

disobedient *adj* disubbidiente *dee·zoob·bee·dyen·te*

disobey *vt* disubbidire *dee·zoob·bee·dee·re*

dispatch *vt* spedire *spe·dee·re*

disposable *adj* da gettare via *da jet·tah·ray vee·a* C19

dispute *vt* (*fact*) contestare *kon·te·stah·ray* □ *n* la disputa *dee·spoo·ta*; (*industrial*) il conflitto *kon·fleet·toh*

disqualify *vt* squalificare *skwa·lee·fee·kah·ray*

dissolve *vt* sciogliere* *shol·ye·re* □ *vi* sciogliersi *shol·yer·see*

distance *n* la distanza *dee·stan·tsa*; in the distance in lontananza *een lon·ta·nan·tsa*

distant *adj* distante *dee·stan·te*

distilled water *n* l'acqua distillata (*f*) *ak·kwa dee·steel·lah·ta*

distillery *n* la distilleria *dee·steel·le·ree·a*

distinct *adj* (*clear*) distinto(a) *dee·steen·to(a)*

distinguish *vt* distinguere* *dee·steen·gwe·re*; to distinguish something from something distinguere* qualcosa da qualcosa *dee·steen·gwe·re kwal·ko·sa da kwal·ko·sa*

distract *vt* distrarre* *dee·strar·re*

distress *n* l'angoscia (*f*) *an·go·sha*; a ship in distress una nave in pericolo *oo·na nah·ve een pe·ree·ko·loh*

distributor *n* (*in car*) il distributore *dee·stree·boo·toh·re*; (*commercial*) il grossista *gro·sees·ta*

district *n* (*of town*) il quartiere *kwar·tye·re*; (*in country*) la regione *re·joh·ne*; (*administrative*) la circoscrizione *cheer·ko·skree·tsyoh·ne*

disturb *vt* (*interrupt*) disturbare *dee·stoor·bah·ray*; do not disturb pregasi non disturbare *pre·ga·see nohn dee·stoor·bah·ray*

ditch *n* il fossato *fos·sah·toh*

divan *n* il divano *dee·vah·noh*

dive *vi* tuffarsi *toof·far·see* □ *n* il tuffo *toof·foh*

diversify *vt/i* diversificare *dee·ver·see·fee·kah·ray*

diversion *n* (*traffic*) la deviazione *de·vee·a·tsyoh·ne*

divert *vt* deviare *de·vee·ah·ray*

divide *vt* (*separate*) separare *se·pa·rah·ray*; (*apportion*) dividere* *dee·vee·de·re*; to divide 8 by 4 dividere* 8 per 4 *dee·vee·de·re 8 payr 4*

divided highway *n* la carreggiata doppia *kar·rej·jah·ta dop·pya*

dividend *n* il dividendo *dee·vee·den·doh*

divingboard *n* il trampolino *tram·po·lee·noh*

divorce *n* il divorzio *dee·vor·tsyoh*

divorced *adj* divorziato(a) *dee·vor·tsyah·to(a)*

dizzy *adj* (*person*) preso(a) da vertigine *pray·so(a) da ver·tee·jee·ne*

do *vt/i* fare* *fah·ray*; will it do? (*be enough*) basta cosi? *ba·sta ko·see*; (*be suitable*) conviene? *kon·vye·ne*; you know him, don't you? lo conosce, non è vero? *lo ko·no·she, nohn e vay·ro*; he didn't come, did he? non è venuto, vero? *nohn e ve·noo·to, vay·ro*

dock *n* il bacino *ba·chee·noh*

doctor *n* il medico *me·dee·koh*; it's Doctor Smith è il dottor/la dottoressa Smith *e eel dot·tohr/la dot·toh·res·sa Smith* 16f

doctor's office *n* il gabinetto medico *ga·bee·nayt·toh me·dee·ko*

document *n* il documento *do·koo·mayn·toh* Bm22, T121

dog *n* il cane *kah·ne*

do-it-yourself *n* il fatelo da voi *fah·te·lo da voy*

doll *n* la bambola *bam·bo·la*

dollar *n* il dollaro *dol·la·roh* M23

dollar bill *n* la banconota da un dollaro *ban·ko·no·ta da oon dol·la·roh*

donate *vt* (*funds*) donare *do·nah·ray*

donation *n* (*money*) il dono *doh·noh*

done *adj* (*cooked*) cotto(a) *kot·to(a)*

donkey *n* l'asino (*m*) *ah·see·noh*

door *n* la porta *por·ta* A60

doorbell *n* il campanello *kam·pa·nel·loh*

door handle, doorknob *n* la maniglia *ma·neel·ya*

doorman *n* (*in hotel*) il portiere *por·tye·re*

doormat *n* lo zerbino *dzer·bee·noh*

doorstep *n* il gradino della porta *gra·dee·noh del·la por·ta*

door-to-door salesman *n* il venditore a domicilio *ven·dee·toh·re a do·mee·cheel·yoh*

dormitory *n* (*room*) il dormitorio *dor·mee·to·ryoh*; (*of college*) la casa dello studente *kah·sa del·lo stoo·den·te*

dosage *n* il dosaggio *do·zaj·joh*

dose *n* la dose *do·ze*

dot *n* il punto *poon·toh*

dotted line *n* la linea punteggiata *lee·ne·a poon·tej·jah·ta*

double *vt* raddoppiare *rad·dop·pyah·ray* □ *adv* to cost double costare il doppio *ko·stah·ray eel dop·pyoh* □ *adj* double doppio(a) *dop·pyo(a)*; a double whisky un whisky doppio *wee·skee dop·pyo*

double bed *n* il letto matrimoniale *let·toh ma·tree·mo·nyah·le* A4

double bend *n* la curva a S *koor·va a es·se*

double-parking *n* il parcheggio in doppia fila *par·kayj·joh een dop·pya fee·la*

double room *n* la camera matrimoniale *kah·me·ra ma·tree·mo·nyah·le* A4

doubt *n* il dubbio *doob·byoh*; no doubt senza dubbio *sen·tsa doob·byoh*; without (a) doubt senza alcun dubbio *sen·tsa al·koon doob·byoh* □ *vt* doubt dubitare *doo·bee·tah·ray*; I doubt it ne dubito *ne doo·bee·to*

doubtful *adj* incerto(a) *een·cher·to(a)*

dough *n* la pasta *pa·sta*

doughnut *n* il bombolone *bom·bo·loh·ne*

dove *n* la colomba *ko·lohm·ba*

down *n* (*fluff*) il piumino *pyoo·mee·noh* □ *adv* to come down venire* giú *ve·nee·re joo*; to go down scendere* *shayn·de·re* □ *prep* down giú per *joo payr*

downhill *adv* in discesa *een dee·shay·sa*; to go downhill scendere* *shayn·de·re*

down payment *n* l'acconto (*m*) *ak·kohn·toh*

downstairs *adv* di sotto *dee soht·to*

downstream *adv* a valle *a val·le*

downtown *adv* in centro *een chen·troh* □ *adj* downtown Chicago il centro di Chicago *chen·troh dee shee·kah·go*

downward(s) *adv* in basso *een bas·so*

doze *vi* sonnecchiare *son·nek·kyah·ray*

dozen *n* la dozzina *dodz·dzee·na*; 4 dozen eggs 4 dozzine di uova *4 dodz·dzee·ne dee wo·va*

drab *adj* scialbo(a) *shal·bo(a)*

draft *n* (wind) la corrente d'aria *kor·ren·te dah·ree·a*; (financial) la cambiale *kam·bee·ah·le*; (rough outline) l'abbozzo (*m*) *ab·bots·tsoh*

draft beer *n* la birra alla spina *beer·ra al·la spee·na*

draftsman *n* il disegnatore *dee·sen·ya·toh·re*

drag *vt* trascinare *tra·shee·nah·ray*

drain *n* la fogna *fohn·ya* □ *vt* (land) prosciugare *pro·shoo·gah·ray*; (vegetables) scolare *sko·lah·ray*; (sump, pool) svuotare *zvwo·tah·ray*

drainboard, draining-board *n* lo scolapiatti *sko·la·pyat·tee*

drainpipe *n* il tubo di scolo *too·boh dee skoh·loh*

drama *n* (art) il teatro *te·ah·troh*

dramatic *adj* drammatico(a) *dram·ma·tee·ko(a)*

drape *n* la tenda *ten·da*

drastic *adj* drastico(a) *dra·stee·ko(a)*

draught *n* (wind) la corrente d'aria *kor·ren·te dah·ree·a*

draught beer *n* la birra alla spina *beer·ra al·la spee·na*

draughts *pl* il gioco della dama *jo·koh del·la dah·ma*

draughtsman *n* il disegnatore *dee·sen·ya·toh·re*

draw *vt* (picture) disegnare *dee·sen·yah·ray*; to draw out (money) ritirare *ree·tee·rah·ray*; to draw up (document) redigere* *re·dee·je·re*

drawer *n* il cassetto *kas·sayt·toh*

drawing *n* il disegno *dee·sayn·yoh*

drawing pin *n* la puntina *poon·tee·na*

dread *vt* temere *te·may·ray*

dream *n* il sogno *sohn·yoh* □ *vi* sognare *son·yah·ray*; to dream of or about sognare di *son·yah·ray dee*

dress *n* il vestito *ve·stee·toh* □ *vt* (child) vestire *ve·stee·re* □ *vi* (oneself) vestirsi *ve·steer·see* S56, S8

dress circle *n* la prima galleria *pree·ma gal·le·ree·a*

dressing *n* (salad) il condimento *kon·dee·mayn·toh*; (stuffing) il ripieno *ree·pye·noh*

dressing gown *n* la vestaglia *ve·stal·ya*

dressing table *n* la tavola da toeletta *tah·vo·la da to·e·let·ta*

dried *adj* (fruit, beans) secco(a) *sayk·ko(a)*; dried milk il latte in polvere *lat·te een pohl·ve·re*

drift *vi* (boat) andare* alla deriva *an·dah·ray al·la de·ree·va*

drill *n* (tool) il trapano *tra·pa·noh* □ *vt* (hole) perforare *payr·fo·rah·ray*

drink *vt* bere* *bay·re* □ *n* la bevanda *be·van·da*; have a drink! prenda qualcosa da bere! *pren·da kwal·ko·sa da bay·re* L53, B52

drinking water *n* l'acqua potabile (*f*) *ak·kwa po·tah·bee·le* A88

drip *n* la goccia *gohch·cha* □ *vi* gocciolare *goch·cho·lah·ray*

drip-dry *vt* lasciare ad asciugarsi *la·shah·ray ad a·shoo·gar·see* □ *adj* (shirt etc) che non si stira *ke nohn see stee·ra*

drive *vt* (car etc) guidare *gwee·dah·ray* □ *vi* andare* in macchina *an·dah·ray een mak·kee·na*; do you drive? sa guidare? *sa gwee·dah·ray* □ *n* drive

(journey) il viaggio *vee·aj·joh*; (driveway) l'ingresso (*m*) *een·gres·soh*; to go for a drive fare* un giro in macchina *fah·ray oon jee·roh een mak·kee·na*; left-hand drive la guida a sinistra *gwee·da a see·nee·stra*; front-wheel drive la trazione anteriore *tra·tsyoh·ne an·te·ryoh·re* T110

driver *n* (of car) il guidatore *gwee·da·toh·re*; (of taxi, bus) il conducente *kon·doo·chen·te*

driver's license, driving licence *n* la patente di guida *pa·ten·te dee gwee·dah* T10

drizzle *n* la pioviggine *pyo·veej·jee·ne*

drop *n* (of liquid) la goccia *gohch·cha* □ *vt* (let fall) lasciare cadere *la·shah·ray ka·day·re* □ *vi* (fall) cadere* *ka·day·re*

drought *n* la siccità *seech·chee·ta*

drown *vi* annegare *an·ne·gah·ray*

drug *n* (medicine) il medicinale *me·dee·chee·nah·le*; (narcotic) la droga *dro·ga* 144

druggist *n* il/la farmacista *far·ma·chee·sta*

drugstore *n* la farmacia *far·ma·chee·a*

drum *n* il tamburo *tam·boo·roh*

drumstick *n* (of chicken) la coscia *ko·sha*

drunk *adj* ubriaco(a) *oo·bree·ah·ko(a)*

dry *adj* secco(a) *sayk·ko(a)* □ *vt* asciugare *a·shoo·gah·ray*

dry-clean *vt* lavare a secco *la·vah·ray a sayk·ko*

dry-cleaner's *n* la tintoria *teen·to·ree·a*

dual carriageway *n* la strada a doppia carreggiata *strah·da a dohp·pya kar·rej·jah·ta*

duck *n* l'anatra (*f*) *ah·na·tra*

due *adj* (owing) da pagarsi *da pa·gar·see*; when is the train due? quando deve arrivare il treno? *kwan·do de·ve ar·ree·vah·ray eel tre·no*

duke *n* il duca *doo·ka*

dull *adj* (day, weather) uggioso(a) *ooj·joh·so(a)*; (boring) noioso(a) *no·yoh·so(a)*

dumb *adj* muto(a) *moo·to(a)*; (stupid) stupido(a) *stoo·pee·do(a)*

dummy *n* (baby's) il succhietto *sook·kyayt·toh*

dump *n* (for rubbish) il luogo di scarico *lwo·go dee skah·ree·ko*

dumping *n* (of goods) il dumping *dum·peeng*

dumpling *n* lo gnocco *nyok·ko*

dune *n* la duna *doo·na*

dungarees *pl* la tuta *too·ta*

dungeon *n* la prigione sotterranea *pree·joh·ne sot·ter·rah·ne·a*

durable *adj* (fabric, article) resistente *re·see·sten·te*

during *prep* durante *doo·ran·te*

dusk *n* il crepuscolo *kre·poo·sko·lo*

dust *n* la polvere *pohl·ve·re* □ *vt* (furniture) spolverare *spol·ve·rah·ray*

dustbin *n* il bidone *bee·doh·ne* A71

dustpan *n* la paletta *pa·layt·ta*

dusty *adj* polveroso(a) *pol·ve·roh·so(a)*

Dutch *adj* olandese *o·lan·day·se* □ *n* l'olandese (*m*) *o·lan·day·se*

duty *n* (obligation) il dovere *do·vay·ray*; (function) il compito *kohm·pee·to*; (tax) il dazio *da·tsyoh*; on duty (doctor) in servizio *een sayr·vee·tsyoh*; off duty fuori servizio *fwo·ree sayr·vee·tsyoh*

duty-free *adj* esente da dogana *e·zen·te da do·gah·na* T41, S10

duvet *n* il piumino *pyoo·mee·no*

dye n la tinta *teen·ta* □ vt tingere* *teen·je·re*

dyke n la diga *dee·ga*

dynamic adj (person) dinamico(a) *dee·na·mee·ko(a)*

dynamo n la dinamo *dee·na·mo*

E

each adj ogni *ohn·yee* □ pron ciascuno(a) *cha·skoo·no(a)*

eager adj desideroso(a) *de·see·de·roh·so(a)*; to be eager to do something essere* impaziente di fare qualcosa *es·se·re eem·pa·tsyen·te dee fah·ray kwal·ko·sa*

eagle n l'aquila (f) *ah·kwee·la*

ear n l'orecchio (m) *o·rayk·kyoh*

earache n il mal d'orecchi *mal do·rayk·kee*; to have earache avere* mal d'orecchi *a·vay·re mal do·rayk·kee*

earlier adj precedente *pre·che·den·te* □ adv prima *pree·ma*

early adj primo(a) *pree·mo(a)*; you're early Lei è in anticipo *lay è een an·tee·chee·poh* □ adv early presto *pre·sto*

earn vt guadagnare *gwa·dan·yah·ray*

earnings pl gli introiti *een·troy·tee*

earplugs pl i tappi per gli orecchi *tap·pee payr lyee o·rayk·kee*

earring n l'orecchino (m) *o·rek·kee·noh*

earth n la terra *ter·ra*

earthquake n il terremoto *ter·re·mo·toh*

ease vt (pain) alleviare *al·le·vyah·ray*

easily adv facilmente *fah·cheel·mayn·te*

east n l'est (m) *est*; the East l'Oriente (m) *o·ree·en·te* □ adv east ad est *ad est*

Easter n Pasqua (f) *pa·skwa*

Easter egg n l'uovo di Pasqua (m) *wo·voh dee pa·skwa*

eastern adj orientale *o·ree·en·tah·le*

East Germany n la Germania Orientale *jer·mah·nya o·ree·en·tah·le*

easy adj facile *fah·chee·le*

eat vt mangiare *man·jah·ray*

eau-de-Cologne n l'acqua di Colonia (f) *ak·kwa dee ko·lon·ya*

eccentric adj eccentrico(a) *ech·chen·tree·ko(a)*

echo n l'eco (m/f) *e·koh*

éclair n il cannolo *kan·no·loh*

economic adj economico(a) *e·ko·no·mee·ko(a)*

economical adj (use, method) economico(a) *e·ko·no·mee·ko(a)*

economics n l'economia (f) *e·ko·no·mee·a*

economist n l'economista (m/f) *e·ko·no·mee·sta*

economy n (of country) l'economia (f) *e·ko·no·mee·a*

eczema n l'eczema (m) *ek·ze·ma*

edge n il bordo *bohr·doh*; (of blade) il filo *fee·loh*

edition n l'edizione (f) *e·dee·tsyoh·ne*

educate vt istruire *ee·stroo·ee·re*

education n l'istruzione (f) *ee·stroo·tsyoh·ne*

E.E.C. n la C.E.E. *che·e*

eels pl le anguille *an·gweel·lay*

effect n l'effetto (m) *ef·fet·toh*; to take effect avere* effetto *a·vay·re ef·fet·toh*

effective adj (remedy etc) efficace *ef·fee·kah·che*

efficient adj efficiente *ef·fee·chen·te*

effort n lo sforzo *sfor·tsoh*

e.g. abbrev p.es. *payr e·zaym·pyoh*

egg n l'uovo (m) *wo·voh* S31

egg cup n il portauovo *por·ta·wo·voh*

eggplant n la melanzana *me·lan·dzah·na*

Egypt n Egitto (m) *e·jeet·toh*

Egyptian adj egiziano(a) *e·jee·tsyah·no(a)*

eiderdown n il piumino *pyoo·mee·noh*

eight num otto *ot·to*

eighteen num diciotto *dee·chot·to*

eighth adj ottavo(a) *ot·tah·vo(a)*

eighties pl (decade) gli anni ottanta *an·nee ot·tan·ta*

eighty num ottanta *ot·tan·ta*

either pron □ either of you o l'uno o l'altro di voi *o loo·noh o lal·troh dee voy*; which one? - either quale? - o l'uno o l'altro *kwah·le - o loo·noh o lal·troh* □ adj on either side a tutti e due i lati *a toot·tee e doo·e ee lah·tee* □ conj either ... or ... o ... o ... o ... o

elaborate adj complicato(a) *kom·plee·kah·to(a)*

elastic n l'elastico (m) *e·la·stee·koh*

elastic band n l'elastico (m) *e·la·stee·koh*

elbow n il gomito *goh·mee·toh*

elder adj maggiore *maj·joh·re*

eldest adj il/la maggiore *maj·joh·re*

elect vt eleggere* *e·lej·je·re*

election n l'elezione (f) *e·le·tsyoh·ne*

electric(al) adj elettrico(a) *e·let·tree·ko(a)*

electric blanket n la coperta elettrica *ko·per·ta e·let·tree·ka*

electrician n l'elettricista (m) *e·let·tree·chee·sta*

electricity n l'elettricità (f) *e·let·tree·chee·ta* A62

electronic adj elettronico(a) *e·let·tro·nee·ko(a)*

electronics n l'elettronica (f) *e·let·tro·nee·ka*

elegant adj elegante *e·le·gan·te*

element n l'elemento (m) *e·le·mayn·toh*

elephant n l'elefante (m) *e·le·fan·te*

elevator n l'ascensore (m) *a·shen·soh·re* A30

eleven num undici *oon·dee·chee*

eleventh adj undicesimo(a) *oon·dee·che·zee·mo(a)*

elm n l'olmo (m) *ohl·moh*

else adj □ somewhere else altrove *al·troh·ve*; someone else qualcun altro *kwal·koon al·troh*

embankment n il terrapieno *ter·ra·pye·noh*

embargo n l'embargo (m) *em·bar·goh*

embark vi imbarcarsi *em·bar·kar·see*

embarrassed adj imbarazzato(a) *eem·ba·rats·tsah·to(a)*

embassy n l'ambasciata (f) *am·ba·shah·ta*

embrace vt abbracciare *ab·brach·chah·ray*

embroidered adj ricamato(a) *ree·ka·mah·to(a)*

embroidery n il ricamo *ree·kah·moh*

emerald n lo smeraldo *zme·ral·doh*

emergency n l'emergenza (f) *e·mer·jen·tsa* E8

emergency exit n l'uscita di sicurezza (f) *oo·shee·ta dee see·koo·rayts·tsa*

emergency landing n l'atterraggio di emergenza (m) *a·ter·raj·joh dee e·mer·jen·tsa*

emery board n la limetta di carta smerigliata *lee·mayt·ta dee kar·ta zme·reel·yah·ta*

emigrate vi emigrare *e·mee·grah·ray*

emotion n l'emozione (f) *e·mo·tsyoh·ne*

emotional adj (person) impressionabile *eem·pres·syoh·nah·bee·le*

emperor n l'imperatore (m) *eem·pe·ra·toh·re*

emphasis n l'enfasi (f) *en·fa·zee*; **emphasis on something** l'enfasi su qualcosa *len·fa·zee soo kwal·ko·sa*

emphasize vt sottolineare *sot·to·lee·ne·ah·ray*; (syllable etc) accentuare *ach·chen·too·ah·ray*

empire n l'impero (m) *eem·pe·roh*

employ vt (worker) impiegare *eem·pye·gah·ray*

employee n l'impiegato(a) (m/f) *eem·pye·gah·to(a)*

employer n il datore di lavoro *da·toh·re dee la·voh·roh*

employment n l'impiego (m) *eem·pye·goh*

empty adj vuoto(a) *vwo·to(a)* □ vt vuotare *vwo·tah·ray*

enamel n lo smalto *zmal·toh*

enclosure n (in letter) l'allegato (m) *al·le·gah·toh*

encore n il bis *bees*; **encore!** bis! *bees*

encyclop(a)edia n l'enciclopedia (f) *en·chee·klo·pe·dee·a*

end n la fine *fee·ne*; (of table) il capo *kah·poh* □ vt terminare *ter·mee·nah·ray* □ vi finire *fee·nee·re*

endive n (smooth) l'indivia (f) *een·dee·vya*; (curly) la cicoria *chee·ko·rya*

endorse vt (document) firmare *feer·mah·ray*

enemy n il nemico *ne·mee·koh*

energetic adj energico(a) *e·ner·jee·ko(a)*

energy n l'energia (f) *e·ner·jee·a*

engaged adj (betrothed) fidanzato(a) *fee·dan·tsah·to(a)*; (busy) occupato(a) *ok·koo·pah·to(a)*

engagement n (betrothal) il fidanzamento *fee·dan·tsa·mayn·toh*

engagement ring n l'anello di fidanzamento (m) *a·nel·loh dee fee·dan·tsa·mayn·toh*

engine n (motor) il motore *mo·toh·re*; (of train) la locomotiva *lo·ko·mo·tee·va* T178

engineer n l'ingegnere (m) *een·jen·ye·re*

England n Inghilterra (f) *een·geel·ter·ra*

English adj inglese *een·glay·se* □ n l'inglese (m) *een·glay·se*; **in English** in inglese *een een·glay·se* B29, 30, 61

enjoy vt (concert, outing) gustare *goo·stah·ray*; **to enjoy oneself** divertirsi *dee·ver·teer·see*

enjoyment n il piacere *pya·chay·re*

enlarge vt ingrandire *een·gran·dee·re*

enormous adj enorme *e·nor·me*

enough pron abbastanza *ab·ba·stan·tsa*; **have you enough?** ne ha abbastanza? *nay a ab·ba·stan·tsa* □ adj enough time/books abbastanza tempo/libri *ab·ba·stan·tsa tem·poh/lee·bree* □ adv big enough abbastanza grande *ab·ba·stan·tsa gran·de* S38

ensemble n (clothes) l'insieme (m) *een·sye·me*

enter vt (room) entrare in *en·trah·ray een* □ vi entrare *en·trah·ray*

enterprise n l'impresa (f) *eem·pray·sa*

entertain vt (amuse) intrattenere* *een·trat·te·nay·re*; (give hospitality) ricevere *ree·chay·ve·re*

entertainment n (show) lo spettacolo *spet·ta·ko·loh* L42

enthusiasm n l'entusiasmo (m) *en·too·zee·a·zmoh*

enthusiast n l'entusiasta *en·too·zee·a·sta*

enthusiastic adj entusiasta *en·too·zee·a·sta*

entrance n (way in) l'ingresso (m) *een·gres·soh*

entrance fee il prezzo d'ingresso *prets·tsoh deen·gres·soh*

entrée n il primo piatto *pree·mo pyat·toh*

entry n (way in) l'ingresso (m) *een·gres·soh*

envelope n la busta *boo·sta* S92

envious adj invidioso(a) *een·vee·dyoh·so(a)*

environment n l'ambiente (m) *am·byen·te*

envy vt invidiare *een·vee·dyah·ray* □ n l'invidia (f) *een·vee·dya*

epidemic n l'epidemia (f) *e·pee·de·mee·a*

epilepsy n l'epilessia (f) *e·pee·les·see·a*

equal adj uguale *oo·gwah·le*

equator n l'equatore (m) *e·kwa·toh·re*

equipment n l'equipaggiamento (m) *e·kwee·paj·ja·mayn·toh* L36

equivalent adj equivalente *e·kwee·va·len·te*

erase vt cancellare *kan·chel·lah·ray*

eraser n la gomma per cancellare *gohm·ma payr kan·chel·lah·ray*

ermine n (fur) la pelliccia di ermellino *pel·leech·cha dee er·mel·lee·noh*

erotic adj erotico(a) *e·ro·tee·ko(a)*

errand n la commissione *kom·mees·syoh·ne*; **to do** or **run an errand** fare* una commissione *fah·ray oo·na kom·mees·syoh·ne*

error n l'errore (m) *er·roh·re*; **in error** per sbaglio *payr zbal·yoh*

escalator n la scala mobile *skah·la mo·bee·le*

escalope n la scaloppina *ska·lop·pee·na*

escape vi scappare *skap·pah·ray*

escort vt accompagnare *ak·kom·pan·yah·ray* □ n l'accompagnatore (m) *ak·kom·pan·ya·toh·re*

especially adv specialmente *spe·chal·mayn·te*

Esperanto n l'esperanto (m) *e·spe·ran·toh*

espresso (coffee) n l'espresso (m) *e·spres·soh* E60

essay n il saggio *saj·joh*

essential adj (necessary) essenziale *es·sen·tsyah·le*

establish vt stabilire *sta·bee·lee·re*; (business) fondare *fon·dah·ray*

estate n (property) la tenuta *te·noo·ta*; (housing) la zona residenziale *dzo·na re·see·den·tsyah·le*

estate agent n l'agente immobiliare (m) *a·jen·te eem·mo·bee·lyah·re*

estate (car) n la giardinetta *jar·dee·nayt·ta*

estimate vt stimare *stee·mah·ray* □ n la stima *stee·ma* Bm23

etc abbrev ecc *ech·che·te·ra*

ethical adj etico(a) *e·tee·ko(a)*

ethnic adj etnico(a) *et·nee·ko(a)*

etiquette n l'etichetta (f) *e·tee·kayt·ta*

Europe n Europa (f) *e·oo·ro·pa*

European adj europeo(a) *e·oo·ro·pe·o(a)*

evaporate vi evaporare *e·va·po·rah·ray*

evaporated milk n il latte evaporato *lat·te e·va·po·rah·to*

even adj (level) piano(a) *pyah·no(a)*;

(*equally matched*) uguale *oo·gwah·le*; an even number un numero pari *oon noo·me·roh pah·ree* □ *adv* even faster ancor piú veloce *an·kohr pyoo ve·loh·che*; even a child could do it anche un bambino potrebbe farlo *an·ke oon bam·bee·noh po·treb·be far·lo*; even so tuttavia *toot·ta·vee·a*

evening *n* la sera *say·ra*; in the evening la sera *la say·ra* L45, Mc44

evening dress *n* (*woman's*) l'abito da sera (*m*) *ah·bee·toh da say·ra*; (*man's*) lo smoking *smo·keeng*

evening paper *n* il giornale della sera *johr·nah·le del·la say·ra*

event *n* l'avvenimento (*m*) *av·ve·nee·mayn·toh*

eventually *adv* alla fine *al·la fee·ne*

ever *adv* sempre *sem·pre*; have you ever been to London? è mai stato a Londra? *e my stah·to a lohn·dra*; ever since he... da quando egli... *da kwan·do eyl·yee*; he's been there ever since da allora è sempre lí *da al·loh·ra e sem·pre lee*

every *adj* ogni *ohn·yee*; every other day ogni due giorni *ohn·yee doo·e johr·nee*; every 6th day ogni sei giorni *ohn·yee se·ee johr·nee*

everybody, everyone *pron* tutti *toot·tee*

everything *pron* tutto *toot·to*

everywhere *adv* dappertutto *dap·per·toot·to*

evidence *n* (*proof*) la prova *pro·va*; (*of witness*) la testimonianza *te·stee·mo·nyan·tsa*

evil *adj* cattivo(a) *kat·tee·vo(a)*

evolution *n* l'evoluzione (*f*) *e·vo·loo·tsyoh·ne*

ex- *pref* ex- *eks*

exact *adj* (*correct*) esatto(a) *e·zat·to(a)*; (*detailed*) preciso(a) *pre·chee·zo(a)*

exactly *adv* precisamente *pre·chee·za·mayn·te*

exaggerate *vt/i* esagerare *e·za·je·rah·ray*

exaggeration *n* l'esagerazione (*f*) *e·za·je·ra·tsyoh·ne*

examination *n* (*exam*) l'esame (*m*) *e·zah·me*; (*inspection*) l'ispezione (*f*) *ee·spe·tsyoh·ne*; (*medical*) la visita *vee·zee·ta*

examine *vt* (*inspect*) ispezionare *ee·spe·tsyoh·nah·ray*

example *n* l'esempio (*m*) *e·zem·pyoh*; for example per esempio *payr e·zem·pyoh*

exceed *vt* superare *soo·pe·rah·ray*

excellent *adj* eccellente *ech·chel·len·te*

except (for), except(ing) *prep* tranne *tran·ne*

exception *n* l'eccezione (*f*) *ech·che·tsyoh·ne*

exceptional *adj* eccezionale *ech·che·tsyoh·nah·le*

excess *n* l'eccedenza (*f*) *ech·che·den·tsa*

excess baggage *n* il bagaglio eccedente *ba·gal·yoh ech·che·den·te*

exchange *vt* cambiare *kam·byah·ray*; to exchange something for something cambiare qualcosa per qualcos'altro *kam·byah·ray kwal·ko·sa payr kwal·ko·sal·tro* □ *n* exchange (*between currencies*) il cambio *kam·byoh*; (*telephone*) la centrale *chen·trah·le*

exchange rate *n* il tasso di cambio *tas·soh dee kam·byoh* M23

excise duties *pl* le imposte sul consumo *eem·poh·ste sool kon·soo·moh*

excited *adj* commosso(a) *kom·mos·so(a)*

excitement *n* l'eccitazione (*f*) *ech·chee·ta·tsyoh·ne*

exciting *adj* emozionante *e·mo·tsyoh·nan·te*

exclaim *vi* esclamare *e·skla·mah·ray*

exclude *vt* escludere* *e·skloo·de·re*

exclusive *adj* (*club, shop*) esclusivo(a) *e·skloo·zee·vo(a)*; exclusive rights l'esclusiva (*f*) *e·skloo·zee·va*; exclusive of... ... non compresa *nohn kom·pray·sa*

excursion *n* la gita *jee·ta*; to go on an excursion fare* una gita *fah·ray oo·na jee·ta* L6

excuse *vt* scusare *skoo·zah·ray*; excuse me mi scusi *mee skoo·zee* □ *n* excuse (*pretext*) la scusa *skoo·za*

ex-directory *adj* che non figura nell'elenco telefonico *ke nohn fee·goo·ra nel·le·len·koh te·le·fo·nee·ko*

execute *vt* (*kill*) giustiziare *joo·stee·tsyah·ray*

executive *n* il direttore *dee·ret·toh·re*

exercise *n* l'esercizio (*m*) *e·zer·chee·tsyoh*

exercise book *n* il quaderno *kwa·der·noh*

exhaust *n* (*fumes*) il gas di scappamento *gas dee skap·pa·mayn·toh*; (*pipe*) il tubo di scappamento *too·bo dee skap·pa·mayn·toh* T184

exhausted *adj* esausto(a) *e·zow·sto(a)*

exhibition *n* la mostra *moh·stra*

exist *vi* esistere* *e·zee·ste·re*

existence *n* l'esistenza (*f*) *e·zee·sten·tsa*

exit *n* l'uscita (*f*) *oo·shee·ta*

exit permit *n* il permesso di uscita *per·mays·soh dee oo·shee·ta*

exotic *adj* esotico(a) *e·zo·tee·ko(a)*

expand *vt* (*material*) dilatare *dee·la·tah·ray*; (*business*) sviluppare *zvee·loop·pah·ray* □ *vi* (*material*) dilatarsi *dee·la·tar·see*; (*business*) svilupparsi *zvee·loop·par·see*

expect *vt* (*anticipate*) aspettare *a·spet·tah·ray*; I expect he'll come suppongo che verrà *soop·pohn·go ke ver·ra*; I expect so credo di sí *cre·do dee see*; she's expecting a baby attende un bambino *at·ten·de oon bam·bee·noh* Bm4

expedition *n* la spedizione *spe·dee·tsyoh·ne*

expenditure *n* le spese *spay·se*

expense *n* (*cost*) la spesa *spay·sa*; expenses le spese *spay·se*

expensive *adj* costoso(a) *ko·stoh·so(a)*

experience *n* l'esperienza (*f*) *e·spe·ree·en·tsa*

experienced *adj* esperto(a) *e·sper·to(a)*

experiment *n* l'esperimento (*m*) *e·spe·ree·mayn·toh*

expert *n* l'esperto (*m*) *e·sper·toh*

expire *vi* scadere* *ska·day·re*

explain *vt* spiegare *spye·gah·ray*

explanation *n* la spiegazione *spye·ga·tsyoh·ne*

explode *vi* esplodere* *e·splo·de·re*

explore *vt* esplorare *e·splo·rah·ray*

explosion *n* l'esplosione (*f*) *e·splo·zyoh·ne*

export *n* l'esportazione (*f*) *e·spor·ta·tsyoh·ne* □ *vt* esportare *e·spor·tah·ray*

exporter *n* l'esportatore (*m*) *e·spor·ta·toh·re*

express *vt* esprimere* *e·spree·me·re* □ *adv* to send something express mandare qualcosa per espresso *man·dah·ray kwal·ko·sa payr e·spres·so*

expression *n* l'espressione (*f*) *e·spres·syoh·ne*

express letter *n* l'espresso (*m*) *e·spres·so*

express train *n* il rapido *ra·pee·doh* T54

expressway *n* l'autostrada (*f*) *ow·to·strah·da*

extension *n* (building) l'annesso (*m*) *an·nes·so*; (phone) il telefono interno *te·le·fo·noh een·ter·no*

exterior *adj* esterno(a) *e·ster·no(a)*

external *adj* esterno(a) *e·ster·no(a)*

extra *adj* supplementare *soop·ple·men·tah·re*; postage extra le spese postali *pyoo le spay·se po·stah·lee* □ *adv* extra in più *een pyoo* M3, A18

extraordinary *adj* straordinario(a) *stra·or·dee·nah·ree·o(a)*

extravagant *adj* stravagante *stra·va·gan·te*

extremely *adv* estremamente *e·stre·ma·maynte*

eye *n* l'occhio (*m*) *ok·kyoh*

eyebrow *n* il sopracciglio *so·prach·cheel·yoh*

eyelash *n* il ciglio *cheel·yoh*

eyelid *n* la palpebra *pal·pe·bra*

eyeliner *n* l'eye-liner (*m*) *eye·line·er*

eyeshadow *n* l'ombretto (*m*) *om·brayt·toh*

eyesight *n* la vista *vee·sta*

F

fabric *n* il tessuto *tes·soo·toh* Sn68

face *n* il viso *vee·zoh*

facecloth *n* la manopola di spugna *ma·no·po·la dee spoon·ya*

face cream *n* la crema per il viso *kre·ma payr eel vee·zoh*

facilities *pl* i servizi *ser·vee·tsee*

facing *prep* di fronte a *dee frohn·te a*

fact *n* il fatto *fat·toh*; in fact infatti *een·fat·tee*

factor *n* il fattore *fat·toh·re*

factory *n* la fabbrica *fab·bree·ka*

faculty *n* (university) la facoltà *fa·kol·ta*

fade *vi* affievolirsi *af·fye·vo·leer·see*; (colour) sbiadire *zbee·a·dee·re*

Fahrenheit *adj* Fahrenheit *fah·ren·hite*

fail *vi* (person) non riuscire* *nohn ree·oo·shee·re*; (plan) fallire *fal·lee·re*; (brakes) guastarsi *gwa·star·see* □ *vt* (exam) non superare *nohn soo·pe·rah·ray* □ *n* without fail senza fallo *sen·tsa fal·loh*

failure *n* l'insuccesso (*m*) *een·sooch·ches·soh*; (person) il/la fallito(a) *fal·lee·to(a)*; (mechanical) l'avaria (*f*) *a·va·ree·a*; (of brakes) il guasto *gwa·stoh*

faint *vi* svenire* *zve·nee·re* □ *adj* (sound etc) debole *day·bo·le*; I feel faint mi sento venir meno *mee sen·to ve·neer may·no*

fair *adj* (just) giusto(a) *joo·sto(a)*; (hair) biondo(a) *byohn·do(a)*; (average) discreto(a) *dee·skray·to(a)* □ *adv* to play fair giocare secondo le regole *jo·kah·ray se·kohn·do le re·go·le* □ *n* fair (funfair) il luna-park *loo·na·park*; (commercial) la fiera *fye·ra*

fairground *n* il campo della fiera *kam·poh del·la fye·ra*

fairly *adv* (rather) piuttosto *pyoot·to·sto*

fairy *n* la fata *fah·ta*

faith *n* la fede *fay·de*

faithfully *adv* □ yours faithfully distinti saluti *dee·steen·tee sa·loo·tee*

fake *adj* falso(a) *fal·so(a)*

fall *vi* (person) cadere* *ka·day·re*; (prices etc) ribassare *ree·bas·sah·ray*; to fall down cadere* *ka·day·re*; to fall in love innamorarsi *een·na·mo·rar·see* □ *n* fall la caduta *ka·doo·ta*; (decrease) la diminuzione *dee·mee·noo·tsyoh·ne*; (season) l'autunno (*m*) *ow·toon·noh*

false *adj* (name etc) falso(a) *fal·so(a)*; false teeth la dentiera *den·tye·ra*

familiar *adj* (impertinent) sfacciato(a) *sfach·chah·to(a)*; to be familiar with something conoscere* bene qualcosa *ko·noh·she·re be·ne kwal·ko·sa*

family *n* la famiglia *fa·meel·ya* A2

famous *adj* famoso(a) *fa·moh·so(a)*

fan *n* (folding) il ventaglio *ven·tal·yoh*; (electric) il ventilatore *ven·tee·la·toh·re*; (in car) la ventola *ven·to·la*; (supporter) il tifoso *tee·foh·soh*

fanbelt *n* la cinghia della ventola *cheen·gya del·la ven·to·la* T183

fancy *adj* di lusso *dee loos·soh*

fancy dress *n* il costume *ko·stoo·me*

far *adv* lontano *lon·tah·no*; (much) di gran lunga *dee gran loon·ga*; how far is it to...? quanto dista da qui a...? *kwan·to dee·sta da kwee a*; as far as the station fino alla stazione *fee·no al·la sta·tsyoh·ne*; as far as I know per quanto io sappia *payr kwan·to ee·o sap·pya*; the Far East l'Estremo Oriente (*m*) *e·stre·mo o·ryen·te* F12

farce *n* la farsa *far·sa*

fare *n* il prezzo del biglietto *prets·tsoh del beel·yayt·toh*; (in taxi) il prezzo della corsa *prets·tsoh del·la kohr·sa*

farm *n* la fattoria *fat·to·ree·a*

farmer *n* l'agricoltore (*m*) *a·gree·kol·toh·re*

farmhouse *n* la casa colonica *kah·sa ko·lo·nee·ka*

farmyard *n* l'aia (*f*) *a·ya*

farther *adv* più lontano *pyoo lon·tah·no*

farthest *adj* il più lontano *eel pyoo lon·tah·no*

fascinating *adj* affascinante *af·fa·shee·nan·te*

fashion *n* la moda *mo·da*; the latest fashions l'ultima moda *lool·tee·ma mo·da*

fashionable *adj* di moda *dee mo·da*

fast *adj* (speedy) veloce *ve·loh·che*; (dye) solido(a) *so·lee·do(a)*; my watch is fast il mio orologio va avanti *eel mee·o o·ro·lo·joh va a·van·tee* □ *adv* fast velocemente *ve·loh·che·mayn·te*; to be fast asleep essere* profondamente addormentato(a) *es·se·re pro·fohn·da·mayn·te ad·dor·men·tah·to(a)* T52, 200

fasten *vt* attaccare *at·tak·kah·ray*; fasten seat belts allacciate le cinture di sicurezza *al·lach·chah·te le cheen·too·re dee see·koo·rayts·tsa*

fat *adj* (person) grasso(a) *gras·so(a)* □ *n* il grasso *gras·soh*

fatal *adj* fatale *fa·tah·le*

father *n* il padre *pah·dre*

father-in-law *n* il suocero *swo·che·roh*

faucet *n* il rubinetto *roo·bee·nayt·toh*

fault *n* (defect) il difetto *dee·fet·toh*; (blame) la colpa *kohl·pa*; whose fault is it? di chi è la colpa? *dee kee e la* *kohl·pa*; it's not my fault non è colpa mia *nohn e kohl·pa mee·a*

faulty *adj* difettoso(a) *dee·fet·toh·so(a)*

favour *n* il favore *fa·voh·re*; to do someone a favour fare* un favore a qualcuno *fah·ray oon fa·voh·re a kwal·koo·no*; I'm not in favour of that idea non sono a favore di quell'idea *nohn soh·no a fa·voh·re dee kwayl·lee·de·a*

favourite *adj* favorito(a) *fa·vo·ree·to(a)*

fawn *adj* fulvo(a) *fool·vo(a)*

fear *n* la paura *pa·oo·ra*

feasibility *n* la fattibilità *fat·tee·bee·lee·ta*

feasibility study *n* lo studio della fattibilità *stoo·dyoh del·la fat·tee·bee·lee·ta*

feast *n* il banchetto *ban·kayt·toh*

feather *n* la piuma *pyoo·ma*

feature film *n* il lungometraggio *loon·go·me·traj·joh*

features *pl* le fattezze *fat·tayts·tse*

February *n* febbraio *(m) feb·bra·yoh*

federal *adj* federale *fe·de·rah·le*

fed up *adj* stufo(a) *stoo·fo(a)*

fee *n* l'onorario *(m) o·no·rah·ryoh*

feed *vt* nutrire *noo·tree·re* □ *vi* mangiare *man·jah·ray*

feedback *n* il feed-back *feed·bak*

feel *vt* (touch) toccare *tok·kah·ray*; I feel that… penso che… *pen·so ke* □ *vi* it feels soft è soffice al tatto *e sof·fee·che al tat·toh*; I feel hungry ho fame *o fah·me*; I feel that I feel better mi sento meglio *mee sen·to mel·yoh*; I feel like a beer gradirei una birra *gra·dee·rey oo·na beer·ra*

feeling *n* la sensazione *sen·sa·tsee·oh·ne*; (emotion) il sentimento *sen·tee·men·toh*

fellow *n* il tizio *tee·tsyoh*; **fellow countryman** il/la connazionale *kon·na·tsyoh·nah·le*

felt *n* (cloth) il feltro *fayl·troh*

felt-tip pen *n* il pennarello *pen·na·rel·loh*

female *adj* (animal) femmina *faym·mee·na*; the female sex il sesso femminile *eel ses·soh fem·mee·nee·le*

feminine *adj* femminile *fem·mee·nee·le*

fence *n* il recinto *re·cheen·toh*

fender *n* (on car) il paraurti *pa·ra·oor·tee*

fern *n* la felce *fayl·che*

ferry *n* (small) il traghetto *tra·gayt·toh*; (large) la nave-traghetto *nah·ve·tra·gayt·toh*

fertile *adj* (land) fertile *fer·tee·le*

festival *n* il festival *fe·stee·val* L4

fetch *vt* andare* a prendere *an·dah·ray a pren·de·re*

fête *n* la festa *fe·sta*

fever *n* la febbre *feb·bre*

few *adj* pochi(e) *po·kee(·ke)*; **a few books** pochi libri *po·kee lee·bree* □ *pron* there are very few ce ne sono pochissimi(e) *che nay soh·no po·kees·see·mee(·me)*; there are quite a few ce ne sono abbastanza *che nay soh·no ab·ba·stan·tsa*

fiancé(e) *n* il/la fidanzato(a) *fee·dan·tsah·to(a)*

fibre *n* la fibra *fee·bra*

fibre-glass *n* la lana di vetro *lah·na dee vay·troh*

fiction *n* la narrativa *nar·ra·tee·va*

field *n* il campo *kam·poh*

field glasses *pl* il binocolo *bee·no·ko·loh*

fierce *adj* feroce *fe·roh·che*

fifteen *num* quindici *kween·dee·chee*

fifth *adj* quinto(a) *kween·to(a)*

fifty *num* cinquanta *cheen·kwan·ta*

fig *n* il fico *fee·koh*

fight *vi* lottare *lot·tah·ray* □ *n* il combattimento *kom·bat·tee·mayn·toh*

figure *n* (of human) la figura *fee·goo·ra*; (number) la cifra *chee·fra*; to have a nice figure essere* ben fatta *es·se·re ben fat·ta* □ *vt* figure (suppose) supporre* *soop·pohr·re*

file *n* (tool) la lima *lee·ma*; (dossier) l'archivio *(m) ar·kee·vyoh*

filing cabinet *n* l'archivio *(m) ar·kee·vyoh*

fill *vt* riempire* *ree·em·pee·re*; to fill in/out/up riempire* *ree·em·pee·re*; fill it up! (car) il pieno, per favore! *eel pye·noh payr fa·voh·re*

fillet *n* (of meat, fish) il filetto *fee·layt·toh*

filling *adj* (food) sostanzioso(a) *so·stan·tsyoh·so(a)* □ *n* (in tooth) l'otturazione *(f) ot·too·ra·tsyoh·ne* I58

filling station *n* la stazione di servizio *sta·tsyoh·ne dee ser·vee·tsyoh* F9

film *n* (movie) il film *feelm*; (for camera) la pellicola *pel·lee·ko·la* L44, S47f

filter *n* il filtro *feel·troh* S95

final *adj* finale *fee·nah·le*

finally *adv* finalmente *fee·nal·mayn·te*

finals *pl* (sports) la finale *fee·nah·le*

finance *n* la finanza *fee·nan·tsa* □ *vt* finanziare *fee·nan·tsyah·ray*

Finance Minister *n* il Ministro delle Finanze *mee·nee·stroh del·le fee·nan·tse*

financial *adj* finanziario(a) *fee·nan·tsy·ah·ryo(a)*

find *vt* trovare *tro·vah·ray*; to find out scoprire* *sko·pree·re*

fine *adj* (delicate) fino(a) *fee·no(a)*; (weather) bello(a) *bel·lo(a)*; (that's) fine! molto bene! *mohl·to be·ne* □ *n* la multa *mool·ta* T196

finger *n* il dito *dee·toh*

finish *vt/i* finire *fee·nee·re*

Finland *n* la Finlandia *(f) feen·lan·dya*

Finnish *adj* finlandese *feen·lan·day·se* □ *n* il finlandese *feen·lan·day·se*

fire *n* il fuoco *fwo·koh*; (accident) l'incendio *(m) een·chen·dyoh*; the house is on fire la casa è in fiamme *la kah·sa e een fyam·me*; to set fire to appiccare il fuoco a *ap·pee·kah·ray eel fwo·koh a* □ *vt* to fire a gun sparare un colpo di fucile *spa·rah·ray oon kohl·poh doo foo·chee·le*; to fire someone (dismiss) licenziare qualcuno *lee·chen·tsyah·ray kwal·koo·no* A72, Ea4

fire alarm *n* l'allarme antincendio *(m) al·lar·me an·teen·chen·dyoh*

firearm *n* l'arma da fuoco *(f) ar·ma da fwo·koh*

fire brigade *n* i vigili del fuoco *vee·jee·lee del fwo·koh* Ea7

fire engine *n* l'autopompa *(f) ow·to·pohm·pa*

fire escape *n* l'uscita di sicurezza *(f) oo·shee·ta dee see·koo·rayts·tsa*

fire extinguisher *n* l'estintore *(m) e·steen·toh·re*

fireman *n* il pompiere *pom·pye·re*

fireplace *n* il focolare *fo·ko·lah·re*

fire station *n* la caserma dei pompieri *ka·zer·ma dey pom·pye·ree*

fireworks *pl* i fuochi d'artificio *fwo·kee dar·tee·fee·choh*

firm n la ditta *deet·ta* □ adj (*object, material*) stabile *stah·bee·le*; (*person*) fermo(a) *fayr·mo(a)* Bm15, 17

first adj primo(a) *pree·mo(a)* □ adv prima *pree·ma* □ **in first** (*gear*) in prima *een pree·ma*; **at first** dapprima *dap·pree·ma*

first aid n il pronto soccorso *prohn·to sok·kohr·soh*

first-aid kit n la cassetta di pronto soccorso *kas·sayt·ta dee prohn·to sok·kohr·soh*

first-class adj (*work etc*) di prima classe *dee pree·ma klas·se*; **to travel first class** viaggiare in prima classe *vyaj·jah·ray een pree·ma klas·se* T61

first floor n il primo piano *pree·mo pya·noh* A5

first name n il nome *noh·me*

fir (tree) n l'abete (*m*) *a·bay·te*

fiscal adj fiscale *fee·skah·le*

fiscal year n l'anno fiscale (*m*) *an·noh fee·skah·le*

fish n il pesce *pay·she* E28

fishing n la pesca *pay·ska*; **to go fishing** andare* a pesca *an·dah·ray a pay·ska* L35

fishing rod n la canna da pesca *kan·na da pay·ska*

fishmonger n il pescivendolo *pe·shee·vayn·do·loh*

fist n il pugno *poon·yoh*

fit adj (*strong, healthy*) in forma *een fohr·ma*; (*suitable*) adatto(a) *a·dat·to(a)* □ vt/i **it fits me** mi sta bene *mee sta be·ne* □ n **fit** (*seizure*) l'accesso (*m*) *ach·ches·soh*

five num cinque *cheen·kwe*

fix vt fissare *fees·sah·ray*; (*mend*) riparare *ree·pa·rah·ray*; (*prepare*) preparare *pre·pa·rah·ray*

fizzy adj gassoso(a) *gas·soh·so(a)*

flag n la bandiera *ban·dye·ra*

flake n la scaglia *skal·ya*; (*of snow*) il fiocco *fyok·koh*

flame n la fiamma *fyam·ma*

flan n la torta di frutta *tohr·ta dee froot·ta*

flannel n (*facecloth*) la manopola di spugna *ma·no·po·la dee spoon·ya*

flap n la patta *pat·ta* □ vi (*sail*) sventolare *zven·to·lah·ray*

flash n il bagliore *bal·yoh·re*; (*on camera*) il flash *flash* □ vi (*light*) balenare *ba·le·nah·ray* S55

flashbulb n il flash *flash*

flashcube n il cubo flash *koo·boh flash*

flashlight n la lampadina tascabile *lam·pa·dee·na ta·skah·bee·le*

flask n il thermos *ter·mos*

flat adj piatto(a) *pyat·to(a)*; (*deflated*) sgonfio(a) *zgohn·fyo(a)*; (*battery*) scarico(a) *skah·ree·ko(a)*; (*beer*) stantio(a) *stan·tee·o(a)*; **B flat** (*music*) il si bemolle *see be·mol·le*; **flat rate** il prezzo fisso *prets·tsoh fees·so* □ n **flat** (*apartment*) l'appartamento (*m*) *ap·par·ta·mayn·toh*

flavo(u)r n il sapore *sa·poh·re*

flea n la pulce *pool·che*

flea market n il mercato delle pulci *mer·kah·toh del·le pool·chee*

fleet n la flotta *flot·ta*; **fleet of vehicles** il parco macchine *par·koh mak·kee·ne*

Flemish adj fiammingo(a) *fyam·meen·go(a)* □ n il fiammingo *fyam·meen·goh*

flesh n la carne *kar·ne*

flexible adj flessibile *fles·see·bee·le*

flight n il volo *voh·loh*; **flight of steps** la scalinata *ska·lee·nah·ta* T2f, 39, 48

flight attendant n la hostess *ho·stess*

flint n (*in lighter*) la pietra focaia *pye·tra fo·ka·ya*

flippers pl (*for swimming*) le pinne *peen·ne*

flirt vi flirtare *fleer·tah·ray* □ n (*for swimming, fishing*) il galleggiante *gal·lej·jan·te*

float vi galleggiare *gal·lej·jah·ray* □ n (*for swimming, fishing*) il galleggiante *gal·lej·jan·te*

flock n il gregge *grayj·je*

flood n l'inondazione (*f*) *een·on·da·tsyoh·ne*

floodlight n il riflettore *ree·flet·toh·re*

floodlit adj illuminato(a) *eel·loo·mee·nah·to(a)*

floor n il pavimento *pa·vee·mayn·toh*; **1st floor** (*Brit*), **2nd floor** (*US*) il primo piano *pree·mo pyah·noh*

florist n il/la fioraio(a) *fyoh·ra·yo(a)*

flour n la farina *fa·ree·na*

flow vi scorrere* *skohr·re·re*; (*traffic*) circolare *cheer·ko·lah·ray*

flow chart n l'organigramma (*m*) *or·ga·nee·gram·ma*

flower n il fiore *fyoh·re* L41

flowerbed n l'aiuola (*f*) *a·yoo·wo·la*

flu n l'influenza (*f*) *een·floo·en·tsa*

fluent adj □ **he speaks fluent French** parla francese correntemente *par·la fran·chay·ze kor·ren·te·mayn·te*

fluorescent light n il tubo fluorescente *too·boh floo·o·re·shen·te*

fluoride n il fluoruro *floo·o·roo·roh*

flush vt □ **to flush the toilet** tirare lo sciacquone *tee·rah·ray lo shak·kwoh·ne*

flute n il flauto *flow·toh*

fly n la mosca *moh·ska* □ vi volare *vo·lah·ray*

flying n il volare *vo·lah·re*

flyover n (*road*) il cavalcavia *ka·val·ka·vee·a*

foam n la schiuma *skyoo·ma*

focus vt mettere* a fuoco *mayt·te·re a fwo·koh*

fog n la nebbia *nayb·bya*

foggy adj nebbioso(a) *neb·byoh·so(a)*; **it's foggy** c'è della nebbia *che del·la nayb·bya*

fog-lamp n il proiettore fendinebbia *pro·yet·toh·re fen·dee·nayb·bya*

foil n (*for food*) la stagnola *stan·yo·la*

fold vt piegare *pye·gah·ray*

folding chair n la sedia pieghevole *se·dya pye·gay·vo·le*

folding table n la tavola pieghevole *tah·vo·la pye·gay·vo·le*

folk dance n il ballo folcloristico *bal·loh fol·klo·ree·stee·ko*

folk song n il canto folcloristico *kan·toh fol·klo·ree·stee·ko*

follow vt/i seguire *se·gwee·re*

following adj seguente *se·gwen·te*

food n il cibo *chee·boh* Mc1, Mc41

food poisoning n l'intossicazione alimentare (*f*) *een·tos·see·ka·tsyoh·ne a·lee·men·tah·re*

foot n (*of person, measurement*) il piede *pye·de*; (*of animal*) la zampa *tsam·pa*

football n (*game*) il calcio *kal·choh*; (*ball*) il pallone *pal·loh·ne*

footbrake n il freno a pedale *fre·noh a pe·dah·le*

footpath n il sentiero *sen·tye·roh*

for prep per *payr*; **to sell something for L.5000** vendere qualcosa per L.5000 *vayn·de·re kwal·ko·sa payr L5000*; **to leave for London** partire per Londra *par·tee·re payr lohn·dra*; to walk for an hour camminare un'ora *kam·mee·nah·ray oo·noh·ra*; what is the Italian for "dog"? come si dice "dog" in italiano? *koh·me see dee·che dog een ee·ta·lyah·no*; it's warm for March fa caldo per marzo *fa kal·do payr mar·tsoh*

forbid *vt* vietare *vee·e·tah·ray*; to forbid someone to do something proibire a qualcuno di fare qualcosa *pro·ee·bee·re a kwal·koo·no dee fah·ray kwal·ko·sa*; it is forbidden è vietato(a) *e vee·e·tah·to(a)*

force *n* (*violence*) la forza *for·tsa* □ *vt* (*compel*) costringere* *ko·streen·je·re*

ford *n* il guado *gwah·doh*

forecast *n* il pronostico *pro·no·stee·koh*; (*weather*) la previsione del tempo *pre·vee·zyoh·ne del tem·poh*

forehead *n* la fronte *frohn·te*

foreign *adj* straniero(a) *stran·ye·ro(a)*

foreigner *n* lo/la straniero/a *stran·ye·ro(a)* T191

foreign exchange market *n* il mercato delle valute estere *mer·kah·toh del·le va·loo·te e·ste·re*

foreign policy *n* la politica estera *po·lee·tee·ka e·ste·ra*

foreman *n* il caposquadra *kah·po·skwa·dra*

forename *n* il nome *noh·me*

forest *n* la foresta *fo·re·sta*

forever *adv* per sempre *payr sem·pre*

forgery *n* la falsificazione *fal·see·fee·ka·tsyoh·ne*

forget *vt* dimenticare *dee·men·tee·kah·ray* B68

forgive *vt* perdonare *per·do·nah·ray*

fork *n* la forchetta *for·kayt·ta*; (*in road*) il bivio *bee·vyoh*

form *n* la forma *fohr·ma*; (*document*) il modulo *mo·doo·loh*; in good form in forma *een fohr·ma*

formal *adj* formale *for·mah·le*

fortnight *n* una quindicina di giorni *oo·na kween·dee·chee·na dee johr·nee*

fortune *n* (*wealth*) la fortuna *for·too·na*

forty *num* quaranta *kwa·ran·ta*

forward *vt* (*letter*) fare* proseguire *fah·ray pro·se·gwee·re* A25

forward(s) *adv* avanti *a·van·tee*; the seat is too far forward il sedile è troppo in avanti *eel se·dee·le e trop·po een a·van·tee*

fountain *n* la fontana *fon·tah·na*; (*for drinking*) la fontanella *fon·ta·nel·la*

fountain pen *n* la penna stilografica *payn·na stee·lo·gra·fee·ka*

four *num* quattro *kwat·troh*

fourteen *num* quattordici *kwat·tor·dee·chee*

fourth *adj* quarto(a) *kwar·to(a)*

fox *n* la volpe *vohl·pe*

fracture *n* (*of arm etc*) la frattura *frat·too·ra*

fragile *adj* fragile *frah·jee·le*

frame *n* (*of picture*) la cornice *kor·nee·che*; frames (*of eyeglasses*) la montatura *mon·ta·too·ra*

France *n* Francia (*f*) *fran·cha*; in/to France in Francia *een fran·cha*

free *adj* libero(a) *lee·be·ro(a)*; (*costing nothing*) gratuito(a) *gra·too·ee·to(a)* Bm10

freeway *n* l'autostrada (*f*) *ow·to·strah·da*

freeze *vi* gelare *je·lah·ray* □ *vt* (*food*) congelare *kon·je·lah·ray*

freezer *n* il congelatore *kon·je·la·toh·re*

freight *n* (*goods*) le merci *mayr·chee*

freight train *n* il treno merci *tray·noh mayr·chee*

French *adj* francese *fran·chay·ze* □ *n* il francese *fran·chay·ze*

french fried potatoes, french fries *pl n* le patatine fritte *pa·ta·tee·ne freet·te*

frequent *adj* frequente *fre·kwen·te*

fresh *adj* fresco(a) *fray·sko(a)*; (*impudent*) insolente *een·so·len·te*

Friday *n* venerdì (*m*) *ve·ner·dee*

fridge *n* il frigo *free·goh*

fried *adj* fritto(a) *freet·to(a)*

friend *n* l'amico(a) (*m/f*) *a·mee·ko(a)*

friendly *adj* amichevole *a·mee·kay·vo·le*

frighten *vt* spaventare *spa·ven·tah·ray*

fringe *n* la frangia *fran·ja*

fritter *n* la frittella *freet·tel·la*

frog *n* la rana *rah·na*

frogs legs *pl* i cosciotti di rana *ko·shot·tee dee rah·na*

from *prep* da *da*; from London da Londra *da lohn·dra*; from 8 o'clock dalle otto in poi *dal·le ot·to een poy*; water from the tap l'acqua di rubinetto *ak·kwa dee roo·bee·nayt·toh*

front *adj* anteriore *an·te·ryoh·re* □ *n* (*foremost part*) la parte anteriore *par·te an·te·ryoh·re*; (*seaside*) il lungomare *loon·go·mah·re*; at the front davanti *da·van·tee*; to sit in front sedersi* davanti *se·dayr·see da·van·tee*

frontier *n* la frontiera *fron·tye·ra*

front-wheel drive *n* la trazione anteriore *tra·tsyoh·ne an·te·ryoh·re*

frost *n* il gelo *je·loh*

frozen *adj* (*food*) congelato(a) *kon·je·lah·to(a)*

fruit *n* la frutta *froot·ta*

fruit salad *n* la macedonia *ma·che·don·ya*

fry *vt* friggere* *freej·je·re*

fry(ing) pan *n* la padella *pa·del·la*

fuel *n* il carburante *kar·boo·ran·te*

fuel pump *n* la pompa del carburante *pom·pa del kar·boo·ran·te*

full *adj* pieno(a) *pye·no(a)*; full of pieno(a) di *pye·no(a) dee*; full up (*bus etc*) completo(a) *kom·ple·to(a)*

full stop *n* il punto *poon·toh*

full-time *adj, adv* a tempo pieno *a tem·po pye·noh*

fun *n* □ it was great fun è stato molto divertente *e stah·to mohl·to dee·ver·ten·te*

funds *pl* i fondi *fohn·dee*

funeral *n* il funerale *foo·ne·rah·le*

funny *adj* (*amusing*) divertente *dee·ver·ten·te*; (*strange*) curioso(a) *koo·ryoh·so(a)*

fur *n* il pelo *pay·loh*

fur coat *n* la pelliccia *pel·leech·cha*

furnish *vt* (*room etc*) ammobiliare *am·mo·bee·lyah·ray*

furniture *n* i mobili *mo·bee·lee*

further *adv* più lontano *pyoo lon·tah·no*

furthest *adj* il più lontano *eel pyoo lon·tah·no*

fuse *n* il fusibile *foo·zee·bee·le* T180, A77

fuss *n* le storie *sto·rye*; to make a fuss fare* delle storie *fah·ray del·le sto·rye*

future *n* il futuro *foo·too·roh*

G

gadget *n* il dispositivo *dees·po·see·tee·vo* S15

gain *vt* (*obtain*) guadagnare *gwa·dan·yah·ray* □ *vi* (*clock*) andare* avanti *an·dah·ray a·van·tee*

gala *n* la gala *gah·la*

gale *n* il vento forte *ven·toh for·te*

gallery *n* la galleria *gal·le·ree·a*; (*in theatre*) il loggione *loj·joh·nay*

gallon *n* il gallone *gal·loh·nay*

gallop *vi* galoppare *ga·lop·pah·ray* □ *n* il galoppo *ga·lop·poh*; **to go at a gallop** andare* al galoppo *an·dah·ray al ga·lop·poh*

gamble *vi* giocare *jo·kah·ray*

gambler *n* il giocatore d'azzardo *jo·ka·toh·ray dadz·dzar·doh*

gambling *n* il gioco d'azzardo *jo·ko dadz·dzar·doh*

game *n* il gioco *jo·ko*; (*hunting*) la cacciagione *kach·cha·joh·nay*; **a game of tennis** una partita di tennis *oo·na par·tee·ta dee ten·nees*

gang *n* la banda *ban·da*

gangster *n* il gangster *gang·ster*

gangway *n* (*passage*) il passaggio *pas·saj·joh*; (*bridge*) la passerella *pas·se·rel·la*

gap *n* lo spazio vuoto *spats·yoh vwo·toh*

garage *n* (*for parking*) l'autorimessa (*f*) *ow·toh·ree·mes·sa*; (*service station*) il garage *ga·raj* T168

garbage *n* le immondizie *eem·mon·dee·tsee·ay*

garbage can *n* la pattumiera *pat·too·mye·rah* A71

garden *n* il giardino *jar·dee·noh*

garden centre *n* il centro per il giardinaggio *chen·troh payr eel jar·dee·naj·joh*

gardener *n* il giardiniere *jar·dee·nye·ray*

gargle *vi* fare* gargarismi *fah·ray gar·ga·reez·mee*

garlic *n* l'aglio (*m*) *al·yoh*

garlic sausage *n* il salame all'aglio *sa·lah·may al·lal·yoh*

garment *n* l'indumento (*m*) *een·doo·mayn·toh*

gas *n* il gas *gas*; **gas cooker** la cucina a gas *koo·chee·na a gas* A94

gasket *n* la guarnizione *gwar·nee·tsee·oh·nay*

gas(oline) *n* la benzina *ben·dzee·na* T155

gas station *n* la stazione di servizio *sta·tsyoh·ne dee ser·vee·tsyoh* F9

gate *n* (*of garden*) il cancello *kan·chel·loh*; (*of building*) la porta *por·ta* T40

gateau *n* la torta *tohr·ta*

gather *vt* (*assemble*) raccogliere* *rak·kol·ye·ray* □ *vi* (*crowd*) radunarsi *ra·doo·nahr·see*

gathered *adj* arricciato(a) *ar·reech·chah·toh(a)*

gauge *n* (*device*) l'indicatore (*m*) *een·dee·ka·toh·ray*

gauze *n* la garza *gar·dza*

gay *adj* (*merry*) allegro(a) *al·lay·groh(a)*

gear *n* (*equipment*) l'equipaggiamento (*m*) *e·kwee·paj·ja·mayn·toh*; (*of car*) la marcia *mahr·cha*; **in gear** innestato(a) *een·ne·stah·toh(a)*; **2nd/3rd gear** seconda/terza marcia *se·kon·da/tayr·tsa mahr·cha*; **top/bottom gear** quarta/prima marcia *kwar·ta/pree·ma mahr·cha*

gearbox *n* la scatola del cambio *skah·to·la del kam·byoh*

gearlever, gearshift *n* la leva del cambio di marcia *lay·va del kam·byoh dee mahr·cha*

gem *n* la gemma *jem·ma*

gender *n* il genere *je·ne·ray*

general *adj* generale *je·ne·rah·lay* □ *n* (*soldier*) il generale *je·ne·rah·lay*; **in general** in generale *een je·ne·rah·lay*

general election *n* le elezioni politiche *e·lets·ee·oh·nee po·lee·tee·kay*

general knowledge *n* la cultura generale *kool·too·ra je·ne·rah·lay*

generally *adv* generalmente *je·ne·rahl·mayn·tay*

general practitioner, G.P. *n* il medico generico *me·dee·koh je·ne·ree·koh*

generation *n* la generazione *je·ne·ra·tsee·oh·nay*

generator *n* (*electrical*) il generatore *je·ne·ra·toh·ray*

generous *adj* (*person*) generoso(a) *je·ne·roh·soh(a)*; (*gift*) splendido(a) *splen·dee·doh(a)*

Geneva *n* Ginevra (*f*) *jee·ne·vra*

gentle *adj* mite *mee·tay*

gentleman *n* il signore *seen·yoh·ray*

genuine *adj* autentico(a) *ow·ten·tee·koh(a)*

geography *n* la geografia *jay·oh·gra·fee·a*

geology *n* la geologia *jay·oh·loh·jee·a*

geometry *n* la geometria *jay·oh·me·tree·a*

geranium *n* il geranio *je·rah·nee·oh*

germ *n* il microbo *mee·kro·boh*

German *adj* tedesco(a) *te·day·skoh(a)* □ *n* il tedesco *te·day·skoh*

Germany *n* Germania (*f*) *jer·mah·nya*; **in/to Germany** in Germania *een jer·mah·nya*

gesture *n* il gesto *jes·toh*

get *vt* (*obtain*) ottenere* *ot·te·nay·ray*; (*fetch*) prendere* *pren·de·ray*; (*receive*) ricevere *re·chay·ve·ray*; (*prepare: food*) preparare *pray·pa·rah·ray*; (*catch: illness*) prendere* *pren·de·ray*; **to have got(ten)** (*possess*) avere* *a·vay·ray*; **to get tired** stancarsi *stan·kahr·see*; **to get ready** prepararsi *pray·pa·rahr·see*; **how do we get there?** come ci si arriva? *koh·may chee see ar·ree·va*; **to get home** arrivare a casa *ar·ree·vah·ray a kah·sa*; **get off the grass** non calpestate l'erba! *non kal·pes·tah·tay ler·ba*; **to get one's hair cut** farsi* tagliare i capelli *far·see tal·yah·ray ee ka·pel·lee*; **to get away** (*escape*) fuggire *fooj·jee·ray*; **how are you getting on?** come va? *koh·may va*; **to get onto a road** entrare su una strada *en·trah·ray soo oo·na strah·da*; **to get through** (*on phone*) ottenere* la linea *ot·te·nay·ray la lee·nay·a*; **to get up** alzarsi *al·tsahr·see*

gherkin *n* il cetriolino *che·tree·oh·lee·noh*

ghetto *n* il ghetto *get·toh*

ghost *n* il fantasma *fan·taz·ma*

giant *n* il gigante *jee·gan·tay*

gift *n* il regalo *re·gah·loh*; (*ability*) il talento *ta·len·toh*

gifted *adj* dotato(a) *do·tah·toh(a)*

gift token *n* il buono-regalo *bwo·noh·re·gah·loh*

gift-wrap *vt* incartare con carta di regalo *een·kahr·tah·ray kon kahr·ta da re·gah·loh*

gin *n* (*drink*) il gin *jeen*

ginger n lo zenzero tsen·tse·roh

ginger ale n la bibita allo zenzero bee·bee·ta al·loh tsen·tse·roh

gingerbread n il pan di zenzero pahn dee tsen·tse·roh

gingham n la percallina a quadretti payr·kal·lee·na a kwa·dret·tee

gipsy n lo zingaro tseen·ga·roh

girdle n (corset) il corsetto kor·sayt·toh

girl n (child) la bambina bam·bee·na; (young woman) la ragazza ra·gats·tsa S106

girlfriend n la ragazza ra·gats·tsa

giro n (post office) il postagiro po·sta·jee·roh; **bank giro** (system) il banco-giro ban·ko·jee·roh

give vt dare* dah·ray; **to give a party** dare* una festa dah·ray oo·na fes·ta; **to give someone something** dare qualcosa a qualcuno dah·ray kwal·koh·sa a kwal·koo·no; **to give away** regalare ray·ga·lah·ray; **to give back** restituire re·stee·too·ee·ray; **to give in** (yield) cedere che·de·ray; **to give up** (abandon hope) abbandonare ab·ban·do·nah·ray; **to give up smoking** smettere* di fumare zmayt·te·ray dee foo·mah·ray; **to give way** (traffic) dare* la precedenza dah·ray la pre·che·den·tsa

glacé adj glacé gla·say

glad adj felice fe·lee·chay; **I was glad to hear...** ero lieto di sapere... e·roh lee·yay·toh dee sa·pay·ray

glamorous adj affascinante af·fa·shee·nan·tay

glance n lo sguardo zgwar·doh □ vi to glance at dare* uno sguardo a dah·ray oo·no zgwar·doh·a

gland n la ghiandola gee·an·doh·la

glare n (of light) il bagliore bal·yoh·ray

glass n il vetro vay·troh; (tumbler) il bicchiere beek·kye·ray; (glassware) gli articoli di vetro ar·tee·ko·lee dee vay·troh B54, 66, E13

glasses pl gli occhiali ok·kyah·lee B68

glide vi scivolare shee·voh·lah·ray

glider n l'aliante (m) a·lee·an·tay

gliding n (sport) il volo a vela voh·loh a vay·la L34

global adj globale glo·bah·le

globe n (map) il globo glo·boh

globe artichoke n il carciofo kar·cho·foh

glove n il guanto gwan·toh

glove compartment n il vano portaoggetti vah·noh por·ta·oj·jet·tee

glow vi essere* incandescente es·se·ray een·kan·de·shen·tay

glue n la colla kol·la □ vt incollare een·kol·lah·ray

glycerin(e) n la glicerina glee·che·ree·na

gnat n il moscerino mo·she·ree·noh

go vi andare* an·dah·ray; (leave) partire par·tee·ray; (clock, machine) funzionare foon·tsyoh·nah·ray; **to go shopping** fare* la spesa fah·ray la spay·sa; **to go bad** marcire mar·chee·ray; **how did it go?** come è andato? koh·may e an·dah·toh; **the books go here** i libri vanno qui ee lee·bree van·noh kwee; **it won't go** in non ci sta nohn chee sta; **all our money's gone** è finito tutto il nostro denaro e fee·nee·toh toot·toh eel no·stroh de·nah·roh; **I'm going to do it** lo faccio io loh fach·choh ee·oh; **go ahead!** faccia pure! fach·cha poo·ra!; **to go away** partire par·tee·ray; **to go back** tornare tor·nah·ray; **to go down** scende-

re* shayn·de·ray; **to go in** entrare en·trah·ray; **to go out** uscire* oo·shee·ray; **to go out with somebody** uscire con qualcuno oo·shee·ray kon kwal·koo·noh; **this goes with your dress** questo s'intona con il Suo vestito kwes·toh seen·toh·na kon eel soo·oh ves·tee·toh; **we will have to go without milk** dovremo fare a meno del latte do·vray·moh fah·ray a may·noh del lat·tay

goal n (sport) la rete ray·tay; (aim) lo scopo sko·poh

goat n la capra kah·pra

god n il dio dee·oh; **God** Dio (m) dee·oh

godfather n il padrino pa·dree·noh

godmother n la madrina ma·dree·na

goggles pl gli occhiali ok·kyah·lee

gold n l'oro (m) o·roh □ adj d'oro do·roh; **gold-plated** placcato d'oro plak·kah·toh do·roh S88, 89

golden adj dorato(a) do·rah·toh(a)

goldfish n il pesce rosso pay·she rohs·soh

golf n il golf golf L33

golf ball n la palla da golf pal·la da golf

golf club n la mazza da golf mats·tsa da golf; (association) il club da golf kloob dee golf

golf course n il campo di golf kam·poh dee golf

golfer n il giocatore di golf jo·ka·toh·ray dee golf

good adj buono(a) bwo·noh(a); (weather) bello(a) bel·loh(a); (well-behaved) educato(a) e·doo·kah·toh(a); **to be good at golf** essere* forte nel golf es·se·ray for·tay nel golf; **spinach is good for you** gli spinaci fanno bene alla salute lyee spee·nah·chee fan·no be·nay al·la sa·loo·tay; **it'll do you good** le farà bene lay fa·ra be·nay; **good morning/afternoon!** buon giorno! bwon johr·noh; **good evening!** buona sera! bwo·na say·ra; **good night!** buona notte! bwo·na not·tay

goodbye excl arrivederci ar·ree·ve·dayr·chee

Good Friday n venerdì santo ve·ner·dee san·toh

goods pl le merci mayr·chee

goose n l'oca (f) o·ka

gooseberry n l'uva spina (f) oo·va spee·na

go-slow n lo sciopero bianco sho·pe·roh byan·koh

gossip vi chiacchierare kya·kye·rah·ray □ n (chatter) la chiacchiera kya·kye·ra

goulash n il gulasch goo·lash

gourmet n il buongustaio bwon·goos·ta·ee·yoh

govern vt (country) governare go·vayr·nah·ray

government n il governo go·vayr·noh

governor n (of colony) il governatore go·vayr·na·toh·ray; (of institution) il direttore dee·ret·toh·ray, la direttrice dee·ret·tree·cha

gown n (dress) la veste ves·tay; (academic) la toga to·ga

grab vt afferrare af·fer·rah·ray

graceful adj grazioso(a) gra·tsyoh·soh(a)

grade n il grado grah·doh; (class) la classe klas·say

grade crossing n il passaggio a livello pas·saj·joh a lee·vel·loh

grade school n la scuola elementare *skwo·la e·le·men·tah·ray*

gradual adj graduale *gra·dwa·lay*

gradually adv gradualmente *gra·doo·al·men·tay*

graduate n (*from university*) il/la laureato(a) *low·ray·ah·toh(a)* □ vi laurearsi *low·ray·ar·see*

grain n (*cereal crops*) il grano *grah·noh*; (*in wood*) la venatura *vay·na·too·ra*

gram n il grammo *gram·moh*

grammar n la grammatica *gram·ma·tee·ka*; **grammar** (*book*) il libro di grammatica *lee·broh dee gram·ma·tee·ka*

gramme n il grammo *gram·moh*

grand adj magnifico(a) *ma·nyee·fee·koh(a)*

grandchild n il/la nipotino(a) *nee·po·tee·noh(a)*

granddaughter n la nipote *nee·poh·tay*

grandfather n il nonno *non·noh*

grandfather clock n l'orologio a pendolo (m) *o·ro·lo·joh a pen·do·loh*

grandmother n la nonna *non·na*

grand piano n il pianoforte a coda *pya·no·for·tay a koh·da*

Grand Prix n il Gran Premio *gran pre·myoh*

grandson n il nipote *nee·poh·tay*

grant n (*to student*) la borsa di studio *bohr·sa dee stoo·dee·oh*; (*to institution*) la sovvenzione *sov·ven·tsyoh·nay* □ vt (*wish*) accordare *ak·kor·dah·ray*

grapefruit n il pompelmo *pom·pel·moh*

grapefruit juice n il succo di pompelmo *sook·koh dee pom·pel·moh*

grapes pl l'uva (f) *oo·va*

graph n il grafico *gra·fee·koh*

grasp vt (*seize*) afferrare *af·fer·rah·ray*

grass n l'erba (f) *er·ba*

grate n la grata *grah·ta* □ vt (*food*) grattugiare *grat·too·jah·ray*

grateful adj grato(a) *grah·toh(a)*

grater n la grattugia *grat·too·jah*

grave n la tomba *tohm·ba*

grave (accent) n l'accento grave (m) *ach·chen·toh grah·vay*

gravel n la ghiaia *ghee·a·ya*

graveyard n il camposanto *kam·po·san·toh*

gravy n la salsa *sal·sa*

gray adj grigio(a) *gree·joh(a)*

graze n la scalfittura *skal·feet·too·ra* □ vt (*skin*) scalfire *skal·fee·ray*

grease n il grasso *gras·soh*; (*lubricant*) il lubrificante *loo·bree·fee·kan·tay*

greasy adj grasso(a) *gras·soh(a)*

great adj grande *gran·day*; (*excellent*) magnifico(a) *ma·nyee·fee·koh(a)*

Great Britain n Gran Bretagna (f) *gran bre·tan·ya*

Greece n Grecia (f) *gray·cha*

greedy adj goloso(a) *go·loh·soh(a)*

Greek adj greco(a) *gre·koh(a)* □ n il greco *gre·koh*

green adj verde *vayr·day*

green card n la carta verde *kar·ta vayr·day*

greengrocer n il fruttivendolo *froot·tee·vayn·do·loh*

greenhouse n la serra *ser·ra*

green salad n l'insalata verde (f) *een·sa·lah·ta vayr·day*

greet vt salutare *sa·loo·tah·ray*

greeting n il saluto *sa·loo·toh*

greetings card n la cartolina *kar·to·lee·na*

grey adj grigio(a) *gree·joh(a)*

grief n il dolore *do·loh·ray*

grill n (*gridiron*) la griglia *greel·ya* □ vt cuocere* ai ferri *kwo·che·ray ai fer·ree*

grillroom n la rosticceria *ro·steech·che·ree·a*

grimace n la smorfia *zmor·fee·a*

grin vi sorridere* *sor·ree·de·re* □ n il sorriso *sor·ree·soh*

grind vt macinare *ma·chee·nah·ray*

grip n afferrare *af·fer·rah·ray* □ n (*case*) la valigetta *va·lee·jayt·ta*

grit n la ghiaia *ghee·a·ya*

groan vi gemere *je·me·ray* □ n il gemito *je·mee·toh*

grocer n il droghiere *dro·gye·ray*

groceries pl i generi alimentari *je·ne·ree a·lee·men·tah·ree*

grocery shop n la drogheria *dro·ge·ree·a*

gross n la grossa *gros·sa* □ adj (*before deductions*) lordo(a) *lohr·doh(a)*

gross national product, GNP n il prodotto nazionale lordo *pro·doht·toh na·tsyoh·nah·le lohr·do*

grotesque adj grottesco(a) *grot·tay·skoh(a)*

ground n la terra *ter·ra* □ adj (*coffee*) macinato(a) *ma·chee·nah·toh(a)*; **ground beef** la carne tritata *kahr·nay tree·tah·ta*

ground floor n il pianterreno *pyan·ter·ray·noh* A5

groundnut n l'arachide (f) *a·ra·kee·day*

grounds pl (*land*) i terreni *ter·ray·nee*; (*of coffee*) i fondi di caffè *fon·dee dee kaf·fe*

groundsheet n la tela impermeabile *tay·la eem·payr·may·ah·bee·lay*

group n il gruppo *groop·poh*

grouse n (*bird*) la pernice *te·tra·oh·nay*

grow vi crescere* *kre·she·ray* □ vt (*plants*) coltivare *kol·tee·vah·ray*; **to grow up** crescere* *kre·she·ray*

growl vi ringhiare *reen·gyah·ray*

grown-up adj adulto(a) *a·dool·toh(a)* □ n il/la adulto(a) *a·dool·toh(a)*

growth n la crescita *kray·shee·ta*; (*in amount etc*) l'aumento (m) *ow·men·to*; (*anatomical*) l'escrescenza (f) *es·kre·shen·tsa*

grumble vi brontolare *bron·to·lah·ray*

grunt vi grugnire *groon·yee·ray*

guarantee n la garanzia *ga·ran·tsee·a* □ vt garantire *ga·ran·tee·ray*

guard n (*prisoner*) custodire *koo·sto·dee·ray*; (*protect*) proteggere* *pro·tej·je·ray* □ n (*sentry*) la sentinella *sen·tee·nel·la*; (*soldiers*) la guardia *gwar·dya*; (*on train*) il capotreno *kah·poh·tre·noh*

guardian n il tutore *too·toh·ray*, la tutrice *too·tree·chay*

guess vt indovinare *een·do·vee·nah·ray* □ vi congetturare *kon·jet·too·rah·ray*

guest n l'ospite (m/f) *o·spee·tay*; (*at hotel*) il/la cliente *klee·en·tay*

guest-house n la pensione *pen·see·oh·nay*

guest-room n la camera degli ospiti *kah·me·ra del·yee o·spee·tee*

guide n la guida *gwee·da* L10

guidebook n la guida *gwee·da* L3

guide dog n il cane per ciechi *kah·nay payr che·kee*

guided tour n la visita con guida *vee·zee·ta kohn gwee·da* L5

guilt n la colpevolezza *kol·pay·vo·layts·tsa*

guilty adj colpevole *kol·pay·vo·lay*

guinea fowl *n* la gallina faraona *gal·lee·na fa·ra·oh·na*

guitar *n* la chitarra *kee·tar·ra*

gum *n* (*of teeth*) la gengiva *jen·jee·va*; (*chewing gum*) la gomma da masticare *gohm·ma da ma·stee·kah·ray* I63

gun *n* il fucile *foo·chee·lay*

gunman *n* il bandito *ban·dee·toh*

gust *n* la raffica *raf·fee·ka*

gusty *adj* (*wind*) burrascoso(a) *boor·ras·koh·so(a)*

gutter *n* (*in street*) la cunetta *koo·nayt·ta*; (*on building*) la grondaia *gron·da·ya*

gym(nasium) *n* la palestra *pa·le·stra*

gymnastics *n* la ginnastica *jeen·nas·tee·ka*

gypsy *n* lo zingaro *tseen·ga·roh*

H

haberdashery *n* la merceria *mer·che·ree·a*

habit *n* l'abitudine (*f*) *a·bee·too·dee·ne*

haddock *n* l'eglefino (*m*) *ay·glay·fee·noh*

haemorrhoids *pl* le emorroidi *e·mor·roy·dee*

Hague (the) *n* l'Aia (*f*) *la·ya*

hail *n* la grandine *gran·dee·ne* □ *vi* it's hailing grandina *gran·dee·na*

hair *n* i capelli *ka·payl·lee*; (*single strand*) il capello *ka·payl·loh* Sn37

hairbrush *n* la spazzola per capelli *spats·tso·la payr ka·payl·lee*

haircut *n* (*style*) il taglio dei capelli *tal·yoh dey ka·payl·lee*; to have a haircut farsi* tagliare i capelli *far·see tal·yah·ray ee ka·payl·lee*

hairdresser *n* il parrucchiere *par·rook·kye·re* Sn36f

hair-drier *n* l'asciugacapelli (*m*) *a·shoo·ga·ka·payl·lee* Sn43

hairpin *n* la forcina *for·chee·na*

hairpin bend *n* la curva a gomito *koor·va a goh·mee·toh*

hair spray *n* la lacca *lak·ka*

hair-style *n* l'acconciatura (*f*) *ak·kon·cha·too·ra*

half *n* la metà *me·ta*; half an hour una mezz'ora *medz·dzoh·ra*; two and a half due e mezzo *doo·e ay medz·dzoh*; to cut something in half tagliare qualcosa in due *tal·yah·ray kwal·ko·sa een doo·e* □ *adj* a half dozen una mezza dozzina *oo·na medz·dza dodz·dzee·na*; three and a half kilometers tre chilometri e mezzo *tray kee·lo·me·tree ay medz·dzo* □ *adv* half a metà *a me·ta*; half open semiaperto(a) *se·mee·a·per·to(a)*

half-fare *n* la tariffa ridotta *ta·reef·fa ree·doht·ta*

half holiday *n* il mezzo giorno di festa *medz·dzo johr·noh dee fe·sta*

half-hour *n* la mezz'ora *medz·dzoh·ra*

half-price *adj* a metà prezzo *a me·ta prets·tsoh*

half-time *n* l'intervallo (*m*) *een·ter·val·loh*

halfway *adv* a metà strada *a me·ta strah·da*

hall *n* (*entrance*) il vestibolo *ve·stee·bo·loh*; (*room*) la sala *sah·la*

hallmark *n* il marchio *mar·kyoh*

halve *vt* (*divide in two*) dividere* a metà *dee·vee·de·re a me·ta*; (*reduce by half*) ridurre* alla metà *ree·door·re al·la me·ta*

ham *n* il prosciutto *pro·shoot·toh* S31

hamburger *n* l'hamburger (*m*) *ham·bur·gur*

hammer *n* il martello *mar·tel·loh*

hammock *n* l'amaca (*f*) *a·mah·ka*

hamper *n* la cesta *chay·sta*

hand *n* la mano *mah·noh*; (*of clock*) la lancetta *lan·chayt·ta*; by hand a mano *a mah·noh* □ *vt* to hand someone something dare* qualcosa a qualcuno *dah·ray kwal·ko·sa a kwal·koo·no*

handbag *n* la borsa *bohr·sa*

handbook *n* il manuale *ma·noo·ah·le*

hand-brake *n* il freno a mano *fre·noh a mah·noh*

hand cream *n* la crema per le mani *kre·ma payr le mah·nee*

handcuffs *pl* le manette *ma·nayt·te*

handicap *n* lo svantaggio *zvan·taj·joh*; (*golf*) l'handicap (*m*) *han·dee·kap*

handkerchief *n* il fazzoletto *fats·tso·layt·toh*

handle *n* (*of door*) la maniglia *ma·neel·ya*; (*of cup, knife*) il manico *mah·nee·koh*; (*for winding*) la manovella *ma·no·vel·la* □ *vt* (*touch*) toccare *tok·kah·ray*; (*deal with*) trattare *trat·tah·ray*; handle with care fragile *frah·jee·le*

handlebar(s) *n* il manubrio *ma·noo·bryoh*

hand-luggage *n* il bagaglio a mano *ba·gal·yoh a mah·noh*

handmade *adj* fatto(a) a mano *fat·to(a) a mah·noh* S107

handrail *n* (*on stairs*) il corrimano *kor·ree·mah·noh*

handsome *adj* (*person*) bello(a) *bel·lo(a)*

handy *adj* (*convenient*) pratico(a) *pra·tee·ko(a)*

hang *vt* appendere* *ap·pen·de·re*; (*criminal*) impiccare *eem·peek·kah·ray* □ *vi* pendere *pen·de·re*; hang on! (*on phone*) aspetti! *a·spet·tee*; to hang up (*phone*) deporre* il ricevitore *de·pohr·re eel ree·che·vee·toh·re*

hangover *n* il mal di testa dopo una sbornia *mal dee te·sta doh·po oo·na zbor·nya*; to have a hangover avere* mal di testa dopo una sbornia *a·vay·re mal dee te·sta doh·po oo·na zbor·nya*

happen *vi* succedere* *sooch·che·de·re*; what happened to him? che cosa gli è successo? *ke ko·sa lyee e sooch·ches·so*

happiness *n* la felicità *fe·lee·chee·ta*

happy *adj* contento(a) *kon·tayn·to(a)*

harbo(u)r *n* il porto *por·toh*

harbo(u)r master *n* il capitano di porto *ka·pee·tah·noh dee por·toh*

hard *adj* (*not soft*) duro(a) *doo·ro(a)*; (*difficult*) difficile *deef·fee·chee·le* □ *adv* (*work*) sodo *so·do*

hard-boiled *adj* sodo(a) *so·do(a)*

hard shoulder *n* la corsia di emergenza *kor·see·a dee e·mer·jen·tsa*

hardware *n* le ferramenta *fer·ra·mayn·ta*; (*computing*) il hardware *hard·wer*

hard-wearing *adj* resistente *re·see·sten·te*

hare *n* la lepre *le·pray*

haricot beans *pl* i fagioli *fa·jo·lee*

harmful *adj* nocivo(a) *no·chee·vo(a)*

harmless *adj* innocuo(a) *een·no·kwo(a)*

harness *n* i finimenti *fee·nee·mayn·tee*

harp *n* l'arpa (*f*) *ar·pa*

harsh *adj* (*severe*) severo(a) *se·ve·ro(a)*

harvest *n* (*of grain*) il raccolto *rak·kol·*

toh; (of grapes) la vendemmia *ven·daym·mya* □ vt (grain) mietere *mye·te·re*; (grapes) fare* la vendemmia di *fah·ray la ven·daym·mya dee*

haste n la fretta *frayt·ta*

hat n il cappello *kap·pel·loh* S12

hatch n (for serving) la portella *por·tel·la*

hatchback n (car) la macchina a cinque porte *mak·kee·na a cheen·kwe por·te*

hate vt odiare *o·dyah·ray*

hatred n l'odio (m) *o·dyoh*

hat stand n l'attaccapanni (m) *at·tak·ka·pan·nee*

have vt avere* *a·vay·re*; (meal) fare* *fah·ray*; **to have a shower** fare* una doccia *fah·ray oo·na dohch·cha*; **to have a drink** prendere* qualcosa da bere *pren·de·re kwal·ko·sa da bay·re*; **she has to do it** deve farlo *de·ve far·lo*; **to have something done** far* fare qualcosa *far fah·ray kwal·ko·sa*

hay n il fieno *fye·noh*

hay fever n la febbre da fieno *feb·bre da fye·noh* S40

he pron egli *ayl·yee*; **here he is!** eccolo! *ek·ko·lo*

head n la testa *te·sta*; (chief) il capo *kah·poh*

headache n il mal di testa *mal dee te·sta*; **to have a headache** avere* mal di testa *a·vay·re mal dee te·sta* S40

headlamp, headlight n il faro *fah·roh*

headline n il titolo *tee·to·loh*

headmaster n il preside *pre·see·de*

headmistress n la preside *pre·see·de*

head office n la sede centrale *se·de chen·trah·le*

head-on adj frontale *fron·tah·le*

headphones pl la cuffia *koof·fya*

headrest n il poggiatesta *poj·ja·te·sta*

heal vi (wound) guarire *gwa·ree·re*

health n la salute *sa·loo·te*

health foods pl i cibi naturali *chee·bee na·too·rah·lee*

health service n il servizio sanitario *ser·vee·tsyoh sa·nee·tah·ryo*

healthy adj (person) sano(a) *sah·no(a)*

heap n il mucchio *mook·kyoh*

hear vt/i sentire *sen·tee·re*; **I can't hear (you)** non La sento *nohn la sen·to*

hearing aid n l'apparecchio acustico (m) *ap·pa·rayk·kyoh a·koo·stee·ko*

heart n il cuore *kwo·re*; **by heart** a memoria *a me·mo·ree·a*; **hearts** (cards) i cuori *kwo·ree* I1

heart attack n l'attacco cardiaco (m) *at·tak·koh kar·dee·a·ko*

heartburn n il bruciore di stomaco *broo·choh·re dee sto·ma·koh*

hearth n il focolare *fo·ko·lah·re*

heat n il calore *ka·loh·re*; (sports) la batteria *bat·te·ree·a*

heater n il riscaldatore *ree·skal·da·toh·re*

heating n il riscaldamento *ree·skal·da·mayn·toh* A44f, 66

heavy adj pesante *pe·san·te*

hedge n la siepe *sye·pe*

heel n il tallone *tal·loh·ne*; (of shoe) il tacco *tak·koh*

height n (of object) l'altezza (f) *al·tayts·tsa*; (of person) la statura *sta·too·ra*

helicopter n l'elicottero (m) *e·lee·kot·te·roh*

hello excl ciao *chow*

helmet n il casco *ka·skoh*

help n l'aiuto (m) *a·yoo·toh*; **help!** aiuto! *a·yoo·toh* □ vt **help** aiutare a-

yoo·tah·ray; **can you help me?** mi può aiutare? *mee pwo a·yoo·tah·ray*; **help yourself** si serva *see ser·va*; **I can't help it** non posso farci nulla *nohn pos·so far·chee nool·la* B60, T78

helping n la porzione *por·tsyoh·ne*

hem n l'orlo (m) *ohr·loh* Sn76

hemorrhoids pl le emorroidi *e·mor·roy·dee*

hen n la gallina *gal·lee·na*

her pron lei *lay*; **it's her** è lei *e lay*; **give it to her** glielo dia *lye·lo dee·a* □ adj her suo *soo·o*, sua *soo·a*, suoi *swoy*, sue *soo·e*; **her brothers** i suoi fratelli *ee swoy fra·tel·lee*; **her sisters** le sue sorelle *le soo·e so·rel·le*

herbs pl le erbe *er·be*

here adv qui *kwee*; **here's my sister** ecco mia sorella *ek·ko mee·a so·rel·la*; **here she comes** eccola che viene *ek·ko·la ke vye·ne*

hernia n l'ernia (f) *er·nee·a*

herring n l'aringa (f) *a·reen·ga*

hers pron il suo *eel soo·o*, la sua *la soo·a*; (plural) i suoi *ee swoy*, le sue *le soo·e*

herself pron lei stessa *lay stays·sa*; **she did it herself** l'ha fatto lei stessa *la fat·to lay stays·sa*; **she dressed herself** si è vestita *see e ve·stee·ta*

hesitate vi esitare *e·zee·tah·ray*; **to hesitate to do something** esitare a fare qualcosa *e·zee·tah·ray a fah·ray kwal·ko·sa*

hiccup n il singhiozzo *seen·gyots·tsoh*; **to have (the) hiccups** avere* il singhiozzo *a·vay·re eel seen·gyots·tsoh*

hide n (leather) la pelle *pel·le* □ vt nascondere* *na·skohn·de·re* □ vi nascondersi* *na·skohn·der·see*

hi-fi adj ad alta fedeltà *ad al·ta fe·del·ta* □ n il sistema hi-fi *see·ste·ma hi-fi*

high adj alto(a) *al·to(a)*; (pitch, voice) acuto(a) *a·koo·to(a)* □ adv in alto *een al·to*; **6 metres high** alto(a) 6 metri *al·to(a) 6 me·tree*

highchair n il seggiolone *sej·jo·loh·ne* C3

high-class adj di prim'ordine *dee pree·mohr·dee·ne*

higher adj più alto(a) *pyoo al·to(a)*

high-heeled adj a tacchi alti *a tak·kee al·tee*

high-rise (block) n il grattacielo *grat·ta·che·loh*

high school n il liceo *lee·che·oh*

high season n l'alta stagione (f) *al·ta sta·joh·ne*

high-speed adj rapido(a) *ra·pee·do(a)*

high street n la strada principale *strah·da preen·chee·pah·le*

high tide n l'alta marea (f) *al·ta ma·re·a*

highway n la strada statale *strah·da sta·tah·le*

Highway Code n il codice stradale *ko·dee·che stra·dah·le*

hijack vt dirottare *dee·rot·tah·ray*

hijacker n il dirottatore *dee·rot·ta·toh·re*

hike n l'escursione a piedi (f) *e·skoor·syoh·ne a pye·dee*

hiking n l'escursionismo a piedi (m) *e·skoor·syoh·nee·zmoh a pye·dee*; **to go hiking** fare* delle escursioni a piedi *fah·ray del·le e·skoor·syoh·nee a pye·dee*

hill n la collina *kol·lee·na*; (slope) il pendio *pen·dee·oh*

hilly adj collinoso(a) *kol·lee·noh·so(a)*

him pron lo lo; it's him è lui e loo·ee;
give it to him glielo dia lye·lo dee·a

himself pron lui stesso loo·ee stays·so;
he did it himself l'ha fatto lui stesso
la fat·to loo·ee stays·so; he dresses
himself si veste see ve·ste

hip n l'anca (f) an·ka

hire vt noleggiare no·lej·jah·ray; to
hire something out noleggiare qualcosa no·lej·jah·ray kwal·ko·sa T108f

hire car n la macchina noleggiata mak·
kee·na no·lej·jah·ta T108

hire purchase n la vendita a rate vayn·
dee·ta a rah·te

his adj suo soo·o, sua soo·a, suoi swoy,
sue soo·e; his brothers i suoi fratelli
ee swoy fra·tel·lee; his sisters le sue
sorelle le soo·e so·rel·le □ pron his il/
la suo(a) eel/la soo·o(a); (plural) i
suoi ee swoy, le sue le soo·e

history n la storia sto·ree·a

hit vt (with hand) battere bat·te·re;
(with bat) colpire kol·pee·re; (with
car) urtare oor·tah·ray □ n (blow) il
colpo kohl·poh

hitchhike vi fare* l'autostop fah·ray
low·to·stop

hitchhiker n l'autostoppista (m/f) ow·
to·stop·pee·sta

hobby n il passatempo pas·sa·tem·poh

hock n il vino del Reno vee·noh del re·
noh

hockey n l'hockey (m) ho·kee

hold vt tenere* te·nay·re; (contain)
contenere* kon·te·nay·re; (support)
sostenere* so·ste·nay·re; hold him
still lo tenga fermo lo ten·ga fayr·
mo; hold on! (on phone) aspetti! a·
spet·tee; to hold up (delay) trattene-
re* trat·te·nay·re

holdall n la borsa bohr·sa

hold-up n (traffic) l'ingorgo (m) een·
gohr·goh

hole n il buco boo·koh

holiday n (day) la festa fe·sta; (period)
le vacanze va·kan·tse; on holiday in
vacanza een va·kan·tsa Mc19

holiday-maker n il/la villeggiante veel·
lej·jan·te

Holland n Olanda (f) o·lan·da

hollow adj cavo(a) ka·vo(a)

holy adj santo(a) san·to(a)

home n la casa kah·sa; (institution) l'a-
silo (m) a·zee·loh; at home a casa a
kah·sa; to go home andare* a casa
an·dah·ray a kah·sa

home address n l'indirizzo di casa (m)
een·dee·reets·tsoh dee kah·sa

homesick adj □ to be homesick provare la nostalgia pro·vah·ray la no·
stal·jee·a

homework n i compiti kohm·pee·tee

homogenized adj omogeneizzato(a) o·
mo·je·ne·eedz·dzah·to(a)

honest adj onesto(a) o·ne·sto(a)

honey n il miele mye·le

honeymoon n la luna di miele loo·na
dee mye·le; we're on our honeymoon
siamo in viaggio di nozze syah·mo
een vyaj·joh dee nots·tse

hood n il cappuccio kap·pooch·choh;
(of car) il cofano ko·fa·noh

hook n l'uncino (m) oon·chee·noh;
(fishing) l'amo (m) ah·moh; hook
and eye il gancio ad occhiello gan·
choh ad ok·kyel·loh

hoop n il cerchio chayr·kyoh

hoot vi (sound horn) suonare il clacson
swo·nah·ray eel klak·son

hop vi saltare su un piede solo sal·tah·
ray soo oon pye·de soh·lo

hope n la speranza spe·ran·tsa □ vi
sperare spe·rah·ray; I hope so/not
spero di sì/no spe·ro dee see/no

horizon n l'orizzonte (m) o·reedz·
dzohn·te

horizontal adj orizzontale o·reedz·
dzon·tah·le

horn n (of animal) il corno kor·noh;
(of car) il clacson klak·son

horrible adj orribile or·ree·bee·le

horror film, horror movie n il film
d'orrore feelm dor·roh·re

hors d'œuvre n l'antipasto (m) an·tee·
pa·stoh

horse n il cavallo ka·val·loh

horse-racing n le corse ippiche kohr·se
eep·pee·ke

horse-riding n l'equitazione (f) e·kwee·
ta·tsyoh·ne; to go horse-riding fare*
dell'equitazione fah·ray del·le·kwee·
ta·tsyoh·ne

hose n (pipe) il tubo flessibile too·boh
fles·see·bee·le

hospital n l'ospedale (m) o·spe·dah·le
I52, Ea6

hospitality n l'ospitalità (f) o·spee·ta·
lee·ta

host n l'ospite (m) o·spee·te

hostage n l'ostaggio (m) o·staj·joh; to
take someone hostage prendere* qualcuno come ostaggio pren·de·re
kwal·koo·no koh·me o·staj·joh

hostel n l'ostello (m) o·stel·loh

hostess n l'ospite (f) o·spee·te

hot adj caldo(a) kal·do(a); (spicy) piccante peek·kan·te

hot dog n il hot-dog hot-dog

hotel n l'albergo (m) al·ber·goh B59,
A6, 29

hotplate n la piastra riscaldante pya·
stra ree·skal·dan·te

hot-water bottle n la borsa di acqua
calda bohr·sa dee ak·kwa kal·da

hour n l'ora (f) oh·ra

hourly adv ogni ora ohn·yee oh·ra

house n la casa kah·sa; on the house
offerto(a) dalla casa of·fer·to(a) dal·
la kah·sa A56f

housecoat n la vestaglia ve·stal·ya

household n la famiglia fa·meel·ya

housekeeper n la governante go·ver·
nan·te

housewife n la casalinga ka·sa·leen·ga

housework n il lavoro domestico la·
voh·roh do·me·stee·ko

housing n l'alloggio (m) al·loj·joh

hovercraft n l'hovercraft ho·ver·kraft

how adv come koh·me; how long?
quanto tempo? kwan·to tem·po; how
long have you been here? da quanto è
qui? da kwan·to e kwee; how many?
quanti(e)? kwan·teel·(te); how much?
quanto(a)? kwan·to(a); how many
people? quante persone? kwan·te
per·soh·ne; how much milk? quanto
latte? kwan·to lat·te

however conj tuttavia toot·ta·vee·a

hug vt abbracciare ab·brach·chah·ray

hullo excl ciao chow

human adj umano(a) oo·mah·no(a)

hump n (on road) il dosso dos·soh

humpback bridge n il ponte con dosso
pohn·te kohn dos·soh

hundred num cento chen·to; a hundred
and one centuno chen·too·no; a hundred and two centodue chen·to·doo·
e; a hundred (and) eighty five centot-
tantacinque chen·tot·tan·ta·cheen·
kwe; a hundred people cento persone
chen·to per·soh·ne; hundreds of

books centinaia di libri *chen·tee·na·ya dee lee·bree*

hundredth *adj* centesimo(a) *chen·te·zee·mo(a)*

Hungarian *adj* ungherese *oon·ge·ray·se* □ *n* ungherese (*m*) *oon·ge·ray·se*

Hungary *n* Ungheria (*f*) *oon·ge·ree·a*

hunger *n* la fame *fah·me*

hungry *adj* affamato(a) *af·fa·mah·to(a)*; to be hungry avere* fame *a·vay·re fah·me*

hunt *vt* cacciare *kach·chah·re*

hurricane *n* l'uragano (*m*) *oo·ra·gah·noh*

hurry *vi* affrettarsi *af·fret·tar·see*; hurry up! faccia presto! *fach·cha pre·sto* □ *n* to be in a hurry avere* fretta *a·vay·re frayt·ta* B63, Ea10

hurt *vi* dolere* *do·lay·re*; that hurts! quello fa male! *kwayl·lo fa mah·le*; to hurt oneself farsi* male *far·see mah·le*

husband *n* il marito *ma·ree·toh* T115, S103

hut *n* (*shed*) la capanna *ka·pan·na*; (*on mountain*) il rifugio *ree·foo·joh*

hygienic *adj* igienico(a) *ee·je·nee·ko(a)*

hymn *n* l'inno (*m*) *een·noh*

hypermarket *n* l'ipermercato (*m*) *ee·per·mer·kah·toh*

hyphen *n* il trattino *trat·tee·noh*

hysterical *adj* isterico(a) *ee·ste·ree·ko(a)*

I

I *pron* io *ee·o*

ice *n* il ghiaccio *gyach·choh* A90

icebox *n* la ghiacciaia *gyach·cha·ya*

ice cream *n* il gelato *je·lah·toh*

ice cube *n* il cubetto di ghiaccio *koo·bayt·toh dee gyach·choh*

ice hockey *n* l'hockey su ghiaccio (*m*) *ho·kee soo gyach·choh*

Iceland *n* Islanda (*f*) *ee·slan·da*

ice lolly *n* il ghiacciolo *gyach·cho·loh*

icing *n* (*on cake*) la glassa *glas·sa*

idea *n* l'idea (*f*) *ee·de·a*

ideal *adj* ideale *ee·de·ah·le*

identical *adj* identico(a) *ee·den·tee·ko(a)*

identify *vt* identificare *ee·den·tee·fee·kah·ray*

identity card *n* la carta d'identità *kar·ta dee·den·tee·ta*

idiot *n* l'idiota (*m*/*f*) *ee·dyo·ta*

if *conj* se *say*

ignition *n* (*car*) l'accensione (*f*) *ach·chen·syoh·ne*

ignition key *n* la chiave dell'accensione *kyah·ve del·lach·chen·syoh·ne* T182

ignorant *adj* ignorante *een·yo·ran·te*

ignore *vt* (*person*) ignorare *een·yo·rah·ray*

ill *adj* malato(a) *ma·lah·to(a)*

illegal *adj* illegale *eel·le·gah·le*

illegitimate *adj* illegittimo(a) *eel·lay·jeet·tee·moh(a)*

illness *n* la malattia *ma·lat·tee·a*

illuminations *pl* l'illuminazione (*f*) *eel·loo·mee·na·tsyoh·ne*

illustration *n* l'illustrazione (*f*) *eel·loo·stra·tsyoh·ne*

imagination *n* l'immaginazione (*f*) *eem·ma·jee·na·tsee·oh·nay*

imagine *vt* immaginare *eem·ma·jee·nah·ray*

imitate *vt* imitare *ee·mee·tah·ray*

immediate *adj* immediato(a) *eem·me·dyah·to(a)*

immediately *adv* subito *soo·bee·to*

immersion heater *n* lo scaldabagno *skal·da·ban·yoh*

immigrant *adj* l'immigrante (*m*/*f*) *eem·mee·gran·te*

impatient *adj* impaziente *eem·pa·tsyen·te*

imperfect *adj* difettoso(a) *dee·fet·toh·so(a)*

impersonal *adj* impersonale *eem·per·so·nah·le*

import *n* l'importazione (*f*) *eem·por·ta·tsyoh·ne* □ *vt* importare *eem·por·tah·ray*

importance *n* l'importanza (*f*) *eem·por·tan·tsa*

important *adj* importante *eem·por·tan·te*

importer *n* l'importatore (*m*) *eem·por·ta·toh·re*

impossible *adj* impossibile *eem·pos·see·bee·le*

impress *vt* (*win approval*) impressionare *eem·pres·syoh·nah·ray*

impression *n* l'impressione (*f*) *eem·pres·syoh·ne*

impressive *adj* impressionante *eem·pres·syoh·nan·te*

improve *vt*/*i* migliorare *meel·yo·rah·ray*

improvement *n* il miglioramento *meel·yo·ra·mayn·toh*

in *prep* in *een*; put it in the box lo metta nella scatola *lo mayt·ta nel·la skah·to·la*; in May in maggio *een maj·joh*; he did it in 2 days l'ha fatto in 2 giorni *la fat·to een 2 johr·nee*; he'll be back in 2 days tornerà fra 2 giorni *tor·ne·ra fra 2 johr·nee*; in town/France in città/Francia *een cheet·ta/fran·cha*; in Italian in italiano *een ee·ta·lyah·noh* □ *adv* is he in? è a casa? *e a kah·sa*; the train is in il treno è arrivato *eel tre·noh e ar·ree·vah·to*

incentive *n* l'incentivo (*m*) *een·chen·tee·voh*

inch *n* il pollice *pol·lee·che*

incident *n* (*event*) l'avvenimento (*m*) *av·ve·nee·mayn·toh*

incinerator *n* l'inceneritore (*m*) *een·che·ne·ra·toh·re*

include *vt* includere* *een·kloo·de·re*

including *prep* compreso(a) *kom·pray·so(a)*

inclusive *adj* (*costs*) globale *glo·bah·le*; from 6th to 12th inclusive dal 6 al 12 incluso *dal 6 al 12 een·kloo·zo* □ *adv* inclusive of service servizio compreso *ser·vee·tsyoh kom·pray·so*

income *n* il reddito *red·dee·toh*

income tax *n* l'imposta sul reddito (*f*) *eem·poh·sta sool red·dee·toh*

incomplete *adj* incompleto(a) *een·kom·play·toh(a)*

inconvenient *adj* poco pratico(a) *po·ko pra·tee·ko(a)*; (*time, place*) scomodo(a) *sko·mo·do(a)*

incorrect *adj* sbagliato(a) *zbal·ya·toh(a)*

increase *vt*/*i* aumentare *ow·men·tah·ray* □ *n* (*in size*) l'accrescimento (*m*) *ak·kre·shee·mayn·toh*; (*in number*) l'aumento (*m*) *ow·mayn·toh*

incredible *adj* incredibile *een·kre·dee·bee·le*

indecent *adj* indecente *een·day·chen·tay*

independence *n* l'indipendenza (*f*) *een·dee·pen·den·tsa*

independent *adj* indipendente *een·dee·pen·den·te*

index *n* l'indice (*m*) *een·dee·che*
index-linked *adj* (*interest rates etc*) legato(a) all'indice del costo della vita *le·gah·to(a) al·leen·dee·che del ko·stoh del·la vee·ta*
India *n* l'India (*f*) *een·dee·a*
Indian *adj* indiano(a) *een·dee·ah·no(a)* □ l'indiano(a) (*m/f*) *een·dee·ah·no(a)*
indicator *n* (*of car*) la freccia *fraych·cha*
indigestible *adj* indigesto(a) *een·dee·je·sto(a)*
indigestion *n* l'indigestione (*f*) *een·dee·je·styoh·ne*
indirect *adj* (*route*) indiretto(a) *een·dee·ret·to(a)*
individual *adj* individuale *een·dee·vee·doo·ah·le*
individually *adv* singolarmente *seen·go·lar·mayn·te*
indoor *adj* (*games*) al coperto *al ko·per·to*
indoors *adv* (*be*) in casa *een kah·sa*; (*go*) dentro *dayn·tro*
industrial *adj* industriale *een·doo·stree·ah·le*
industry *n* l'industria (*f*) *een·doo·stree·a*
inedible *adj* immangiabile *eem·man·jah·bee·le*
inefficient *adj* inefficiente *een·ef·fee·chen·te*
inevitable *adj* inevitabile *een·e·vee·tah·bee·le*
inexpensive *adj* poco costoso(a) *po·ko ko·stoh·so(a)*
infection *n* l'infezione (*f*) *een·fe·tsyoh·ne*
infectious *adj* infettivo(a) *een·fet·tee·vo(a)*
inferior *adj* inferiore *een·fe·ryoh·re*
inflammable *adj* infiammabile *een·fyam·mah·bee·le*
inflammation *n* l'infiammazione (*f*) *een·fyam·ma·tsyoh·ne* 127
inflatable *adj* gonfiabile *gon·fyah·bee·le*
inflate *vt* gonfiare *gon·fee·ah·re*
inflation *n* (*economic*) l'inflazione (*f*) *een·fla·tsyoh·ne* Bm26
influence *n* l'influenza (*f*) *een·floo·en·tsa*
inform *vt* avvisare *av·vee·zah·ray*
informal *adj* (*party*) informale *een·for·mah·le* S57
information *n* le informazioni *een·for·ma·tsyoh·nee*
information desk/office *n* l'ufficio informazioni (*m*) *oof·fee·choh een·for·ma·tsyoh·nee*
ingredients *pl* gli ingredienti *een·gre·dyen·tee*
inhabit *vt* abitare in *a·bee·tah·ray een*
inhabitant *n* l'abitante (*m/f*) *a·bee·tan·te*
inherit *vt* ereditare *e·re·dee·tah·ray*
initials *pl* le iniziali *ee·nee·tsyah·lee*
injection *n* l'iniezione (*f*) *een·ye·tsyoh·ne*
injure *vt* ferire *fe·ree·re*
injured *adj* ferito(a) *fe·ree·to(a)* I16
injury *n* la ferita *fe·ree·ta*
ink *n* l'inchiostro (*m*) *een·kyo·stroh*
Inland Revenue *n* il fisco *fee·skoh*
inn *n* la locanda *lo·kan·da*
innocent *adj* innocente *een·no·chen·te*
inoculation *n* la vaccinazione *vach·chee·na·tsyoh·nay*
input *n* (*computing*) l'input (*m*) *een·poot*

insect *n* l'insetto (*m*) *een·set·toh* S40
insect repellent *n* l'insettifugo (*m*) *een·set·tee·foo·goh*
inside *n* l'interno (*m*) *een·ter·noh* □ *adj* the inside wall la parete interna *la pa·ray·te een·ter·na* □ *prep* inside the box dentro la scatola *dayn·tro la skah·to·la* □ *adv* to be/go inside stare*/andare* dentro *stah·ray/an·dah·ray dayn·tro*; to turn something inside out rivoltare qualcosa *ree·vol·tah·ray kwal·ko·sa*
insist *vi* insistere* *een·see·ste·re*; to insist on something insistere* su qualcosa *een·see·ste·re soo kwal·ko·sa*
insolent *adj* insolente *een·so·len·te*
inspect *vt* ispezionare *een·spe·tsyoh·nah·ray*; (*ticket*) controllare *kon·trol·lah·ray*
inspector *n* (*police*) l'ispettore di polizia (*m*) *ee·spet·toh·re dee po·lee·tsee·a*; (*of tickets*) il controllore *kon·trol·loh·re*
instal(l)ment *n* la rata *rah·ta* M11
instant *adj* immediato(a) *eem·me·dyah·to(a)*; instant coffee il caffè solubile *kaf·fe so·loo·bee·le* □ *n* instant l'istante (*m*) *ee·stan·te*
instead *adv* invece *een·vay·che*; instead of invece di *een·vay·che dee*
institute *n* l'istituto (*m*) *ee·stee·too·toh*
instructions *pl* le istruzioni *ee·stroo·tsyoh·nee*
instructor *n* l'istruttore (*m*) *ee·stroot·toh·re*
instructress *n* l'istruttrice (*f*) *ee·stroot·tree·chay*
instrument *n* lo strumento *stroo·mayn·toh*
insulin *n* l'insulina (*f*) *een·soo·lee·na*
insult *n* l'insulto (*m*) *een·sool·toh* □ *vt* insultare *een·sool·tah·ray*
insurance *n* l'assicurazione (*f*) *as·see·koo·ra·tsyoh·ne* T116, 189
insurance company *n* la compagnia di assicurazione *kom·pan·yee·a dee as·see·koo·ra·tsyoh·ne* T213
insurance policy *n* la polizza di assicurazione *po·leets·tsa dee as·see·koo·ra·tsyoh·ne*
insure *vt* assicurare *as·see·koo·rah·ray* □ *vi* to insure against something assicurarsi contro qualcosa *as·see·koo·rar·see kohn·tro kwal·ko·sa*
insured *adj* assicurato(a) *as·see·koo·rah·to(a)*
intelligence *n* l'intelligenza (*f*) *een·tel·lee·jen·tsa*
intelligent *adj* intelligente *een·tel·lee·jen·te*
intend *vt* destinare *de·stee·nah·ray*; to intend to do something avere* l'intenzione di fare qualcosa *a·vay·re leen·ten·tsyoh·ne dee fah·ray kwal·ko·sa*
intention *n* l'intenzione (*f*) *een·ten·tsyoh·ne*
interchange *n* (*on roads*) l'incrocio (*m*) *een·kroh·choh*
intercom *n* il citofono *chee·to·foh·noh*
interest *n* l'interesse (*m*) *een·te·res·se*; (*hobby*) il passatempo *pas·sa·tem·poh* □ *vt* interessare *een·te·res·sah·ray*
interested *adj* interessato(a) *een·te·res·sah·to(a)*; to be interested in interessarsi a *een·te·res·sar·see a*
interesting *adj* interessante *een·te·res·san·te*
interest rate *n* il tasso d'interesse *tas·soh deen·te·res·se*

interfere vi intromettersi* een·tro·mayt·ter·see

interior adj interiore een·te·ryoh·re

internal adj interno(a) een·ter·no(a)

Internal Revenue n il fisco fee·skoh

international adj internazionale een·ter·na·tsyoh·nah·le Sn16

interpret vt interpretare een·ter·pre·tah·ray □ vi fare* da interprete fah·ray da een·ter·pre·te

interpreter n l'interprete (m/f) een·ter·pre·te

interrupt vt/i interrompere* een·ter·rohm·pe·re

intersection n (of roads) l'incrocio (m) een·kroh·choh

interval n (in performance) l'intervallo (m) een·ter·val·loh L51

interview n (for job) il colloquio kol·lo·kwee·oh

into prep in een

introduce vt (person) presentare pre·zen·tah·ray Mc27

introduction n (in book) l'introduzione (f) een·tro·doo·tsyoh·ne; (social) la presentazione pre·zen·ta·tsyoh·ne

invalid n l'invalido (m) een·va·lee·doh

invent vt inventare een·ven·tah·ray

invention n l'invenzione (f) een·ven·tsyoh·ne

inventory n l'inventario (m) een·ven·tah·ryoh

invest vt/i investire een·ve·stee·re

investment n l'investimento (m) een·ve·stee·mayn·toh

investor n l'azionista (m/f) a·tsyoh·nee·sta

invisible adj invisibile een·vee·zee·bee·lay

invitation n l'invito (m) een·vee·toh

invite vt invitare een·vee·tah·ray

invoice n la fattura fat·too·ra

iodine n lo iodio ee·oh·dee·oh

Iran n Iran (m) ee·ran

Iraq n Irak (m) ee·rak

Ireland n Irlanda (f) eer·lan·da

Irish adj irlandese eer·lan·day·se

iron n (metal, golf club) il ferro fer·roh; (for clothes) il ferro da stiro fer·roh da stee·roh □ vt stirare stee·rah·ray

ironmonger n il negoziante in ferramenta ne·go·tsyan·te een fer·ra·mayn·ta

is vi è she/he is è

island n l'isola (f) ee·zo·la; (traffic) il salvagente pedonale sal·va·jen·te pe·do·nah·le

Israel n Israele (m) ee·zra·e·le

issue n (matter) la questione kwe·styoh·ne; (of magazine) il numero noo·me·roh; (of stocks) l'emissione (f) e·mees·syoh·ne

it pron □ it's blue è azzurro(a) e adz·dzoor·ro(a); take it lo/la prenda lo/la pren·da; it's me sono io soh·no ee·o; it's raining piove pyo·ve; it's 5 kilometres sono 5 chilometri soh·no 5 kee·lo·me·tree

Italian adj italiano(a) ee·ta·lyah·no(a) □ n l'italiano (m) ee·ta·lyah·noh Mc28

Italy n l'Italia (f) ee·ta·lya

itch n il prurito proo·ree·toh □ vi prudere* proo·de·re

item n l'articolo (m) ar·tee·ko·loh

itemized adj (bill etc) dettagliato(a) dayt·tal·ya·toh(a)

its adj suo soo·o, sua soo·a; (with plural noun) suoi swoy, sue soo·e

ivory n l'avorio (m) a·vo·ryoh

J

jack n (for car) il cric kreek; (cards) il fante fan·te

jacket n la giacca jak·ka

jail n la prigione pree·joh·nay; in jail in prigione een pree·joh·nay

jam vi (machine) bloccarsi blok·kar·see □ n la marmellata mar·mel·lah·ta; (in traffic) l'ingorgo (m) een·gohr·goh

janitor n il portiere por·tye·re

January n gennaio (m) jen·na·yoh

Japan n il Giappone jap·poh·ne

Japanese adj giapponese jap·po·nay·se □ n il giapponese jap·po·nay·se

jar n il barattolo ba·rat·to·loh

jaw n la mascella ma·shel·la

jazz n il jazz jazz L43

jealous adj geloso(a) je·loh·so(a)

jeans pl n i blue-jeans bloo·jeens

jeep n la jeep jeep

jello, jelly n la gelatina je·la·tee·na

jellyfish n la medusa me·doo·za

jerkin n la giacca a vento jak·ka a ven·toh

jersey n (fabric) il jersey jer·zee; (sweater) la maglia mal·ya

jet n (plane) l'avietto (m) a·vyo·jet·toh

jetty n il pontile pon·tee·le

Jew n l'ebreo (m) e·bre·oh

jewel n il gioiello jo·yel·loh

jeweller n il gioielliere jo·yel·lye·re

jewellery n i gioielli jo·yel·lee S84

Jewish adj ebreo(a) e·bre·o(a)

jigsaw (puzzle) n il puzzle puz·zuhl

jingle n (advertising) la cantilena kan·tee·le·na

job n (employment) l'impiego (m) eem·pye·goh; (task) il compito kohm·pee·toh Mc39

jockey n il fantino fan·tee·noh

jogging n il footing foo·teeng; to go jogging fare* del footing fah·ray del foo·teeng

join vt unire oo·nee·re; (club) diventare socio di dee·ven·tah·ray so·cho dee; do join us venga pure con noi ven·ga poo·re kohn noy

joint n (of body) la giuntura joon·too·ra; (of meat) la trancia di carne tran·cha dee kar·ne

joint ownership n la comproprietà kom·pro·pree·e·ta

joint-stock company n la società per azioni so·che·ta payr a·tsyoh·nee

joke n lo scherzo skayr·tsoh

joker n (cards) il jolly jol·lee

journalist n il/la giornalista johr·na·lee·sta

journey n il viaggio vyaj·joh

joy n la gioia jo·ya

jubilee n il giubileo joo·bee·le·oh

judge n il giudice joo·dee·che □ vt giudicare joo·dee·kah·ray

judo n il judo joo·doh

jug n la brocca brok·ka

juice n il succo sook·koh E63

jukebox n il juke-box jook·boks

July n luglio (m) lool·yoh

jumbo jet n il jumbo joom·boh

jump vt/i saltare sal·tah·ray; to jump (over) a wall saltare un muricciolo sal·tah·ray oon moo·reech·cho·loh

jumper n (dress) lo scamiciato ska·mee·chah·toh; (sweater) il maglione mal·yoh·ne

jump leads pl i conduttori elettrici ee·kon·doot·toh·ree e·let·tree·chee

junction n (in road) l'incrocio (m) een·kroh·choh; (railway) il nodo ferroviario no·doh fer·ro·vee·ah·ree·oh

June n giugno (m) joon·yoh

junior adj (class, pupil) elementare e·le·men·tah·ray

junket n la giuncata joon·kah·ta

just adv □ just here proprio qui pro·pree·o kwee; he's just left è appena partito e ap·pay·na par·tee·to; it was just a mistake non era che un errore nohn e·ra ke oon er·roh·re; I just managed it ci sono appena riuscito chee so·no ap·pay·na ree·oo·shee·to; just above the elbow poco sopra il gomito po·ko soh·pra eel go·mee·toh; it only just missed è mancato per poco e man·kah·to payr po·ko; he arrived just now è arrivato proprio ora e ar·ree·vah·to pro·pree·o oh·ra

justice n la giustizia joo·stee·tsya

K

karate n il karatè ka·rah·te

kebab n il kebab ke·bab

keen adj (swimmer, reader) appassionato(a) ap·pas·syoh·nah·to(a)

keep n il sostentamento so·sten·ta·mayn·toh; to earn one's keep guadagnarsi la vita gwa·dar·yar·see la vee·ta □ vt keep (retain) tenere* te·nay·re; (feed and clothe) mantenere* man·te·nay·re; to keep something till later tenere* qualcosa per piú tardi te·nay·re kwal·ko·sa payr pyoo tar·dee; to keep something in the fridge tenere* qualcosa nel frigo te·nay·re kwal·ko·sa nel free·goh; keep the change! tenga il resto! ten·ga eel re·stoh; to keep something tidy tenere* qualcosa in ordine te·nay·re kwal·ko·sa een ohr·dee·ne □ vi milk doesn't keep very well il latte non si conserva molto bene eel lat·te nohn see kon·ser·va mohl·to be·ne

Kenya n Kenia (m) ken·ya

kerb n il bordo della strada bohr·doh del·la strah·da

kerosene n il cherosene ke·ro·ze·ne

ketchup n il ketchup ke·chup

kettle n il bollitore bol·lee·toh·re

key n la chiave kyah·ve; (of piano, typewriter) il tasto ta·stoh B68, A41, 60

keyhole n il buco della serratura boo·koh del·la ser·ra·too·ra

key ring n il portachiavi por·ta·kyah·vee

kick n il calcio kal·choh □ vt (person) dare* un calcio a dah·ray oon kal·choh a; (ball) calciare kal·chah·ray

kid n (leather) il capretto ka·prayt·toh

kidnap vt rapire ra·pee·re

kidney n (of person) il rene re·ne; (to eat) il rognone ron·yoh·ne

kidney beans pl i fagioli rossicci fa·jo·lee ros·seech·chee

kill vt uccidere* ooch·chee·de·re

killer n l'assassino (m) as·sas·see·noh

kilo n il chilo kee·loh S31

kilogram(me) n il chilogrammo kee·lo·gram·moh

kilometer, kilometre n il chilometro kee·lo·me·troh T197

kilowatt n il chilowatt kee·lo·vat

kilt n il kilt keelt

kind n (type) il genere je·ne·re; a kind of bean una specie di fagiolo oo·na spe·che dee fa·jo·loh □ adj kind gentile jen·tee·le

king n il re ray

kiosk n (for newspapers) l'edicola (f) e·dee·ko·la; (telephone) la cabina ka·bee·na

kirsch n il kirsch keersh

kiss vt baciare ba·chah·ray; to kiss (each other) baciarsi ba·char·see □ n kiss il bacio bah·choh

kit n (sports) l'equipaggiamento (m) e·kwee·paj·ja·mayn·toh

kitchen n la cucina koo·chee·na

kite n l'aquilone (m) a·kwee·loh·ne

kleenex n il fazzolettino di carta fats·tso·let·tee·noh dee kar·ta

knee n il ginocchio jee·nok·kyoh; to sit on someone's knee sedersi* sul·le ginocchia di qualcuno se·dayr·see sool·le jee·nok·kya dee kwal·koo·no

kneel vi inginocchiarsi een·jee·nok·kyar·see; to kneel down mettersi* in ginocchio mayt·ter·see een jee·nok·kyoh

knife n il coltello kol·tel·loh

knit vt/i lavorare a maglia la·vo·rah·ray a mal·ya; to knit a sweater fare* un maglione fah·ray oon mal·yoh·ne

knitting needle n il ferro da calza fer·roh da kal·tsa

knitwear n la maglieria mal·ye·ree·a

knob n (on door) il pomo poh·moh; (on radio etc) la manopola ma·no·po·la

knock vt colpire kol·pee·re; to knock (at) the door bussare alla porta boos·sah·ray al·la por·ta; to knock down abbattere ab·bat·te·re; to knock out mettere* k.o. mayt·te·re kappa·oh □ vi knocking (engine) picchiare peek·kyah·ray

knot n annodare an·no·dah·ray □ n il nodo no·doh; to tie a knot fare* un nodo fah·ray oon no·doh

know vt (person) conoscere* ko·noh·she·re; (fact, subject) sapere* sa·pay·re; to know how to do something sapere* fare qualcosa sa·pay·re fah·ray kwal·ko·sa

knowledge n la conoscenza ko·no·shen·tsa

knuckle n la nocca nok·ka

kohlrabi n il cavolo rapa kah·vo·loh rah·pa

kosher adj kasher kah·sher

L

label n l'etichetta (f) e·tee·kayt·ta □ vt etichettare e·tee·ket·tah·ray

laboratory n il laboratorio la·bo·ra·to·ryoh

labo(u)r n la manodopera mah·no·do·pe·ra

labo(u)rer n il manovale ma·no·vah·le

labo(u)r force n la manodopera mah·no·do·pe·ra

lace n il pizzo peets·tsoh; (of shoe) il laccio lach·choh

lacquer n (for hair) la lacca lak·ka

ladder n la scala skah·la; (in stocking) la smagliatura zmal·ya·too·ra

ladle n il ramaiolo ra·ma·yo·loh

lady n la signora seen·yoh·ra

lager n la birra chiara beer·ra kyah·ra

lake n il lago lah·goh

lamb n l'agnello (m) an·yel·loh S37

lambswool n la lana d'agnello lah·na dan·yel·loh

lamp n la lampada lam·pa·da

lamppost n il lampione lam·pyoh·ne

lampshade n il paralume pa·ra·loo·me

land n (opposed to sea) la terra ter·ra;

(*country*) il paese *pa·ay·ze*; (*soil*) la terra *ter·ra*; (*property*) la proprietà *pro·pree·e·ta* □ *vi* (*from ship*) sbarcare *zbar·kah·ray*; (*plane*) atterrare *at·ter·rah·ray*

landing *n* (*of plane*) l'atterraggio (*m*) *at·ter·raj·joh*; (*on stairs*) il pianerottolo *pya·ne·rot·to·loh*

landing stage *n* il pontile *pon·tee·le*

landing strip *n* la pista d'atterraggio *pee·sta dat·ter·raj·joh*

landlady *n* la padrona *pa·droh·na*

landlord *n* il padrone *pa·droh·ne*

landmark *n* il punto di riferimento *poon·toh dee ree·fe·ree·mayn·toh*

landslide *n* la frana *frah·na*

lane *n* (*in country*) il viottolo *vee·ot·to·loh*; (*in town*) il vicolo *vee·ko·loh*; (*of road*) la corsia *kor·see·a*

language *n* la lingua *leen·gwa*; (*way one speaks*) il linguaggio *leen·gwaj·joh*

language laboratory *n* il laboratorio linguistico *la·bo·ra·to·ryoh leen·gwee·stee·ko*

lanolin *n* la lanolina *la·no·lee·na*

lap *n* (*of track*) il giro *jee·roh*; (*of person*) il grembo *grem·boh*

lard *n* il lardo *lar·doh*

larder *n* la dispensa *dee·spen·sa*

large *adj* grande *gran·de*

laryngitis *n* la laringite *la·reen·jee·te*

last *adj* ultimo(a) *ool·tee·mo(a)*; **last night** stanotte *sta·not·te*; **last week** la settimana scorsa *la set·tee·mah·na skohr·sa* □ *adv* last per ultimo *payr ool·tee·mo*; **at last** alla fine *al·la fee·ne* □ *vi* durare *doo·rah·ray*

latch *n* il saliscendi *sa·lee·shayn·dee*

late *adj* (*not on time*) in ritardo *een ree·tar·doh* □ *adv* tardi *tar·dee*; **late in the day** tardi *tar·dee*; **the latest news** le ultime notizie *le ool·tee·me no·tee·tsye*; **the late king** il fu re *eel foo re*

lately *adv* recentemente *re·chen·te·mayn·te*

later *adj* (*date etc*) posteriore *po·ste·ree·oh·re*; (*version*) piú recente *pyoo re·chen·te* □ *adv* (*to come etc*) piú tardi *pyoo tar·dee*

Latin *n* il latino *la·tee·noh* □ *adj* latino(a) *la·tee·no(a)*

Latin America *n* l'America Latina (*f*) *a·me·ree·ka la·tee·na*

Latin American *adj* latinoamericano(a) *la·tee·no·a·me·ree·kah·no(a)*

laugh *vi* ridere* *ree·de·re*; **to laugh at somebody** ridere* di qualcuno *ree·de·re dee kwal·koo·no* □ *n* laugh il riso *ree·soh*

laughter *n* le risa *ree·sa*

launch *n* la motolancia *mo·to·lan·cha* □ *vt* (*ship*) varare *va·rah·ray*; (*product*) lanciare *lan·chah·ray*

launderette *n* la lavanderia automatica *la·van·de·ree·a ow·to·ma·tee·ka* Sn71

laundry *n* (*place*) la lavanderia *la·van·de·ree·a*; (*clothes*) il bucato *boo·kah·toh* A52, Sn72

lavatory *n* la toeletta *to·e·let·ta*

law *n* la legge *layj·je*; **law and order** l'ordine pubblico (*m*) *ohr·dee·ne poob·blee·ko*

lawn *n* (*grass*) il prato rasato *prah·toh ra·sah·to*

lawn mower *n* la falciatrice *fal·cha·tree·che*

lawn tennis *n* il tennis su erba *ten·nees soo er·ba*

lawyer *n* l'avvocato (*m*) *av·vo·kah·toh* Sn83

laxative *n* il lassativo *las·sa·tee·voh*

lay *vt* posare *po·sah·ray*; **to lay the table** apparecchiare la tavola *ap·pa·rek·kyah·ray la tah·vo·la*; **to lay the fire** preparare il fuoco *pre·pa·rah·ray eel fwo·koh*; **to lay down** deporre* *de·pohr·re*; (*wine*) mettere* in cantina *mayt·te·re een kan·tee·na*; **to lay off** (*workers*) licenziare *lee·chen·tsyah·ray*

lay-by *n* la piazzola *pyats·tso·la*

layer *n* lo strato *strah·toh*

lazy *adj* pigro(a) *pee·gro(a)*

lead¹ *vt* condurre* *kon·door·re* □ *vi* (*in contest*) essere* in testa *es·se·re een te·sta*; **this door leads into the garden** questa porta dà sul giardino *kway·sta por·ta da sool jar·dee·noh* □ *n* **lead** (*electrical*) il filo *fee·loh*; (*dog's*) il guinzaglio *gween·tsal·yoh*

lead² *n* il piombo *pyohm·boh*; (*in pencil*) la mina *mee·na*

leaf *n* la foglia *fol·ya*

leak *n* (*water*) la perdita *per·dee·ta*; (*gas*) la fuga *foo·ga* □ *vi* fare* acqua *fah·ray ak·kwa* T179, Sn50

lean *adj* (*meat*) magro(a) *ma·gro(a)* □ *vi* pendere *pen·de·re*; **to lean against something** appoggiarsi a qualcosa *ap·poj·jar·see a kwal·ko·sa*

learn *vt* imparare *eem·pa·rah·ray*

learner(-driver) *n* il guidatore principiante *gwee·da·toh·re preen·chee·pyan·te*

lease *n* l'affitto (*m*) *af·feet·toh*

leash *n* il guinzaglio *gween·tsal·yoh*

least *adj* □ **the least money** il meno denaro *eel may·no de·nah·roh*; **the least amount** la minima quantità *la mee·nee·ma kwan·tee·ta* □ *adv* **the least expensive** il meno caro *eel may·no kah·ro* □ *n* **he has the least** ha il meno *a eel may·no*; **at least** almeno *al·may·no*; **not in the least** per niente *payr nyen·te*

leather *n* il cuoio *kwo·yoh*

leave *n* (*holiday*) il congedo *kon·je·doh*; **on leave** in congedo *een kon·je·doh* □ *vi* partire *par·tee·re* □ *vt* (*room*) uscire* da *oo·shee·re da*; (*club, school, object, message*) lasciare *la·shah·ray*; **leave it to me** lasci fare a me *la·shee fah·ray a may*; **to leave out** (*omit*) omettere* *o·mayt·te·re*

lecture *n* la conferenza *kon·fe·ren·tsa*

ledger *n* il mastro *ma·stroh*

leek *n* il porro *por·roh*

left *adv* □ **there's some cream left** ci avanza un po' di panna *chee a·van·tsa oon po dee pan·na*; **to turn left** girare a sinistra *jee·rah·ray a see·nee·stra* □ *adj* **the left side** il lato sinistro *lah·to see·nee·stro* T104

left-handed *adj* mancino(a) *man·chee·no(a)*

left luggage office *n* il deposito bagagli *de·po·zee·toh ba·gal·yee* T24

leg *n* (*of person*) la gamba *gam·ba*; (*of animal*) la zampa *tsam·pa*; **leg of lamb** il cosciotto d'agnello *ko·shoht·toh dan·yel·loh*; **chicken leg** la coscia di pollo *ko·sha dee pohl·loh* I21

legal *adj* legale *le·gah·le*

leisure *n* l'ozio (*m*) *o·tsyoh*

leisure centre *n* il circolo ricreativo *cheer·ko·loh ree·kre·a·tee·vo*

lemon *n* il limone *lee·moh·ne*

lemonade *n* la limonata *lee·mo·na·ta*

lemon juice n il succo di limone sook·koh dee lee·moh·ne

lemon sole n la sogliola sol·yo·la

lemon-squeezer n lo spremilimoni spre·mee·lee·moh·nee

lend vt prestare pre·stah·ray

length n la lunghezza loon·gayts·tsa

lens n (of glasses) la lente len·te; (of camera) l'obiettivo (m) o·byet·tee·voh

lentils pl le lenticchie len·teek·kye

less adj □ less meat meno carne may·no kar·ne □ adv less quickly meno rapidamente may·no ra·pee·da·mayn·te □ n he has less non ha meno ne a may·no; less than meno di/che may·no deel/kay

lesson n la lezione le·tsyoh·ne

let vt (allow) lasciare la·shah·ray; (rent out) affittare af·feet·tah·ray; to let someone do something permettere* a qualcuno di fare qualcosa payr·mayt·te·re a kwal·koo·no dee fah·ray kwal·ko·sa; let me in mi lasci entrare mee la·shee en·trah·ray; let's go andiamo an·dyah·mo; they let him go lo hanno lasciato andare lo an·no la·shah·to an·dah·ray; to let (house etc) affittasi af·feet·ta·see; to let someone down deludere* qualcuno de·loo·de·re kwal·koo·no

letter n la lettera let·te·ra B71, A25, Sn1

letter box n la buca per le lettere boo·ka payr le let·te·re

lettuce n la lattuga lat·too·ga

level n il livello lee·vel·loh □ adj (surface) piano(a) pyah·no(a); (horizontal) orizzontale o·reedz·dzon·tah·le

level crossing n il passaggio a livello pas·saj·joh a lee·vel·loh

lever n la leva le·va

Levis pl i blue-jeans bloo·jeens

liabilities pl (on balance sheet) il passivo pas·see·voh

library n la biblioteca bee·blee·o·te·ka

Libya n Libia (f) lee·bya

licence, license n (for driving) la patente di guida pa·ten·te dee gwee·da

license plate n la targa d'immatricolazione tar·ga deem·ma·tree·ko·la·tsyoh·ne T207

lick vt leccare lek·kah·ray

licorice n la liquirizia lee·kwee·reet·tsya

lid n il coperchio ko·per·kyoh

lie n (untruth) la bugia boo·jee·a □ vi giacere* ja·chay·re; (tell a lie) mentire* men·tee·re; to lie down sdraiarsi zdra·yar·see

Liechtenstein n Liechtenstein (m) leekh·ten·shtine

life n la vita vee·ta; for life a vita a vee·ta

lifebelt n la cintura di salvataggio cheen·too·ra dee sal·va·taj·joh

lifeboat n (on ship) la scialuppa di salvataggio sha·loop·pa dee sal·va·taj·joh; (from shore) il battello di salvataggio bat·tel·loh dee sal·va·taj·joh

lifeguard n il bagnino ban·yee·noh

life insurance n l'assicurazione sulla vita (f) as·see·koo·ra·tsyoh·ne sool·la vee·ta

life jacket n la giacca di salvataggio jak·ka dee sal·va·taj·joh

life preserver n (belt) la cintura di salvataggio cheen·too·ra dee sal·va·taj·joh; (jacket) la giacca di salvataggio jak·ka dee sal·va·taj·joh

lift vt sollevare sol·le·vah·ray □ n (elevator) l'ascensore (m) a·shen·

soh·re; to give somebody a lift dare* un passaggio a qualcuno dah·ray oon pas·saj·joh a kwal·koo·no A30

light vt (fire, cigarette) accendere* ach·chen·de·re; to light up (car) accendere* i fari ach·chen·de·re ee fah·ree □ n light la luce loo·che; (lamp) la lampada lam·pa·da; (on car) il faro fah·roh; (traffic light) il semaforo se·mah·fo·roh; have you got a light? mi fa accendere? mee fa ach·chen·de·re □ adj light (bright, pale) chiaro(a) kyah·ro(a); (not heavy) leggero(a) lej·je·ro(a); light music la musica leggera moo·zee·ka lej·je·ra; as soon as it was light allo spuntar del giorno al·lo spoon·tar del john·noh

light bulb n la lampadina lam·pa·dee·na

lighter n l'accendino (m) ach·chen·dee·noh S101

lighthouse n il faro fah·roh

light industry n l'industria leggera (f) een·doo·strya lej·je·ra

lighting n (on road) l'illuminazione (f) eel·loo·mee·na·tsyoh·ne; when is lighting-up time? quando accendono le luci? kwan·do ach·chen·do·no le loo·chee

light meter n il fotometro fo·to·me·troh

lightning n il lampo lam·poh

like prep come koh·me □ adj simile see·mee·le; what's it like? com'è? kohm·e □ vt like piacere* a pya·chay·re a; I'd like to go mi piacerebbe andare mee pyah·che·reb·be an·dah·ray; I'd like an ice cream gradirei un gelato gra·dee·re·e oon je·lah·toh; what would you like? che cosa vorrebbe? ke ko·sa vor·reb·be S20, 21

likely adj probabile pro·bah·bee·le; he's likely to come è probabile che venga e pro·bah·bee·le ke ven·ga

lily n il giglio jeel·yoh

lime n (fruit) il cedro chay·droh

lime juice n il succo di cedro sook·koh dee chay·droh

limit n il limite lee·mee·te

limousine n la limousine lee·moo·zeen

limp vi zoppicare tsop·pee·kah·ray

line n la linea lee·ne·a; (railway) il binario ben·nah·ryoh; (telephone) la linea lee·ne·a; (people waiting) la coda koh·da; to stand in line fare* la coda fah·ray la koh·da

linen n (cloth) il lino lee·noh; (for beds, table) la biancheria byan·ke·ree·a

liner n (ship) il transatlantico trans·at·lan·tee·koh

lining n la fodera fo·de·ra

lino(leum) n il linoleum lee·no·le·oom

lint n la garza gar·dza

lion n il leone le·oh·ne

lip n il labbro lab·broh

lipstick n il rossetto ros·sayt·toh

liqueur n il liquore lee·kwoh·re E14

liquid n il liquido lee·kwee·doh □ adj liquido(a) lee·kwee·do(a)

liquid assets pl la liquidità lee·kwee·dee·ta

liquidation n la liquidazione lee·kwee·da·tsyoh·ne; to go into liquidation andare* in liquidazione an·dah·ray oon lee·kwee·da·tsyoh·ne

liquor n gli alcolici al·ko·lee·chee

list n l'elenco (m) e·len·koh □ vt elencare e·len·kah·ray

listen vi ascoltare a·skol·tah·ray; to listen to ascoltare a·skol·tah·ray

list price n il prezzo di catalogo prets·tsoh dee ka·tah·lo·goh

liter n il litro lee·troh

literature n la letteratura let·te·ra·too·ra

litre n il litro lee·troh T155

little adj piccolo(a) peek·ko·lo(a) □ n a little un po' oon po

live[1] adj (alive) vivo(a) vee·vo(a)

live[2] vi vivere· vee·ve·re; (reside) abitare a·bee·tah·ray

lively adj vivace vee·vah·che

liver n il fegato fay·ga·toh

living room n il salotto sa·lot·toh

load n il carico kah·ree·koh □ vt caricare ka·ree·kah·ray

loaf (of bread) n il pane pah·ne

loan n il prestito pre·stee·toh □ vt prestare pre·stah·ray

lobby n (entrance) il vestibolo ve·stee·bo·loh

lobster n l'aragosta (f) a·ra·goh·sta

local adj locale lo·kah·le; the local shops i negozi del quartiere ee ne·go·tsee del kwar·tye·re; a local call (on phone) una chiamata urbana oo·na kya·mah·ta oor·bah·na E10

lock n (on door) la serratura ser·ra·too·ra; (in canal) la chiusa kyoo·sa □ vt chiudere· a chiave kyoo·de·re a kyah·ve; the door's locked la porta è chiusa a chiave la por·ta e kyoo·sa a kyah·ve A47

locker n l'armadietto (m) ar·mah·dyayt·toh

lodger n l'inquilino(a) (m/f) een·kwee·lee·no(a)

lodgings pl l'alloggio (m) al·loj·joh

loft n la soffitta sof·feet·ta

log n (of wood) il ceppo chayp·poh

logbook n (of car) il libretto di circolazione lee·brayt·toh dee cheer·ko·la·tsyoh·ne

lollipop n il lecca-lecca layk·layk·ka

London n Londra (f) lohn·dra

lonely adj (person) solitario(a) so·lee·tah·ryo(a)

long adj lungo(a) loon·go(a); how long is the river? quant'è lungo il fiume? kwan·te loon·go eel fyoo·me; 6 metres long lungo(a) 6 metri loon·go(a) 6 me·tree; how long is the programme? quanto dura il programma? kwan·to doo·ra eel pro·gram·ma; 6 months long che dura 6 mesi ke doo·ra 6 may·see □ adv long a lungo a loon·go; all day long tutta la giornata toot·ta la jor·nah·ta; I shan't be long non prenderò molto tempo nohn pren·de·ro mohl·to tem·poh; as long as (provided that) purché poor·kay

long-distance adj (phone call) interurbano(a) een·tayr·oor·bah·no(a)

long drink n il long drink long dreenk

long-sighted adj presbite prez·bee·te

long-term adj a lunga scadenza a loon·ga ska·den·tsa

long wave n le onde lunghe ohn·de loon·ge

look n lo sguardo zgwar·doh; (appearance) l'aspetto (m) a·spet·toh □ vi guardare gwar·dah·ray; (appear) sembrare sem·brah·ray; to look at guardare gwar·dah·ray; to look like rassomigliare ras·so·meel·yah·ray; to look after curare koo·rah·ray; to look for cercare cher·kah·ray; to look forward to non vedere· l'ora di nohn

ve·day·re loh·ra dee; look out! attenzione! at·ten·tsyoh·ne; to look up (word) cercare cher·kah·ray

loop n il cappio kap·pyoh

loose adj (knot) sciolto(a) shol·to(a); (clothing) ampio(a) am·pyo(a); (stone) fuori posto fwo·ree poh·stoh

lorry n il camion ka·myon

lorry driver n il camionista ka·myo·nee·sta

lose vt perdere· per·de·re; to lose one's way smarrirsi zmar·reer·see si vi lose (clock, watch) ritardare ree·tar·dah·ray Sn82

loss n la perdita per·dee·ta Sn79

lost property office n l'ufficio oggetti smarriti (m) oof·fee·choh oj·jet·tee zmar·ree·tee

lot n (at auction) il lotto lot·toh; lots of or a lot of milk molto latte mohl·to lat·te; lots of or a lot of people molta gente mohl·ta jen·te; a lot better molto meglio mohl·to mel·yo

lotion n la lozione lo·tsyoh·ne

lottery n la lotteria lot·te·ree·a

loud adj (voice) forte for·te

loudly adv fortemente for·te·mayn·te

loudspeaker n l'altoparlante (m) al·to·par·lan·te

lounge n (in house) il salotto sa·lot·toh; (in hotel) il salone sa·loh·ne; (at airport) la sala d'aspetto sah·la da·spet·toh

love vt amare a·mah·ray; to love doing something piacere· molto a qualcuno fare qualcosa pya·chay·re mohl·to a kwal·koo·no fah·ray kwal·ko·sa; I'd love to go mi piacerebbe andare mee pyah·che·reb·be an·dah·ray □ n love l'amore (m) a·moh·re; in love innamorato(a) een·na·mo·rah·to(a); love from (on letter) affettuosamente af·fet·too·oh·sa·mayn·te

lovely adj bello(a) bel·lo(a); we had a lovely time ci siamo divertiti un mondo chee syah·mo dee·ver·tee·tee oon mohn·doh

low adj basso(a) bas·so(a)

Low Countries pl i Paesi Bassi pa·ay·zee bas·see

lower adj inferiore een·fe·ryoh·re

low tide n la bassa marea bas·sa ma·re·a

L.P. n il longplaying long·ple·eeng

Ltd abbrev S.r.l. es·se·er·re·el·le

luck n la fortuna for·too·na; good luck! buona fortuna! bwo·na for·too·na; bad luck la sfortuna sfor·too·na

lucky adj fortunato(a) for·too·nah·to(a)

luggage n i bagagli ba·gal·yee T21f, A24

luggage rack n il portabagagli por·ta·ba·gal·yee

luggage trolley n il carrello per bagagli kar·rel·loh payr ba·gal·yee T25

lump n (on skin) il gonfiore gon·fyoh·re; (in sauce) il grumo groo·moh; lump of sugar la zolletta di zucchero tsol·layt·ta dee tsook·ke·roh

lunch n il pranzo pran·dzoh A26, E6

lunch hour n l'ora di pranzo (f) oh·ra dee pran·dzoh

lung n il polmone pol·moh·ne

Luxemburg n Lussemburgo (m) loos·sem·boor·goh

luxurious adj sontuoso(a) son·too·oh·so(a)

luxury n il lusso loos·soh □ adj (car, hotel) di lusso dee loos·soh

M

macaroni n i maccheroni mak·ke·roh·nee

machine n la macchina mak·kee·na

machinery n il macchinario mak·kee·nah·ryoh

mackerel n lo scombro skohm·broh

mack(intosh) n l'impermeabile (m) eem·payr·may·ah·bee·lay

mad adj (insane) pazzo(a) pats·tsoh(a); (angry) furioso(a) foo·ree·oh·soh(a)

madam n signora (f) seen·yoh·ra

Madeira n (wine) il madera ma·de·ra

made-to-measure adj fatto(a) su misura fat·toh(a) soo mee·zoo·ra

Madrid n Madrid (f) ma·dreed

magazine n (journal) la rivista ree·vee·sta

magic n la magia ma·jee·a □ adj magico(a) ma·jee·koh(a)

magnet n la calamita ka·la·mee·ta

magnetic tape n il nastro magnetico nas·troh man·ye·tee·koh

magnificent adj magnifico(a) man·yee·fee·koh(a)

mahogany n il mogano mo·ga·noh

maid n la domestica do·me·stee·ka A67

maiden name n il cognome da nubile kon·yoh·may da noo·bee·lay

maid service n il servizio della domestica sayr·vee·tsyoh del·la do·mes·tee·ka

mail n la posta pos·ta □ vt mandare per posta man·dah·ray payr pos·ta

mailbox n la cassetta della posta kas·say·ta del·la pos·ta

mailing list n l'elenco di indirizzi (m) e·len·koh dee een·dee·ree·tsee

mailman n il postino po·stee·noh

mail order n □ to buy something by mail order comprare qualcosa per corrispondenza kom·prah·ray kwal·ko·sa payr kor·ree·spon·den·tsa

main adj principale preen·chee·pah·lay □ n to turn the electricity/water off at the mains chiudere* l'elettricità/l'acqua al contatore kyoo·de·re le·let·tree·chee·ta/lak·kwa al kon·ta·toh·re

mainland n il continente kon·tee·nen·tay

mainly adv principalmente preen·chee·pal·mayn·tay

maintenance n la manutenzione ma·noo·ten·tsyoh·nay

maize n il mais ma·ees

major adj principale preen·chee·pah·lay

majority n la maggioranza maj·jo·ran·tsa; elected by a majority of 5 eletto(a) con una maggioranza di 5 voti e·let·toh(a) kon oo·na maj·jo·ran·tsa dee 5 voh·tee

make n (of product) la marca mahr·ka □ vt fare* fah·ray; to make the beds rifare* i letti ree·fah·ray·ee let·tee; to make someone sad rattristare qualcuno rat·tree·stah·ray kwal·koo·noh; to make someone do something far fare* qualcosa a qualcuno fahr fah·ray kwal·koh·sa a kwal·koo·noh; to make do with something arrangiarsi con qualcosa ar·ran·jahr·see kon kwal·koh·sa; to make (oneself) up truccarsi trook·kahr·see

make-up n il trucco trook·koh

male adj maschio mask·yo

mallet n il maglio mal·yo

malt n il malto mal·toh

Malta n Malta (f) mal·ta

malt (whisky) n il whisky di malto wees·kee dee mal·toh

man n l'uomo (m) wo·moh

manage vt (business) dirigere* dee·ree·je·ray; can you manage? ce la fa? chay la fa; to manage to do something riuscire* a fare qualcosa ree·oo·shee·ray a fah·ray kwal·ko·sa

management n la direzione dee·rets·yo·nay

manager n il direttore dee·ret·toh·ray M31

manageress n la direttrice dee·ret·tree·chay

managing director, M.D. n il direttore generale dee·ret·toh·ray je·ne·rah·lay

manicure n la manicure ma·nee·koo·ray

manicure set n il nécessaire per unghie nay·ses·sayr payr oon·gye

man-made adj artificiale ahr·tee·fee·chah·lay

manner n (way) il modo mo·doh; (attitude) l'atteggiamento (m) at·tej·ja·mayn·toh

manners pl le maniere man·ye·ray

manpower n la manodopera mah·noh·do·pe·ra

mansion n il palazzo pa·lats·tsoh

mantelpiece n il caminetto ka·mee·nayt·toh

manual adj manuale ma·nwah·lay □ n (book) il manuale ma·nwah·lay

manufacture vt fabbricare fab·bree·kah·ray

manufacturer n il fabbricante fab·bree·kan·tay

manufacturing n la fabbricazione fab·bree·ka·tsyo·nay

many pron molti mohl·tee □ adj many books molti libri mohl·tee lee·bree

map n (of country) la carta geografica kahr·ta jay·oh·gra·fee·ka; (of town) la pianta pyan·ta F7, L3, S94

marble n (material) il marmo mahr·moh; (ball) la bilia beel·ya

March n marzo (m) mahr·tsoh

march n il marciare mahr·chah·ray □ n la marcia mahr·cha

margarine n la margarina mahr·ga·ree·na

margin n (on page) il margine mahr·jee·nay

marina n il porticciolo por·teech·cho·loh

marjoram n la maggiorana maj·jo·rah·na

mark n il segno sen·yo; (stain) la macchia mak·kya; (currency) il marco mahr·koh; (in school) il voto voh·toh □ vt segnare sen·yah·ray; (stain) macchiare mak·kyah·ray

market n il mercato mayr·kah·toh □ vt (product) vendere vayn·de·ray Bm16

market-day n il giorno di mercato johr·noh dee mayr·kah·toh

marketing n il marketing mahr·ke·ting

marketing manager n il direttore di marketing dee·ret·toh·ray dee mahr·ke·ting

market-place n la piazza del mercato pyats·tsa del mayr·kah·toh

market research n la ricerca di mercato ree·chayr·ka dee mayr·kah·toh

market value n il valore di mercato va·loh·ray dee mayr·kah·toh

marmalade n la marmellata d'arance mahr·mel·lah·tah dar·an·chay

maroon adj bordeaux bor·doh

marriage n il matrimonio ma·tree·mon·yoh

married adj sposato(a) *spo·zah·toh(a)*; they were married yesterday si sono sposati ieri *see so·noh spo·zah·tee ye·ree* Mc42

marrow n (vegetable) la zucca *tsook·ka*

marry vt sposare *spo·zah·ray* □ vi sposarsi *spo·zahr·see*

martini n (Brit) il Martini *mahr·tee·nee*; (US) il gin con Martini *jeen kon mahr·tee·nee*

marvellous adj meraviglioso(a) *me·ra·veel·yoh·soh(a)*

marzipan n il marzapane *mahr·tsa·pah·nay*

mascara n il mascara *mas·ka·ra*

masculine adj maschile *mas·kee·lay*

mash vt schiacciare *skya·chah·ray*

mashed potatoes pl il purè di patate *poo·re dee pa·tah·tay*

mask n la maschera *mas·ke·ra* □ vt mascherare *mas·ke·rah·ray*

mass n (church) la messa *mes·sa*; a mass of blossom una massa di fiori *oo·na mas·sa dee fyo·ri*

massage n il massaggio *mas·saj·joh* □ vt massaggiare *mas·saj·jah·ray*

masseur n il massaggiatore *mas·saj·ja·toh·re*

masseuse n la massaggiatrice *mas·saj·ja·tree·chay*

massive adj massiccio(a) *mas·see·choh(a)*

mass-produce vt fabbricare in serie *fab·bree·kah·ray een ser·ye*

mass production n la produzione in serie *pro·doo·tsyoh·nay een ser·ye*

mast n (ship's) l'albero (m) *al·be·roh*; (radio) l'antenna trasmittente (f) *an·tayn·na tras·meet·ten·tay*

master n il maestro *ma·ay·stroh*

master key n il passe-partout *pas·par·too*

masterpiece n il capolavoro *kah·po·la·voh·roh*

mat n la stuoia *stoo·oy·a*; (place mat) il sottopiatto *sot·toh·pyat·toh*; (under a glass) il sottobicchiere *sot·toh·beek·kyie·ray*

match n il fiammifero *fyam·mee·fe·roh*; (sport) la partita *par·tee·ta* □ vt intonarsi a *een·to·nahr·see* a S99

matchbox n la scatola di fiammiferi *skah·to·la dee fyam·mee·fe·ree*

material n il materiale *ma·te·ryah·lay*; (fabric) la stoffa *stof·fa* S60

maternity dress il pré-maman *pray·ma·man*

maternity hospital n la maternità *ma·tayr·nee·ta*

mathematics n la matematica *ma·te·ma·tee·ka*

matter n □ what's the matter? che c'è? *ke che* □ vi it doesn't matter non fa niente *nohn fa nyen·tay*

mattress n il materasso *ma·te·ras·soh*

mature adj (wine) maturo(a) *ma·too·roh(a)*; (cheese) stagionato(a) *sta·jo·nah·toh(a)*

mauve adj malva *mal·va*

maximize vt portare al limite massimo *por·tah·ray al lee·mee·tay mas·see·moh*

maximum n il massimo *mas·see·moh* □ adj massimo(a) *mas·see·moh(a)*

May n maggio (m) *maj·joh*

may vi □ may I come in? posso entrare? *pos·soh en·trah·ray*; it may rain potrà piovere *po·tra pyo·ve·ray*; we may as well go ci varrebbe andare *chee var·reb·bay an·dah·ray*

Mayday n il segnale di soccorso *sen·yah·lay dee sok·kohr·soh*

mayonnaise n la maionese *ma·yo·nay·say*

mayor n il sindaco *seen·da·koh*

me pron mi *mee*; give it to me me lo dia *may loh dee·a*; he gave it to me me lo diede *may loh dye·day*; it's me sono io *so·noh ee·oh*

meal n il pasto *pas·toh* T42, E47

mean adj (miserly) tirchio(a) *teer·kyoh(a)*; (unkind) meschino(a) *mes·kee·noh(a)* □ vt (signify) significare *seen·yee·fee·kah·ray*; to mean to do avere* l'intenzione di fare *a·vayr·ay leen·ten·tsyo·nay dee fah·ray*

meaning n il significato *seen·yee·fee·kah·toh*

means pl i mezzi *medz·dzee*; by means of per mezzo di *payr medz·dzoh dee*

meanwhile adv intanto *een·tan·toh*

measles n il morbillo *mor·beel·loh*

measure vt/i misurare *mee·zoo·rah·ray*

measurements pl le misure *mee·zoo·ray*

meat n la carne *kahr·nay*

mechanic n il meccanico *mek·kan·ee·koh* T167

media pl i mass media *mass mee·dee·a*

medical adj medico(a) *me·dee·koh(a)*

medicine n (pills etc) la medicina *me·dee·chee·na*

Mediterranean adj mediterraneo(a) *me·dee·ter·rah·nay·oh(a)*; the Mediterranean (Sea) il Mediterraneo *me·dee·ter·rah·nay·oh*

medium adj medio(a) *me·dee·o(a)*; medium wave le onde medie *ohn·day me·dee·ay*

meet vt (encounter) incontrare *een·kon·trah·ray*; (make acquaintance of) fare* la conoscenza di *fah·ray la kon·o·shen·tsa dee*; (demand) rispondere* a *ree·spon·de·ray* a; I'll meet you at the station (go to get) verrò a prenderla alla stazione *ver·roh a pren·dayr·la al·la sta·tsyoh·nay*

meeting n la riunione *ree·oon·yoh·nay*

melon n il melone *me·loh·nay*

melt vi sciogliersi* *shol·yer·see* □ vt fondere* *fohn·de·ray*

member n il socio *so·choh* T5, L57

memo(randum) n la nota *no·ta*

memory n la memoria *me·mo·ree·a*; one of my memories un mio ricordo *oon mee·oh mee·kahr·day*

mend vt riparare *ree·pa·rah·ray*

menswear n l'abbigliamento per uomo (m) *ab·beel·ya·mayn·toh payr wo·moh*

mental hospital n l'ospedale psichiatrico (m) *o·spe·dah·lay psee·kee·a·tree·koh*

mentholated adj al mentolo *al men·to·loh*

mention vt menzionare *men·tsyo·nah·ray*; don't mention it non c'è di che! *nohn che dee kay*

menu n il menù *me·noo* E8

merchant n il mercante *mayr·kan·tay*; (shop keeper) il negoziante *ne·go·tsyan·tay*

merchant bank n la banca commerciale *ban·ka kom·mayr·chah·lay*

merge vi fondersi* *fohn·der·see*

merger n la fusione *foo·zyoh·nay*

meringue n la meringa *me·reen·ga*

merry adj gaio(a) *ga·yoh(a)*

merry-go-round n la giostra *jo·stra*

mess n il disordine *dee·zohr·dee·nay*; to make a mess mettere* in disordine met·te·ray een dee·zohr·dee·nay; to make a mess of (spoil) rovinare ro·vee·nah·ray

message n il messaggio mes·saj·joh

messenger n il messaggero mes·saj·je·roh

metal n il metallo me·tal·loh

meter n il contatore kon·ta·toh·ray; (measure) il metro met·roh

method n il metodo me·to·doh

Methodist n il metodista me·to·dees·sta

methylated spirits pl l'alcool denaturato (m) al·kol day·na·too·rah·toh

metre n il metro met·roh

metric adj metrico(a) met·ree·koh(a)

Mexican adj messicano(a) me·see·ka·noh(a)

Mexico n Messico (m) mes·see·koh

microchip n il microchip mee·kro·chip

microcomputer n il microcomputer mee·kro·kom·poo·tayr

microfiche n la microscheda mee·kro·ske·da

microfilm n il microfilm mee·kro·feelm

microphone n il microfono mee·kro·fo·noh

microprocessor n il microprocessor mee·kro·pro·ches·sohr

microwave oven n il forno a microonde fohr·noh a mee·kro·ohn·day

midday n il mezzogiorno medz·dzo·johr·noh; at midday a mezzogiorno a medz·dzo·johr·noh

middle n il mezzo medz·dzoh; right in the middle nel bel mezzo nel bel medz·dzoh; in the middle of the night nel cuore della notte nel kwo·ray del·la not·tay

middle-aged adj di mezza età dee medz·dza ay·ta

middle-class adj borghese bor·gay·say

Middle East n il Medio Oriente med·yoh o·ree·en·tay

middle management pl i quadri medi kwa·dree me·dee

midnight n la mezzanotte medz·dza·not·tay; at midnight a mezzanotte a medz·dza·not·tay

midwife n la levatrice le·va·tree·chay

might vi □ it might rain potrebbe piovere po·treb·bay pyo·ve·ray; we might as well go tanto vale che andiamo tan·toh vah·lay kay an·dya·moh

migraine n l'emicrania (f) e·mee·krah·nee·a

mild adj (weather) mite mee·tay; (cigarette) leggero(a) lej·je·roh(a); (taste) dolce dohl·chay

mile n il miglio meel·yoh

miles per hour, m.p.h. miglia all'ora meel·ya al·loh·ra

mileage n ≈ il chilometraggio kee·lo·me·traj·joh T113

military adj militare mee·lee·tah·ray

milk n il latte lat·tay E61, S34

milk chocolate n il cioccolato al latte chok·ko·lah·toh al lat·tay

milkman n il lattaio lat·ta·yoh

milkshake n il frullato di latte frool·lah·toh dee lat·tay

mill n il mulino moo·lee·noh; (for coffee) il macinino ma·chee·nee·noh □ vt macinare ma·chee·nah·ray

milligram(me) n il milligrammo meel·lee·gram·moh

millilitre n il millilitro meel·lee·lee·troh

millimetre n il millimetro meel·lee·me·troh

million num il milione mee·lee·oh·nay

millionaire n il milionario mee·lee·o·nah·ree·oh

millionth adj milionesimo(a) mee·lee·o·ne·zee·moh(a)

milometer n ≈ il contachilometri kon·ta·kee·lo·me·tree

mince vt tritare tree·tah·ray □ n (meat) la carne tritata kahr·nay tree·tah·ta

mincer n il tritacarne tree·ta·kahr·nay

mind n la mente mayn·tay; to change one's mind cambiare idea kam·byah·ray ee·de·a; to make up one's mind decidersi* de·chee·der·see □ vt I don't mind the heat non mi dispiace il caldo nohn mee dee·spyah·chay eel kal·doh; I don't mind non mi importa nohn mee eem·por·ta; never mind non importa nohn eem·por·ta; do you mind if...? le spiace se...? le spyah·chay se; mind the step attenzione allo scalino at·ten·tsyoh·nay al·loh ska·lee·noh

mine pron il mio eel mee·oh, la mia la mee·a; (plural) i miei ee me·ay·ee; le mie le mee·ay □ n (for coal etc) la miniera mee·nye·rah

miner n il minatore ma·na·toh·ray

mineral water n l'acqua minerale (f) a·kwa me·ne·rah·lay

minestrone (soup) n il minestrone mee·ne·stroh·nay

minibus n il pullmino pool·mee·noh

minicab n il minitassì mee·nee·tas·see

minicomputer n il minicomputer mee·nee·kom·poo·ter

minimum n il minimo mee·nee·moh □ adj minimo(a) mee·nee·moh(a)

miniskirt n la minigonna mee·nee·gohn·na

minister n (in government) il ministro mee·nee·stroh; (of religion) il pastore pa·stoh·ray S88

ministry n (government) il ministero mee·nee·ste·roh

mink n (fur) il visone vee·zoh·nay

mink coat n il mantello di visone man·tel·loh dee vee·zoh·nay

minor adj (road) secondario(a) se·kon·dah·ree·oh(a); (injury) leggero(a) lej·je·roh(a); minor operation l'intervento minore (m) een·tayr·ven·toh mee·noh·ray

minority n la minoranza mee·no·ran·tsa

mint n (herb) la menta mayn·ta; (confectionery) la caramella alla menta ka·ra·mel·la al·la mayn·ta

minus prep meno may·noh; at minus 2 degrees a 2 gradi sotto zero a 2 grah·dee soht·toh dze·roh

minute n il minuto mee·noo·toh; just a minute un momento oon mo·mayn·toh

mirror n lo specchio spek·kyoh S70

miscarriage n l'aborto (m) a·bor·toh

miserable adj infelice een·fe·lee·chay

misprint n l'errore di stampa (f) er·roh·ray dee stam·pa

Miss n Signorina (f) seen·yo·ree·na

miss vt (target) mancare man·kah·ray; (train) perdere* payr·de·ray; (signpost) non vedere* nohn ve·day·ray; I miss London sento la mancanza di Londra sen·toh la man·kan·tsa dee lohn·dra; to miss out omettere* oh·mayt·te·ray

missing adj (object) smarrito(a) zmar·ree·toh(a); (person) disperso(a) dee·spayr·soh(a); some pages are missing mancano alcune pagine man·ka·noh al·koo·nay pah·jee·nay; my wallet is

missing è sparito il mio portafoglio *e spa·ree·toh eel mee·oh por·ta·fol·yoh*

mist *n* la foschia *fo·skee·a*

mistake *n* lo sbaglio *zbal·yoh*; **by mistake** per sbaglio *payr zbal·yoh*; **to make a mistake** sbagliarsi *zbal·yahr·see* B40, E45

mistress *n* (*lover*) l'amante (*f*) *a·man·tay*; (*school*) la maestra *ma·ay·stra*

mitt(en) *n* la manopola *ma·no·po·la*

mix *vt* mescolare *me·sko·lah·ray*; **to mix up** (*confuse*) confondere* *kon·fohn·de·ray* □ *vi* mix mescolarsi *me·sko·lahr·see*

mixed *adj* (*co-ed*) misto(a) *mee·stoh(a)*; **mixed grill** il misto di carne ai ferri *eel mee·stoh dee kahr·nay a·ee fer·ree*

mixer *n* il frullatore *frool·la·toh·ray*

mixture *n* la mescolanza *me·sko·lan·tsa*

moan *n* il gemito *je·mee·toh* □ *vi* gemere *je·me·ray*

model *n* il modello *mo·del·loh*; (*mannequin*) l'indossatrice (*f*) *een·dos·sa·tree·chay*; **this year's model** il modello di quest'anno *eel mo·del·loh dee kway·stan·noh*; **a model railway** una ferrovia in miniatura *oo·na fer·ro·vee·a een mee·nya·too·ra*

modern *adj* moderno(a) *mo·der·noh(a)* S84

modernize *vt* modernizzare *mo·der·needz·dzah·ray*

modest *adj* modesto(a) *mo·de·stoh(a)*

modification *n* la modifica *mo·dee·fee·ka*

modify *vt* modificare *mo·dee·fee·kah·ray*

mohair *n* il mohair *mo·er*

molasses *n* la melassa *me·las·sa*

molecule *n* la molecola *mo·le·ko·la*

moment *n* il momento *mo·mayn·toh*; **at the moment** in questo momento *een kway·stoh mo·mayn·toh*

mom(my) *n* la mamma *mam·ma*

Monaco *n* Monaco (*f*) *mo·na·koh*

monastery *n* il monastero *mo·na·ste·roh*

Monday *n* lunedí (*m*) *loo·ne·dee*

monetary *adj* monetario(a) *mo·ne·tah·ree·oh(a)*

money *n* il denaro *de·nah·roh*; **to make money** fare* soldi *fah·ray sol·dee* M17, 18

money order *n* il vaglia *val·ya*

monitor *n* (*TV*) il monitore *mo·nee·toh·ray*

monk *n* il monaco *mo·na·koh*

monkey *n* la scimmia *sheem·mya*

mono *adj* mono *mo·noh*; **in mono** in mono *een mo·noh*

monopoly *n* il monopolio *mo·no·po·lyo*

monorail *n* la monorotaia *mo·no·ro·ta·ya*

monster *n* il mostro *moh·stroh*

month *n* il mese *may·say*

monthly *adj* mensile *men·see·lay* □ *n* il mensile *men·see·lay*

monument *n* il monumento *mo·noo·mayn·toh*

mood *n* l'umore (*f*) *oo·moh·ray*; **in a good mood** di buon umore *dee bwon oo·moh·ray*

moon *n* la luna *loo·na*

moor *vt* ormeggiare *or·mej·jah·ray*

mop *n* la scopa di cotone *sko·pa dee ko·toh·ne* □ *vt* asciugare *a·shoo·gah·ray*

moped *n* il ciclomotore *chee·klo·mo·toh·ray*

more *adj* ancora di *an·koh·ra dee*; **more cheese** ancora del formaggio *an·koh·ra del for·maj·joh*; **more people** piú gente *pyoo jen·tay* □ *pron* I'd like (some) more gradirei ancora un po' *gra·dee·ray an·koh·ra oon po* □ *adv* more dangerous than piú pericoloso che/di *pyoo pe·ree·ko·loh·soh kay/dee*; **more or less** piú o meno *pyoo o may·noh*

morning *n* la mattina *mat·tee·na*

Moroccan *adj* marocchino(a) *ma·rok·kee·noh(a)*

Morocco *n* il Marocco *ma·rok·koh*

mortgage *n* l'ipoteca (*f*) *ee·po·te·ka* □ *vt* ipotecare *ee·po·te·kah·ray*

Moscow *n* Mosca (*f*) *moh·ska*

moselle *n* (*wine*) il mosella *mo·zel·la*

mosque *n* la moschea *mo·skay·a*

mosquito *n* la zanzara *dzan·dzah·ra*

mosquito net *n* la zanzariera *dzan·dza·ree·e·ra*

most *adv* □ **the most beautiful** il/la piú bello(a) *eel/la pyoo bel·loh(a)* □ *adj* **most people** i piú *ee pyoo*; **the most cars** il piú grande numero di macchine *eel pyoo gran·day noo·me·roh dee mak·kee·nay* □ *pron* he has the most ne ha la maggior parte *nay a la maj·johr pahr·tay*; **at the most** al massimo al *mas·see·moh*; **to make the most of** sfruttare al massimo *sfroot·tah·ray al mas·see·moh*

motel *n* il motel *mo·tel*

moth *n* la falena *fa·le·na*

mother *n* la madre *mah·dray*

mother-in-law *n* la suocera *swo·che·ra*

motion *n* (*movement*) il movimento *mo·vee·mayn·toh*

motor *n* il motore *mo·toh·ray*

motorbike *n* la motocicletta *mo·to·chee·klayt·ta*

motorboat *n* il motoscafo *mo·to·skah·foh* L29

motorcyclist *n* il/la motociclista *mo·to·chee·klee·sta*

motorist *n* l'automobilista (*m/f*) *ow·to·mo·bee·lee·sta*

motor show *n* il salone dell'automobile *sa·loh·nay del·low·to·mo·bee·lay*

motorway *n* l'autostrada (*f*) *ow·to·strah·da*

mount *vt* montare *mon·tah·ray*

mountain *n* la montagna *mon·tan·ya*

mountaineering *n* l'alpinismo (*m*) *al·pee·nee·zmoh*; **to go mountaineering** fare* dell'alpinismo *fah·ray del·lal·pee·nee·zmoh*

mouse *n* il topo *to·poh*

mousse *n* la mousse *moos*

mouth *n* la bocca *bohk·ka*

move *vt* muovere* *mwo·ve·ray* □ *vi* muoversi* *mwo·ver·see*; (*traffic*) circolare *cheer·ko·lah·ray*; (*move house*) traslocarsi *traz·lo·kahr·see*; **to move in** trasferirsi *ra·sfe·reer·see*; **to move out** cambiare casa *kam·byah·ray kah·sa*

movement *n* il movimento *mo·vee·mayn·toh*

movie *n* il film *feelm*

moving walkway *n* il marciapiede a rulli *mar·cha·pye·day a rool·lee*

mow *vt* falciare *fal·chah·ray*

mower *n* la falciatrice *fal·cha·tree·chay*

Mr *n* Signor (*m*) *seen·yohr*

Mrs *n* Signora (*f*) *seen·yoh·ra*

Ms *n* Signorina (*f*) *seen·yo·ree·na*

much *adv* □ **much better** molto meglio

mohl·toh mel·yoh; much bigger molto piú grande *mohl·toh pyoo gran·day* □ adj much milk molto latte *mohl·toh lat·tay* □ pron have you got much? ne ha molto? *nay a mohl·toh;* not much non molto *nohn mohl·toh*

mud *n* il fango *fan·goh*

muddle *n* il pasticcio *pa·steech·choh;* in a muddle in disordine *een dee·zohr·dee·nay*

muddy *adj* (water) fangoso(a) *fan·goh·soh(a);* (clothes) infangato(a) *een·fan·gah·toh(a)*

mud-flap *n* il paraspruzzi *pa·ra·sproots·tsee*

mudguard *n* il parafango *pa·ra·fan·goh*

muffler *n* (on car) la marmitta *mar·meet·ta*

mug *n* la tazza *tats·tsa* □ vt assalire* *as·sa·lee·ray*

multilingual *adj* multilingue *mool·tee·leen·gway*

multinational *adj* multinazionale *mool·tee·nats·yo·nah·lay*

multiple store *n* il negozio a catena *ne·go·tsyoh a ka·tay·na*

multiplication *n* la moltiplicazione *mol·tee·plee·kats·yoh·nay*

multiply *vt* moltiplicare *mol·tee·plee·kah·ray;* to multiply 9 by 4 moltiplicare 9 per 4 *mol·tee·plee·kah·ray 9 payr 4*

multi-storey *adj* a piú piani *a pyoo pyah·nee*

mum(my) *n* la mamma *mam·ma*

mumps *n* gli orecchioni *o·rek·kyoh·nee*

Munich *n* Monaco di Baviera (f) *mo·na·koh dee Ba·vye·ra*

municipal *adj* municipale *moo·nee·chee·pah·lay*

murder *n* l'omicidio (m) *o·mee·chee·dee·oh* □ vt assassinare *as·sas·see·nah·ray*

muscle *n* il muscolo *moos·ko·loh*

museum *n* il museo *moo·ze·oh* F10, L3

mushroom *n* il fungo *foon·goh*

music *n* la musica *moo·zee·ka*

musician *n* il/la musicista *moo·zee·chee·sta*

Muslim *adj* musulmano(a) *moo·sool·mah·noh(a)* □ *n* il/la musulmano(a) *moo·sool·mah·noh(a)*

mussel *n* la cozza *kots·tsa*

must *vi* □ I must go devo andare *de·voh an·dah·ray;* you must come devo venire *de·vay ve·nee·ray*

mustard *n* la mostarda *mo·stahr·da*

mutton *n* la carne di montone *kahr·nay dee mon·toh·nay*

my *adj* mio(a) *mee·oh(a),* miei *mee·ay·ee,* mie *mee·ay;* my brothers i miei fratelli *ee mee·ay·ee fra·tel·lee;* my sisters le mie sorelle *lay mee·ay so·rel·lay*

myself *pron* io stesso(a) *ee·oh stays·soh(a);* I washed myself mi sono lavato(a) *mee so·noh la·vah·toh(a);* I did it myself l'ho fatto io stesso *loh fat·toh ee·oh stays·soh*

mystery *n* il mistero *mee·ster·oh*

N

nail *n* (human) l'unghia (f) *oon·gya;* (metal) il chiodo *kyo·do* □ vt inchiodare *een·kyo·dah·ray*

nailbrush *n* lo spazzolino da unghie *spats·tso·lee·noh da oon·gyay*

nailfile *n* la limetta *lee·mayt·ta*

nail polish, nail varnish *n* lo smalto *zmal·toh*

naked *adj* nudo(a) *noo·doh(a)*

name *n* il nome *noh·may;* what is your name? come Si chiama? *koh·may see kya·ma;* my name is Paul mi chiamo Paul *mee kya·moh Paul* B16, T212

nap *n* (sleep) il sonnellino *son·nel·lee·noh*

napkin *n* (for table) il tovagliolo *to·val·yo·loh*

nappy *n* il pannolino *pan·no·lee·noh*

narrow *adj* stretto(a) *strayt·toh(a)*

nasty *adj* cattivo(a) *kat·tee·voh(a)*

nation *n* la nazione *na·tsyoh·nay*

national *adj* nazionale *na·tsyoh·nah·lay;* national anthem l'inno nazionale (m) *een·noh na·tsyoh·nah·lay;* national dress il costume nazionale *ko·stoo·may na·tsyoh·nah·lay*

National Health Service ≈ il Servizio Sanitario Statale *sayr·vee·tsyoh sa·nee·tah·ryoh sta·tah·lay*

nationality *n* la nazionalità *na·tsyoh·na·lee·ta*

nationalize *vt* nazionalizzare *na·tsyoh·na·leedz·dzah·ray*

native *adj* nativo(a) *na·tee·voh(a)*

natural *adj* naturale *na·too·rah·lay* S60

naturalized *adj* naturalizzato(a) *na·too·ra·leedz·dzah·toh(a)*

naturally *adv* (of course) naturalmente *na·too·ral·mayn·tay*

nature *n* la natura *na·too·ra;* (type, sort) il genere *je·ne·ray*

naughty *adj* cattivo(a) *kat·tee·voh(a)*

nausea *n* la nausea *now·ze·a*

nave *n* la navata *na·vah·ta*

navy *n* la marina *ma·ree·na*

navy blue *adj* blu scuro *bloo skoo·roh*

near *adv* vicino *vee·chee·noh* □ prep near (to) the house vicino alla casa *vee·chee·noh al·la kah·sa;* near (to) Christmas sotto Natale *soht·toh na·tah·lay*

nearby *adv* qui vicino *kwee vee·chee·noh*

nearly *adv* quasi *kwah·zee*

neat *adj* ordinato(a) *or·dee·nah·toh(a);* (liquor) liscio(a) *lee·shoh(a)*

neck *n* il collo *kol·loh*

necklace *n* la collana *kol·lah·na*

necktie *n* la cravatta *kra·vat·ta*

need *vt* avere* bisogno di *a·vay·ray bee·zohn·yoh dee;* I need to go devo andare *de·voh an·dah·ray;* you needn't come non occorre che lei venga *nohn ok·kohr·ray kay le·ee ven·ga* S9

needle *n* l'ago (m) *ah·goh;* (on dial) la lancetta *lan·chayt·ta*

negative *n* (of photo) la negativa *ne·ga·tee·va*

negotiable *adj* negoziabile *ne·go·tsyah·bee·lay*

negotiate *vi* negoziare *ne·go·tsyah·ray*

negotiations *pl* le trattative *trat·ta·tee·vay*

neighbo(u)r *n* il/la vicino(a) *vee·chee·noh(a)*

neighbo(u)rhood *n* il vicinato *vee·chee·nah·toh*

neither *pron* né l'uno né l'altro *nay loo·noh nay lal·troh* □ adv neither ... nor né .... né *nay ... nay* □ conj I wasn't there and neither was he io non c'ero e nemmeno lui *ee·o nohn che·ro e nem·may·noh loo·ee*

nephew *n* il nipote *nee·poh·tay*

nerve *n* il nervo *ner·voh*; *(courage)* il coraggio *ko·raj·joh*

nervous *adj (person)* nervoso(a) *ner·voh·soh(a)*; **nervous breakdown** l'esaurimento nervoso *(m)* *e·zow·ree·mayn·toh ner·voh·so*

nest *n* il nido *nee·doh*

net *n* la rete *ray·tay* □ *adj (income, price)* netto(a) *nayt·toh(a)*; **net weight** il peso netto *pay·soh nayt·toh*

neutral *adj* neutrale *ne·oo·trah·lay* □ *n (gear)* in neutral in folle *een fol·lay*

never *adv* mai *ma·ee*; **he never comes** egli non viene mai *el·yee nohn vye·nay ma·ee*

new *adj* nuovo(a) *nwo·voh(a)*

news *n* le notizie *no·tee·tsye*

newsagent *n* il giornalaio *johr·na·la·yoh*

newspaper *n* il giornale *johr·nah·lay* S91

newsstand *n* l'edicola *(f)* *e·dee·ko·la*

New Year's Day *n* il Capodanno *kah·po·dan·noh*

New Year's Eve *n* la vigilia di Capodanno *vee·jeel·ya dee kah·po·dan·noh*

next *adj (stop, station, week)* prossimo(a) *pros·see·moh(a)*; **next of kin** il parente stretto *pa·ren·tay strayt·toh*

nice *adj* bello(a) *bel·loh(a)*; *(person)* simpatico(a) *seem·pa·tee·koh(a)*

niece *n* la nipote *nee·poh·tay*

night *n* la notte *not·tay* A8

night club *n* il night-club *nait·kloob* L44

nightdress *n* la camicia da notte *ka·mee·cha da not·tay*

nightmare *n* l'incubo *(m)* *een·koo·boh*

night porter *n* il portiere di notte *por·tye·ray dee not·tay*

night school *n* la scuola serale *skwo·la se·rah·lay*

nil *n* lo zero *dze·roh*

nine *num* nove *no·vay*

nineteen *num* diciannove *dee·chan·no·vay*

ninety *num* novanta *no·van·ta*

ninth *adj* nono(a) *no·noh(a)*

nipple *n (on bottle)* la tettarella *tet·ta·rel·la*

no *adv (as answer)* no *no*

nobody *pron* nessuno *nes·soo·noh*; **I can see nobody** non vedo nessuno *nohn vay·do nes·soo·noh*

noise *n* il rumore *roo·moh·ray*; *(loud)* il fragore *fra·goh·ray*

noisy *adj* rumoroso(a) *roo·mo·roh·soh(a)*

nominal *adj (fee)* simbolico(a) *seem·bo·lee·koh(a)*

non- *pref* non- *nohn-*

nonalcoholic *adj* analcolico(a) *a·nal·ko·lee·koh(a)*

none *pron* nessuno(a) *nes·soo·noh(a)*

nonsense *n* le sciocchezze *shok·kayts·tse*

nonsmoker *n (person)* il non-fumatore *nohn·foo·ma·toh·ray*; *(compartment)* lo scompartimento per non-fumatori *skom·par·tee·mayn·toh payr nohn·foo·ma·toh·ree*

noodles *pl* i taglierini *tal·ye·ree·nee*

noon *n* il mezzogiorno *medz·dzo·johr·noh*

no one *pron* nessuno *nes·soo·noh*; **I can see no one** non vedo nessuno *nohn vay·do nes·soo·noh*

normal *adj* normale *nor·mah·lay*

normally *adv (usually)* normalmente *nor·mal·mayn·tay*

north *n* il nord *nord* □ *adv* a nord *a nord* □ *n* **northeast** il nord-est *nord·est*; **northwest** il nord-ovest *nord·o·vest*

North America *n* l'America del Nord *(f)* *a·me·ree·ka del nord*

northern *adj* settentrionale *set·ten·tree·o·nah·lay*

North Pole *n* il Polo Nord *po·loh nord*

North Sea *n* il Mare del Nord *mah·ray del nord*

nose *n* il naso *nah·soh*

nosebleed *n* l'emorragia nasale *(f)* *e·mor·ra·jee·a na·sah·lay*

not *adv* non *nohn*; **he did not** *or* **didn't do it** egli non l'ha fatto *el·yee nohn la fat·to*; **not at all** non affatto *nohn af·fat·to*; *(don't mention it)* non c'è di che *nohn che dee kay*

note *n (music)* la nota *no·ta*; *(letter)* il biglietto *beel·yayt·toh*; *(banknote)* la banconota *ban·ko·no·ta* M20, 22

notepaper *n* la carta da lettere *kahr·ta da let·te·ray*, S92

nothing *n* niente *nyen·tay*

notice *n (poster)* l'avviso *(m)* *av·vee·zoh*; *(sign)* il cartello *kahr·tel·loh* □ *vt* notare *no·tah·ray*

notice board *n* il tabellone *ta·bel·loh·nay*

notions *pl* la merceria *mayr·che·ree·a*

nougat *n* il torrone *tor·roh·nay*

nought *n* lo zero *dze·roh*

novel *n (book)* il romanzo *ro·man·dzoh*

November *n* novembre *(m)* *no·vem·bre*

now *adv* ora *oh·ra*; **now and then**, **now and again** ogni tanto *on·yee tan·to*

nowadays *adv* oggigiorno *oj·jee·johr·noh*

nowhere *adv* in nessun luogo *een nes·soon lwo·goh*

nuclear *adj (energy, war)* nucleare *noo·klay·ah·ray*

nude *adj* nudo(a) *noo·doh(a)*

nuisance *n* la seccatura *sek·ka·too·ra*; **he's a nuisance** egli è una persona noiosa *el·yee e oo·na payr·soh·na no·yoh·sa*; **it's a nuisance** è un fastidio *e oon fa·stee·dyoh*

null and void *adj* nullo(a) e di nessun effetto *nool·loh(a) e dee nes·soon ef·fet·toh*

numb *adj (with cold)* intirizzito(a) *een·tee·reedz·dzee·toh(a)*

number *n (figure)* il numero *noo·me·roh*

numberplate *n* la targa d'immatricolazione *tahr·ga deem·ma·tree·ko·la·tsyoh·nay* T207

nun *n* la monaca *mo·na·ka*

nurse *n* l'infermiera *(f)* *een·fayr·mye·ra* □ *vt (patient)* curare *koo·rah·ray*

nursery *n* la camera dei bambini *kah·me·ra dey bam·bee·nee*

nursery slope *n* la pista per principianti *pee·sta payr preen·chee·pee·an·tee*

nursing home *n* la casa di cura *kah·sa dee koo·ra*

nylon *n* il nailon *nai·lon*

O

oak *n* la quercia *kwer·cha*

oar *n* il remo *re·moh*

oats *pl* l'avena *(f)* *a·vay·na*

obedient *adj* obbediente *ob·be·dyen·te*

obey *vi* ubbidire *oob·bee·dee·re* □ *vt* to

obey someone ubbidire a qualcuno *oob·bee·dee·re a kwal·koo·no*

object[1] n l'oggetto (m) *oj·jet·toh*

object[2] vi □ **to object to a remark** obiettare ad una osservazione *o·byet·tah·ray ad oo·na os·sayr·va·tsyoh·ne*

objective n l'obiettivo (m) *o·byet·tee·voh*

obligation n l'obbligo (m) *ob·blee·goh*

oblong adj oblungo(a) *o·bloon·go(a)*

obscure adj oscuro(a) *o·skoo·ro(a)*

obsession n l'ossessione (f) *os·ses·syoh·ne*

obstacle n l'ostacolo (m) *o·sta·ko·loh*

obtain vt ottenere* *ot·te·nay·re*

obvious adj ovvio(a) *ov·vyo(a)*

obviously adv ovviamente *ov·vya·mayn·te*

occasion n l'occasione (f) *ok·ka·zyoh·ne*; (*special event*) l'avvenimento (m) *av·ve·nee·mayn·toh*

occasional adj (*event*) casuale *ka·zoo·ah·le*

occasionally adv di quando in quando *dee kwan·do een kwan·do*

occupation n (*job*) l'impiego (m) *eem·pye·goh*

occur vi (*happen*) accadere* *ak·ka·day·re*

ocean n l'oceano (m) *o·che·a·noh*

o'clock n □ **at 3 o'clock** alle tre *al·le tray*; **it's 4 o'clock** sono le 4 *so·no le 4*

October n ottobre (m) *ot·toh·bre*

odd adj (*number*) dispari *dee·spa·ree*; (*strange*) strano(a) *strah·no(a)*

odds pl (*in betting*) la quota *kwo·tah*

of prep di *dee*; **a friend of mine** un mio amico *oon mee·o a·mee·koh*; **3 of them** tre di loro *tray dee loh·ro*; **14th of June** il quattordici giugno *eel kwat·tohr·dee·chee joon·yo*; **made of stone** di pietra *dee pye·tra*

of course adv naturalmente *na·too·ral·mayn·te*

off adj (*machine*) fermo(a) *fayr·mo(a)*; (*radio, light*) spento(a) *spen·to(a)*; (*water supply*) chiuso(a) *kyoo·so(a)*; (*meat*) passato(a) *pas·sah·to(a)*; (*milk*) acido(a) *ah·chee·do(a)* □ adv **a day off** un giorno libero *oon johr·noh lee·be·ro*; **3% off** sconto del 3% *skohn·toh del 3%*; **6 kilometres off** a 6 chilometri *a 6 kee·lo·me·tree* □ prep **to fall off a wall** cadere* da un muro *ka·day·re da oon moo·roh*; **off the main road** fuori dalla strada principale *fwo·ree del·la strah·da preen·chee·pah·le*

offend vt offendere* *of·fen·de·re*

offer vt offrire* *of·free·re*; **to offer to do something** offrire* di fare qualcosa *of·free·re dee fah·ray kwal·ko·sa* □ n offer l'offerta (f) *of·fer·ta*

office n l'ufficio (m) *oof·fee·choh*; (*doctor's*) il gabinetto medico *ga·bee·nayt·toh me·dee·ko* T49

office-block n il palazzo di uffici *pa·lats·tsoh dee oof·fee·chee*

office hours pl le ore d'ufficio *oh·re doof·fee·choh*

officer n (*in army etc*) l'ufficiale (m) *oof·fee·chah·le*; (*police*) l'agente di polizia (m) *a·jen·te dee po·lee·tsee·a* T190

office worker n l'impiegato(a) d'ufficio (m/f) *eem·pye·gah·to(a) doof·fee·choh*

official adj ufficiale *oof·fee·chah·le*

off-season adj di bassa stagione *dee bas·sa sta·joh·ne*

offshore adj (*island*) al largo *al lar·go*; **offshore sailing** la navigazione costiera *na·vee·ga·tsyoh·ne ko·stye·ra*

often adv spesso *spays·so*

oil n l'olio (m) *o·lyoh*; (*petroleum*) il petrolio *pe·tro·lyoh* T158

oil filter n il filtro dell'olio *feel·troh del·lol·yoh*

oil pan n (*in car*) la coppa dell'olio *kop·pa del·lol·yoh*

oil-rig n la piattaforma petroliera *pyat·ta·fohr·ma pe·tro·lye·ra*

oil tanker n la petroliera *pe·tro·lye·ra*

ointment n l'unguento (m) *oon·gwen·toh*

O.K., okay adv (*agreement*) va bene *va be·ne*; **it's OK** va bene *va be·ne*

old adj vecchio(a) *vayk·kyo(a)*; **how old are you?** quanti anni ha? *kwan·tee an·nee a*

old-age-pensioner n il/la pensionato(a) *pen·see·oh·nah·to(a)*

old-fashioned adj antiquato(a) *an·tee·kwah·to(a)*

olive n l'oliva (f) *o·lee·va*

olive oil n l'olio d'oliva (m) *o·lyoh do·lee·va*

omelette n la frittata *freet·tah·ta*

on adj (*machine*) in moto *een mo·toh*; (*light, radio*) acceso(a) *ach·chay·so(a)*; (*water supply*) aperto(a) *a·per·to(a)*; **when is the film on?** quando è in visione il film? *kwan·do e een vee·zee·oh·ne eel feelm* □ prep **on su** *soo*; **on the table** sulla tavola *sool·la tah·vo·la*; **on the train** sul treno *sool tre·noh*; **on the wall** alla parete *al·la pa·ray·te*; **on the left/right** a sinistra/destra *a see·nee·stra/de·stra*; **come on Friday** venga venerdì *ven·ga ve·ner·dee*; **on television** alla televisione *al·la te·le·vee·zee·oh·ne*

once adv una volta *oo·na vol·ta*; **once more** ancora una volta *an·koh·ra oo·na vol·ta*

one num uno(a) *oo·no(a)*; **one day** un giorno *oon johr·noh* □ pron **which one** quale *kwah·le*; **the one on the table** quello(a) sulla tavola *kwayl·lo(a) sool·la tah·vo·la*; **this one** questo(a) *kway·sto(a)*; **one should...** uno dovrebbe... *oo·no do·vreb·be*; **one another** l'un l'altro *loon lal·tro*

one-armed bandit n la macchina mangiasoldi *mak·kee·na man·ja·sol·dee*

oneself pron se stesso(a) *say stays·so(a)*; **to dress oneself** vestirsi *ve·steer·see*

one-way street n la strada a senso unico *strah·da a sen·soh oo·nee·ko*

one-way ticket n il biglietto di solo andata *beel·yayt·toh dee soh·lo an·dah·ta* T57

onion n la cipolla *chee·pohl·la*

only adv solo *soh·lo*; **there are only 4** ce ne sono solo 4 *che ne so·no soh·lo 4* □ adj **the only woman** l'unica donna *loo·nee·ka don·na la*; **an only child** un figlio unico *oon feel·yoh oo·nee·ko*; **not only** non solo *nohn soh·lo*

onto prep su *soo*

OPEC n l'OPEC (f) *oh·pek*

open adj aperto(a) *a·per·to(a)* □ vt (*window etc*) aprire* *a·pree·re* □ vi (*store, bank*) aprire* *a·pree·re*; (*play*) cominciare *ko·meen·chah·ray* L12

open-air adj all'aperto *al·la·per·to*

open-plan adj senza muri divisori *sen·tsa moo·ree dee·vee·zo·ree*

opera n l'opera (f) *o·pe·ra*

operate vt (machine) fare* funzionare *fah·ray foon·tsyoh·nah·ray*

operation n l'operazione (f) *o·pe·ra·tsyoh·ne*

operator n il/la telefonista *te·le·fo·nee·sta*

opinion n l'opinione (f) *o·pee·nyoh·ne*; in my opinion a mio parere *a mee·o pa·ray·re*

opportunity n l'occasione (f) *ok·ka·zee·oh·ne*

opposite adv dirimpetto *dee·reem·pet·to*; the house opposite la casa di fronte *la kah·sa dee frohn·te*; the opposite sex l'altro sesso *lal·tro ses·soh* □ n opposite il contrario *kon·trah·ryoh* □ prep di fronte a *dee frohn·te a*

optician n l'ottico (m) *ot·tee·koh*

optimistic adj ottimista *ot·tee·mee·sta*

option n l'opzione (f) *op·tsyoh·ne*

or conj o *o*

orange n l'arancia (f) *a·ran·cha* □ adj arancione *a·ran·choh·ne*

orangeade n l'aranciata (f) *a·ran·chah·ta* E64

orange juice n la spremuta d'arancia *spray·moo·ta da·ran·cha* E63

orchard n il frutteto *froot·tay·toh*

orchestra n l'orchestra (f) *or·ke·stra*; (in theatre) la platea *pla·te·a*

order n (in shops) l'ordine (f) *ohr·dee·ne*; (for goods) l'ordinazione (f) *ohr·dee·na·tsyoh·ne*; out of order (machine) guasto(a) *gwa·sto(a)*; in order to do something per fare qualcosa *payr fah·ray kwal·ko·sa* □ vt order (goods, meal) ordinare *or·dee·nah·ray*

order-form n il modulo d'ordinazione *mo·doo·loh dor·dee·na·tsyoh·ne*

ordinary adj ordinario(a) *or·dee·nah·ryo(a)*

organ n (instrument) l'organo (m) *or·ga·noh*

organization n l'organizzazione (f) *or·ga·needz·dza·tsyoh·ne*

organize vt organizzare *or·ga·needz·dzah·ray*

oriental adj orientale *o·ree·en·tah·le*

origin n l'origine (f) *o·ree·jee·ne*

original adj originale *o·ree·jee·nah·le* □ n l'originale (m) *o·ree·jee·nah·le*

originally adv (at first) originariamente *o·ree·jee·nah·rya·mayn·te*

ornament n l'ornamento (m) *or·na·mayn·toh*

orphan n l'orfano(a) (m/f) *or·fa·no(a)*

other adj altro(a) *al·tro(a)*; the other day l'altro giorno *lal·tro johr·noh* □ pron the other l'altro(a) *lal·tro(a)* S13, 22

otherwise adv altrimenti *al·tree·mayn·tee*; otherwise engaged occupato(a) con altri impegni *ok·koo·pah·to(a) kohn al·tree eem·pen·yee*

ought vi □ I ought to do it dovrei farlo *do·vre·ee far·lo*; he ought to win dovrebbe vincere *do·vreb·be veen·che·re*; that ought to do quello dovrebbe bastare *kwayl·lo do·vreb·be ba·stah·ray*

ounce n l'oncia (f) *ohn·cha*

our adj nostro(a) *no·stroh(a)*; our brothers/sisters i nostri fratelli/le nostre sorelle *ee no·stree fra·tel·lee/lay no·stray so·rel·lay*

ours pron il nostro *eel no·stroh*, la no-

---

stra *la no·stra*; (plural) i nostri *ee no·stree*, le nostre *lay no·stray*

ourselves pron noi stessi *noy stays·see*; we dressed ourselves ci siamo vestiti *chee syah·mo ve·stee·tee*

out adv (not at home) fuori *fwo·ree*; (team, player) eliminato(a) *e·lee·mee·nah·to(a)*; the tide is out la marea è bassa *la ma·re·a e bas·sa*; the sun is out il sole splende *eel soh·le splen·de*; the light is out la luce è spenta *la loo·che e spayn·ta* □ prep out of (outside) fuori di *fwo·ree dee*; to be out of petrol rimanere* senza benzina *ree·ma·nay·re sen·tsa ben·dzee·na*; made out of wood di legno *dee layn·yoh*; he ran out of the house è uscito di corsa dalla casa *e oo·shee·to dee kohr·sa dal·la kah·sa*

outboard adj fuoribordo *fwo·ree·bohr·doh*

outdoor adj all'aria aperta *al·lah·ree·a a·per·ta*

outdoors adv all'aperto *al·la·per·to*

outfit n (clothes) il completo *kom·ple·toh*

outgoings pl le uscite *oo·shee·te*

outing n la gita *jee·ta*

outlet n (electric) la presa *pray·sa*

outline n (summary) il sommario *som·mah·ree·oh*

outlook n la prospettiva *pro·spet·tee·va*

out-of-date adj (passport, ticket) scaduto(a) *ska·doo·to(a)*

output n la produzione *pro·doo·tsyoh·ne*

outside n l'esterno (m) *e·ster·noh* □ adj the outside wall il muro esterno *eel moo·roh e·ster·no*; the outside lane (in road) la corsia di sorpasso *la kor·see·a dee sor·pas·soh* □ prep outside the house fuori della casa *fwo·ree del·la kah·sa* □ adv to be outside stare* fuori *stah·ray fwo·ree*; to go outside uscire* *oo·shee·re*

outsize adj (clothes) di taglia grande *dee tal·ya gran·de*

outskirts n la periferia *pe·ree·fe·ree·a*

oval adj ovale *o·vah·le*

oven n il forno *fohr·noh*

over adv □ to fall over cadere* *ka·day·ray*; to knock over fare* cadere *fah·ray ka·day·ray*; to turn something over rovesciare qualcosa *ro·ve·shah·ray kwal·ko·sa*; come over here venga qui *ven·ga kwee*; he's over here on holiday è qui in vacanza *e kwee een va·kan·tsa*; the match is over la partita è finita *la par·tee·ta e fee·nee·ta* □ prep to jump over something saltare qualcosa *sal·tah·ray kwal·ko·sa*; it weighs over a kilo pesa più di un chilo *pay·sa pyoo dee oon kee·loh*

overall n la tuta *too·ta*

overalls pl la tuta da lavoro *too·ta da la·voh·roh*

overcoat n il cappotto *kap·pot·toh*

overdose n la dose eccessiva *do·ze ech·ches·see·va*

overdraft n lo scoperto *sko·per·toh*

overdrive n l'overdrive (m) *oh·ver·draiv*

overexposed adj (photo) sovraesposto(a) *soh·vra·e·spoh·sto(a)*

overhead adj (railway) aereo(a) *a·e·re·o(a)* □ adv in alto *een al·to* □ n overheads le spese generali *spay·se je·ne·rah·lee*

overheat vi (engine) surriscaldarsi *soor·ree·skal·dahr·see*

overnight adj (a stay) per una notte payr oo·na not·te □ adv (happen) durante la notte doo·ran·te la not·te

overpass n il viadotto vee·a·doht·toh

overseas adv oltremare ol·tre·mah·re □ adj (market) d'oltremare dol·tre·mah·re; (visitor) straniero(a) stra·nye·ro(a)

overtake vt (car) sorpassare sor·pas·sah·ray

overtime n le ore straordinarie oh·re stra·or·dee·nah·ree·e; to work overtime fare* dello straordinario fah·ray del·lo stra·or·dee·nah·ree·o

overture l'ouverture (f) oo·ver·tōōr

overweight adj (baggage) in eccedenza een ech·che·den·tsa; (person) troppo pesante trop·po pe·san·te

owe vt (money) dovere* do·vay·re; he owes me £5 mi deve £5 mee de·ve £5

own adj proprio(a) pro·pree·o(a) □ n he did it on his own l'ha fatto da sé la fat·to da say □ vt (possess) possedere* pos·se·day·re

owner n il/la proprietario(a) pro·pree·e·tah·ree·o(a)

ownership n la proprietà pro·pree·e·tah

oxygen n l'ossigeno (m) os·see·je·noh

oyster n l'ostrica (f) o·stree·ka

P

pace n il passo pas·soh; to keep pace with tenere* il passo di te·nay·re eel pas·soh dee

Pacific Ocean n l'Oceano Pacifico (m) o·che·a·noh pa·chee·fee·ko

pacifier n la tettarella tet·ta·rel·la

pack vt (goods) imballare eem·bal·lah·ray; to pack one's case fare* la valigia fah·ray la va·lee·ja □ n pack il pacchetto pak·kayt·toh; (of cards) il mazzo mats·tsoh

package n il pacco pak·koh

package deal n l'accordo globale (m) ak·kor·doh glo·bah·le

package holiday n il viaggio organizzato vyaj·joh or·ga·needz·dzah·to

packet n il pacchetto pak·kayt·toh S32, 95

packing n (material) l'imballaggio (m) eem·bal·laj·joh

packing case n la cassa da imballaggio kas·sa da eem·bal·laj·joh

pad n (notepaper) il blocco blok·koh

paddle n (oar) la pagaia pa·ga·ya □ vi sguazzare zgwats·tsah·ray

paddling pool n la piscina per bambini pee·shee·na payr bam·bee·nee

padlock n il lucchetto look·kayt·toh

paediatrician n il/la pediatra pe·dee·at·ra

page n la pagina pah·jee·na □ vt fare* chiamare fah·ray kya·mah·ray

pageboy n il paggio paj·joh

paid adj (vacation) pagato(a) pa·gah·to(a)

pail n il secchio sayk·kyoh

pain n il dolore do·loh·re 128, 29

painful adj doloroso(a) do·lo·roh·so(a)

painkiller n il calmante kal·man·te

paint n la vernice ver·nee·che □ vt dipingere* dee·peen·je·re

painter n il pittore peet·toh·re; (decorator) il decoratore de·ko·ra·toh·re

painting n (picture) il quadro kwa·droh

pair n il paio pa·yoh; (of people) la coppia kop·pya; pair of shoes paio di scarpe pa·yoh dee skar·pe; pair of scissors le forbici for·bee·chee; pair of trousers i pantaloni pan·ta·loh·nee

pajamas pl il pigiama pee·jah·ma

Pakistan n Pakistan (m) pa·kee·stan

Pakistani adj pachistano(a) pa·kee·stah·no(a)

palace n il palazzo pa·lats·tsoh L12

pale adj (face) pallido(a) pal·lee·do(a); (colour) chiaro(a) kyah·ro(a)

Palestine n Palestina (f) pa·le·stee·na

Palestinian adj palestinese pa·le·stee·nay·se

palm n (of hand) il palmo pal·moh

palm-tree n la palma pal·ma

pan n (saucepan) il tegame te·gah·me; (frying pan) la padella pa·del·la

pancake n la frittella freet·tel·la

pane il vetro vay·troh

panic n il panico pa·nee·koh; in a panic preso(a) dal panico pray·so(a) dal pa·nee·koh □ vi panic allarmarsi al·lar·mar·see

pant vi ansimare an·see·mah·ray

panties pl le mutandine moo·tan·dee·ne

pantomime n lo spettacolo natalizio per bambini spet·ta·ko·loh na·ta·lee·tsyo payr bam·bee·nee

pants pl i pantaloni pan·ta·loh·nee; (undergarment: men's) le mutande moo·tan·de; (women's) le mutandine moo·tan·dee·ne

pant(s) suit n il tailleur-pantalone tye·yur·pan·ta·loh·ne

panty hose n il collant kol·lon

paper n la carta kar·ta; (newspaper) il giornale johr·nah·le; papers (passport etc) i documenti do·koo·mayn·tee □ vt paper (wall) tappezzare tap·pets·tsah·ray S94

paperback n il libro tascabile lee·broh ta·skah·bee·le S94

paper clip n la graffetta graf·fayt·ta

paprika n la paprica pa·pree·ka

par n (golf) la norma nor·ma; (business) la pari pah·ree; above par sopra la pari soh·pra la pah·ree

parachute n il paracadute pa·ra·ka·doo·te

parade n il corteo kor·te·oh

paraffin n la paraffina pa·raf·fee·na

paragraph n il paragrafo pa·ra·gra·foh

parallel adj parallelo(a) pa·ral·le·lo(a)

paralysed adj paralizzato(a) pa·ra·leedz·dzah·to(a)

parasol n il parasole pa·ra·soh·le

parcel n il pacco pak·koh Sn3

pardon excl scusate skoo·zah·te; pardon me?, (I beg your) pardon? prego? pre·go

parents pl i genitori je·nee·toh·ree

Paris n Parigi (f) pa·ree·jee

park n il parco par·koh □ vt parcheggiare par·kej·jah·ray □ vi can I park here? posso parcheggiare qui? pos·so par·kej·jah·ray kwee T122f

parka n la giacca a vento jak·ka a ven·toh

parking disk n il disco orario dee·skoh o·rah·ryo T131

parking lights pl i fanali di posizione fa·nah·lee dee po·zee·tsyoh·ne

parking-lot n il parcheggio par·kayj·joh T125, 126

parking meter n il parchimetro par·kee·me·troh

parking-ticket n la multa per sosta vietata mool·ta payr so·sta vye·tah·ta

parliament n il parlamento par·la·mayn·toh

Parmesan n il parmigiano par·mee·jah·noh

parsley n il prezzemolo *prets·tsay·mo·loh*

parsnip n la pastinaca *pa·stee·nah·ka*

part n la parte *par·te*; (of machine) il pezzo *pets·tsoh* □ vt (separate) separare *se·pa·rah·ray* T187

participate vi partecipare *par·te·chee·pah·ray*

participation n la partecipazione *par·te·chee·pa·tsyoh·ne*

particular adj particolare *par·tee·ko·lah·re*; (special) speciale *spe·chah·le* □ n in particular in particolare *een par·tee·ko·lah·re*

particularly adv particolarmente *par·tee·ko·lar·mayn·te*

parting n (in hair) la scriminatura *skree·mee·na·too·ra*

partition n (wall) il tramezzo *tra·medz·dzoh*

partly adv in parte *een par·te*

partner n (in business) il socio *so·choh*; (dancing) il cavaliere *ka·va·lye·re*, la dama *dah·ma*

partridge n la pernice *per·nee·che*

part-time adj a tempo parziale *a tem·poh par·tsyah·le*

party n (celebration) la festa *fe·sta*; (group) il gruppo *groop·poh*; (political) il partito *par·tee·toh* T5f

pass n (permit) il permesso *per·mays·soh*; (in mountains) il passo *pas·soh* □ vt (place) passare *pas·sah·ray*; (car) sorpassare *sor·pas·sah·ray*; (exam) essere* promosso(a) *a es·se·re pro·mos·so(a) a*; (time) trascorrere* *tra·skohr·re·re*; (hand on: object) passare *pas·sah·ray*; please pass the sugar mi passa lo zucchero per favore *mee pas·sa lo tsook·ke·roh payr fa·voh·re*

passage n il passaggio *pas·saj·joh*

passenger n il/la passeggero(a) *pas·sej·je·ro(a)*

passenger seat n il sedile del passeggero *se·dee·le del pas·sej·je·roh*

passion n la passione *pas·syoh·ne*

passport n il passaporto *pas·sa·por·toh* T11f, Sn82

past adj passato(a) *pas·sah·to(a)* □ n il passato *pas·sah·toh* □ adv to run past passare correndo *pas·sah·ray kor·ren·do* □ prep he ran past me mi ha passato di corsa *mee a pas·sah·to de kohr·sa*; he's past forty ha oltre quarant'anni *a ohl·tre kwa·ran·tan·nee*

pasta n la pasta *pa·sta*

paste n (glue) la colla *kol·la*; meat paste l'impasto di carne (m) *eem·pa·stoh dee kar·ne*

pasteurized adj pastorizzato(a) *pa·sto·reedz·dzah·to(a)*

pastille n la pastiglia *pa·steel·ya*

pastry n la pasta *pa·sta*

pat vt carezzare *ka·rets·tsah·ray*

patch n (of material) la pezza *pets·tsa*; (for eye) la benda *ben·da*; (spot) la macchia *mak·kya*

pâté n il pâté *pa·tay*

patent n il brevetto *bre·vayt·toh*

patent leather n il cuoio verniciato *kwo·yoh ver·nee·chah·toh*

path n il sentiero *sen·tye·roh*

patience n la pazienza *pa·tsyen·tsa*

patient adj paziente *pa·tsyen·te* □ n il/la paziente *pa·tsyen·te*

patio n il patio *pa·tyoh*

pattern n il disegno *dee·sayn·yoh*; (dressmaking) il patron *pa·tron*; (knitting) le istruzioni *ee·stroo·tsyoh·nee*

pause n la pausa *pow·za* □ vi fare* una pausa *fah·ray oo·na pow·za*

pavement n (sidewalk) il marciapiede *mar·cha·pye·de*; (roadway) il lastricato *la·stree·kah·toh*

paw n la zampa *tsam·pa*

pay n la paga *pah·ga* □ vt pagare *pa·gah·ray*; to pay back (money) rimborsare *reem·bohr·sah·ray*; to pay for pagare *pa·gah·ray*; to pay off (workers) licenziare *lee·chen·tsyah·ray* M9f

payable adj pagabile *pa·gah·bee·le*

payee n il beneficiario *be·ne·fee·chah·ryoh*

paying guest n l'ospite pagante (m/f) *o·spee·te pa·gan·te*

payment n il pagamento *pa·ga·mayn·toh*

payroll n il libro paga *lee·broh pah·ga*

peace n la pace *pah·che*; (calm) la calma *kal·ma*

peaceful adj tranquillo(a) *tran·kweel·lo(a)*

peach n la pesca *pe·ska*

peak n (of cap) la visiera *vee·zye·ra*; (of mountain) la cima *chee·ma*

peak hours pl le ore di punta *oh·re dee poon·ta*

peanut n l'arachide (f) *a·ra·kee·de*

pear n la pera *pay·ra*

pearl n la perla *per·la*

peas pl i piselli *pee·sel·lee*

pebble n il ciottolo *chot·to·loh*

peck vt beccare *bek·kah·ray*

peculiar adj (strange) strano(a) *strah·no(a)*

pedal n il pedale *pe·dah·le*

pedalo n il pattino a pedali *pat·tee·noh a pe·dah·lee*

pedestrian n il pedone *pe·doh·ne*

pedestrian crossing n il passaggio pedonale *pas·saj·joh pe·do·nah·le*

pedestrian precinct n l'isola pedonale (f) *ee·zo·la pe·do·nah·le*

pediatrician n il/la pediatra *pe·dya·tra*

peel vt sbucciare *zbooch·chah·ray* □ vi (person) spellarsi *spel·lar·see* □ n la buccia *booch·cha*

peg n il picchetto *peek·kayt·toh*; (for coat) l'attaccapanni (m) *at·tak·ka·pan·nee*; (clothes peg) la molletta *mol·layt·ta*

pen n la penna *payn·na* S92

pencil n la matita *ma·tee·ta*

penetrate vt penetrare *pe·ne·trah·ray*

penicillin n la penicillina *pe·nee·cheel·lee·na*

penis n il pene *pe·ne*

penknife n il temperino *tem·pe·ree·noh*

pen pal n il/la corrispondente *kor·ree·spon·den·te*

pension n la pensione *pen·syoh·ne*

pensioner n il/la pensionato(a) *pen·syoh·nah·to(a)*

pension fund n la cassa di pensionamento *kas·sa dee pen·syoh·na·mayn·toh*

penthouse n l'attico (m) *at·tee·koh*

people pl la gente *jen·te* Mc18

pepper n il pepe *pay·pe*; (capsicum) il peperone *pe·pe·roh·ne*; green/red pepper il peperone verde/rosso *pe·pe·roh·ne vayr·de/rohs·so*

peppermint n (confectionery) la caramella di menta *ka·ra·mel·la dee mayn·ta*; (plant) la menta peperita *mayn·ta pe·pe·ree·ta*

pepper pot n la pepaiola *pe·pa·yo·la*

peppery adj pepato(a) *pe·pah·to(a)*

per *prep* per *payr*; **100 km per hour** 100 chilometri all'ora *100 kee·lo·me·tree al·loh·ra*; **to earn £25 per hour** guadagnare £25 all'ora *gwa·dan·yah·ray £25 al·loh·ra*; **£3 per kilo** £3 il chilo *£3 eel kee·loh*; **per person** per persona *payr per·soh·na*; **per day** al giorno *al johr·noh*; **per annum** all'anno *al·lan·noh*; **20 per cent** 20 per cento *20 payr chen·to*

percentage *n* la percentuale *per·chen·too·ah·le*

percolate *vt* (*coffee*) filtrare *feel·trah·ray*

percolator *n* la macchinetta per il caffè *mak·kee·nayt·ta payr eel kaf·fe*

perfect *adj* perfetto(a) *per·fet·to(a)*

perform *vi* (*business*) andare* *an·dah·ray* L47

performance *n* (*of actor*) l'interpretazione (*f*) *een·ter·pre·ta·tsyoh·ne*; (*of play*) la rappresentazione *rap·pre·zen·ta·tsyoh·ne*; (*of car*) il rendimento *ren·dee·mayn·toh* L49, 52

perfume *n* il profumo *pro·foo·moh* S44

perhaps *adv* forse *fohr·se*

period *n* (*of time*) il periodo *pe·ree·o·doh*; (*punctuation*) il punto *poon·toh*; (*menstruation*) le mestruazioni *me·stroo·a·tsyoh·nee* □ *adj* (*furniture*) antico(a) *an·tee·ko(a)*

perm *n* la permanente *per·ma·nen·te* Sn41

permanent *adj* permanente *per·ma·nen·te*

permanently *adv* permanentemente *per·ma·nen·te·mayn·te*

permanent wave *n* la permanente *per·ma·nen·te*

permission *n* il permesso *per·mays·soh*

permit *vt* (*something*) permettere* *per·mayt·te·re*; **to permit someone to do something** permettere* a qualcuno di fare qualcosa *per·mayt·te·re a kwal·koo·no dee fah·ray kwal·ko·sa* □ *n* il permesso *per·mays·soh*

Persian *adj* persiano(a) *per·syah·no(a)*; (*person*) di persona *dee per·soh·na*

personal *adj* personale *per·so·nah·le*; (*private*) privato(a) *pree·vah·to(a)*

personal assistant, P.A. *n* la segretaria(o) particolare *se·gre·tah·ryo(a) par·tee·ko·lah·re*

personality *n* la personalità *per·so·na·lee·ta*

personally *adv* personalmente *per·so·nal·mayn·te*

personnel *n* il personale *per·so·nah·le*

personnel department *n* l'ufficio del personale (*m*) *oof·fee·choh dayl per·so·nah·le*

personnel manager *n* il direttore del personale *dee·ret·toh·re dayl per·so·nah·le*

person-to-person call *n* la telefonata personale *te·le·fo·nah·ta per·so·nah·le* Sn13

Perspex *n* il plexiglas *plek·see·glas*

perspire *vi* traspirare *tra·spee·rah·ray*

persuade *vt* persuadere* *per·swa·day·re*; **to persuade someone to do something** persuadere* qualcuno a fare qualcosa *per·swa·day·re kwal·koo·no a fah·ray kwal·ko·sa*

peseta *n* la peseta *pe·say·ta*

pessimistic *adj* pessimista *pes·see·mee·sta*

pet *n* l'animale domestico (*m*) *a·nee·mah·le do·me·stee·ko*

petrol *n* la benzina *ben·dzee·na* T155, 168, 170

petroleum jelly *n* la vaselina *va·ze·lee·na*

petrol pump *n* il distributore di benzina *dee·stree·boo·toh·re dee ben·dzee·na*

petrol station *n* la stazione di servizio *sta·tsyoh·ne dee ser·vee·tsyoh* F9

petticoat *n* la sottoveste *soht·to·ve·ste*

pharmacist *n* il/la farmacista *far·ma·chee·sta*

pharmacy *n* la farmacia *far·ma·chee·a*

pheasant *n* il fagiano *fa·jah·noh*

phone *n* il telefono *te·le·fo·noh*; **he's on the phone** sta telefonando *sta te·le·fo·nan·do* □ *vt* **phone** telefonare *te·le·fo·nah·ray* Sn11

phone-call *n* la telefonata *te·le·fo·nah·ta* Sn13

photo *n* la foto *fo·toh* L14, S51f

photocopy *n* la fotocopia *fo·to·ko·pya* □ *vt* fotocopiare *fo·to·ko·pyah·ray* Bm13

photograph *n* la fotografia *fo·to·gra·fee·a* □ *vt* fotografare *fo·to·gra·fah·ray* S52

photographer *n* il fotografo *fo·to·gra·foh*

photography *n* la fotografia *fo·to·gra·fee·a*

phrase *n* la frase *frah·ze*

phrase book *n* il libro di fraseologia *lee·broh dee fra·ze·o·lo·jee·a*

physical *adj* fisico(a) *fee·zee·ko(a)*

physics *n* la fisica *fee·zee·ka*

piano *n* il piano *pyah·noh*

pick *n* (*pickaxe*) il piccone *peek·koh·ne* □ *vt* (*flower*) cogliere* *kol·ye·re*; (*choose*) scegliere* *shayl·ye·re*; **to pick up** (*object*) raccogliere* *rak·kol·ye·re*; **to pick up a friend** andare* a prendere un amico *an·dah·ray a pren·de·re oon a·mee·koh*

pickaxe *n* il piccone *peek·koh·ne*

picket *n* il picchetto *peek·kayt·toh*

pickles *pl* i sottaceti *sot·ta·chay·tee*

picnic *n* il picnic *peek·neek*; **to go on a picnic** andare* a fare un picnic *an·dah·ray a fah·ray oon peek·neek* L39

picture *n* (*object*) il quadro *kwa·droh*; (*drawing*) il disegno *dee·sayn·yoh*; (*photo*) la foto *fo·toh*; (*movie*) il film *feelm*

pie *n* la torta *tohr·ta*; (*meat*) il pasticcio *pa·steech·choh*

piece *n* il pezzo *pets·tsoh*; **piece of furniture** il mobile *mo·bee·le*; **a good piece of work** un buon lavoro *oon bwon la·voh·roh*

piecework *n* il lavoro a cottimo *la·voh·roh a kot·tee·moh*

pier *n* il molo *mo·loh*

pierce *vt* trafiggere* *tra·feej·je·re*

pig *n* il maiale *ma·yah·le*

pigeon *n* il piccione *peech·choh·ne*

pigskin *n* la pelle di cinghiale *pel·le dee cheen·gyah·le*

pilchard *n* la sardella *sar·del·la*

pile *n* il mucchio *mook·kyoh* □ *vt* **to pile up** ammucchiare *am·mook·kyah·ray*

pill *n* la pillola *peel·lo·la*; **to be on the pill** prendere* la pillola *pren·de·re la peel·lo·la* I47

pillar *n* il pilastro *pee·la·stroh*

pillow *n* il guanciale *gwan·chah·le* A41

pillowcase, pillowslip *n* la federa *fe·de·ra*

pilot *n* il pilota *pee·lo·ta*

pilot light *n* (*gas*) l'accenditore (*m*) *ach·chen·dee·toh·re*

pimple *n* la bollicina *bol·lee·chee·na*

pin *n* lo spillo *speel·loh*; (*drawing pin*) la puntina *poon·tee·na*; (*safety pin*) lo spillo di sicurezza *speel·loh dee see·koo·rayts·tsa* □ *vt* attaccare con uno spillo *at·tak·kah·ray kohn oo·no speel·loh*

pinball *n* il flipper *fleep·per*

pinch *vt* pizzicare *peets·tsee·kah·ray* □ *n* (*of salt etc*) il pizzico *peets·tsee·koh*

pine *n* il pino *pee·noh*

pineapple *n* l'ananas (*m*) *a·na·nas*

ping-pong *n* il ping-pong *peeng·pong*

pink *adj* rosa *ro·za* □ *vi* (*engine*) picchiare *peek·kyah·ray*

pint *n* la pinta *peen·ta*

pipe *n* (*tube*) il tubo *too·boh*; (*for smoking*) la pipa *pee·pa*; (*musical*) il piffero *peef·fe·roh*; (*bag*)pipes la cornamusa *kor·na·moo·za* A76, S97

pipeline *n* l'oleodotto (*m*) *o·le·o·doht·toh*

piston *n* il pistone *pee·stoh·ne*

pit *n* la fossa *fos·sa*

pitch *vt* (*tent*) piantare *pyan·tah·ray*

pitcher *n* la brocca *brok·ka*

pity *n* la compassione *kom·pas·syoh·ne*; what a pity! che peccato! *ke pek·kah·to*

pizza *n* la pizza *peets·tsa*

place *n* il luogo *lwo·goh*; (*seat*) il posto *poh·stoh*; in place a posto *a poh·stoh*; out of place (*object*) fuori posto *fwo·ree poh·stoh*; come back to our place venga a casa nostra *ven·ga a kah·sa no·stra* □ *vt* place (*put*) mettere* *mayt·te·re*; (*a bet*) fare* *fah·ray*; to place an order with someone collocare un ordine presso qualcuno *kol·lo·kah·ray oon ohr·dee·ne pres·so kwal·koo·no*

place mat *n* il sottopiatto *soht·to·pyat·toh*

place setting *n* il coperto *ko·per·toh*

plaice *n* la passera *pas·se·ra*

plaid *n* il plaid *plahd*

plain *n* la pianura *pya·noo·ra* □ *adj* (*clear*) chiaro(a) *kyah·ro(a)*; (*simple: cooking etc*) semplice *saym·plee·che*; (*not patterned*) con ooo *oo·nee·to(a)*; plain chocolate il cioccolato scuro *chok·ko·lah·toh skoo·ro*; plain yogurt il iogurt naturale *yo·goort na·too·rah·le*

plait *n* (*of hair etc*) la treccia *traych·cha*

plan *n* (*scheme*) il progetto *pro·jet·toh*; (*map*) la pianta *pyan·ta*; (*drawing, design*) il disegno *dee·sayn·yoh* □ *vt* progettare *pro·jet·tah·ray*; (*make a design*) disegnare *dee·sayn·yah·ray*

plane *n* l'aereo (*m*) *a·e·re·oh*; (*tree*) il platano *pla·ta·noh*; (*tool*) la pialla *pyal·la*; by plane in aereo *een a·e·re·oh* B69

planet *n* il pianeta *pya·nay·ta*

planetarium *n* il planetario *pla·ne·tah·ryoh*

plank *n* la tavola *tah·vo·la*

planning *n* (*economic*) la pianificazione *pya·nee·fee·ka·tsyoh·ne*

plant *n* la pianta *pyan·ta*; (*factory*) lo stabilimento *sta·bee·lee·maynt·toh*; (*equipment*) il macchinario *mak·kee·nah·ryoh* □ *vt* piantare *pyan·tah·ray*

plaster *n* (*for wall*) l'intonaco (*m*) *een·to·na·koh*; (*for wound*) il cerotto *che·rot·toh*; (*for limb*) il gesso *jes·soh*; plaster of Paris il gesso *jes·soh*

plastic *n* la plastica *pla·stee·ka* □ *adj* in

plastica *een pla·stee·ka*; plastic surgery la chirurgia plastica *kee·roor·jee·a pla·stee·ka*

plastic bag *n* il sacco in plastica *sak·koh een pla·stee·ka* S25

plate *n* il piatto *pyat·toh*; (*of glass, metal*) la lastra *la·stra*

plated *adj* □ gold plated placcato(a) d'oro *plak·kah·to(a) do·roh*

platform *n* (*in station*) la banchina *ban·kee·na*; (*in hall*) il palco *pal·koh*; (*of oil-rig*) la piattaforma *pyat·ta·fohr·ma* T69, 70

platinum *n* il platino *pla·tee·noh*

play *vt/i* giocare *jo·kah·ray*; to play football giocare al calcio *jo·kah·ray al kal·choh*; to play the violin suonare il violino *swo·nah·ray eel vee·o·lee·noh*; to play with giocare con *jo·kah·ray kohn* □ *n* play (*theatrical*) il dramma *dram·ma*

player *n* (*in sport*) il giocatore *jo·ka·toh·re*, la giocatrice *jo·ka·tree·che*

playground *n* il cortile *kor·tee·le* C9

play-group *n* il nido d'infanzia *nee·doh deen·fan·tsya*

playing card *n* la carta da gioco *kar·ta da jo·koh*

playing field *n* il campo da gioco *kam·poh da jo·koh*

playpen *n* il box *boks*

pleasant *adj* gradevole *gra·day·vo·le*; (*person*) simpatico(a) *seem·pa·tee·ko(a)*

please *adv* per favore *payr fa·voh·re*

pleased *adj* contento(a) *kon·ten·to(a)*

pleasure *n* il piacere *pya·chay·re*

pleasure boat *n* il battello da diporto *bat·tel·loh da dee·por·toh*

pleated *adj* pieghettato(a) *pye·get·tah·to(a)*

plenty *n* □ plenty of milk molto latte *mohl·to lat·te*; thank you, that's plenty grazie, basta così *gra·tsye ba·sta ko·see*

plexiglas *n* il plexiglas *plek·see·glas*

pliers *pl* le pinze *peen·tse*

plimsolls *pl* le scarpette da tennis *skar·payt·te da ten·nees*

plot *n* (*of land*) l'appezzamento (*m*) *ap·pets·tsa·maynt·toh*; (*in play*) la trama *trah·ma*

plough *n* l'aratro (*m*) *a·ra·troh*

plug *n* (*for basin etc*) il tappo *tap·poh*; (*electric*) la spina *spee·na*; (*in car*) la candela *kan·day·la* □ *vt* tappare *tap·pah·ray*; to plug something in attaccare qualcosa *at·tak·kah·ray kwal·ko·sa*

plum *n* la susina *soo·see·na*

plumber *n* l'idraulico (*m*) *ee·drow·lee·koh*

plump *adj* grassoccio(a) *gras·soch·cho(a)*

plus *prep* più *pyoo*

plywood *n* il compensato *kom·pen·sah·toh*

p.m. *adv* di sera *dee say·ra*

pneumonia *n* la polmonite *pol·mo·nee·te*

poached *adj* affogato(a) *af·fo·gah·to(a)*

P.O. Box *n* la casella postale *ka·sel·la po·stah·le*

pocket *n* la tasca *ta·ska*

pocketbook *n* il portafogli *por·ta·fol·yee*

pocketknife *n* il temperino *tem·pe·ree·noh*

pocket money *n* il denaro per le piccole spese *de·nah·roh payr le peek·ko·le spay·se*

poem n la poesia po·e·zee·a

poetry n la poesia po·e·zee·a

point vt (gun) puntare poon·tah·ray □ vi to point at or to something indicare qualcosa een·dee·kah·ray kwal·ko·sa; to point something out (show) mostrare qualcosa mo·strah·ray kwal·ko·sa □ n point il punto poon·toh; (tip) la punta poon·ta; (in time) il momento mo·mayn·toh; (electric outlet) la presa pray·sa; decimal point la virgola veer·go·la; 3 point 4 3 virgola 4 3 veer·go·la 4; he answered him point by point gli ha risposto punto per punto lyee a ree·spoh·sto poon·toh payr poon·toh; what's the point? a che serve? a ke serve

point of view n il punto di vista poon·toh dee vee·sta

poison n il veleno ve·lay·noh

poisonous adj velenoso(a) ve·le·noh·so(a)

poker n (card game) il poker po·ker

Poland n Polonia (f) po·lo·nya

Polaroid adj polaroid po·la·royd

pole n (wooden) il palo pah·loh

Pole n il/la polacco(a) po·lak·ko(a)

police n la polizia po·lee·tsee·a T190f, Sn77

police car n la macchina della polizia mak·kee·na del·la po·lee·tsee·a

policeman n il poliziotto po·lee·tsyot·toh

police station n il commissariato kom·mees·sa·ryah·toh Sn78

policewoman n la donna poliziotto don·na po·lee·tsyot·toh

policy n la politica po·lee·tee·ka; (insurance) la polizza po·leets·tsa

polio n la polio po·lyoh

polish n (for shoes) il lucido loo·chee·doh; (for floor) la cera chay·ra □ vt lucidare loo·chee·dah·ray

Polish adj polacco(a) po·lak·ko(a) □ n il polacco po·lak·koh

polite adj gentile jen·tee·le

political adj politico(a) po·lee·tee·ko(a)

politician n l'uomo politico (m) wo·moh po·lee·tee·ko

politics n la politica po·lee·tee·ka

pollution n l'inquinamento (m) een·kwee·na·mayn·toh

polo n il polo po·loh

polo neck n il collo alto kol·loh al·to

polyester n il poliestere po·lee·e·ste·re

polythene n il polietilene po·lee·e·tee·le·ne

polythene bag n il sacchetto di plastica sak·kay·toh dee pla·stee·ka

pomegranate n la melagrana me·la·grah·na

pond n (natural) lo stagno stan·yoh; (artificial) il bacino ba·chee·noh

pontoon n il ventuno ven·too·noh

pony n il pony poh·nee

pool n (of rain) la pozzanghera pots·tsan·ge·ra; (swimming) la piscina pee·shee·na; (game) il biliardo bee·lyar·doh A11

poor adj povero(a) po·ve·ro(a); (mediocre) mediocre me·dee·o·kre

pop adj (music, art) pop pop

pop concert n il concerto pop kon·cher·toh pop

popcorn n il pop-corn pop·korn

pope n il papa pah·pa

pop group n il complesso pop kom·ples·soh pop

poplar n il pioppo pyop·poh

poplin n la popeline po·pe·leen

popsicle n il lecca-lecca layk·ka·layk·ka

popular adj popolare po·po·lah·ray; (fashionable) di moda dee mo·da

population n la popolazione po·po·la·tsyoh·ne

porcelain n la porcellana por·chel·lah·na

porch n il portico por·tee·koh

pork n la carne di maiale kar·ne dee ma·yah·le S36

porridge n il porridge po·reej

port n il porto por·toh

portable adj portatile por·tah·tee·le

porter n (for luggage) il facchino fak·kee·noh; (doorkeeper) il/la portiere(a) por·tye·re(a) T25

portfolio n il portafoglio por·ta·fol·yoh

porthole n l'oblò (m) o·blo

portion n la porzione por·tsyoh·ne

Portugal n Portogallo (m) por·to·gal·loh

Portuguese adj portoghese por·to·gay·se □ n il portoghese por·to·gay·se

position n la posizione po·zee·tsyoh·ne; (place, job) il posto poh·stoh

positive adj positivo(a) po·zee·tee·vo(a); (definite) preciso(a) pre·chee·zo(a)

possibility n la possibilità pos·see·bee·lee·ta

possible adj possibile pos·see·bee·le

possibly adv forse fohr·se; to do all one possibly can fare* tutto il possibile fah·ray toot·to eel pos·see·bee·le

post n (pole) il palo pah·loh; (mail) la posta poh·sta; by post per posta payr po·sta □ vt post imbucare eem·boo·kah·ray Sn1f

postage n le spese postali spay·se po·stah·lee

postal adj postale po·stah·le

postal district n il distretto postale dee·strayt·toh po·stah·le

postal order n il vaglia val·ya

post-box n la cassetta per le lettere kas·sayt·ta payr le let·te·re

postcard n la cartolina kar·to·lee·na L15, S91, Sn2

post-code n il codice postale ko·dee·che po·stah·le

postdate vt postdatare post·da·tah·ray

poster n il manifesto ma·nee·fe·stoh

poste restante adv fermo posta fayr·mo po·sta Sn7

postman n il postino po·stee·noh

post office n l'ufficio postale (m) oof·fee·choh po·stah·le; the Post Office le Poste po·ste F8, Sn1f

post-office box n la casella postale ka·sel·la po·stah·le

postpone vt rimandare ree·man·dah·ray

pot n (for cooking) la pentola payn·to·la; (for jam) il barattolo ba·rat·to·loh; (for plant) il vaso vah·zoh

potato n la patata pa·tah·ta

pottery n la ceramica che·ra·mee·ka; (workshop) la fabbrica di ceramiche fab·bree·ka dee che·ra·mee·ke

pot(ty) n il vasino va·zee·noh

poultry n il pollame pol·lah·me

pound n la sterlina ster·lee·na; (weight) la libbra leeb·bra

pour vt (tea, milk) versare ver·sah·ray □ vi scorrere* skohr·re·re

powder n la polvere pohl·ve·re; (cosmetic) la cipria chee·prya

powder room n la toeletta to·e·let·ta

power n (of machine) la potenza po·

ten·tsa; (*authority*) il potere *po·tay·re*; (*electricity*) la corrente *kor·ren·te*

power cut *n* la sospensione temporanea dell'erogazione della corrente *so·spen·syoh·ne tem·po·rah·ne·a del·le·ro·ga·tsyoh·ne del·la kor·ren·te*

powerful *adj* potente *po·ten·te*

power point *n* la presa di corrente *pray·sa dee kor·ren·te*

P.R. *n* le pubbliche relazioni *poob·blee·ke re·la·tsyoh·nee*

practical *adj* pratico(a) *pra·tee·ko(a)*

practise *vt/i* □ to practise running esercitarsi nel correre *e·zer·chee·tar·see nel kor·re·re*; to practise the piano esercitarsi al pianoforte *e·zer·chee·tar·see al pya·no·for·te*

Prague *n* Praga (*f*) *prah·ga*

pram *n* il carrozzino *kar·rots·tsee·noh*

prawn *n* il gamberetto *gam·be·rayt·toh*

pray *vi* pregare *pre·gah·ray*

prayer *n* la preghiera *pre·gye·ra*

precinct *n* (*administrative area*) la circoscrizione *cheer·ko·skree·tsyoh·ne*

precious *adj* (*jewel etc*) prezioso(a) *pre·tsyoh·so(a)* S87

precise *adj* preciso(a) *pre·chee·zo(a)*

precision *n* la precisione *pre·chee·zyoh·ne*

predict *vt* predire* *pre·dee·re*

prediction *n* la predizione *pre·dee·tsyoh·ne*

prefer *vt* preferire *pre·fe·ree·re*

preference shares *pl* le azioni privilegiate *a·tsyoh·nee pree·vee·le·jah·te*

pregnant *adj* incinta *een·cheen·ta* 146

prejudice *n* il pregiudizio *pre·joo·dee·tsyoh*

preliminary *adj* preliminare *pre·lee·mee·nah·re*

première *n* la prima *pree·ma*

premises *pl* lo stabile *stah·bee·le*

premium *n* il premio *pre·myoh*

prepaid *adj* prepagato(a) *pre·pa·gah·to(a)*

preparation *n* la preparazione *pre·pa·ra·tsyoh·ne*; preparations (*for trip*) i preparativi *pre·pa·ra·tee·vee*

prepare *vt* preparare *pre·pa·rah·ray* □ *vi* he's preparing to leave si prepara a partire *see pre·pah·ra a par·tee·re*

Presbyterian *adj* presbiteriano(a) *pre·zbee·te·ree·ah·no(a)*

prescription *n* la ricetta *ree·chet·ta*

present *adj* presente *pre·zen·te*; the present king il re attuale *eel ray at·twah·le* □ *n* present (*gift*) il regalo *re·gah·loh*; at present in questo momento *een kway·sto mo·mayn·toh* □ *vt* present (*give*) regalare *re·ga·lah·ray* S6, 103

presentation *n* la presentazione *pre·zen·ta·tsyoh·ne*

preserve(s) *n* la marmellata *mar·mel·lah·ta*

president *n* (*of country*) il presidente *pre·see·den·te*; (*of company*) il direttore *dee·ret·toh·re*

press *n* (*newspapers, journalists*) la stampa *stam·pa*; (*printing machine*) la pressa tipografica *pres·sa tee·po·gra·fee·ka* □ *vt* premere *pre·me·re*; (*iron*) stirare *stee·rah·ray*

press-campaign *n* la campagna giornalistica *kam·pan·ya johr·na·lee·stee·ka*

press-stud *n* il bottone automatico *bot·toh·ne ow·to·ma·tee·ko*

pressure *n* la pressione *pres·syoh·ne* T159

pressure cooker *n* la pentola a pressione *payn·to·la a pres·syoh·ne*

pressure group *n* il gruppo di pressione *groop·poh dee pres·syoh·ne*

prestige *n* il prestigio *pre·stee·joh*

pretax *adj* (*profit*) lordo(a) *lohr·do(a)*

pretend *vi* fingere* *feen·je·re*; to pretend to do something fingere* di fare qualcosa *feen·je·re dee fah·ray kwal·ko·sa*

pretty *adj* (*woman, child*) grazioso(a) *gra·tsyoh·so(a)*; (*dress*) bello(a) *bel·lo(a)*

preview *n* l'anteprima (*f*) *an·te·pree·ma*

previous *adj* precedente *pre·che·den·te*; on the previous day il giorno prima *eel johr·noh pree·ma*

price *n* il prezzo *prets·tsoh* □ *vt* (*goods*) fissare il prezzo di *fees·sah·ray eel prets·tsoh dee* Bm25

price list *n* il listino prezzi *lee·stee·noh prets·tsee*

price range *n* la gamma di prezzi *gam·ma dee prets·tsee*

prick *vt* pungere* *poon·je·re*

pride *n* l'orgoglio (*m*) *or·gohl·yoh*

priest *n* il prete *pre·te* Sn88

primary *adj* (*education*) primario(a) *pree·mah·ryo(a)*

prime minister, P.M. *n* il primo ministro *pree·mo mee·nee·stroh*

prince *n* il principe *preen·chee·pe*

princess *n* la principessa *preen·chee·pays·sa*

principal *n* (*of school etc*) il/la preside *pre·see·de*

print *vt* (*book, newspaper*) stampare *stam·pah·ray*; (*write in block letters*) scrivere* a stampatello *skree·ve·re a stam·pa·tel·loh* □ *n* la stampa *stam·pa*; (*photographic*) la copia *ko·pya*; out of print esaurito(a) *e·zow·ree·to(a)* S50

printer *n* il tipografo *tee·po·gra·foh*

printout *n* lo stampato *stam·pah·toh*

prison *n* la prigione *pree·joh·ne*; in prison in prigione *een pree·joh·ne*

prisoner *n* il/la prigioniero(a) *pree·joh·nye·ro(a)*

private *adj* privato(a) *pree·vah·to(a)*; (*secluded*) isolato(a) *ee·zo·lah·to(a)*; (*confidential*) confidenziale *kon·fee·den·tsyah·le*; in private in privato *een pree·vah·to* A37, E5

private enterprise *n* l'impresa privata (*f*) *eem·pray·sa pree·vah·ta*

private limited company *n* la società a responsabilità limitata *so·che·ta a re·spon·sa·bee·lee·ta lee·mee·tah·ta*

private sector *n* il settore privato *set·toh·re pree·vah·to*

prize *n* il premio *pre·myoh*

probable *adj* probabile *pro·bah·bee·le*

probably *adv* probabilmente *pro·ba·beel·mayn·te*

problem *n* il problema *pro·ble·ma* A69

procedure *n* il procedimento *pro·che·dee·mayn·toh*

process *n* il processo *pro·ches·soh*; (*method*) il procedimento *pro·che·dee·mayn·toh* □ *vt* trattare *trat·tah·ray*; (*application, order*) occuparsi di *ok·koo·par·see dee*

produce *vt* produrre* *pro·door·re*; (*play*) mettere in scena *mayt·te·re een she·na* □ *n* (*products*) i prodotti *pro·doht·tee*

producer *n* il produttore *pro·doot·toh·re*; (*of play*) il/la regista *re·jee·sta*

product n il prodotto *pro·doht·toh* Bm21

production n la produzione *pro·doo· tsyoh·ne*; (*of play*) la rappresentazione *rap·pre·zen·ta·tsyoh·ne*

productivity n la produttività *pro·doot· tee·vee·ta*

profession n la professione *pro·fes· syoh·ne*

professional adj professionale *pro·fes· syoh·nah·le*

professor n il professore *pro·fes·soh·re*

profit n il profitto *pro·feet·toh*

profitability n il rendimento *ren·dee· mayn·toh*

profitable adj vantaggioso(a) *van·taj· joh·so(a)*

profiterole n la profiterole *pro·fee·te· rohl*

profit-making adj a scopo di lucro *a sko·poh dee loo·kroh*

profit margin n il margine di profitto *mar·jee·ne dee pro·feet·toh*

profit-sharing n la compartecipazione agli utili *kom·par·te·chee·pa·tsyoh·ne al·yee oo·tee·lee*

program(me) n il programma *pro· gram·ma* □ vt programmare *pro· gram·mah·ray* L50

programmer n (*person*) il programmatore *pro·gram·ma·toh·re*, la programmatrice *pro·gram·ma·tree·che*

programming n (*computer*) la programmazione *pro·gram·ma·tsyoh·ne*

progress n il progresso *pro·gres·soh*; to make progress fare* progressi *fah· ray pro·gres·see*

prohibit vt proibire *pro·ee·bee·re*

project n (*plan*) il progetto *pro·jet·toh*; (*venture*) l'impresa (*f*) *eem·pray·sa*

projector n il proiettore *pro·yet·toh·re*

promenade n (*by sea*) il lungomare *loon·go·mah·re*

promise n la promessa *pro·mays·sa* □ vt promettere* *pro·mayt·te·re*

promote vt promuovere* *pro·mwo· ve·re*

promotion n la promozione *pro·mo· tsyoh·ne*

pronounce vt pronunciare *pro·noon· chah·ray*

pronunciation n la pronuncia *pro· noon·cha*

proof n la prova *pro·va*; a 70° proof whisky un whisky di 40 gradi *oon wee·skee dee 40 grah·dee*

proper adj (*appropriate*) adatto(a) *a· dat·to(a)*; (*correct*) corretto(a) *kor· ret·to(a)*; (*respectable*) conveniente *kon·ve·nyen·te*

properly adv correttamente *kor·ret·ta· mayn·te*

property n la proprietà *pro·prye·ta*; (*estate*) il patrimonio *pa·tree·mo· nyoh*

proposal n (*suggestion*) la proposta *pro·poh·sta*

propose vt (*suggest*) proporre* *pro· pohr·re*; to propose a toast to someone brindare a qualcuno *breen· dah·ray a kwal·koo·no*

proposition n (*proposal*) la proposta *pro·poh·sta*

prospect n la prospettiva *pro·spet· tee·va*

prospectus n il prospetto *pro·spet·toh*

prosperous adj prospero(a) *pro·spe· ro(a)*

protect vt proteggere* *pro·tej·je·re*

protein n la proteina *pro·te·ee·na*

protest n la protesta *pro·te·sta* □ vi protestare *pro·te·stah·ray*

Protestant adj protestante *pro·te· stan·te* Sn86

prototype n il prototipo *pro·to·tee·poh*

proud adj orgoglioso(a) *or·goh·lyoh· so(a)*; proud of fiero(a) di *fye·ro(a) dee*

prove vt provare *pro·vah·ray*

provide vt fornire *for·nee·re*; to provide someone with something fornire qualcuno di qualcosa *for·nee·re kwal·koo·no dee kwal·ko·sa* □ vi to provide for someone provvedere* a qualcuno *prov·ve·day·re a kwal· koo·no*

provided, providing conj purché *poor· kay*; provided (that) he comes purché venga *poor·kay ven·ga*

province n (*region*) la provincia *pro· veen·cha*

provincial adj provinciale *pro·veen· chah·le*

proviso n la condizione *kon·dee· tsyoh·ne*

prune n la prugna secca *proon·ya sayk· ka*

P.S. abbrev P.S. *pee·es·se*

psychiatric adj psichiatrico(a) *psee·kee· a·tree·ko(a)*

psychiatrist n lo/la psichiatra *psee·kee· a·tra*

psychological adj psicologico(a) *psee· ko·lo·jee·ko(a)*

psychologist n lo/la psicologo(a) *psee· ko·lo·go(a)*

psychology n la psicologia *psee·ko·lo· jee·a*

P.T.O. abbrev Vedi retro

pub n il bar *bar*

public adj pubblico(a) *poob·blee·ko(a)* □ n il pubblico *poob·blee·koh*; in public in pubblico *een poob·blee·koh*

public conveniences pl i gabinetti *ga· bee·nayt·tee*

publicity n la pubblicità *poob·blee· chee·ta*

publicity campaign n la campagna di pubblicità *kam·pan·ya dee poob· blee·chee·ta* Bm17

public relations n le pubbliche relazioni *poob·blee·ke re·la·tsyoh·nee*

public relations officer n l'incaricato delle pubbliche relazioni (*m*) *een·ka· ree·kah·toh del·le poob·blee·ke re·la· tsyoh·nee*

public school n (*in Britain*) la scuola privata *skwo·la pree·vah·ta*

public sector n il settore pubblico *set· toh·re poob·blee·ko*

publish vt pubblicare *poob·blee·kah· ray*

publisher n l'editore (*m*) *e·dee·toh·re*, l'editrice (*f*) *e·dee·tree·che*

pudding n il dolce *dohl·che*

puddle n la pozzanghera *pots·tsan· ge·ra*

pull vt/i tirare *tee·rah·ray*; to pull something out cavare qualcosa *ka· vah·ray kwal·ko·sa*; to pull out of a deal ritirarsi da un affare *ree·tee·rar· see da oon af·fah·re*; the car pulled in la macchina si è accostata *la mak· kee·na see e ak·ko·stah·ta*; he pulled out to overtake the car fece manovra per superare la macchina *fay·che ma·no·vra payr soo·pe·rah·ray la mak·kee·na*; to pull something off strappare qualcosa *strap·pah·ray kwal·ko·sa*

pullover n il pullover *pool·lo·ver*

pump n la pompa *pohm·pa* □ vt pompare *pohm·pah·ray*

pumpkin n la zucca *tsook·ka*

punch n (blow) il pugno *poon·yoh*; (drink) il ponce *pon·che* □ vt (with fist) dare* un pugno a *dah·ray oon poon·yoh a*; (ticket etc) forare *fo·rah·ray*

punctual adj (person) puntuale *poon·too·ah·le*; (train) in orario *een o·rah·ryoh*

puncture n la foratura *fo·ra·too·ra*

punish vt punire *poo·nee·re*

punishment n la punizione *poo·nee·tsyoh·ne*

pupil n l'alunno(a) (m/f) *a·loon·no(a)*

purchase n l'acquisto (m) *ak·kwee·stoh* □ vt comprare *kom·prah·ray*

pure adj puro(a) *poo·ro(a)*

purée n il purè *poo·re*

purple adj purpureo(a) *poor·poo·re·o(a)*

purpose n lo scopo *sko·poh*; on purpose apposta *ap·po·sta*

purse n (for money) il borsellino *bor·sel·lee·noh*; (lady's bag) la borsa *bohr·sa*

push vt spingere* *speen·je·re*; (button) premere *pre·me·re*; (product) lanciare *lan·chah·ray*; push it in lo spinga dentro *lo speen·ga dayn·tro*

push-chair n il passeggino *pas·sej·jee·noh*

put vt mettere* *mayt·te·re*; to put a question fare* una domanda *fah·ray oo·na do·man·da*; to put one's things away mettere* le cose a posto *mayt·te·re le ko·se a poh·stoh*; to put back (replace) rimettere* *ree·mayt·te·re*; to put down a parcel deporre* un pacco *de·pohr·re oon pak·koh*; to put on a dress indossare un abito *een·dos·sah·ray oon ah·bee·toh*; to put on the light accendere* la luce *ach·chen·de·re la loo·che*; to put on the brakes frenare *fre·nah·ray*; to put the light spegnere* la luce *spen·ye·re la loo·che*; he put out his hand ha allungato la mano *a al·loon·gah·to la mah·noh*; to put someone through (on phone) mettere* qualcuno in comunicazione *mayt·te·re kwal·koo·no een ko·moo·nee·ka·tsyoh·ne*; to put up a notice affiggere* un avviso *af·feej·je·re oon av·vee·zoh*; to put up capital fornire del capitale *for·nee·re del ka·pee·tah·le*

puzzle n il rompicapo *rom·pee·kah·poh*; (jigsaw) il puzzle *pa·zel*

pyjamas pl il pigiama *pee·jah·ma*

pyramid n la piramide *pee·ra·mee·de*

Pyrenees pl i Pirenei *pee·re·ne·ee*

Q

quail n la quaglia *kwal·ya*

quaint adj curioso(a) *koo·ryoh·so(a)*

qualification n (diploma etc) il titolo *tee·to·loh*; (restriction) la riserva *ree·ser·va*

qualified adj qualificato(a) *kwa·lee·fee·kah·to(a)*

qualify for vt (grant etc) corrispondere* ai requisiti per *kor·ree·spohn·de·re a·ee re·kwee·zee·tee payr*; (in sports) qualificarsi per *kwa·lee·fee·kar·see payr*

quality n la qualità *kwa·lee·ta*; quality goods gli articoli di qualità *ar·tee·ko·lee dee kwa·lee·ta*

quantity n la quantità *kwan·tee·ta*

quarantine n la quarantena *kwa·ran·te·na*

quarrel n la lite *lee·te* □ vi litigare *lee·tee·gah·ray*

quarry n la cava *kah·va*

quart n due pinte *doo·e peen·te*

quarter n il quarto *kwar·toh*; a quarter of an hour un quarto d'ora *oon kwar·toh doh·ra*; (a) quarter to 4 le 4 meno un quarto *le 4 may·no oon kwar·toh*; (a) quarter past 4 le 4 e un quarto *le 4 e oon kwar·toh*

quartz n il quarzo *kwar·tsoh*

quay n la banchina *ban·kee·na*

quayside n la banchina *ban·kee·na*

queen n la regina *re·jee·na*

queer adj (strange) strano(a) *strah·no(a)*

question n la domanda *do·man·da*; (subject discussed) la questione *kwe·styoh·ne*; to ask a question fare* una domanda *fah·ray oo·na do·man·da*; it's a question of è questione di *e kwe·styoh·ne dee*; out of the question fuori discussione *fwo·ree dee·skoos·syoh·ne*

question mark n il punto interrogativo *poon·toh een·ter·ro·ga·tee·vo*

questionnaire n il questionario *kwe·styoh·nah·ryoh*

queue n la coda *koh·da* □ vi fare* la coda *fah·ray la koh·da*

quiche n la quiche *keesh*

quick adj rapido(a) *ra·pee·do(a)*; be quick! faccia presto! *fach·cha pre·sto*

quickly adv rapidamente *ra·pee·da·mayn·te*

quiet adj tranquillo(a) *tran·kweel·lo(a)*; be quiet! zitto(a)! *tseet·to(a)* A5

quietly adv (speak) piano *pyah·no*; (walk, speak) silenziosamente *see·len·tsyoh·sa·mayn·te*

quilt n la trapunta *tra·poon·ta*; (duvet) il piumino *pyoo·mee·noh*

quit vt (leave) abbandonare *ab·ban·do·nah·ray* □ vi (give up) rinunciare *ree·noon·chah·ray*

quite adv (fairly) piuttosto *pyoot·to·sto*; (absolutely) del tutto *del toot·toh*; quite a few abbastanza *ab·ba·stan·tsa*

quiz n il quiz *kweez*

quota n (of goods) la quota *kwo·ta*

quotation n (passage) la citazione *chee·ta·tsyoh·ne*; (price) la quotazione *kwo·ta·tsyoh·ne*

quote vt (passage) citare *chee·tah·ray*; (price) quotare *kwo·tah·ray*

R

rabbi n il rabbino *rab·bee·noh*

rabbit n il coniglio *ko·neel·yoh*

rabies n la rabbia *rab·bya*

race n la razza *rats·tsa*; (sport) la corsa *kohr·sa*; the races le corse *kohr·se*

racecourse n l'ippodromo (m) *eep·po·dro·moh*

racehorse n il cavallo da corsa *ka·val·loh da kohr·sa*

race relations pl i rapporti interrazziali *rap·por·tee een·tayr·rats·tsyah·lee*

race track n la pista *pee·sta*

racial adj razziale *rats·tsyah·lay*

rack n (for luggage) il portabagagli *por·ta·ba·gal·yee*; (for wine) il portabottiglie *por·ta·bot·teel·yay*; (for dishes) lo scolapiatti *sko·la·pyat·tee*

racket n (tennis) la racchetta *rak·kayt·ta*

radar n il radar ra·dar

radar trap n il controllo radar kon·trol· loh ra·dar

radial(-ly) adj cinturato(a) cheen·too· rah·to(a)

radiator n il radiatore ra·dya·toh·ray T179

radio n la radio ra·dyoh; on the radio alla radio al·la ra·dyoh

radish n il ravanello ra·va·nel·loh

rag n lo straccio strach·choh

ragged adj (clothes) a brandelli a bran· del·lee

raid n (military) l'attacco (m) at·tak· koh; (by police) l'irruzione (f) eer· roo·tsyoh·nay; (by criminals) la raz· zia rats·tsee·a

rail n (on stairs) il corrimano kor·ree· mah·noh; (on bridge, balcony) la ringhiera reen·gye·ra; rails (for train) le rotaie ro·ta·ye; by rail per ferrovia payr fer·ro·vee·a

railings pl n la cancellata kan·chel·lah·ta

railroad, railway n la ferrovia fer·ro· vee·a T69f

railway station n la stazione sta·tsyoh· nay T69f

rain vi piovere* pyo·ve·re; it's raining piove pyo·ve Mc8

rainbow n l'arcobaleno (m) ar·ko·ba· lay·noh

raincoat n l'impermeabile (m) eem· payr·me·ah·bee·lay

rainy adj piovoso(a) pyo·voh·so(a)

raise vt sollevare sol·le·vah·ray; (price) rialzare ree·al·tsah·ray; (family) alle· vare al·le·vah·ray; (amount) l'aumento ow·mayn·toh

raisins pl l'uva passa (f) oo·va pas·sa

rake n il rastrello ra·strel·loh

rally n (political) la manifestazione ma·ne·fe·sta·tsyoh·nay; (sporting) il rally ral·lee

ramp n (slope) la rampa ram·pa; (in garage) l'elevatore (m) e·le·va·toh· ray

ranch n il ranch ranch

random adj fatto(a) a caso fat·to(a) a kah·zo; at random a caso a kah·zo

range n (variety) la scelta shayl·ta; (of mountains) la catena ka·tay·na; (of missile) la gittata jeet·tah·ta □ vi to range from X to Y andare* da X a Y an·dah·ray da X a Y

range finder n (on camera) il telemetro te·le·me·troh

rank n (status) il rango ran·goh; (for taxis) il posteggio di tassì po·stayj· joh dee tas·see

rare adj raro(a) rah·ro(a); (steak) al sangue al san·gwe

rash n l'eruzione (f) e·roo·tsyoh·nay

raspberry n il lampone lam·poh·nay

rat n il ratto rat·toh

rate n (price) la tariffa ta·reef·fa; at the rate of al ritmo di al reet·moh dee; rate of inflation il tasso d'inflazione tas·soh deen·fla·tsyoh·ne; rate of ex· change il cambio kam·byoh M23, Sn21, Bm26

rates pl (local tax) le tasse comunali tas·se ko·moo·nah·lee

rather adv (quite) piuttosto pyoot·to· sto; I'd rather go to the cinema prefe· rirei andare al cinema pre·fe·ree·ray an·dah·ray al chee·ne·ma

ratio n il rapporto rap·por·toh

rationalization n la razionalizzazione ra·tsyoh·na·leedz·dza·tsyoh·nay

rationalize vt razionalizzare ra·tsyoh· na·leedz·dzah·ray

ravioli n i ravioli ra·vee·o·lee

raw adj (uncooked) crudo(a) kroo· do(a); (unprocessed) grezzo(a) graydz·dzo(a)

raw material n le materie prime ma·te· ree·e pree·me

ray n il raggio raj·joh

razor n il rasoio ra·soh·yo A42

razor blade n la lametta da barba la· met·ta da bar·ba

reach vt (arrive at) arrivare a ar·ree· vah·ray a; (with hand) raggiungere* raj·joon·je·ray; (contact) contattare kon·tat·tah·ray □ n out of reach fuori portata fwo·ree por·tah·ta; within easy reach of the sea a poca distanza dal mare a po·ka dee·stan·tsa dal mah·re

reaction n la reazione re·a·tsyoh·nay

reactor n il reattore re·at·toh·ray

read vt/i leggere* lej·je·re

readdress vt fare* proseguire fah·ray pro·se·gwee·ray

reading n la lettura let·too·ra

ready adj pronto(a) prohn·to(a); ready to do something pronto(a) a fare qualcosa prohn·to(a) a fah·ray kwal· ko·sa Sn56

ready-cooked adj precotto(a) pre·kot· to(a)

ready-made adj (clothes) confeziona· to(a) kon·fe·tsyoh·nah·to(a)

ready-to-wear adj prêt-à-porter preh· ta·por·tay

real adj vero(a) vay·roh(a); it's a real problem è un vero problema e oon vay·roh pro·ble·ma; in real terms realmente re·al·mayn·tay

real estate n la proprietà fondiaria pro·pree·e·ta fon·dee·ah·ree·a

realize vt rendersi* conto di ren·der· see kohn·toh dee; (assets) realizzare re·a·leedz·dzah·ray

really adv veramente ve·ra·mayn·tay

realtor n l'agente immobiliare (m) a· jen·tay eem·mo·beel·yah·ray

rear adj posteriore po·ste·ryoh·ray □ vt (children, cattle) allevare al·le·vah· ray

rear-view mirror n lo specchietto re· trovisore spek·kyayt·toh re·tro·vee· zoh·ray

reason n la ragione ra·joh·nay

reasonable adj ragionevole ra·joh·nay· vo·lay

receipt n la ricevuta ree·che·voo·ta; (for parcel) la ricevuta di spedizione ree·che·voo·ta dee spe·dee·tsyoh·nay; receipts (income) gli introiti een·tro· ee·tee M14

receive vt (letter) ricevere ree·chay·ve· ray; (guest) accogliere* ak·kol·ye·ray

receiver n (phone) il ricevitore ree· che·vee·toh·ray

recent adj recente re·chen·tay

recently adv recentemente re·chen·te· mayn·tay

reception n il ricevimento ree·che·vee· mayn·toh

reception desk n il ricevimento ree· che·vee·mayn·toh

receptionist n (in hotel) l'addetto(a) al ricevimento (m/f) ad·dayt·to(a) al ree·che·vee·mayn·toh

recession n la recessione re·ches·syoh· nay

recipe n la ricetta ree·chet·ta

recognize vt riconoscere* ree·ko·noh· she·ray

recommend vt raccomandare rak·ko· man·dah·ray E10, 17

record n (*register*) la documentazione *do·koo·men·ta·tsyoh·nay*; (*file*) l'archivio (*m*) *ar·kee·vyoh*; (*disk*) il disco *dee·skoh*; (*in sports*) il primato *pree·mah·toh* □ adj (*production, crop etc*) record *re·kord* □ vt registrare *re·je·strah·ray*

recorded delivery n □ **by recorded delivery** con ricevuta di ritorno *kohn ree·che·voo·ta dee ree·tohr·noh*

record-player n il giradischi *jee·ra·dee·skee*

recover vi (*from illness*) rimettersi* *ree·mayt·ter·see*

recruit vt (*personnel*) assumere* *as·soo·me·ray* □ n la recluta *re·kloo·ta*

recruitment n il reclutamento *re·kloo·ta·mayn·toh*

red adj rosso(a) *rohs·so(a)*

red currant n il ribes rosso *ree·bes rohs·so*

red-haired adj dai capelli rossi *dai ka·pel·lee rohs·see*

redirect vt (*letter*) fare* proseguire *fah·ray pro·se·gwee·ray*

redistribute vt ridistribuire *ree·dee·stree·boo·ee·ray*

redistribution n la ridistribuzione *ree·dee·stree·boo·tsyoh·nay*

red light n (*traffic light*) la luce rossa *loo·che rohs·sa*; **to go through a red light** passare con il rosso *pas·sah·ray kohn eel rohs·soh*

red light district n il quartiere luce rossa *kwar·tyay·ray loo·che rohs·sa*

red tape n la burocrazia *boo·ro·kra·tsee·a*

reduce vt ridurre* *ree·door·ray* □ vi (*lose weight*) dimagrire *dee·ma·gree·ray*

reduction n la riduzione *ree·doo·tsyoh·nay*; (*in price*) il ribasso *ree·bas·soh*; **to buy something at a reduction** comprare qualcosa a prezzo ridotto *kom·prah·ray kwal·ko·sa a prets·tsoh ree·doht·to* I3

redundant adj (*worker*) licenziato(a) *lee·chen·tsyah·to(a)*

referee n (*sports*) l'arbitro (*m*) *ar·bee·troh*

reference n (*mention*) la menzione *men·tsyoh·nay*; (*testimonial*) le referenze *re·fe·ren·tse*; **his reference to this matter** la sua menzione di quest'affare *la soo·a men·tsyoh·nay dee kway·staf·fah·ray*; **with reference to your letter** in riferimento alla vostra lettera *een ree·fe·ree·mayn·toh al·la vo·stra let·te·ra*

refer to vt (*allude to*) alludere* a *al·loo·de·ray a*; (*consult*) consultare *kon·sool·tah·ray*

refine vt raffinare *raf·fee·nah·ray*

refinery n la raffineria *raf·fee·ne·ree·a*

reflect vt riflettere* *ree·flet·te·ray*

reflector n (*on cycle, car*) il catarifrangente *ka·ta·ree·fran·jen·tay*

refreshments pl i rinfreschi *reen·fray·skee*

refrigerator n il frigorifero *free·go·ree·fe·roh*

refund vt rimborsare *reem·bor·sah·ray* □ n il rimborso *reem·bohr·soh*

refusal n il rifiuto *ree·fyoo·toh*

refuse vt rifiutare *ree·fyoo·tah·ray*; **to refuse to do something** rifiutarsi di fare qualcosa *ree·fyoo·tar·see dee fah·ray kwal·ko·sa*

regarding prep per quanto riguarda *payr kwan·to ree·gwar·da*

regardless of prep senza riguardo a *sen·tsa ree·gwar·do a*

regatta n la regata *re·gah·ta*

region n la regione *re·joh·nay*

register n il registro *re·jee·stroh*

registered letter n la lettera raccomandata *let·te·ra rak·ko·man·dah·ta* Sn6

registered trademark n il marchio di fabbrica depositato *mar·kyoh dee fab·bree·ka de·po·zee·tah·to*

registration number n (*on car*) il numero di immatricolazione *noo·me·roh dee eem·ma·tree·ko·la·tsyoh·nay*

regret vt rincrescere* *reen·kray·she·ray*

regular adj regolare *re·go·lah·ray*; (*usual*) abituale *a·bee·too·ah·le*; (*ordinary*) normale *nor·mah·le*; (*size*) normale *nor·mah·le*

regulation n (*rule*) il regolamento *re·go·la·mayn·toh*

rehearsal n la prova *pro·va*

rein n la briglia *breel·ya*

reject vt respingere* *re·speen·je·ray*; (*goods in manufacture*) rifiutare *ree·fyoo·tah·ray* □ n l'articolo difettoso (*m*) *ar·tee·ko·loh dee·fet·toh·so*

relation n il/la parente *pa·ren·te*

relative n il/la parente *pa·ren·te* □ adj relativo(a) *re·la·tee·vo(a)*

relax vi rilassarsi *ree·las·sar·see*

release vt (*prisoner*) liberare *lee·be·rah·ray*; (*book, film*) fare* uscire *fah·ray oo·shee·ray*

relevant adj relativo(a) *re·la·tee·vo(a)*; **relevant to** pertinente a *payr·tee·nen·te a*

reliability n (*of person*) la serietà *se·ree·e·ta*; (*of car*) l'affidabilità (*f*) *af·fee·da·bee·lee·ta*

reliable adj (*person*) fidato(a) *fee·dah·to(a)*; (*car*) solido(a) *so·lee·do(a)*

relief n (*from pain, anxiety*) il sollievo *sol·lye·voh*

relief road n la strada sussidiaria *strah·da soos·see·dee·ah·ree·a*

relief train n il treno supplementare *tre·noh soop·ple·men·tah·ray*

religion n la religione *re·lee·joh·nay*

religious adj (*person*) religioso(a) *re·lee·joh·so(a)*

rely on vt (*person*) contare su *kon·tah·ray soo*

remain vi rimanere* *ree·ma·nay·ray*; (*be left over*) avanzare *a·van·tsah·ray*

remark n l'osservazione (*f*) *os·sayr·va·tsyoh·nay*

remarkable adj notevole *no·tay·vo·lay*

remedy n il rimedio *ree·me·dyoh*

remember vt ricordarsi di *ree·kor·dar·see dee*

remind vt ricordare *ree·kor·dah·re*; **to remind someone of something** ricordare qualcosa a qualcuno *ree·kor·dah·ray kwal·ko·sa a kwal·koo·no*

remittance n la rimessa *ree·mays·sa*

remote control n il telecomando *te·le·ko·man·doh*

removal van n il camion di traslochi *ka·myon dee tra·zlo·kee*

remove vt spostare *spo·stah·ray*; (*stain*) togliere* *tol·ye·re*

renew vt (*subscription, passport*) rinnovare *reen·no·vah·ray*

rent n l'affitto (*m*) *af·feet·toh* □ vt (*house etc*) affittare *af·feet·tah·ray*; (*car*) noleggiare *no·lej·jah·ray* A56f, L29

rental n il noleggio *no·layj·joh* A61

rental car n la macchina noleggiata *mak·kee·na no·lej·jah·ta* T108f

reorder vt (*goods*) riordinare *ree·or·dee·nah·ray*

reorganization n la riorganizzazione *ree·or·ga·needz·dza·tsyoh·nay*

reorganize vt riorganizzare *ree·or·ga·needz·dzah·ray*

repair vt riparare *ree·pa·rah·ray* T186f, Sn46f

repay vt (*sum*) ripagare *ree·pa·gah·ray*; (*person*) rimborsare *reem·bor·sah·ray*

repeat vt ripetere *ree·pe·te·ray*

repeat order n l'ordine successivo (*m*) *ohr·dee·ne soo·ches·see·vo*

repetition n la ripetizione *ree·pe·tee·tsyoh·nay*

replace vt (*put back*) rimettere* *ree·mayt·te·ray*; (*substitute*) sostituire *so·stee·too·ee·ray*

replacement n la sostituzione *so·stee·too·tsyoh·nay* Sn54

reply vi rispondere* *ree·spohn·de·ray*; **to reply to a question** rispondere* a una domanda *ree·spohn·de·ray a oo·na do·man·da* □ n **reply** la risposta *ree·spoh·sta*

report vt riportare *ree·por·tah·ray* □ n il rapporto *rap·por·toh*; (*in press*) il servizio *sayr·vee·tsyoh*

reporter n (*press*) il/la cronista *kro·nee·sta*

represent vt rappresentare *rap·pre·zen·tah·ray*

representative n il/la rappresentante *rap·pre·zen·tan·te* T18, Bm19

republic n la repubblica *re·poob·blee·ka*

republican adj repubblicano(a) *re·poob·blee·kah·no(a)*

reputation n la fama *fah·ma*

request n la richiesta *ree·kye·sta*

request stop n la fermata facoltativa *fayr·mah·ta fa·kol·ta·tee·va*

require vt (*need*) avere* bisogno di a·vay·ray bee·zohn·yoh dee*

requirement n l'esigenza (*f*) *e·zee·jen·tsa*

reroute vt deviare *de·vee·ah·ray*

resale n □ **not for resale** rivendita proibita *ree·vayn·dee·ta pro·ee·bee·ta*

rescue vt salvare *sal·vah·ray* □ n il salvataggio *sal·va·taj·joh*

research n la ricerca *ree·chayr·ka*

resell vt rivendere *ree·vayn·de·ray*

resemble vt rassomigliare *ras·so·meel·yah·ray*; **he resembles his father** rassomiglia a suo padre *ras·so·meel·ya a soo·o pah·dre*

reservation n (*of seats, rooms etc*) la prenotazione *pre·no·ta·tsyoh·nay*; (*doubt*) la riserva *ree·ser·va* A57

reserve vt (*seat, room*) riservare *ree·ser·vah·ray* B35, A13, E2, L46

reserve price n il prezzo minimo *prets·tsoh mee·nee·mo*

reserves pl le riserve *ree·ser·ve*

residence n la residenza *re·see·den·tsa*

residence permit n il permesso di soggiorno *payr·mays·soh dee soj·johr·noh*

residential adj (*area*) residenziale *re·see·den·tsyah·le*

resign vi dimettersi* *dee·mayt·ter·see*

resignation n le dimissioni *dee·mees·syoh·nee*

resist vt resistere* *re·see·ste·ray*

resistance n (*to illness*) la resistenza *re·see·sten·tsa*

resort n il luogo di villeggiatura *lwo·go dee veel·lej·ja·too·ra*; **in the last resort** in ultimo *een ool·tee·mo* □ vi **to**

resort to ricorrere* a *ree·kohr·re·ray a*

resources pl le risorse *ree·sohr·se*

respect n il rispetto *ree·spet·toh* □ vt rispettare *ree·spet·tah·ray*

respectable adj rispettabile *ree·spet·tah·bee·lay*

responsibility n la responsabilità *re·spon·sa·bee·lee·ta*; **this is your responsibility** questo è di Sua responsabilità *kway·stoh e dee soo·a re·spon·sa·bee·lee·ta*

responsible adj responsabile *re·spon·sah·bee·lay*; **responsible for** (*to blame*) responsabile di *re·spon·sah·bee·lay dee*; **he's responsible for the department** è lui il responsabile del dipartimento *e loo·ee eel re·spon·sah·bee·lay del dar·par·tee·mayn·toh*

rest n il riposarsi *ree·po·sar·see* □ n (*repose*) il riposo *ree·po·soh*; **all the rest** tutto il resto *toot·to eel re·sto*

restaurant n il ristorante *ree·sto·ran·te* B59, E1

restaurant car n il vagone ristorante *va·goh·nay ree·sto·ran·te*

restrict vt limitare *lee·mee·tah·ray*

restriction n la restrizione *ree·stree·tsyoh·nay*

restroom n la toeletta *to·e·let·ta*

result n il risultato *ree·sool·tah·toh*

retail n la vendita al minuto *vayn·dee·ta al mee·noo·toh*; **to sell something retail** vendere qualcosa al minuto *vayn·de·re kwal·ko·sa al mee·noo·toh* □ vt **retail** vendere al minuto *vayn·de·re al mee·noo·toh*

retailer n il dettagliante *det·tal·yan·te*

retail price n il prezzo al minuto *prets·tsoh al mee·noo·toh* Bm25

retire vi andare* in pensione *an·dah·ray een pen·syoh·nay*

retired adj in pensione *een pen·syoh·nay*

retirement n il ritiro *ree·tee·ro*

retrain vt riaddestrare *ree·ad·de·strah·ray* □ vi riaddestrarsi *ree·ad·de·strar·see*

retraining n il riaddestramento *ree·ad·de·stra·mayn·toh*

retread n lo pneumatico rimodellato *pne·oo·ma·tee·koh ree·mo·del·lah·toh*

retrieve vt (*data*) ricuperare *ree·koo·pe·rah·ray*

retrospect n □ **in retrospect** retrospettivamente *re·tro·spet·tee·va·mayn·tay*

return vi tornare *tor·nah·ray* □ vt (*give back*) restituire *re·stee·too·ee·ray*; (*send back*) rinviare *reen·vee·ah·ray* □ n (*going/coming back*) il ritorno *ree·tohr·noh*; (*profit*) il guadagno *gwa·dan·yoh*

return ticket n il biglietto di andata e ritorno *beel·yayt·toh dee an·dah·ta e ree·tohr·noh* T58, 59

rev n (*in engine*) il giro *jee·roh* □ vt imballare *eem·bal·lah·ray*

revenue n il reddito *red·dee·toh*

reverse n (*gear*) la retromarcia *re·tro·mar·cha*; **in reverse** (*gear*) in retromarcia *een re·tro·mar·cha* □ vt **to reverse the charges** telefonare ad onere del destinatario *te·le·fo·nah·ray ad o·ne·re del de·stee·na·tah·ree·oh* □ vi **to reverse into the garage** entrare nel garage in retromarcia *en·trah·ray nel ga·raj een re·tro·mar·cha*

reversed charge call n la telefonata con la R *te·le·fo·nah·ta kohn la er·re* Sn13

review *n* la revisione *re·vee·zee·oh·nay*; *(of book etc)* la recensione *re·chen·syoh·nay* □ *vt* riesaminare *ree·e·za·mee·nah·ray*

revise *vt (estimate etc)* rivedere* *ree·ve·day·re*; *(school work)* ripassare *ree·pas·sah·ray*

revive *vt (person)* rianimare *ree·a·nee·mah·ray* □ *vi* riprendere* i sensi *ree·pren·de·re ee sen·see*

revolution *n (political)* la rivoluzione *ree·vo·loo·tsyoh·nay*

revue *n* la rivista *ree·vee·sta*

reward *n* la ricompensa *ree·kom·pen·sa*

rheumatism *n* il reumatismo *re·oo·ma·tee·zmoh*

Rhine *n* il Reno *re·no*

Rhone *n* il Rodano *ro·da·no*

rhubarb *n* il rabarbaro *ra·bar·ba·roh*

rhythm *n* il ritmo *reet·moh*

rib *n* la costola *ko·sto·la*

ribbon *n* il nastro *na·stroh*

rice *n* il riso *ree·soh*

rich *adj* ricco(a) *reek·ko(a)*; *(food)* pesante *pe·san·te*

ride *n (in vehicle)* il percorso *payr·kohr·soh*; *(on horse)* la cavalcata *ka·val·kah·ta*; **to go for a ride** *(by car)* fare* un giro in macchina *fah·ray oon jee·roh een mak·kee·na*; **to give someone a ride into town** dare* un passaggio in città a qualcuno *dah·ray oon pas·saj·joh een cheet·ta a kwal·koo·noh*; **it's only a short ride** non è che un breve percorso *nohn e ke oon bre·ve payr·kohr·soh* □ *vt* **to ride a horse** cavalcare *ka·val·kah·ray*; **to ride a bicycle** andare* in bicicletta *an·dah·ray een bee·chee·klayt·ta*

ridge *n* il giogo *joh·goh*

ridiculous *adj* ridicolo(a) *ree·dee·ko·lo(a)*

riding *n* la cavalcata *ka·val·kah·ta*; **to go riding** cavalcare *ka·val·kah·ray* L35

rifle *n* il fucile *foo·chee·le*

right *adj (correct)* corretto(a) *kor·rayt·to(a)*; *(morally good)* giusto(a) *joo·sto(a)*; *(not left)* destro(a) *de·stro(a)*; **yes, that's right** sì, giusto *see joo·sto* □ *adv* **to turn right** girare a destra *jee·rah·ray a de·stra*; **right in the middle** proprio nel mezzo *pro·pree·o nel medz·dzoh* □ *n* **right** *(right-hand side)* la destra *de·stra*; *(entitlement)* il diritto *dee·reet·toh*; **on/to the right** a destra *a de·stra* B34, T104

right-handed *adj* chi usa di preferenza la mano destra *kee oo·za dee pre·fe·ren·tsa la mah·no de·stra*

right of way *n (on road)* la precedenza *pre·che·den·tsa*

ring *n (on finger)* l'anello *(m)* *a·nel·loh*; *(circle)* il cerchio *chayr·kyoh*; *(wedding ring)* la fede *fay·de* □ *vt* **to ring the (door)bell** suonare *swo·nah·ray* □ *vi* **ring** suonare *swo·nah·ray*; *(telephone)* squillare *skweel·lah·ray*; **to ring off** riattaccare il telefono *ree·at·tak·kah·ray eel te·le·fo·no*; **to ring back** ritelefonare *ree·te·le·fo·nah·ray*; **ring me tomorrow** mi telefoni domani *mee te·le·fo·nee do·mah·nee*

ring road *n* la circonvallazione *cheer·kon·val·la·tsyoh·nay*

rink *n* la pista di pattinaggio *pee·sta dee pat·tee·naj·joh*

rinse *vt* risciacquare *ree·shak·kwah·ray* □ *n (hair tint)* la tintura *teen·too·ra*

riot *n* il tumulto *too·mool·toh*

rip *vt* strappare *strap·pah·ray* □ *vi* strapparsi *strap·par·see*

ripe *adj (fruit)* maturo(a) *ma·too·ro(a)*; *(cheese)* stagionato(a) *sta·joh·nah·to(a)*

rise *vi (go up)* salire* *sa·lee·ray*; *(prices)* aumentare *ow·men·tah·ray*; *(person)* alzarsi *al·tsar·see*; *(sun)* sorgere* *sohr·je·re* □ *n (in prices, wages)* il rialzo *ree·al·tsoh*

risk *n* il rischio *ree·skyoh* □ *vt* rischiare *ree·skyah·ray*

risotto *n* il risotto *ree·sot·toh*

rival *n* il/la rivale *ree·vah·le*; **a rival firm** una ditta concorrente *oo·na deet·ta kon·kor·ren·te*

river *n* il fiume *fyoo·me*

Riviera *n* la Costa Azzurra *ko·sta adz·dzoor·ra*

road *n* la strada *strah·da* T133f, F21

road block *n* la barricata *bar·ree·kah·ta*

road map *n* la carta stradale *kar·ta stra·dah·le*

road sign *n* il segnale *sen·yah·le* T143f

road test *n* la prova su strada *pro·va soo strah·da*

road works *pl* i lavori stradali *la·voh·ree stra·dah·lee*

roar *vi (person)* urlare *oor·lah·ray*; *(lion)* ruggire *rooj·jee·ray*; *(engine)* rimbombare *reem·bom·bah·ray* □ *n (of person)* l'urlo *(m)* *oor·loh*; *(of lion)* il ruggito *rooj·jee·toh*; *(of engine)* il rombo *rohm·boh*

roast *vt* arrostire *ar·ro·stee·ray*; **roast meat** l'arrosto *(m)* *ar·ro·stoh*

rob *vt (person)* derubare *de·roo·bah·ray*; *(bank)* svaligiare *zva·lee·jah·ray*

robbery *n* il furto *foor·toh*

robe *n (after bath)* l'accappatoio *(m)* *ak·kap·pa·toh·yoh*

robot *n* il robot *ro·bot*

rock *n* la roccia *roch·cha*; **on the rocks** *(with ice)* con ghiaccio *kohn gyach·choh* □ *vt* **rock** cullare *kool·lah·ray*

rocket *n* il razzo *radz·dzoh*

rock ('n' roll) *n* il rock and roll *rok and rol*

rod *n (metallic)* la barra *bar·ra*; *(fishing)* la canna da pesca *kan·na da pay·ska*

roll *n* il rotolo *ro·to·loh*; *(bread)* il panino *pa·nee·noh* □ *vt (on wheels)* fare* rotolare *fah·ray ro·to·lah·ray*; **to roll up** *(newspaper etc)* arrotolare *ar·ro·to·lah·ray* □ *vi* **roll** rotolare *ro·to·lah·ray*

roller skates *pl* i pattini a rotelle *pat·tee·nee a ro·tel·le*

rolling pin *n* il matterello *mat·te·rel·loh*

Roman *adj* romano(a) *ro·mah·no(a)*; **Roman Catholic** cattolico(a) *kat·to·lee·ko(a)*

romantic *adj* romantico(a) *ro·man·tee·ko(a)*

Rome *n* Roma *(f)* *roh·ma*

roof *n* il tetto *tayt·toh*

roof rack *n* il portabagagli *por·ta·ba·gal·yee*

room *n (in house)* la stanza *stan·tsa*; *(in hotel)* la camera *kah·me·ra*; *(space)* lo spazio *spa·tsyoh* A4f

room service *n* il servizio di camera *sayr·vee·tsyoh dee kah·me·ra*

root *n* la radice *ra·dee·chay*

rope *n* la corda *kor·da*

rose *n* la rosa *ro·za*

rosé *n* il rosé *ro·zay*

rot *vi* marcire *mar·chee·ray*

rotten *adj* (wood etc) marcio(a) *mar·cho(a)*

rough *n* (golf) l'erba lunga (f) *er·ba loon·ga* □ *adj* (surface) ruvido(a) *roo·vee·do(a)*; (weather) burrascoso(a) *boor·ra·skoh·so(a)*; (sea) agitato(a) *a·jee·tah·to(a)*; (not gentle) violento(a) *vee·o·len·to(a)*; **a rough estimate** un calcolo approssimativo *oon kal·ko·loh ap·pros·see·ma·tee·vo*

roughly *adv* rudemente *roo·de·mayn·tay*; (approximately) approssimativamente *ap·pros·see·ma·tee·va·mayn·tay*

roulette *n* la roulette *roo·let*

round *adj* rotondo(a) *ro·tohn·do(a)* □ *n* (circle) il cerchio *chayr·kyoh*; (in competition) la partita *par·tee·ta*; (in boxing) il round *rownd*; (of golf) il giro *jee·roh*; (of talks) la serie *se·ree·e* □ *prep* intorno a *een·tohr·no a*; **to go round the shops** fare* un giro dei negozi *fah·ray oon jee·roh de·ee ne·go·tsee*; **it's round the corner** è dietro l'angolo *è dye·tro lan·go·loh* □ *adv* to turn something round girare qualcosa *jee·rah·ray kwal·ko·sa*

roundabout *n* la rotonda *ro·tohn·da*; (fairground) la giostra *jo·stra*

round figure/number *n* la cifra tonda *cheef·ra tohn·da*

round trip *n* il viaggio di andata e ritorno *vyaj·joh dee an·dah·ta e ree·tohr·noh*

round trip (ticket) *n* il biglietto di andata e ritorno *beel·yayt·toh dee an·dah·ta e ree·tohr·noh* T58

route *n* l'itinerario (m) *ee·tee·ne·rah·ryoh* T133, F18

routine *n* la routine *roo·teen* □ *adj* comune *ko·moo·ne*

row[1] *n* la fila *fee·la* □ *vi* (sport) remare *re·mah·ray*

row[2] *n* (noise) lo schiamazzo *skya·mats·tsoh*

rowing (sport) il canottaggio *ka·not·taj·joh*

royal *adj* reale *re·ah·le*

R.S.V.P. *abbrev* R.S.V.P.

rub *vt* fregare *fre·gah·ray*; **to rub out** cancellare *kan·chel·lah·ray*

rubber *n* (material) la gomma *gohm·ma*; (eraser) la gomma da cancellare *gohm·ma da kan·chel·lah·ray*

rubber band *n* l'elastico (m) *e·la·stee·koh*

rubbish *n* i rifiuti *ree·fyoo·tee*; (nonsense) le sciocchezze *shok·kayts·tse*

ruby *n* il rubino *roo·bee·noh*

rucksack *n* lo zaino *dzy·noh*

rudder *n* il timone *tee·moh·nay*

rude *adj* (person) grossolano(a) *gros·so·lah·no(a)*; (remark) scortese *skor·tay·zay*

rug *n* il tappetino *tap·pe·tee·noh*

rugby *n* il rugby *roog·bee*

ruin *n* la rovina *ro·vee·na* □ *vt* rovinare *ro·vee·nah·ray*

ruins *pl* le rovine *ro·vee·ne*

rule *n* (regulation) la regola *re·go·la*; (for measuring) il regolo *re·go·loh* □ *vt* governare *go·vayr·nah·ray*

ruler *n* (leader) il capo *kah·poh*; (for measuring) il regolo *re·go·loh*

rum *n* il rum *room*

Rumania *n* la Romania *ro·ma·nee·a*

Rumanian *adj* romeno(a) *ro·me·no(a)* □ *n* (language) il romeno *ro·me·noh*

rumble *vi* rombare *rom·bah·ray* □ *n* il rombo *rohm·boh*

rump steak *n* la bistecca di girello *bee·stayk·ka dee jee·rel·loh*

run *n* (outing) la gita *jee·ta*; (in stocking) la smagliatura *zmal·ya·too·ra* □ *vi* (person, animal) correre* *kohr·re·re*; (liquid) scorrere* *skohr·re·re*; (machine, engine) funzionare *foon·tsyoh·nah·ray*; **the trains run every hour** i treni partono ogni ora *ee tre·nee par·to·no ohn·yee oh·ra*; **the road runs past the house** la strada passa davanti alla casa *la strah·da pas·sa da·van·tee al·la kah·sa*; **this car runs on diesel** questa macchina funziona a nafta *kway·sta mak·kee·na foon·tsyoh·na a naf·ta*; **to run after someone** correre* dietro a qualcuno *kohr·re·re dye·tro a kwal·koo·no*; **to run away** fuggire *fooj·jee·re*; **to run down** or **over** (car etc) investire *een·ve·stee·ray*; **we've run out of milk** siamo rimasti senza latte *syah·mo ree·ma·stee sen·tsa lat·te* □ *vt* run (a business, country) dirigere* *dee·ree·je·ray*; **to run in** (engine, car) rodare *ro·dah·ray*

runner beans *pl* i fagiolini *fa·jo·lee·nee*

running costs *pl* il costo di esercizio *ko·stoh dee e·zayr·chee·tsyoh*

runway *n* la pista *pee·sta*

rural *adj* rurale *roo·rah·le*

rush *vi* precipitarsi *pre·chee·pee·tar·see* □ *vt* (goods) mandare con urgenza *man·dah·ray kohn oor·jen·tsa* □ *n* la fretta *frayt·ta*; **we had a rush of orders** siamo stati inondati di ordinazioni *syah·mo sta·tee een·on·dah·tee dee or·dee·na·tsyoh·nee*

rush hour *n* l'ora di punta (f) *oh·ra dee poon·ta*

Russia *n* Russia (f) *roos·sya*

Russian *adj* russo(a) *roos·so(a)* □ *n* (language) il russo *roos·soh*

rust *n* la ruggine *rooj·jee·ne* □ *vi* arrugginirsi *ar·rooj·jee·neer·see*

rustproof *adj* inossidabile *een·os·see·dah·bee·lay*

rusty *adj* arrugginito(a) *ar·rooj·jee·nee·to(a)*

rye *n* la segale *say·ga·le*; **rye** (whisky) il whisky di segale *wee·skee dee say·ga·le*

rye bread *n* il pane di segale *pa·ne dee say·ga·le*

S

saccharin(e) *n* la saccarina *sak·ka·ree·na*

sachet *n* la bustina *boo·stee·na*

sack *n* il sacco *sak·koh* □ *vt* (dismiss) licenziare *lee·chen·tsyah·ray*

sad *adj* triste *tree·ste*

saddle *n* la sella *sel·la*

safe *adj* (out of danger) salvo(a) *sal·vo(a)*; (not dangerous) innocuo(a) *een·no·kwo(a)* □ *n* la cassaforte *kas·sa·for·te* A34

safeguard *n* la salvaguardia *sal·va·gwar·dya*

safety *n* la sicurezza *see·koo·rayts·tsa*

safety belt *n* la cintura di sicurezza *cheen·too·ra dee see·koo·rayts·tsa*

safety pin *n* lo spillo di sicurezza *speel·loh dee see·koo·rayts·tsa*

sage *n* (herb) la salvia *sal·vya*

sail *n* la vela *vay·la* □ *vi* veleggiare *ve·lej·jah·ray* L30

sail(ing) boat *n* il veliero *ve·lye·roh* L29

sailor *n* il marinaio *ma·ree·na·yoh*

saint n il/la santo(a) *san·to(a)*

sake n □ for my sake per me *payr may*

salad n l'insalata (f) *een·sa·lah·ta* E39

salad cream n la maionese *ma·yo·nay·se*

salad dressing n il condimento per l'insalata *kon·dee·mayn·toh payr leen·sa·lah·ta*

salary n lo stipendio *stee·pen·dyoh*

sale n la vendita *vayn·dee·ta*; (*cheap prices*) i saldi *sal·dee*; on sale or return da vendere o rimandare *da vayn·de·re o ree·man·dah·ray*

sales pl (*cheap prices*) i saldi *sal·dee*

sales assistant n il/la commesso(a) *kom·mays·so(a)*

salesman n (*rep*) il commesso viaggiatore *kom·mays·soh vyaj·ja·toh·re*

sales manager n il direttore delle vendite *dee·ret·toh·re del·le vayn·dee·te*

saliva n la saliva *sa·lee·va*

salmon n il salmone *sal·moh·ne*

saloon n (*bar*) il bar *bar*; (*car*) la berlina *ber·lee·na*

salt n il sale *sah·le* S32

salt cellar n la saliera *sa·lye·ra*

salty adj salato(a) *sa·lah·to(a)*

same adj stesso(a) *stays·so(a)*; the same book as (*similar*) lo stesso libro di/che *lo stays·so lee·broh dee/kay* □ pron all the same nondimeno *nohn·dee·may·no*; (the) same again please! lo stesso, per favore *lo stays·soh payr fa·voh·re*

sample n (*of goods*) il campione *kam·pyoh·ne* □ vt (*wine*) degustare *de·goo·stah·ray* Bm21

sanatorium n il sanatorio *sa·na·to·ryoh*

sanctions pl le sanzioni *san·tsyoh·nee*

sand n la sabbia *sab·bya*

sandal n il sandalo *san·da·loh*

sandbank n il banco di sabbia *ban·koh dee sab·bya*

sandwich n il panino imbottito *pa·nee·noh eem·bot·tee·to*; a ham sandwich un panino al prosciutto *oon pa·nee·noh al pro·shoot·toh* E70

sandy adj (*beach*) sabbioso(a) *sab·byoh·so(a)*

sanitary towel n l'assorbente igienico (m) *as·sor·ben·te ee·je·nee·ko*

sarcastic adj sarcastico(a) *sar·ka·stee·ko(a)*

sardine n la sardina *sar·dee·na*

Sardinia n Sardegna (f) *sar·dayn·ya*

satellite n il satellite *sa·tel·lee·te*

satin n il raso *rah·soh*

satire n (*play*) la satira *sa·tee·ra*

satisfactory adj soddisfacente *sod·dee·sfa·chen·te*

satisfy vt soddisfare* *sod·dee·sfah·ray*

saturate vt (*market*) saturare *sa·too·rah·ray*

Saturday n sabato (m) *sah·ba·toh*

sauce n la salsa *sal·sa*

saucepan n la pentola *payn·to·la*

saucer n il piattino *pyat·tee·noh*

sauna n la sauna *sow·na* A11

sausage n la salsiccia *sal·seech·cha*

sausage roll n il rustico con salsiccetta *roo·stee·koh kohn sal·see·chayt·ta*

sauté adj saltato(a) *sal·tah·to(a)*

save vt (*person*) salvare *sal·vah·ray*; (*money*) risparmiare *ree·spar·myah·ray*

savings bank n la cassa di risparmio *kas·sa dee ree·spar·myoh*

savo(u)ry adj (*not sweet*) salato(a) *sa·lah·to(a)*

say vt dire* *dee·re*; could you say that

again? può ripetere quello? *pwo ree·pe·te·re kwayl·lo*

scab n la crosta *kro·sta*

scald vt scottarsi *skot·tar·see*

scale n la scala *skah·la*; (*of fish*) la scaglia *skal·ya*; scale of charges la tariffa *ta·reef·fa*

scales pl (*for weighing*) la bilancia *bee·lan·cha*

scallop n il pettine *pet·tee·ne*

scalp n il cuoio capelluto *kwo·yoh ka·pel·loo·to*

scampi n gli scampi *skam·pee*

Scandinavia n Scandinavia (f) *skan·dee·nah·vya*

Scandinavian adj scandinavo(a) *skan·dee·nah·vo(a)*

scar n la cicatrice *chee·ka·tree·che*

scarce adj raro(a) *rah·ro(a)*

scarcely adv appena *ap·pay·na*

scared adj □ to be scared avere* paura *a·vay·re pa·oo·ra*

scarf n la sciarpa *shar·pa*

scarlet adj scarlatto(a) *skar·lat·to(a)*

scene n la scena *she·na*; (*sight*) la veduta *ve·doo·ta*

scenery n il paesaggio *pa·e·zaj·joh*

scenic route n l'itinerario turistico (m) *ee·tee·ne·rah·ryoh too·ree·stee·ko* F19

scent n (*smell*) l'odore (m) *o·doh·re*; (*perfume*) il profumo *pro·foo·moh* S45

schedule n il programma *pro·gram·ma*; (*of trains etc*) l'orario (m) *o·rah·ryoh*; on schedule (*train*) in orario *een o·rah·ryoh*

scheduled flight n il volo di linea *voh·loh dee lee·ne·a*

scheme n (*plan*) il progetto *pro·jet·toh*

school n la scuola *skwo·la*

science n la scienza *shen·tsa*

science fiction n la fantascienza *fan·ta·shen·tsa*

scientific adj scientifico(a) *shen·tee·fee·ko(a)*

scientist n lo/la scienziato(a) *shen·tsyah·to(a)*

scissors pl le forbici *for·bee·chee*

scooter n lo scooter *skoo·ter*

scope n □ within the scope of entro le possibilità di *ayn·tro le pos·see·bee·lee·ta dee*

score n il punteggio *poon·tayj·joh* □ vt (*goal*) segnare *sayn·yah·ray*

Scot n lo/la scozzese *skots·tsay·se*

Scotch n (*liquor*) il whisky scozzese *wee·skee skots·tsay·se*

Scotland n Scozia (f) *sko·tsya*

Scottish adj scozzese *skots·tsay·se*

scourer n la spugnetta abrasiva *spoon·yayt·ta a·bra·zee·va*

scrap n (*bit*) il pezzettino *pets·tset·tee·noh*

scrape vt strisciare *stree·shah·ray*

scratch vt graffiare *graf·fyah·ray*

scream vi strillare *streel·lah·ray*

screen n (*partition*) il paravento *pa·ra·ven·toh*; (*TV, movie*) lo schermo *skayr·moh*

screw n la vite *vee·te*

screwdriver n il cacciavite *kach·cha·vee·te*

sculpture n la scultura *skool·too·ra* L16

sea n il mare *mah·re*; to go by sea andare* per mare *an·dah·ray payr mah·re*

seafood n i frutti di mare *froot·tee dee mah·re*

seafront n il lungomare *loon·go·mah·re*

sea level n il livello del mare *lee·vel·loh del mah·re*

seam n la costura *ko·stoo·ra*

search vt perquisire *payr·kwee·zee·re*; to search for cercare *cher·kah·ray*

seasick adj □ to be seasick avere* mal di mare *a·vay·re mal dee mah·re*

seaside n il mare *mah·re*; seaside resort la stazione balneare *sta·tsyoh·ne bal·ne·ah·re*

season n la stagione *sta·joh·ne*; the holiday season la stagione di villeggiatura *la sta·joh·ne dee veel·lej·ja·too·ra*; strawberries are in season è la stagione delle fragole *e la sta·joh·ne del·le frah·go·le*

seasoning n il condimento *kon·dee·mayn·toh*

season ticket n l'abbonamento (m) *ab·bo·na·mayn·toh*

seat n il posto *poh·stoh*; take a seat si accomodi see *ak·ko·mo·dee* T9, 44, 62, L45

seat belt n la cintura di sicurezza *cheen·too·ra dee see·koo·rayts·tsa*

seaweed n le alghe *al·ge*

second n (time) il secondo *se·kohn·doh* □ adj secondo(a) *se·kohn·do(a)*

secondary adj (importance) secondario(a) *se·kon·dah·ryo(a)*

secondary school n la scuola media *skwo·la me·dya*

second-class adj di seconda classe *dee se·kohn·da klas·se*

second floor n il secondo piano *se·kohn·do pyah·noh*

secondhand adj (car etc) di seconda mano *dee se·kohn·da mah·noh* S14

secret adj segreto(a) *se·gray·to(a)* □ n il segreto *se·gray·toh*

secretary n il/la segretario(a) *se·gre·tah·ryo(a)* Bm7, 12

secretary of state n il Segretario di Stato *se·gre·tah·ryoh dee stah·toh*

sector n (economy) il settore *set·toh·re*

security n (at airport) la sicurezza *see·koo·rayts·tsa*; (for loan) la cauzione *kow·tsyoh·ne*

sedative n il sedativo *se·da·tee·voh*

see vt/i vedere* *ve·day·re*; to see someone off at the station accompagnare qualcuno alla stazione *ak·kom·pan·yah·ray kwal·koo·no al·la sta·tsyoh·ne*; to see someone home accompagnare qualcuno a casa *ak·kom·pan·yah·ray kwal·koo·no a kah·sa*; to see to something occuparsi di qualcosa *ok·koo·par·see dee kwal·ko·sa*

seed n il seme *say·me*

seem vi sembrare *sem·brah·ray*

seersucker n il crespo di cotone *kray·spoh dee ko·toh·ne*

seesaw n l'altalena (f) *al·ta·lay·na*

seldom adv raramente *rah·ra·mayn·te*

selection n la scelta *shayl·ta* S44, Bm21

self-catering adj con cucina *kohn koo·chee·na*

self-contained adj (apartment) indipendente *een·dee·pen·den·te*

self-employed adj autonomo(a) *ow·to·no·mo(a)*

selfish adj egoistico(a) *e·go·ee·stee·ko(a)*

self-service adj self-service *self·ser·vees*

sell vt vendere *vayn·de·re* S7

sellotape n il nastro adesivo *na·stroh a·de·zee·vo*

semifinal n la semifinale *se·mee·fee·nah·le*

semiskilled adj semispecializzato(a) *se·mee·spe·cha·leedz·dzah·to(a)*

senate n (political) il senato *se·nah·toh*

senator n il senatore *se·na·toh·re*

send vt mandare *man·dah·ray*

sender n il/la mittente *meet·ten·te*

senior adj (in rank) superiore *soo·pe·ryoh·re*; (in age) maggiore *maj·joh·re*

sense n (feeling) il senso *sen·soh*; (common sense) il senso comune *sen·soh ko·moo·ne*; sense of humour la vena d'umorismo *vay·na doo·mo·ree·zmoh*; to make sense avere* senso *a·vay·re sen·soh*

sensible adj ragionevole *ra·jo·nay·vo·le*

sentence n la frase *frah·ze*

separate adj separato(a) *se·pa·rah·to(a)*

September n settembre (m) *set·tem·bre*

serious adj serio(a) *se·ryo(a)*

serve vt servire *ser·vee·re*

service n il servizio *ser·vee·tsyoh*; (for car) la revisione *re·vee·zyoh·ne*; (in church) l'ufficio (m) *oof·fee·choh*

service area n l'area di servizio (f) *ah·re·a dee ser·vee·tsyoh*

service charge n il servizio *ser·vee·tsyoh* M4, E44

service industry n l'industria terziaria (f) *een·doo·stree·a ter·tsyah·rya*

service station n la stazione di servizio *sta·tsyoh·ne dee ser·vee·tsyoh*

serviette n il tovagliolo *to·val·yo·loh*

set n (collection) la collezione *kol·le·tsyoh·ne* □ vt (alarm) mettere* *mayt·te·re*; to set the table apparecchiare la tavola *ap·pa·rek·kyah·ray la tah·vo·la*; to have one's hair set farsi* fare la messa in piega *far·see fah·ray la mays·sa een pye·ga*; to set off or out avviarsi *av·vee·ar·se*

settle vt (argument) regolare *re·go·lah·ray*; (bill) saldare *sal·dah·ray* □ vi (wine) depositare *de·po·zee·tah·ray*; to settle out of court conciliare una causa in via amichevole *kon·chee·lyah·ray oo·na kow·za een vee·a a·mee·kay·vo·le*; to settle in installarsi *een·stal·lar·see*

settled adj (weather) stazionario(a) *sta·tsyoh·nah·ryo(a)*

seven num sette *set·te*

seventeen num diciassette *dee·chas·set·te*

seventeenth adj diciassettesimo(a) *dee·chas·set·te·zee·mo(a)*

seventh adj settimo(a) *set·tee·mo(a)*

seventy num settanta *set·tan·ta*

several adj parecchi(ie) *pa·rayk·kee (·kye)* □ pron several of us parecchi di noi *pa·rayk·kee dee noy*

sew vi cucire *koo·chee·re* Sn76

sewing machine n la macchina per cucire *mak·kee·na payr koo·chee·re*

sex n il sesso *ses·soh*

sexual intercourse n i rapporti sessuali *rap·por·tee ses·soo·ah·lee*

sexy adj sexy *sek·se*

shade n l'ombra (f) *ohm·bra*; (for lamp) il paralume *pa·ra·loo·me*

shades pl (sunglasses) gli occhiali da sole *ok·kyah·lee da soh·le*

shadow n l'ombra (f) *ohm·bra*

shake vt agitare *a·jee·tah·ray*; to shake hands with someone stringere* la mano a qualcuno *streen·je·re la mah·noh a kwal·koo·no* □ vi shake tremare *tre·mah·ray*

shall *vi* □ I shall do it lo farò *lo fa·ro*; shall I do it? lo faccio io? *lo fach·cho ee·o*; shall we come tomorrow? veniamo domani? *ve·nyah·mo do·mah·nee*

shallot *n* lo scalogno *ska·lohn·yoh*

shallow *adj* poco profondo(a) *po·ko pro·fohn·do(a)*

shame *n* la vergogna *ver·gohn·ya*; what a shame! che peccato! *ke pek·kah·toh*

shampoo *n* lo sciampo *shahm·poh* Sn41

shandy *n* la birra con limonata *beer·ra kohn lee·mo·nah·ta*

shape *n* la forma *fohr·ma*

share *n* (part) la parte *par·te*; (finance) l'azione (f) *a·tsyoh·ne* □ *vt* (money, room) dividere* *dee·vee·de·re*

shareholder *n* l'azionista (m/f) *a·tsyoh·nee·sta*

shark *n* il pescecane *pe·she·kah·ne*

sharp *adj* (knife) affilato(a) *af·fee·lah·to(a)*; (bend) brusco(a) *broo·sko(a)*; (intelligent) sveglio(a) *zvayl·yo(a)*

sharp practice *n* la prassi disonesta *pras·see dee·zo·ne·sta*

shave *vi* radersi* *rah·der·see*

shaver *n* il rasoio elettrico *ra·soh·yoh e·let·tree·ko*

shaving brush *n* il pennello da barba *pen·nel·loh da bar·ba*

shaving cream *n* la crema per barba *kre·ma payr bar·ba*

shaving soap *n* il sapone da barba *sa·poh·ne da bar·ba*

shawl *n* lo scialle *shal·le*

she *pron* lei *ley*; here she is eccola *ek·ko·la*

sheath *n* (contraceptive) il preservativo *pre·ser·va·tee·voh*

shed *n* la capanna *ka·pan·na*

sheep *n* la pecora *pe·ko·ra*

sheepskin *n* la pelle di montone *pel·le dee mon·toh·ne*

sheer *adj* (stockings) sottile *sot·tee·le*

sheet *n* il lenzuolo *len·tswo·loh*; (of paper) il foglio *fol·yoh*

shelf *n* lo scaffale *skaf·fah·le*

shell *n* (of egg) il guscio *goo·shoh*; (of fish) la conchiglia *kon·keel·ya*

shellfish *n* (on menu) i frutti di mare *froot·tee dee mah·re*

shelter *n* (for waiting under) la tettoia *tet·toh·ya* □ *vi* (from rain etc) ripararsi *ree·pa·rar·see*

shelve *vi* (beach) digradare *dee·gra·dah·ray* □ *vt* (project) rinviare *reen·vyah·ray*

sheriff *n* lo scerriffo *she·reef·foh*

sherry *n* lo sherry *sher·ree*

shift *n* (change) il cambiamento *kam·bya·mayn·toh*; (of workmen) il turno *toor·noh* □ *vt* to shift gear cambiare marcia *kam·byah·ray mar·cha*

shin *n* lo stinco *steen·koh*

shine *vi* (sun etc) splendere *splen·de·re*; (metal) brillare *breel·lah·ray*

shingles *n* (illness) l'erpete zoster (m) *er·pe·te zo·ster*

shiny *adj* splendente *splen·den·te*

ship *n* la nave *nah·ve* □ *vt* (goods) spedire *spe·dee·re*

shipbuilding *n* la costruzione navale *ko·stroo·tsyoh·ne na·vah·le*

shipment *n* il carico *kah·ree·koh*

shipping agent *n* l'agente marittimo (m) *a·jen·te ma·reet·tee·mo*

shipping company *n* la compagnia di navigazione *kom·pan·yee·a dee na·vee·ga·tsyoh·ne*

shipyard *n* il cantiere navale *kan·tye·re na·vah·le*

shirt *n* la camicia *ka·mee·cha* S58, Sn65

shiver *vi* rabbrividire *rab·bree·vee·dee·re*

shock *n* lo shock *shok*; (electric) la scossa elettrica *skos·sa e·let·tree·ka*

shock absorber *n* l'ammortizzatore (m) *am·mor·teedz·dza·toh·re*

shoe *n* la scarpa *skar·pa*; (of brake) il ceppo del freno *chayp·poh del fre·noh* S11, 59, 62

shoelace *n* la stringa *streen·ga*

shoeshop *n* il negozio di calzature *ne·go·tsyoh dee kal·tsa·too·re*

shoot *vt* (injure) sparare *spa·rah·ray*; (kill) uccidere* con un colpo di fucile *ooch·chee·de·re kohn oon kohl·poh dee foo·chee·le* □ *vi* sparare *spa·rah·ray*

shop *n* il negozio *ne·go·tsyoh*

shop assistant *n* il/la commesso(a) *kom·mays·so(a)*

shoplifting *n* il taccheggio *tak·kayj·joh*

shopping *n* gli acquisti *ak·kwee·stee*; to go shopping fare* la spesa *fah·ray la spay·sa*

shopping bag *n* la borsa per la spesa *bohr·sa payr la spay·sa*

shopping centre *n* il centro commerciale *chen·troh kom·mer·chah·le*

shop-soiled *adj* sciupato(a) *shoo·pah·to(a)*

shop steward *n* il rappresentante sindacale *rap·pre·zen·tan·te seen·da·kah·le*

shop window *n* la vetrina *ve·tree·na*

shore *n* (of sea) la spiaggia *spyaj·ja*; (of lake) la riva *ree·va*

short *adj* corto(a) *kohr·to(a)*; (person) basso(a) *bas·so(a)*; to be short of something essere* a corto di qualcosa *es·se·re a kohr·to dee kwal·ko·sa*; he gave me short change non mi ha dato tutto il resto *nohn mee a dah·to toot·to eel re·stoh*

shortage *n* la carenza *ka·ren·tsa*

shortbread *n* il biscotto di pasta frolla *bee·skot·toh dee pa·sta frol·la*

short cut *n* la scorciatoia *skor·cha·toh·ya* T134

short drink *n* l'alcolico forte (m) *al·ko·lee·koh for·te*

shorten *vt* accorciare *ak·kor·chah·ray*

shortfall *n* la deficienza *de·fee·chen·tsa*

shorthand *n* la stenografia *ste·no·gra·fee·a*

shorthand typist *n* lo/la stenodattilografo(a) *ste·no·dat·tee·lo·gra·fo(a)*

short list *n* la lista dei candidati *lee·sta dey kan·dee·dah·tee*

shortly *adv* (soon) fra poco *fra po·ko*

shorts *pl* i calzoncini *kal·tson·chee·nee*; (underwear) le mutande *moo·tan·de*

shortsighted *adj* miope *mee·o·pe*

short-staffed *adj* □ to be short-staffed avere* una mancanza di personale *a·vay·re oo·na man·kan·tsa dee per·so·nah·le*

short term *adj* a breve termine *a bre·ve ter·mee·ne*

short wave *n* le onde corte *ohn·day kohr·tay*

shot *n* (from gun) il colpo *kohl·poh*

should *vi* □ we should buy it dovremmo comprarlo *do·vrem·mo kom·prar·lo*; I should like a... gradirei un(a)... *gra·dee·rey oon(a)*

shoulder *n* la spalla *spal·la*

shout n il grido *gree·doh* □ vi gridare *gree·dah·ray*

shovel n la pala *pah·la*

show n (exhibition) la mostra *moh·stra*; (in theatre) lo spettacolo *spet·ta·ko·loh* □ vt mostrare *mo·strah·ray*; (movie) proiettare *pro·yet·tah·ray*; **to show someone out** accompagnare qualcuno alla porta *ak·kom·pan·yah·ray kwal·koo·no al·la por·ta* □ vi **show** (be visible) vedersi* *ve·dayr·see* L52

show business n il mondo dello spettacolo *mohn·doh del·lo spet·ta·ko·loh*

shower n (rain) l'acquazzone (m) *ak·kwats·tsoh·ne*; (bath) la doccia *dohch·cha* A4, 87

showroom n la sala d'esposizione *sah·la de·spo·zee·tsyoh·ne*

shrewd adj astuto(a) *a·stoo·to(a)*

shrimp n il gamberetto *gam·be·rayt·toh*

shrink vi restringersi* *re·streen·jer·see*

shrinkage n la diminuzione *dee·mee·noo·tsyoh·ne*

Shrove Tuesday n martedì grasso (m) *mar·te·dee gras·so*

shrub n l'arbusto (m) *ar·boo·stoh*

shrug vi stringersi* nelle spalle *streen·jer·see nel·le spal·le*

shut adj chiudere* *kyoo·de·re*; **to be shut** (door) essere* chiuso(a) *es·se·re kyoo·so(a)* □ vi **shut** (door, window) chiudersi* *kyoo·der·see*

shutter n (on window) l'imposta (f) *eem·po·sta*; (in camera) l'otturatore (m) *ot·too·ra·toh·re*

shuttle (service) n (airline) il servizio di spola *ser·vee·tsyoh dee spo·la*

shy adj timido(a) *tee·mee·do(a)*

Sicily n Sicilia (f) *see·chee·lya*

sick adj (ill) malato(a) *ma·lah·to(a)*; **to be sick** (vomit) vomitare *vo·mee·tah·ray*; **I feel sick** mi sento male *mee sen·to mah·le* T45

sickly adj (cake etc) stucchevole *stook·kay·vo·le*

sickness n (illness) la malattia *ma·lat·tee·a*; (nausea) la nausea *now·ze·a*

side n il lato *lah·toh*; **the right side** (of cloth etc) il diritto *dee·reet·toh*; **the wrong side** il rovescio *ro·ve·shoh*; **this side up** *al·to*

sideboard n la credenza *kre·den·tsa*

sidelights pl (on car) i fanali di posizione *fa·nah·lee dee po·zee·tsyoh·ne*

side-road, side-street n la strada secondaria *strah·da se·kohn·dah·rya*

sidewalk n il marciapiede *mar·cha·pye·de*

siesta n la siesta *sye·sta*

sieve n il setaccio *se·tach·choh* □ vt setacciare *se·tach·chah·ray*

sift vt (sieve) setacciare *se·tach·chah·ray*

sigh vi sospirare *so·spee·rah·ray*

sight n □ **to have poor sight** avere* la vista debole *a·vay·re la vee·sta day·bo·le*; **a lovely sight** una bella vista *oo·na bel·la vee·sta*; **to see the sights** visitare le cose interessanti *vee·zee·tah·ray le ko·se een·te·res·san·tee*

sightseeing n il turismo *too·ree·zmoh*

sign n il segno *sayn·yoh*; (notice) l'insegna (f) *een·sayn·ya* □ vt (document) firmare *feer·mah·ray* T194

signal n il segnale *sen·yah·le* T192

signature n la firma *feer·ma*

signpost n il palo indicatore *pah·loh een·dee·ka·toh·re*

silence n il silenzio *see·len·tsyoh*

silencer n (on car) la marmitta *mar·meet·ta*

silent adj silenzioso(a) *see·len·tsyoh·so(a)*

silk n la seta *say·ta*; **a silk dress** un vestito di seta *oon ve·stee·toh dee say·ta*

silly adj stupido(a) *stoo·pee·do(a)*

silver n (metal) l'argento (m) *ar·jen·toh*; (money) la moneta *mo·nay·ta*; (ware) l'argenteria (f) *ar·jen·te·ree·a*; **a silver bracelet** un braccialetto d'argento *oon brach·cha·layt·toh dar·jen·toh* S88, 89

similar adj simile *see·mee·le*; **to be similar to** somigliare a *so·meel·yah·ray a*

simmer vi sobbollire *sob·bol·lee·re*

simple adj semplice *saym·plee·che*

since prep da *da*; **I've been here since 4 o'clock** sono qui dalle 4 *soh·no kwee dal·le 4* □ conj **since we arrived** da quando siamo arrivati *da kwan·do syah·mo ar·ree·vah·tee*; **since he's ill** poiché è malato *poy·kay e ma·lah·to*

sincere adj sincero(a) *seen·che·ro(a)*

sincerely adv □ **yours sincerely** cordialmente *kor·dyal·mayn·te*

sing vt/i cantare *kan·tah·ray*

single adj (not double) singolo(a) *seen·go·lo(a)*; (not married: man/woman) celibe/nubile *che·lee·be/noo·bee·le*; **a single bed** un letto a una piazza *oon let·toh a oo·na pyats·tsa*; **a single room** una camera singola *oo·na kah·me·ra seen·go·la*; **a single ticket** un biglietto semplice *oon bel·yayt·toh saym·plee·che* T57, A4

sink n (basin) l'acquaio (m) *ak·kwa·yoh* □ vi (in water) affondare *af·fohn·dah·ray*; (currency) calare *ka·lah·ray*

sir n Signore (m) *seen·yoh·re*

siren n la sirena *see·re·na*

sirloin n la lombata di manzo *lom·bah·tah dee man·dzoh*

sister n la sorella *so·rel·la*

sister-in-law n la cognata *kon·yah·ta*

sit vi sedersi* *se·dayr·see*; **we were sitting at the table** eravamo seduti alla tavola *e·ra·vah·mo se·doo·tee al·la tah·vo·la*; **to sit down** sedersi* *se·dayr·see*

site n (of building) il sito *see·toh*

sitting room n il salotto *sa·lot·toh*

situation n (place) l'ubicazione (f) *oo·bee·ka·tsyoh·ne*; (circumstances) la situazione *see·too·a·tsyoh·ne*

six num sei *sey*

sixteen num sedici *say·dee·chee*

sixteenth adj sedicesimo(a) *say·dee·che·zee·mo(a)*

sixth adj sesto(a) *se·sto(a)*

sixty num sessanta *ses·san·ta*

size n le dimensioni *dee·men·syoh·nee*; (of clothes) la taglia *tal·ya*; (of shoes) il numero *noo·me·roh* S61, 62

skate n il pattino *pat·tee·noh*; (fish) la razza *radz·dza* □ vi pattinare *pat·tee·nah·ray*

skateboard n lo skateboard *skeyt·bord*

skating rink n la pista di pattinaggio *pee·sta dee pat·tee·naj·joh*

sketch n (drawing) il bozzetto *bots·tsayt·toh* □ vt abbozzare *ab·bots·tsah·ray*

skewer n lo spiedino *spye·dee·noh*

ski n lo sci *shee* □ vi sciare *shee·ah·ray* L38

ski boot n lo scarpone da sci *skar·poh·ne da shee*

skid n lo slittamento *zleet·ta·mayn·toh* □ vi slittare *zleet·tah·ray*

skier n lo sciatore *shee·a·toh·re*, la sciatrice *shee·a·tree·che*

skiing n lo sci *shee*; **to go skiing** fare* dello sci *fah·ray del·lo shee*

ski lift n la sciovia *shee·o·vee·a*

skill n l'abilità (f) *a·bee·lee·ta*

skilled adj (workers) specializzato(a) *spe·cha·leedz·dzah·to(a)*

skillet n la padella *pa·del·la*

skim(med) milk n il latte scremato *lat·te skre·mah·to*

skin n la pelle *pel·le* I10

ski pants pl i pantaloni da sci *pan·ta·loh·nee da shee*

skirt n la gonna *gon·na* Sn65

ski run n la pista da sci *pee·sta da shee*

skull n il teschio *te·skyoh*

sky n il cielo *che·loh*

skyscraper n il grattacielo *grat·ta·che·loh*

slack adj (loose) lento(a) *len·to(a)*; (business) fiacco(a) *fyak·ko(a)*

slacks pl i calzoni *kal·tsoh·nee*

slam vt sbattere *zbat·te·re*

slang n il gergo *jer·goh*

slap vt schiaffeggiare *skyaf·fej·jah·ray*

slate n l'ardesia (f) *ar·de·zya*

Slav n lo slavo(a) *zlah·vo(a)*

slave n lo/la schiavo(a) *skyah·vo(a)*

sledge n (toboggan) la slitta *zleet·ta*

sleep n il sonno *sohn·noh* □ vi dormire *dor·mee·re* □ vt **the apartment sleeps three** l'appartamento ha tre letti *lap·par·ta·mayn·toh a tray let·tee*

sleeper n (berth) la cuccetta *kooch·chayt·ta*; (train) il treno con cuccette *tre·noh kohn kooch·chayt·te*

sleeping bag n il sacco a pelo *sak·koh a pay·loh*

sleeping car n il vagone letto *va·goh·ne let·to* T62

sleeping pill n il sonnifero *son·nee·fe·roh*

sleet n il nevischio *ne·vee·skyoh*

sleeve n la manica *mah·nee·ka*

sleigh n la slitta *zleet·ta*

slice n la fetta *fayt·ta* □ vt affettare *af·fayt·tah·ray* S31

slide vi scivolare *shee·vo·lah·ray* □ n (chute) lo scivolo *shee·vo·loh*; (photo) la diapositiva *dee·a·po·zee·tee·va*

slide rule n il regolo calcolatore *re·go·loh kal·ko·la·toh·re*

slight adj (small) leggero(a) *lej·je·ro(a)*

slim adj snello(a) *znel·lo(a)*

sling n (for arm) la benda al collo *ben·da al kol·loh*

slip vi (slide) scivolare *shee·vo·lah·ray*; (trip) inciampare *een·cham·pah·ray* □ n (underskirt) la sottana *sot·tah·na*; (of paper) la scheda *ske·da*

slipper n la pantofola *pan·to·fo·la*

slippery adj sdrucciolevole *zdrooch·cho·lay·vo·le*

slip-road n lo svincolo *zveen·ko·loh*

slogan n lo slogan *zlo·gan*

slope n (angle) la pendenza *pen·den·tsa*; (sloping ground) il pendio *pen·dee·oh*

slot n la fessura *fes·soo·ra*

slot machine n il distributore automatico *dee·stree·boo·toh·re ow·to·mah·tee·ko*

slow adj lento(a) *len·to(a)*; **my watch is slow** il mio orologio va indietro *eel mee·o o·ro·lo·joh va een·dye·tro* □ vi **to slow down** or **up** rallentare *ral·len·tah·ray*

slump n il crollo *krol·loh* □ vi crollare *krol·lah·ray*

smack vt schiaffeggiare *skyaf·fej·jah·ray* □ n lo schiaffo *skyaf·foh*

small adj piccolo(a) *peek·ko·lo(a)* A15

smallpox n il vaiolo *va·yo·loh*

smart adj (elegant) elegante *e·le·gan·te*; (clever) intelligente *een·tel·lee·jen·te*

smash vt frantumare *fran·too·mah·ray*

smell n l'odore (m) *o·doh·re* □ vt sentire *sen·tee·re* □ vi **to smell of garlic** sapere* di aglio *sa·pay·re dee al·yoh*

smile n il sorriso *sor·ree·soh* □ vi sorridere* *sor·ree·de·re*

smock n la blusa *bloo·za*

smoke n il fumo *foo·moh* □ vt/i fumare *foo·mah·ray*; **do you smoke?** lei fuma? *ley foo·ma* Mc25

smoked adj (salmon etc) affumicato(a) *af·foo·mee·kah·to(a)*

smoker n (person) il fumatore *foo·ma·toh·re*; (compartment) lo scompartimento per fumatori *skom·par·tee·mayn·toh payr foo·ma·toh·ree*

smooth adj liscio(a) *lee·sho(a)*

smuggle vt contrabbandare *kon·trab·ban·dah·ray*

snack n lo spuntino *spoon·tee·noh*

snack bar n lo snack-bar *znak·bar*

snail n la chiocciola *kyoch·cho·la*

snake n il serpente *ser·pen·te*

snap vi (break) spezzarsi *spets·tsar·see*

snatch vt afferrare *af·fer·rah·ray*

sneakers pl le scarpette *skar·payt·te*

sneeze n lo starnuto *star·noo·toh* □ vi starnutire *star·noo·tee·re*

snob n lo/la snob *znob*

snobbish adj snobistico(a) *zno·bee·stee·ko(a)*

snooker n il biliardo *beel·yar·doh*

snore vi russare *roos·sah·ray*

snorkel n il tubo di respirazione *too·boh dee re·spee·ra·tsyoh·ne*

snow n la neve *nay·ve* □ vi nevicare *ne·vee·kah·ray*; **it's snowing** nevica *nay·vee·ka*

snowball n la palla di neve *pal·la dee nay·ve*

snowdrift n il cumulo di neve *koo·moo·loh dee nay·ve*

snowman n il pupazzo di neve *poo·pats·tsoh dee nay·ve*

snowplow, snowplough n lo spazzaneve *spats·tsa·nay·ve*

snuff n il tabacco da fiuto *ta·bak·koh da fyoo·toh*

so adv □ **so pleased that…** così contento(a) che… *ko·see kon·ten·to(a) ke*; **I hope so** spero di sì *spe·ro dee see*; **so many** tanti(e) *tan·tee('te)*; **so much** tanto(a) *tan·to(a)* □ conj and **so we left** e così siamo partiti e *ko·see syah·mo par·tee·tee*; **so do I** anch'io *an·kee·oh*; **so is he** anche lui *an·ke loo·ee*; **he did it so that I would go** l'ha fatto perché io andassi *la fat·to payr·kay ee·oh an·das·see*

soak vt (washing) mettere* a mollo *mayt·te·re a mol·loh*

soap n il sapone *sa·poh·ne* A41

soap-flakes pl il sapone in scaglie *sa·poh·ne een skal·ye*

soap powder n il detersivo *de·ter·see·voh*

sober adj (not drunk) non ubriaco(a) *nohn oo·bree·ah·ko(a)*

soccer n il calcio *kal·choh*

social adj sociale *so·chah·le*

socialism n il socialismo *so·cha·lee·zmoh*

socialist n il/la socialista *so·cha·lee·sta* □ adj socialista *so·cha·lee·sta*

social security n la sicurezza sociale *see·koo·rayts·tsa so·chah·le*

social services pl i servizi sociali *ser·vee·tsee so·chah·lee*

social worker n l'assistente sociale (m/f) *as·see·sten·te so·chah·le*

society n la società *so·che·ta*; (association) l'associazione (f) *as·so·cha·tsyoh·ne*

sock n il calzino *kal·tsee·noh*

socket n (electrical) la presa *pray·sa* A42

soda n (chemical) la soda *so·da*; **a whisky and soda** un whisky con selz *oon wee·skee kohn selts*

soda water n il selz *selts*

sofa n il divano *dee·vah·noh*

soft adj (not hard) morbido(a) *mor·bee·do(a)*; (not loud) basso(a) *bas·so(a)*; (drink) analcolico(a) *a·nal·ko·lee·ko(a)*

soft-boiled adj □ **a soft-boiled egg** un uovo la coque *oon wo·voh a la kok*

software n il software *soft·wayr*

soil n il suolo *swo·loh*

solar adj solare *so·lah·re*

soldier n il soldato *sol·dah·toh*

sold out adj esaurito(a) *e·zow·ree·to(a)*

sole n (of foot) la pianta *pyan·ta*; (of shoe) la suola *swo·la*; (fish) la sogliola *sol·yo·la*

solicitor n l'avvocato (m) *av·vo·kah·toh*

solid adj solido(a) *so·lee·do(a)*; **in solid gold** in oro massiccio *een o·roh mas·seech·cho*

solution n la soluzione *so·loo·tsyoh·ne*

solve vt (problem) risolvere* *ree·sol·ve·re*

some adj □ **some apples** alcune mele *al·koo·ne may·le*; **some bread** del pane *del pah·ne*; **some people** alcune persone *al·koo·ne per·soh·ne* □ pron **some (of it) was left** ne avanzava un po' *nay a·van·tsah·va oon po*; **some (of them) were...** alcuni (di loro) erano... *al·koo·nee (dee loh·ro) e·ra·no*

somebody, someone pron qualcuno *kwal·koo·no*

something pron qualcosa *kwal·ko·sa*; **something bigger** qualcosa di piú grande *kwal·ko·sa dee pyoo gran·de*

sometimes adv qualche volta *kwal·ke vol·ta*

somewhere adv in qualche luogo *een kwal·ke lwo·goh*

son n il figlio *feel·yoh* Sn84, C10

son et lumière n lo spettacolo di suoni e luci *spet·ta·ko·loh dee swo·nee e loo·chee*

song n la canzone *kan·tsoh·ne*

son-in-law n il genero *je·ne·roh*

soon adv presto *pre·sto*

sophisticated adj sofisticato(a) *so·fee·stee·kah·to(a)*

sore adj (painful) doloroso(a) *do·lo·roh·so(a)*

sorry adj spiacente *spya·chen·te*; **(I'm) sorry** mi dispiace *mee dee·spyah·che*

SOS n l'S.O.S. (m) *es·se·o·es·se*

soufflé n il soufflé *soo·flay*

soul n l'anima (f) *ah·nee·ma*

sound n il suono *swo·noh* □ vi **it sounds like a car** sembra il rumore di una macchina *saym·bra eel roo·moh·re dee oo·na mak·kee·na* □ vt **to**

sound one's horn suonare il clacson *swo·nah·ray eel klak·son*

sound track n la colonna sonora *ko·lohn·na so·no·ra*

soup n la zuppa *tsoop·pa* E35

sour adj (sharp) acerbo(a) *a·cher·bo(a)*; (milk) acido(a) *ah·chee·do(a)*; **sour(ed) cream** la panna agra *pan·na a·gra*

source n la fonte *fohn·te*

south n il sud *sood* □ adv al sud *al sood* □ n **southeast** il sud-est *sood·dest*; **southwest** il sud-ovest *soo·do·vest*

South Africa n il Sud-Africa *soo·da·free·ka*

South African adj sudafricano(a) *soo·da·free·kah·no(a)*

South America n l'America del Sud (f) *a·me·ree·ka del sood*

South American adj sudamericano(a) *soo·da·me·ree·kah·no(a)*

southern adj meridionale *me·ree·dyo·nah·le*

South Pole n il Polo Sud *po·loh sood*

souvenir n il ricordo *ree·kor·doh*

Soviet adj sovietico(a) *so·vye·tee·ko(a)*

Soviet Union n l'Unione Sovietica (f) *oo·nyoh·ne so·vye·tee·ka*

soya beans pl la soia *so·ya*

soy(a) sauce n la salsa di soia *sal·sa dee so·ya*

spa n la stazione termale *sta·tsyoh·ne ter·mah·le*

space n lo spazio *spa·tsyoh*

spacecraft n l'astronave (f) *a·stro·nah·ve*

spade n la vanga *van·ga*; **spades** (cards) le picche *peek·ke*

spaghetti n gli spaghetti *spa·gayt·tee* E22

Spain n Spagna (f) *span·ya*

Spaniard n lo/la spagnolo(a) *span·yo·lo(a)*

Spanish adj spagnolo(a) *span·yo·lo(a)* □ n lo spagnolo *span·yo·loh*

spanner n la chiave *kyah·ve*

spare adj □ **spare wheel** la ruota di scorta *rwo·ta dee skor·ta*; **spare time** il tempo libero *tem·poh lee·be·ro* □ n **spare (part)** il pezzo di ricambio *pets·tsoh dee re·kam·byoh* T187

spare rib n la cotoletta di maiale *ko·to·layt·ta dee ma·yah·le*

spark n la scintilla *sheen·teel·la*

sparking plug n la candela *kan·day·la*

sparkle vi scintillare *sheen·teel·lah·ray*

sparkling adj (wine) spumante *spoo·man·te*

sparrow n il passero *pas·se·roh*

spatula n la spatola *spa·to·la*

speak vt/i parlare *par·lah·ray*; **do you speak English?** parla inglese? *par·la een·glay·se*; **to speak to someone about something** parlare a qualcuno di qualcosa *par·lah·ray a kwal·koo·no dee kwal·ko·sa* B24

speaker n (electrical) l'altoparlante (m) *al·to·par·lan·te*

special adj speciale *spe·chah·le*

specialize vi specializzarsi *spe·cha·leedz·dzar·see* Bm15

specific adj specifico(a) *spe·chee·fee·ko(a)*

specifications pl le specificazioni *spe·chee·fee·ka·tsyoh·nee*

specify vt specificare *spe·chee·fee·kah·ray*

specimen n il campione *kam·pyoh·ne*

speech n il modo di parlare mo·doh dee par·lah·ray; (oration) il discorso dee·skohr·soh

speed n la velocità ve·lo·chee·ta □ vi to speed up accelerare ach·che·le·rah·ray

speedboat n il fuoribordo fwo·ree·bohr·doh

speeding n (in car) l'eccesso di velocità (m) ech·ches·soh dee ve·lo·chee·ta

speed limit n il limite di velocità lee·mee·te dee ve·lo·chee·ta T138

speedometer n il tachimetro ta·kee·me·troh

spell vt (in writing) scrivere* skree·ve·re □ n (period) il breve periodo bre·ve pe·ree·o·doh

spend vt (money) spendere* spen·de·re; (time) trascorrere* tra·skor·re·re

spice n le spezie spe·tsye

spicy adj piccante peek·kan·te

spider n il ragno ran·yoh

spill vt rovesciare ro·ve·shah·ray □ vi rovesciarsi ro·ve·shar·see B67

spin vi (rotate) girare jee·rah·ray □ vt (wool) filare fee·lah·ray

spinach gli spinaci spee·nah·chee

spin(-dry) vt asciugare nell'asciuga-panni a·shoo·gah·ray nel·la·shoo·ga·pan·nee

spine n (backbone) la spina dorsale spee·na dor·sah·le

spirit n (soul) lo spirito spee·ree·toh; spirits (alcohol) i liquori lee·kwoh·ree; in good spirits di buon umore dee bwon oo·moh·re

spit vi sputare spoo·tah·ray □ n (for roasting) lo spiedo spye·doh

spite n il dispetto dee·spet·toh; in spite of malgrado mal·grah·do

splash n il tonfo tohn·foh □ vt schiz-zare skeets·tsah·ray □ vi sguazzare zgwats·tsah·ray

splint n la stecca stayk·ka

splinter n (wood) la scheggia skayj·ja

split vt (tear) lacerare la·che·rah·ray; (divide, share) dividere* dee·vee·de·re □ vi (tear) strapparsi strap·par·see □ n (tear) la spaccatura spak·ka·too·ra

spoil vt (damage) danneggiare dan·nej·jah·ray; (child) viziare vee·tsyah·ray

spokesman n il portavoce por·ta·voh·che

sponge n la spugna spoon·ya; (cake) il pan di Spagna pan dee span·ya

sponge-bag n la borsa da toletta bohr·sa da to·layt·ta

spoon n il cucchiaio kook·kee·a·yoh

spoonful n la cucchiaiata kook·kee·a·yah·ta

sport n lo sport sport L31, Mc24

sports car n la macchina sportiva mak·kee·na spor·tee·va

sports coat, sports jacket n la giacca sportiva jak·ka spor·tee·va

sportswear n gli indumenti da sport een·doo·mayn·tee da sport

spot n (patch) la macchia mak·kya; (dot) il punto poon·toh; (pimple) la pustola poo·sto·la; (locality) il luogo lwo·goh; on the spot sul luogo sool lwo·goh

spot check n il controllo improvviso kon·trol·loh eem·prov·vee·zo

spotlight n il riflettore ree·flet·toh·re

sprain n la distorsione dee·stor·syoh·ne □ vt to sprain one's ankle slogarsi la caviglia zlo·gar·see la ka·veel·ya

spray n (of liquid) lo spruzzo sproots·tsoh; (container) la bombola spray bohm·bo·la spray □ vt (liquid) spruz-zare sproots·tsah·ray

spread vt (butter) spalmare spal·mah·ray; (news) diffondere* deef·fohn·de·re; (payments) rateizzare ra·te·eedz·dzah·ray; to spread something out spiegare qualcosa spye·gah·ray kwal·ko·sa

spring n (season) la primavera pree·ma·ve·ra; (coil) la molla mol·la; (of water) la sorgente sor·jen·te

spring onion n la cipollina chee·pol·lee·na

sprinkle vt □ to sprinkle with water spruzzare con acqua sproots·tsah·ray kohn ak·kwa; to sprinkle with sugar cospargere* di zucchero ko·spar·je·re dee tsook·ke·roh

sprouts npl i cavolini di Bruxelles kah·vo·lee·nee dee broo·sel

spy n la spia spee·a

square n il quadrato kwa·drah·toh; (in town) la piazza pyats·tsa □ adj qua-drato(a) kwa·drah·to(a); a square metre un metro quadrato oon me·troh kwa·drah·to; 3 metres square 3 metri per 3 3 me·tree payr 3 L2

squash vt (crush) schiacciare skyach·chah·ray □ n (sport) lo squash skwosh; (gourd) la zucca tsook·ka; lemon/orange squash la spremuta di limone/d'arancia spre·moo·ta dee lee·moh·ne/da·ran·cha

squeeze vt (lemon) spremere spre·me·re; (hand) stringere* streen·je·re □ n (financial) la restrizione economica re·stree·tsyoh·ne e·ko·no·mee·ka

squirrel n lo scoiattolo sko·yat·to·loh

stab vt pugnalare poon·ya·lah·ray

stable n la stalla stal·la □ adj stabile stah·bee·le

stadium n lo stadio sta·dyoh

staff n il personale per·so·nah·le

stage n (in theatre) il palcoscenico pal·ko·she·nee·koh; (point) la tappa tap·pa; in stages a tappe a tap·pe

stain n la macchia mak·kya □ vt mac-chiare mak·kyah·ray Sn 67

stained glass window n la vetrata di-pinta ve·trah·ta dee·peen·ta

stainless adj (steel) inossidabile een·os·see·dah·bee·le

stair n il gradino gra·dee·noh

staircase n la scala skah·la

stairs pl le scale skah·le I4

stake n (in gambling) la posta po·sta; to be at stake essere* in gioco es·se·re een jo·koh

stale adj (bread) raffermo(a) raf·fayr·mo(a); the room smells stale la stanza sa di rinchiuso la stan·tsa sa dee reen·kyoo·so

stall n (stand) la bancarella ban·ka·rel·la □ vi (car engine) fermarsi fer·mar·see

stalls pl (in theatre) la platea pla·te·a L46

stamp n (postage) il francobollo fran·ko·bohl·loh; (rubber) il timbro teem·broh □ vt (letter) affrancare af·fran·kah·ray; (visa) vistare vee·stah·ray Sn2

stand n (stall) la bancarella ban·ka·rel·la □ vi stare* in piedi stah·ray een pye·dee; to stand up alzarsi al·tsar·see □ vt stand (put) porre* pohr·re; (bear) sopportare sop·por·tah·ray; to stand for (signify) significare seen·yee·fee·kah·ray; to stand out spiccare speek·kah·ray

standard n il grado grah·doh □ adj standard stan·dard

standard lamp n la lampada a stelo lam·pa·da a ste·loh

standard of living n il tenore di vita te·noh·re dee vee·ta

standing order n l'ordine di pagamento automatico (m) ohr·dee·ne dee pa·ga·mayn·toh ow·to·ma·tee·ko

staple n la graffetta graf·fayt·ta

stapler n la cucitrice koo·chee·tree·che

star n la stella stayl·la; (celebrity) il/la divo(a) dee·vo(a)

starch n l'amido (m) ah·mee·doh

stare vi fissare fees·sah·ray; to stare at somebody fissare qualcuno fees·sah·ray kwal·koo·no

start vt/i cominciare ko·meen·chah·ray □ n (beginning) l'inizio (m) ee·nee·tsyoh

starter n (in car) il motorino d'avviamento mo·to·ree·noh dav·vya·mayn·toh; (hors d'œuvre) l'antipasto (m) an·tee·pa·stoh

starve vi morire* di fame mo·ree·re dee fah·me

state vt dichiarare dee·kya·rah·ray □ n (condition) lo stato stah·toh; the State lo Stato stah·toh; the States gli Stati Uniti stah·tee oo·nee·tee

statement n la dichiarazione dee·kya·ra·tsyoh·ne

station n la stazione sta·tsyoh·ne; (radio) la stazione radio sta·tsyoh·ne ra·dyoh F3

stationer's (shop) n la cartoleria kar·to·le·ree·a

stationery n la cancelleria kan·chel·le·ree·a

station wagon n la giardinetta jar·dee·nayt·ta

statistic n la statistica sta·tee·stee·ka

statistical adj statistico(a) sta·tee·stee·ko(a)

statistics n la statistica sta·tee·stee·ka

statue n la statua sta·too·a

stay n (period) il soggiorno soj·johr·noh □ vi rimanere* ree·ma·na·re; (reside) stare* stah·ray; to stay the night pernottare per·not·tah·ray; to stay with friends alloggiare da amici al·loj·jah·ray da a·mee·chee; to stay in rimanere* a casa ree·ma·na·re a kah·sa; to stay up (at night) vegliare vel·yah·ray A3, 55

S.T.D. n la teleselezione te·le·se·le·tsyoh·ne

steady adj fermo(a) fayr·mo(a); (pace) regolare re·go·lah·re

steak n la bistecca bee·stayk·ka E23

steal vt rubare roo·bah·ray; to steal something from someone rubare qualcosa a qualcuno roo·bah·ray kwal·ko·sa a kwal·koo·no Sn81

steam n il vapore va·poh·re □ vt (food) cuocere* a vapore kwo·che·re a va·poh·re

steamer n (ship) il piroscafo pee·ro·ska·foh

steel n l'acciaio (m) ach·cha·yoh

steep adj ripido(a) ree·pee·do(a)

steer vt (car) guidare gwee·dah·ray; (boat) governare go·ver·nah·ray

steering n (in car) lo sterzo ster·tsoh

steering column n la colonna dello sterzo ko·lohn·na del·lo ster·tsoh

steering-wheel n il volante vo·lan·te

stem n lo stelo ste·loh

stenographer n lo/la stenodattilografo(a) ste·no·dat·tee·lo·gra·fo(a)

step n (pace) il passo pas·soh; (stair) il gradino gra·dee·noh; to take steps to do something prendere* le misure per fare qualcosa pren·de·re le mee·zoo·re payr fah·ray kwal·ko·sa

stepbrother n il fratellastro fra·tel·la·stroh

stepdaughter n la figliastra feel·ya·stra

stepfather n il patrigno pa·treen·yoh

stepladder n la scala portatile skah·la por·tah·tee·le

stepmother n la matrigna ma·treen·ya

stepsister n la sorellastra so·rel·la·stra

stepson n il figliastro feel·ya·stroh

stereo(phonic) adj stereofonico(a) ste·re·o·fo·nee·ko(a) □ n lo stereo ste·re·oh

sterile adj sterile ste·ree·le

sterilize vt (disinfect) sterilizzare ste·ree·leedz·dzah·ray

sterling n la sterlina ster·lee·na M23

stew n lo stufato stoo·fah·toh

steward n il cameriere di bordo ka·me·rye·re dee bohr·doh; (at club) l'intendente (m) een·ten·den·te

stewardess n la hostess ho·stes

stick n il bastone ba·stoh·ne □ vt (with glue etc) incollare een·kol·lah·ray

sticking-plaster n il cerotto che·rot·toh

sticky adj appiccicoso(a) ap·peech·chee·koh·so(a)

stiff adj rigido(a) ree·jee·do(a); a stiff neck il torcicollo tor·chee·kol·loh

stiletto heels pl i tacchi a spillo tak·kee a speel·loh

still adj (motionless) immobile eem·mo·bee·le; (wine etc) non gassoso(a) nohn gas·soh·so(a) □ adv (up to this time) ancora an·koh·ra; (nevertheless) tuttavia toot·ta·vee·a

sting vt/i pungere* poon·je·re □ n la puntura poon·too·ra

stipulate vt stipulare stee·poo·lah·ray

stipulation n la stipula stee·poo·la

stir vt rimescolare ree·me·sko·lah·ray

stitch n (sewing) il punto poon·toh; (pain) il fitta feet·ta

stock vt (have in shop) avere* a·vay·re □ n (supply) la riserva ree·ser·va; (in shop) lo stock stok; (for soup etc) il brodo bro·doh; stocks (financial) i titoli tee·to·lee; in stock in magazzino een ma·gadz·dzee·noh; out of stock esaurito(a) e·zow·ree·to(a)

stockbroker n l'agente di cambio (m) a·jen·te dee kam·byoh

stock exchange n la Borsa bohr·sa

stocking n la calza kal·tsa

stockist n il grossista gros·see·sta

stock market n la Borsa bohr·sa

stocktaking n l'inventario (m) een·ven·tah·ryoh

stole n (wrap) la stola sto·la

stomach n lo stomaco sto·ma·koh

stomach ache n il mal di stomaco mal dee sto·ma·koh; I have (a) stomach ache ho mal di stomaco o mal dee sto·ma·koh S40

stone n la pietra pye·tra; (in fruit) il nocciolo noch·cho·loh; (weight) ≈ 6,35 chili

stony adj sassoso(a) sas·soh·so(a)

stool n lo sgabello zga·bel·loh

stop n (bus stop) la fermata fer·mah·ta □ vi fermarsi fer·mar·see; to stop doing something smettere* di fare qualcosa zmayt·te·re dee fah·ray kwal·ko·sa □ vt stop fermare fer·mah·ray; to stop someone doing something impedire a qualcuno di fare qualcosa eem·pe·dee·re a kwal·koo·no di fah·ray kwal·ko·sa; to stop a cheque bloccare un assegno *blok·kah·ray oon as·sayn·yoh* T73, 94, 201

stopcock *n* il rubinetto di arresto *roo·bee·nayt·toh dee ar·re·stoh*

stoplights *pl* i fanali dei freni *fa·nah·lee dey fre·nee*

stopover *n* (*air travel*) lo scalo *skah·loh*

stopper *n* (*air travel*) lo scalo *skah·loh*

stopper *n* il tappo *tap·poh*

stop watch *n* il cronometro *kro·no·me·troh*

store *vt* immagazzinare *eem·ma·gadz·dzee·nah·ray* □ *n* (*stock*) la provvista *prov·vee·sta*; (*shop*) il negozio *ne·go·tsyoh*; (*big shop, warehouse*) il magazzino *ma·gadz·dzee·noh*

store room *n* il magazzino *ma·gadz·dzee·noh*

storey *n* il piano *pyah·noh*

storm *n* la tempesta *tem·pe·sta*

stormy *adj* tempestoso(a) *tem·pe·stoh·so(a)*

story *n* la storia *sto·rya*

stove *n* la cucina *koo·chee·na* A70

straight *adj* diritto(a) *dee·reet·to(a)*; (*drink*) liscio(a) *lee·sho(a)* □ *adv* (*shoot, write etc*) diritto *dee·reet·to*; **to go straight home** andare* direttamente a casa *an·dah·ray dee·reet·ta·mayn·te a kah·sa*; **straight away** subito *soo·bee·to* F23

strain *n* (*tea etc*) colare *ko·lah·ray*; (*muscle*) stirarsi *stee·rar·see*

strainer *n* il colino *ko·lee·noh*

strange *adj* (*unknown*) sconosciuto(a) *sko·no·shoo·to(a)*; (*unusual*) strano(a) *strah·no(a)*

stranger *n* lo/la sconosciuto(a) *sko·no·shoo·to(a)*

strangle *vt* strangolare *stran·go·lah·ray*

strap *n* la cinghia *cheen·gya*

strapless *adj* senza spalline *sen·tsa spal·lee·ne*

straw *n* la paglia *pal·ya*

strawberry *n* la fragola *frah·go·la*

streak *n* la striscia *stree·sha*

stream *n* il ruscello *roo·shel·loh*

streamlined *adj* (*car*) aerodinamico(a) *a·e·ro·dee·na·mee·ko(a)*

street *n* la via *vee·a* F27

streetcar *n* il tram *tram*

streetlamp *n* il lampione *lam·pyoh·ne*

strength *n* la forza *for·tsa*; (*of girder, rope etc*) la resistenza *re·see·sten·tsa*

strengthen *vt* rinforzare *reen·for·tsah·ray*

stress *n* (*emphasis*) l'enfasi (*f*) *en·fa·zee*; (*tension*) la tensione *ten·syoh·ne*

stretch *vt* (*fabric etc*) tendere* *ten·de·re* □ *vi* stirarsi *stee·rar·see*

stretcher *n* la barella *ba·rel·la*

strict *adj* severo(a) *se·ve·ro(a)*

strike *vt* (*hit*) colpire *kol·pee·re*; **to strike a match** accendere* un fiammifero *ach·chen·de·re oon fyam·mee·fe·roh*; **the clock struck three** l'orologio ha battuto le tre *lo·ro·lo·joh a bat·too·to le tray* □ *vi* strike (*workers*) scioperare *sho·pe·rah·ray* □ *n* (*industrial*) lo sciopero *sho·pe·roh*; **on strike** in sciopero *een sho·pe·roh*

strikebound *adj* paralizzato(a) da uno sciopero *pa·ra·leedz·dzah·to(a) da oo·no sho·pe·roh*

strike-breaker *n* il crumiro *kroo·mee·roh*

striker *n* lo/la scioperante *sho·pe·ran·te*

string *n* lo spago *spah·goh*; (*of instrument*) la corda *kor·da*

string bag *n* la rete *ray·te*

strip *n* (*stripe, length*) la striscia *stree·sha*

stripe *n* la striscia *stree·sha*

strip-lighting *n* l'illuminazione al neon (*f*) *eel·loo·mee·na·tsyoh·ne al ne·on*

stripper *n* la spogliarellista *spol·ya·rel·lee·sta*

striptease *n* lo spogliarello *spol·ya·rel·loh*

stroke *vt* accarezzare *ak·ka·rets·tsah·ray* □ *n* (*swimming*) la bracciata *brach·chah·ta*; (*golf*) il colpo *kohl·poh*; (*illness*) il colpo apoplettico *kohl·poh a·po·plet·tee·koh*

stroll *n* la passeggiatina *pas·sej·ja·tee·na*; **to go for a stroll** fare* quattro passi *fah·ray kwat·tro pas·see*

stroller *n* il passeggino *pas·sej·jee·noh*

strong *adj* (*person*) forte *for·te*; (*structure, material*) solido(a) *so·lee·do(a)*; **it has a strong smell** ha un odore forte *a oon o·doh·re for·te*

strongbox *n* la cassaforte *kas·sa·for·te*

strongroom *n* la camera blindata *kah·me·ra bleen·dah·ta*

structure *n* la struttura *stroot·too·ra*; (*building*) l'edificio (*m*) *e·dee·fee·choh*

struggle *n* la lotta *lot·ta* □ *vi* (*physically*) lottare *lot·tah·ray*; **to struggle to do something** sforzarsi di fare qualcosa *sfor·tsar·see dee fah·ray kwal·ko·sa*

stub *n* (*counterfoil*) la matrice *ma·tree·che*

stubborn *adj* testardo(a) *te·star·do(a)*

stuck *adj* bloccato(a) *blok·kah·to(a)*

stud *n* il chiodo *kyo·doh*; (*for collar*) il bottoncino da colletto *bot·ton·chee·noh da kol·layt·toh*

student *n* lo studente *stoo·den·te*, la studentessa *stoo·den·tays·sa* M5

studio *n* lo studio *stoo·dyoh*

study *vt/i* studiare *stoo·dyah·ray* □ *n* (*room*) lo studio *stoo·dyoh*; **to enjoy one's studies** provare piacere negli studi *pro·vah·ray pya·chay·re ne·lye stoo·dee*

stuff *n* (*things*) la roba *ro·ba*; (*substance*) la sostanza *so·stan·tsa*

stuffed *adj* (*cushion*) imbottito(a) *eem·bot·tee·to(a)*; (*chicken*) farcito(a) *far·chee·to(a)*

stuffing *n* (*in chicken etc*) il ripieno *ree·pye·noh*

stuffy *adj* soffocante *sof·fo·kan·te*

stun *vt* stordire *stor·dee·re*

stupid *adj* stupido(a) *stoo·pee·do(a)*

style *n* lo stile *stee·le*

stylish *adj* elegante *e·le·gan·te*

subcommittee *n* la sottocommissione *soht·to·kom·mees·syoh·ne*

subcontract *n* il subappalto *soo·bap·pal·toh*

subcontractor *n* il subappaltatore *soo·bap·pal·ta·toh·re*

subject *n* (*topic*) l'argomento (*m*) *ar·go·mayn·toh*; (*person*) il/la suddito(a) *sood·dee·to(a)*; (*in school*) la materia *ma·te·rya* □ *adj* **subject to** soggetto(a) a *soj·jet·to(a) a*

submarine *n* il sommergibile *som·mer·jee·bee·le*

submit *vt* (*proposal*) sottoporre* *soht·to·pohr·re*

subordinate *adj* subordinato(a) *soo·bor·dee·nah·to(a)* □ *n* il/la subordinato(a) *soo·bor·dee·nah·to(a)*

subscriber *n* l'abbonato (*m/f*) *ab·bo·nah·to(a)*

subscribe to vt (*periodical*) abbonarsi a *ab·bo·nar·see a*

subscription n (*to periodical*) l'abbonamento (*m*) *ab·bo·na·mayn·toh*; (*to club*) la quota *kwo·ta*

subsidiary adj affiliato(a) *af·fee·lyah·to(a)* □ n (*company*) la filiale *fee·lyah·le*

subsidize vt sovvenzionare *sov·ven·tsyo·nah·ray*

subsidy n la sovvenzione *sov·ven·tsyo·ne*

substance n la sostanza *so·stan·tsa*

substandard adj inferiore *een·fe·ryoh·re*

substitute n il sostituto *so·stee·too·toh* □ vt to substitute something for something else sostituire qualcosa a qualcos'altro *so·stee·too·ee·re kwal·ko·sa a kwal·ko·sal·tro*

subtitle n (*of movie*) il sottotitolo *soht·to·tee·to·loh*

subtle adj sottile *sot·tee·le*

subtotal n il subtotale *soob·to·tah·le*

subtract vt sottrarre* *sot·trar·re*

suburb n il sobborgo *sob·bohr·goh*; the suburbs la periferia *pe·ree·fe·ree·a*

suburban adj suburbano(a) *soo·boor·bah·no(a)*

subway n (*underground passage*) il sottopassaggio *soht·to·pas·saj·joh*; (*railway*) la metropolitana *me·tro·po·lee·tah·na*

succeed vi riuscire* *ree·oo·shee·re*; he succeeded in doing it è riuscito a farlo *e ree·oo·shee·to a far·lo*

success n il successo *sooch·ches·soh*

successful adj (*venture*) che ha buon esito *ke a bwon e·zee·toh*; (*businessman*) prospero(a) *pro·spe·ro(a)*

such adj tale *tah·le*; such a lot of tanto(a) *tan·to(a)*; such a book un libro *oon tah·le lee·broh*; such books tali libri *tah·lee lee·bree*; such kindness tale gentilezza *tah·le jen·tee·layts·tsa*

suck vt succhiare *sook·kyah·ray*

sudden adj improvviso(a) *eem·prov·vee·zo(a)*

suddenly adv improvvisamente *eem·prov·vee·za·mayn·te* T203

sue vt citare *chee·tah·ray*

suede n la pelle scamosciata *pel·le ska·mo·shah·ta*

suet n la sugna *soon·ya*

suffer vt/i soffrire* *sof·free·re*

sugar n lo zucchero *tsook·ke·roh* S31

sugar bowl n la zuccheriera *tsook·ke·rye·ra*

suggest vt suggerire *sooj·je·ree·re*

suggestion n il suggerimento *sooj·je·ree·mayn·toh*

suicide n il suicidio *soo·ee·chee·dyoh*

suit n (*men's*) il completo *kom·ple·toh*; (*women's*) il tailleur *tay·yur*; (*cards*) il seme *say·me*; (*astronaut, diver*) la tuta *too·ta* □ vt that hat suits you quel cappello ti sta bene *kwayl kap·pel·loh tee sta be·ne*; does Thursday suit you? Le conviene giovedì? *le kon·vye·ne jo·ve·dee* S59

suitable adj adatto(a) *a·dat·to(a)*; (*fitting*) appropriato(a) *ap·pro·pree·ah·to(a)* S106

suitcase n la valigia *va·lee·ja* T30f, Sn52

sultanas pl l'uva sultanina (*f*) *oo·va sool·ta·nee·na*

sum n (*total amount*) la somma *sohm·ma*; (*problem*) il calcolo *kal·ko·loh*

summary n il sommario *som·mah·ryoh*

summer n l'estate (*f*) *e·stah·te*

summons n la citazione *chee·ta·tsyoh·ne*

sump n (*in car*) la coppa dell'olio *kop·pa del·lo·lyoh*

sun n il sole *soh·le*

sunbathe vi fare* un bagno di sole *fah·ray oon ban·yoh dee soh·le*

sunburn n (*painful*) la scottatura *skot·ta·too·ra* S40

sunburnt adj abbronzato(a) *ab·bron·dzah·to(a)*; (*painfully*) scottato(a) *skot·tah·to(a)*

Sunday n domenica (*f*) *do·me·nee·ka*

sun dress n il vestito da spiaggia *ve·stee·toh da spyaj·ja* S58

sunglasses pl gli occhiali da sole *ok·kyah·lee da soh·le* S7

sun-hat n il cappello da sole *kap·pel·loh da soh·le*

sunlamp n la lampada a raggi ultravioletti *lam·pa·da a raj·jee ool·tra·vyo·layt·tee*

sunny adj soleggiato(a) *soh·lej·jah·to(a)*

sunrise n il sorgere del sole *sohr·je·re del soh·le*

sunroof n il tetto mobile *tayt·toh mo·bee·le*

sunset n il tramonto *tra·mohn·toh*

sunshade n (*over table*) l'ombrellone (*m*) *om·brel·loh·ne*

sunshine n il sole *soh·le*

sunstroke n l'insolazione (*f*) *een·so·la·tsyoh·ne*

suntan n l'abbronzatura (*f*) *ab·bron·dza·too·ra*

sun-tanned adj abbronzato(a) *ab·bron·dzah·to(a)*

suntan oil n l'olio solare (*m*) *o·lyoh so·lah·re* S9

sun visor n (*in car*) la visiera *vee·zye·ra*

superannuation n la pensione *pen·syoh·ne*

superior adj (*quality*) superiore *soo·pe·ryoh·re* □ n il superiore *soo·pe·ryoh·re*

supermarket n il supermercato *soo·per·mer·kah·toh*

superstition n la superstizione *soo·per·stee·tsyoh·ne*

superstore n l'ipermercato (*m*) *ee·per·mer·kah·toh*

supertanker n la superpetroliera *soo·per·pe·tro·lye·ra*

supervise vt sorvegliare *sor·vel·yah·ray*

supervisor n il/la sorvegliante *sor·vel·yan·te*

supper n (*main meal*) la cena *chay·na*; (*snack*) lo spuntino *spoon·tee·noh*

supply vt (*goods*) fornire *for·nee·re*; to supply someone with something fornire qualcosa a qualcuno *for·nee·re kwal·ko·sa a kwal·koo·no* □ n supply (*stock*) la provvista *prov·vee·sta*; supply and demand l'offerta e la domanda *lof·fer·ta e la do·man·da*

support vt (*hold up*) reggere* *rej·je·re*; (*financially*) mantenere* *man·te·nay·re*; (*party, view etc*) sostenere* *so·ste·nay·re* □ n (*moral, financial*) il sostegno *so·stayn·yoh*

suppose vt supporre* *soop·pohr·re*; he's supposed to be an engineer lo si ritiene un ingegnere *lo see ree·tye·ne oon een·jen·ye·re*; you're supposed to do it today dovreste farlo oggi *do·vreb·be far·lo oj·jee*

suppository n la supposta *soop·poh·sta*

surcharge n la soprattassa *soh·prat·tas·sa*

sure adj (person) sicuro(a) *see·koo·ro(a)*; (fact) certo(a) *cher·to(a)*; it's sure to work sicuro che funzionerà *see·koo·ro ke foon·tsyoh·ne·ra*; he's sure to come verrà sicuramente *ver·ra see·koo·ra·mayn·te*

surely adv sicuramente *see·koo·ra·mayn·te*

surface n la superficie *soo·per·fee·che*

surface mail n □ to send something surface mail spedire qualcosa per posta ordinaria *spe·dee·re kwal·ko·sa payr po·sta or·dee·nah·rya*

surf board n la tavola da surfing *tah·vo·la da soor·feeng*

surfing il surfing *soor·feeng*; to go surfing fare* del surfing *fah·ray del soor·feeng*

surgeon n il chirurgo *kee·roor·goh*

surgery n (operation) la chirurgia *kee·roor·jee·a*; (place) il gabinetto medico *ga·bee·nayt·toh me·dee·ko*

surname n il cognome *kon·yoh·me*

surplus n l'eccedenza (f) *ech·che·den·tsa*

surprise vt sorprendere* *sor·pren·de·re* □ n la sorpresa *sor·pray·sa*

surprised adj sorpreso(a) *sor·pray·so(a)*; surprised at sorpreso(a) da *sor·pray·so(a) da*

surround vt circondare *cheer·kon·dah·ray*

surroundings pl i dintorni *deen·tohr·nee*

survey n (of land) il rilievo *ree·lye·voh*; (of building) la perizia *pe·ree·tsya*

surveyor n (of land) il geometra *je·o·me·tra*; (of building) l'ispettore (m) *ee·spet·toh·re*

survive vi sopravvivere* *soh·prav·vee·ve·re*

suspend vt (worker) sospendere* *so·spen·de·re*

suspenders pl (for stockings) le giarrettiere *jar·ret·tye·re*

suspension n (on car) la sospensione *so·spen·syoh·ne*

swallow vt/i inghiottire *een·gyot·tee·re*

swamp n la palude *pa·loo·de*

swan n il cigno *cheen·yoh*

sway vi (person) barcollare *bar·kol·lah·ray*; (building, bridge) oscillare *o·sheel·lah·ray*

swear vi (curse) bestemmiare *be·stem·myah·ray*; he swears that... giura che... *joo·ra ke*

sweat n il sudore *soo·doh·re* □ vi sudare *soo·dah·ray*

sweater n il pullover *pool·lo·ver*

sweatshirt n la blusa *bloo·zah*

Swede n lo/la svedese *zve·day·se*

swede n la rapa svedese *rah·pa zve·day·se*

Sweden n Svezia (f) *zve·tsya*

Swedish adj svedese *zve·day·se* □ n lo svedese *zve·day·se*

sweep vt (floor) scopare *sko·pah·ray*

sweet n (candy) la caramella *ka·ra·mel·la*; (dessert) il dolce *dohl·che* □ adj (taste, food) dolce *dohl·che*; (smell) fragrante *fra·gran·te*; (music) armonioso(a) *ar·mo·nyoh·so(a)*; (cute, pretty) grazioso(a) *gra·tsyoh·so(a)*; (kind) carino(a) *ka·ree·no(a)*

sweet corn n il granturco dolce *gran·toor·koh dohl·che*

sweet potato n la patata dolce *pa·tah·ta dohl·che*

swell (up) vi (limb etc) gonfiarsi *gon·fyar·see*

swelling n (lump) la tumefazione *too·me·fa·tsyoh·ne* I26

swerve vi sbandare *zban·dah·ray*

swim vi nuotare *nwo·tah·ray* □ vt to swim the Channel attraversare la Manica a nuoto *at·tra·ver·sah·ray la mah·nee·ka a nwo·toh* L26

swimming n il nuoto *nwo·toh*; to go swimming andare* a nuotare *an·dah·ray a nwo·tah·ray*

swimming pool n la piscina *pee·shee·na* A11

swimming trunks pl il costume da bagno *ko·stoo·me da ban·yoh*

swimsuit n il costume da bagno *ko·stoo·me da ban·yoh*

swing n l'altalena (f) *al·ta·lay·na* □ vt/i dondolare *don·do·lah·ray*

Swiss adj svizzero(a) *zveets·tse·ro(a)*

switch n l'interruttore (m) *een·ter·root·toh·re* □ vt to switch on accendere* *ach·chen·de·re*; to switch off spegnere* *spen·ye·re* B66, A62

switchboard n il centralino *chen·tra·lee·noh*

switchboard operator n il/la centralinista *chen·tra·lee·nee·sta*

Switzerland n Svizzera (f) *zveets·tse·ra*; in/to Switzerland in Svizzera *een zveets·tse·ra*

swollen adj gonfio(a) *gohn·fyo(a)*

sword n la spada *spah·da*

syllable n la sillaba *seel·la·ba*

syllabus n il programma *pro·gram·ma*

symbol n il simbolo *seem·bo·loh*

symmetrical adj simmetrico(a) *seem·me·tree·ko(a)*

sympathetic adj comprensivo(a) *kom·pren·see·vo(a)*

sympathy n la compassione *kom·pas·syoh·ne*

symphony n la sinfonia *seen·fo·nee·a*

symposium n il simposio *seem·po·zyoh*

symptom n il sintomo *seen·to·moh*

synagogue n la sinagoga *see·na·go·ga*

synchromesh n il cambio sincronizzato *kam·byoh seen·kro·nedz·dzah·to*

syndicate n il sindacato *seen·da·kah·toh*

synthetic adj sintetico(a) *seen·te·tee·ko(a)*

Syria n Siria (f) *see·rya*

Syrian adj siriano(a) *see·ryah·no(a)*

syrup n lo sciroppo *shee·rop·poh*; (golden) syrup la melassa raffinata *me·las·sa raf·fee·nah·ta*

system n il sistema *see·ste·ma*

systematic adj sistematico(a) *see·ste·ma·tee·ko(a)*

systems analyst n l'analista-programmatore (m) *a·na·lee·sta·pro·gram·ma·toh·re*

T

tab n l'etichetta (f) *e·tee·kayt·ta*

table n la tavola *tah·vo·la*; (list) la tabella *ta·bel·la* E2f

tablecloth n la tovaglia *to·val·ya*

table-mat n il sottopiatto *soht·to·pyat·toh*

tablespoon n la cucchiaia *kook·kee·a·ya*; (measure) la cucchiaiata *kook·kee·a·yah·ta*

tablet n (medicine) la pastiglia *pa·steel·ya*

table tennis n il tennis da tavolo *ten·nees da tah·vo·loh*

tack n (nail) la bulletta *bool·layt·ta*

□ *vi* (*sailing*) virare di bordo *vee·rah·ray dee bohr·doh*

tackle *vt* (*problem*) affrontare *af·fron·tah·ray*; (*in sports*) placcare *plak·kah·ray* □ *n* (*gear*) l'attrezzatura (*f*) *at·trets·tsa·too·ra*

tactics *pl* la tattica *tat·tee·ka*

tag *n* l'etichetta (*f*) *e·tee·kayt·ta*

tail *n* la coda *koh·da*

tailback *n* la coda *koh·da*

tailcoat *n* la marsina *mar·see·na*

tailgate *n* (*of car*) il portellone posteriore *por·tel·loh·ne po·ste·ryoh·re*

tailor *n* il sarto *sar·toh*

take *vt* prendere* *pren·de·re*; (*win: prize*) vincere* *veen·che·re*; he took it from me me lo ha preso *me lo a pray·so*; to take someone to the station portare qualcuno alla stazione *por·tah·ray kwal·koo·no al·la sta·tsyoh·ne*; take this to the post office porti questo alla posta *por·tee kway·sto al·la po·sta*; to take a photo scattare una foto *skat·tah·ray oo·na fo·to*; I'm taking French at school studio il francese a scuola *stoo·dyo eel fran·chay·ze a skwo·la*; to take an exam dare* un esame *dah·ray oon e·zah·me*; it takes a lot of effort/an hour ci vuole un grande sforzo/un'ora *chee vwo·le oon gran·de sfor·tsoh/oo·noh·ra*; to take something away togliere* qualcosa *tol·ye·re kwal·ko·sa*; to take something back (*return*) restituire qualcosa *re·stee·too·ee·re kwal·ko·sa*; to take off (*clothes*) togliersi* *tol·yer·see*; (*plane*) decollare *de·kol·lah·ray*; to take someone out to the theatre portare qualcuno a teatro *por·tah·ray kwal·koo·no a te·ah·troh*; to have a tooth taken out farsi* togliere un dente *far·see tol·ye·re oon den·te*; to take over a firm assumere* il controllo di una ditta *as·soo·me·re eel kon·trol·loh dee oo·na deet·ta*; to take up a sport cominciare a praticare uno sport *ko·meen·chah·ray a pra·tee·kah·ray oo·no sport*

take-away *adj* (*food*) da portar via *da por·tar vee·a*

take-home pay *n* lo stipendio netto *stee·pen·dyoh nayt·to*

takeoff *n* (*of plane*) il decollo *de·kol·loh*

takeover *n* l'acquisto (*m*) *ak·kwee·stoh*

take-over bid *n* l'offerta di acquisto (*f*) *of·fer·ta dee ak·kwee·stoh*

talc(um powder) *n* il talco *tal·koh*

talent *n* il talento *ta·len·toh*

talk *vi* parlare *par·lah·ray*; to talk to someone about something parlare a qualcuno di qualcosa *par·lah·ray a kwal·koo·no dee kwal·ko·sa*; to talk something over discutere* di qualcosa *dee·skoo·te·re dee kwal·ko·sa* □ *vt* to talk nonsense dire* sciocchezze *dee·re shok·kayts·tse* □ *n* talk (*conversation*) la conversazione *kon·ver·sa·tsyoh·ne*; (*lecture*) la conferenza *kon·fe·ren·tsa*; talks (*negotiations*) le trattative *trat·ta·tee·ve*

tall *adj* alto(a) *al·to(a)*; how tall are you? quanto è alto lei? *kwan·to e al·to ley*

tame *adj* (*animal*) domestico(a) *do·me·stee·ko(a)*

tan *adj* marrone rossiccio *mar·roh·ne ros·seech·cho* □ *n* (*on skin*) l'abbronzatura (*f*) *ab·bron·dza·too·ra* □ *vi* (*in sun*) abbronzarsi *ab·bron·dzar·see*

tangerine *n* il mandarino *man·da·ree·noh*

tangle *vt* aggrovigliare *ag·gro·veel·yah·ray*

tango *n* il tango *tan·goh*

tank *n* (*of car*) il serbatoio *ser·ba·toh·yoh*; (*military*) il carro armato *kar·roh ar·mah·to*

tanker *n* (*ship*) la nave cisterna *nah·ve chee·ster·na*; (*truck*) il camion cisterna *ka·myon chee·ster·na*

tap *n* (*for water*) il rubinetto *roo·bee·nayt·toh* □ *vt* colpire leggermente *kol·pee·re lej·jer·mayn·te* A31

tape *n* il nastro *na·stroh*; (*magnetic*) il nastro magnetico *na·stroh man·ye·tee·ko* □ *vt* (*record*) registrare *re·jee·strah·ray*

tape measure *n* il metro a nastro *me·troh a na·stroh*

tape record *vt* registrare *re·jee·strah·ray*

tape recorder *n* il magnetofono *man·ye·to·fo·noh*

tap-water *n* l'acqua di rubinetto (*f*) *ak·kwa dee roo·bee·nayt·toh* A31

tar *n* il catrame *ka·trah·me*

target *n* il bersaglio *ber·sal·yoh*; (*sales etc*) l'obiettivo (*m*) *o·byet·tee·voh*

tariff *n* (*list of charges*) la tariffa *ta·reef·fa*; (*tax*) la tariffa doganale *ta·reef·fa do·ga·nah·le*

tarmac *n* il macadam *ma·ka·dam*

tart *n* la crostata *kroh·stah·ta*

tartan *n* il tartan *tar·tan*; a tartan skirt una gonna scozzese *oo·na gohn·na skots·tsay·se*

tartar sauce *n* la salsa tartara *sal·sa tar·ta·ra*

task *n* il compito *kohm·pee·toh*

taste *n* il sapore *sa·poh·re*; in poor/good taste di cattivo/buon gusto *dee kat·tee·vo/bwon goo·stoh* □ *vt* tasse gustare *goo·stah·ray*; (*try*) assaggiare *as·saj·jah·ray*; I can't taste the garlic non sento l'aglio *nohn sen·to lal·yoh* □ *vi* it tastes like fish sa di pesce *sa de pay·she*

tax *n* (*on goods*) la tassa *tas·sa*; (*on income*) l'imposta (*f*) *eem·poh·sta* □ *vt* (*goods*) imporre* una tassa su *eem·pohr·re oo·na tas·sa soo*; (*income*) tassare *tas·sah·ray* A9, M4

taxable *adj* imponibile *eem·po·nee·bee·le*

taxation *n* la tassazione *tas·sa·tsyoh·ne*

tax-free *adj* esente da tasse *e·zen·te da tas·se*

taxi *n* il tassì *tas·see*; to go by taxi andare* in tassì *an·dah·ray een tas·see* T96f

taxi rank *n* il posteggio per tassì *po·stayj·joh payr tas·see*

tea *n* il tè *te*; (*meal*) la merenda *me·ren·da*; mint tea il tè alla menta *el·la mayn·ta* E61

tea bag *n* la bustina di tè *boo·stee·na dee te*

tea-break *n* la pausa per il tè *pow·za payr eel te*

teach *vt* insegnare *een·sen·yah·ray*; to teach someone something insegnare qualcosa a qualcuno *een·sen·yah·ray kwal·ko·sa a kwal·koo·no*

teacher *n* (*secondary school*) il professore *pro·fes·soh·re*, la professoressa *pro·fes·sor·res·sa*; (*primary school*) il/la maestro(a) *ma·e·stro(a)*

tea-cloth *n* il canovaccio *ka·no·vach·choh*

teacup *n* la tazza da tè *tats·tsa da te*

team n la squadra *skwa·dra*

teapot n la teiera *te·ye·ra*

tear¹ vt (rip) strappare *strap·pah·ray* □ n lo strappo *strap·poh* Sn76

tear² n la lacrima *la·kree·ma*; in tears in lacrime *een la·kree·me*

tea-shop n la sala da tè *sah·la da te*

teaspoon n il cucchiaino *kook·kya·ee·noh*

tea strainer n il colino da tè *ko·lee·noh da te*

teat n (for bottle) la tettarella *tet·ta·rel·la*

technical adj tecnico(a) *tek·nee·ko(a)*

technician n il/la tecnico(a) *tek·nee·ko(a)*

technique n la tecnica *tek·nee·ka*

technological adj tecnologico(a) *tek·no·lo·jee·ko(a)*

technology n la tecnologia *tek·no·lo·jee·a*

tee n (in golf) il tee *tee*

teenager n l'adolescente (m/f) *a·do·le·shen·te*

tee shirt n la maglietta *mal·yayt·ta*

telecommunications pl le telecomunicazioni *te·le·ko·moo·nee·ka·tsyoh·nee*

telegram n il telegramma *te·le·gram·ma* Sn3

telegraph vt telegrafare *te·le·gra·fah·ray*

telephone n il telefono *te·le·fo·noh*; to be on the telephone essere* al telefono *es·se·re al te·le·fo·noh*; by telephone per telefono *payr te·le·fo·noh* □ vt telephone (person) telefonare a *te·le·fo·nah·ray a* T166, A35, Sn11

telephone booth n la cabina telefonica *ka·bee·na te·le·fo·nee·ka*

telephone call n la telefonata *te·le·fo·nah·ta* Sn11

telephone directory n l'elenco telefonico (m) *e·len·koh te·le·fo·nee·ko* Sn25

telephone exchange n la centrale telefonica *chen·trah·le te·le·fo·nee·ka*

telephone number n il numero telefonico *noo·me·roh te·le·fo·nee·ko* Sn12, 24

telephonist n il/la telefonista *te·le·fo·nee·sta*

telephoto lens n il teleobiettivo *te·le·o·byet·tee·voh*

telescope n il telescopio *te·le·sko·pyoh*

televise vt teletrasmettere* *te·le·tra·zmayt·te·re*

television n la televisione *te·le·vee·zyoh·ne*; (set) il televisore *te·le·vee·zoh·re*; on television alla televisione *al·la te·le·vee·zyoh·ne*

telex n il telex *te·lex*; by telex per telex *payr te·lex* □ vt telex mandare un telex a *man·dah·ray oon te·lex a* A35, Bm14

tell vt (fact, news) dire* *dee·re*; (story) raccontare *rak·kon·tah·ray*; to tell someone something dire* qualcosa a qualcuno *dee·re kwal·ko·sa a kwal·koo·no*; to tell someone to do something dire* a qualcuno di fare qualcosa *dee·re a kwal·koo·no dee fah·ray kwal·ko·sa*; I can't tell the difference between them non posso distinguere tra di loro *nohn pos·so dee·steen·gwe·re tra dee loh·ro*

teller n il/la cassiere(a) *kas·sye·re(a)*

temper n □ in a bad temper di cattivo umore *dee kat·tee·vo oo·moh·re*; to lose one's temper andare* in collera *an·dah·ray een kol·le·ra*

temperature n la temperatura *tem·pe·ra·too·ra*; to have a temperature (fever) avere* la febbre *a·vay·re la feb·bre*; to take someone's temperature prendere* la temperatura a qualcuno *pren·de·re la tem·pe·ra·too·ra a kwal·koo·no* I31

temple n (building) il tempio *tem·pyoh*

temporary adj provvisorio(a) *prov·vee·zo·ryo(a)*

tempt vt tentare *ten·tah·ray*

ten num dieci *dye·chee*

tenant n l'inquilino(a) (m/f) *een·kwee·lee·no(a)*

tend vi □ to tend to do something tendere* a fare qualcosa *ten·de·re a fah·ray kwal·ko·sa*

tender adj tenero(a) *te·ne·ro(a)* □ vi to tender for something fare* un'offerta per qualcosa *fah·ray oo·nof·fer·ta payr kwal·ko·sa*

tennis n il tennis *ten·nees* L33

tennis court n il campo da tennis *kam·poh da ten·nees*

tennis racket n la racchetta da tennis *rak·kayt·ta da ten·nees*

tense adj teso(a) *tay·so(a)*

tent n la tenda *ten·da* A81

tenth adj decimo(a) *de·chee·mo(a)*

tent peg n il picchetto *peek·kayt·toh*

tent pole n il palo da tenda *pah·loh da ten·da*

term n (of school etc) il trimestre *tree·me·stre*; (word) il termine *ter·mee·ne*; during his term of office durante il suo periodo di carica *doo·ran·te eel soo·o pe·ree·o·doh dee kah·ree·ka*; terms (of contract) le condizioni *kon·dee·tsyoh·nee*

terminal n (air terminal) il terminal *ter·mee·nal*; (buses) il capolinea *kah·po·lee·ne·a*; (electricity, computer) il terminale *ter·mee·nah·le*

terrace n (of café) la terrazza *ter·rats·tsa*

terrible adj terribile *ter·ree·bee·le*

territory n il territorio *ter·ree·to·ryoh*

terrorism n il terrorismo *ter·ro·ree·zmoh*

terrorist n il/la terrorista *ter·ro·ree·sta*

terylene n il terilene *te·ree·le·ne*

test n la prova *pro·va*; (medical) la visita *vee·zee·ta*; (driving test) l'esame di guida (m) *e·zah·me dee gwee·da* □ vt (product) collaudare *kol·low·dah·ray*; (sight, hearing) esaminare *e·za·mee·nah·ray*; (ability) mettere* alla prova *mayt·te·re al·la pro·va*

test-drive n la prova su strada *pro·va soo strah·da* □ vt to test-drive a car provare una macchina su strada *pro·vah·ray oo·na mak·kee·na soo strah·da*

text n il testo *te·stoh*

textbook n il libro di testo *lee·broh dee te·stoh*

textiles pl i tessili *tes·see·lee*

texture n la tessitura *tes·see·too·ra*

than conj che *ke*; better than him meglio di lui *mel·yo dee loo·ee*; more than 10 più di 10 *pyoo dee 10*

thank vt ringraziare *reen·gra·tsyah·ray*; thank you grazie *gra·tsye*; thanks to grazie a *gra·tsye a*

that adj quel(la) *kwayl(·la)*; that one quello(a) *lf kwayl·lo(a) lee* □ pron that quello *kwayl·lo*; give me that il mi dia quello *mee dee·a kwayl·lo*; that's what I want ecco quello che voglio *ek·ko kwayl·lo ke vol·yo*; what's that? che cos'è quello? *ke ko·se*

kwayl·lo; who's that? chi è? *kee e*; that is (to say)... cioè *cho·e*; the photo that I gave you la foto che Le ho dato *la fo·to ke le o dah·to* □ *conj* I hope that... spero che... *spe·ro ke*

thaw *vi* (ice) sgelare *zje·lah·ray*; (frozen food) disgelare *dee·zje·lah·ray* □ *vt* (food) fare* disgelare *fah·ray dee·zje·lah·ray*

the *art* □ the boy il ragazzo *eel ra·gats·tsoh*; the woman la donna *la don·na*; the boys i ragazzi *ee ra·gats·tsee*; the women le donne *le don·ne*

theater, theatre *n* il teatro *te·ah·troh*; to go to the theatre andare* a teatro *an·dah·ray a te·ah·troh* Mc44

their *adj* loro *loh·ro*; their father il loro padre *eel loh·ro pah·dre*; their mother la loro madre *la loh·ro mah·dre*; their brothers/sisters i loro fratelli/le loro sorelle *ee loh·ro fra·tel·lee/le loh·ro so·rel·le*

theirs *pron* il/la loro *eel/la loh·ro*; (plural) i/le loro *eel/le loh·ro*

them *pron* li(le) *lee(le)*; buy them li (le) compri *lee (le) kohm·pree*; show them the books mostri loro i libri *moh·stree loh·ro ee lee·bree*; he spoke to them ha parlato loro *a par·lah·to loh·ro*; it's them! sono loro! *soh·no loh·ro*

themselves *pron* □ they wash themselves si lavano *see lah·va·no*; they did it themselves l'hanno fatto loro stessi(e) *lan·no fat·to loh·ro stays·see(·se)*

then *adv* poi *poy*; then it must be true allora dev'essere vero *al·loh·ra de·ves·se·re vay·ro*; from then on d'allora in poi *dal·loh·ra een poy*

theory *n* la teoria *te·o·ree·a*

there *adv* lí *lee*; there is c'è che; there are ci sono *chee soh·no*; is there anyone there? c'è qualcuno là? *che kwal·koo·no la*; he went there ci è andato *chee e an·dah·to*; there he/she is! eccolo/a! *ek·ko·lo(a)*

thermometer *n* il termometro *ter·mo·me·troh*

Thermos (flask) *n* il termos *ter·mos*

these *adj, pron* questi(e) *kway·stee (·ste)*; these are what I want ecco quelli(e) che voglio *ek·ko kwayl·lee (·le) ke vol·yo*

they *pron* loro *loh·ro*; they say that... (people in general) si dice che... see *dee·che ke...*; there they are eccoli(e) *ek·ko·lee(·le)*

thick *adj* spesso(a) *spays·so(a)*; (soup) denso(a) *den·so(a)*; 3 metres thick spesso(a) 3 metri *spays·so(a) 3 me·tree*

thief *n* il ladro *la·droh* Ea2

thin *adj* (line) sottile *sot·tee·le*; (person) magro(a) *ma·gro(a)*; (material) fine *fee·ne*; (liquid) poco denso(a) *po·ko den·so(a)*

thing *n* la cosa *ko·sa*; the best thing would be... la cosa migliore sarebbe... *la ko·sa meel·yoh·re sa·reb·be*; where are your things? dove sono le Sue cose? *doh·ve soh·no le soo·e ko·se*

think *vi* pensare *pen·sah·ray*; to think of something pensare a qualcosa *pen·sah·ray a kwal·ko·sa*; to think about someone pensare a qualcuno *pen·sah·ray a kwal·koo·no*; I think so credo di sí *kre·do dee see*; to think something over riflettere* su qualcosa *ree·flet·te·re soo kwal·ko·sa*

third *adj* terzo(a) *ter·tso(a)* □ *n* third (gear) la terza (marcia) *ter·tsa (mar·cha)*

third party insurance *n* l'assicurazione contro terzi (f) *as·see·koo·ra·tsyoh·ne kohn·tro ter·tsee*

Third World *n* il Terzo Mondo *ter·tso mohn·doh*

thirsty *adj* assetato(a) *as·se·tah·to(a)*; to be thirsty avere* sete *a·vay·re say·te*

thirteen *num* tredici *tray·dee·chee*

thirteenth *adj* tredicesimo(a) *tre·dee·che·zee·mo(a)*

thirtieth *adj* trentesimo(a) *tren·te·zee·mo(a)*

thirty *num* trenta *trayn·ta*

this *adj, pron* questo(a) *kway·sto(a)*; this one questo(a) *kway·sto(a)*; this is what I want ecco quello che voglio *ek·ko kwayl·lo ke vol·yo*

thorough *adj* (work) coscienzioso(a) *ko·shen·tsyoh·zo(a)*

those *adj* quelli(e) *kwayl·lee(·le)*; those boys quei ragazzi *kway ra·gats·tsee*; those women quelle donne *kwayl·le don·ne* □ *pron* those quelli(e) *kwayl·lee(·le)*; those are what I want ecco quelli(e) che voglio *ek·ko kwayl·lee (·le) ke vol·yo*

though *conj, adv* □ though you may think... sebbene Lei possa pensare... *seb·be·ne lay pos·sa pen·sah·ray*; he's happy, though è contento, comunque *e kon·tayn·to, ko·moon·kwe*

thought *n* il pensiero *pen·sye·roh*; (idea) l'idea (f) *ee·de·a*

thousand *num* mille *meel·le*

thousandth *adj* millesimo(a) *meel·le·zee·mo(a)*

thread *n* il filo *fee·loh*

threat *n* la minaccia *mee·nach·cha*

threaten *vt* minacciare *mee·nach·chah·ray*

three *num* tre *tray*

thriller *n* (film) il thriller *threel·ler*; (book) il giallo *jal·loh*

throat *n* la gola *goh·la* S40

throttle *n* (in car) l'acceleratore (m) *ach·che·le·ra·toh·re*

through *prep* attraverso *at·tra·ver·so*; (all) through the year durante tutto l'anno *doo·ran·te toot·to lan·no*; Monday through Friday da lunedí a venerdí *da loo·ne·dee a ve·ner·dee*; I couldn't get through (on phone) non sono riuscito ad ottenere la comunicazione *nohn soh·no ree·oo·shee·to ad ot·te·nay·re la ko·moo·nee·ka·tsyoh·ne*; put me through to Mr X mi passi il Signor X *mee pas·see eel seen·yohr X*; when I'm through with my work quando avrò finito il mio lavoro *kwan·do a·vro fee·nee·to eel mee·o la·voh·roh*

through train *n* il treno diretto *tre·noh dee·ret·to* T74

throw *vt* gettare *jet·tah·ray*; (rider) disarcionare *dee·zar·cho·nah·ray*; to throw a 6 (dice) fare* 6 *fah·ray 6*; to throw away buttare via *boot·tah·ray vee·a*

thumb *n* il pollice *pol·lee·che* □ *vt* to thumb a lift fare* l'autostop *fah·ray low·to·stop*

thumbtack *n* la puntina *poon·tee·na*

thump *n* (noise) il tonfo *tohn·fo*

thunder *n* il tuono *two·noh*

thunderstorm *n* il temporale *tem·po·rah·le*

Thursday *n* giovedí (m) *jo·ve·dee*

thus adv (*in this way*) così ko·see

thyme n il timo tee·moh

tick n (*mark*) il segno sayn·yoh □ vt segnare sen·yah·ray □ vi (*clock*) fare* tic-tac fah·ray teek·tak

ticket n il biglietto beel·yayt·toh; (*label*) l'etichetta (f) e·tee·kayt·ta; (*parking*) la contravvenzione kon·trav·ven·tsyoh·ne

ticket office n la biglietteria beel·yet·te·ree·a T49

tickle vt solleticare sol·le·tee·kah·ray

tide n la marea ma·re·a; the tide is in/out c'è alta/bassa marea che al·ta/bas·sa ma·re·a

tidy adj ordinato(a) or·dee·nah·to(a)

tie n la cravatta kra·vat·ta □ vt (*string, ribbon*) annodare an·no·dah·ray; to tie a dog to a post attaccare un cane ad un palo at·tak·kah·ray oon kah·ne ad oon pah·loh; to tie up a parcel legare un pacco le·gah·ray oon pak·koh; to tie up capital immobilizzare del capitale eem·mo·bee·leedz·dzah·ray del ka·pee·tah·le

tiger n la tigre tee·gre

tight adj (*rope*) teso(a) tay·so(a); (*clothes*) stretto(a) strayt·to(a); (*schedule*) impegnativo(a) eem·pen·ya·tee·vo(a)

tights pl il collant ko·loñ

tile n (*on floor, wall*) la piastrella pya·strel·la; (*on roof*) la tegola tay·go·la

till prep fino a fee·no a □ conj till he comes finché verrà feen·kay ver·ra □ n till (*cash register*) la cassa kas·sa

time n il tempo tem·poh; what's the time? che ora è? ke oh·ra e; the time is 5 o'clock sono le 5 soh·no le 5; the first time la prima volta la pree·ma vol·ta; how many times? quante volte? kwan·te vol·te; a short/long time poco/molto tempo po·ko/mohl·to tem·poh; in times past nei tempi passati nay tem·pee pas·sah·tee; to have a good time divertirsi dee·ver·teer·see; for the time being per il momento payr eel mo·mayn·toh; from time to time di tanto in tanto dee tan·to een tan·to; just in time giusto in tempo joo·sto een tem·poh; on time puntualmente poon·too·al·mayn·te B45, T4, L12

timetable n (*for trains etc*) l'orario (m) o·rah·ryoh T49

time zone n il fuso orario foo·soh o·rah·ryoh

tin n (*substance*) lo stagno stan·yoh; (*can*) il barattolo ba·rat·to·loh S33

tin foil n la stagnola stan·yo·la

tinned adj (*food*) in scatola een skah·to·la

tin-opener n l'apriscatole (m) a·pree·skah·to·le

tip n (*end*) la punta poon·ta; (*money given*) la mancia man·cha □ vt (*tilt*) inclinare een·klee·nah·ray M4

tipped adj (*cigarettes*) con filtro kohn feel·troh

tire n lo pneumatico pne·oo·ma·tee·koh

tired adj stanco(a) stan·ko(a); I'm tired of it ne sono stufo(a) nay soh·no stoo·fo(a)

tissue n (*handkerchief*) il fazzolettino di carta fats·tso·let·tee·noh dee kar·ta

tissue paper n la velina ve·lee·na

title n il titolo tee·to·loh

T-junction n (*on road*) l'incrocio a T (m) een·kroh·choh a tee

to prep a a; to the station alla stazione

al·la sta·tsyoh·ne; to London a Londra a lohn·dra; to France in Francia een fran·cha; to school a scuola a skwo·la; to town in città een cheet·ta; give it to me me lo dia me lo dee·a; he wants to leave vuole partire vwo·le par·tee·re; I forgot to do... ho dimenticato di fare... o dee·men·tee·kah·to dee fah·ray; the key to my room la chiave della mia camera la kyah·ve del·la mee·a kah·me·ra

toast n il pane tostato pah·ne to·stah·to; to propose a toast to someone proporre* un brindisi a qualcuno pro·pohr·re oon breen·dee·zee a kwal·koo·no

toaster n il tostapane to·sta·pah·ne

tobacco n il tabacco ta·bak·koh S97

tobacconist n il/la tabaccaio(a) ta·bak·ka·yoh(a)

tobacconist's (shop) n la tabaccheria ta·bak·ke·ree·a S95f

today adv oggi oj·jee

toe n il dito del piede dee·toh del pye·de

toffee n la caramella ka·ra·mel·la

together adv insieme een·sye·me

toilet n la toeletta to·e·let·ta A4, 89

toilet paper n la carta igienica kar·ta ee·je·nee·ka A51

toiletries pl gli articoli da toeletta ar·tee·ko·lee da to·e·let·ta

toilet water n l'acqua di Colonia (f) ak·kwa dee ko·lon·ya

token n (*voucher*) il buono bwo·noh; (*for machine*) il gettone jet·toh·ne Sn18

toll n (*on road etc*) il pedaggio pe·daj·joh T139

toll bridge n il ponte a pedaggio pohn·te a pe·daj·joh

tomato n il pomodoro po·mo·do·roh S31

tomorrow adv domani do·mah·nee T1, A19

ton n la tonnellata ton·nel·lah·ta

tone n il tono to·noh

tongue n la lingua leen·gwa

tonic n (*medicine*) il tonico to·nee·koh

tonic water n l'acqua tonica (f) ak·kwa to·nee·ka

tonight adv stasera sta·say·ra

tonne n la tonnellata ton·nel·lah·ta

tonsillitis n la tonsillite ton·seel·lee·te

too adv (*also*) anche an·ke; he's too big è troppo grande e trop·po gran·de; too much troppo trop·po; too many books troppi libri trop·pee lee·bree

tool n l'arnese (m) ar·nay·se

tooth n il dente den·te 157

toothache n il mal di denti mal del den·tee; to have toothache avere* il mal di denti a·vay·re eel mal dee den·tee

toothbrush n lo spazzolino da denti spats·tso·lee·noh da den·tee

toothpaste n il dentifricio den·tee·free·choh

top n (*of mountain, ladder*) la cima chee·ma; (*of table*) la superficie soo·per·fee·che; (*lid*) il coperchio ko·per·kyoh; (*of bottle*) il tappo tap·poh; on top of su soo; top (*gear*) la quarta (marcia) kwar·ta (mar·cha) □ adj top superiore soo·pe·ryoh·re; (*in rank*) primo(a) pree·mo(a); (*best*) migliore meel·yoh·re L22

top hat n il cappello a cilindro kap·pel·loh a chee·leen·droh

topic n l'argomento (m) ar·go·mayn·toh

torch n la lampadina tascabile *lam·pa·dee·na ta·skah·bee·le*
toss vt (salad) rimescolare *ree·me·sko·lah·ray*; to toss a coin fare* a testa e croce *fah·ray a te·sta e kroh·che*
total n il totale *to·tah·le* □ adj totale *to·tah·le*
touch vt toccare *tok·kah·ray* □ n in touch with in contatto con *een kon·tat·toh kohn*
tough adj (meat etc) duro(a) *doo·ro(a)*; (material) resistente *re·see·sten·te*
tour n il giro *jee·roh* □ vt (town) visitare *vee·zee·tah·ray* L5, 7
tourism n il turismo *too·ree·zmoh*
tourist n il/la turista *too·ree·sta*
tourist class n la classe turistica *klas·se too·ree·stee·ka*
tourist office n l'ufficio turistico (m) *oof·fee·choh too·ree·stee·ko* F5
tourist trade n il turismo *too·ree·zmoh*
tow vt (trailer) rimorchiare *ree·mor·kyah·ray*; on tow a rimorchio *a ree·mor·kyoh* T168
toward(s) prep verso *ver·so*; to come towards someone venire* incontro a qualcuno *ve·nee·re een·kohn·tro a kwal·koo·no*; his attitude towards others il suo atteggiamento nei confronti altrui *eel soo·o at·tej·ja·mayn·toh ne·ee kon·frohn·tee al·troo·ee*
tow-bar n (on car) il gancio per rimorchio *gan·choh payr ree·mor·kyoh*
towel n l'asciugamano (m) *a·shoo·ga·mah·noh* A41
tower n la torre *tohr·re*
town n la città *cheet·ta*; to go to town andare* in città *an·dah·ray een cheet·ta* T100, L3, F4
town hall n il municipio *moo·nee·chee·pyoh*
toy n il giocattolo *jo·kat·to·loh*
toyshop n il negozio di giocattoli *ne·go·tsyoh dee jo·kat·to·loh*
trace n (mark) la traccia *trach·cha*
track n (of animal) la traccia *trach·cha*; (pathway) il sentiero *sen·tye·roh*; (on record) il solco *sohl·koh*; (for trains) il binario *bee·nah·ryoh*; (sports) la pista *pee·sta*
track suit n la tuta *too·ta*
tractor n il trattore *trat·toh·re*
trade n il commercio *kom·mer·choh*
trade-in n □ as a trade-in come pagamento parziale *koh·me pa·ga·mayn·toh par·tsyah·le*
trade mark n il marchio di fabbrica *mar·kyoh dee fab·bree·ka*
trade name n il marchio depositato *mar·kyoh de·po·zee·tah·to*
trader n il/la commerciante *kom·mer·chan·te*
trade union n il sindacato *seen·da·kah·toh*
trading estate n la zona industriale *dzo·na een·doo·stryah·le*
trading stamp n il buono premio *bwo·noh pre·myoh*
tradition n la tradizione *tra·dee·tsyoh·ne*
traffic n (cars) il traffico *traf·fee·koh* T133
traffic jam n l'ingorgo stradale (m) *een·gohr·goh stra·dah·le*
traffic lights pl il semaforo *se·mah·fo·roh*
traffic warden n il vigile urbano *vee·jee·le oor·bah·no*
trailer n (for goods) il rimorchio *ree·mor·kyoh*; (home on wheels) la roulotte *roo·lot*

train n il treno *tre·noh*; (on dress) lo strascico *stra·shee·koh*; by train in treno *een tre·noh* □ vt train (apprentice) addestrare *ad·de·strah·ray*; (dog) ammaestrare *am·ma·e·strah·ray* □ vi (sportsman) allenarsi *al·le·nar·se*; to train as a teacher abilitarsi all'insegnamento *a·bee·lee·tar·see al·leen·sen·ya·mayn·toh* T2f, 51f
trainee n l'apprendista (m/f) *ap·pren·dee·sta*
training n (for job) la formazione *for·ma·tsyoh·ne*; (for sports) l'allenamento (m) *al·le·na·mayn·toh*
tram(car) n il tram *tram*
tramp n il/la vagabondo(a) *va·ga·bohn·doh(a)*
tranquillizer n il tranquillante *tran·kweel·lan·te*
transaction n la transazione *tran·sa·tsyoh·ne*
transatlantic adj transatlantico(a) *tran·sat·lan·tee·ko(a)*
transfer vt (money) trasferire *tras·fe·ree·re*; to transfer the charges (on phone) telefonare con la R *te·le·fo·nah·ray kohn la er·re* M28
transistor n il transistore *tran·see·stoh·re*
transit n □ in transit in transito *een tran·see·toh*
transit lounge n la sala di transito *sah·la dee tran·see·toh*
transit visa n il visto di transito *vee·stoh dee tran·see·toh*
translate vt tradurre* *tra·door·re*
translation n la traduzione *tra·doo·tsyoh·ne*
transmission n (of car) la trasmissione *tra·zmees·syoh·ne*
transmitter n il trasmettitore *tra·zmet·tee·toh·re*
transparent adj trasparente *tra·spa·ren·te*
transport n il trasporto *tra·spor·toh* □ vt trasportare *tra·spor·tah·ray*
transport café n il ristorante per camionisti *ree·sto·ran·te payr kam·yo·nee·stee*
trap n la trappola *trap·po·la*
trash n le immondizie *eem·mon·dee·tsye*
trash can n la pattumiera *pat·too·mye·ra* A71
travel n i viaggi *vee·aj·jee* □ vi viaggiare *vyaj·jah·ray* □ vt (a distance) percorrere* *per·kohr·re·re*
travel agency n l'agenzia di viaggi (f) *a·jen·tsee·a dee vee·aj·jee*
travel agent n l'agente di viaggi (m) *a·jen·te dee vee·aj·jee*
travel(l)er n il viaggiatore *vyaj·ja·toh·re*
travel(l)er's cheque n l'assegno per viaggiatori (m) *as·sayn·yoh payr vyaj·ja·toh·ree* M12, 22, A23
tray n il vassoio *vas·soh·yoh*
treacle n la melassa *me·las·sa*
treasure n il tesoro *te·zo·roh*
Treasury n il Ministero del Tesoro *mee·nee·ste·roh del te·zo·roh*
treat vt trattare *trat·tah·ray*; (medically) curare *koo·rah·ray*; I'll treat you to an ice cream Le offrirò un gelato *lay of·free·ro oon je·lah·toh* □ n a little treat un piacere *oon pya·chay·re*
treatment n il trattamento *trat·ta·mayn·toh*; (medical) la cura *koo·ra*
tree n l'albero (m) *al·be·roh*

trend n (tendency) la tendenza *ten·den·tsa*

trial n (test) la prova *pro·va*; (in law) il processo *pro·ches·soh*

triangle n il triangolo *tree·an·go·loh*

tribe n la tribù *tree·boo*

trick n (clever act) il trucco *trook·koh*; (malicious) l'inganno (m) *een·gan·noh*; (in cards) la mano *mah·no* □ vt ingannare *een·gan·nah·ray*

trifle n (dessert) la zuppa inglese *tsoop·pa een·glay·se*

trim vt (hedge) potare *po·tah·ray*; (hair) spuntare *spoon·tah·ray*; (decorate) ornare *or·nah·ray*

trip n (journey) il viaggio *vyaj·joh*; (excursion) la gita *jee·ta*; to go on a trip to the seaside fare* una gita al mare *fah·ray oo·na jee·ta al mah·re* □ vi trip (stumble) inciampare *een·cham·pah·ray*

tripe n la trippa *treep·pa*

tripod n il treppiede *trep·pye·de*

trivial adj insignificante *een·seen·yee·fee·kan·te*

trolley n il carrello *kar·rel·loh*

troop n la truppa *troop·pa*

tropical adj tropicale *tro·pee·kah·le*

tropics pl i tropici *tro·pee·chee*

trot vi (horse) trottare *trot·tah·ray*

trouble n (problems) i guai *gwy*; the troubles in this country i guai di questo paese *ee gwy dee kway·sto pa·ay·ze*; to take trouble over something darsi* pena di fare qualcosa *dar·see pay·na dee fah·ray kwal·ko·sa*; stomach trouble i disturbi allo stomaco *dee·stoor·bee al·lo sto·ma·koh*; engine trouble il guasto al motore *gwa·stoh al mo·toh·re*; to be in trouble essere* nei guai *es·se·re nay gwy* Sn47, T169

trouble-shooter n (political) il conciliatore *kon·chee·lya·toh·re*; (technical) il perito *pe·ree·toh*

trousers pl i pantaloni *pan·ta·loh·nee* Sn65

trouser-suit n il tailleur-pantalone *tye·yur·pan·ta·loh·ne*

trout n la trota *tro·ta*

truck n (vehicle) il camion *ka·myon*

true adj vero(a) *vay·ro(a)*

truffle n (fungus) il tartufo *tar·too·foh*

truly adv □ yours truly distinti saluti *dee·steen·tee sa·loo·tee*

trump n (cards) l'atout (m) a·too □ vi giocare una briscola *jo·kah·ray oo·na bree·sko·la*

trumpet n la tromba *trohm·ba*

trunk n (of tree) il tronco *trohn·koh*; (for clothes etc) il baule *ba·oo·le*; (in car) il bagagliaio *ba·gal·yah·yoh*

trunk-call n la comunicazione interurbana *ko·moo·nee·ka·tsyoh·ne een·ter·oor·bah·na*

trunk-road n la strada statale *strah·da sta·tah·le*

trust vt (person) fidarsi di *fee·dar·see dee* □ n (company) il trust *trust*

truth n la verità *ve·ree·ta*

try vt provare *pro·vah·ray*; (in law) processare *pro·ches·sah·ray*; to try to do something cercare di fare qualcosa *cher·kah·ray dee fah·ray kwal·ko·sa*; to try on a dress provare un vestito *pro·vah·ray oon ve·stee·toh*

T-shirt n la maglietta *mal·yayt·ta*

tube n il tubo *too·boh*

Tuesday n martedì (m) *mar·te·dee*

tulip n il tulipano *too·lee·pah·noh*

tuna(-fish) n il tonno *tohn·noh*

tune n l'aria (f) *a·ree·a* □ vt (engine) mettere* a punto *mayt·te·re a poon·toh*; (instrument) accordare *ak·kor·dah·ray*

tunic n (of uniform) la tunica *too·nee·ka*

Tunisia n Tunisia (f) *too·nee·see·a*

tunnel n la galleria *gal·le·ree·a*

turbot n il rombo *rohm·boh*

turkey n il tacchino *tak·kee·noh*

Turkey n Turchia (f) *toor·kee·a*

Turkish adj turco(a) *toor·ko(a)* □ n il turco *toor·ko*

Turkish coffee n il caffè alla turca *kaf·fe al·la toor·ka*

Turkish delight n il Turkish delight

turn n (bend in road) la curva *koor·va*; it's your turn tocca a Lei *tok·ka a lay*; in turn a vicenda *a vee·chen·da* □ vi turn (person, car) girare *jee·rah·ray*; he turned (round) si è voltato *see e vol·tah·to*; to turn back tornare sui propri passi *tor·nah·ray soo·ee pro·pree pas·see*; to turn professional diventare professionista *dee·ven·tah·ray pro·fes·syoh·nee·sta* □ vt turn girare *jee·rah·ray*; to turn on (light) accendere* *ach·chen·de·re*; (water) aprire* *a·pree·re*; to turn off (light) spegnere* *spayn·ye·re*; (water) chiudere* *kyoo·de·re*; to turn down (heat) ridurre* *ree·door·re*; (volume) abbassare *ab·bas·sah·ray*; to turn up (heat) alzare *al·tsah·ray*; (volume) aumentare *ow·men·tah·ray*; to turn something over rovesciare qualcosa *ro·ve·shah·ray kwal·ko·sa* T104, 205

turnip n la rapa *ra·pa*

turnover n (money) il giro d'affari *jee·roh daf·fah·ree*; (in goods) il movimento delle merci *mo·vee·mayn·toh del·le mer·chee*

turnpike n l'autostrada a pedaggio (f) *ow·to·strah·da a pe·daj·joh*

turn signal n la freccia *fraych·cha*

turquoise adj color turchese *ko·lohr toor·kay·se*

turtle soup n la zuppa di tartaruga *tsoop·pa dee tar·ta·roo·ga*

tutor n l'insegnante privato(a) (m/f) *een·sen·yan·te pree·vah·to(a)*

tuxedo n lo smoking *smo·keeng*

TV n la TV *tee·voo*

tweed n il tweed *tweed*

tweezers pl le pinzette *peen·tsayt·te*

twelfth adj dodicesimo(a) *do·dee·che·zee·mo(a)*

twelve num dodici *doh·dee·chee*

twenty num venti *vayn·tee*

twice adv due volte *doo·e vol·te*

twig n il ramoscello *ra·mo·shel·loh*

twill n la saia *sa·ya*

twin beds pl i letti gemelli *let·tee je·mel·lee* A4

twins pl i gemelli *je·mel·lee*, le gemelle *je·mel·le*

twin set n il completo *kom·ple·toh*

twin towns pl le città gemelle *cheet·ta je·mel·le*

twist vt torcere* *tor·che·re* □ vi (road) serpeggiare *ser·pej·jah·ray*

two num due *doo·e*

two-piece n il completo *kom·ple·toh*

tycoon n il magnate *man·yah·te*

type n (sort) il tipo *tee·poh* □ vt (letter) dattilografare* *dat·tee·lo·skree·ve·re*

typewriter n la macchina da scrivere *mak·kee·na da skree·ve·re*

typewritten adj dattiloscritto(a) *dat·tee·lo·skreet·to(a)*

typical adj tipico(a) *tee·pee·ko(a)*

typist n il/la dattilografo(a) *dat·tee·lo·gra·fo(a)* Bm12

tyre n lo pneumatico *pne·oo·ma·tee·koh* T176

U

U-bend n (in road) la curva a gomito *koor·va a go·mee·to*

ugly adj (object, person) brutto(a) *broot·toh(a)*

ulcer n l'ulcera (f) *ool·che·ra*

ultimatum n l'ultimatum (m) *ool·tee·mah·toom*

umbrella n l'ombrello (m) *om·brel·loh*; (on table) l'ombrellone (m) *om·brel·loh·ne*

umbrella stand n il portaombrelli *por·ta·om·brel·lee*

umpire n l'arbitro (m) *ahr·bee·troh*

unable adj □ to be unable to do something non potere* fare qualcosa *nohn po·tay·re fah·ray kwal·ko·sa*

unanimous adj (decision) unanime *oo·nah·nee·may*; we were unanimous eravamo tutti d'accordo *e·ra·vah·mo toot·tee dak·kor·doh*

unarmed adj (person) disarmato(a) *dee·zar·mah·toh(a)*

unavoidable adj inevitabile *een·e·vee·tah·bee·lay*

unbearable adj (pain) insopportabile *een·sop·por·tah·bee·lay*

unbeatable adj (offer) imbattibile *eem·bat·tee·bee·lay*

unbiased adj imparziale *eem·par·tsee·ah·lay*

unbreakable adj infrangibile *een·fran·jee·bee·lay*

uncertain adj (fact) incerto(a) *een·cher·toh(a)*

unchanged adj immutato(a) *eem·moo·tah·toh(a)*

uncle n lo zio *tsee·oh*

uncomfortable adj scomodo(a) *sko·mo·doh(a)*

unconditional adj (offer) incondizionato(a) *een·kon·dee·tsyoh·nah·toh(a)*

unconscious adj privo(a) di sensi *pree·vo(a) dee sen·see*

uncover vt scoprire* *sko·pree·ray*

under prep sotto *soht·toh*; under a kilometre un chilometro *oon kee·lo·me·troh*; under repair in riparazione *een re·pa·ra·tsyoh·nay*; children under 10 i minori di 10 anni *ee mee·noh·ree dee 10 an·nee*

underclothes pl la biancheria intima *byan·ke·ree·a een·tee·ma*

undercooked adj insufficientemente cotto(a) *een·soof·fee·chen·te·mayn·tay kot·toh(a)*

underdeveloped adj (country) sottosviluppato(a) *soht·to·zvee·loop·pah·toh(a)*

underdone adj (steak) al sangue *al san·gwe*; (food in general) insufficientemente cotto(a) *een·soof·fee·chen·te·mayn·tay kot·toh(a)*

underexposed adj sottoesposto(a) *soht·to·e·spoh·stoh(a)*

undergraduate n lo studente universitario *stoo·den·te oo·nee·vayr·see·tah·ryo*, la studentessa universitaria *stoo·den·tays·sa oo·nee·vayr·see·tah·rya*

underground adj (pipe etc) sotterraneo(a) *soht·ter·rah·ne·oh(a)* □ n underground railway la metropolitana *me·tro·po·lee·tah·na*; to go by underground andare* con la metropolitana *an·dah·ray kohn la me·tro·po·lee·tah·na*

underline vt sottolineare *soht·to·lee·ne·ah·ray*

underneath prep sotto *soht·to* □ adv it's underneath sta di sotto *sta dee soht·to*

underpaid adj mal pagato(a) *mal pa·gah·to(a)*

underpants pl le mutande *moo·tan·day*

underpass n (for pedestrians) il sottopassaggio *soht·to·pas·saj·joh*; (for cars) la sottovia *soht·to·vee·a*

undershirt n la canottiera *ka·not·tye·ra*

understand vt/i capire *ka·pee·ray*; we understand that... capiamo che... *ka·pyah·mo ke* B21f

understanding n la comprensione *kom·pren·syoh·nay*; (agreement) l'intesa (f) *een·tay·sa*

undertake vt intraprendere* *een·tra·pren·de·ray*; to undertake to do impegnarsi a fare *eem·pen·yar·see a fah·ray*

undertaking n (enterprise) l'impresa (f) *eem·pray·sa*; (promise) l'impegno (m) *eem·payn·yoh*

undervalue vt sottovalutare *soht·to·va·loo·tah·ray*

underwear n la biancheria intima *byan·ke·ree·a een·tee·ma*

underwrite vt (insurance) assicurare *as·see·koo·rah·ray*; (finance) garantire *ga·ran·tee·ray*

underwriter n l'assicuratore (m) *as·see·koo·ra·toh·ray*

undo vt slacciare *zlach·chah·ray*

undress vt svestire *zve·stee·ray* □ vi spogliarsi *spol·yar·see*

unearned income n la rendita *ren·dee·ta*

uneconomic adj antieconomico(a) *an·tee·e·ko·no·mee·ko(a)*

uneconomical adj non economico(a) *nohn e·ko·no·mee·ko(a)*

unemployed adj disoccupato(a) *dee·zok·koo·pah·to(a)*; the unemployed i disoccupati *ee dee·zok·koo·pah·tee*

unemployment n la disoccupazione *dee·zok·koo·pa·tsyoh·nay*

UNESCO n l'UNESCO (f) *oo·ne·sko*

unfair adj ingiusto(a) *een·joo·sto(a)*; (competition) sleale *zle·ah·lay*

unfasten vt slacciare *zlach·chah·ray*

unfold vt spiegare *spee·e·gah·ray*

unfortunate adj (event) sfortunato(a) *sfor·too·nah·to(a)*

unfortunately adv sfortunatamente *sfor·too·nah·ta·mayn·tay*

unhappy adj infelice *een·fe·lee·chay*

uniform n la divisa *dee·vee·za*

unilateral adj unilaterale *oo·nee·la·te·rah·lay*

union n l'unione (f) *oo·nyoh·nay*; (trade union) il sindacato *seen·da·kah·toh*

unique adj unico(a) *oo·nee·ko(a)*

unisex adj unisex *oo·nee·sex*

unit n (of machinery, furniture) l'elemento (m) *e·le·mayn·toh*; (department, squad) il reparto *re·par·toh*; (of measurement) l'unità (f) *oo·nee·ta*

unite vt unire *oo·nee·ray*

United Kingdom, U.K. n il Regno Unito *rayn·yoh oo·nee·to*

United Nations Organization, UN, UNO n le Nazioni Unite *na·tsyoh·nee oo·nee·tay*

United States (of America), US(A) n

gli Stati Uniti (d'America) *stah·tee·oo·nee·tee (da·me·ree·ka)*
unit price n il prezzo unitario *prets·tsoh oo·nee·tah·ree·oh*
universal adj universale *oo·nee·vayr·sah·lay*
universe n l'universo (m) *oo·nee·ver·soh*
university n l'università (f) *oo·nee·ver·see·ta*
unkind adj (person) scortese *skor·tay·zay*; (remark) cattivo(a) *kat·tee·voh(a)*
unknown adj sconosciuto(a) *sko·no·shoo·toh(a)*
unless conj □ unless we come a meno che noi non veniamo *a may·no ke noy nohn ve·nya·mo*
unlikely adj improbabile *eem·pro·bah·bee·lay*
unlimited adj illimitato(a) *eel·lee·mee·tah·to(a)*
unlined adj (clothes) sfoderato(a) *sfo·de·rah·to(a)*
unload vt scaricare *ska·ree·kah·ray*
unlock vt aprire* (con chiave) *a·pree·ray (kohn kyah·ve)*
unlucky adj sfortunato(a) *sfor·too·nah·to(a)*
unnatural adj non naturale *nohn na·too·rah·lay*
unnecessary adj inutile *ee·noo·tee·lay*
unofficial adj ufficioso(a) *oof·fee·choh·so(a)*; unofficial strike lo sciopero non ufficiale *sho·pe·roh nohn oof·fee·chah·lay*
unpack vt (case) disfare* *dee·sfah·ray*; (clothes) togliere* da una valigia *tol·ye·ray da oo·na va·lee·ja*
unpaid adj (debt) non pagato(a) *nohn pa·gah·to(a)*
unpleasant adj sgradevole *zgra·day·vo·le*
unprofitable adj poco redditizio(a) *po·ko red·dee·tee·tsyo(a)*
unreasonable adj (demand, price) irragionevole *eer·ra·joh·nay·vo·le*
unripe adj acerbo(a) *a·cher·bo(a)*
unsalted adj (butter) non salato(a) *nohn sa·lah·to(a)*
unscrew vt svitare *zvee·tah·ray*
unskilled labo(u)r n il lavoro manuale *la·voh·ro ma·nwah·le*
unsuitable adj inadatto(a) *een·a·dat·to(a)*
untidy adj (room) disordinato(a) *dee·zor·dee·nah·to(a)*; (hair) arruffato(a) *ar·roof·fah·to(a)*
untie vt slegare *zle·gah·ray*
until prep fino a *fee·no a* □ conj until he comes finché egli verrà *feen·kay el·yee ver·ra*
unusual adj insolito(a) *een·so·lee·to(a)* S108
unwrap vt disfare* *dee·sfah·ray*
up prep □ to go up a hill salire* su una collina *sa·lee·ray soo oo·na kol·lee·na*; up till now finora *fee·noh·ra*; up to 6 fino a 6 *fee·no a 6* □ adv up there lassù *las·soo*; he isn't up yet (out of bed) egli non si è ancora alzato *el·yee nohn see e an·koh·ra al·tsah·to*
update vt aggiornare *aj·johr·nah·ray*
uphill adv in su *een soo*; to go uphill salire* *sa·lee·ray*
upkeep n la manutenzione *ma·noo·ten·tsyoh·nay*
upon prep su *soo*
upper adj superiore *soo·pe·ryoh·re*; the upper class la classe alta *klas·se al·ta*

upside down adv sottosopra *soht·to·soh·pra*; to turn something upside down rovesciare qualcosa *ro·ve·shah·ray kwal·ko·sa*
upstairs adv di sopra *dee soh·pra*
upturn n (in business) il rialzo *ree·al·tso*
upward(s) adv in alto *een al·to*
urban adj urbano(a) *oor·bah·no(a)*
urgent adj urgente *oor·jen·te*
urgently adv urgentemente *oor·jen·te·mayn·te*
us pron ci *chee*; noi *noy*; it's us siamo noi *syah·mo noy*
use n l'uso (m) *oo·zo*; in use in uso *een oo·zo*; it's no use è inutile *e ee·noo·tee·lay* □ vt use usare *oo·zah·ray*
used adj (car etc) usato(a) *oo·za·toh(a)*; to get used to abituarsi a *a·bee·twar·see a* □ vi we used to go andavamo *an·da·vah·mo*
useful adj utile *oo·tee·lay*
useless adj inutile *ee·noo·tee·lay*
U.S.S.R. n l'U.R.S.S. (f) *loo·erre·esse·esse*
usual adj abituale *a·bee·too·ah·le*
usually adv di solito *dee so·lee·to*
U-turn n (in car) l'inversione (f) *een·vayr·syoh·nay*

V

vacancy n (job) il posto vacante *poh·sto va·kan·tay*; (in hotel etc) la camera libera *kah·me·ra lee·be·ra*; no vacancies al completo *al kom·ple·toh* A12
vacant adj (seat, toilet) libero(a) *lee·be·roh(a)*
vacation n le vacanze *va·kan·tse*; on vacation in vacanza *een va·kan·tsa* Mc19
vacationer n il/la villeggiante *veel·lej·jan·te*
vaccination n la vaccinazione *vach·chee·na·tsyoh·nay*
vacuum cleaner n l'aspirapolvere (m) *a·spee·ra·pohl·ve·re*
vacuum flask n il termos *ter·mos*
vague adj vago(a) *va·go(a)*
vain adj vanitoso(a) *va·nee·toh·so(a)*; in vain invano *een·vah·no*
valet n (in hotel) il cameriere *ka·me·rye·re*
valid adj valido(a) *vah·lee·do(a)*
valley n la valle *val·le*
valuable adj di gran valore *dee gran va·loh·ray*
valuables pl gli oggetti di valore *oj·jet·tee dee va·loh·ray*
value n il valore *va·loh·ray* □ vt valutare *va·loo·tah·ray*
value-added tax n l'imposta sul valore aggiunto (f) *eem·po·sta sool va·loh·ray aj·joon·toh* M4
valve n la valvola *val·vo·la*
van n il furgone *foor·goh·nay*
vandal n il teppista *tep·pee·sta*
vanilla n la vaniglia *va·neel·ya*; vanilla ice cream il gelato alla vaniglia *je·lah·toh al·la va·neel·ya*
variable adj variabile *va·ree·ah·bee·lay* □ n la variabile *va·ree·ah·bee·lay*
variation n la variazione *va·ree·a·tsyoh·nay*
variety n la varietà *va·ree·e·ta*
variety show n lo spettacolo di varietà *spet·ta·ko·lo dee va·ree·e·ta*
various adj vario(a) *va·ree·oh(a)*
varnish n la vernice *vayr·nee·chay*
vary vi variare *va·ree·ah·ray*

vase n il vaso *vah·zoh*
vaseline n la vaselina *va·ze·lee·na*
V.A.T. n l'I.V.A. (f) *ee·va* M4
Vatican n il Vaticano *va·tee·kah·noh*
veal n il vitello *vee·tel·loh*
vegetables pl gli ortaggi or *taj·jee* E25
vegetarian adj vegetariano(a) *ve·je·ta·ree·ah·no(a)*
vehicle n il veicolo *ve·ee·ko·loh*
veil n il velo *vay·loh*
vein n la vena *vay·na*
velvet n il velluto *vel·loo·toh*
vending machine n il distributore automatico *dee·stree·boo·toh·ray ow·to·ma·tee·ko*
vendor n il venditore *ven·dee·toh·ray*
Venice n Venezia (f) *ve·ne·tsya*
venison n la carne di cervo *kar·nay dee cher·voh*
ventilator n il ventilatore *ven·tee·la·toh·ray*
venture n l'impresa (f) *eem·pray·sa*
veranda n la veranda *ve·ran·da*
verbal adj (agreement) verbale *vayr·bah·lay*
verdict n il verdetto *vayr·dayt·toh*
verge n l'orlo (m) *ohr·loh*
vermouth n il vermut *ver·moot*
version n la versione *vayr·syoh·nay*
versus prep contro *kohn·tro*
vertical adj verticale *vayr·tee·kah·lay*
very adv molto *mohl·to*; the very last l'ultimissimo *lool·tee·mees·see·mo*; I like it very much mi piace molto *mee pyah·che mohl·to*; I haven't very much non ho molto *nohn o mohl·to*
vest n (undergarment) la canottiera *ka·not·tye·ra*
vet(erinary surgeon) n il/la veterinario(a) *ve·te·ree·nah·ryoh(a)*
veto vt mettere* il veto a *mayt·te·ray eel ve·toh a* □ n il veto *ve·toh*
V.H.F. abbrev V.H.F. *voo·akka·effe*
via prep via *vee·a*
viaduct n il viadotto *vee·a·doht·toh*
vicar n il curato *koo·rah·toh*
vice chairman n il vicepresidente *vee·che·pre·se·den·te*
vice president n il vicepresidente *vee·che·pre·see·den·te*
vice versa adv viceversa *vee·che·ver·sa*
victim n (of accident etc) la vittima *veet·tee·ma*
victory n la vittoria *veet·to·ree·a*
video n il video *vee·de·oh*; on video alla televisione *al·la te·le·vee·zyoh·nay*
videocassette n la videocassetta *vee·de·o·kas·sayt·ta*
videocassette recorder n il videoregistratore a cassetta *vee·de·o·re·jee·stra·toh·ray a kas·sayt·ta*
videotape n il videonastro *vee·de·o·na·stroh*
Vienna n Vienna (f) *vee·en·na*
view n la vista *vee·sta*; (opinion) il parere *pa·ray·ray* A5
villa n la villa *veel·la*
village n il paesino *pa·e·zee·noh*
vinaigrette (sauce) n la salsa vinaigrette *sal·sa vee·nay·gret*
vine n la vite *vee·te*
vinegar n l'aceto (m) *a·chay·toh*
vineyard n la vigna *veen·ya*
vintage n l'annata (f) *an·nah·ta*; a vintage wine un vino di qualità *oon vee·noh dee kwa·lee·ta*
vinyl n il vinile *vee·nee·le*
violence n la violenza *vee·o·len·tsa*
violin n il violino *vee·o·lee·noh*
V.I.P. n il V.I.P. *voo·ee·pee*

visa, visé n il visto *vee·stoh*
visible adj visibile *vee·zee·bee·lay*
visit vt visitare *vee·zee·tah·ray* □ n la visita *vee·zee·ta*; (stay) il soggiorno *soj·johr·noh* Mc31
visitor n il visitatore *vee·zee·ta·toh·ray*, la visitatrice *vee·zee·ta·tree·chay*
visual aids pl i sussidi visivi *soos·see·dee vee·zee·vee*
vital adj (essential) vitale *vee·tah·lay*
vitamin n la vitamina *vee·ta·mee·na*
V-neck n il collo a V *kol·loh a vee*
vocabulary n il vocabolario *vo·ka·bo·lah·ree·oh*
vodka n la vodka *vod·ka*
voice n la voce *voh·che*
void adj (contract) nullo(a) *nool·loh(a)*
vol-au-vent n il vol-au-vent *vol·ó·voñ*
volcano n il vulcano *vool·kah·noh*
volleyball n la pallavolo *pal·la·voh·loh*
voltage n la tensione *ten·syoh·nay*
volume n il volume *vo·loo·me*
vomit vi vomitare *vo·mee·tah·ray*
vote n il voto *voh·to* □ vi votare *vo·tah·ray*
voucher n il buono *bwo·noh*

W

wafer n il wafer *va·fer*
waffle n la cialda *chal·da*
wag vt (tail) dimenare *dee·me·nah·ray*
wage, wages n il salario *sa·lah·ryoh*
wage earner n il salariato *sa·la·ree·ah·toh*
wage freeze n il blocco dei salari *blok·koh de·ee sa·lah·ree*
wag(g)on n (rail) il vagone *va·goh·ne*
wagon-lit n il vagone letto *va·goh·ne let·toh*
waist n la vita *vee·ta*
waistcoat n il panciotto *pan·chot·toh*
wait vi aspettare *a·spet·tah·ray*; to wait for someone aspettare qualcuno *a·spet·tah·ray kwal·koo·no*; to keep someone waiting fare* aspettare qualcuno *fah·ray a·spet·tah·ray kwal·koo·no*; no waiting (road sign) divieto di sosta *dee·vye·toh dee so·sta*
waiter n il cameriere *ka·me·rye·re* E42
waiting list n la lista d'attesa *lee·sta dat·tay·sa*
waiting room n (at station) la sala d'aspetto *sah·la da·spet·toh*
waitress n la cameriera *ka·me·rye·ra*
wake vt svegliare *zvel·yah·ray* □ vi to wake up svegliarsi *zvel·yar·see*
Wales n Galles (m) *ga·les*
walk vi camminare *kam·me·nah·ray*; (for pleasure) passeggiare *pas·sej·jah·ray* □ vt to walk 10 km fare* 10 km a piedi *fah·ray 10 km a pye·dee* □ n walk la passeggiata *pas·sej·jah·ta*; to go for a walk fare* una passeggiata *fah·ray oo·na pas·sej·jah·ta* L37
walking n il camminare *kam·me·nah·ray*
walking stick n il bastone *ba·stoh·ne*
walkout n lo sciopero *sho·pe·roh*
wall n (inside) la parete *pa·ray·te*; (outside) il muro *moo·roh*
wallet n il portafogli *por·ta·fol·yee* Sn81
wallpaper n la carta da parati *kar·ta da pa·rah·tee*
wall-to-wall carpet(ing) n la mochetta *mo·kayt·ta*
walnut n la noce *noh·che*
waltz n il valzer *val·tser*
wander vi errare *er·rah·ray*

want vt (wish for) volere* vo·lay·re; (need) avere* di bisogno di a·vay·re bee·zohn·yoh dee; **to want to do something** volere* fare qualcosa vo·lay·re fah·ray kwal·ko·sa

war n la guerra gwer·ra

ward n (in hospital) la corsia kor·see·a

wardrobe n (furniture) il guardaroba gwar·da·ro·ba

warehouse n il magazzino ma·gadz·dzee·noh

warm adj caldo(a) kal·do(a); **it's warm today** fa caldo oggi fa kal·do oj·jee; **I'm warm** ho caldo o kal·do □ vt **to warm** scaldare skal·dah·ray Mc10

warn vt avvertire av·vayr·tee·re

warrant(y) n la garanzia ga·ran·tsee·a

Warsaw n Varsavia (f) var·sah·vya

was vi □ **I was** ero e·ro; **he was** era e·ra

wash vt lavare la·vah·ray □ vi **to wash (oneself)** lavarsi la·var·see; **to wash up** (dishes) lavare le stoviglie la·vah·ray le sto·veel·ye A91

washable adj lavabile la·vah·bee·le S81

washbasin n il lavabo la·vah·boh A49

washcloth n il guanto di spugna gwan·toh dee spoo·nya

washing n (clothes) il bucato boo·kah·toh; **to do the washing** il bucato fah·ray eel boo·kah·toh A91

washing machine n la lavatrice la·va·tree·che A93

washing powder n il detersivo de·ter·see·voh

washroom n la stanza da bagno stan·tsa da ban·yoh A89

waste n lo spreco spre·koh; (rubbish) i rifiuti ree·fyoo·tee □ vt sprecare spre·kah·ray; **to waste one's time** perdere* tempo per·de·re tem·poh

waste paper basket n il cestino che·stee·noh

watch n l'orologio (m) o·ro·lo·joh □ vt guardare gwar·dah·ray; (spy on) sorvegliare sor·vel·yah·ray S86

water n l'acqua (f) ak·kwa B67, A31, E66, Mc10

watercress n il crescione kre·shoh·ne

waterfall n la cascata ka·skah·ta

water heater n lo scaldabagno skal·da·ban·yoh

water ice n la granita gra·nee·ta

watermelon n il cocomero ko·koh·me·roh

waterproof adj impermeabile eem·payr·me·ah·bee·le

water-skiing n lo sci nautico shee now·tee·ko; **to go water-skiing** fare* dello sci nautico fah·ray del·lo shee now·tee·ko L30

watt n il watt vat

wave vi agitare la mano a·jee·tah·ray la ma·noh □ n l'onda (f) ohn·da

wavy adj (hair) ondulato(a) on·doo·lah·to(a)

wax n la cera chay·ra; (in ear) il cerume che·roo·me

way n (manner) il modo mo·doh; (in) a different way in un modo diverso een oon mo·doh dee·ver·so; **which is the way to London?** qual'è la strada per Londra? kwah·le la strah·da payr lohn·dra; **to ask the way to Paris** chiedere* la strada per Parigi kyay·de·re la strah·da payr pa·ree·jee; **it's a long way** è lontano e lon·tah·no; **to be in the way** bloccare il passaggio blok·kah·ray eel pas·saj·joh; **on the way** strada facendo strah·da fa·chen·

do; this way please di qua, per favore dee kwa payr fa·voh·re; **by the way** a proposito a pro·po·see·to; **to give way** (when driving) dare* la precedenza dah·ray la pre·che·den·tsa F1f

we pron noi noy

weak adj (person) debole day·bo·le; (tea) leggero(a) lej·je·ro(a)

wealth n la ricchezza reek·kayts·tsa

wealthy adj ricco(a) reek·ko(a)

weapon n l'arma (f) ar·ma

wear vt (clothes) portare por·tah·ray □ vi (fabric) logorarsi lo·go·rar·see; **to wear something out** logorare qualcosa lo·go·rah·ray kwal·ko·sa; **wear and tear** il logoramento lo·go·ra·mayn·toh

weather n il tempo tem·poh

weather forecast n le previsioni del tempo pre·vee·zyoh·nee del tem·poh

weave vt tessere tes·se·re

wedding n il matrimonio ma·tree·mo·nyoh

wedding dress n l'abito da sposa (m) ah·bee·toh da spo·za

wedding present n il regalo di nozze re·gah·loh dee nots·tse

wedding ring n la fede fay·de

Wednesday n mercoledì (m) mayr·ko·le·dee

weed n l'erbaccia (f) er·bach·cha

week n la settimana set·tee·mah·na T112

weekday n il giorno feriale johr·noh fe·ree·ah·le

weekend n il week-end week·end

weekly adv settimanalmente set·tee·mah·nal·mayn·te □ adj settimanale set·tee·ma·nah·le □ n (periodical) il settimanale set·tee·ma·nah·le

weigh vt pesare pe·sah·ray

weight n (mass) il peso pay·soh

welcome adj benvenuto(a) ben·ve·noo·to(a) □ n l'accoglienza (f) ak·kol·yen·tsa □ vt accogliere* ak·kol·ye·re

weld vt saldare sal·dah·ray

well n (for water) il pozzo pohts·tsoh □ adv bene be·ne; **to be well** stare* bene stah·ray be·ne; **get well soon** si ristabilisca presto see ree·sta·bee·lee·ska pre·sto; **well!** bene! be·ne

wellington boot n lo stivalone di gomma stee·va·loh·ne dee gohm·ma

Welsh adj gallese gal·lay·se □ n il gallese gal·lay·se

were vi □ **you were** voi eravate voy e·ra·vah·te; **we were** eravamo e·ra·vah·mo; **they were** erano e·ra·no

west n l'ovest (m) o·vest; **the West** l'Occidente (m) loch·chee·den·te □ adv west all'ovest al·lo·vest

western adj occidentale och·chee·den·tah·le □ n (movie) il western wes·tern

West Germany n la Germania Occidentale jer·mah·nya och·chee·den·tah·le

wet adj (clothes) bagnato(a) ban·yah·to(a); (weather, day) piovoso(a) pyo·voh·so(a); (paint) fresco(a) fray·sko(a); (climate) umido(a) oo·mee·do(a); **to get wet** bagnarsi ban·yar·see

whale n la balena ba·lay·na

wharf n la banchina ban·kee·na

what adj quale kwah·le; **what book?** qual libro? kwahl lee·broh; **what languages?** quali lingue? kwah·lee leen·gwe □ pron what che ke; **what's happened?** che cos'è successo? ke ko·se

sooch·ches·so; what do you want? cosa vuole? *ko·sa vwo·le*; I saw what happened ho visto quello che è successo *o vee·sto kwayl·lo ke e sooch·ches·so*; I saw what you did ho visto quello che ha fatto *o vee·sto kwayl·lo ke a fat·to*; what's it called? come si chiama? *koh·me see kyah·ma*; what a mess! (*in room*) che disordine! *ke dee·zohr·dee·ne*; what? (*please repeat*) come? *koh·me*

wheat *n* il frumento *froo·mayn·toh*

wheel *n* la ruota *rwo·ta*; (*steering wheel*) il volante *vo·lan·te*

wheelbarrow *n* la carriola *kar·ryo·la*

wheelchair *n* la sedia a rotelle *se·dya a ro·tel·le* I5

when *conj* quando *kwan·do*; the day when we... il giorno in cui noi... *eel johr·noh een koo·ee noy*

where *conj* dove *doh·ve*; where are you from? di dove è? *dee doh·ve e*

whether *conj* se *say*

which *adj* quale *kwah·le*; which book? qual libro? *kwahl lee·broh*; which languages? quali lingue? *kwah·lee leen·gwe*; which one of you? chi di voi? *kee dee voy* □ *pron* the book, which is long il libro, che è lungo *eel lee·broh ke e loon·go*; the apple which you ate la mela che ha mangiato *la may·la ke a man·jah·to*; I don't know which to take non so quale prendere *nohn so kwah·le pren·de·re*; after which dopo di che *doh·po dee ke*; the chair on which the sedia sulla quale *la se·dya sool·la kwah·le*

while *n* il momento *mo·mayn·toh* □ *conj* mentre *mayn·tre*

whip *n* la frusta *froo·sta* □ *vt* (*cream, eggs*) montare *mon·tah·ray*

whipped cream *n* la panna montata *pan·na mon·tah·ta*

whirlpool *n* il vortice *vor·tee·che*

whirlwind *n* il turbine *toor·bee·ne*

whisk *n* il frullino *frool·lee·noh* □ *vt* (*cream, eggs*) sbattere *zbat·te·re*

whisky *n* il whisky *wee·skee*

whisper *vi* sussurrare *soos·soor·rah·ray*

whist *n* il whist *weest*

whistle *n* (*sound*) il fischio *fee·skyoh*; (*object*) il fischietto *fee·skyayt·toh* □ *vi* fischiare *fee·skyah·ray*

white *adj* bianco(a) *byan·ko(a)*

whitebait *n* i bianchetti *byan·kayt·tee*

White House *n* la Casa Bianca *kah·sa byan·ka*

whiting *n* il merlano *mayr·lah·noh*

Whitsun *n* la Pentecoste *pen·te·ko·ste*

Whitsunday *n* la Pentecoste *pen·te·ko·ste*

who *pron* chi? *kee*; the man who... l'uomo che... *lwo·moh kay*

whole *adj* (*complete*) intero(a) *een·te·ro(a)*

wholemeal bread *n* il pane integrale *pah·ne een·te·grah·le*

wholesale *n* la vendita all'ingrosso *vayn·dee·ta al·leen·gros·soh* □ *adj, adv* all'ingrosso *al·leen·gros·soh* Bm25

wholesaler *n* il/la grossista *gros·sees·ta*

whom *pron* chi? *kee*; the man whom you see l'uomo che vede *lwo·moh ke ve·de*; the boy with whom... il ragazzo con cui... *eel ra·gats·tsoh kohn koo·ee*

whooping cough *n* la pertosse *payr·tohs·se*

whose *adj* □ whose book is this? di chi è questo libro? *dee kee e kway·sto lee·broh*; the man, whose son l'uomo, il cui figlio *lwo·moh, eel koo·ee feel·yoh*; I know whose it is io so di chi è *ee·o so dee kee e*

why *adv* perché *payr·kay*

wick *n* (*of cigarette lighter*) lo stoppino *stop·pee·noh*

wicked *adj* malvagio(a) *mal·va·jo(a)*

wicker *n* il vimine *vee·mee·ne*

wide *adj* (*broad*) largo(a) *lar·go(a)*; (*range*) grande *gran·de*; 4 cm. wide largo(a) 4 cm. *lar·go(a) 4 cm.*

wide-angle lens *n* l'obiettivo grandangolare (*m*) *o·byet·tee·voh gran·dan·goh·lah·re*

widow *n* la vedova *vay·do·va*

widower *n* il vedovo *vay·do·voh*

width *n* la larghezza *lar·gayts·tsa*

wife *n* la moglie *mohl·ye* T115, A2, S103

wig *n* la parrucca *par·rook·ka*

wild *adj* (*animal, tribe*) selvaggio(a) *sel·vaj·jo(a)*; (*flower*) selvatico(a) *sel·va·tee·ko(a)*

wildlife *n* la fauna *fow·na* L40

will *n* (*testament*) il testamento *te·sta·mayn·toh* □ *vi* he will do it lo farà *lo fa·ra*

willing *adj* □ willing to do something disposto(a) a fare qualcosa *dee·spoh·sto(a) a fah·ray kwal·ko·sa*

win *vi* vincere* *veen·che·re* □ *vt* vincere* *veen·che·re*; (*contract*) ottenere* *ot·te·nay·re*

windmill *n* il mulino a vento *moo·lee·noh a ven·toh*

window *n* (*in house*) la finestra *fee·ne·stra*; (*in car, train*) il finestrino *fee·ne·stree·noh*; (*of shop*) la vetrina *ve·tree·na*

window shade *n* la tendina *ten·dee·na*

window shopping *n* il guardare le vetrine *gwar·dah·ray le ve·tree·ne*

windscreen *n* il parabrezza *pa·ra·brayts·tsa*

windscreen washer *n* il lavacristallo *la·va·kree·stal·loh*

windscreen wiper *n* il tergicristallo *ter·jee·kree·stal·loh*

windshield *n* il parabrezza *pa·ra·brayts·tsa*

windshield washer *n* il lavacristallo *la·va·kree·stal·loh*

windshield wiper *n* il tergicristallo *ter·jee·kree·stal·loh*

windsurfing *n* il surfing a vela *soor·feeng a vay·la*; to go windsurfing fare* del surfing a vela *fah·ray del soor·feeng a vay·la*

windy *adj* (*place*) esposto(a) al vento *e·spo·sto(a) al ven·toh*; it's windy tira vento *tee·ra ven·toh*

wind¹ *n* (*breeze*) il vento *ven·toh*; (*in stomach*) la flatulenza *fla·too·len·tsa*

wind² *vt* avvolgere* *av·vol·je·re*; to wind a bandage round something avvolgere* una benda intorno a qualcosa *av·vol·je·re oo·na ben·da een·tohr·no a kwal·ko·sa*; to wind up a clock caricare un orologio *ka·ree·kah·ray oon o·ro·lo·joh*

wine *n* il vino *vee·noh* B54, E10f, S35

wine cellar *n* la cantina *kan·tee·na*

wineglass *n* il bicchiere da vino *beek·kye·re da vee·noh*

wine list *n* la lista dei vini *lee·sta de·ee vee·nee* E9

wine waiter *n* il sommelier *so·muh·lyay*

wing n l'ala (f) *ah·la*; (of car) il parafango *pa·ra·fan·goh*

wink vi strizzare l'occhio *streets·tsah·ray lok·kyoh*

winner n il vincitore *veen·chee·toh·re*, la vincitrice *veen·chee·tree·che*

winter n l'inverno (m) *een·ver·noh*

winter sports pl gli sport invernali *sport een·ver·nah·lee*

wipe vt asciugare *a·shoo·gah·ray*; to wipe off cancellare *kan·chel·lah·ray*

wire n il filo di ferro *fee·loh dee fer·roh*; (electrical) il filo elettrico *fee·loh e·let·tree·ko*; (telegram) il telegramma *te·le·gram·ma*

wise adj (person) saggio(a) *saj·jo(a)*; (decision) prudente *proo·den·te*

wish n il desiderio *de·see·de·ryoh*; with best wishes con i migliori auguri *kohn ee meel·yoh·ree ow·goo·ree* □ vt/i I wish I could... vorrei potere... *vor·re·e po·tay·re*; to wish for something desiderare qualcosa *de·see·de·rah·ray kwal·ko·sa*

witch n la strega *stray·ga*

with prep con *kohn*; red with anger rosso(a) di collera *rohs·so(a) dee kol·le·ra*; filled with water pieno(a) d'acqua *pye·no(a) dak·kwa*

withdraw vt (money) ritirare *ree·tee·rah·ray*

without prep senza *sen·tsa*

witness n il testimone *te·stee·mo·ne* □ vt (signature) firmare come testimone *feer·mah·ray koh·me te·stee·mo·ne* T215

wobble vi (chair etc) dondolare *don·do·lah·ray*

wolf n il lupo *loo·poh*

woman n la donna *don·na*

womb n l'utero (m) *oo·te·roh*

wonder vi □ to wonder whether... domandarsi se... *do·man·dar·see say*

wonderful adj meraviglioso(a) *me·ra·veel·yoh·so(a)*

wood n (material) il legno *layn·yoh*; (forest) il bosco *bo·skoh*

wooden adj di legno *dee layn·yoh*

wool n la lana *lah·na*

wool(l)en adj di lana *dee lah·na*

word n la parola *pa·ro·la*; word for word parola per parola *pa·ro·la pay pa·ro·la*

work n il lavoro *la·voh·roh*; (art, literature) l'opera (f) *o·pe·ra* □ vi lavorare *la·vo·rah·ray*; (clock, mechanism) funzionare *foon·tsyoh·nah·ray*; (medicine) agire *a·jee·re*; to work out (problem) risolvere *ree·sol·ve·re* A65, Sn55

worker n il lavoratore *la·vo·ra·toh·re*, la lavoratrice *la·vo·ra·tree·che*

work force n la manodopera *mah·no·do·pe·ra*

working capital n il capitale d'esercizio *ka·pee·tah·le de·zer·chee·tsyoh*

working-class adj operaio(a) *o·pe·ra·yo(a)*

working day n il giorno feriale *johr·noh fe·rya·le*

working hours pl le ore di lavoro *oh·re dee la·voh·roh*

working order n □ to be in working order funzionare *foon·tsyoh·nah·ray*

workman n l'operaio (m) *o·pe·ra·yoh*

work of art n l'opera d'arte (f) *o·pe·ra dar·te*

works pl (mechanism) il meccanismo *mek·ka·nee·zmoh*; (factory) la fabbrica *fab·bree·ka*

workshop n l'officina (f) *of·fee·chee·na*

work-to-rule n lo sciopero bianco *sho·pe·roh byan·ko*

world n il mondo *mohn·doh*

world power n il potere mondiale *po·tay·re mon·dee·ah·le*

world war n la guerra mondiale *gwer·ra mon·dee·ah·le*

worm n il verme *ver·me*

worn adj logoro(a) *loh·go·ro(a)*

worn-out adj (object) logoro(a) *loh·go·ro(a)*; (person) sfinito(a) *sfee·nee·to(a)*

worried adj preoccupato(a) *pre·ok·koo·pah·to(a)*

worry n la preoccupazione *pre·ok·koo·pa·tsyoh·ne*

worse adj □ it's worse (than the other) è peggiore (dell'altro) *e pej·joh·re (del·lal·tro)* □ adv to do something worse fare* qualcosa di peggio *fah·ray kwal·ko·sa dee pej·jo*

worst adj □ the worst book il peggiore libro *eel pej·joh·re lee·broh* □ adv he did it worst l'ha fatto il peggio *la fat·to eel pej·jo*

worth adj □ to be worth £5 valere* £5 *va·lay·re £5*; L.20000 worth of petrol/gas L.20000 di benzina *L20000 dee ben·dzee·na*; it's worth it vale la pena *vah·le la pay·na*

worthwhile adj (activity) che vale la pena *ke vah·le la pay·na*

would vi □ she would come if... ella verrebbe se... *ayl·la ver·reb·be say*; would you like a cup of coffee? gradirebbe una tazza di caffè? *gra·dee·reb·be oo·na tats·tsa dee kaf·fe*

wound n (injury) la ferita *fe·ree·ta*

wrap vt avvolgere* *av·vol·je·re*; to wrap up a parcel imballare un pacco *eem·bal·lah·ray oon pak·koh* □ n wrap (shawl) lo scialle *shal·le* S23

wrapper n (paper) la copertina *ko·per·tee·na*

wrapping paper n la carta d'imballaggio *kar·ta deem·bal·laj·joh*

wreck n (ship) il naufragio *now·frah·joh* □ vt fare* naufragare *fah·ray now·fra·gah·ray*; (plans) rovinare *ro·vee·nah·ray*

wrestling n la lotta *lot·ta*

wring vt (clothes) strizzare *streets·tsah·ray*

wrinkle n la ruga *roo·ga*

wrist n il polso *pohl·soh*

write vt/i scrivere* *skree·ve·re*; to write down annotare *an·no·tah·ray*; to write off a debt cancellare un debito *kan·chel·lah·ray oon de·bee·toh* B28

writer n lo scrittore *skreet·toh·re*, la scrittrice *skreet·tree·che*

writing n la scrittura *skreet·too·ra*; in writing per iscritto *payr ee·skreet·to*

writing case n l'astuccio con il necessario per scrivere (m) *a·stooch·choh kohn eel ne·ches·sah·ryoh payr skree·ve·re*

writing paper n la carta da scrivere *kar·ta da skree·ve·re*

wrong adj sbagliato(a) *zbal·yah·to(a)*; you're wrong ha torto *a tor·toh*; what's wrong? che c'è? *ke che*; to go wrong (machine) guastarsi *gwa·star·see*

X

Xerox n la xerocopia *kse·ro·ko·pya* □ vt fotocopiare *fo·to·ko·pyah·ray*

X-ray n (photo) la radiografia *ra·dyo·*

gra·fee·a □ *vt* radiografare *ra·dyo·gra·fah·ray*

Y

yacht *n* lo yacht *yot*
yachting *n* lo yachting *yo·teeng*; **to go yachting** fare* dello yachting *fah·ray del·lo yo·teeng*
yard *n* (*of building*) il cortile *kor·tee·le*; (*measure*) la iarda *yar·da*
yawn *vi* sbadigliare *zba·deel·yah·ray*
year *n* l'anno (*m*) *an·noh*; (*as duration*) l'annata (*f*) *an·nah·ta*
yearly *adj* annuale *an·noo·ah·le* □ *adv* annualmente *an·noo·al·mayn·te*
yeast *n* il lievito *lye·vee·toh*
yellow *adj* giallo(a) *jal·lo(a)*
yes *adv* sí *see*
yesterday *adv* ieri *ye·ree*
yet *adv* ancora *an·koh·ra*
yield *n* il rendimento *ren·dee·mayn·toh*; (*financial*) il reddito *red·dee·toh* □ *vt* (*investment*) rendere* *ren·de·re* □ *vi* (*to traffic*) dare* la precedenza *dah·ray la pre·che·den·tsa*
yoga *n* lo yoga *yo·ga*
yoghurt *n* lo yogurt *yo·goort*
you *pron* (*familiar form*) tu *too*; (*polite form*) (*plural form*) voi *voy*; **he's watching you** ti/La/vi guarda *tee/la/vee gwar·da*; **milk is good for you** il latte ti fa bene *eel lat·te tee fa be·ne*
young *adj* giovane *joh·va·ne*
your *adj* (*familiar form*) tuo *too·o*, tua *too·a*, tuoi *twoy*, tue *too·e*; (*polite form*) Suo *soo·o*, Sua *soo·a*, Suoi *swoy*, Sue *soo·e*; (*plural form*) vostro *vo·stro*, vostra *vo·stra*, vostri *vo·stree*, vostre *vo·stre*; **your sisters** le tue/Sue/vostre sorelle *le too·e/soo·e/vo·stre so·rel·le*
yours *pron* (*familiar form*) il tuo *eel too·o*, la tua *la too·a*; (*polite form*) il Suo *eel soo·o*, la Sua *la soo·a*; (*plural form*) il vostro *eel vo·stro*, la vostra *la vo·stra*; **where are yours?** dove

sono i tuoi/i Suoi/i vostri? *doh·ve soh·no ee twoy/ee swoy/ee vo·stree*; dove sono le tue/le Sue/le vostre? *doh·ve soh·no le too·e/le soo·e/le vo·stre*; **these are yours** questi sono tuoi/Suoi/vostri *kway·stee soh·no twoy/swoy/vo·stree*; queste sono tue/Sue/vostre *kway·ste soh·no too·e/soo·e/vo·stre*
yourself *pron* (*familiar form*) te stesso(a) *tay stays·so(a)*; (*polite form*) Lei stesso(a) *lay stays·so(a)*; **you've hurt yourself** Sí è fatto male *see e fat·to mah·le*; **you did it yourself** l'ha fatto Lei stesso(a) *la fat·to lay stays·so(a)*
yourselves *pron* voi stessi(e) *voy stays·see('se)*; **you've hurt yourselves** vi siete fatti male *vee sye·te fat·tee mah·le*; **you did it yourselves** l'avete fatto voi stessi(e) *la·vay·te fat·to voy stays·see('se)*
youth *n* (*period*) la gioventú *jo·ven·too*
youth club *n* il circolo della gioventú *cheer·ko·loh del·la jo·ven·too*
youth hostel *n* l'ostello della gioventú (*m*) *o·stel·loh del·la jo·ven·too*
Yugoslavia *n* Iugoslavia (*f*) *yoo·go·slah·vya*
Yugoslav(ian) *adj* iugoslavo(a) *yoo·go·slah·vo(a)*

Z

zebra *n* la zebra *dze·bra*
zero *n* lo zero *dze·roh*
zinc *n* lo zinco *tseen·koh*
zip code *n* il codice postale *ko·dee·che po·stah·le*
zip(-fastener), zipper *n* la cerniera lampo *cher·nye·ra lam·poh* S78, Sn76
zone *n* la zona *dzo·na*
zoo *n* lo zoo *dzo*
zoom lens *n* lo zoom *zoom*
zucchini *pl* gli zucchini *tsook·kee·nee*